ALSO BY GEORGE BUSH

LOOKING FORWARD (with Victor Gold)

A WORLD TRANSFORMED (with Brent Scowcroft)

ALL THE BEST,

MY LIFE IN LETTERS
AND OTHER WRITINGS

GEORGE BUSH

A TOUCHSTONE BOOK
PUBLISHED BY SIMON & SCHUSTER
NEW YORK LONDON TORONTO SYDNEY SINGAPORE

TOUCHSTONE
Rockefeller Center
1230 Avenue of the Americas
New York, NY 10020

First Touchstone Edition 2000
TOUCHSTONE and colophon are registered trademarks of Simon & Schuster, Inc.

DESIGNED BY ERICH HOBBING
Set in Adobe Garamond

Manufactured in the United States of America

1   3   5   7   9   10   8   6   4   2

The Library of Congress has cataloged the Scribner edition as follows:
Bush, George, 1924–
All the best, George Bush : My life in letters
and other writings / George Bush.
p.   cm.
"George Bush" in the title appears as his signature.
"A Lisa Drew Book"
Includes index.
1. Bush, George, 1924– Correspondence.
2. Presidents—United States Correspondence. I. Title.
E838.5.B872   1999
973.928'092—dc21   99-40440
CIP

ISBN 0-684-83958-X
0-7432-0041-1 (Pbk)

To Barbara
and all my family,
who have given so much love
and support through these many years

EDITOR'S NOTE

The letters and other entries in this book appear in their original form with the following exceptions: 1. Some letters were edited for length; 2. For the sake of clarity, typos were corrected; punctuation and grammar were not; 3. For consistency, the format of the letters (position of date, spacing, paragraphing, etc.) are uniform; 4. To protect the privacy of letter recipients, street addresses and P.O. box numbers were removed from inside addresses.

CONTENTS

GLOSSARY OF NAMES

Aga Khan, His Highness Prince Sadruddin—I first met Sadruddin when I was at the United Nations and Sadri was the U.N. high commissioner for refugees. We became close friends, and Barbara and I have stayed with him and his charming wife, Kate, in Geneva. He is a member of the royal Aga Khan family.

Allday, Martin—Martin and I became close friends when we lived in Midland during the fifties. Now a lawyer in Austin, Texas, Martin served as my chairman of the Federal Energy Regulatory Commission.

Allin, The Reverend Jack—Jack served as presiding bishop of the Episcopal Church, after which he became the winter pastor of my mother's church in Hobe Sound, Florida, and our summer pastor at St. Ann's in Kennebunkport. He was a friend and an adviser, and it was a great loss when he died of cancer in 1998.

Allison, James, Jr.—A newspaperman from Midland, Jimmy was one of my closest political confidants and friends. He ran my 1966 campaign when I was elected to Congress and moved with me to Washington to run my office. He died in 1978 from cancer. His son Jay worked for me at the White House.

Ashley, Thomas Ludlow (Lud)—We met at Yale and became the closest of friends. From 1955 until 1981, he was a Democratic congressman from Ohio's Ninth District. When I was President, he gave me sound advice, and his loyalty and friendship really mattered. They still do.

Baker, James A., III—Jim was perhaps my closest confidant during my political days. I trusted him completely. His appointment as secretary of state was the first I announced after being elected President. My doubles partner in tennis, my friend of close to forty years, Jim has served our country with great distinction and honor.

11

Bartlett, Charles—A Pulitzer Prize–winning journalist and columnist, Charles and his wife, Martha, used to invite us to their home for movies all through our Washington days. Charlie was a close friend and adviser to President Kennedy and certainly was the same for me.

Bates, David—David became my traveling aide in 1979 and together we saw every airport in America. He also was my able tennis partner and adviser. He served in the White House as secretary of the cabinet before going over to Commerce. He's now a successful lawyer and businessman in San Antonio.

Bemiss, FitzGerald (Gerry)—We became the best of friends before 1930 since his family came from Richmond, Virginia, every summer to Kennebunkport. Gerry served for years in the Virginia legislature and became one of the state's leading environmentalists and outdoors enthusiasts.

Blake, Robert—A successful rancher and oilman from Lubbock, Texas, Bob helped in all my elections, and when I was President, he stayed in close touch, keeping me informed of the grassroots opinions of the people in the West Texas area. He is a great and loyal friend and supporter.

Blanton, Taylor—Taylor, an early campaign worker, was almost a son to us. He worked on all my early campaigns, later joining the Foreign Service, where he served with distinction for twenty-four years. He is currently in the real estate business in Austin, Texas.

Brady, Nicholas—A longtime friend, Nick was head of Dillon, Read & Co. until he was bitten by the public service bug. He served for a brief time in the U.S. Senate and was appointed secretary of the treasury by President Reagan in 1988, a position he kept throughout my administration.

Bush, Dorothy Walker—My mother, raised in St. Louis, Missouri, was born in Kennebunkport in 1901. She was my guiding light and led us all by example. She excelled in athletics and had a strong faith in God. She was unfailingly kind and gave us all love until the day she died in 1992, just a few weeks after I lost the election.

Bush, George Walker—Our oldest child was born July 6, 1946, in New Haven, Connecticut, but grew up in Texas, where he is now in his second term as governor. Before that he was successful in the oil business and was managing partner of the Texas Rangers. George was one of my best political advisers. He married Midland native Laura Welch in 1977. They have twin daughters, Jenna and Barbara, soon to turn eighteen.

Bush, John Ellis (Jeb)— Our son Jeb was born February 11, 1953, in Midland. He and his wife, Columba (they met in Mexico during a summer internship), moved to Florida in 1981, where he helped start a real estate development company and later established a pioneer charter school. He is serving his first term as governor of Florida. He and Colu have three children: George P., twenty-three; Noelle, twenty-two; and Jeb Jr., fifteen.

Bush, Jonathan—My younger brother by seven years, Jon and his wife, Jody, live in Killingworth, Connecticut. A graduate of Yale, Jon was very successful in the investment advisory business, selling his company, J. Bush & Co., to Riggs Bank in Washington, D.C. He is very musically talented and a great joke teller.

Bush, Marvin Pierce—Our son Marvin also was born in Midland, on October 22, 1956. He graduated from the University of Virginia, where he met his wife, Margaret Molster. Marvin, the undisputed tennis champ of the family, is managing director and founder of Winston Partners, L.P. He and Margaret live in Alexandria, Virginia, with their two children: Marshall, thirteen; and Walker, almost ten.

Bush, Neil Mallon—Born January 22, 1955, in Midland, our son Neil met his wife, Sharon, while campaigning for me in New Hampshire in 1980. His siblings nicknamed him Mr. Perfect. He and his wife live in Houston where Neil is chairman of Interlink Management Corporation, a firm focused on education, high tech, and biomedical business development. They have three children: Lauren, fifteen; Pierce, thirteen; and Ashley, ten.

Bush, Prescott S.—An imposing man of six feet four inches, my father was perhaps the most powerful influence in my life. By example he taught all five of his kids a great deal about character. He did it through action, not words. He was a managing partner of Brown Bros. Harriman & Co. In 1952 he was elected U.S. senator from Connecticut, serving for ten years. He died of cancer in 1972.

Bush, Prescott S., Jr.—Two years older than I am, my brother Pres and I roomed together as kids and were very close. His successful business life was largely spent with Johnson & Higgins, a leader in the insurance field. He and his wife, Beth, live in Greenwich, Connecticut.

Bush, Robin—Our second child, Robin, was born December 20, 1949 while Barbara and I were living for a short time in California. When Robin was three, she was diagnosed as having leukemia and died six months later, in 1953. She will always be a part of our life.

Bush, William H.T. (Bucky)—Bucky, the youngest of my siblings, was a successful banker in both Hartford, Connecticut, and St. Louis, Missouri, before starting his own financial advisory firm in St. Louis, Bush-O'Donnell & Co. He and his wife, Patty, live in St. Louis. Like all my siblings, he is a true Point of Light.

Chambers, C. Fred—We met Fred and Marion Chambers in Midland in the early 1950s. We did some oil deals together, but more importantly, became good friends, which continued when we all moved to Houston. Bar named one of our dogs in Fred's honor, C. Fred. In our family, that's quite an honor.

Crichton, Flo—Flo has been a leader in the Republican Party in Texas and served as a national committeewoman. She was one of my earliest, strongest supporters. Today, she and her husband, John, live in San Antonio where she is active in the community.

Eagleburger, Larry—A seasoned Foreign Service officer, Larry served as Jim Baker's number two at the State Department, then followed Jim as secretary of state. He was very close to Brent Scowcroft, my national security adviser, which made for smooth relations between the National Security Council (NSC) and State.

Ellis, Nancy—My only sister is twenty months younger than I am, born right in the middle of the Bush boys. She is full of energy and has a real zest for life that inspires us all. She campaigned tirelessly for me and now campaigns for my boys, her nephews. Her husband, Sandy, died in 1989. She lives in Boston.

Fitzwater, Marlin—In my opinion, Marlin is the best press secretary the White House has ever seen. He was and is a valued counselor and friend. I tried to include him on all serious deliberations, and that trust was never compromised. He also earned the universal respect of the tough White House press corps.

Foley, Tom—Although as Speaker of the House Tom opposed me on many of the domestic initiatives we took to Congress and is a tough opponent in many ways, I had great respect for his integrity. I always felt our personal relationship was such that I could talk frankly to him on any and all problems.

Fuller, Craig—Craig was one of the brightest and most effective staffers in the Reagan White House and then became my chief of staff in 1985. He played a key role in the 1988 campaign, then decided to go back into the private sector where he has been very successful.

Gates, Robert—Bob was number two at the NSC until I named him director of Central Intelligence in 1991. Knowledgeable on world affairs and a man of the highest integrity, Bob is now the interim dean of the George Bush School of Government and Public Service at Texas A&M University.

Gregg, Hugh—The former governor of New Hampshire and father of the former governor and the current senator, Judd Gregg, Hugh killed himself for me in 1980 as we crisscrossed the state in his old station wagon. Loyal and dedicated, he was at my side in all my campaigns.

Harlow, Bryce—Trusted friend and adviser to Republicans, Bryce served President Nixon as a speechwriter and a top assistant in the White House. With his great propensity for humor, wisdom, and sound judgment, he had the respect and confidence of all who knew him.

Koch, Dorothy (Doro)—Born August 18, 1959, in Houston, our only daughter is particularly close to her dad. She worked at the National Rehabilitation Hospital in Washington, D.C., before resigning to major in carpooling. She and her husband, Bobby, live in Bethesda, Maryland, where they are raising four children: Sam, fifteen; Ellie, almost thirteen; Robert, six; and Gigi, three, the youngest of fourteen grandchildren.

Lias, Thomas L.—One of the best political operatives I have ever known, Tom was my right-hand man at the Republican National Committee and my executive assistant at the United Nations. He went on to work in both the Ford and Nixon administrations. My loyal friend died in 1988.

Liedtke, J. Hugh—We met Hugh and his brother Bill in Midland and became close friends. Together, with my partner, John Overbey, we started Zapata Petroleum Corp. Years later, after I was out of the oil business, under Hugh's creative and brilliant leadership Zapata eventually became Pennzoil. Hugh resides in Houston.

Mallon, Neil—Yale classmate of my dad's, Neil was an intimate family friend. He founded Dresser Industries and built it into a huge manufacturing company. He gave me my first job after college, as an equipment clerk in one of Dresser's subsidiaries, in Odessa, Texas.

McKenzie, William A. and Sally—Billy Mac (as everyone calls him) and Sally were among my earliest political supporters in Texas. Billy Mac is a former chairman of the Texas A&M University Board of Regents and was instrumental in getting me to locate my presidential library on that wonderful campus.

Michel, Robert—The House minority leader was perhaps my most loyal and dependable supporter in the House. Often under attack by some in his own party, he brought maturity, total integrity, and strong, stable leadership to the House Republicans. He is now retired and enjoying private life.

Moore, Dick—A close friend and adviser, I named Dick ambassador to Ireland, where he served with distinction. He was a close adviser to Richard Nixon but was unscathed by Watergate. He was a wonderful writer with a great sense of humor and contributed to many of my major speeches. He died in 1995.

Mosbacher, Robert—A highly successful businessman, Bob was one of my earliest supporters. His specialty was fund-raising, but his business acumen led me to ask him to serve as secretary of commerce, a post he held with great distinction. He's now back in Houston and is one of my closest friends.

Murphy, Admiral Daniel—Dan, former commander of the Sixth Fleet in the Mediterranean, was one of my two deputies at the CIA. He subsequently became my chief of staff when I was elected Vice President.

Overbey, John—John, a native Texan, became my business partner in 1952 when we formed Bush-Overbey Oil Development Company. He was a knowledgeable land man, and I learned a great deal about the royalty, leasing, and production business from John. Today he lives in Austin, Texas.

Pierce, Marvin—Barbara's father was president and chairman of the board of the McCall Corporation. The family lived in Rye, New York, where Barbara grew up adoring her father. Tragically, Barbara's mother, Pauline, was killed in an auto accident in 1949. Mr. Pierce died in 1969.

Presock, Patty—Patty was a career civil servant who came to work in my vice presidential office, and she ended up being my right-hand person in the Oval Office. She was imaginative, considerate, and had a wonderful sense of values. We called her Miss Perfect.

Rendon, Paula—Paula has lived with us in our house since 1959, coming to us from Mexico. She is more than a housekeeper. She is a trusted friend and a confidante to our four sons and daughter. She lived in the Vice President's house and in the White House, making our life easier every day.

Rhodes, Don—Don first came into our lives in 1964 when he volunteered for my Senate campaign. When I was elected to Congress in 1966, Don went with us to Washington and has been an integral part of our family ever since. He has been my right-hand man for thirty-three years, and I know no man who is more honest or principled.

Rostenkowski, Dan—As a Democratic congressman from Illinois, Dan rose to be chairman of the powerful House Ways and Means Committee. We became friends when I served on that committee from 1967 to 1970. Although he did not vote with me on many issues, we respected each other's views, and we remain good friends.

Roussel, Peter—Son of a prominent Houston newspaper columnist, Pete was at my side in most of my early political battles. He was my press secretary in Congress, at the United Nations, and at the Republican National Committee. He now has his own public relations firm in Houston and still helps me on various projects.

Scowcroft, Brent—When I became President, Brent was my first and only choice to head the NSC. He handled that job with total dedication and skill. One of my closest friends and today my closest adviser on all things, he and I coauthored the book *A World Transformed,* which was published by Knopf in 1998.

Shevardnadze, Eduard—The former foreign minister of the Soviet Union will go down in history as one of the people directly responsible for the peaceful end to the Cold War. He worked closely with Jim Baker and often helped bring Gorbachev along on difficult issues. He is now the President of Georgia.

Siller, Raymond—Ray was the lead joke writer for Johnny Carson for many years, and he would help me with speech material along the way. His one-liners saved the day—or at least the speech—many times. He remains a close friend and is now freelancing and living in New York City.

Simpson, Alan K.—The former senator from Wyoming, whose sense of humor is legendary, became one of my closest friends. As the number two Republican in the Senate, he was a great leader and I depended on him for advice. He is now in Boston and director of Harvard's Institute of Politics.

Skinner, Samuel—Sam was secretary of transportation in my cabinet and then became chief of staff in late 1991. Now living in Chicago, he remains a close friend.

Smith, Aleene—I first met Aleene when I ran for chairman of the Harris County Republican Party in 1963. Aleene was a loyal Republican and savvy in the ways of politics. When I was elected to Congress, Aleene came with me to Washington to be my secretary, then on to New York while I was at the United Nations.

Steel, Jack—Jack was one of the people who encouraged me to get into politics, way back in 1963. When he retired in 1980 from his "day" job, working for the Prudential Insurance Company, he worked for me full-time in Houston, but always as a volunteer. I relied on him always and lost a close friend when he died in 1996.

Steiger, William—Bill was elected to Congress from Wisconsin on the same day I was elected from Texas in 1966. He was exceptionally bright and talented, a leader in our large class. We were close friends, and I felt a great loss when he died in 1978. I named his wife, Janet, chairwoman of the Federal Trade Commission.

Straus, Joci and Joe —When I ran for the Senate in 1964, Joci was one of the earliest Republican workers at my side. She and Joe worked hard in the Republican vineyards way back in the days when the party hardly existed in Texas. True philanthropists, they are among San Antonio's greatest civic leaders.

Sununu, John—The former governor of New Hampshire is one of the brightest men I know, and his all-out support was critical in helping me win the New Hampshire primary in 1988. He was a logical choice to be my White House chief of staff, and he did a first-rate job until he left in late 1991.

Teeter, Robert—Bob, one of the most respected political pollsters in the country, has given me sound advice through many campaigns, and when I was in the White House, he helped me understand public opinion on various issues. He was my campaign chairman in 1992.

Untermeyer, Charles (Chase)—Chase, starting as a volunteer in 1966, has worked for me off and on over the years. When I was elected President, he played a key role in staffing our entire administration as director of presidential personnel. He also was assistant secretary of the navy and director of the Voice of America.

Walker, G. H., Jr. (Herbie)—My mother's oldest brother headed G. H. Walker & Co. of St. Louis and New York. After his father died, Herbie became the Walker family patriarch. His financial support and advice were key to getting me started in the oil business. An original stockholder in the New York Mets, he died in 1977.

Weintraub, Jerry and Jane Morgan—World-class singer Jane Morgan still owns a home in Kennebunkport where she and I became friends as children. She later married our friend Jerry Weintraub, music, movie, and TV producer. They have been great friends and supporters throughout the years.

Zeder, Fred—Fred was one of my earliest political supporters when he lived in Dallas and then later when he moved to Hawaii. He was my ambassador to Micronesia and then head of the government agency Overseas Private Investment Corp. He remains a close friend.

PREFACE

Dear Reader,

When I left office and returned to Texas in January 1993, several friends suggested I write a memoir. "Be sure the historians get it right" seemed to be one common theme. Another: "The press never really understood your heart-beat—you owe it to yourself to help people figure out who you really are."

I was unpersuaded. Barbara, in her best-selling *Barbara Bush: A Memoir,* wrote a wonderful book about our days together both in and out of public life and about our family. Then last year General Brent Scowcroft and I finished our book, *A World Transformed,* which dealt with the many historic changes that took place in the world when we were in the White House.

I felt these two books "got it right" both on perceptions of the Bushes as a family and on how my administration tried to handle the foreign-policy problems we faced.

But then along comes my friend and editor Lisa Drew, who suggested that what was missing is a personal book, a book giving a deeper insight into what my own heartbeat is, what my values are, what has motivated me in life. And then she said something that got me interested: "You already have done such a book. I am talking about a book of letters already written."

But there was a major sticking point. The private life I have returned to is challenging and rewarding and chockablock full of things to do. I have never been busier; nor, might I add, happier. I knew I did not have the time to do the research necessary to find, edit, and then publish the letters—letters that start when I was eighteen years old and go right on up through the present time.

So I turned to my trusted friend Jean Becker, who had helped Barbara with her memoir. We became partners, Jean and I. I told her, I have done my part—I wrote all these letters. Now it's your turn.

Jean spent endless hours contacting people whom I had written, digging through endless boxes of letters now in the archives at the George Bush Presidential Library at Texas A&M University, going through my records from my United Nations and CIA days, listening to pathetic little scratchy tapes I had made for my spotty diary. She dug, and edited. She cajoled and pleaded

21

for letters. She pushed me for my ideas as to what to include, what to leave out. She never gave up. I will never be able to properly express my gratitude to Jean Becker.

So what we have here are letters from the past and present. Letters that are light and hopefully amusing. Letters written when my heart was heavy or full of joy. Serious letters. Nutty letters. Caring and rejoicing letters.

Along the way we expanded our original mission and decided also to include diary entries, mainly to fill in some blank spaces. Please keep in mind, as you read some of these disjointed entries, that I dictated my diaries to a tape recorder. The diary entries are really me thinking out loud.

This book is not meant to be an autobiography. It is not a historical documentation of my life. But hopefully it will let you, the reader, have a look at what's on the mind of an eighteen-year-old kid who goes into the Navy and then at nineteen is flying a torpedo bomber off an aircraft carrier in World War II; what runs through the mind of a person living in China, halfway around the world from friends and family; what a President is thinking when he has to send someone else's son or daughter into combat.

It's all about heartbeat.

It took me fifty-seven years to write this book. If you enjoy reading it even just a tenth as much as I've enjoyed living it, then that is very good indeed.

All the best,

G. Bush

CHAPTER 1

Love and War

When Japan bombed Pearl Harbor on December 7, 1941, I was a seventeen-year-old high school senior at Phillips Academy, Andover. I could hardly wait to get out of school and enlist. Six months later, Secretary of War Henry Stimson delivered our commencement address and advised my class to go to college. He predicted it would be a long war, and there would be plenty of time for us to serve. My dad, Prescott Bush, with whom it was not easy to disagree, hoped I would listen to Secretary Stimson and go on to Yale. After the ceremony, Dad asked me if I had changed my mind. I told him no, I was "joining up." Dad simply nodded his okay. On my eighteenth birthday, June 12, 1942, I enlisted in the Navy's flight training program as a seaman second class.

My mother kept all the letters I wrote to her and Dad during World War II, so most of these come from her collection. You will find only one letter to a Barbara Pierce of Rye, New York. Barbara lost her "love" letters during one of our many moves after we got married.

This first group of letters was written from Chapel Hill, North Carolina, where I was enrolled in Naval Aviation Pre-Flight School. For some reason I did not date these letters, but I was stationed there from August to October of 1942.

———

Dear Mum and Dad,

. . . Today I felt better than I have since I've been here. It was hot but not unbearable. One fellow fainted at drill just to remind us that it was still hot. It is amazing how our moods change here. So many little things affect us. A cold Coke after drill can do more for one than you can imagine. I have never appreciated little things before. Ice cream, movies, a 15 minute rest, a letter, a compliment to our platoon. All these little things amount to so much in your mind and it is fun. Spirits go way up and way down, but when they're up you feel so wonderful . . .

I have gotten to know most of the fellows in the platoon. They are a darn good-hearted bunch . . . There are so many different types here. We have a pretty friendly platoon—also good spirit . . .

On our 5 hr. hike tomorrow my heart'll be with you in the "docks."* So drink a sip of water for me. It is our greatest luxury—a swallow of cold water. I think I'm really going to get a lot out of this place. Already we have learned a lot about people & discipline and tired muscles.

Much love,
Pop†

This is a letter to my sister, Nancy, who was two years my junior. I was one of five children: Prescott (whom we called Pres or Pressy), myself, Nancy, Jonathan, and William (nicknamed Bucky), who was only four years old when I joined the Navy.

Dear Nance,

. . . There is not much "news" here. We live by the day—a wholesome life, at times seemingly futile, but looking at it philosophically I wouldn't change positions with any fellow in civilian life. The Navy itself is great, but what we are here for is even greater, and if at all times I can keep my objective in view I am hopeful of a successful conclusion to this one year course. After having been here just one month my desire to win my wings and become an officer is tremendous. I'm afraid if I fail for any reason my disappointment will be very deep. I am proud to be here, Nance, and as I said before wouldn't change for the world.

. . . I have to write Bobsie‡ now. I miss her more than she knows, Nance. I don't know why but she seems so perfect a girl—beautiful, gentle, a wonderful sense of humor, so much fun etc. I think of her all the time and would love to see her.

Give her my love especially—

Much love to you and write if you get another minute—so long,

Pop

*"Docks" refers to Kennebunkport, Maine, where my mother's side of the family, the Walkers, had spent their summers since 1901, when my grandfather bought the property that would eventually become known as Walker's Point.

†Most of my early letters will be signed "Pop" or "Poppy." My mother's brothers gave me the nickname Poppy when I was born. I was named for their father, my maternal grandfather, George Herbert Walker, whom they called Pop. So they called me Little Pop or Poppy.

‡I don't ever remember calling Barbara "Bobsie," but that's whom I'm talking about here.

Dear Mum and Dad,

. . . The only thing wrong with this place is, they don't realize the average intelligence. They hand out so much crude propaganda here. It is really sickening—Many of the men here realize it—also the intelligent officers. Stuff like "Kill the Japs—hate—murder" and a lot of stuff like "you are the cream of American youth." Some fellows swallow it all. These are the fellows many whom are below average intelligence, 2 of my roommates, for example, get a big kick out of hearing it. Maybe it is good. All the well educated fellows know what they are fighting for—why they are here and don't need to be "brainwashed" into anything . . .

> Much love,
> Pop

Dear Mum,

Well the war strikes home, as it were, doesn't it—c.c. with the very sad news of George Mead.* I didn't know him very well, but from all sides all you could hear was praise. He died the way all of us would like to die when our time comes—Mum, it's a very funny thing. I have no fear of death now. Maybe it's because I am here safely on the ground that I say this. I do not think I will change. All heroics aside, I feel, and every fellow here I'm sure feels, that the only part of the whole thing of any worry would be the sorrow it might cause to our families. I cannot express myself as clearly as I see it in my own mind. Once in the air death may strike at any time, but I shall not fear it. Perhaps with this fleet it will be different—God grant it won't! . . .

> Much, much love,
> Pop

Dear Mum,

Well today sure was wonderful.

. . . I met Barbara at the Inn at 12. She took a cab over from Raleigh. She looked too cute for words—really beautiful. We had a sandwich in town and then walked. I showed her the plant and then we walked over to Keenan Stadium. When we started it was clear, but once there it poured—just buckets. We got some protection from the canvas covered press box, but couldn't leave

---

*George Mead was a Marine, killed in combat. His sister, Louise, married my mother's brother Dr. John Walker.

there. . . . Not thrilling but such fun just seeing her. We laughed at everything. I had formation at six so we went back to the Inn. She took a bus for
Raleigh where she is staying overnight with a girl from school. She was so
swell to come way over here. I sure am glad you said "grand idea" to Mrs.
Pierce.* . . .

                                        Much love to all,
                                        Pop

———————

*This next group of letters were written from Wold-Chamberlain Naval Air Sta-
tion, Minneapolis, where I was based from November 1942 to February 1943. It
was here that I finally began to learn how to fly.*

Dear Mum,

Well today was the big day—in fact one of the biggest thrills of my life, I
imagine. We marched down to the #1 hanger and they read out the names for
the first hop. I was in. I went down, got my gear, and then consulted the
board. Plane P-18 1st hop—2nd hop Plane P-18 check pilot Boyle. I immediately went around trying to find out what kind of a check Boyle is. All I got
was "pretty tough". This was quite disheartening. I then went out and
warmed up the ship waiting for Ens. Crume (CRUME pronounced croom)†
to arrive. . . . The fog was pretty thick but they let us go up. Crume came and
we were off. I did it all myself and everything went O.K. However, I was so
nervous, that in the beginning my legs were shivering around. Once in the air
I was completely cool much to my surprise. We did some emergencies and
landings and then came in. I gave him one poor landing so I wasn't sure about
my "up", but when we got out he told me "O.K." Then for the real check.
Ens. Boyle came out. Once in the plane we didn't say a word. I taxied out,
revved up the engine, locked the tailwheel, adjusted my goggles & seat,
checked the instruments & the tower, swung into the wind and we were off.
For about one turn of the field I was pretty nervous. First he signaled (would-
n't talk) to make 2 landings (When I speak of landings I mean "touch and go"
except for this final one before the plane stops rolling, gun her and take off
again.) The first landing was swell—the 2nd rather rough. We then dove into
the fog and went off and did 2 1,000-foot emergencies. (That is he cuts the

———————

*At the time, Barbara was a high school student at Ashley Hall, a boarding school in
Charleston, South Carolina. Mum had helped convince Barbara's mother, Mrs. Marvin Pierce,
that it would be fine for Barbara to come visit me in Chapel Hill.

†Ensign James Charles Crume Jr. was my primary flight instructor. Ensign J. A. Boyle was
another instructor I occasionally flew with.

gas, and I have to establish a glide, get going into the wind to land on a field which I select—we don't actually land, just go down to about 75 feet) Once I picked out a good field but the other time I'm afraid it'd have been a pretty rough procedure if I had had to land. He then indicated to head back to the field—For a minute I was lost—couldn't see the field through the mist, but luckily I located it. I did 2 more landings and taxied in. My nervousness, which had subsided after the first takeoff, came on again. As he climbed out I looked for the verdict. "Did you get an up from your instructor," he said. "O.K.—then take it up yourself," and off he walked. There I was alone in the plane: I gave the "thumbs up" to the plane captain, he removed the chocks and I was off. I wasn't shaky on the controls, and was completely confident for some reason. I had to taxi way down between rows of army bombers to get to my take off point. My solo was just "2 landings"—that's your first solo assignment. Off I zoomed—climbed to 300 ft at 65 knots; level off—pass under the traffic circle. Nobody was there saying all this, this time yet I did it—The needle seemed to stay right at 500—whereas with the instructors I'd drop or gain. Everything seemed so free and easy and really wonderful. My landings weren't good—I bounced and didn't cut quite soon enough, but I didn't worry as I have before. This was the thing that made it so much fun. I turned back in and it was over—just as quickly as it had come. I felt good though—Mum, It was the first time I have climbed out of the plane without worrying or having a touch of discouragement. Yes, tonight I am very happy.

When we leave here we want to specify the type of flying we want to do. I have been considering the Marines (I'd be commissioned 2nd Lt. instead of Ensign) The reason is they fly a lot in attack bombers—fly low and strafe as well as bomb. They clear the way for advancing troops. This or long range bombing appeals to me more than anything else, and from all I can gather, the Marines do more of it than the Navy. I have 2 months before I choose anyway, and besides you don't always get your choice. I'll let you know what I decide as soon as I know more about flying and find out what I'd be best in . . .

Well, Mum, I better go back and get some sleep—Much love to all,

Pop

———————

Dear Mum,

. . . Thanksgiving comes tomorrow. I guess that I will hardly notice it here—that is outwardly as we can't leave the base and just get 1 hr. off, but it won't just be a regular day Mum. We all do have something to be thankful for, even though the days are darker than when we could all be together. I guess I'm the most thanks-giving fellow here, because even though I'm a couple of thousand miles off I'm lucky, Mum—Lucky for you and Dad and all the family and so many other things. I thought when I was away at school I understood it all, but being away in the Navy for this long and with so many different types of fellows has made me see more clearly still how much I do have to be thankful for. . . .

> Much love, Mum dear
> Pop

Dear Mum,

Gosh it was wonderful hearing your voice today—It was swell of you to call. I got the message just after I came back from church. . . .

It was interesting to see a lot of these fellows, today. Some tough ones, some common, other grand fellows. We all are up to our beds for a few minutes after church, and most of the fellows were quiet—thinking of other Thanksgiving days. For many it was the first time away and it was a bit strange. It will always be strange to me, to be away on a day like this, at least until I have my own home. It's days like this that makes me anxious to be out fighting—though I know I can never become a killer, I will never feel right until I have actually fought. Being physically able and young enough I belong out at the front and the sooner there, the better. The job seems so tremendous, yet it must end and when it does and we have won perhaps days like this will once again be symbolic of happiness and freedom and the ironic note added by a brutal war will be far removed. . . .

> Much love,
> Pop

Dear Dad and Mum,

. . . Yesterday a friend of mine cracked up. His motor cut on him and all landing sites were poor. He managed to get it fairly well down but then he nosed over, flipped onto his back, and was hanging by his safety belt—about 1 ft. from the ground (his head). The tail was wiped right off the plane. Luckily he unhooked his belt and could slip out O.K. Poor Ed. He hasn't been doing too well anyway and this may be just what he doesn't need. The motors are apt to cut on cold days—Once I started looking for a field but the thing got going O.K. again . . .

Barbara knitted me a pair of socks which she claims don't look at all like socks but she's sending them anyway. Maybe I can make a neck protector out of 'em if they are too big. . . .

> Much love,
> Pop

Dear Mum and Dad,

Well my first Xmas away is over and gone, but I don't believe I'll ever forget it. I missed you all very much, yet I wasn't homesick. Your lovely presents are wonderful. I've got the bracelet on and it'll never be taken off permanently until I'm back for good.* It's beautiful, Mum, and it means an awful lot to me. The goggles I wore today and they are wonderful. I'm surprised you could get such grand ones. They are just what I needed—good protection by that rubber and it holds my face mask firmly in place and also they don't hurt across the nose. The bathrobe is swell, too. Thank you so much—oh yes, the stocking too—I only hope that we'll never think we're too old for them . . .

. . . My Xmas take was good. $25 from Gampy, and numerous socks and the like. Got a big box of food from the Pierces and Barbara is sending me soon what I asked for; namely a decent picture of her . . .

As always,
Pop

Occasionally in my letters home I would include diagrams to illustrate what I was learning. This is a typical example:

Dear Mum,

Well the sky is clear today and it looks like I'll get my hop in . . .

My inverted spins were really pretty good fun. You are really thrown outward with terrific force and if it weren't for the belt you'd fly through space. I also had immelman's and falling leaf.† An immelman's starts off like a loop. Dive to pick up your 125 knots, pull back to upside down—now here's the difference—instead of coming on around you do a slow roll from the upside down position and fly on out:

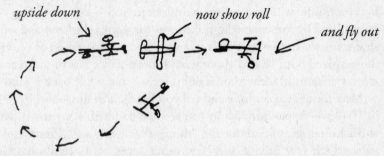

upside down   *now show roll*   *and fly out*

*Today the bracelet is on display at my presidential library.
†Terms used to describe two special maneuvers.

They are about the hardest but are also good fun. . . .

                                                    Pop

———————

Please keep in mind as you read this letter that I was a very innocent eighteen-year-old, and it was 1942. Things were very different way back then. Having said that, I do not think it would be a bad thing if more eighteen-year-olds today were just as innocent. As to the reference to my sister, Nancy, I suspect Mum had caught her kissing a beau.

Dearest Mum,

Now about your question, Mum. I do love to kid you and did this summer but I agree with you in part. I would <u>hate</u> to have Nancy a necker at heart. Nothing could be worse. Kissing is <u>not</u> an <u>obligation</u> a girl <u>owes</u> a boy regardless of how often he takes her out or how much money he spends . . . <u>but</u> I don't think that it is entirely wrong for a girl to be kissed by a boy. Let us take this famous case Pierce vs. Bush summer '42. I kissed Barbara and am glad of it. I don't believe she will ever regret it or resent it, and I certainly am not ashamed of it. I'd tell you, Mrs. Pierce, or anybody but at the same time I might as well tell you I have never felt towards another girl as I do towards her. Whether the feeling is mutual I cannot say. To get back to my example, however, if Barbara sort of forgets me, which is not unlikely, as I have no chance to see her at all, I don't believe she will ever dislike me more for having kissed her. She knows how I felt towards her and she must have shared some of the same feeling or she would not have allowed me to kiss her. I have never kissed another girl—this making myself just as much of an oddity as Nancy, since most of the boys do not stop with kissing—(how terribly true that is here, more than home, but then again most of these fellows are grown men—also men with different background.) It's not because I have honestly disapproved of it, however. If I said it were I would be lying. In conclusion a Mrs. Simmons kiss, both sides willing, I believe harmless; to neck—entirely wrong—for a girl to be kissed by someone whom she loves (or <u>thinks</u> she love) and who—she is sure cares for her—O.K. This is a very uncoordinated piece of writing and unorganized but I've said about what I mean. For a kiss to mean engagement is a very beautiful idea, Mama, but it went out a while back I guess.

Now for me to continue and tell you the facts of life—of the life I'm living in 1940's— Apparently Mum you seemed so terribly surprised when Pressy and I hinted around about the "things that went on?" Pressy and I share a view which few others, <u>very few</u> others even in Greenwich share. That's regarding intercourse before marriage. I would hate to find that my wife had known some other man, and it seems to me only fair to her that she be able to expect the same standards from me. Pres agrees as I said before, but not many others our age will. Daddy has never discussed such things with us—of this I am very glad. But we have learned as the years went on by his character what is right and what is wrong. Most fellows here—true some are engaged and some believe as I do—but most fellows take sex as much they can get. This town in particular seems full of girls (working in offices etc.) rather attractive girls at that, who after a couple of drinks would just as soon go to bed with some cadet. They are partly uniform conscious I suppose, but the thing is they, as well as the cadet, have been brought up differently. They believe in satisfying any sexual urge by contact with men. They all say "I'm not that type of girl, but all-right—just for you!" Every single girl says this. These girls are not prostitutes, but just girls without any morals at all. Somehow it does seem a little worse for girls to me, I suppose it shouldn't but it does. Leading the life we lead one cannot help but feel the desire for a woman. I would be most facetious were I to deny ever having experienced said feelings. The difference is entirely in what we have been taught; not only in "what" but in "how well" we have been taught it.

This pertains not only to the N.A.S. [Naval Air Station] Minneapolis, Minn., but to every town in the country, to college campuses—yes, even to Yale University. Boys you know—boys I like very much—and even boys I admire have had intercourse with women. . . .

Some guys, you know one perfect example in New Haven, because they love a girl believe in relationships before marriage. This seems to me more excusable than just plain sex—sex to satisfy physical biological emotions— yet I know it is not right.

Most of this you have probably known, but this is how I feel. I hope that this letter does not seem presumptuous. To think all this was brought on by your asking me what I thought about kissing.

> Much love,
> Pop
> professor "sexology" Ph.D.

───────

Dear Mum,

Last night I really had quite a scare in night flying. I finished all my night flying last night. I just had one solo yesterday. The wind was almost from south—a little southwest, but they had the runway laid out west. This meant we were landing somewhat crosswind to start with—an undesirable setup. Furthermore they had the runway much narrower than usual. It was like landing on a pin. All the instructors were griping about how narrow the runway was. You see with the crosswind there was considerable drift. In other words you'd have your plane pointing one way, and you'd be making true a different course over the ground. It was quite tough, but I surprised myself and really made some nice landings (Night flying is much easier alone as you can see all the signals more clearly and command a better view of the runway.) Well, I was coming in for my last landing. I got all "squared away" and even got a green light from the truck. Suddenly I heard this scraping noise—I had hit a tree—Well you can imagine my feelings. I didn't know whether the next second I'd hit one with my prop instead of my wheels. I gave full throttle and climbed up—flew across the field and came in again. It turned out later that two instructors also hit this tree. The runway was too close to the woods on the east side of the field. I just thanked my lucky stars I wasn't 2 or 3 feet lower or I'd have hit the prop and then, well I don't really know. It's a funny thing— you don't ever get scared till afterwards. Same with a dangerous landing or something. . . .

> So long for now, Mum
> Much much love,
> Pop

———————

Dear Mum,

Yesterday was one of the—if not <u>the</u>—most unpleasant days of my life— at least 1¼ hours of it. I had my "D" check with Ensign Warren. He was very nice on the ground, but no sooner did we get in the plane than he started yelling. In no time in my life have I ever felt so uncomfortable. According to him I just couldn't do a thing right. Frankly, before my check I was confident but once in that plane I was lost. Taxing, climbing—even on fundamentals like that—he bellowed. I was so flustered I couldn't think. (How I pity guys with instructors like that) Well we got on the ground and I was beat. But after it was over he gave me a very weak "up" nevertheless it's an "up." It was an experience I'll probably have to undergo again. But I sure hope not. That must be the philosophy of some pilots to make you fly under tough condi-tions. The fact remains however, that I got an up. . . .

. . . The realization came upon me yesterday that I'm ⅔ on the way to my commission and wings almost. It is a wonderful feeling and I just hope that in 3 months more I'll actually get through . . .

> Much love to all,
> Pop

———————

This next series of letters were written from the U.S. Naval Air Station in Corpus Christi, Texas, where I was stationed from February to June 1943.

Dear Mum,

    . . . Today I went to church here. There were only about 12 cadets and 8 others there but it was very nice. The Chaplain was an awfully young fellow with a most appealing nature. It was held in ground school. I was very poor about churching in Mpls. . . .

    I got a letter from F. Von Stade.* He was on a 14 day furlough at Aiken [S.C.] recovering from pneumonia—what a break. Anyway he called up Barbara . . . He claims Barbara said she was glad I was in Texas where the girls are lousy so maybe I still am in. I sure so hope so. If she "fluffed me off" without warning I would be absolutely sick no kidding. Every day practically guys are getting "fluffed off" from girls they've left. . . . All the time it happens. You know Mum it's funny being thrown in with a bunch of guys so much older— They don't seem older, but here they are, all thinking and talking about getting married etc. Everyone asks me, after looking at Barbara's picture, when I'm going to marry her. Good heaven's! To think that last year at this time I was thinking along lines of prep school proms and stuff seems unbelievable. That's the hard part. Being around guys averaging 22 about it's only natural to think as they do on general things, and yet my 18 years keep coming up. I wish I were 20 or 21. It's not that I feel younger or anything, but I just wish I were. The fellows whose lives may be better for this thing are those who graduated last fall or Xmas from college. They have a degree and can probably get a decent job after the war and still will profit from having had military experience. Say the war ends in 2 years and I go to college. I'll feel like the old man . . . all my friends'll be through. That'll all straighten out though, and if you think I'd change with any of those fellows at Yale, you're sadly mistaken. I still would like to be 21—have a million dollars, and a beautiful wife. I can remember how I once said I wasn't going to get married.

    . . . I do still <u>love</u> (I honestly feel sure of it) Barbara, Mum, yet I know that there is such a chance of her meeting some other guy. She is so very young and so darn attractive and I could hardly expect her to keep caring about me for years. ENOUGH OF THIS!!!!!!!! You both must think I'm crazy! . . .

Much love,
Pop

Dear Mum and Dad,

    Today was the big day and after a great deal of confusion it seems that your loving son is a torpedo bomber selectee. Yes I got my first choice and tomorrow morning, unless some unforeseen circumstances arise, I pack my belong-

*Fred Von Stade, a family friend and uncle to the opera singer Frederica Von Stade.

ings and move out to nearby (3 miles) Waldron Field, new home of the Torpedo squadron. I really am delighted with my lot and provided all goes well I should be home with you all in <u>less</u> than 6 weeks.

. . . John Buckby, one of my roommates now, 19 years old (the only other fellow I've met that young) is going to get married when he graduates. Naturally we all talk about these things, and he is convinced that he should—however, he has no money aside from the $250 he'll be making and then his future is a bit of a "?" I don't quite see how these guys get married when they know that they have no means of support and probably will be out of this country in a short time. . . .

Much love,
Pop

Dear Mum,

. . . Barbara knit me another pair of socks. The last ones, except for the shape, were really swell. These, she says, are too heavy and miles too big. At the last minute she always gets embarrassed and won't send them until I persuade her.

. . . Mum, I don't know why, but I can hardly believe that I'll be an officer soon. It just is something I've really wanted and now that it looks like I'm going to get it, I find it hard to believe. From what I can gather I will be the youngest flying officer (maybe officers) in the Navy. I'm not proud of being young—but it's a fact so I've been told. The youngest in the Army is 19. . . .

Much much love,
Pop

Mum, De-ah,

. . . Mum, I'm really worried. I hope it's one of her lapses which she falls in occasionally either because she's busy or just to keep me anxious and interested; but I haven't gotten but 1 letter in 3½ weeks. Before there were a couple of 2 week famines but never this. I don't know, hope it's not the "fluff." Being away from <u>all</u> nice girls I worry more than usual over Barb. It's silly but that's how its been. As I've said before Barb is really a smart girl in that she can be sweet and all that without committing herself to any great degree—Oh well, not much I can do now. . . .

Much love,
Pop

I received my wings on June 9, 1943, in Corpus Christi, three days before my nine-teenth birthday. After a short leave at home, I reported to the U.S. naval air station in Fort Lauderdale, Florida, where I would learn how to fly torpedo bombers.

Dear Mum,

First of all and mainly is the matter of a glorious 5 days. Never in the world could any son ever have been given such a welcome. You and Dad just did too much for me. Not much else I can say about it, except that those short 5 days have made all my time away from home seem worthwhile. Trite though it may be, it's a short stay with those you love which re-clarifies in one's mind exactly what you're fighting for. From now on it will be no picnic. Two months here (no more). A week or so at Chicago and then as quickly as one squadron can form at either San Diego or Norfolk or Oklahoma, we head overseas. That takes perhaps a week, perhaps 2 months, depending on the men available. Being here and seeing these monstrous ships in their battle paint brings home the point that it won't be long now. I cannot wait—not because of the glamour or of the thrills—for heaven's knows I love my home like few others—but because it is my job, clearly defined and it must be done. . . .

One last thing, sweet Mama! The way you and Dad both were so wonderful about Barbara probably meant more to me than anything. After all you hadn't seen me in ages and yet you didn't object to my running off. I needn't bother to tell you how much Barbara means to me—pretty evident I guess—knowing this you must know how happy you made me by being so marvelous about having her up etc.

Goodnight and much, much love,

Pop

———————

Dear Mum and Dad,

. . . I saw a Henry Aldrich movie here at the base tonight. Also heard Fred* & am now back listening to Marian Anderson. I have used this radio almost incessantly. . . .

I sent Barbara an alligator; he ate Mrs. Pierce's frog in her pool, and finally beat an escape into the woods. If you would like a 'gator' at home—give me the word and he's as good as yours.

Much love,
Pop

———————

*Fred Waring, a music maestro and glee club leader, who was a friend of my father's.

I finished my training in Fort Lauderdale in August 1943 and then headed for the huge naval base in Norfolk, Virginia. For the next few months, as I entered my final stage of training, I bounced around quite a bit—to the naval air station at Chincoteague, Virginia; back to Norfolk; up to Hyannis, Massachusetts; to Charlestown, Rhode Island; then back to Norfolk. During this period my squadron was formed, VT-51. (For some reason, I also started dating my letters about this time.)

Monday, Nov. 1

Dear Dad,

I've thought this over and I wasn't quite sure whether I should write or not, but I wanted to tell someone about it, and I think it wiser to tell you, cause Mum might do some unnecessary worrying. I hope you won't worry about me after hearing it. I wanted to tell you all about it though.

Today on my last flight I was coming in for my final landing when I hit a vicious slipstream from 2 recently landed TBF's.* I was ready to land but I shoved on full throttle to go around again—by that time, however, the slipstream had one wing down on the runway. I swerved to that (the left side) going off the runway. As I went off—my wheels hit and one gave way—This sent me careening sort of half sideway on one wing and the belly over the ground. Everything happened so quickly that I can't exactly remember it all. The prop hit and stopped. I was scared we'd tip over, but luckily we didn't. As soon as she stopped—I snapped off the switch, gas, and battery and leapt out and to the stern. My crewmen were scurrying out as I opened the back door. Luckily none of the 3 of us was injured at all. The plane is a <u>total</u> loss. Both wings smashed, fuselage slightly buckled etc.-etc. It gave me quite a feeling. While careening speedily and recklessly across the runway a feeling of helplessness <u>not</u> fear seized me. Then there flashed thru my mind the question "will we go over?"—then she stopped and I leapt. Funny I never really was scared. After it was over I had that excited feeling in the pit of my stomach. We were terribly lucky that the ship didn't burn.

The skipper was very understanding & nice about the whole thing. Nothing will happen to me, I'll just sign a report. It really was something—one of the things that make flying dangerous is the slipstream, and I really got hit bad.

I feel perfectly now and am anxious to get back in the air tomorrow, so don't give it another thought. I just wanted to let you know about it.

---

*This was the plane I ultimately flew into combat. Called the Avenger, *TB* stood for "Torpedo bomber," and the *F* was the symbol for the manufacturer, Grumman. (The plane was later built by General Motors and designated TBM.) It was huge; the largest single-engine plane in the Navy.

It was really great seeing you all again this weekend, and I'm now looking forward to the next one—

Ever devotedly,
Pop

———————

Dear Mum,

. . . Now, Mum, I may have quite a secret to tell you in a few days—are you wiser at all? Maybe you can guess—maybe not.

It was such fun seeing you, Mum. It really wasn't for long—I feel badly about it after; came home and then see you so little. Must be love Mum—No longer am I confused though—I'm just so convinced that Barbara is <u>the</u> girl for me. The only thing that bothers me is the future. I feel certain that right now I could hold down a job as well as men with an educational advantage over me. I have associated for the most part with college fellows since I've been in the Navy and in my own heart I know I could do a job as well—The question is <u>what</u>—I wouldn't want to fly all my life for a living—any job where I could make enough money to have the few basic things I desire would be most welcome. I often think and worry about it—I now know exactly what I want. No college, I'll have to do without, just a job anywhere with a fairly decent salary. The war will probably last at least 2 years more so my problem is not as imminent as it might be, but it worries me a little. Why this outburst I don't know—anyway lots of people will need a good butler when this is over. . . .

Ever lovingly,
Pop

———————

This letter was written after I had been home on leave, during which I told my mother that Barbara and I were "secretly" engaged.

Dear Mum,

. . . I'm glad I told you all about Bar & me. You probably knew already; but do tell Dad! I found two letters from Barbara here today. I think she has told her family. She said she was going to and she told me to tell <u>all</u> my family— Poor child doesn't quite know what "<u>all</u>" means in this case I'm afraid. I do think I'll write Ganny & Flash* sometime soon about it. I don't quite know how to go about it all. As things stand now I'll probably wait about a year to

———

*Ganny was my maternal grandmother, Loulie Wear Walker. Flash was her daughter, my mother's sister, Nancy Walker.

announce it, but things do so change—I think Barbara is partial to the present—I'll have to see her soon again and talk it all over. She agreed to my suggestion of waiting till after the fleet, but I can't be sure her heart feels that way until I see her. As for me, the present would be fine, but somehow the other seems wiser . . .

Incidentally if you see any shiny rocks on our driveway collect them—Seriously though, Mum just for interests sake what does a fairly decent looking ring cost? . . .

Much love,
Pop

———

As I mentioned at the beginning of this chapter, Barbara lost all my letters to her during the war—except for this one, which she kept in her engagement scrapbook.

Dec. 12, 1943

My darling Bar,

This should be a very easy letter to write—words should come easily and in short it should be simple for me to tell you how desperately happy I was to open the paper and see the announcement of our engagement, but somehow I can't possibly say all in a letter I should like to.

I love you, precious, with all my heart and to know that you love me means my life. How often I have thought about the immeasurable joy that will be ours some day. How lucky our children will be to have a mother like you—

As the days go by the time of our departure draws nearer. For a long time I had anxiously looked forward to the day when we would go aboard and set to sea. It seemed that obtaining that goal would be all I could desire for some time, but, Bar, you have changed all that. I cannot say that I do not want to go—for that would be a lie. We have been working for a long time with a single purpose in mind, to be so equipped that we could meet and defeat our enemy. I do want to go because it is my part, but now leaving presents itself not as an adventure but as a job which I hope will be over before long. Even now, with a good while between us and the sea, I am thinking of getting back. This may sound melodramatic, but if it does it is only my inadequacy to say what I mean. Bar, you have made my life full of everything I could ever dream of—my complete happiness should be a token of my love for you.

Wednesday is definitely the commissioning and I do hope you'll be there. I'll call Mum tomorrow about my plan. A lot of fellows put down their parents or wives and they aren't going so you could pass as a Mrs.—Just say you lost the invite and give your name. They'll check the list and you'll be in. How proud I'll be if you can come.*

I'll tell you all about the latest flying developments later. We have so much to do and so little time to do it in. It is frightening at times. The seriousness of this thing is beginning to strike home. I have been made asst. gunnery officer and when Lt. Houle leaves I will be gunnery officer. I'm afraid I know very little about it but I am excited at having such a job. I'll tell you all about this later too.

The wind of late has been blowing like mad and our flying has been cut to a minimum. My plane, #2 now, is up at Quonset, having a camera installed.† It is Bar #2 but purely in spirit since the Atlantic fleet won't let us have names on our planes.

Goodnite, my beautiful. Everytime I say beautiful you about kill me but you'll have to accept it—

I hope I get Thursday off—there's still a chance. All my love darling—

Poppy
public fiancé as of 12/12/43

———

December 29

Dear Mum,

. . . I changed my allotment check, so starting either at the end of January or the end of February the check for 143 dollars will come to you every month. The reason for this is because if I left it made out to the bank and I should become lost the payments would immediately be stopped. If it is made out to you and I am lost the checks will continue to come in until it is definitely established that I am safely in heaven. . . .

all love
[not signed]

———

Jan. 11

Dear Mum,

. . . I miss Bar something terrific but I suppose it's only natural. It's really agony—so close and yet so far away. I think of her every minute and know that

---

*I was referring to the commissioning of the USS *San Jacinto* (CVL 30), the ship to which my squadron was assigned, which took place on December 15, 1943, at the Philadelphia Naval Yard. Mom and Barbara did attend.

†I was having a camera installed on my plane because I was training to become VT-51's aerial photographer.

I will be completely happy only when I am with her again. I will be so pleased when she is mine for keeps. When that will be it is hard to guess. I certainly hope we can get married before she finishes Smith. As far as her wanting to, that's settled. We both want to be married, but it's so clear to see that our wants are not the determining factor in this case. What do you both think I should have to offer Bar before we can get married? She does not expect us to have a thing, but I wonder if it would be fair to her to get married with what I have saved, say in a year after I get back I will have well over $2,000 by then.

Perhaps I'd be sent back out again a few months after we were married. There are so many considerations. The one thing I really want is to have Barbara for my wife and naturally I want that as soon as possible. . . . I have talked to Bar a good deal about it and we both want to get married when I come back from the fleet next year. Please tell me what you think. Mr. Pierce would like Barbara to finish Smith, but I don't think he'd disapprove of our getting married next year—I don't know for sure. Mrs. Pierce probably would hate to lose her daughter but she does want her to be happy so that's the way that stands. Perhaps I should have a talk with Mr. P after shakedown.*

Much love to all,

Pop

———

Jan. 25

Dear Mum,

Yesterday we went and landed aboard the San [*Jac*] for the first time . . . We, the TBF's, landed first. The ship looked really swell steaming along in her battle camouflage. We made a few practice passes down wind and then she swung around into the wind and we came aboard. She was moving at a good clip and the air was nice and smooth, facilitating landings. We each made 3 landings and then cut our motors on the deck. We taxied into position before cutting the motors. On Carriers it is necessary to utilize every inch of deck space. The result is that the line-men taxi you right up to the very edge of the deck. They put me right on the starboard bow and I thought I was going to fall over any minute. With the water rushing by over the side etc. it is quite scary. This putting the planes where they want them is called spotting and it's very important. The loudspeakers announced that the pilots had 7 minutes so then 3 of us went below for coffee. Everyone aboard welcomed us and was swell to us. These are the first landings a lot of the crew had seen so they were quite excited. Soon the loudspeaker boomed and we manned our planes,

*Every new ship takes what is called a shakedown cruise to break in the new crew and make sure all systems are go.

started the engines etc. We were catapulted off. In fact I made the first catapult shot ever made from the USS San Jacinto—I was mighty glad the machine worked. I think I'd rather be catapulted than make a full deck take off. . . .

Pop

———————

After a two-week shakedown cruise to Trinidad, British West Indies, the San Jac *set sail March 25, 1944, heading for San Diego first, then to the South Pacific. The next group of letters was written from the ship.*

Wed. April 12, 1944

Dear Mum and Dad,

. . . I wish I could tell you where we are, what we're doing etc. I can't of course mainly because we aren't allowed to, secondly because I really can't be sure I know.

I finished the 4 books you gave me Mum and loved them all. I'm going to pick up a couple of more. I am trying to read a few on Russia, because I have become pretty much interested in that end of our diplomatic relations. Then, too, I know so little about it all that a couple of books wouldn't hurt anyway. . . .

Well, so long for now and much, much love to all,

Pop

———————

April 27, 1944

Dearest Mum and Dad,

I haven't written for several days but still there is little to write about—at least little which I am allowed to write. I wish I could tell all because it is interesting and will be plenty exciting no doubt.

Have piled up quite a few hours lately and have boosted my total landings aboard up to about 47. One of them (my second to last to be exact) really was a scary devil. I came in high and a little fast—I got the cut & nosed once but not enough—I then hauled back and made a real hard landing, blowing out my right tire and stopping precariously near the catwalk. How I hate to make a terrible landing—I get to worrying about it and also it's not good for the crewmen. Everyday someone at least gets a tire or 2; so it's not serious, but I don't like it.

. . . From now on it's going to be plenty rugged duty—in a way I'm glad, cause I probably need the experience—maybe you should have been a little bit mean so I would relish the thought of killing etc. When my time is up all I ask for is to get married and be able to be with my wife for some sort of a decent amount of time. How I miss my Barbara—It's such fun at nite after the hectic turmoil of carrier flight operations is over to lie in my upper and let my mind relax, think of you both, all at home, and of Bar—our wedding.

> Much love,
> Pop

May 24, 1944

Dear Mum and Dad,

. . . I can say that I have been in battle against the enemy. It is quite a feeling, Mum to be shot at I assure you. The nervousness which is with you before a game of some kind, was extremely noticeable but no great fear thank heavens. I wish I could tell you more about it. Probably will be able to later. Must stop now—

> Much much love,
> Pop

May 26, 1944

Dear Mum and Dad,

Here is some distressing news which I hate to report. Jim Wykes is officially missing. It has affected those of us who knew him very deeply as he was a fellow whom everyone liked. I personally, have far from given up hope, and as I write this can't help but feel that he will turn up. He may fall into enemy hands, but at least he'll still have his life. All we can do is hope. His family has been notified, so it's O.K. to mention it now. He disappeared on a search mission—good men [his crew], one of whom had just become a father shortly before leaving the states. News like this is unpleasant, but I guess I'll just have to learn to take it. Jim was my closest friend on the ship—a fellow whom I was very fond of. There is a definite hope—perhaps he will even turn up soon.

Well, I must stop for now and get up on security watch. With much love to all the family I am—

> Devotedly yours,
> Pop

June 4, 1944

My Dear Mrs. Wykes,

For the past year your son, Jim, and I have been very close friends. We have been together at all our various stations, joined the squadron together, and have roomed together for a year now, even aboard this ship. I know your son well and have long considered myself fortunate to be one of his intimate friends. His kindly nature and all around goodness have won for him the friendship and respect of every officer and enlisted man in the squadron.

I realize that the news of his being missing has undoubtedly brought into your home a good deal of grief and sorrow—but however difficult it may be, you must never give up hope. All of us out here firmly believe that there is an excellent chance that Jim and his 2 crewmen are still alive. I am not saying this merely to console you, for I would not want to give you false hope. You have lost a loving son, we have lost a beloved friend; so let us be brave—let us keep faith and hope in our hearts and may our prayers be answered.

God bless you and your family
Sincerely yours,
George Bush

June 10th

Dear Mum and Dad,

I suppose this is the first letter you've received from me in a long time, but in my last I told you it would be a while between so I hope you haven't worried at all.

. . . We have received flashes on the invasion of Europe and eagerly await any further news. Every day our ship puts out a sort of newspaper. The news in it is gathered for the most part from aboard ship, but there are a few short wave radioed messages. I am eager to receive your letters telling about how the news was received at home, but I will have to wait a while more for any letters I'm afraid.

. . . As much as I hate to admit it, and though I'd never tell Bar for fear she'd misconstrue what I said, I really think we did the right thing in not getting married. A couple of fellows' wives in our outfit are having babies now. The guys worry a lot and I imagine it must be hell on the poor girls. No it wouldn't have been fair to Bar to have gotten married. When I return I certainly hope we can, however. I will have saved $3000 by next fall. I have learned a good deal out here—lots that's not practical by a long shot, but it all goes to making a man out of one. As far as elapsed time making a difference in my feeling toward Bar I was sure when I left I'd never change, and now as each day passes I am never more sure. . . .

Your ever devoted son,
Pop

June 22, 1944

Dear Mum and Dad,

Things have been happening so fast that I have forgotten when I wrote you last. 3 days ago I had to make a forced landing in the water.* It was my first water landing and when my engine acted up I was a bit nervous. It went off o.k. however. All three of us got out safely and into our raft. We were rescued by a destroyer. I'm afraid I can tell you no more details than that.

As I write this I have not gotten back to my own ship. Yesterday I was transferred from the destroyer by "breeches buoy"† to this ship. When I will get back I do not know. I am getting a rest here so I don't care too much, though I would rather be back with my own squadron.

The transfer on the breeches buoy was quite a thrill. I really enjoyed my stay aboard the destroyer. They all treated me and my crewmen like kings. I slept a good deal read a lot and generally enjoyed myself. When they picked us out of the water the Doc administered us some brandy. The crewmen were always surrounded by an attentive group of listeners and they would have liked to stay there. . . .

Some of the experiences that fellows out here have had lately would really amaze you. The "braid"‡ will go thru almost anything to rescue pilots and crews, and believe me, it's a real comforting feeling. Well that's about all for now—with much love to all—

Pop

———————

Mon. June 26th

Dear Mum and Dad,

Once more back aboard my own ship and really glad to be back. Before actually getting back I was transferred from 3 different ships, 2 destroyers and one carrier. (I am assuming you got my letter telling you about my crash landing in the water.) It was certainly nice to get the clean clothes back on and get in my own sack. Two new pilots joined our squadron and came aboard with me. By then I was an old hand at being transferred by breeches buoy.

The high point of my return was 4 letters—2 Bar, 1 Mum, 1 Aunt Nance . . .

Bar's two letters (and yours of course) were a Godsend. I miss her so des-

---

*Our ship was about to come under attack from Japanese planes, so we hastily launched all our planes. Mine developed engine problems with four five-hundred-pound depth charges (used to sink submarines) in the plane's belly. I had to make a forced landing in the water.

†We were rescued by the destroyer *C. K. Bronson,* then transferred several times before getting back to the *San Jac.* A "breeches buoy" transfer was pretty dicey—all ropes and pulleys while you dangled between ships over the water.

‡A nickname for high-ranking officers.

perately and love to think of getting home to her. She is so marvelous to me, and now she is the object of prime importance in my life. After these hectic, often frightening days, it is indeed a comfort to lie in my upper and think of those marvelous days ahead with Barbara. If only I could see her—look into those lovely eyes, hear her laugh, and watch her playing with Bucky. Enough of that for now.

. . . Have you read this gov't education Bill? Looks to me like it might be a nice 2 or 3 year rest at college. I'll have saved some money and then they pay you, too, it seems. It's just a passing fancy—probably because right now the lazy routine of college would appeal to me. We could live in some swell apartment and I could study—Bar too if she wanted—Well, it's just something to think about. My mind grasps onto any and every possibility since it's so much fun planning and wondering. Barbara's letters are so wonderful. I do hope she is happy at Smith. I'm afraid she misses out on some fun by being engaged, but she's always been cute about it. . . .

We've been flying a good deal midst lots of excitement. The initial shakiness has left me before the battles, but the intensity of fire over the objectives will always scare me—of that I'm sure. Keeps you a good Christian anyway.

. . . For the most part I am relatively happy. The time has seemed endless since we parted. However when all's said, I'll have to admit I'm glad I am here—though I do wish this phase of it were behind me and I was home again, having been through it. At last I feel that I am at least doing my part and when I get back I'll have no feeling of guilt about being in the States.

Oh Mum I hope John and Buck and my own children never have to fight a war. Friends disappearing, lives being extinguished. It's just not right. The glory of being a carrier pilot has certainly worn off. True it's always a thrill to land successfully aboard, to return and see your ship steaming along, there's lots of thrills; but I mean it's mostly work.

I have mumbled on pages and have said very little I'm afraid—I love you all very much—

Your ever devoted son,
Pop

P.S. While I remember—don't ever send me any packages. They take ages and always get crushed.

July 12, 1944

Dear Mum and Dad,

. . . First while I remember I am enclosing a copy of a letter from Jim Wykes' mother, Mrs. Anna Wykes (don't know husband's name). Please save it for me, Mum. It is to me a beautiful letter, perhaps not eloquent or verbose, but one written from the depths of a loving mother's heart. How my heart aches for them. Jim has 2 brothers, both in service, and then his Mother and Father. Still no word of him and though I have not given up all hope, it is a bit discouraging. Today Bush Daniels, Lou Grab & I were standing at the small boat landing when a dark-skinned fellow jumped out of a little landing boat. He looked an awful lot like Jim and the 3 of us just stared. Unfortunately it wasn't he at all. I told you that Bob Whalen, Wykes' gunner, is married and his wife is with child. That, too, is terribly sad. I didn't mean to dwell on this subject for so long, but Jim was very close to me, and I feel his loss more each day. He has not been the only fellow I know that has been lost—not by a long shot—but I knew him so well. . . .

Lots of love,
Pop

———

July 21st

Dear Mum and Dad,

. . . During these last few hectic days, I have had little time for reading or the like—most fun when you get the chance is to stretch out on the sack or in a ready room chair and think. I also try to figure out what I'll do after the war.

One thing which appeals to me, is a job like Pressy's—go to S. America for a year (not much more).* It would be fun provided, of course, Bar were with me. The whole fun of it would lie in our being together—laughing and stumbling along in Portuguese, Espanol or what have you. . . . Barbara with her Northampton Spanish, me with none at all—live in some small cottage. The only thing I'd be scared of would be that she'd be lonely—miles away from her family and friends. I wouldn't care what kind of work I did.

So far I haven't been able to make up my mind on what I want to do. . . . Further education isn't out of my mind by a long shot. If I went to college I'd definitely find plenty to interest me—of that I am sure now. Before, I couldn't see that. It took the war, and the Navy to show me how advantageous a good education can be. I say advantageous and not necessary, for I do feel that I would get along with a bit of initiative and honest endeavor provided I could get some employer to give me a chance. I am prepared and fully cognizant of the fact that my salary will not be near what it is now. Barbara, too knows what to expect. When I return next fall I'll have saved $3000—we can make that last awhile anyway. Besides the S. Amer. and college plans—there

*Because of his poor eyesight, Pressy was 4-F, which was a huge disappointment for him. He took a job working for Pan-American Airlines in Brazil.

is a third—a regular job in the U.S. . . . It would be nice to know I could get a job for sure—a job which would not require me to dig a ditch—merely because I don't have a "college education." . . .

Much love to all,
Pop

––––––

July 22nd

My Dear Mrs. Wykes,

I received your letter one week ago. We had been at sea for a long time—that accounts for the delay. I was very touched by your kind words.

I wish I could tell you exactly what happened to Jim, but I do not know—nor does anyone, I'm afraid. He just never returned from a search flight. We all felt certain that when we returned to port he would be there; However, when we did get back there was no trace of him. A search had been launched by another carrier, and everyone around that area was notified. It is entirely possible that at this very minute he is on some island. I know how hard it must be for you to keep your spirits up, but all of us must keep saying to ourselves that Jim is still alive. At times, I feel "oh what's the use", but then I check myself. As long as there is a thread of hope I think we should cling to it. Some of islands in the vicinity were enemy held, as there is always that possibility to consider. Others were practically uninhabited!

. . . I wish this letter could give you some new hope, some evidence that your loving son is all right, but I'm afraid I don't have such tidings. Lets just keep that ray of hope in our hearts and in our prayers, and perhaps our faith will be rewarded.

My sincerest affection to you and your family—

George Bush

[Jim Wykes was never found.]

––––––

Sunday July 30th

Dear Mum and Dad,

. . . I wrote the Pierces a few days ago asking them how they felt about a wedding when I get back. I have been thinking about it so much and wondering how they felt that I just had to write. I don't ever like to think how it will be if they say "No". I have counted on it so much, even thought imaginary plans so often, and in fact just based my whole future around it, that I shall be very disappointed if they choose to make us wait.

. . . Incidentally, Dad, I would appreciate it, if you would let me know what you feel I should do after the war. As I have said before I do think I can get a job—a modest one at first of course, irregardless of my lack of college education. I wonder if you agree with me on this point. . . .

Much love to one and all,
Pop

[My father definitely did not *agree with my plan of not going to college.]*

Aug. 13th Sunday

Dear Mum and Dad,
. . . People are talking a good deal about the election. It's hard to say what the consensus of opinion is—I think most feel FDR will win, but then most of the people I know around here seem to be Dewey voters. The southern boys will support Roosevelt. The ones I've talked with seem to think he's some sort of a god—I don't believe they look too closely at what the New Deal administration has done or has not done. . . .

Much love to all,
Pop

Aug. 19th

Dear Mum and Dad,
. . . Got a letter from Mr. Pierce telling me that they did approve of our plans. I felt sure they would, but now that I have that definite 'yes' I feel terribly glad. From what he said, Bar is going to leave Smith since she wouldn't have time to complete the term. It will be nice for her to be with her family for a while anyway. I hope she comes up to Maine with you. If only I could snap my fingers and have these next months shoot swiftly by—I have so much to look forward to now—so very much!
. . . Mrs. GHWB—long but very nice! We are going to be the happiest Mr. & Mrs. going—or shall I say the happiest young Mr. & Mrs. going?
. . . Will stop now as it is almost time for dinner. Steak tonite I think. Usually the steaks have a great deal in common with an old sneaker sole, but occasionally a good one slips past the cook and the mess boys and gets as far as one of the tables.
Of course you heard about the muscular fellow who got himself a job at the zoo. He applied to be a trainer but when they told him they only needed an ape (since theirs had died) he volunteered to act as an ape. They gave him a costume and for several days he thrilled the customers with his ape-like antics. One day he did a terrific somersault, but unfortunately he landed in the lions cage. As the ferocious lion began to draw near him, the fellow started to

holler and yell and run for the door. Suddenly the lion spoke up and said, "Take it easy, buddy, do you want to get us both fired?!

Much love to all the family,

Ever devotedly,

Pop

———————

August 24th

Dear Mum and Dad,

. . . Gosh I'd like to see you all now—I miss you so much. Give all the family my love. John'll be going back for his 8th and last year soon I imagine and William should be about ready to battle his way into grade 1. I get such a kick out of Buck—I picture him so clearly at all times—He is sort of a symbol to me in a way. I remember how Bar & I used to play with him. We'd pretend he was our little boy. I don't know why, but little old Buck so often is brought to my mind—even when I'm up flying I'll burst out laughing at times. . . . Perhaps it's because he's so young and innocent. . . .

Today Rumania quit the war, according to a press release we received. That is indeed a good sign that that phase of this war should be over before too long. I hope the guilty receive treatment they deserve. I feel so strongly that the Nazis, fascist, or whatever moniker they use, should all be dealt with severely. The leaders—those responsible for murder, famine, treachery, etc. must be <u>killed.</u> I hope our government and our allies act boldly and powerfully and mete out severe but just penalties. If this is not done with all leaders who have collaborated with the Nazis, whether they be recognized heads of government or quislings ruling in conquered countries, I fear these 4 years of bloodshed will have been for naught. . . .

Ever devotedly,

Pop

———————

September 3, 1944

Dear Mother and Dad,

This will be the first letter you have gotten from me in a good long while. I wish I could tell you that as I write this I am feeling well and happy. Physically I am O.K., but I am troubled inside and with good cause. Here is the whole story at least as much of it as I am allowed to relate right now.

Yesterday was a day which will long stand in my memory. I was on a bombing hop with Delaney as my radioman* and Lt. (j.g.) Ted White as my gunner. He did not usually fly, but I asked him if he would like to go with me and he wanted to. We had the usual joking around in the ready room about

———

*My two regular crewmates were John Delaney and Leo Nadeau, who was the gunner.

having to bail out etc.—at that time it all seemed so friendly and innocent but now it seems awful and sinister.

I will have to skip all the details of the attack as they would not pass the censorship, but the fact remains that we got hit. The cockpit filled with smoke and I told the boys in back to get their parachutes on. They didn't answer at all, but I looked around and couldn't see Ted in the turret so I assumed he had gone below to get his chute fastened on. I headed the plane out to sea and put on the throttle so as we could get away from the land as much as possible. I am not too clear about the next parts. I told them to bail out, and then I called up the skipper and told him I was bailing out. My crewmen never acknowledged either transmission, and yet the radio gear was working—at least mine was and unless they had been hit back there theirs should have been, as we had talked not long before. I heard the skipper say something but things were happening so fast that I don't quite remember what it was. I turned the plane up in an attitude so as to take pressure off the back hatch so the boys could get out. After that I straightened up and started to get out myself. At that time I felt certain that they had bailed out. The cockpit was full of smoke and I was choking from it. I glanced at the wings and noticed that they were on fire. I still do not know where we got hit and never will. I am now beginning to think that perhaps some of the fragments may have either killed the two in back, or possibly knocked out their communications.

Fortunately I had fastened all my straps before the dive and also I had left my hatch open, something I hadn't been doing before. Just the day before I had asked the skipper and he advised leaving it open in a dive. The jump itself wasn't too bad. I stuck my head out first and the old wind really blew me the rest of the way out. I do remember tugging at my radio cord which I had forgotten to unplug. As I left the plane my head struck the tail. I now have a cut head and bruised eye but it is far from serious. After jumping, I must have pulled the ripcord too soon for when I was floating down, I looked up at the canopy and several of the panels were all ripped out. Just as I got floating down, I saw the plane strike the water. In the meantime, I noticed there was a liferaft down in the water. Not until later did I discover that it was mine that was supposed to be attached to my lifejacket. I had forgotten to hook it on, and when I left the plane it had come loose and had fallen into the water. Fortunately, the wind didn't carry me too far away from the raft. The entrance into the water was not too bad. I had unloosened several of my chute straps so that when it came to getting out of the harness I wouldn't have too many buckles to undo under the water. I went fairly deep under when I hit, but not deep enough to notice any pressure or anything. I shook the harness and the wind carried the chute away on the water. The wind was blowing towards shore, so I made every effort to head the other way. The skipper saw me and he saw my raft, so he made a pass over it to point it out to me. I had inflated my mae west* and then started swimming towards the raft. Fortunately, the fall hadn't injured the boat, so it inflated easily and I struggled into it. I then realized that I had overexerted myself swimming, because suddenly I felt quite tired. I was still afraid that the wind would take me in closer so I began paddling. It was a hell of a job to keep the water out of the raft. In fact I never did get it bailed out completely. At first I was scared that perhaps a boat would put out from the shore which was very close by, but I guess our planes made them think twice about that. A few fighter planes stayed nearby the whole time until I was rescued and you can imagine how comfortable that was.† One of them came right over me and dropped me some medical supplies which were most welcome, since I had no idea how badly cut up I was. It turned out to be slight, but did use the iodine anyway. I had some dye marker attached to my life jacket and also there was some in the raft so I sprinkled a bit of that on the water so the planes could see me easily. I took inventory of my supplies and discovered that I had no water. The water had broken open when the raft fell from the plane I imagine. I had a mirror and some other equipment, and also was wearing my own gun and knife.

There was no sign of Del or Ted anywhere around. I looked as I floated down and afterwards kept my eye open from the raft, but to no avail. The fact that our planes didn't seem to be searching anymore showed me pretty clearly that they had not gotten out. I'm afraid I was pretty much of a sissy about it cause I sat in my raft and sobbed for awhile. It bothers me so very much. I did tell them and when I bailed out I felt that they must have gone, and yet now I feel so terribly responsible for their fate, Oh so much right now. Perhaps as the days go by it will all change and I will be able to look upon it in a different light.

I floated around for a couple of hours during which time I was violently sick to my stomach. and then the planes started zooming me, pointing out my position to my rescuers. You can imagine how happy I was when I saw this submarine hove into view. They pulled me out of the raft and took me below where they fixed me up in grand style. As I write this I am aboard the sub— don't know how long I will be here, or when I will get back to the squadron.

As I said physically I am o.k. The food aboard here is unequaled anywhere I have ever seen. I am getting plenty of sleep and am even standing watches so that I will get the air occasionally. My back ached as did my leg last nite, and also my seat was a bit sore from the chute straps, but the pharmacist mate rubbed me down and today I feel much better. Last nite I rolled and tossed. I kept reliving the whole experience. My heart aches for the families of those

*Our inflatable yellow life vests were called Mae Wests.
†Later I learned that a Japanese boat did start out for me only to be strafed by one of our planes.

two boys with me. Delaney had always been a fine loyal crewman. His devotion to duty was at all times highly commendable and his personality most pleasing. I shall most certainly write to his family after I am sure they have been notified by the Bureau.

As for Ted White, I have spoken of him several times in my letters before. He was the fellow from Yale, one class ahead of Stu Clement.* He comes from St. Paul Minn. White Bear Lake to be exact. Perhaps Dad, you know the family. If so do not write them until you get the word from me or elsewhere that the family has been officially notified. There is a possibility that they parachuted and I didn't see them, but I am afraid it is quite remote as we received a message aboard here last nite saying that only one chute opened.† All in all it is terribly discouraging and frankly it bothers me a good deal.

As time goes by I shall add bits to this letter and will mail it at my earliest possible convenience. I shall do the same by Bar, but shall not go into detail like this over my experience so please read her the parts of this letter which might interest her. It's a funny thing how much I thought about Bar during the whole experience. What I wouldn't give to be with her right now. Just to see that lovely face and those beautiful eyes and to know she was by my side. Right now I long to be with you so much. To be with you both and to be with Bar is my main desire—at least it won't be too long, the time is going by quite rapidly.

Please excuse all my misspellings—they are caused not from ignorance but from carelessness in operating this machine.

much much love to you all,
your ever devoted and loving son,
Pop

[I was shot down off the island of Chichi Jima, in the Bonins, and rescued by the USS Finback. *I am still humbled by how lucky and blessed I was that an American submarine was patrolling the area and picked me up before the Japanese. I will also always be grateful to fellow pilot Doug West, who stuck with me as long as he could, strafing the Japanese boats and pointing his wing at my life raft so the* Finback *could find me. Years later we learned from the Japanese report of the incident that two parachutes were seen leaving the plane. That means a great deal to me—that at least one of my crewmates made it out of the plane—although he was never found. Right after the war, the Japanese commander in charge of Chichi Jima was tried and executed for eating the livers of captured American pilots. I like to tease Barbara that I almost ended up becoming an hors d'oeuvre.]*

*Stuart Clement was a first cousin.
†We later learned from an American pilot, and then confirmed years later after we obtained the Japanese records of the incident, that two chutes did open.

Sept. 5th

Dear Mum and Dad,

I have just finished writing Bar a long letter so I will add a bit more to this one for you. I did tell Bar all about what happened, so disregard the part I wrote in the first part of this.

I am now standing Junior officer of the Deck watches and I really love them. I am not in any way a qualified submariner as you can well imagine, but armed with a pair of binoculars and dark glasses if I need them I can sweep the sea and skies pretty well. After my griping about the security watches aboard the ship it may seem funny my enjoying any watches, but here it is different. These watches afford me a good chance to get up topside and grab some of that fresh air. When we are submerged, I am utterly useless to them, but when on the surface I stand two watches a day—6-8PM and 4-6AM. just a nice length.

The food continues to be excellent, with steaks, ice cream, chicken etc. in abundance. You actually can't believe how good the chow is. Of course they have a much smaller complement of officers to prepare for, but still the food is so much better that there is no comparison. As for sleep, I have been "claiming more than my fair share".* I usually sleep all morning and also all nite until my watch comes up. The sacks are comfortable and so darn inviting. I'd love to see 'The Big One' trying to get in and out of some of them. Dad, you just couldn't do it. All the beds are fine once you get in—that is until you have to get out. I sort of get half way in and then have to pull the rest of me in like a worm. The boat is now overcrowded, having three extra officers aboard. But since two men are on watch all the time there is always a bed for everyone. The fellow coming off watch just crawls into the bed which his relief had been sleeping in. . . .

So far diving and submerging haven't hurt my ears at all, and everything about this life agrees with me. I think I would still prefer flying, since you are out in the open so much more, but this would be my second choice.

All the officers, and crew too, are just as nice as they can be. The Captain is a peach.† He eats his meals with us in the wardroom and is just as good a guy as you'd want to meet. Yesterday I got a hunk of liferaft and stamped the name

---

*This was an expression used a lot by my parents. It was taken from the Greenwich Country Day School's report card, where there was a line for "Claims more than his fair share of time and attention in class." If this was checked on our card, we were in big trouble. I was a student at GCDS until age twelve.

†Commander Robert R. Williams Jr., who was awarded a Silver Star for enemy ships sunk on this very patrol.

of the ship and the date on it and then all the officers signed it. They also took some pictures the day they brought me aboard which I will try to get hold of to bring.* Will quit now.

much love,
Pop

September 8th

Dear Mum and Dad,

. . . Haven't been doing a great deal out of the ordinary—just daydreaming the time away. It is such fun to think about getting home, the wedding and all that. I find myself bursting forth into song up on the bridge. I am not sure the others up there appreciate my efforts too much, but if they ever complain I am going to tell them that my mother feels I am potentially a second Caruso—and I don't mean Frank Caruso† either. . . .

One thing I do miss aboard here is my daily shower which I loved aboard the ship. Water cannot be produced as abundantly aboard this boat, so naturally we have to conserve whenever and wherever possible. One shower per week is the ration. Tomorrow I can take mine—wow do I need it (unattractive). . . . The clothes situation is far from serious since all we wear is sandals, undies and pants—no shirts, just undershirts for meals.

I hope you have not been worrying up till the time you received these letters. This may be the first you have heard of my experience, I don't know. I try to think about it as little as possible, yet I cannot get the thought of those two boys out of my mind. It is so different, reading about people getting killed etc. Even when Jim and Dick Houle were lost, though I did feel it deeply, it did not affect me as this has. Oh, I am O.K.—I do want to fly again and I shall not be scared of it, but I know I shall never be able to shake the memory of this incident, and I don't believe I want to completely. They were both such fine people. . . .

Pop

I spent thirty days aboard the Finback *while she completed her war patrol, getting off at Midway and flying to Pearl Harbor where I spent a couple of days on R&R. I could have rotated home, but I wanted to get back with my squadron. So eight*

---

*Ensign Bill Edwards of the *Finback* filmed my rescue. Years later, when I was a candidate for Vice President, he contacted me and told me he had the film. It is now on display in my presidential library.

†Our garbage collector.

weeks after being shot down, and after hitchhiking on various planes, I finally rejoined the San Jac *at Ulithi in the Caroline Islands.*

Nov. 3rd

Dear Mum and Dad,

I have so much to write about that I hardly know where to start.

Yesterday I arrived back aboard, and it was one of the happiest moments of my life—I really mean that. The first guy I saw in the squadron was the skipper—He came down to the quarterdeck and greeted me. After that all the boys came around. I was so glad to see them—they are a good bunch alright. Lately (since I've been away) they have been thru hell. Almost everyone has been decorated for some deed or other and believe me they deserve it. They have had it tough and I am sorry I wasn't here to do my part. . . .

The only sad part was to find that Tom Waters has been killed in action—a bombing attack. Tom roomed with Doug West, Jack,* and I and we all liked him a lot. . . .

First of all about the accident. It seems that someone else did get out of the plane, but his chute didn't open. I am sorry over that, but am glad that someone at least got out of the plane besides myself. I wrote Delaney's sister (Mary J. Delaney 34 Somerset St. Providence R.I.) and also Ted White's parents. I am afraid the letters weren't very good but I do hope they know how I feel about the accident. Bush Daniels told me about how bravely the Whites received the news and I must say I do admire them, even though I don't know them.

. . . I am a little anxious over my first flight off the ship. I have flown so little lately that I will probably be rusty as can be.

I'm afraid you are wrong about my not having to come out again, though I hope you are right. This war is so big and so damn hard that you can never realize it fully unless you have actually studied it or been out here a while.

Your ever loving,
Pop

———

Nov. 9th

Dear Mum and Dad,

Quite a few days have elapsed since my first letter written from here upon my return. Since that first letter I have gotten back into the swing of things pretty much, having had 2 hops so far. Both went off o.k., and it was a relief to me, as I had been a bit anxious about landing aboard again after such a long lay-off.

---

*This is Jack Guy, with whom I'm still good friends today. Jack found and had refurbished an exact replica of my Avenger airplane to hang in my presidential library.

. . . Everyone talks of only one thing and that is getting home. We are supposed to be relieved soon, but no one knows <u>when</u>; and then after we are relieved it will take a few weeks to actually get home. . . . The vagueness must be hard on Bar. She has been so good about waiting and has never complained

. . . The election has come and gone and we now face 4 more years of FDR. There was hardly any talk of it on the 7th, probably cause most have felt that Dewey didn't have much of a chance. I know how discouraged you must be about it, and I feel the same way. My knowledge of the campaign etc. is not extensive, but from all reports it was not a pleasant one.

Much love,
Pop

Dean Spratlin was one of my crewmates aboard the USS Finback.

Friday, Nov. 17th

Dear Dean,

Just a note to let you know I finally did get back here to my original squadron and to thank you for everything you did for me aboard the Finback

Since my return I have been flying quite a bit—seems the boys want me to catch up with them.

We are heading home shortly—when exactly we don't know, but we're hoping it will be within the next couple of weeks at the most.

I still have a "SPRAT" undershirt and one mouldy "SPRAT" sock which you may receive thru the mail some day. Thanks again, Dean, for all you did for me. I really do appreciate it. Hope the new job is a good one and has gotten you back to the States—

Best of luck from a Goddamned zoomie—*

very sincerely,
George

Nov. 23rd

Dear Mum and Dad,

. . . This morning we had a combination Thanksgiving & Memorial service. The memorial part was for all the fellows who have lost their lives— They read off all their names, and had several prayers. It was a nice service and I am glad they had it before we leave.

---

*A term used—rather derisively—by submariners to describe pilots.

. . . I hope you all had a wonderful Thanksgiving day—I can picture each of you at the table now—John, Buck, and Nance. I hope Pres got home, but I have my doubts about this.

. . . This year Thanksgiving has more significance for me than ever; for heavens knows I have more to be thankful for than ever before—mainly all of you, my loving family and my own precious Bar and the happiness which will soon be ours; and then too my own life which has been guarded and protected during these last few months.

So long, Mum & Dad. I love you both so deeply and am ever thankful that God gave me two such wonderful parents.

> Your ever loving and middle-sized,*
> Pop

                                                                    Dec. 1st

Dear Mum and Dad,

This is the letter I have wanted to write to you for a long long time. At last I can tell you that we're coming home. I am all thru flying, combat complete, off the ship, and ready for a nice long leave. After you get this letter, it will still be quite a while before I reach the states and can call you up; but, nevertheless, I feel pretty damned happy. I wrote Bar this A.M., but in case her letter got waylaid, please call her and tell her.

Mum, when I do get back I shall call up both you & Bar. I'll give her a safe date when I'll definitely be in Greenwich, and she can set the wedding date . . .

> Much, much love,
> Pop

Barbara had wedding invitations printed for December 17, but she had to scratch out that date as I did not make it home until Christmas Eve. We were married January 6, 1945, and after a short honeymoon, I went back into training. We jumped from base to base, among them Grosse Ile Air Station in Michigan. You will notice that after I got married, my letters home became rather sparse.

Dear Mum,

. . . Bar probably told you we had one room . . . It is a nice room and we were lucky to get it the first day; but it costs $14 per week and we don't get kitchen privileges, so now that we have time we are looking around for something else. Out at the base they help us find places. . . . It's about 4½ miles to

*A nickname of mine when Pres, Nancy, and I were the only children.

the base and about ½ mile to the center of town. Bar walks in for lunch and then we walk in together for supper. They have one small-townish restaurant, but it's not too bad. It is sort of a lonely existence for poor Bar, but she doesn't complain at all, and I am just in heaven having her here.

. . . Bar has returned from the laundering and is now sitting at this table making a puzzle. Tomorrow she is going out to check on a new place to live.

. . . Our landlady has a electric massager which I love—I have had a sore shoulder for a week now, but it's well on its way to recovery. Bar is in good health, and is a perfect wife. It is such fun to come home and find her here— She always is in a good humor and when worryin' Pop appears on the scene she always cheers him up. . . .

Your ever loving,
Pop

Monday

Dear Mum,

. . . Our landlady is funny—nice and friendly and I feel fine having Bar with her all day, but she is so odd. She thinks she is being so patriotic having these 2 rooms for rent, when actually she is making a mint on us. She even thinks she's making a huge sacrifice when she lets Bar use the laundry.

. . . Bar is quite the wife—launders, irons, cleans well etc. The only thing she hasn't tried is cooking but perhaps she'll get a chance at that soon. . . .

Much love,
Pop

Monday—2/26/

Dear Mum and Dad,

Time seems to be whipping right by, but still no orders. . . . There are rumors going around that a big _nite_ Torpedo outfit is forming—may get stuck in that. I wouldn't like it too much, since I find it enough work flying off a carrier during the day. Worse than the nite part though is the possibility that it _may_ form way down in the Florida Keys where you can't take wives. That would be too much to take. . . .

Yesterday was my day off. Bar and I stayed in the whole day—just rested and read the papers and Newsweek.

. . . Bar had a little cold a few days ago but she is now completely cured. She is really a good cook now. The other day we had fancy shirred eggs. She is good on vegetables, too. Yesterday we had sausage, beets, and mashed potatoes, a real good lunch. She always has the ice box full of milk. We drink about 3½ quarts a day, and that counts my eating lunch out here. . . .

Your ever loving,

Pop

On that rather dramatic statement about Barbara's cooking, the World War II letters end. My mother did not have any other letters in her collection.

Barbara and I bounced around the country for eight months, finally landing back at the Navy base in Norfolk, Virginia. My squadron had received orders to ship back out to the South Pacific, to participate in the invasion of Japan, when Japan surrendered and World War II ended on August 14, 1945. (Germany had surrendered in May.) Suddenly, it was over, and along with it, my three-year Navy career. Because I had flown fifty-eight combat missions and won the Distinguished Flying Cross, I had enough "points" to get an early discharge from the Navy.

As I look back on these letters, I realize how protected my life had been until I joined the Navy. In addition, although my childhood was very happy, my upbringing was also strict—indeed, puritanical. As a result, my vision of the world was narrow, and I was a little judgmental at age eighteen. Like most young people, my horizon needed expanding.

Most troubling, of course, was what happened to me on September 2, 1944. Although I am confident that I followed all the procedures necessary for getting my crew and myself out of my burning plane, it still haunts me today that I lived and my two crewmen died. Both John's and Ted's sisters visited me in the White House nearly fifty years later and were very kind to me. Unfortunately, my letters written to their families in 1944 have been lost.

All in all these are letters written from the heart from a loving son to his parents—letters from a kid sometimes homesick, sometimes scared; and certainly from a kid who was madly in love with the woman who has now been his wife for nearly fifty-five years.

ZAPATA OFF-SHORE COMPANY
1701 HOUSTON CLUB BUILDING
HOUSTON, TEXAS 77002

CHAPTER 2

"Texas, Our Texas"*

Despite my earlier misgivings about going to college, I had come to my senses by the end of the war, and like millions of other discharged veterans, I headed to college on the G.I. Bill. Next stop for Barbara and me was New Haven, Connecticut, and Yale University. We were all anxious to get on with our lives, so most of us went through school on a fast track, receiving some credit for military service. It took me just two and a half years to get a bachelor's degree in economics. In addition to a heavy class load, I was fairly active on campus, including playing first base for the baseball team and serving as team captain my senior year. And last but certainly not least, our first child, George W. Bush, was born July 6, 1946. No wonder there's no record of any letters I wrote in 1946 or 1947.

This chapter begins with one written in June 1948, right before graduation, to my good friend FitzGerald (Gerry) Bemiss, who lived then (and now) in Richmond, Va. Gerry and I had become great friends in Kennebunkport where both our families spent their summers. This letter was written on "Hotel Robert E. Lee" stationery, from Winston-Salem, North Carolina, where I had traveled with the Yale baseball team.

———————

Fri P.M.

Dear Gerry,

We have a while this afternoon before train time so I shall respond to your interesting letter. I can't imagine where you ever heard that I was going into the ministry. I have never even thought about the cloth—only a table-

*Title of the state song.

61

cloth or a loincloth. Seriously I would be curious to know where you heard about it.

Right now I am bewildered to say the least. My mind is in a turmoil. I want to do something of value and yet I have to and want to make money—after Georgie goes through 3 squares every day, one's wallet becomes thin and worn. I have thought of teaching, but right now it seems to me that it would be confining and not challenging enough. Besides teaching would require further study almost immediately, and I am not prepared to study textbooks right now—perhaps later but not now.

So where does that leave me—no cloth, no books, perhaps a briefcase. I could work for Herby Walker* in St. Louis—GH Walker & Co. investments etc. Some are fascinated, and genuinely so, by such a business. Perhaps I would be. Right now I do not know. It's not a basic business and yet it is important as long as we are living under a relatively free economic system. I am uncertain—I want to know and understand people, but the people I'd be doing business with in the investment business, I know to some degree now. I am not sure I want to capitalize completely on the benefits I received at birth—that is on the bene-fits of my social position. Such qualities as industriousness, integrity, etc. which I have or at least hope I have had inculcated into me by my parents, at least to some degree, (I hope) I do want to use, but doing well merely because I have had the opportunity to attend the same debut parties as some of my cus-tomers, does not appeal to me.

This may sound frightfully confused. Don't get me wrong. I am not preaching redistribution of wealth etc.; rather I am saying that I would hate to get caught in what could be a social and somewhat unproductive eddy. Per-haps I shall go with Walkers. If I go I shall work hard and long. Financially it would be fine—good starting pay, and fairly nice sledding ahead; but once again I just don't know.

Lastly I have this chance to go with Neil Mallon's† Dresser Industries—per-haps to Texas. They make equipment for the oil and gas industries. They are basic. Texas would be new and exciting for a while—hard on Bar perhaps—and heavens knows many girls would bitch like blazes about such a proposed move—Bar's different though, Gerry. She lives quite frankly for Georgie and myself. She is wholly unselfish, beautifully tolerant of my weaknesses and idio-syncrasies, and ready to faithfully follow any course I chose. . . . I haven't had a chance to make many shrewd moves in my young life, but when I married Bar I hit the proverbial jackpot. Her devotion overcomes me and I must

*G. H. Walker Jr., the oldest of my mother's four brothers. Most people called him Herbie, which I often spelled "Herby."
†A close friend of the family and a classmate of my father's.

often stop in my mad whirl around college etc. to see if I am considering her at all. . . .

Anyway—the Dresser job at the moment has great appeal. I would be seeing new people, learning something of basic importance. What stands in the way of my flying headlong into it, is first—(I have to see Neil this month in Cleveland about pay and other not so minor details) and secondly the old question of is business what I want?

Well from all the above you can see that I don't know what I am going to do. Graduation is on Monday—then we go to Kalamazoo Michigan for the college world series in baseball. Down here at W. Salem we have just won the Eastern Championship . . . We were thrilled to win—It was all night baseball quite a change from day, but we played our best ball of the year and came through. . . .

> your clerical maybe
> but not clergical
> friend—
> Pop

I accepted the job from Neil Mallon and drove our 1947 Studebaker (a graduation gift from my parents) to Odessa, Texas, to start my career at one of Dresser Industries' subsidiaries, IDECO (short for the International Derrick and Equipment Company). I started at the very bottom of the corporate ladder, as an equipment clerk. Barbara and George W. joined me as soon as I found us a place to live—a tiny two-room duplex. There was only one bathroom, which we shared with our neighbors: a woman and her daughter, both of whom seemed to make their living by questionable means. Let's just say they had a lot of male visitors at all hours of the day and mostly night. Many a night they locked us out of the bathroom. Anyway, I wrote Gerry Bemiss:

August 28th

Dear Gerry,

As I sit here writing this letter in our store the wind is whistling around outside and I am seeing my first real powerful West Texas sand storm.

. . . Speaking of Golf—they have a course here. The other day Bar and I were driving by and we saw four players seated on a small jeep-like vehicle with an umbrella raised over it. They were driving between shots, and when they arrived beside one's ball the player claiming the pellet would climb down, take a shot, and then remount the vehicle. It was so damned hot that they really couldn't have made it around without this car. We laughed over the looks of the damn thing but had to secretly admire the ingenuity of the gents. The course is beautifully adapted to such a machine, since the only hills on it are those made by cows or ants.

My job is progressing O.K. I am doing nothing which requires any brain-work, but I am learning a bit about the oil business, so far principally the supply end of it. I understand that in a while I shall be going into the fields more to see our equipment in action. I am eagerly awaiting this phase of my training. I have been to the fields on several occasions but not as much as I should like. The store gives one a sound basis though and I certainly have a lot to learn here. In my spare minutes I find plenty of oil journals etc. to look at. It is surprising how much you can learn merely by reading the ads in these papers. You begin to recognize equipment that you have seen lying around the store, and gradually the whole thing takes on some central theme. . . .

You should see Georgie now, nothing like bragging about one's own kid. He is really cute, I feel. Whenever I come home he greets me and talks a blue streak, sentences disjointed of course but enthusiasm and spirit boundless. He is a real blond and pot-bellied. He tries to say everything and the results are often hilarious. How he would love to be there at K'port. The great thing is that he seems to be very happy wherever he is and he is very good about amusing himself in the small yard we have here. . . .

We miss you Beam—

as ever,
Pop

———————

October 20—Wed.

Dear Mum,

As I wrote you last weekend poor little Googen felt punk, had a fever etc. Well right now he is still sick and not feeling much better. Yesterday we got tired of the old doctor. He told us nothing, took no interest in what we at least thought was a real problem, and generally disturbed me. . . . Mrs. Miller across the street recommended this new doctor and we threw medical etiquette or ethics out the window and called Dr. Thornton. . . . he diagnosed Georgie's case as inflamed tonsils and a chest congestion. The fever was nothing to worry about and it was quite normal for it to jump around. He gave us a prescription for penicillin pills and also for cod liver oil. We had stopped giving Georgie cod liver oil, foolishly, and he now is in need of it badly—slight case of rickets said frank Dr. Thornton. . . . We gave it to Georgie and he went off to sleep. Three hours or less later he awoke and vomited absolutely everything. He had done same a couple of times during the day. Then all during the nite he vomited. Today his fever was still 104. The doctor came again this time armed with a long needle destined to be shot into

Georgie. The doctor felt he should have penicillin and since the pills didn't work the needle would do it. Well today Georgie stayed in all day long. He hardly moved, just lying in my bed, falling asleep off and on and then listening to his records, played faithfully by Bar. . . .

He has been such a good little fellow in his sickness. When he vomited he looked up pathetically one time and said "Sorry, Mum, sorry". His little face is bright red and he is so hot to the touch. He just lies in bed next to us and sort of dozes off. Tonight I was playing his records for him, (the girl next door is wonderfully generous with her vic,) He sort of had his eyes half closed and then he looked up at me and said "No man hurt Georgie, No Man!" Referring of course to the needle. . . . He is so wonderful, Mum, so cute and bright. Oh he has his mischievous and naughty spells, but I just can't picture what we would do without him.

Bar is still not quite up to par. She gets little rest now with Georgie sick, but she is feeling better, and I think the worst of her troubles are over. I think that physically the last few days have been rough on her, and I know that her disappointment over this miscarriage was large. As I told you before we both are sort of hoping that we will have another child before too long. Bar thinks about it a lot, and foolishly worries too much. I don't like to have her upset. She is something, Mum, the way she never ever complains or even suggests that she would prefer to be elsewhere. She is happy, I know, but anyone would like to be around her own friends, be able to take at least a passing interest in clothes, parties etc. She gets absolutely none of this. It is different for me, I have my job all day long with new things happening, but she is here in this small apt. with people whose interests cannot be at all similar to Bar's because they have never had any similar experiences. I continue to be amazed at her unselfishness, her ability to get along with absolutely anyone, and her wonderful way with Georgie. She never becomes cross or irritable at him, and never complains in any way about anything that we don't have, don't get to enjoy right now. It is one thing for her to be far from her home and friends, but it is still another and greater thing to be able to live happily with people from such different backgrounds. I am so very lucky, Mum; I am grateful and I must always work to make Bar happy. She has made my life full and complete; she has given so much and never asked a [sic] return. How lucky I am! . . .

Monday night I went out for the whole night again. This time I went with Horn and Pewitt our two servicemen up to Jal, New Mexico. They were changing clutches and brakes on the Sabine Drilling Co.'s Clark rig. I worked on the clutch for two hours till midnight and then watched for three hours. I slept in the front seat of the car till 4:45. Then watched, then slept another hour, then headed for home at 6:30, arriving at about 9. . . . These all night trips give me some idea of some of the problems faced on a rig floor. I have seen many techniques etc., but only by staying with a rig for hours on a row can one grasp the overall picture of certain phases of drilling. These night trips poop me out, though, and I shan't do it too much. . . .

Mum, about Xmas. I don't get Saturdays off as it is anyway. I work every Saturday except one in three I get the afternoon off. Therefore, saving Saturdays will do no good . . . I just couldn't ask to get off. None of the other people in the store get anytime off at all Xmas, and I wouldn't feel right asking. If directed to go, then it would be different. Perhaps between Odessa and our next move they will give us a week. Can we save our Xmas present for such a chance? This we'd love.

We three send our love, and allow as how we'd love to be cruising up the Grove Lane* drive in our Study, eagerly craning for a glimpse of the boysies, and awaiting the old who-hoo call. We do miss you both so much, and though we don't know when it'll be we always plan and talk about our next trip home.

Much Love
Pop

————————

This next series of letters to Gerry Bemiss document a lot of changes in our life—moves, babies, and unfortunately, a death.

Jan. 11, 1949

Dear Gerry,

Thanks so much for your kind letter. . . . We did have a nice Xmas—very quiet and too far from any family or friends, but nevertheless a happy one. Our "take" was far too large for three people who have so much, but we didn't let it bother us to the extent of turning anything back. My prize was an electric blanket—a marvelous invention which I love. . . . Georgie was the center of attraction for us of course. This was his first year of understanding and he really was excited. Modesty does not prevent my enclosing a Xmas day snap of Georgie and yours truly taken in front of our tree.

The big excitement now is that Mum and Dad are coming down here in a week or so. Dad is on a Dresser inspection trip and Mum is hitching a ride with him in the company plane. We are counting the days till they get here. We know very few people here and there won't be any great activity but it will be fun having them here. Dad will only stay a day or two whereas Mum will be with us for 5 or 6 days we are hoping.

. . . The job continues in a interesting fashion, although I am selling or supposed to be, and am frankly very sad at it. I drive around to rigs and small

*My parents lived on Grove Lane in Greenwich, Connecticut.

company offices, and so far have sold nothing. In this business to sell you have to be able to supply pipe to your customers. Up till now we haven't been able to get enough pipe at all. Many of our competitors have their own pipe mills etc., so they get a lot. . . .

This West Texas is a fabulous place, Gerry. Fortunes can be made in the land end of the oil business, and of course can be lost. Commissions paid to land brokers are tremendous, prices asked for proven land are equally as high. If a man could go in and get just a few acres of land which later turned out to be good he would be fixed for life. I might say that the supply business while a bit more stable is not the field to be in if you expect to make some money. . . .

How are you getting along Bemo. How about starting a third party and running for office next election. I have in the back of my mind a desire to be in politics, or at least the desire to do something of service to this country. Think it over and let me know what to run for. . . . In the meantime I shall continue peddling pig iron here in the oil fields and trying to absorb not only facts pertinent to the oil industry, but helpful hints on human nature and life in general. . . .

> Yours truly,
> Pop

––––––––

April 3, 1949

Dear Bemo,

. . . Bemiss, I leave here Wednesday for California. We are going to work for Security Engineering Co. out there, another Dresser subsidiary, manufacturers of rock bits, packers, etc. They are a smaller outfit than IDECO, but a good company. I will be in the plant for about five months in Whittier Calif. outside L.A.,* then home for two weeks I hope, and then back to West Texas somewhere for more field experience. They are moving me a lot, but each is worthwhile, of that I am sure, and the field experience is invaluable. One trip to our Dallas office convinced me of that. At times I wish I had a little responsibility of a little thinking to do, but maybe that will come later. In any case we are excited over the move. We plan to drive our Studebaker out there, and store our furniture here, seeking a furnished place on the coast. . . .

Love to all the family.

> Poppy

––––––––

*In addition to Whittier, we also lived in Bakersfield, Ventura, and Compton during our one year in California.

Oct. 21, '49

Dear Gerry,

Just a line to let you know we're still alive. I was sorry to have missed you at K'port, but did have a great time with the Senator and wife.* What a refreshing feeling to catch that all too fleeting glimpse of them—marvelous really marvelous.

We're living at the above address, working for Pacific Pumps, a Dresser company, at Huntington Park, Cal. I am a laborer, assemblyman to be exact and a dues paying CIO steelworker. The work is long and at times tedious but the experience is marvelous. Last week we worked 7 days—same this week. This part I don't like. The union meetings are most interesting. The problems of labor, the basic problems of insecurity lay-offs etc. Economics teach one thing but the welfare of a man and his peace of mind often cannot exist at the right level if the rudiments of economics are strictly adhered to. In other words I feel sorry as hell for men getting laid off, not knowing from one week to the next whether they'll be at work and yet business cannot survive if labor is considered more than a "cost". Working in the plant gives one much food for thought.

Bar and GWB are well and the big excitement, new baby, arrives in a couple of months.

Did you know Bar's mother was killed in an auto accident 3 weeks ago while driving Mr. Pierce to the station?

Our life here is socially non-existent but we are happy, very much so.

Best to you and drop me a line—

Pop

———

Nov. 9, 1949

Dear Mr. O'Connor,†

Since our conversation last August I have been a member of the Testing, Assembly, and Hydrostatic Testing departments in the Pacific Pumps East Plant. At present I am working in the Production Control department learning some of the "flow" procedure. I believe that I was moved into this department temporarily because there has been a slack period in the shop. Mr. Prust, the plant superintendent, is sort of letting me map out my own program but he has suggested a short stay in the cost department, in order to fol-

———

*The "Senator" is Gerry's father, Samuel Bemiss. He was not really a senator, but he was a true Virginia gentleman of the old school, and we called him Senator.

†John O'Connor, to whom I reported from time to time, was executive vice president of Dresser Industries.

low through the paper work originated in the plant. I realize that this is not actual plant work, but it might prove of value. I definitely want to return to my status of laborer, and especially I want to get some machine experience which has been okayed by Prust, but since work is slack right now this other move has immediate attraction. I would appreciate your advising me if you do not want me to spend time in the cost department.

My work in the plant has proved very interesting in many ways, not the least of which has been my membership in the CIO steelworkers. I elected to join the union even though we have an open shop and I have not been disappointed in this decision. Now that I am in production control, even though I work in the plant, I cannot remain in the union, but upon my return to actual floor work I will be readmitted.

Very Sincerely,
George H. W. Bush

———————

In April 1950, I was transferred back to IDECO, this time to Midland, Texas, which was just down the road from Odessa. Three of us moved to California; four of us moved back to Texas: Pauline Robinson Bush had been born December 20, 1949. We called her Robin. A few months after moving back to Texas, I received a job offer from Brown Brothers Harriman, my father's Wall Street firm. The letter came from Mr. Tom McCance, who assured me in his letter, "This suggestion did not originate with your father and, in fact, he has nothing to do with it. . . . Others of us here [feel] this would be an excellent move for us and are most hopeful that you will react favorably to the suggestion." My reply:

June 25, 1950

Dear Mr. McCance,

I hope that you will excuse this long period of silence. I assure you that it has not been caused by any lack of interest in your offer—on the contrary, ever since receiving your letter of May 4th my wife and I have thought about nothing else. My trip back East satisfied me that your business is a fascinating one. In addition to that, many personal factors tended to make us lean towards moving back. The decision has been a most difficult one to make for the choice was between two wonderful jobs.

We have decided to remain with Dresser Industries. I have a great feeling of loyalty to Dresser and to Mr. Mallon; and I am convinced that there is a real opportunity here. It will mean living out here in West Texas for perhaps a year more, and then moving in to Dallas.

I should like to thank you and the others there at Brown Bros. Harriman for making me this offer. It came as a surprise and indeed a thrill and I shall always have a deep feeling of appreciation.

> Gratefully Yours,
> George Bush

January 1, 1951

Joyous New Years, oh Bemiss!

. . . Midland is a fine town—there are more congenial young people in this place than in any town of near its size that I have ever seen. We really love it. I am selling oilfield equipment and supplies, a task which is great as far as gaining experience goes, but which I do not particularly relish. I am a poor salesman, that has been rather conclusively demonstrated. I don't know exactly what the Dresser plans are for me, but they do involve moving to Dallas eventually—maybe in a few months, maybe in a year or so.

Have you had any greetings from the Navy dept. as yet. I would, of course, hate to go back in the Navy again, hate to leave the family and all yet I suppose that if this becomes an all out thing my whole attitude will change.*

We have had a fine year—we like Texas, the kids have been well. Robin is now walking around and Georgie has grown to be a near-man, talks dirty once in a while and occasionally swears, aged 4½. He lives in his cowboy clothes.

The only thing I feel real badly about is that I did nothing, absolutely nothing, towards helping Dad in his campaign. We felt terribly about the outcome after the way Dad worked at it. I do feel that he made a lot of friends though and I think he will be hard to beat if he runs again in 1952.† . . .

Love to all the family,

> devotedly,
> Pop

By the spring of 1951, I became too restless in my job with IDECO/Dresser and decided to strike out on my own. I joined up with our good friend and neighbor John Overbey, and together we founded Bush-Overbey Oil Development Co. Leaving my job was a tough decision, not only because it meant lost security, but especially because of my great respect for Neil Mallon. However, he was supportive and even encouraged me to try to start my own business.

---

*I was referring to the war in Korea. Since I was not a member of the Navy Reserves, chances were slim I would be called back, but everyone at least thought about it.

†Dad ran for the U.S. Senate in 1950, but lost by just a few votes to Democrat William Benton.

April 12, 1951

Mr. H.N. Mallon
Dresser Industries
Dallas, Texas
Dear Neil,

This will let you know that we are in business. . . . we do have a little office here which will suffice until we can make permanent connections. . . .

Overbey is good—he knows the business well and has demonstrated an excellent knowledge of prices, values, etc. I am happy about our arrangement with him, and I hope it will turn out to be a good thing for John.

. . . Midland is full of dust at this season—such sandstorms. I keep telling Bar she never had it so good—three square meals and a sack every nite, but I occasionally detect a lack of conviction as she nods agreement.

. . . Neil I want to thank you once again for your advice and interest in this little project. I shall always be grateful to you, not only for the wonderful training which I had with Dresser, but also for everything which you personally have done for me and for the family. I hated to leave the company, sincerely—maybe someday I will really regret my move, but this too is a challenge and something which I really felt I had to tackle.

My love to all the family, to Dale, and my best wishes and many many thanks to you—

[copy unsigned]

———————

I'm afraid in many of my letters during this time, I bored friends and family with details of the oil business. But it was an exciting time in West Texas, and I'd like to share with you some of those letters so you can get the flavor of what it was like.

June 30, 1951

Dear Gerry:

It has been ages since I have last written to you and much has transpired in that long period. The main thing in our small lives is the new business venture in which I find myself. . . .

So far we have been concentrating in the royalty business*—at this stage our corporation can stand short-term income (any income for that matter) and we feel that the most conservative way and yet a lucrative way if fortu-

———

*The royalty is the interest retained by the owner (the lessor) of the land or minerals—in those days it usually was one-eighth of the production. The operator (the lessee) owns the remaining seven-eighths but pays the full amount of drilling, development, and operating costs. Both types of interest are actively traded.

nate, is to play royalty. You eliminate many risks by playing royalty. After we start building up a large income, if we do, then we will start drilling wells or taking interest deals in wells. We still can promote wells now, but we don't want to put much of our capital into this type of venture for the present.

The business is fascinating—always exciting. We have bought a good deal of royalty, a lease or two and some minerals. I have taken trips into North Dakota and Wyoming—Nebraska—Colorado on certain plays.

Most of our stockholders are from New York. My belief is that if we can show them some earnings they will all want to participate as individuals on what I would consider a large scale. Tax-wise the oil business is hard to beat, and I think we are in a position to give them very fair deals, without loading it on like so many people here do in dealing with the Easterners. Many East-erners are trying to get in the oil business but they refrain from it for fear of being "promoted but good". Our objective now is to get our own situation going and then take on larger deals with ourselves participating but others working in as partners. In this way our stockholders can get the individual benefits such as intangible drilling cost deductions, depletion allowance, etc. whereas in our set-up the corporate entity gets it but not the individuals. . . .

Give my warmest regards to your family.

Write!

> Best Wishes,
> Pop

August 22, 1951

Mr. G.H. Walker Jr.
Kennebunkport, Maine
Dear Herby:

I can't thank you enough for the wonderful two days at K'port. It was great fun from the cunner fishing to the links to the boat to the tremendous chow and to seeing the family.

Bar and the kids and I got back here Monday night after a tiring but uneventful flight. The kids behaved fairly well on the plane—only occasional screams and gripes. It is nice to be back in a way and the desk is stacked high with things to do. This business is so darned exciting that when away for a lit-tle while only many new developments have taken place. . . .

I enjoyed our talks up there Herby. There are many ways for us to expand when we think the time is ripe. The Delaware Basin thing has tremen-dous appeal to me; and I am convinced we could make some money for any investor we might find as well as for our company. When the time becomes riper to get after this thing, I'll write to you for some advice. The

Liedtkes,* our good friends here, might be interested in some kind of joint deal whereby they provide half the capital and we provide the other half, both sharing in the expenses of some qualified employee—this might be a good approach with the new company being a partly owned subsidiary . . .

Another avenue which we have not entered, of course, is the drilling business. We have stayed away from this because we cannot afford the tax write-off; but here again we could possibly get additional money from people who have spoken to me about getting into drillings deals . . .

In any case there are plenty of places to go from here—the only trouble is that the 'here' is keeping us busy as it is right at the present.

Much Love to Mary and many many thanks again to the whole family for a wonderful visit and for the many kindness' bestowed.

[copy unsigned]

Dear Sir:

On Nov. 18, 1951 I was apprehended by a Weatherford [Texas] officer for speeding—his charge that I was doing 50 in a 30 mile zone. I should like to settle this matter with your court. I do not feel I was doing 50, nor does my companion, but I do admit I was exceeding 30. For this I am very sorry. There was little traffic, but nevertheless I do realize I was wrong.

I hope that you will consider my feeling of not doing 50, and I assure you I will be more considerate of Weatherford's laws in the future.

Will you please advise as to what I am to do.

Yours Truly,
George H Bush

[I lost my appeal and paid my $10 fine.]

January 21, 1952

Mr. Dave Hershey†
Cornell College
Ithaca, N.Y.
Dear Moose:

I can't thank you enough for the chair, which appeared here last week. It is really a beauty and is far too big a gift for you to have sent us. You can well

---

*Brothers Hugh and Bill Liedtke, originally from Oklahoma.

†If I remember right, Moose was a young kid who had worked for us in the oil fields the previous summer.

imagine the pleasure that it is giving us right now. We have it situated in our little den in our new house and it is just perfect.

In a way the chair has brought us very good luck, for the day it arrived Barbara was out in the yard working on some shrubbery. It was the delivery of the chair which brought her into the house where she smelled smoke. She rushed into Robin's room where she found the little darling feeding plastic toys into the heater and cackling with joy at the flames. We lost an antique rug, $3.95 at Penny's, and almost lost Robin. Only the heroic efforts of the delivery man who threw the rug and heater out the window saved the day. Now you can see we feel particularly attached to the chair.

Seriously, Moose, it was most thoughtful of you to send this wonderful present and we really appreciate it. Let me know your plans for the summer and if I can be of help to you. Many thanks from the four of us to all of you.

Yours truly,

[copy unsigned]

Dear Herby:

. . . I am working locally on the Ike thing, being head of the publicity committee for newspaper work and on the finance comm. Our main job is to get the word spread about Ike making no reference to the word REPUBLI-CAN—it is surprising how strong the prejudice against the Republicans is, and yet I am more and more impressed by the number of people who express their preference for IKE for this year. It is hard to grasp the full meaning of all the hot air put out, but if you can believe half of what you read here I believe IKE can carry Texas.

Your efforts on Dad's behalf are terrific. I'll bet Neil will be able to help a lot in this connection. I am attaching a small donation—its size in no way reflects my interest, for I find myself thinking all the time about things up there in Conn.—Dad just has to win this time.

Love to all the clan:

[copy unsigned]

October 8, 1952

Mr. H. N. Mallon
Dresser Industries
Dallas, Texas
Dear Neil:

Barbara and I will not be able to come into Dallas for the Oklahoma game like we were planning. I hope that letting you know at this late date will not foul up your weekend plans. As you may have heard, Barbara is expecting again and just does not feel up to making the long drive. The baby is not due until February, but she feels pretty punk if she has to travel for long distances.

. . . Bar is urging me to take her to Dallas sometime this fall for a Christmas shopping trip. My check book keeps insisting that we not make this trip, but somehow I have a feeling that Barbara may win out. If this is the case, we will have the gall to hit you up for a couple of free sacks.

Love to all the family.

[copy unsigned]

[You must find it curious that Barbara did not feel up to driving to Dallas for a football game but did want to go there to shop. The truth is, she was suffering from morning sickness, which we knew would go away later in the pregnancy.]

————

Obviously I preferred to do my Christmas shopping the easy way . . .

October 9, 1952

Parker Brothers Inc.
Salem, Massachusetts
Dear Sirs:

Would you please send me a Winnie the Pooh game at the above address. I would appreciate your including a statement of your charges at that time.

Yours very truly,
George H. W. Bush

————

October 14, 1952

Q-T Novelty Co., Inc.
Murray Hill Station
New York 16, N. Y.
Dear Sirs:

Attached herewith is a check in the amount of $1.00 for one set of your wooden "Seven Little Indians".

Would you please send this set to me at the above address.

Yours very truly,
George H. W. Bush

————

The beginning of 1953 was eventful, highlighted by the birth of our third child, John Ellis Bush, called Jeb. Dad did win his election, so was sworn in as a U.S. sen-

ator from Connecticut. I entered into yet another business venture: Bush-Overbey officially joined forces with the Liedtke brothers, calling our new company Zapata. We took the name from the Midland movie marquee; Marlon Brando's Viva Zapata! *was playing at the time. But then, among all the excitement, came the most dreaded news: we learned that spring that Robin, age three, was suffering from advanced leukemia. Our doctor in Midland advised us to take her home to die, but refusing to give up, Barbara and I took her to Memorial Hospital at Sloan-Kettering in New York City. For the next few months, Barbara stayed in New York with Robin while I went back and forth between New York and Texas, trying to look after business and the boys. I wrote this letter to Thomas "Lud" Ashley, a class-mate from Yale and one of my best friends. He served for years as a Democratic con-gressman from Ohio, but at this time, he was a bachelor living in New York.*

May 26, 1953

Dear Lud:

. . . I cannot begin to tell you here just how much we appreciate all that you did for Bar and myself. I know how busy you were, but you let that make no difference and you devoted your time to us when we needed you. It is funny what friendships can mean in times of stress. When thinking about Robin's illness, I cannot help but get philosophical—I have stopped asking "why". One thing I do know is that when one is worried or suffering or troubled that there are only two things which help, friendships (love) and faith. I will say no more, but you have helped us both in a time of need. A few tougher days will probably lie ahead, Lud, but I don't believe many will be rougher than those first couple of weeks. We will have many wonderful memories of people who helped us and tried to help us, but none will exceed in my mind your many gestures of true friendship. . . .

———————

August 19, 1953

Mr. Fitzgerald Bemiss
Richmond, Virginia
Dear Gerry:

. . . I hope that your honeymoon was all that you expected and that we will have the opportunity of seeing you before long. I am hoping that Barbara and Robin will come back to Texas in the next couple of days. Robin apparently is making headway, or at least has not lost ground. While you were in Europe she went through a crisis during which she was flown to New York and given radically different treatments that saved her life, and once again she is back to normal, at least to what we have come to accept as normal. She is still full of fun and we hope that she will have many more months of active life. I have

been back here with our youngest boy for several weeks and am eagerly awaiting Barbara's return. . . .

Best regards,
Pop

*[Robin's suffering ended on Columbus Day, 1953, with Barbara and me at her
bedside.]*

————

October 22, 1953

Senator Prescott S. Bush
Grove Lane
Greenwich, Conn.
Dear Dad:

Just a note to let you know that I saw Senator Lyndon Johnson yesterday at
the hotel here in Midland.

He was making a speech yesterday evening to the Lions Club, and he
walked in as I was walking out. I introduced myself to him as your son and
received a very warm greeting. He announced that you were the best thing
that had happened to the 83rd Congress. I countered with the statement that
I was glad to hear that coming from a staunch Democrat, to which he replied,
"Your father and I don't like to be thought of as Republican or Democrat,
rather as good Americans!" All I could do was nod enthusiastically and hum a
few verses of the Star Spangled Banner. . . .

All is well here, and we are settling back into our normal life. At times I
think we are just beginning to miss Robin, but I also know that in time we
will only have pleasant memories to look back on.

Devotedly,
[copy unsigned]

————

December 27, 1954

Mr. Marvin Pierce
The McCall Corporation
New York, New York
Dear Mr. Pierce:

I am sending you a copy of our recent press release on our off-shore
drilling project and a glossy print of the proposed barge. Zapata has taken this
deal and we have hired the personnel and set up the organization. We will end
up with partners undoubtedly, in fact we are now talking about a public
financing since it is too big for us to handle alone.

The main part of our business has done fairly well this year. We now have a one-third interest in seventy wells and it looks like we have about one hundred more to drill next year. As a result of this development program our company's income is going up pretty well. I will send you a statement when we get it out in a couple of months. . . .

Your Christmas presents were the hit of the day. My suit case is just perfect, Jebby never took his eyes off the record player and George was most enthusiastic over his German cars.

Please give my love to Willa* and many thanks for such a wonderful Christmas.

Best regards,
[copy unsigned]

January 24, 1955

Honorable Thomas Ludlow Ashley
House of Representatives
Washington, D.C.
Dear Lud:

Just a line to let you know that Henry Mallon Bush, weighing 9 lbs. 9 oz., was born Saturday night. Bar is fine and we are very happy with our third giant boy. I was afraid she might be a little disappointed at not having a girl, but I know now that she couldn't be more happy.

I am glad to have your observation on Congressman Alger and if we can ever pay off some of the money we owe in our business here, I might actually try to join him in that telephone booth.†

Best regards,
[copy unsigned]

[A few days later we changed the name of our third son from Henry to Neil. We wanted to name him for Neil Mallon, whose name was really Henry, but everyone called him Neil.]

---

*Barbara's father had remarried, to a woman named Willa Martin from Greenville, South Carolina.

†Alger was the only Republican congressman from Texas. There were so few Republicans in Texas in those days that we used to joke we held our meetings in phone booths.

April 7, 1955

Mr. Marvin Pierce
The McCall Corporation
New York, New York
Dear Mr. Pierce:

So that you can see where what little bread your daughter gets comes from, I am attaching annual reports on Walker-Bush Corp. and Zapata as well as a prospectus which pretty well sums up the off-shore picture. . . .

The weather has started warming up, and now if the sand would stop blowing we would get in some golf. The kids are fine. Georgie aggravates the hell out of me at times (I am sure I do the same to him), but then at times I am so proud of him I could die. He is out for Little league—so eager. He tries so very hard. It makes me think back to all the times I tried out, etc. He has good fast hands and even seems to be able to hit a little. I get as much kick out of watching him trying out as I do out of all our varied business efforts.

Jeb, the clown, is fine and Neil brings us nothing but happiness. We still miss our Robin. At times Bar and I each find ourselves vividly recalling the beauty and charm of our little girl. Time has not dulled these happy memories at all. I guess if we had Robin now we would just have too darn much happiness. . . .

Give my love to Willa,

Ever devotedly,
[copy not signed]

———

Mr. Fitzgerald Bemiss
Richmond, Virginia
Dear Gerry:

Impressed am I by the Commonwealth of Virginia stationery.* It looks like you have enough committee assignments to keep any delegate busy for the rest of his life. It was wonderful to hear from you.

Since your letter, the Zapata Petroleum Corporation stock quoted at 14 moved up to 17 and is now, as I understand it, gone back to around 15. There is no one that I had rather have as a stockholder than you, Bemiss, and yet I am reluctant to advise you to purchase the stock. I, of course, have great confidence in it, but I hate to be put in the role of touting something that is so near and dear to my heart. I do think that the stock will go higher and if you could buy some at around 14, prepared to hold it for several years, I would certainly hope you would make some money. We are working on a lot of deals and if we could make a good-sized one the stock should go up.

Bar and I have just returned from Galveston where we attended the

*Gerry had been elected to the state legislature.

launching of our new drilling barge, the Scorpion. This, you may recall, is our $3 million piece of off-shore equipment. The attached invitation is not sent along to point out to you that you weren't invited, but is enclosed to give you some idea of what this monstrous piece of equipment looks like.* Needless to say, I do not expect an R.S.V.P . . .

> Best regards and love to all,
> Pop

––––––––––

July 11, 1957

Mr. Donald K. Walker
Yale University 703-A Yale Station
New Haven, Connecticut
Dear Don:

There is a boy in Midland named Bob Connery who has just completed his Junior year in high school. This boy is very interested in attending Yale, and I am most hopeful that he can go there.

Briefly, here is the story. This boy is a straight "A" student in high school. In fact, he has never had anything but one "B" since he has been in school. Everything else has been a 'A'.

. . . He is interested in swimming and all sports although he is not big enough to letter at the school in these things. He is a good all-around boy and one of the few kids of this age I have met who seems to be intellectually curious. His main interest seems to be in math and chemistry.

This boy has had a most unhappy family life. His father, who is a doctor in Midland, married the family baby-sitter two weeks after divorcing Bob's mother. The kid has had to face all kinds of problems which few adults are called upon to solve. It is my belief he will need a full scholarship to Yale, although he may be able to come up with some expense money. There is some question as to whether he will be able to stay in Midland next year because of his broken home, but he is determined to remain even if he has to live alone. He is 16 years old. I have taught this boy in Sunday School and I feel that my confidence in him is not misplaced.

I would consider it a personal favor if you would advise me as to what steps should be taken to give this kid every chance for admission to Yale. . . .

> Yours very truly,
> George H. W. Bush

[Bob was accepted and attended Yale.]

*R.G. LeTourneau was revolutionizing the off-shore oil drilling business with his invention of the three-legged drilling barge. Zapata signed up as one of his first customers.

_____

This letter was found among my mother's things after she died in 1992. It was not dated, but based on the ages of the boys, it was probably written during the summer of 1958.

Dear Mum,

I have jotted down some words about a subject dear to your heart and mine. It is fun to fool around and try in one form or another to express thoughts that suddenly come up from way down deep in one's heart. Last night I went out on the town and on my way home—late—I said to myself, "You could well have gone to Greenwich tonight"*. . . this thought struck me out of the blue, but I felt no real sense of negligence. The part I like is to think of Robin as though she were a part, a living part, of our vital and energetic and wonderful family of men and Bar. Bar and I wonder how long this will go on. We hope we will feel this genuine closeness when we are 83 and 82. Wouldn't it be exciting at that age to have a beautiful 3½ year-old daughter . . . she doesn't grow up. Now she's Neil's age. Soon she'll be Marvin's†—and beyond that she'll be all alone, but with us, a vital living pleasurable part of our day-to-day life. I sometimes wonder whether it is fair to our boys and to our friends to "fly-high" that portrait of Robin which I love so much; but here selfishness takes over because every time I sit at our table with just our candlelight, I somehow can't help but glance at this picture you gave us and enjoy a renewed physical sensation of closeness to a loved one.

This letter . . . is kind of like a confessional . . . between you and me, a mother and her little boy—now not so little but still just as close, only when we are older, we hesitate to talk from our hearts quite as much.

There is about our house a need. The running, pulsating restlessness of the four boys as they struggle to learn and grow; the world embraces them . . . all this wonder needs a counter-part. We need some starched crisp frocks to go with all our torn-kneed blue jeans and helmets. We need some soft blond hair to off-set those crew cuts. We need a doll house to stand firm against our forts and rackets and thousand baseball cards. We need a cut-out star to play alone while the others battle to see who's "family champ." We even need someone . . . who could sing the descant to "Alouette," while outside they scramble to catch the elusive ball aimed ever roofward, but usually thudding against the screens.

We need a legitimate Christmas angel—one who doesn't have cuffs beneath the dress.

We need someone who's afraid of frogs.

*I was in New York on a business trip. Robin was buried in a Greenwich, Connecticut, cemetery.

†Our fourth boy, Marvin Pierce Bush, had been born October 22, 1956.

We need someone to cry when I get mad—not argue.

We need a little one who can kiss without leaving egg or jam or gum.

We need a girl.

We had one once—she'd fight and cry and play and make her way just like the rest. But there was about her a certain softness.

She was patient—her hugs were just a little less wiggly.

Like them, she'd climb in to sleep with me, but somehow she'd fit.

She didn't boot and flip and wake me up with pug nose and mischievous eyes a challenging quarter-inch from my sleeping face.

No—she'd stand beside our bed till I felt her there. Silently and comfortable, she'd put those precious, fragrant locks against my chest and fall asleep.

Her peace made me feel strong, and so very important.

"My Daddy" had a caress, a certain ownership which touched a slightly different spot than the 'Hi Dad" I love so much.

But she is still with us. We need her and yet we have her. We can't touch her, and yet we can feel her.

We hope she'll stay in our house for a long, long time.

Love
Pop

———————

In 1959 the Liedtkes and I decided to split Zapata into two companies: I was more interested in the offshore business, so we spun off Zapata Off-Shore of which I was president. (Under Hugh Liedtke's creative leadership, the original Zapata eventually merged into South Penn Oil Co., later changing its name to Pennzoil.) We loved our life in Midland but there was a problem: Midland is nowhere near the Gulf of Mexico, where all our drilling rigs were operating. So a very pregnant Barbara, myself, and four boys packed up and moved to Houston.

August 20, 1959

Mr. J. Hugh Liedtke
Zapata Petroleum Corp.
Midland, Texas
Dear Hugh:

We are tremendously thrilled over our new girl, Dorothy Walker. We can hardly believe it is true and just to top matters off we will be moving into our new house this week-end. Now if we could stumble into 150 ft. of gas sand we would feel grand.

Best regards and good luck on your new move.

Very truly yours,
George H. W. Bush

August 24, 1959

Mr. & Mrs. Geza Kapus
Zapata Petroleum Corp.
Midland, Texas
Dear Geza and Giesella:

How very thoughtful of you to remember Barbara in the hospital and then today Eva's lovely present came in the mail. You can imagine how thrilled we are to have a baby girl in the family. Barbara came home yesterday and the boys all gathered around and looked over the new baby with great concern. She looks just like all the others.

Best regards,
George H. W. Bush

June 15, 1960

Mr. Cornelius Ryan
New York, N.Y.
Dear Connie:

It has been a long time since our paths have crossed. Yesterday morning at the airport I picked up your terrific book* and yesterday evening I was almost through it. I never thought I would be writing a fan letter to a reprobate such as you but I must say that I don't believe I ever enjoyed reading a book more. I think in this day and age many of us are inclined to view all of our international problems without due consideration to the human aspects of a total war. We have short memories in this connection. Your forthright and sensitive treatment of D-Day is going to be crammed down the throats of each of my four boys as soon as they are old enough to digest the importance of this fine book.

The offshore business is rocking along. Actually things have improved somewhat and today our business is better than it has been in anytime during the last three or four years. Our stock is acting rather doggy but I like to think that part of this at least is due to the generally sad oil market. I note with some satisfaction that you are still a stockholder. . . .

Very truly yours,
George H. W. Bush

* *The Longest Day,* which went on to be made into an award-winning and popular movie.

December 19, 1960

Senator Prescott S. Bush
Senate Office Building
Washington, D. C.
Dear Dad,

Christmas fever has struck out at our house and the little lads'* excitement cannot be told. A large box of presents arrived from Mom the other day and please tell her that we got a beautiful guitar for Georgie at the price she mentioned. We have kept it hidden but the only thing Georgie has mentioned that he wants (and he mentions it all the time) is a guitar, so this will make his Christmas for him. . . .

Devotedly,
[copy unsigned]

The next few years were consumed with family and the new business, but by 1963 I was beginning to get a political itch. I decided to start small—very small—by running for chairman of the Harris County Republican Party. Obviously my name recognition was not very high.

February 12, 1963

Mr. Alfred Mansell
THE HOUSTON CHRONICLE
Houston, Texas
Dear Mr. Mansell:

I am taking the liberty of sending you a personal photograph. The other day the CHRONICLE published a story on Republican politics. My name was mentioned but some other character's face showed up. I would appreciate your passing this along to the proper department.

It was nice talking to you on the phone the other day and should I become Chairman of the Republican Party I would like very much to sit down and have lunch with you. Win, lose or draw I would like to do this but I would hate to waste your time so let's see how it goes and I will give you a ring when the issue has been decided.

Very truly yours,
George H. W. Bush

Lads was a term my father used a lot.

2-13-63

Dear Lud,

Long before now I should have answered your Christmas card letter. All is well with the Bush clan. Georgie is an upper-middler (class of 64) at Andover. He's doing OK there. The three other boys fight and go all the time—they're really active—Dorothy is enchanting. She is a wild dark version of Robin. They look so much alike that Mum & Dad both called Dorothy "Robin" all last week when Bar went to visit at Hobe Sound.*

I am running—yes for Chairman of the Republican Party of Harris County . . . Promise not to endorse me, OK? . . . I think I'll win—though I now have misgivings. Actually it is a challenging job and one which, if done right, could show results. . . .

Pop

_____

March 18, 1963

The Honorable T. Ludlow Ashley
House of Representatives
Washington, D.C.
Dear Lud:

. . . My opponent withdrew before the election so I recorded an overwhelming victory at the polls. I am rather immodestly enclosing a clipping from the HOUSTON CHRONICLE. This is an exciting job and tremendously interesting. We have a paid staff, 270 odd precincts in the county and Houston was the largest city in the country to carry for Nixon.† My job is primarily an organizational job since the Republican Party has quite a few unorganized precincts. So far I like it a lot and although it takes a tremendous amount of time I think it is worthwhile. . . .

Best regards,
Poppy

_____

One of my goals as county GOP chairman was to reach out to minority voters. The term big tent had not yet been invented, but I believed strongly the Republican Party should make room for every American. Some of my constituents did not agree.

_____

*My parents had a home in Hobe Sound, Florida.
†In Nixon's 1960 loss to John F. Kennedy.

July 29, 1963

Mr. William N. Michels
Houston 3, Texas
Dear Mr. Michels,

. . . I was certainly pleased to hear from you that you had been instrumental in fighting the Republican battle back in the 20's.

In working to obtain some of the Negro vote we are not trying to out promise the Democrats, nor are we trying to say one thing on one side of town and another on the other side. We have contacted certain responsible leaders, Negroes who have been Republicans for a long time and who own their own businesses. These men believe strongly in economic conservatism, freedom of the individual and in general in all the things that you and I believe in.

I do not think that we can leave 30,000–50,000 votes unsolicited in this county. I think we should make an honorable appeal to the Negro vote, realizing that we are working against very difficult odds. As long as we maintain our principles and do not try to out promise anybody I think the effort is worthwhile.

Thank you for your letter and rest assured we are trying to do a constructive job for you and other Republicans in this county.

Very truly yours,
George H. W. Bush

September 6, 1963

Dear [sister] Nance,
After talking at length with John Tower* and other State leaders this week, I have decided to go ahead and make my announcement around the middle of next week for the United States Senate. Please keep your fingers crossed for me.

Best regards,
[copy unsigned]

This letter is to a newspaper reporter working on a profile and wanting to visit one of my offshore rigs.

*John represented Texas in the U.S. Senate.

June 13, 1964

Mr. Ed Johnson
Fort Worth Star-Telegram
Fort Worth, Texas
Dear Ed,

... The only time before the Republican National Convention that I could do the offshore trip would be during the week of June 21st–June 26th ...

Barbara and I leave on the 26th for a vacation at the World's Fair and if you don't tell General Walker's boys about it, we may be going up to that rib-rocked Yankee strong-hold Maine. Following this leisurely visit with my Cape Cod heiress (the visit will get her tantalizing close to Cape Cod but I just don't dare let her put foot there)* we will then go to the National Convention where I hope to be in prominence on national TV handing the gavel to somebody.

Following the national convention we return to Texas at which point I would be delighted to make one of the first orders of business a trip to the Maverick. ...

Let me know what your desires are. I will be at the Statler Hotel in Dallas occupying, I'm sure, a smoke filled suite.

Yours truly,
George Bush

————

June 22, 1964

Congressman T.W.L. Ashley
House of Representatives
Washington, D.C.
Dear Lud,

Thanks so much for your letter. It was great hearing from you. I was pleased to win the Primary. As you may or may not have heard, I took on General Walker, The National Indignation Council and the rest of those people—it got most unpleasant as you can imagine.

Frankly, Lud, I like Goldwater. I find him far more reasonable than one would believe from reading the newspapers about him. I think he will be a greater threat to Johnson than many people feel right now, particularly in the South and West. This goes for Texas, too.

*All of this is in reference to the ultraconservative John Birch Society, which did not like me. A man named General Walker, an extremist, was one of their leaders. Among the nasty propaganda they put out was a letter saying that Barbara was "an heiress who spent all her time on the Cape." At that point in her life, Barbara was fairly certain she had never set foot on Cape Cod, but she immediately wrote her father and inquired if she was "an heiress." She was disappointed in the answer.

Ralph Yarborough* is unpopular in the State, and even though the President comes from Texas, I think there will be many people who will want to see Yarborough bumped off.

In any event, I am going to work as hard as possible and do my very best. . . . campaigning in Texas on a Statewide basis is more exhausting than anything I have ever done. . . .

Pop

———————

Earlier that summer Congress had passed the controversial Civil Rights Bill of 1964—the Senate had debated a record-breaking eighty-three days before voting. It was a difficult issue for me. I opposed discrimination of any kind and abhorred racism. Changes obviously needed to be made, but I agreed with Barry Goldwater and others who supported the concept of civil rights but felt strongly this bill was unconstitutional and threatened more rights than it protected. I decided I could not support the bill and said so in my campaign. Yarborough had voted for it, which would not help him in Texas. But I was not comfortable using that in the campaign because my reasons for not supporting the bill were very different from those who hated the bill for racist reasons. I wrote this letter to my friend and supporter Marjorie Arsht, who was a leader in Houston's Jewish community.

7-28

Dear Marjorie—
. . . My heart is heavy—I have traveled the state for 2 weeks. The civil rights issue can bring Yarborough to sure defeat. I know this now for certain—but I am not sure that a <u>fair</u> and <u>moderated</u> debate on civil rights can do it. Goldwater's position is correct (and parenthetically so is mine)—for Texas and for the USA. We must develop this position reasonably, prudently, sensitively—we must be sure we don't inflame the passions of unthinking men to garner a vote; yet it is essential that the position I believe in be explained. I believe I am right—I know we must have restraint, yet I don't want this restraint to prevent right from prevailing—My heart aches for Tom D† . . .

What shall I do? How will I do it? I want to win but not at the expense of justice, not at the expense of the dignity of any man—not at the expense of hurting a friend nor teaching my children a prejudice which I do not feel. . . .

I want and need the advice of one who can perhaps understand what troubles me!

George

*My Democratic opponent, the incumbent senator.
†Tom Dixon, a friend and supporter, and an African-American.

Sunday, 8-16

Dear Ike,*

. . . Things are shaping up. The schedule is now <u>full</u> blast Sundays included. We are broadened out past the ladies coffee set—have now reached the Bar B Que and Rotary stage—somehow I miss the intimacy of the former.

. . . R.Y. is getting mean . . . hope to generate an idea for sticking a telling blow on Ralph—preferably above the belt, but as your note suggested, maybe I can find a way to gently nudge him in the groin—oh not really!!!

Many thanks,

G Bush

I resoundingly lost that election. The entire Republican Party took a drubbing because of Lyndon Johnson's landslide win over Barry Goldwater. The cause was especially hopeless in Texas, where the popular Texas President's coattails were long. So I decided to give up politics—at least momentarily—and go back to being an oilman. First, however, I had to thank some of the people who had supported me, both those inside and outside Texas.

November 10, 1964

Mr. Richard M. Nixon
Nixon, Mudge, Rose, Guthrie & Alexander
New York 5, N.Y.
Dear Dick,

November 3rd has come and gone and we got whipped, and whipped soundly, but out of the gloom on November 3rd there are some bright spots. It is too early to analyze the election here in the state but I think objectivity dictates that we were caught in the landslide. Johnson beat Goldwater by some 700,000 votes and Yarborough beat me by 300,000 votes. Actually we received more votes than any other Republican has ever gotten in Texas, polling over 1,100,000 but with the Johnson landslide it was not in the cards to be enough vote splitting. The minority groups, principally the Negroes went to the polls and voted 98.5% to 1.5% against me. It was not my position on civil rights because they also gave the same margin they gave Johnson to people like Joe Pool, Bob Casey and to all congressmen who voted against the Civil Rights Bill. Nineteen of Texas' congressmen voted against the Bill

---

*Ike Kampmann of San Antonio. He and his wife, Flo, were among my early supporters in Texas.

and all the Democrats in the delegation got this type of percentage from the Negroes. The Negro went to the poll and "voted her straight".

We had a good campaign with the best people in Texas involved; a wonderfully dedicated spirit; a sense of humor, something I'm afraid the Goldwater campaign did not have; and a lot of dedication. I think we have a base for a future race should the opportunity present itself.

I am anxious to stay active in the Party and this I intend to do. I talked to Pete O'Donnell, our State Chairman, the other day and told him that I felt that the immediate job would be to get rid of some of the people in the Party who [permit] no difference, who through their overly dedicated conservatism are going to always keep the Party small. I have great respect for Barry Goldwater. In fact, most of his positions are totally acceptable to me. The only criticism is that his campaign, in many areas, in our State anyway, got taken over by a bunch of "nuts" whose very presence at a rally would shake up a plain fellow coming in to make up his mind. When they discovered a "doubtful" voter, instead of giving him some pro Goldwater literature they would hand him a bunch of hate stuff on Johnson. This, of course, is not the reason Goldwater lost, by a long shot, but there is too much of it and responsible people are now going to have to stand up and do something about it.

Now after giving you this background let me tell you the purpose of this letter. It is first to thank you again for your wonderful visit here in Houston. It helped immeasurably. You really got under Ralph's skin and he kept going around after this visit saying "I really am effective" and "my colleagues really do like me". In fact he ran in a few left-wing colleagues to prove his point. Your visit was great and all of us here appreciate it. It was a terrific help in fund raising.

Secondly, I have followed your comments about Nelson Rockefeller and others in the paper and I am in whole-hearted accord. Under no circumstances will Texas take Nelson Rockefeller. He would get beaten here far worse than Barry Goldwater. Goldwater's philosophy was not rejected. It was the false image that people had about Goldwater and the Johnson presence on the ticket. More particularly the latter I believe. Rockefeller's brand of liberalism just won't hunt here. You said some things that had to be said in pointing out that he sat on the sidelines and didn't hit a constructive lick. It's so true. If there is ever any way in which I can be helpful to you here in Texas let me know. I am anxious to see the Party grow and I believe the ideas that you spelled out in the papers last week make a hell of a lot of sense.

I am now back at work in the offshore drilling business where things from a business standpoint are very exciting. I must say its still hard to concentrate after the intensity of the Senate campaign. I get to New York once in a while and would like to drop by and say hello to you because I will always be indebted for the help you gave me.

Yours truly,
George Bush

––––––––––

November 13, 1964

Mrs. Brad Streeter
Wichita Falls, Texas
Dear Virginia,

The tears have dried, the dogs have stopped barking at me, the kids have let me back in the house and the people here at Zapata are beginning to recognize that they are going to have to put up with me once again. A certain normalcy is returning to things. One which, frankly on November 4th, I doubted would ever come back.

Now I can tell you just how much I appreciate the job which you and Brad did for me over the past year. You worked with a dedication and a selflessness that is rare and in addition you made every visit to Wichita Falls extremely pleasant. I just doubt the campaign, though arduous, could have been more fun. We had such terrific people around the State putting in so much work.

To you both my heartfelt thanks and deepest affection. You are terrific and someday, some way I hope I can tell you in person how deeply I feel.

Yours truly,
George Bush

––––––––––

After the thrashing the Republican Party took in 1964, I was concerned (as were most Republicans) about what the party could and should do to get back on track. I wrote this letter to Peter O'Donnell, a good friend and chairman of the Texas State Republican Party, and Texas senator John Tower.

Dec. 16, 1964

Mr. Peter O'Donnell
Dallas, Texas
Senator John G. Tower
#142, Old Senate Office Bldg.
Washington, D.C.
Dear Peter and John,

I am writing this letter to urge on you two courses of action which I feel will be beneficial to the Party and to winning elections.

First . . . I think it is essential that the State Executive Committee go on record in favor of responsibility and as opposed to Birchism (whether by name or not is debatable). This is no move towards liberalism—it simply takes some long overdue action in favor of right and against these mean, negative, super-patriots who give Texas Republicans the unfortunate image of total irresponsibility.

. . . The second point is with reference to Dean Burch.* All of us have admitted that the last campaign was a disaster. Burch didn't run it, but presumably he had a lot to do with it. He's a good guy but unfortunately in the eyes of the people, he is the symbol of defeat.

I realize that both of you are on record as favoring the retention of Burch; however, I think it is important that a difference of opinion be permitted to exist on this point without pressure. I feel Burch should step aside . . . I think he should be replaced by a man of predominantly conservative persuasion . . . I am not for changing the Party's philosophy as outlined in the platform. I am for broadening the base of the Party, permitting differences to exist, etc.

. . . How I hope we can learn a lesson from the past so as to win in the future!

Yours very truly,
George Bush

I tried to keep focused on business in 1965— and I had doubts whether I wanted to run again for public office anyway—but it wasn't long before friends started talking to me about another race, this one for Congress. I wrote this note to my extraordinarily able friend Charles Untermeyer, who would work for me in various capacities for years to come.

July 20, 1965

Mr. Charles Untermeyer
Houston, Texas 77024
Dear Charles,

. . . Regarding the congressional race in the 7th District, it is way too early to make up one's mind on something like this although there is a possibility that I will run. I am going to think about it, but so many factors enter into a decision of this nature, such as business, family life, etc., that I just can't decide this far in advance.

---

*Dean Burch was put in by Barry Goldwater as head of the Republican National Committee, and he did resign soon after this. At this point I had never even met Burch. Later on he became one of my closest friends and supporters. I found him to be broad-minded and certainly able. The lesson here is "Do not judge others without knowing them personally."

Should I run, I would most certainly welcome your support next summer. Thanks again for your thoughtful letter and please excuse my delay in answering it.

Yours very truly,
George Bush

———

En route K'port to Houston
Dear Gerry & Margaret,

That was a real nice clam bake—In fact that was a nice summer. We're now somewhere between Newark (god it was hot during that long stay on the ground there) and Atlanta—last stop before Houston. The kids are reaching that kind of restless stage—you know the pinch that's just a little harder and the whine—just a touch more penetrating—but I don't care. My thoughts are back near the beach busy with some wily ones on the hook, or in the cold water, or on the links or courts, or in the sack on a cold Maine night, and no fight or tease can divert me now.

What fun we had, and how much you have contributed to it. After you left it wasn't as great. We had a good big storm come through so we got some great rock pounding surf and some real cold days. We had a couple of hot tennis and golfs and some rebelling*—no mackerel at all—they left. John [Bush] brought Dina, his girl down . . . We had a cocktail party on the point, John & Bucky did—planning as to food was poor—John at 10 came to our house for some scraps of ham and some frozen English muffins—He cooked this all together—result: English muffins black on the outside—ice cold in; ham, pretty scraggly—No one cared . . .

Today was a perfect Maine day—crisp, clear—we crowded all the action in we could and then took off in a Grapes of Wrath like scene—

I am sad to be going home in a way—yet also glad. That great and wonderful feeling that K'port gives. We are happy you were there—it made our summer perfect—and as we now again start in to compete in business, as we now start to try to figure out where we are and where we go . . . we do it all refreshed and with much happiness for having seen you all . . .

Adios and love,

Poppy

———

Storms were always one of the biggest enemies of the offshore oil industry, and I had become accustomed to dealing with battered and washed-up oil rigs. How-

---

*This refers to my boat, Rebel.

ever, the worst happened in 1965, probably best explained in this "chairman's letter" in the 1965 annual report:

In the history of our company the year 1965 will be remembered both as a year of progress and a year of disappointment. I believe you will find the progress clearly spelled out in the following report on our activities and in the financial statements. The disappointment came in the loss of our large and highly successful drilling barge MAVERICK which disappeared in Hurricane Betsy.

On September 9th, the day Hurricane Betsy struck, MAVERICK was located 20 miles off the Louisiana Coast in 220 feet of water. The following day an inspection showed Zapata's three other rigs were undamaged, but the MAVERICK had vanished.* This was the largest single loss that the domestic offshore drilling industry sustained in this or any other hurricane. Another rig, identical to the MAVERICK, drilling less than 40 miles from it, came through the storm with no damage. The unpredictability of hurricanes was borne out by the freak occurrence.

. . . The MAVERICK loss was a substantial one for Zapata. This was our newest rig and one of our very best contracts; but in spite of this loss we posted record earnings. Fortunately, we have two other rigs under construction and the earning power generated by this new equipment should assure Zapata's future growth. . . .

Respectfully submitted,
George H. W. Bush
Chairman

———————

The political bug bit me once again and I decided to run for Congress. I realized I could not pursue both a career in politics and do justice to our public shareholders of Zapata. I made the agonizing decision to sell my shares in Zapata, being sure any shareholders wanting to sell were offered the same price I received. Anyone who has started and run a company can appreciate what a tough move this was, but I felt it was best for all involved. I wrote family friend Tom Devine, who had been an investor and supporter:

Feb. 6th

Dear T:

. . . There are so many trying days that I remember well—bent legs, no work, storms, financial crises, personnel problems—you name it—and through them all you were there to give me so darn much help and so much good advice.

---

*Fortunately, the rig had been totally evacuated and no lives were lost.

I feel like I am selling a baby. I am sure that it is right, but I have a strong feeling for the individuals at Zapata. I will miss them, I will miss their problems. . . . (you remember the one with the sex problem after her husband was killed in a plane crash) through the rest of the office types, to Hoyt, and Buster* and the others who have made Zapata click on a day to day basis.

I think, Tom, that you more than any other Zapata director understood the business and knew the enormity of our problems, or when they were not so big you were the first to size this up too. . . .

I am lucky to have your friendship, your wonderful loyal friendship; and the happy thing about all this is that I know it.

Cheers,
G. Bush

———————

In the end, I guess selling Zapata was worth it. I became the first Republican elected from Texas's Seventh Congressional District, beating conservative Democrat Frank Briscoe.

Nov. 13th

Dear Bemi,

Thanks for your wire and your great letter. Needless to say we were thrilled. The margin turned out to be almost 58% so this may bode well for the future. I was running against their supposed best vote getter. The hard-hitting crusading D.A. type. He proved to be less formidable on national issues than we had thought and he pitched his campaign way over in right field—near the Birchers—strongly anti Lyndon and a subtle appeal to the back-lash. . . . In any event he has been done in (saying after the election that Bush's money and LBJ cost him the election—not too gracious in defeat) . . .

So where now. Bar and I are going to D.C. Wednesday for two days to apartment hunt. We have decided to leave the lads here in school until June and Bar will be here a lot. I'll commute—unsatisfactory but no other plan seems as good . . . Thursday night we go to Hobe for four days with Mum and Dad—the unwinding department. John Bush came down for the election and was, as you can imagine, something else again.

Love to all . . .

Pop

———————

*Hoyt Taylor was one of the company vice presidents and chief engineer; Buster Whittington was the drilling superintendent and in charge of all the rigs.

So after eighteen years in Texas (minus a year in California), Barbara and I headed for Washington. Though Texas remained our home—our base—we had no idea then that it would be twenty-six years before we would come back to stay put for good. Just as my World War II experience taught me a lot about life, so did my years in the Texas oil fields. I learned the honor system of doing business—just a simple handshake sealed many of our deals. I learned what it meant to take risks, and how to start over when you failed. I learned the true meaning of grief when Robin died. Sometimes when a child dies, the parents drift apart; but miraculously, her passing strengthened our faith and our love for each other.

We made some of our best friends in Midland, and later in Houston. We really grew up together and raised our children together. Our Texas friends have stuck with us all these years, through losing and winning. It's only appropriate that in 1999 we're all together again, living just down the street or across town from each other—just as we did in the fifties and sixties. They are the reason why, after the 1992 election, we never thought twice about what to do next: go home to Texas, of course.

CHAPTER 3

Potomac Fever

The task of becoming a congressman began almost immediately, although it would be two months before I took office. The first order of business was vying for committee assignments. The key person to lobby was Gerald Ford, then a congressman from Michigan and House minority leader.

———————

November 26, 1966

The Honorable Gerald Ford
U. S. House of Representatives
Washington, D.C.
Dear Gerry,*

In reply to your letter of November 14th, and keeping in mind our 'phone conversation of Wednesday of this week, I am attaching a Request For Committee Assignment.

I put down, as you will see, a strong plea for Appropriations. I noticed that the Democrats did put a Freshman on this committee last year. I hope that I have not tried to "oversell" on this matter.

I know you are swamped with all kinds of grandiose requests—perhaps this ranks as the grandiosest of them all, but whatever you decide will be fine with me; and I promise to work like hell to be a good member of whatever committee I get. . . .

I have been delighted with your comments I have been reading in the papers. I hope we'll be able to be "for" a bunch of things in 90th. It is so

———————

*He actually spells his name "Jerry," but I had not figured that out yet.

important, particularly coming from Texas, that we offer solutions to problems and that we dispel the image of Republicans as aginners.*

Best regards.

Sincerely,
George Bush

––––––––––

November 25, 1966

The Honorable Melvin R. Laird†
U. S. House of Representatives
Washington, D.C.
Dear Mel,

I am very sorry to have missed you when I was up house hunting. Incidentally, we bought Milward Simpson's‡ house in Spring Valley so at least we have a roof for January occupancy.

I am taking the liberty of sending you a copy of a request for committee assignment which I sent to Gerry Ford at his request. Before mailing it, I talked to Gerry lest the request for Appropriations Committee be misinterpreted as an awful grabby thing for a Freshman Congressman.

. . . I don't want you or any of the others in the leadership to feel that I expect any special consideration,§ but Gerry said to go ahead, under the circumstances, and write it up, so this I have done.

. . . If the idea has any possibility of working out, I'd like to touch the right bases but I want desperately not to offend any of the wiser and older hands around the House. Should such a paper be sent to the Chairman of the Committee on Committees?

Please call me . . . or drop me a line if you care to give me any advice on any of this.

Very truly yours,
George Bush

*Being in the minority, Republicans had the image in some quarters of being "against" everything, or in slang terms, *aginners*. The reference to "the 90th" means that I would be a member of the Ninetieth Congress.

†Mel was then a congressman from Wisconsin and chairman of the Republican Conference; he was later secretary of defense in the Nixon administration.

‡The retiring senator from Wyoming and the father of the future senator and my good friend Alan Simpson. We had decided to go ahead and buy a house and move the family to Washington. However, George W. was already a student at Yale, and Jeb stayed in Houston to finish school there, living with our good friends Baine and Mildred Kerr.

§This was less about my dad and more about the fact that a Republican from Texas was still a rarity.

_____

Before I was even sworn in, I began to be swamped with constituent mail. My most faithful pen pal was a Houston gentleman named Paul Dorsey, who worked as a photographer. Much to my staff's dismay, I took time every Saturday morning to answer his letters. He was no fan of mine in the beginning, but during our fifteen-month relationship, we actually became friends (although his criticism never stopped). The next group of letters are to Mr. Dorsey, and looking back on them more than thirty years later, I find that they almost provide a diary of my first year in Congress.

December 16, 1966

Dear Mr. Dorsey,

. . . I want to make a confession. When I saw your first letter in the newspaper, pro Briscoe–anti Bush, I immediately said to myself, "There's a damn crackpot." Then came your letter with the advice on how to conduct myself in the Congress. I gave it to my very pro-Bush secretary who has also had a lot of experience in politics. She said, "Well, I guess we've got this guy all wrong." She also pointed out, and I agree, that P. Dorsey knows a lot about the Congress and the affairs of the Country.

You're right about Adam Clayton Powell. Negro or white, no one should flaunt the laws as openly as he has and sit in the Congress of the United States.* You're wrong about being for Briscoe over me. You're right about giving me a chance to show what I can do.

But, lets have a Holiday armistice. Leave the cudgels on the shelf, keep the needle ready, blunt and ready, but don't use it on me until after January 10th, when the Congress convenes.

I hope you have a great Christmas and prosperous New Year. I know I'll be hearing from you in '67, but in spite of the needle, in spite of the cudgels, in spite of your poor political judgment in being for Briscoe instead of me, I must say I'm kinda looking forward to getting the letters. I have somewhat reluctantly concluded, as you can see, that you probably know what you're talking about and are right more than you're wrong. After all, isn't this what it's all about?

Merry, Merry Christmas,

Sincerely,
George Bush

_____

*Powell, a Democratic congressman from New York, was eventually denied his seat because of charges he misused government funds.

January 14, 1967

Dear Mr. Dorsey:

We have to establish some ground rules. I know that text books on this job say answer every letter—in your case, tho I'd like to, for your letters are provocative, I can't answer 'em all. You studied Civics 2 well and when they said write your congressman you sure do . . . Hell, if I were as rich as the papers say I'd pay to get a jet to bring you up here just to sit down . . .

Things I do like from Dorsey:

1. view on state of union message—you can say more personal things about LBJ than I can but the points I find to be totally acceptable.*
2. knowledge of Washington scene—some day you must tell me where you got all this background.
3. Frankness, even when in disagreement with my mighty views.

Things I don't like from Dorsey:

1. Suggestion that the astute statesman who sent in letter saying Bush should be President might be on my payroll—surely, sir, you can recognize that bestirring of the grass roots. No, Mr. Jungman must indeed be a shrewd unpaid observer of the national big picture.
2. Canning Secretary—this upset us. Not too much and no action has been taken but what it did was cast a pall over our normally bubbling office staff—"If Mrs. Brown† can receive the wrath of Dorsey, what about me" kind-of-thing.
3. Criticism for applauding President. There is such a thing as manners. Most of the GOP including yours truly sat on hands much of time. I don't like LBJ programs, but he's not wrong on everything—so I clap when I think he's right and throw stuff when he's wrong . . .
4. criticism of Kennedy‡ Hairdo—It's swingin', man. I think it'll prove to be his undoing. . . .

General Comments on Dorsey

1. He must be quite a guy. . . . We can argue politics, and we can and will agree and disagree—but all this is beside the point. I now have a treasured personal view of a man who obviously can think and feel, and who's trying to reach for something. . . .

---

*Dorsey had blasted LBJ's State of the Union message, both the substance and style. He thought LBJ wanted to spend too much of the taxpayers' dollar and give the federal government too much power over the states. I agreed with him on both counts. He also thought LBJ's delivery was boring.

†My secretary's name was Aleene Smith, but Paul insisted on calling her Mrs. Brown. For some reason, he also decided he didn't like her and suggested she be fired.

‡Senator Robert Kennedy of New York.

2. I hope he continues to eat me out or holler in rage as I vote or who knows even agree at times. . . .

> Best regards,
> George Bush

——————

January 27, 1967

Dear Paul:*

. . . I hope you approved of my committee assignment. Let's face it. There's a lot of luck involved in this, and I was at the right place at the right time. But no matter how you skin it, it's a real good break for a freshman Congressman to be on the Ways and Means Committee.†

Life has been hectic. I've been briefed by every department on the Hill, and though it's a liability in Texas, I find that the Ivy League bit is not too big a liability around some of these agencies. I have been favorably impressed by some of the people and rather dismally impressed by others. But isn't this the way life is?

More later. Best regards.

> George Bush, M.C.‡

——————

February 3, 1967

Dear Paul:

Thank you for your letter of the 30th about the committee. . . . it takes plenty of time. For the first two days on the debt ceiling we met for six and a half hours a day, and I sat there up to my neck in tables and graphs. Wilbur Mills§ appears to be fair-minded and will give everybody a chance, though I must say, when it came my time to take a shot at the Secretary of the Treasury, I decided to listen rather than talk.

. . . You won the battle of the mouthwash.** Now what can you do for the armpit sufferers?

> Best regards,
> George Bush

* It was about time we were on a first-name basis.

†Instead of getting my first choice, the Appropriations Committee, I was appointed to the more powerful Ways and Means Committee.

‡Member of Congress.

§The powerful chairman of the Ways and Means Committee for whom I had great respect; respect that he earned simply by knowing more about the subjects before Ways and Means than anyone else.

**He had written Johnson & Johnson complaining that their mouthwash commercials were irritating, especially when viewed while eating.

I wrote this letter after Mr. Dorsey told me he had been diagnosed with cancer. A short time later he called me at home for the first time. Barbara answered the phone and he showered her with praise; she had no idea who he was.

April 8, 1967

Dear P.D.,

Say—what are you trying to do to my wife—she was teary and grateful and very happy. She was embarrassed about the lack of recognition on the phone, but I took her our correspondence file and let her read it—something I never do, because I keep my business and politics separate from my home life—usually that is. She is not informed on issues and intrigue—perhaps this is selfish on my part but we have a close, close relationship with the kids, et al, and I just want to have that oasis of privacy. However, where friendship is involved we have a new ballgame. Suffice it to say she is your admirer and friend.

No more politics in this letter. I am not happy with the news you sent me. I don't like the pain, I don't like the whole damn thing. . . . You must keep me advised on the progress—you must also remember that in this field there is change—there is radical discovery—there is hope. I will never forget when they told me Robin had leukemia—age 4—beautiful, sinless, full of vitality. The lady doctor, our friend, when I asked what we should do—said "Let nature take its course—spare yourself the agony of treatment for this is an advanced case"—then with broken heart I called my uncle at Memorial Hospital in N.Y.

He was a great cancer surgeon, who had been stricken with polio.* A strong and purposeful man. I told him of our local doc's advice and he said "You have no choice—none at all—you must treat this child. You must do all you can to keep her alive" and he went on to tell me of the strides in the field and of the importance of hope. So we treated her, and we watched her die before our eyes, but we also saw the wonders of remission and the dedication of the nurses and doctors, and we saw progress and we knew his advice was right. Six months later when it was all over—I thought back with gratitude for this sensible advice—it was tough on Barbara—I guess the toughest assignment a mother could have—for she was there for the bone marrow tests—the ordeals of blood. Someone had to look into Robin's eyes and give her comfort and love and somehow, Paul, I didn't have the guts. My point I guess is this—today a kid with leukemia has a much greater chance—and so tomorrow perhaps a gutsy guy with carcinoma might well have it made.

If there is anything a far away friend can do to make this possible you

*My mother's brother Dr. John Walker.

should tell him—you should not hold back for embarrassment sake—you should not be afraid to tell a friend, for you owe it to yourself to battle it with all you've got. Never forget that friends, true friends, get pleasure—pure selfish pleasure—from being around when they are needed. Let me know what it is I can do—when-where-what.

Adios,
George Bush

April 21, 1967

Dear Paul,

I got your note about the license plates. I used to have those personal plates but traded them in on ones that say House and also U.S. Congress. They get a good deal of notoriety around town and I guess it's a good thing except when one of my kids starts to speed.

Things are getting along pretty good here. I have been spending at least four hours a day in the Ways and Means hearings (executive sessions) on the social security legislation. It is tedious and long but I'm sure I'll have a much better understanding of the problems after these weeks in hearings.

Last night you would have been pleased. I attended a Teamsters' Banquet . . . How's this for getting "grass-rootsy"? . . . I learned one thing pretty quick—that is, don't say anything against Hoffa at a Teamsters' meeting. I didn't, but there was a great deal of obvious sentiment for him there.* The Teamsters have a unique way of campaigning. They send their wives around to the offices laden with tough questions. My approach is to be very frank with them and tell them where I agree with them and where I don't.

Hope things are getting along good for you there. I don't like sending this to the hospital. I'd rather have you out there at your own place with your own typewriter and your own wealth of documents.

Best regards,
George Bush

August 23, 1967

Dear Paul:

It was good hearing from you.

As usual, you are screwed up on some of your political thinking, but it almost sounds like you're your same old mean self again.

You are right about the poverty program and the votes. You are wrong

---

*This was before Jimmy Hoffa disappeared. That would not happen until 1975.

about my comments on the TSU* rioters. All I was saying was that the innocent should be promptly processed and released. This is the American system, and I'm sure you would agree.

You are right about the midnight program being boring. But look at it this way. There was always Channel 11 or Channel 13 to switch to. You are partially wrong about Francis Williams, the head of the Poverty program.† He is to some degree a victim of circumstances. I agree that he's wrong about those indicted for murder. Technically, they are not murderers until convicted. But he has been right in trying to keep the black power elements from taking over the Poverty Program. You are wrong about my wife. She's not nearly as great as you think she is. Oh well, maybe, on balance, she is. You are right on some of your comments about public stature—not all. I am worried about trying to build a constructive record here and it isn't too easy.

Get well quick—In spite of your rightness and wrongness, it was terrific hearing from you. Mrs. Smith Brown is fine and so is Jim Allison‡ and we talk about you often.

Best regards,
George

[Paul Dorsey died in January 1968. We did finally meet, when I went to visit him in the hospital.]

———

I sent a copy of this letter to all my friends and supporters. This particular copy went to one of my closest friends and advisers, Jim Baker, a friend from Houston.

January 11, 1968

Mr. James A. Baker, III
Houston, Texas
Dear Jim:

Before making a public announcement of my intentions, I wanted to let you know that I plan to run for reelection to the Congress.

This has not been an easy decision. Many of my friends have urged me to consider the governor's race, but I feel that I have just begun my work in the congress, to which you helped elect me, and so I have decided against making the race for governor.

---

*Texas Southern University, a historically black college in Houston.

†Francis Williams got a lot of bad press in those days, including being accused of putting murderers on his payroll.

‡Jimmy was my campaign manager, then organized my congressional office and served as administrative assistant.

I want to thank you again for all you have done, and I hope that I can count on your help and support this year. I am looking forward to being closely associated with you in the campaign ahead.

Very truly yours,
George Bush, M.C.

————————

The day after Christmas 1967, I left on a fact-finding trip to Vietnam. This was during the height of the war, and our country was continuing to sink into this quagmire. Following are some letters I wrote when I returned home:

January 12, 1968

Mrs. R. L. Murray
Alexandria, Virginia 22308
Dear Mrs. Murray:

I am just back from Vietnam. Last week I had breakfast with your husband and then he took me on a tour of some hamlets.

I thought you might like to have these pictures. They are pretty good of him. My feelings will not be hurt if you clip me out. They were taken at Swinwa Village.

The General looked well and gave me a great time. The respect his men have for him was evident. I particularly noted his warmth and affection for those beguiling Vietnamese children in the hamlets.

Don't bother to acknowledge. I simply wanted to give you this firsthand report on your far away husband. Let's hope he will be home soon.

Very truly yours,
George Bush, M.C.

————————

January 16, 1968

Major General F. K. Mearns
Headquarters 25th Infantry Division
APO San Francisco 96225
Dear General Mearns:

Thanks so much for your letter of January 10th and those wonderful pictures which I am delighted to have. I do appreciate your kind words.

I called Mrs. Mearns this morning and had a nice chat with her on the phone . . . to give her a firsthand report on you and to tell her how cordial you had been to me. She sounded great, full of pep. She, too, had gotten the pictures from you taken out in the rice cache.

Thanks again for a great day out there. I was particularly interested in the

P.S. on your letter about the Mustang Battalion fight. I follow the war with a great deal more interest now, having seen so many of the places involved. I am concerned about the spirit here at home and about the lack of understanding of the kind of job you and your troops are doing. Perhaps in some small way I can help offset this feeling of discontent.

Again, my warmest regards.

Yours very truly,
George Bush, M.C.

———————

Those of you who are old enough to remember the 1960s—no matter your age at the time—have to agree it was a challenging time for America. The Vietnam War was tearing our country apart. The protests were often ugly, violent, and personal. Furthermore, I felt—as did many of my generation—that too many young people used the war as an excuse to break the law, practice free sex, take drugs, and eschew responsibility of any kind. The personal values I had been taught as a child were threatened and, at least for a time, seemed lost. I wrote this note to my friend Bob Blake, an early political supporter.

February 6, 1968

Mr. Robert W. Blake
Lubbock, Texas 79408
Dear Bob:

It was great to get your recent letter and to hear from you, even if what you had to say was sobering.

Things here in Washington look even more glum than the way you see them in Lubbock. The whole list of things you mentioned—the Pueblo, the war, de Gaulle, and the Great Society*—is compounding its horrors at a rate exceeded only by the credibility gap. I fully agree that we Republicans had better come up with a good ticket to take advantage of the situation—and start cleaning up the mess.

. . . Thanks again for your note and please write more often.

Yours very truly,
George Bush, M.C.

———————

*The North Koreans had seized the USS *Pueblo* and its eighty-three-man crew in the Sea of Japan (they were released in December); de Gaulle, president of France, had been bashing America; the Great Society was President Johnson's domestic program, which Republicans generally disliked because of its huge cost.

The most controversial vote of my four years in the House of Representatives was the Open Housing Bill of 1968, which was an extension of the 1964 Civil Rights Bill. Almost all of my constituents were opposed to it, as were most in the Texas congressional delegation. I still had some constitutional concerns about the bill, just as I did in 1964, but the problem of discrimination troubled me deeply. I became particularly passionate on the issue after my tour in Vietnam, where I saw young black soldiers fighting and dying for love of their country while affluent white kids ran away or got deferred, letting others go in their place. Were we supposed to tell these black soldiers when they came home that they couldn't buy houses in our neighborhood? The day Martin Luther King died, I scribbled this note to Chase Untermeyer, who had urged me to vote for the bill.

April 4, 1968

Dear CGU,

I am most grateful for your "unsolicited views" on open housing.

. . . I'll vote for the bill on final passage—Have misgivings—giant political misgivings—also constitutional—also I know it won't solve much . . . but I'm <u>for</u> much of the bill and in my heart I know you're right on the <u>symbolism</u> of open housing.

The mail is more on this than any subject since I've been in Congress—all against except 2 letters—500 to 2 I'd guess.

But this will be my character builder and friend antagonizer—and your letter helped me decide—

Thanks,
GB

_____

April 11, 1968

Charlie-me-boy [Untermeyer]:

. . . Yesterday, I voted for the Civil Rights bill. Today, I am being fitted for my lead underwear. And Sunday, I go back to Houston.

Adios,
GB

_____

I did go back to Houston to face my angry constituents. When I arrived at an open meeting, I was greeted with catcalls and boos, and at first they wouldn't even let me speak. Eventually they calmed down enough so I could at least be heard. No one was more shocked than I when, at the end, they gave me a standing ovation. This is the speech I gave:

And now I'd like to frankly discuss my recent vote of the civil rights bill, a vote which has brought some approval and much concern. . . .

On this bill I received over 1100 letters—most of it against the bill, much of it centered on the discriminatory real estate agent provisions* and much of it in response to advertisements both locally and across the state.

The real estate mail was good mail—it was forceful and factual and most of it stated the powerful case well.

Much of the other mail was persuasive and well done—some of it was filled with hatred.

Since the vote, there has been quite a lot of mail—Some of it is favorable—

A lot of it disagrees with my vote and tells me why in a forceful but extremely fair way.

But much of it was filled with venom and vitriol.

The unsigned letter.

The threat.

The "sell-out" approach

The phone call

The "nigger-lover"—this in 1968 with our country ripped apart at the seams.

The base and mean emotionalism that makes me bow my head in sadness.

There is an irony here—much of the mail comes from people who have written me in favor of the Dirksen amendment for prayer in schools—an amendment I have introduced in the House—and you should see what it says about Senator Dirksen, who supported this Bill in the Senate, and of course what it says about me.

Much of it says the Congress succumbed to pressure in the light of the riots, though the Bill passed the Senate almost 1½ months ago by almost 4 to 1 with but 3 Republicans voting against it—and it was scheduled in the House for April 10th—3 weeks before the riots and the tragic assassination of Dr. Martin Luther King.

Some thought the house should change its schedule because of the riots—and they have a point but, I don't feel this great body should change its schedule under pressure of any kind.

It has been suggested that were it not for the riots, the Bill would have lost in the House—this is not true—look at the Senate majorities.

Here is my position—

I liked some of the provisions—I didn't like others—

---

*I felt the bill was unfair to real estate agents, since it forced them to play under different rules from homeowners who sold their houses directly, without an agent.

I liked the provisions making it a federal offense to interfere with a man exercising his Constitution given rights to peacefully petition and peacefully demonstrate.

I like the part making it unlawful to exclude people from schools because of race, color, creed or natural origin—or to keep people from voting—or attending school.

I liked the provisions to bring the full power of Federal law against those who teach others to make, or who ship firearms, or Molotov cocktails or similar devices "knowing they will be used in a civil disorder"—a riot if you will.

I like the part protecting firemen and policemen as they try to quell riots—

If ever we needed full protection in the Law for these men, it is now. I especially like the part making it a federal crime to cross state lines or to use interstate communications (TV, radio, telephone) to incite a riot, or organize a riot or to aid people in rioting. . . .

On open housing—I voted first to send the Bill to conference where it could be amended. (The only section I received mail on) So did the leadership.

Under the Bill the individual home owner is exempt—most of my mail does not reflect a knowledge of this important fact.

My view is that the Bill discriminates against the real estate people. After December 31, 1969, it prohibits individual owners, free to discriminate under the Bill, from using a real estate agent to sell as he wishes.

I opposed this and wanted to see the Bill amended.

When the vote to send the Bill to conference failed and the Bill passed, I promptly introduced legislation (HR 16626) to correct this major inequity—I hope this makes some headway . . .

Many fear that this new legislation will radically alter their living pattern in Houston. I understand this concern, but I urge you to look at the 20 plus states which have more sweeping legislation on the books than this Bill— New York, Pennsylvania, Indiana, just to name three. There is no drastic change in their pattern of living.

What this Bill does do in this area is to remove an obstacle—what it does do is try to offer a promise or a hope—a realization of The American Dream.

In Vietnam I chatted with many Negro soldiers. They were fighting, and some were dying, for the ideals of this Country; some talked about coming back to get married and to start their lives over.

Somehow it seems fundamental that this guy should have a hope. A hope that if he saves some money, and if he wants to break out of a ghetto, and if he is a good character and if he meets every requirement of purchaser—the door will not be slammed solely because he is a Negro, or because he speaks with a Mexican accent.

In these troubled times, fair play is basic. The right to hope is basic. And so I suggest that there are things wrong with this Bill and there are things right with it.

I have been accused of killing the Republican Party. With one of the more conservative voting records in the House, I am now accused by some of killing the Republican party by this one vote.

But I don't believe it. All Republican Senators voting except 3 voted for this Bill—

100 out of 184 Republicans in the House voted for it.

Richard Nixon and about every national Republican leader advocated its passage. . . .

I may not be right on this vote—only time will tell—

But I voted from conviction.

I see the shortcomings of the Law—but I also see its strengths.

I see its invasions of property, but I see its strong provisions against inciting civil disorders.

I see its discrimination against the real estate business but, I see its several riot control provisions—and I see a ray of hope—not a handout—not a gift—but a ray of hope for the Negroes locked in by habit and sometimes regrettably by prejudice alone.

And so I voted . . . not out of intimidation or fear, not stampeded by riots—but because of a feeling deep down in my heart that this was the right thing for me to do. That this was the right thing for America.

I know it was not a popular vote—the strong and fair protest in the mail tells me this.

But, as I read this hatred—as I hear a great leader of our party ridiculed for going to a man's funeral*—as the venom surfaces and the veneer is torn away from some—showing a base and ugly prejudice, I feel a deep sadness in my heart.

I don't ask agreement on this or any issue—I worried and struggled about this vote.

I knew it would be unpopular—I knew it would be emotional—but I did what I thought was right—what more can I tell you!

———

This letter I wrote to Jimmy Allison on the plane back to Washington showed just how violent some of the reaction was.

———

*I'm likely referring to Martin Luther King's funeral, but I don't remember now which Republican leader was being criticized for attending.

Dear Jimmy,

. . . I never dreamed the reaction would be so violent. Seething hatred—the epithets—the real chicken shit stuff in spades—to our [office] girls: "You must be a nigger or a Chinaman"—and on and on—and the county crowd disowning me and denouncing me and wondering if they could "still continue to support me"—and at the Gridiron Dinner the snubs by legislative candidates who were wanting my support and fawning all over me a couple of months ago . . .

Tonight I got on this plane and this older lady came up to me. She said, "I'm a conservative Democrat from the district, but I'm proud, and will always vote for you now" . . . and suddenly somehow I felt that maybe it would all be OK—and I started to cry—with the poor lady embarrassed to death—I couldn't say a word to her . . .

[copy unsigned]

———————

I wrote this letter to a friend, Richard Mack, who had written me a very antiwar letter.

Easter Sunday

Dear Dick,

I am writing this at home—self typed I'll have you know—and at a great big loss because I regret to say I have lost your magnificent letter, and thus cannot give you the detailed reply that a concerned letter like that deserves. I put the letter in my brief case to answer on the plane, but it has been lost—probably amongst the literally hundreds of letters I have gotten on the Civil Rights Bill. I voted for the bill and the roof is falling in—boy does the hatred surface. I have had more mail on this subject than on Viet Nam and Taxes and sex all put together. Most of the mail has been highly critical of my vote—emotional and mean—but a little has been reassuring. Anyway, your letter on War and Peace is buried somewhere and this makes me sad for I wanted to send you a respectable reply.

Let me make a few points. I think you are wrong on the immorality aspect of it all. I just don't buy that this is an immoral war on our part. If you want to argue that all war is immoral—fine; but this selectivity and this blind willingness to emphasize the weaknesses of the South Viet Nam government while totally overlooking the terror of the VC and the past slaughters by Ho* and the boys I can't buy.

. . . If I felt we were seeking permanent ground in this country I might buy

———————

*Ho Chi Minh, the president of North Vietnam. *VC* stands for the Viet Cong.

the immorality theory—but I don't feel that. From a military standpoint I think we are fighting the wrong war. I think in retrospect that we should have learned from the history books; but this is not a comment on the war's morality or lack thereof.

I think the peace talks might well lead to peace—these efforts are deep and there is private evidence that Ho wants to stop the level of fighting—so let us hope the problem is further on its way to solution than when your letter was written. I am convinced that the military pressure has compelled Ho to take a look at least at peace talks—it wasn't the fact that the country is divided. It wasn't the fact that there were voices here for unilaterally turning this country over to the North Vietnamese—rather it was the cruel and hard fact that Ho was getting hurt.

. . . I am hopeful that the Geneva Accords can provide a basis for understanding which will move the talks along faster than they moved in Korea. The situation is so taut though that the whole talk thing could blow sky high—I of course hope it doesn't.

. . . In summary all I ask is an objective look. I can recognize the lack of viability of the government in the south but I recognize its improvement. Bobby Kennedy, knowing damn well they start drafting 18 year olds in May—talks about their failure to draft 18 year olds. He doesn't mention the percentage of their youth in the military, he doesn't talk about the vast improvement* . . . He as much says they are lousy fighters and cowards and yet everyone I talked to over there—not the big brass—but the little American sergeant who is risking getting his ass shot off side by side with these troops, say they are good fighters—who have improved considerably and who will continue to improve.

I think the biased reporting on this stinks . . . In this regard all I call for is balance—fairness—but no, the emphases is on our round that falls short—or the brutality of the South Vietnamese—or the civilians killed by our napalm. When I went to V.Nam I thought every hamlet had been devastated by our napalm—how grossly unfair this turned out to be. . . .

And so when we want the war over, we can want it over for different reasons. We can want it over because we don't want to fight ourselves—or because we think it is immoral . . . or because we think it is diverting funds from other purposes, or because this country shouldn't involve ourselves in this type of massive effort in a country not suited to resisting guerrilla and terror tactics. The thing that amazes me often is the arrogance and total lack of compassion on the part of some doves who suggest that those who don't want

*This is in reference to comments Senator Kennedy had made saying the South Vietnamese military was not doing its part.

to turn tail and quit really don't want the war to end—Hey hey LBJ how many kids did you kill today*—how brutal can a critic be . . . I detest this suggestion that the President really doesn't care about human lives. Look, I don't go [for] LBJ, I vote against him all the time, but I'm not going to take that mean step which strips the man of any feeling and assigns to him unthinkable motives—and all the time these smart critics are immune to the repeated abuses, the sheer terror and torture of the VC. Good god Dick there must be some fair play somewhere in all this.

Lastly you get all over the Congress—all I can tell you, and you can believe it or not, is that there is deep concern. Not many congressmen want to haul ass—to quit—some few did but very few, but I don't know any who want to see these peace talks fail and I know a hell of a lot who feel that only by keeping the pressure up as long as we have could we get any kind of reasonable chance for talks—most felt and I think rightly so, that to pull back or retreat would only further strengthen the resolve of Hanoi. The protests at home (and I'm not saying here they shouldn't be) have definitely strengthened Hanoi's will, but the pressure remained on and it hurt and now maybe they will try for a peace—not that they'll go away for they may try to gain at the table which they couldn't gain in the field, but at least we can stop the slaughter and the spending and hopefully we'll learn from the past.

I have concluded there is no easy answer. And that is where we differ—you think there is. I am not a "Communism is monolithic"† man; but nor am I one who feels the Communists have renounced their clearly stated goals for world revolution or world takeover. I am hopeful over the split between Russia and China and I'd like to see it widen; but I am not about to believe that either suddenly thinks we're OK and that they will support this. The next struggle will be in the Middle East. Let us then hear from those on the campuses who say war is immoral or perhaps their selectivity will apply—time will tell.

I've gone on too long . . . As I close I know I am leaving unanswered many of the excellent points you raised in your letter, and this depresses me.

Let me give you a word of unsolicited advice—if you think the Congress is so screwed up—why don't you get in there and do something about it—run I mean—I'll send the first campaign contribution and I'll come out to your district and wage an aggressive campaign against you, which should guarantee your election. I am serious, though—get involved. The water's great . . .

My concluding statement—in spite of the riots and the dissent and the fis-

*This was the chant of protesters in Lafayette Park, across the street from the White House.
†I did not believe that all communists were engaged in a *united* effort to overthrow all non-communist governments.

cal problems and the worries—POGO* put it very well when he said "We are faced by insurmountable opportunity"—The opportunity is here that is for sure.

> Best Ever
> Poppy

Now I solicit your views on the riots. If you were Pres. What would you do. Please sit down and write. GB

———

In the midst of all the turmoil, I tried not to forget to make time for what truly counts in life, including staying in touch with old friends. I sent this telegram to my Yale baseball coach, Ethan Allen, the day he announced his retirement:

> May 15, 1968

All of us .300 hitters read today's Times with mixed emotions. Regret Yale will be losing a great coach but happiness is knowing that you will continue to make a significant contribution to American sports in whatever you decide to do. Regret that "time marches on" but great happiness in the many wonderful memories we will always have of baseball at Yale under your coaching. One of the great experiences of my own was playing at Yale during your first three years. I will never forget the spirit we had, the pure enjoyment of it all, and the great benefits I felt that I got as a person in playing for a wonderful coach, a real gentleman, and most important a warm and close friend. Bar joins me in sending our love to Doris. On this significant occasion my thanks to you for everything you did for me and for Yale baseball.

> Congratulations and warmest regards.
> George Bush Member of Congress.

———

In May I went to visit Resurrection City, the encampment on the Mall in Washington of tens of thousands of people who were in town as part of the Poor People's March. After my visit, I wrote this letter to one of the leaders, the Reverend Ralph Abernathy.

> May 28, 1968

Dear Reverend Abernathy:

On my recent visit to your encampment I was impressed with the attitudes you expressed concerning law and order and the nature of your legislative program. However, this is not what is quoted in the press nor is this how your people sometimes act when away from the camp.

———

*The comic strip character.

These forays into the public schools, the demonstrations on Capitol Hill and the incident yesterday in the Department of Agriculture cafeteria* are inexcusable. On our visit to your camp, one of my colleagues asked a lieutenant what would happen if your camping permit was not renewed past June 15. He replied that you would stay anyway in violation of the permit. Yet this is a direct contradiction to your desire to obey the law. I was surprised when one leader was quoted in the press as being critical of my visit to the camp. Concerned Members of Congress should see what is going on.

I went to the camp with an open mind, but regretfully I am much more concerned now than before my visit. These incidents and pronouncements are alienating people of good will who want to help poor people. I am most disturbed by the powder keg atmosphere of the whole march. And I can't get over the feeling that there are those on your side now who want to see you fail—both inside and outside of your camp.

You told me that your fundamental concern was jobs. I continue to be troubled by the fact that you are widely quoted as advocating legislative goals in direct conflict with this objective. You are asking for a $2.50 minimum wage, one million federal make-work jobs, and a guaranteed annual income. These goals are counter-productive to permanent employment. Statistics indicate that every time the minimum wage is increased the unemployment rate of teen-agers, particularly non-white teen-agers, rises substantially. As to make-work jobs, I would prefer to see legislation which will put people to work in permanent private industry jobs.

The Human Investment Act would give the private sector tax credits for more efficient job training. Moreover, your people would be guaranteed a job at the end of training.

The Percy-Widnall Home Ownership Act can help people own decent homes.

The Rural Job Development Act of 1968 would encourage private industry to locate outside the ghettoes, to help the poverty stricken in rural areas find jobs, and to reverse the flow of poor people to the cities.

A National Skill Survey would match up existing jobs with available able-bodied workers.

Technological Education for the Future is a clean new look at vocational education.

I could go on and on down the list. There are so many exciting new ideas which can work if given the chance, but they will never have the chance unless we realize that the present programs are not working.

---

*The protesters targeted the Agriculture Department, demanding more food stamps for the poor. The demonstrations were often ugly and violent.

I urge you to set and publicize a termination date for this march, to repudiate those who preach or practice breaking of the law, and to exclude the possibility of violence as a weapon.

I further urge you to appoint from your Committee of One Hundred a top level committee to work for new legislative answers. Explore the alternatives I have suggested. The people who have authored this legislation would be delighted to discuss it with you and would welcome any constructive criticism and support.

Do not let the honest poor people who have come all this way be used by the special interest seekers within your camp. Accept the challenge of changing the system within the law by shifting the emphasis of this crusade, after your forthcoming major meeting, from camping and demonstration to seeking new answers. Put all the brain power you have available towards seeking workable programs.

This Congress will not buy threats. It will not condone violence. It will not accept legislative goals which are financially impossible and which lack inventiveness and stifle the initiative of the individual.

On the other hand, it will consider new approaches. It will protect a citizen's right to peacefully and lawfully petition. And, contrary to some of the statements coming from those around you, the Members of Congress are for the most part vitally interested in the welfare of those honest poor people you represent.

I hope you will consider these suggestions and will favor me with an immediate reply.

Yours very truly,
George Bush, M.C.

[He never answered my letter.]

I wrote a weekly newspaper column for the constituents back home. I felt that this one, dated July 8, 1968, summed up very well the principles that guided me throughout my political career.

The more I contemplate the problems of fair play and opportunity in this country, the more convinced I become that in the independent sector associations, such as LULAC,* Planned Parenthood† and the American Heart Association, we have real hope for the future. They appear so much more effective than the government programs in helping our underprivileged and alienated citizens.

---

*League of United Latin American Citizens.

†This was long before Planned Parenthood began emphasizing abortion as a form of family planning. At that point we had a parting of the ways.

The people of this country want a part in molding their own future. And the more I talk with constituents in the 7th District and the more I read the thousands of letters that come into my office a week, the more this truth becomes apparent.

The people I talk with, the people who write all are a part of a new wave that is sweeping the country—Dick Nixon called it the "quiet revolution." "Let us have a role in solving our problems." "Let us be a part." "The Government is too big." They are not saying that we should turn our backs on the underprivileged and not face our problems.

The answer that I have always favored—the answer that is so eloquently being espoused by Dick Nixon and other progressive leaders of the Republican Party—is that we must seek new ways to transfer functions from government to private enterprise and to the private sector—those voluntary organizations which have been so successful. In the case of Planned Parenthood in Houston, we find the interesting situation of an organization that did its job so well that the demands for their services become more than they could provide. This is where the federal government can participate for it is the most efficient tax collector in the country. But it is NOT the most efficient dispenser of services.

This is why it is so important that we enlist the energies of those millions of Americans who stand ready and eager to serve and to help in the best traditions of this country. . . .

The centralized philosophy of government tends to drive private charity and private philanthropy out of the market. We need a change of philosophy in Washington which recognizes this basic fact and, at the same time, encourages the independent sector.

Richard Nixon won the GOP nomination for President in 1968, and there was a great deal of speculation at the GOP convention in Miami about whom his running mate might be. My name started popping up on some of the "short" lists. I was both surprised and flattered.

August 20, 1968

Mr. Bob Connery*
Denver, Colorado 80202
Dear Bob:
     . . . We did have a little somewhat abortive run for the vice presidency. When I saw Nixon in San Diego last week he confirmed that he gave it very

---

*Bob was a Texas supporter who moved to Colorado.

serious consideration, but decided against it because of my short service in the House. I hope the ticket does well and I feel that Agnew, off to a shaky start, has only one way to go and that's up. I will say that in visiting with him in person he comes across a lot better than the public image to date. I think we have to keep in focus that the race is going to be between Humphrey and Nixon, and I can't see the American people turning to Humphrey right now—though maybe this is wishful thinking.

I do hope our paths cross soon. I have found my service in the House frustrating but tremendously interesting and if I had to do it all over again I'd take the same course of action I have taken to date. Call me if you ever get near Houston or Washington. I really did appreciate your wonderful letter.

Yours very truly,
George Bush, M.C.

————————

September 10, 1968

Mrs. Nancy Palm, County Chairman
Harris County Republican Party
Houston, Texas 77006
Dear Nancy,

I was pleased when someone suggested that the first issue of the new BANNER* be dedicated to me, and then I read the paper and I could hardly believe my eyes when I saw on Page 8 the article titled "The Scene at Miami Beach."

I was so shocked and so terribly hurt that a contributing editor would print such an ethnic-prejudiced article. In this day and age when the times cry out for justice, fair play and a renewal of trust, it was a real crusher to see Marjorie Shepherd's comments.†

I doubt that there is any remedial action that can be taken, but I just would not feel right if I didn't express to you in the strongest possible terms my total revulsion at the anti-Jewish references in this article. They are not fair, they are not accurate. They are just plain vicious.

I express myself in this manner so that there can be no misunderstanding as to how I personally feel and how, I am sure, a majority of Republicans feel about this kind of journalism.

I know that many there at County Headquarters view me as a meddling

---

*The Harris County GOP newsletter.
†The outrageous article referred to "filthy rich Hebrews with tall willowy blondes on either arm."

critic, but, Nancy, I simply can't remain silent in the face of this obnoxious prejudice. I do hope you understand.

> Yours very truly,
> George Bush, M.C.

[This letter was printed in the Banner, *which brought on more hate mail. One constituent wrote in and said I was "doing too much stupid popping off about social and ethnic subjects which you have no control over and which show you is some kind of jackass."]*

January 8, 1969

Mr. Jack Steel*
Office of George Bush, M.C.
Houston, Texas 77002
Dear Jack:

Knowing that you will have tons of room in your luggage (I always love people who make this type of request), would you please bring Neil's binoculars when you come? I was so pleased that Neil wanted the binoculars I gave him for Christmas but, lo, it turns out he stashed some cash away in the case. If you could bring them, it would be great but there is no crisis since I will be down there in February.

> Yours very truly,
> George

The following letter, written to one of my staff people, Allie Page Matthews, is undated. It had to have been written sometime between November 1968 and November 1969, the time when George W. was flying fighter jets for the Texas Air National Guard.

Friday

En route to Houston
Dear Allie,

. . . My brief case is filled with official looking papers. . . .

Tucked away, devilishly and fiendishly (for all good representatives should

---

*Jack, an insurance agent in Houston, had become one of our best friends when we moved to Houston. He encouraged me to get into politics, then became my most loyal supporter. He worked for me for years and never accepted a dime in payment.

be serious and well briefed so they can talk about taxes and wars and ghettoes and governments) were your selected Marshall* quotes. . . .

Last weekend our son came home leaving his frightening "jet" behind in Georgia. And he had lots of college friends there, for a wedding weekend. Some had the long hair and the bell bottoms, all seemed close and concerned.

Yesterday we got a letter from George and it thanked us for having his friends—and then it went on to say "Someday Jeb, and Neil, Marvin, and Doro will know how lucky they are—someday they'll know what it is to be surrounded by love"—and we thought back to Yale and turmoil as we watched George try to figure which way to go— how far to reach—and we wiped back our tears and we said, "We are very lucky to have a boy today who understands." (and I put aside that growing concern I often feel as I think of his flying those awful planes and quietly I realized that he'd be fine.)

And now tonight I reread some of Peter Marshall—his tenderness, his deep commitment.

But the thought I have now is not of his words, but of the fact that you plucked them out and sent them on.

And suddenly in a world congested, in a life cluttered, in a day without a moment to stop—it has come to me that I am surrounded by values that somehow in the press of the country's problems I am oft inclined to feel have fled the scene.

I don't know why I am writing this except to say thank you. For through your choice of quotes, you let me stop—and reach for that butterfly.

You let me escape not from the real life but to it—

Thanks, Allie—don't change.

GB

———————

May 1, 1969

Mr. Mickey Herskowitz
Houston Post
Houston, Texas
Dear Mickey:

Through my uncle, Herbie Walker, one of the minority owners of the Mets, I met Commissioner Bowie Kuhn in Washington—in fact, I gave a little luncheon for him here at the Capitol with ten baseball oriented Congressmen and Senators. I found him delightful.

. . . When the Republicans play the Democrats on June 17th I hope the

---

*Peter Marshall, a minister well known for his inspirational words.

Commissioner will be on hand. The game is always held just before the Senators* game.

I know this will seem hard for you to believe and I hope you will not interpret it as lacking in propriety or modesty but last year I "wuz" robbed in the game. A tremendous blast, definitely destined for the left field stands, was hauled down by Lee Hamilton, a Congressman from Indiana, who theretofore I had always respected in a kind of quiet way. This year, though, with "Vinegar Bend" Mizell† on the mound, and with renewed determination burning inside of me, things should go better. Last year we won 19 to 1. Somehow in these critical times that's just not enough.

Warmest regards,
George Bush, M.C.

———————

As I mentioned in an earlier letter, I did find my House experience frustrating because as a junior member of the minority party, it was difficult to get much of anything accomplished. After owning and running my own business, I found it hard not to be able to make decisions, then immediately execute them. That's not how government works, especially in the large House of Representatives. That is one reason why I started thinking again about running for the Senate in 1970, assuming that my opponent would be the same as in 1964, Ralph Yarborough.

May 8, 1969

The Honorable Richard M. Nixon
The White House
Washington, D.C.
Re: 1970 Senate Race in Texas
Dear Mr. President,

In June or early July, I would like a 15-minute appointment with you to discuss briefly the forthcoming Senate race. . . .

The purpose of this meeting, to which I would like to bring one person, would be to ask your candid advice on this race and to inquire as to what support the Administration might be free to give in such a battle.

I remember our brief conversation in San Diego about a possible Senate race. I am reluctant to give up my seat on Ways and Means to gamble excessively, but a key to the whole ball game could be, depending on events, the Administration's role.

---

*The Senators was Washington's major league baseball team, which is now known as the Texas Rangers.

†Representative Wilmer Mizell from North Carolina, who was a former major league player for the Pittsburgh Pirates and St. Louis Cardinals.

More than all of this, I have always valued your advice.

I recognize the limits on your time, but I am hopeful this meeting can be arranged.

Respectfully,
George Bush, M.C.

[Nixon did invite me to the White House and encouraged me to run.]

———————

When sportswriter Mickey Herskowitz went on vacation that summer, he invited various people to write guest columns for the Houston Post. *Here was my draft column:*

On Tuesday evening June 17th the place to be in D.C. was at Kennedy Stadium. That's where the action was at.

If President Kennedy were living he could have found a few more examples for "Profiles in Courage".

It took guts for those 5 Democratic Congressmen that had to face Vinegar Bend Mizell to even walk to the plate. But walking up there wasn't the bad part. In fact it wasn't the fact that all of them struck out that was bad.

It was the fact they had to be <u>told</u> by Commissioner Bowie Kuhn, the plate umpire, that they had struck out. "Go back to the dugout—you just struck out". . . .

The Republicans won the 5 inning game 7-2. Rep. Bob Michel of Illinois started for the GOP and chalked up his 7th straight victory.

Rep Henry B. Gonzalez [Texas] went the route for the Democrats—Really Henry B. didn't have too much but he worked his heart out—and wow! did his infield plummer things for Henry B. In a way, Gonzalez was the game's real star. He ripped a crisp double down the left field line. In the 4th, wary of the support he had received in the 1st three innings, he charged almost to the dugout to backhand a pop fly. . . .

Who starred—well let's see

Senator Birch Bayh [Indiana] hit a long clean double to center field. He handled a lot of chances at short with real pizzazz. He booted one—but who can blame him, he had just returned from Houston . . . Bayh was still a little dazed after his exposure to Texas politics.

The Republican infield was great—superlative—the Republican first baseman George Bush went 2 for 2 (would you believe 1 for 2) against Gonzalez. He batted 4th.

Rep Pete McClosky [California], the guy who in the GOP primary crushed Shirley Temple like a boycotted grape hit a long blast to deep left field, but was robbed by Rep. Mo Udall a one-eyed Mormon from Arizona. Udall pitched last year but after his 10–1 defeat decided to play centerfield and also to run against John McCormack for Speaker.

He lost to McCormack but he made that catch and he got two fouls off Mizell. That's not a bad year so far. Bowie Kuhn umpired. . . .

Rep. Jim Symington [Missouri] asked me why we took Mizell out after 5 hitters—"We were just beginning to get to him" suggested Pres. Johnson's former protocol chief—"After all I clearly fouled one off and Udall got 2 foul tips."

Ted Williams* suggested next year's game be played on a Sunday afternoon "After seeing you guys out there, I think we'll pack the place". This remark was the subject of much partisan debate.

In the locker room winners and losers alike seemed happy and relieved. Vinegar hadn't stuck a fast one in a Democrat's ear.

No one got really hurt.

. . . I wondered where is the justice of it all—We Republicans can always beat these guys in America's greatest sport—baseball.

But they can usually beat us in the worlds second greatest sport—bull throwing!

––––––––––––

Mr. Russell U. Smith
Baton Rouge, Louisiana 70808
Dear Russell:

Because of your thoughtfulness in offering your support should I decide to enter the race for the U. S. Senate, I wanted to write you before the public announcement on my decision is made.

There is a possibility that Republicans can win control of the Senate in 1970—a condition that is vital to the Administration and to the country.

We are moving into a new decade. The tired, old answers of the past are not good enough for the 70's. Texas needs a positive and constructive voice that will be respected by President Nixon whether in support of his programs or in criticism.

After much study, I have decided to enter the Senate race. It will be a long, tough, uphill battle. However, I am convinced I can win. But, I desperately need and want your help.

Best regards,
George Bush, M.C.

––––––––––––

*My good friend and former superstar of the Boston Red Sox was managing the Senators at that time.

While in Congress I served as chairman of the House Republican Research Committee Task Force on Earth Resources and Population. Population control was an important cause for me. I thought it was essential if we were to have any success at all in the fight against poverty and in protecting the environment. However, I am convinced that years later my work on this committee would lead to some misunderstanding regarding my stand on abortion. I was and am for family planning; I am not for abortion. Unfortunately, I could not find any correspondence or other notes regarding this topic, so instead I would like to share with you part of what I said in a news release when we finished a task force report on Federal Government Family Planning Programs—Domestic and International.

December 22, 1969
EARTH RESOURCES AND POPULATION
House Republican Research Committee Task Force

This report and its recommendations . . . are the result of five months of hearings and research.

. . . This report will, we believe, be of assistance in the achievement of President Nixon's goal . . . of providing these services in the next five years to all Americans who want these services but cannot afford them or do not know where to find them.

There is great urgency in providing these services. So many of our poor and near poor American women have been frustrated and discouraged over their inability to control their fertility, their inability to prevent unwanted children. . . .

This is not a sensational report. The subject of family planning should not be considered sensational. The subject has certainly been a sensitive one, but we have found that the public in general is way ahead of legislators and policy makers in recognizing the need of providing these health care services. Birth control is a very private and personal matter. There is a big job to be done in providing dignified services to the estimated 5.3 million American women who want to avail themselves of family planning services in order to have the knowledge necessary to make a personal choice of birth control methods, whether it be the pill, an IUD, or the rhythm method. Family planning is a public health matter and it is also an answer to alleviating poverty. To deny this right to any American because of the lack of health services, poorly administered health services, or because of the sensitivity of the subject is not only foolish but negligent.

It is important to note our emphasis on the need to rely heavily on the private sector of our society in solving this problem. No one on the Task Force believes that the Federal and State governments alone can do the job. Leadership and funds are necessary from all levels of government, but the ultimate difference between success and failure in these programs will depend on the private sector's contribution of money and people. . . .

———————

February 16, 1970

Dear Charles [Untermeyer],

. . . Things are hectic. I am traveling extensively in the state and I find it difficult to be both a Congressman and candidate. The mean parts of the campaign are already starting. Yarborough is saying nasty things but, I swear to God, I yet have to make my first tough comment about him. We've vowed to stay completely off him, at least till after the primary. Lloyd Bentsen,* the Connally anointed conservative Democrat, is running all out against Yarborough and is hitting him pretty hard. He is hurting me with the money; but, all the pros at the Capitol press room simply inquire how much did you pay Bentsen to get into the race. . . .

I'm not sure I can survive the next nine months; but, I'm going to give it everything I've got. Keep those cards and letters coming.

Best regards,
George Bush, M.C.

———————

As you've seen already, there were many emotional issues in the 1960s. The next three letters deal with three: gun control, POWs, and busing.

June 4, 1970

Mr. Stephen Melinder
Houston, TX 77024
Dear Mr. Melinder:

Thanks so much for your recent letter concerning gun legislation . . .

I am opposed to federal registration and licensing of firearms and my voting record is quite clear on that point. I have never been pleased with all the aspects of the Gun Control Act of 1968. I did vote for it, but only because I feel that a state, if it so wishes, should be permitted to control the flow of weapons within its borders and should not be harassed by importation of weapons across state lines.

*Bentsen, the future vice-presidential nominee and secretary of the treasury, had shocked everyone by challenging the incumbent for his party's nomination. Bentsen had served in Congress, but at the time he ran for the Senate, he was an executive in the insurance industry in Houston. The "Connally" is John Connally, the former Texas governor.

Frankly, Mr. Melinder, I am extremely concerned about the prevalence of "Saturday Night Specials" in the Houston area. I think the state should review its gun laws very carefully with the idea of cutting down on this kind of weapon. I don't believe this is an area for federal legislation. Police Chief Herman Short of Houston, one of the best law enforcement officers in the country, feels quite strongly that local action is required to solve this problem. I agree. . . .

Yours very truly,
George Bush, M.C.

_____

July 9, 1970

Dear Mr. President:

The horror of the treatment American Prisoners of War are receiving at the hands of the Viet Cong and the North Vietnamese has been vividly brought to light in our nation's Capital in a display made available by Mr. Ross Perot.* I believe that anyone who has taken the time to view the replica of a North Vietnamese bamboo prison cage, and accompanying photos realizes the message it contains—that North Vietnam is ignoring the Geneva Convention it signed in 1957. Surely, many of those who have seen the display have been moved, as I was, to write the leaders of North Vietnam and ask they respect the Geneva accords which that country has signed. I am convinced that American public opinion could influence the North Vietnamese to respect the Geneva agreements concerning Prisoners of War.

But, in spite of all that has been done to bring the problem to the attention of the public, I believe something additional is needed. I therefore request that you earnestly consider designating a certain day, or hour within that day, as a time for Americans to remember our Prisoners of War. In this manner the problem of enemy neglect of our captured soldiers would receive the national attention it deserves. I feel certain that when the public is fully aware of the Prisoner of War problem, tens if not hundreds of thousands will be moved to take the time to write the leaders of North Vietnam expressing dismay for treatment of captured Americans and asking the Geneva accords be respected.

With warm regards,
George Bush, M.C.

_____

*Perot's number one cause for years was the release of American prisoners in Vietnam. I was sympathetic to this cause and even suggested to Jerry Ford that Congress hold a special session to address the POW problem. However, years down the road, I believe it is this same issue that drove a wedge between Perot and me.

July 23, 1970

Mrs. William S. Dixon
Houston, Texas 77017
Dear Mrs. Dixon:

Thank you very much for your concerned letter and I just wish I had an easy and simple answer.

. . . I am a strong advocate of the neighborhood school concept . . . It seems ridiculous to go ahead and juggle the students around from one school to another when there are no racial problems involved. There have been great inconveniences to many of my constituents under this plan.

I hope my record in human rights is a sensitive one—I think it is; but, I can assure you that I do not favor bussing to achieve racial balance and I do not favor quotas. What I want to see is every student in Houston have a quality education in a quality plant by quality teachers. We are not at that point yet; but, we can do it without sweeping revisions of our sweeping court orders.

Best regards,
George Bush, M.C.

————

At some point during the 1970 campaign, I jotted down some notes (perhaps for a speech) on how I felt about the relationship between Congress and the President. Obviously I was irritated, but I don't remember now what sparked it. I did find my notes interesting, because I would feel exactly the same way when the tables were turned years later.

. . . As I said repeatedly in my 1966 campaign for Congress, I will support the President when I think he's right but I'll battle against him when I think he's wrong.

I don't believe in kicking the President. I didn't do it when Pres Johnson was in office and I won't do it now.

C.Q. [Congressional Quarterly] shows I support Pres Nixon 64% of the time . . . but when I differ I don't do it in a way to increase the personal burden on the President.

One of my real regrets about the Johnson presidency was the personal abuse that was heaped on the President—the name calling. The direct allegations, usually chanted in epithet, that he wanted war or encouraged killing. How gross! How unfair.

It is ironic that the steadfastness of Pres Johnson at certain critical times laid a groundwork for the Nixon plan which is winding down the war.

Just as some kick Pres Nixon on the economy, some still kick Pres Johnson on the war.

My plea is this: criticism "yes" but continually trying to blame the President "no." . . .

––––––––––

Bentsen ended up beating Yarborough in the Democratic primary, then beat me in the general election. I think I could have beaten Yarborough; Bentsen proved much tougher and was also aided by a "liquor by the drink" vote that brought out Democratic voters in rural Texas in record numbers. Not only did I lose the election, I lost my job, since I had given up my House seat to run. The first order of business was to write some of my campaign staff and volunteers: Pete Roussel, a young man from Houston who had been my press secretary for several years; Carl Warwick, a major league baseball player who had supported me back home; and Vivian Flynn, a family friend and supporter.

November 1970

Dear Pete—

You showed us Bushes a lot of class in the time you've been around us.

Perhaps you more than anyone else understood how desperately I wanted to win the race. You understood it because you became almost a part of our family.

You've given us a lot Pete— a lot to be grateful for, a lot to be happy about, a lot to be proud of.

God it hurts to lose to Bentsen after all our work and trying and caring.

I've never seen a guy [Pete] remain so cool—so fair—so "hanging in there" when the schedule got tough.

My love to your family and my family's gratitude—lasting gratitude to you—

George

––––––––––

Nov. 8th

Carl Warwick
Houston, Texas 77069
Dear Carl,

There was this guy standing on a manhole cover—oh God the campaign was fun and exciting. It moved a lot of people——young people seemed to give a damn. I am truly grateful to you for taking all that time and for working so hard.

Our paths will cross again—I'll make sure of that, but in the meantime thanks for so very much.

The future—I don't know maybe public life in D.C. maybe back to Texas. My main balloon has burst—we didn't win the pennant. But today it's clear that the world will keep turning. Tuesday night with those great kids in tears* I wasn't a bit sure.

Thanks,
George Bush

November 20, 1970

Miss Vivian Flynn
Houston, Texas 77005
Dear Vivian:

. . . Things look a lot brighter now. It's still too early to know what we're going to do, but the future looks pretty darned exciting. We're torn between staying in politics in some way, or moving back to Houston and getting fairly immersed in business. Whatever we do, I'm sure it will be challenging. . . .

Best regards,
George Bush, M.C.

*Doro, then in the fifth grade, had cried almost uncontrollably, telling her mother, "I'm the only girl in my class whose father doesn't have a job."

CHAPTER 4

International Waters

The first order of business after the election was to decide what to do next. Before I committed to running for the Senate, President Nixon had subtly made clear to me that should I lose, he would want me to continue serving in government. However, although no job offers had been made, I did not feel that President Nixon owed me a thing.

Another interesting political twist at this time was the relationship between Nixon and former Texas governor John Connally. Nixon was high on Connally, convincing him to become a Republican and then appointing him secretary of the treasury. (Nixon really thought Connally should eventually become President.) Given my Texas Republican base, they both felt I should "be taken care of" before the Connally appointment was announced.

However, I had no interest in staying in Washington unless the job was right. Barbara and I had decided we would much rather go home to Texas. That was not to be. In early December, I began keeping a diary, by dictating into a tape recorder, on how I went from Capitol Hill to the United Nations.

December 11, 1970

On Wednesday, the 9th of December, Bob Haldeman* called me to come to the White House. I had previously talked to him and I had previously talked to Secretary of State [William] Rogers. In both these discussions, the subject of the U.N. came up. Rogers seemed very

---

*H. R. Haldeman was Nixon's chief of staff. I liked Bob and felt my relationship with him was good. He was straightforward with me at all times.

131

much interested in my doing it, but he pointed out that there were a lot of pitfalls and a lot of problems involved with the U.N. that I really needed to know about before getting thoroughly involved. . . .

On the 9th, then, I went back to Haldeman's office and he told me they'd decided they wanted me on the White House staff as an Assistant to the President . . . He indicated he felt the President thought this would be better for me than the U.N. job or certainly the National Committee job which was under active consideration.

We chatted for awhile and he started to define the duties of the job of one of the President's assistants when the President called for Haldeman to go into his office. He returned in five minutes and took me into the Oval Office where he and I and the President chatted for some forty minutes. During the course of the conversation, the President began to outline the staff job, saying that it would give us real flexibility. He told me that he understood that I did not want the National Committee job, and I told him that I didn't want it under the existing circumstances.* We didn't go into the details of it. He pointed out that he knew that people around there were somewhat abrasive and that he felt I could do a good job for him in the White House presenting the positive side of the issues. . . .

We then started talking about the U.N. and I told him that I thought the U.N. would have some real appeal because I could spell out his programs with some style and we could preempt that mass news media area—that he was operating almost in a vacuum, John Lindsay, Goldberg† and others being critics and not supporters; that perhaps the U.N. job was not the greatest for getting something done, but that I felt I could really put forward an image there that would be very helpful to the Administration. The President stopped and told Haldeman something like this, "Wait a minute, Bob, this makes some sense. George would be in the Cabinet, and I'm not putting much emphasis on that, but given that, he'd be coming down here every couple of weeks, getting briefed and having an input on domestic policy and all of this makes a good deal of sense to me."

"Let's announce tomorrow that Bush will be Assistant to the President, with general duties, and that he will start right after the Congress reconvenes. Tell Rogers to put a "hold" on the U.N. job. In this

---

*Several White House staff, especially Chuck Colson, constantly called on the Republican National Committee to do their bidding, such as being the main "attack dog" against the press.

†John Lindsay was mayor of New York City; Arthur Goldberg was a former ambassador to the United Nations.

way, if Yost* anytime wants out, we can still have the option open on the U.N., but go ahead with the staff position." . . .

We then went into Haldeman's office and started talking about how it would all work. . . . The President called for him again and so I went back to the Hill. Haldeman called me 15 minutes later and told me they'd decided to go with the U.N. job. . . . "You've sold the President, and he wants to move with it now. He's talked to Rogers and they're ready to go." . . .

My feelings now are kind of mixed. I'll miss the Congress, but it's going to be a tremendously exciting challenge . . .

It will be interesting to see what the Texas reaction is.

We called a lot of our friends after the President's statement at the press conference—Will Farish, Fred Chambers, and others. All these fellows felt it was really great. A couple of them said, "Well, if this is really what you want," meaning that I guess they were somewhat disappointed.

At this early stage, the more I think about it, the more I'm inclined to think it's just ideal.

. . . This idea originally was the idea of Charles Bartlett,† a great friend of mine. He called me right after the election when I was in the depths of despair about the election and Charley Bartlett said you'd be amazed what this campaign did for your image up here. A lot of people are thinking of you in national terms. I thought he was just going overboard as a polite, decent, warm guy trying to cheer me up, but he said, "I think out of this will come some real opportunity," and he said I want to talk to you about one. I went over and talked to him when I got back to Washington and he talked about the U.N. as the greatest thing. I talked to him just before I went over to the White House and he told me it was marvelous for Nixon and I was the one guy who could bring it together and have new ideas and all this kind of thing. He was very excited and he's got a lot of ideas that might help. Nobody's ever been able to sell the country on the U.N., he says, and he thinks I might be able to do that, and he's very pleased and, of course, I'm very much indebted to him. . . .

---

*The current U.N. ambassador, Charles Yost, who had been appointed by President Johnson. He was a senior career Foreign Service officer and had never been close to President Nixon.

†Charles Bartlett was a Pulitzer Prize–winning journalist, savvy in Washington ways. He had been a close friend of John F. Kennedy's, and was at my side in Washington through good times and bad.

December 17, 1970

I went up to the U.N. headquarters for the first time. People's reaction ranged from the chauffeur to the woman at the entrance— you could see they were looking me over carefully. Ted Schottke, the administrative guy, seemed amazed when I asked him to have lunch . . . but he is a down to earth kind of guy and I was determined to get his confidence early on. The woman was waiting, holding the elevator as we were walking into the building, and I glanced back over my shoulder and noticed her looking me over carefully as we got on. . . .

Despite my excitement over the new job, I was nostalgic about leaving Congress. I wrote this letter to Jack Steel the day I closed my office.

Dear Jack—

We've cleaned out the desk . . . It's been a sad day. All our projects up in smoke. The pictures gone, the little plaques . . . things without life—out of a happy past; but now just kind of there.

But there's more than faded pictures of happy days—there really is—deep happy memories of unselfish people who shared with me some happy times—shared in helping people or trying at least—shared in my life with its excitement and its ups and downs. And now it's kind of over—at least these 4 happy years are clearly gone . . .

I now move on to a near summit slot in a life full of new challenges; but I know full well that this fate would not be mine were it not for that sensitivity that for me you conveyed to all who called for help. I get credit for caring, and I do, but it was you and the others who implemented things, who conveyed the concern through action.

. . . I couldn't walk out of this office where we lived and fought so hard without trying to tell you what's in my heart Thanks, my dear friend—

George

January 11, 1971

I was with President Lyndon Johnson. I flew down on an Air Force Convair with a large group . . . going down to the Johnson Library.

. . . I visited with the President. The main reaction was there can only be one cook. He used the example you can put in the potatoes and know all about proteins but you won't know all the rest of it. You have got to rely on the President. You cannot have two State Departments. You must have trust in the President. . . . He spoke with great reservation about U Thant.* He was not very fond of him I think. He indicated that [Dean] Rusk† clearly didn't think much of him either. He pointed out that Goldberg always wanted his ear and so did [Adlai] Stevenson. They both tried to go around the Secretary of State. I had the feeling he felt they were wasting his time an awful lot of the time. . . .

If I had to draw a conclusion, perhaps President Johnson was preoccupied, but I don't believe he really felt all that great about the U.N. His two analogies—you're just a slice of the apple, an important slice but just one slice—you put the potato in and you know about the proteins, but you don't know the final taste of the stew for only the President is the cook and he alone understands all that is happening . . .

The main thing I got from President Johnson was that you should entertain these people, be good to them, show them the best in America, let the President have some exposure to them which will be good for both the President and the ambassadors and that was about it. He did not seem to rely too heavily on the U.N. to solve the problems and he certainly had a reservation about the way Stevenson and Goldberg kept bugging him, calling him on matters that he felt were trivial. . . .

———

January 19, 1971
I have been invited to my first Cabinet meeting. Things are shaping up. It was a very interesting session. Rog Morton‡ and I were the two new guys there. We sat at the front table and heard a presentation of the president's message. I was surprised at a couple of little things. The President graciously worked me into the conversation a time or two—"Now, George, this will be of interest to you up at the U.N." He seemed to be including me in the official family which is a very helpful thing. I didn't get a chance to visit with him. I am determined this kind of meeting is going to be terribly important.

On Thursday night [National Security Adviser] Henry Kissinger came out to the House for dinner with his secret service man and incidentally instead of staying outside we invited the secret service

*Secretary general of the United Nations.
†Secretary of state in the Johnson administration.
‡Rogers Morton had just been appointed secretary of the interior.

man in and he was promptly defeated in Tiddley Winks. He won four games but lost a total of twenty-four. He was heard to remark as he got into the car, "Well, the boys told me I at least have a great long shot." They indeed confirmed he had a long shot but the rest of his game was not too fantastic. This was the first time the guy ever played however, but I kind of like the concept of the secret service man down playing Tiddley Winks.*

I had a long talk with Kissinger. We talked about the right relationship between me and the President, and he told me I had the confidence of the President, that the President wanted to work through the U.N. That day the Secretary General had just made a statement criticizing the Government of Saigon and Kissinger remarked that the President wished George Bush were up there because at least he could respond and point out that compared to Hanoi, Saigon was a pretty good government. We set up lines of communication for me to get directly to him if there was any major problem. . . .

He said there are about four ambassadors that have this confidence of the President. I told him I am glad to know I have it, and I am determined to keep it. I also told him I did not want to "go around" Secretary Rogers, but I felt that we could keep a balance here. Kissinger has, I think, a rather low regard for the paperwork and bureaucratic foul-up at the State Department, but he was not critical or down on any particular individual here. I probed for the President's true feeling on the U.N. . . . I am determined that to do this job right we have got to have the right relationships. I told Henry this. I told him that I wanted to be an advocate for the President's positions with which I agree. If we differ I want to be in a position to tell him. . . . The conversation could not have been more productive from delineating the ground rules standpoint. Kissinger is a very interesting guy . . .

January 25, 1971
 . . . Little things—My office† has no pictures of the President or Secretary of State. I am taking care of that. I am also going to get some

---

*The President had provided Secret Service protection for Kissinger because of some threats made against him. Tiddleywinks was a game all Bushes played growing up. Mother was the champion. It was a real icebreaker. With a large plastic shooter chip, the goal is to flick smaller chips into a little jar. Thumb control is the key.

†I'm talking about my temporary office at the State Department since I had not yet been confirmed by the Senate. I did not take charge of the U.N. post until March 1.

White House Pictures up in the New York mission. There seems to be an avoidance of President Nixon around here. Some of it may be that the people here are Democrats or maybe it's the apolitical nature of the place. I don't know which but certainly there doesn't seem to be any great enthusiasm or advocacy for the President and yet many of his positions seem to have good loyal support which I think is probably the main thing. I am beginning to see how important it is to keep the lines of communication open on personnel . . . SHW* is a case of a political appointee who is so bad that you can see why the pros would be upset. He stays loaded. He calls Negroes niggers and all in all he is apparently bad news. I am determined to ease him out of here just as soon as possible. He made the mistake of telling me in the one conversation I have had with him that he is willing to resign. He shall be given the opportunity. . . .

I think the best policy around here is to demonstrate your willingness to "go to others," to ask advice, to be grateful, to get here earlier and leave later than the rest of the people. This will be the way I plan to do it at the Mission. Set the pace. I think we need to lower the median age up there. It needs to be revitalized. . . .

February 2, 1971

On the first of February I had a call from Ambassador Yost talking about whether the March 1 take over date was firm. I assured him it was as far as I knew and sure enough the Secretary confirmed it later on that day. He did ask that he be permitted to stay on in the apartment for another 10 days.† I had offered this earlier when I thought we were going to take this up the first of February. I assured him it would not be a problem. He said he would be out in a week or ten days afterwards. He said they were having a lot of farewell parties and it would make it easier for them. Barbara Bush was not overly excited about this. She said I wouldn't permit her to do this, to be there 5 minutes over the time. That may be true but it is better to bend over backwards on this kind of small thing. What's a week over a span of what might be several years.

---

*I would rather not use his full name. He was dismissed.

†The official residence of the U.S. ambassador to the United Nations was an apartment in the Waldorf Towers.

February 5, 1971

I had a long briefing on the Senate hearings. Everyone says that the Senate committee gives very perfunctory questions and that the hearings should be over fast—30 or 45 minutes at the most. The questions are pretty general. I must confess I feel a certain uneasiness although the pros all say you're a Member of Congress, don't worry, etc. . . . it all ought to go well, but even at 46 years old, one gets a little nervous about encounters of this sort. . . .

————

February 8, 1971

. . . Hearings were held today. They went well. Senator [William] Fulbright was very courteous . . . [Stuart] Symington dug in on the relationship between Kissinger and Rogers. . . . There were several questions on peace-keeping but for the most part the hearings went well indeed.

————

March 11, 1971

Dear Congressman:*

This is just a note to have you know that the welcome mat is out for you here at the United States Mission to the United Nations.

I know from my own experience in the House that I never really took a good look at the operation here in New York, and I want to be sure you realize that I would like to have you stop in at any time. If we can ever help with answering questions from constituents please call on us.

The Mission is located just across the street from United Nations Headquarters. Several people from Washington days are with me and along with a first-class staff which I inherited, we are looking forward to showing you around and visiting with you whenever business, or pleasure, brings you to town.

Sincerely,
George Bush
Ambassador

————

March 28, 1971

. . . I had a meeting last week at which the financial people from the United Nations came over and they were talking about having to take out of trust funds in order to pay the salaries. This is depressing,

*I sent a copy of this letter to many of my former House colleagues.

and it certainly reflects terrible management. I don't know what the answer is going to be, but we must take a real hard look at it.

. . . After the Four Power Meetings Malik* was talking about whom we wanted for Secretary General. It was a very general conversation, both of us fencing back and forth, neither of us saying anything. It will be interesting to see how this one works out, but the more I look at the financial management problems facing the United Nations, the more I realize the importance of having some kind of forceful administrator at the top of all this. I like U Thant personally very much, but I don't think he is strong or tough enough in this administrative field. . . .

Social whirl—I am going to have to sort out some priorities. The long deadly luncheons given for people by the Secretary General and the others are too much. They are having a series of going away luncheons for Ambassador Farra of Jordan. The cocktails, the wine, the heavy meal, the whole thing consumes a couple of hours and they are a total waste of time. It is going to be difficult drawing the line between being polite and courteous and yet not wasting time. On the other hand, the U.N. dinners can be productive. At the dinner given by [British Ambassador] Colin Crowe I had a chance to visit intimately with two or three of the ambassadors in a rather relaxed surrounding. This week we took the Ambassador of Madagascar to a hockey game with one of his boys and then Ambassador Ogbu of Nigeria brought his boy to go to a basketball game. I think this kind of thing will be important to do, and I think it demonstrates a certain friendliness that the U.N. ambassadors should show to other people. . . .

Prisoners of War—I hope we can do more to emphasize the plight of the prisoners here. . . . Ross Perot was here by chance. He is a difficult fellow to figure out. He has always been very friendly to me, and he and his wife Margo are great, but he is a very complicated man. I think he now pictures himself as totally non-partisan.

———

April 5, 1971

. . . I got into a big fight with Malik at the Four Powers Meeting today. He accused the U.S. of being tools of the Zionist conspiracy which is nothing new. . . . I climbed on Malik very firmly and told

*Yakov Malik, the Soviet Union's ambassador to the United Nations and a true cold warrior who could make my life difficult. The Four Powers Meetings included the U.N. ambassadors from the United States, Great Britain, France, and the Soviet Union.

him that I felt he was smearing names of good men and that there was no excuse for this and that he could not possibly justify it. I really gave my strongest smash at him and he did not come back quite as strongly. Afterwards I went up and shook hands with him and he was fairly jovial. His text during the first round of the Four Talks was a long political harangue harassing the United States, harassing Israel . . . I am amazed at this "obvious" propaganda that he resorts to, but he does it over and over again. I just wish those who think the Russians have completely changed could listen to these outlandish claims and comments. It would do the world good to have all of this on TV. It would bore them to death, but this propaganda that seems so overt and obvious and base is resorted to at every meeting. I simply can't get over it. . . .

The most difficult issue I had to deal with as U.N. ambassador concerned China's representation in the United Nations, especially who would sit in China's seat on the smaller, powerful U.N. Security Council. For years Taiwan had held China's seat as the Republic of China while the People's Republic of China (the mainland) was not represented. As each year went by, it became increasingly clear that it was unrealistic to have the PRC excluded from the United Nations. Rather than expelling Taiwan, the United States adopted a policy of "dual representation"—a One China policy but with both sides being represented. I wrote the following letter to Henry Kissinger outlining the challenges ahead. (I apologize for the acronyms; that is how we talked.)

April 17th, 1971

Dear Henry,

The Security Council (SC) question is fundamental. It will be impossible to consider Peking's (PRC) coming into the General Assembly (GA) without considering the SC question.

I have not talked to a single person around the U.N. who feels that a Dual Representation (DR) would have a chance unless the SC went to PRC. As we ask the official of GRC [Taiwan] to consider a policy shift on our part they must face this basic fact.

A DR resolution could in fact include a paragraph recommending that PRC hold the China seat on the SC; but at a minimum there would be an unwritten understanding. Any effort to obscure the SC seat question will be viewed as an effort to keep the PRC out of the U.N. Alas, I wish it weren't so. . . .

My recommendations:

1. Any emissary discussing U.N. representation with GRC must not avoid facing up to the SC question. It is a regrettable fact of life.

2. Pres. Nixon would be ill served by any policy that appears to be "selling out" the GRC. It is argued by the elite—"PRC is a reality"— It is but so is GRC and we must not appear to "sell out" a little reality in order to face up to a big reality. It may happen, but we must not be its advocate.

3. Time is important. As soon as things shape up, we should be able to get you a lot more dope as to how viable a DR plan is, but we will have to be able to hustle up some votes, and we will need some insight into the GRC final position.

[copy unsigned]
Self-typed—apologies . . . GB

April 19, 1971

. . . The social whirl is too much. We are going to have to cut down on some of these useless evenings. Tonight it was the Stuttgart ballet. Actually it was great fun, but it didn't help the job any, it didn't help the President any, and it didn't help my ulcers any. I am very tired. I have never seen a job where there is such constant activity. There are so many things to do. There is one appointment after the other and very little time to do any reading.

The Host Country problems are beginning to bug me. It's a shame to have to spend any time at all at these crazy things, but they must be done . . . Malik raised hell with me about "throwing away frogs" in the Amtorg* office. The crazy JDL† let loose a bunch of frogs and mice which terrified the people in the building. Today the South African Consulate was bombed by black extremists. New York is a miserable place to have the U.N. This is heretical to say in the Mission, but it is. . . .

I am very much concerned about the attack on the institutions in this country. One gets a tremendously distorted view of America from New York. I am convinced of this. The drumbeat of attacks on Hoover‡ are in the news right now. My own personal view is that Hoover should have gotten out a long time ago, but to degrade him and to give him a "bum rap" is not correct . . .

I have never seen such a distorted impression of America, and I

---

*This was the Soviet trading company headquartered in New York City.

†The Jewish Defense League, led by the outrageous and radical Meir Kahane, continually used disruptive, radical tactics against the Soviet Union while protesting the treatment of Soviet Jews.

‡J. Edgar Hoover, the powerful director of the FBI.

am afraid it is not good for the U.N. to see all of this. Continually at the Four Meetings Malik quotes back to me things that are wrong with our country, things that he has read in the paper. The <u>Times</u> is quoted all the time. . . .

There is a lot of Vice President speculation, mainly among close friends who are wishful thinkers. I have told them, people such as [Peter] O'Donnell, [Bob] Mosbacher, Jimmy Allison, Will Farish, that we don't need money now and that I do not want to do anything to appear as if I am campaigning for Vice President. The essential thing is to do this job and to do it well, and to make clear that I am not running for anything. There has been a lot of speculation in the papers, mainly in Texas, although Newsweek and couple of others up here had mention of this. This kind of speculation is no good at all . . .

At this point in time I would have to think twice about whether I'd rather have this job or be in the Senate. Two months ago or three it wouldn't have been any choice at all, but now I find this work so fascinating that it is hard to tell. I worry sometimes about the lack of accomplishment on the political or diplomatic side. It seems to me a lot of times we are simply following out orders in the Four Power meeting, although I feel the talks with Kissinger on China and the Middle East have been more substantive than that. In time I hope to move more into the policy end of things. In the meantime it is better to do my homework, not bother the President or Secretary, and learn the business cold.

———

May 2, 1971

I am continually impressed by how unrealistic a place New York is. I find it very difficult to be polite when people ask me how I like New York. It is an unrepresentative city. There are tremendous host country problems. There are tremendous intensified urban problems that are not "the real America." . . . I am continually amazed at the arrogance of the intellectual elite in New York. They are so darn sure they are right on everything. It's unbelievable. Having lived in Texas for 23 years I had forgotten how concentrated this problem is, but it's sure there . . .

I got the Mission together the other day and told them that we are reacting. If somebody blows up a bomb there are protests and then we get on the ball with host country problems. Somebody says something against us in the economic field and we react then. It is essential that we sit down and plan where we want to be a year from now or five years from now and then try to implement it. The financial problems still have me bugged. I met with Phil Klutznick, an Adlai Stevenson man, and he gave me some good advice. Don't knuckle in. Don't make concessions to the Russians. If you do, they'll only consider it a sign of weakness and take that as a point of departure. We are facing a major financial crisis, and I think Klutznick is right. We have to be absolutely firm. I am convinced if we are not, we cannot get support from our Congress so we might as well start from that realistic point.

Private—I worry about the family situation. The boys are in good shape. Jebby is going to need some help I am sure. He is a free and independent spirit and I don't want him to get totally out of touch with the family. He doesn't want to be. But I am just worried with our strange hectic life and Jeb going back to Texas this summer that we may lose touch with him. The other boys seem to be in good shape. Jeb will be staying with George and this is good. George will be a good influence on him. Jebby is a deep sensitive kid with lots of compassion and love in his heart, but I worry that he might take on some crazy idea. He has not so far nor is there a sign of it but it just plagues me a little bit.

May 11, 1971

Brigadier General Alexander M. Haig, Jr.
Deputy Assistant to the President for National Security Affairs
Washington, DC 20500
Dear Al:

The subject of Vietnam, Cambodia, Laos is not in front of the U.N., but it permeates the corridors and is all around us. I am wondering if anyone at the NSC has ever drawn up a paper that shows the things we have offered and the rejections we have received. I have in mind things like: 1. Stop the bombing, 2. Cease-fire, 3. Statements of prisoner release, 4. Withdraw if they withdraw. There is little understanding at the U.N. on these things, and I would like to have a definitive paper showing the history of our offers—offers which have not been accepted.

The reason I am writing you is that Dr. Kissinger has mentioned to me on several occasions that we have done all the things many of the severest critics have suggested in the past. It would be useful for me to study any information like this which you might have and then be sure that our own top people that are dealing with ambassadors across the street are fully versed in all of this, No rush. Thanks a lot.

Yours very truly,
George Bush

May 20, 1971

We have just about completed a series of dinners at the Waldorf. The dinners have been pretty good. We tried to keep the men and women from going off into separate rooms at the end of the dinner. We tried to keep it informal. At the last one Bryce Harlow* attended and gave a marvelous talk about the "real President Nixon." He was very articulate, very able and did an excellent job. Charlotte Reid† sang and she was most attractive. I am confident that these ambassadors find this kind of evening an improvement over just sitting around yakking and smoking cigars . . .

The President has seemed rather tense to me lately at the Cabinet meetings. We talked about the youth and I could see that he was concerned about some of the outrageous youth statements. He talked about the demonstrators. We just had the veterans demonstration. He was concerned of course about how they were behaving. I think he would like to be a lot tougher, but I think he is conscious of public opinion and wants to appear to be concerned. I think his own gut reaction is to crack down on these people. I must say I concur with him on that.

There have been a lot of rumors around. On the CBS morning program they asked about whether I would serve as Vice President. These questions are designed strictly to put one on the spot. They are impossible to answer. I did call up the Republican State Chairman in Texas, George Willeford, and told him under no conditions would I be a candidate for governor. It's funny how quickly one gets out of touch with the political scene there. I have a good strong feeling for Texas but I really don't have much judgment on exactly what's happening there. . . .

I attended Dad's 76th birthday in Greenwich. All five of us were there and all the in-laws were there except Bar. It was a very touching occasion. I think how lucky we are as a family to feel so very, very close. I look around at our friends and there are very few that have this same closeness in their families during these peculiar times.‡ I am hoping our children will have it but there is no way one can guarantee how these things work. . . .

---

*Bryce was a counselor to Nixon and a close confidant. He was respected and well liked by everyone.

†A congresswoman from Illinois.

‡I really mean the *turbulent* times—war protests, civil unrest, our troubled college campuses.

June 3, 1971

His Excellency Mr. Yakov Aleksandrovich Malik
Permanent Representative of the USSR
to the United Nations
New York, New York 10021
Dear Mr. Ambassador:

I have your letter of May 31. I cannot help but note that it follows the May 18 article in the Soviet Government newspaper Izvestiya accusing me of "trembling with delight" at the sight of damages caused by the Jewish Defense League.

I will continue to fight against the illegal harassment of Soviet officials in New York, but I will also continue to speak out in the United Nations, as well as to responsible groups of American citizens, whenever I believe your Government's record demands criticism. In this connection, I would note that were I to protest every time you or a member of your delegation made a statement "unfriendly" to the United States, I would have little time left for other work.

I have noted your statement that the right to enter or leave a country is purely an internal matter. This is, as you know, at variance with the United Nations Declaration on Human Rights, which states, "Everyone has the right to leave any country, including his own, and to return to his country."

Respectfully,
George Bush

June 12, 1971

On the eleventh I had a very interesting luncheon with Yakov Malik up at his apartment. I am told this is rather unusual. . . .

Vodka before, vodka during, wine during, offer of cognac after, long philosophical discussion about what the people in Russia thought about us and what the people in our country thought about them. He repeated all the cold war rhetoric—that we were imperialists. He told me one interesting thing when I questioned him about the fact that in the elections in the Soviet Union there was no opposition. "Yes, but you don't have to vote for the man, thus you can register your disapproval." I told him that would never get by in a country like ours with open press. He keeps accusing the press in our country of being Zionist-controlled. Then he made this interesting point. He himself as ambassador has to sit in a commune-like gathering in his own Mission while they all criticize him, and during those meetings he is not the ambassador. He is just one more person. I told him it didn't seem likely to me that they would give him the full treatment of criticism but he assured me that they did. His deputy kept nodding all the while. . . . We talked about the Vietnam war, and I reassured him we want no territory there. He jumped on me about the aggression. We talked about the Middle East. I talked about Hungary and Czechoslovakia. He did not want to talk about the budget. He did not want to talk about the Secretary General's succession. He was in a very likable, expansive mood, and yet he could be very tough and doctrinaire. I am sure in the next Four Power meeting he will act totally cold and tough, but these contacts must be kept up. . . .

The battle is on for the succession of Secretary General. I went over and had a very frank discussion with [U Thant], laying it on the line, telling him that I did not want to be going around his back talking about succession unless he made clear to me that he did want to move out. He seemed to appreciate this frankness, although I was later told that the inscrutable [eastern] way is to be not quite so direct. This was passed along to me by Ambassador Shahi of Pakistan. . . . I find U Thant fascinating. He is obviously against us on the war and things like this, but I must say he impresses me. He is a man totally dedicated to peace. He is a philosopher and not an administrator. The U.N. desperately needs administration at this critical point, but U Thant cannot, will not, does not want to provide it.

I am increasingly concerned about the overlay of inefficiency that I am told exists there. Everyone knows it, but nobody does much about it. . . .

Another incident—Teddy Kennedy made a speech on the floor of the Senate during the week of June 4 in which he said that Nixon wanted to prolong the end of the war until 1972 for political purposes to help get re-elected. To me this was one of the crassest, cruelest statements I had ever heard. When I gave a speech to the Andover Chamber of Commerce with a good press conference beforehand, I denounced the statement as cruel and mean. I can understand debate on the war, but I cannot understand somebody making a statement like that and yet the press let Teddy get away with it. They simply don't jump him out as they would somebody else. It was irresponsibility at its worst, and yet he wasn't damaged a bit by it, I am sure. . . .

I'm continually besieged by host country problems—Yugoslavian ambassador's daughter robbed, coat slashed with a razor—another ambassador's car stolen—harassment of the Soviet ambassador by the Jewish Defense League. One darn thing after another. We have been working closely with the White House trying to get more done in the way of protection for missions in New York. Something may happen on this. . . .

Nixon-Cox wedding—We were very pleased to be included. The Cabinet had assigned seats as did a few family friends. The rest of the people were all seated wherever there was a chair in the Rose Garden. It rained and the ceremony was held in between rain and clouds. They got away with it, and it was a terrifically beautiful occasion. The President looked happy. . . .

I talked with Billy Graham at the wedding, who said there were lots and lots of young people coming to his crusades. He really felt a change coming about in the country away from the wild stuff, away from the outrages of the dissent. I hope like heck he is right. . . .

The U.N. job is an interesting job. People are "rooting for you"— Democrats, Republicans, all people. Some, because of the illustrious predecessors, have an inflated idea about what the job is. My assessment at this point is that the job is broad, interesting, fantastic but that it is not as "important" as some think because we have less policy input at this point than I would like to see it have. I am still convinced that the way to get that is to earn it, not go down and demand it as Goldberg did. I'll never get over Goldberg telling me how he planted phone calls. People come in and hand him a note that the President is calling. Goldberg gets up and leaves and of course the President wouldn't be calling. I think the problem was that some of the ambassadors might have thought the President was calling, but most people that followed the U.S. Mission knew he wasn't. . . .

I watched Agnew at the Cabinet meetings with some interest. He speaks his piece and to me makes sense. I have respect for Agnew. He cannot help but get on the press. Even at the Cabinet meetings he'll mention media etc. but his point of view, where he is positioned on the issues, all is pretty darn sensible. It's almost as though nobody listens to him, but he is always very forthright, speaks his mind, doesn't claim too much time, and then shuts up. He is much more impressive in this kind of gathering than he is ever given credit for publicly. . . .

About this time I jotted down the following notes for a speech about my new job:

Every day I go to work I have that inner exhilarating feeling that comes from having the challenge of working for peace.

Sure the vehicle has problems but is that reason to give up—Must we because of obvious difficulties give up, turn back—

The answer, perhaps idealistic is a reassuring "No"—

We must be critics—constructive critics—if the U.N. is to fulfill its potential.

But let's not be hand wringing, carping critics

———

TELEGRAM
Action: SEC-STATE
SUBJ: Protest by SOV PERM REP Malik
Following ad appeared page 68 NY times June 22 under Merchandise Offerings:

Going Out of Business
Must sell all office furn. Desks, file cabinets, chairs, office machines. No reasonable offer refused. 1st come first serve.
Mr. Malik UN 1-4900.

I received a strong telephone protest from AMB Malik June 23 regarding . . . the advertisement placed in NY Times re selling of Malik's furniture.

Publisher [Arthur] Sulzberger had called Malik to apologize.

I called Sulzberger who explained that advertisements of very small amounts are not checked out as to authenticity. Sulzberger instituting new policy at TIMES to try to take care of problem.

I expressed profound regret to Malik. Advised him of our efforts to battle extremism. He was firm and upset.

Bush

———

June 27, 1971

The New York Times disclosed some classified documents. My own feeling is that there will not be much damage to the national security from the release of these documents by themselves. The great problem lies in the damage to the national security if the concept ever gets around that each individual can indeed be his own judge as to what should be classified and what should not be. The press is a very liberal press. People are trying to make a hero out of Ellsberg. It will be interesting to see how the trial comes out if he is given one.*

———

*On June 13, the New York Times began publishing classified documents that became known as the Pentagon Papers detailing U.S. involvement in Vietnam. They were leaked by Dr. Daniel Ellsberg, one of the analysts who helped write the report.

Hypothetical question—Suppose a citizen had given these documents to the Soviet Union directly and it had been found out that he had so conducted himself. What would be the reaction of the American people? What price should he have been asked to pay?

Ellsberg did not do this. What he did do was not very different though. He gave to the <u>New York Times,</u> they published them and of course the Russians have them. The difference is not so easy to see. . . .

———————

[Undated diary entry]

Cabinet meeting of June 29 was a most unusual one. There were no other people in the room except the Cabinet people themselves and Haldeman. The President was tremendously upset about leaks in government. I have never seen him more forceful or more fired-up. He talked about the people in the woodwork who are trying to get the Administration, the people who use their own judgment as to what to leak all in an effort to unseat the President. He seemed firm. The President said that Haldeman would be policing these leaks and not to try to go around Haldeman for he had the full authority of the President.

The point is very well taken. How can a Presidential decision be made if "it is tried in the press" beforehand. Leaks representing the points of view of the newspapers are often encouraged and to the degree the President does not have maximum flexibility his hands are tied. . . .

———————

President Nixon surprised everyone when he announced in July he would visit China in the near future. It was a historic step, and he deserves much credit for opening this long-closed door. I was strongly in favor of the new policy but immediately saw that we would face a real battle in the United Nations in terms of China's representation.

July 19, 1971

Nixon-China visit—The China announcement came with an amazing surprise value particularly in light of the Pentagon papers dispute. At this dictation the U.N. community is very much in favor of it. At this moment I don't know what our China policy in the U.N. will turn out to be, but all the U.N. people feel that the ball game is over, Peking is in and Taiwan is out. Kosciusko Morizet* came up for the weekend in Maine, and we had a long talk about his views on all of this. He thought it was a very good move, that the Russians would be climbing the walls and that it would make for a much more realistic world. I was with Vinci† and Carlos Ortiz De Rozas of Argentina when the announcement was made. They were both elated. They both kept emphasizing what this would do to the Russians. They have got to make clear to the Russians we do not plan to make capital against them with this. This was a brilliant move.

The Cabinet Meeting—the President emphasized over and over again the need for security. He discussed nothing with the Cabinet about policy, gave no indication about whether Vietnam was involved, gave no hint about what the U.N. policy would be. He simply asked for as little speculation as possible due to the sensitivity of the Chinese on this point. In a matter like this it is better not to know so that you don't inadvertently foul up these very difficult negotiations. . . .

General observations—Watching these cabinet meetings and seeing how little decision making goes on there, there is a certain luxury in being out of Washington. You are not under the intense political pressure or fire all the time and yet there is a certain degree of access by being a member of the Cabinet. I am convinced that very little decision-making is done at cabinet meetings. It's usually information, giving instructions, etc. I have not yet sorted out what route should be taken in order to have a real input on decisions, but I am clear it is not through the bureaucracy in the State Department and it is not through the Cabinet meetings themselves. I think it is probably direct personal contact with the Secretary of State and direct personal contact with NSC and Kissinger, mainly Kissinger. Of course in some crisis it would be the President himself. The whole concept though of instructions needs review and work just as the whole classification system in the government needs work. Instructions can really come from so low down as to be meaningless or as to be out of touch with the President in terms of philosophy. Of course too many darn documents are classified. . . .

———

*France's ambassador at the United Nations and later a foreign policy adviser to Paris mayor Jacques Chirac, now president of France.
†Piero Vinci, Italy's engaging ambassador to the United Nations.

August 12, 1971

... I have great respect for Bill Rogers. He is easy to work with, to talk to. I know he finds it hard to battle the State Department bureaucracy at times. He never fails to return a phone call, and I am feeling closer and closer to him. The battle between the White House and the State Department is very clear. . . . There is a cross fire there that it would be well to avoid getting caught in. I'm not sure it's all together possible. . . .

Personal touch—I saw the President at an August 6 meeting. He gave me a golf ball. I told him, "Great, I'll use this in Maine tomorrow." He asked me to fly with him to Maine which I did. On the plane we reminisced a bit about Maine and I told him it was my mother's and dad's fiftieth anniversary and he immediately placed a phone call from Air Force One to my father. Unfortunately Dad was not there at the time. Nixon does nice, gracious things like this but he gets little credit on that score. . . .

Public opinion was strong as the U.N. vote approached on whether to admit the People's Republic of China and keep or expel Taiwan. I wrote this note to Senator Bill Brock after he and some of his Senate colleagues expressed concern over Taiwan being expelled.

September 30, 1971

The Honorable William E. Brock, III
United States Senate
Washington, DC
Dear Bill:

I have read the statement which you and your colleagues issued today on the China policy and I want to say at the outset that I understand how you feel and why you feel that way.

Your position reflects the realities of the situation today. In a very responsible way you are helping the American people know that there have been significant political changes in the world over the past decade.

In 1964 there were 115 member nations in the United Nations and only 39 of them had diplomatic relations with Mainland China. Today there are 130 member nations and some 62 U.N. members have recognized the Mainland Government.

In the last General Assembly the vote on the Albanian Resolution to expel the Nationalists and seat the Communists was 51 to 49 (although a 2/3rds vote was necessary for passage). Since last Fall, 12 more nations have established diplomatic relations, thus the trend has moved towards the PRC and against the ROC. Included among the nations which today maintain diplomatic relations are such friendly countries as Canada, the UK and France. This means they are not free to support us on our present policy. . . .

Nonetheless, I want you and the others in the Congress to know we are leaving no stone unturned here in our effort to win this issue. I have talked personally to some 65 Representatives of foreign nations. My staff is working virtually around the clock making contacts and soliciting support. In the capitals around the world our Ambassadors are contacting governments in behalf of our position.

People always ask "can we win." I feel that we have a winnable proposition—but it will be extremely close.

After living with this problem for several months, I am totally convinced that the President is correct in his approach. Given the changes in the world, our former position would not have been sustained. The votes simply aren't there to support it. The only way Nationalist China can be kept as a U.N. member is for the dual representation approach to succeed. They know it and so do we.

We are working desperately to keep them in the U.N.

Bringing PRC in, in my view, is a move towards reality and I support it, but we must not let a big reality "muscle out" a smaller reality.

ROC is bigger than 92 countries. Expulsion sets a very dangerous precedent. It is this point I am trying so hard to get across to the other U.N. members.

Your statement of interest puts appropriate emphases on this policy.

Yours very truly,
George Bush

October 19, 1971

Mr. Charles Untermeyer
Houston, Texas 77024
Dear Charles:

. . . Right now we are in the midst of the China question here at the United Nations. It is all encompassing—night and day—at every meal—first thing in the morning, last thing at night. I think we can win for a policy that I believe strongly in, but it's going to be terribly close. I am enjoying this experience here at the United Nations tremendously. There are problems that at times seem insurmountable, but there are also some rewarding moments as well. All the kids are fine. Jeb is a freshman at the University of Texas. George is living in Houston. Dorothy is here with us in New York. Neil is boarding at

St. Alban's,* and Marvin is boarding at Andover. Hurriedly, but with warmest regards.

Yours very truly,
George Bush

———————

We lost the China vote. The People's Republic of China was admitted to the United Nations—which we supported—but Taiwan was expelled. In the end, it became more of an anti-American vote than anything else, especially among Third World countries. Some anti-American delegates literally danced in the aisles when the final vote was tallied: 59–55, with fifteen countries abstaining. (Several of those countries had promised to support us.) I felt it was a dark moment for the United Nations and international diplomacy.

October 31, 1971

The China Vote. I am dictating this a week after the vote.

1. When we went into the voting I really thought we could win by one or two votes. The villains are documented in our [file]—ones who simply did not do what they said they would do. Foremost among these is Cyprus. I recall walking back when I heard that Cyprus was slipping during the voting. I asked the Foreign Minister whether we had a problem. He said, "Yes." I said, "I don't understand this. President Makarios has assured us twice that he would vote with us on the important question." He said "You and I have never talked about this." I said, "We have talked about this, but what's important is that your President has assured us of his support." I said, "Go ahead and vote for this, but simply remember that we do not view this lightly, and we feel we have a direct and strong commitment."

2. After the vote there was a tremendous amount of discussion about American arm-twisting. I don't know of a single case where we linked in the question of aid or where we made any direct pledge of any kind. We did make very forcefully clear to other countries what we were doing. All the reports talk about undue U.S. pressure and threats etc. but they simply are not true. We have been battling the news media from the very beginning. All of them at the outset said we had no chance at all and when we got within a gnat's eyebrow of the whole thing, then they started talking about undue pressure. It simply is not fair reporting. It is untrue. . . .

*A boarding school in Washington, D.C.

3. There is no question in my mind that the Kissinger visit [to China] gave our position some incredibility. The minute the President announced his trip to Peking the race to Peking was on, and my list . . . shows which countries tried to beat us in that race, and thus were unavailable for support. The timing of the planning trip was unfortunate. It was thrust on the White House by long-standing negotiations and uncertainty as to when the U.N. vote was going to be. There is no question in my mind that Kissinger feels that the bilateral approach to Peking is much more important than the U.N. I am convinced he did not deliberately sabotage the U.N. vote. Kissinger called me up after he got back from Peking. I have never heard him in such an ugly mood, ending up by saying, "I am not amused." The source of his ire seemed to be the fact that he felt I told him the vote would come later, towards October 28. I distinctly remember discussing it with him in a very private meeting. I told him procedures could not be controlled, and the main thing in my mind was that he did not want the vote while he was in Peking . . .

I think history will show the Nixon initiative to Peking is the thing that lost the U.N. vote, although maybe there are things we should have done differently here. . . .

It was an ugliness in the chamber. I was hissed when I got up to speak on a procedural motion. Many of the ambassadors mentioned how bad it was. U Thant practically had tears in his eyes— so much so that I went to see him the next day to tell him that we were going to continue to support the U.N. and at that point he . . . joined in abhorring the ugly atmosphere. It was not pleasant and it was not glee. It was gladiatorial ugliness at its worst. I can certainly understand a country being happy at winning after many years of frustration, but this mood had more serious implications for the U.N. than that. . . .

———————

November 5, 1971

Mrs. William A. McKenzie*
Dallas, Texas 75202
Dear Sally:

Thanks so much for your thoughtful note. You're great. Life goes on, and there is no question that the U.N. will be a more realistic and vital place with

—————————————
*Sally and Bill McKenzie are good friends and supporters from Dallas.

Peking in here, but I had my heart and soul wrapped up in the policy of keeping Taiwan from being ejected. The withdrawal symptoms have been horrible.

Warmest regards,

George Bush

––––––––––

The new Chinese delegation arrived in New York with much fanfare. They were accompanied by their vice minister of foreign affairs, Chiao Kuan Hua. This was my diary entry after their first U.N. appearance:

November 15, 1971

On Monday the Chinese Vice Minister of Foreign Affairs, Mr. Chiao, gave his blast. We gave a warm welcoming speech, and then he got up and gave his speech which was clearly hostile to the United States, referring to us as bullies etc. It was not a speech that was unexpected and all the great experts, diplomats, news people plus our own people said this was to be expected. After the speech I came over and called the Secretary of State to tell him about the speech. I told him I felt it had to be answered. We were under strict instructions at the time not to answer it. We gave a gracious welcoming speech which received good comment at the U.N. If it weren't for the domestic pressures perhaps it would not be necessary to answer Chiao's speech but I told Rogers that my strongly held view was that if we didn't answer it (the U.N. had just suffered a setback in the Gallup Polls—36 percent support by the American people—an all-time low), the U.N. would vanish off the scale completely.

. . . I think the feeling of the experts was that it was less inflammatory than it might have been. My point was that without any background on how inflammatory they were in the past, this would be grossly misconstrued by the American people, and the President would be ill-served if it appeared that we are unwilling to answer these allegations about our being bullies, super powers trying to dominate the little powers, etc. I told Rogers that the people are interested in the Peking trip, but not just on Peking's terms. If we appear to be pushed around by Peking at every turn, the whole thing can backfire on the President.

. . . I went down to see Kissinger then and had a long and interesting discussion. He started off madder than hell. "I want to treat you as I do four other ambassadors, dealing directly with you, but if you are uncooperative I will treat you like any other ambassador." I reacted very strongly, told him my only interest was in supporting the President, and told him I damn sure had a feel for this country and I felt we had to react.

. . . For 2 or 3 minutes we had a very heated and somewhat spirited exchange. After that he calmed down and was pleasant, charming and most cooperative. . . .

He suggested that it might be productive for me to sit in on some of his meetings on the Chinese thing so we could develop a future line. We talked about telling Red China we will "turn Bush loose" if certain things happen. All in all it was one of the most constructive talks I have ever had with Kissinger. . . . I told him very clearly when he got upset that I was not trying to screw things up, I was trying to serve the President and that it was the only interest I had. He ought to get that through his head. I was not trying to get any power or enter into any dispute between him and the State Department. I said it so forcefully that he seemed taken back and he really cooled down. The conversation ended in a very good way. Kissinger needs allies, and I am one of them. I also must and intend to remain loyal to Rogers. It is not easy, and it is a problem that I am not able to talk to anyone about in order to get advice . . .

[Because I felt caught between Rogers and Kissinger, I totally changed my mind about whether the U.N. ambassador should be a member of the President's cabinet. The answer is absolutely not. Except in rare circumstances when the President personally intervenes, the U.N. ambassador must answer to the secretary of state—as do all ambassadors—and therefore should not be on the same cabinet level as the secretary.]

————————

At the end of 1971, ABC sportscaster Dick Schapp wrote a tongue-in-cheek article for New York *magazine on the ten most overrated men in New York City. A modest man, Schapp did not put himself on the list—a terrible oversight. Besides me, the other "honorees" were McGeorge Bundy, president of the Ford Foundation; Terence Cardinal Cooke, archbishop of New York; Ralph DeNunzio, chairman of the board of governors of the New York Stock Exchange; Sanford Garelik, president of the New York City Council; Senator Jacob Javits; Broadway and Hollywood producer David Merrick: Steve Smith, married to Jean Kennedy Smith, and the man "who managed the clan"; Gabe Pressman from NBC; and Arthur Sulzberger of the* New York Times. *Barbara and I decided to give a party in honor of the "overrated" so we could check each other out. I remember that Ambassador Malik, who attended the party, was confused by it all, and he was overheard asking someone, "Vat is dis 'overrated'?"*

January 4, 1972

Mr. David Merrick
New York, New York
Dear "Most-Overrated" Mr. Merrick:

. . . I was kind of flattered to be included on this list.

I thought it might be fun to get together. I'd like the chance to look you over to see why you are so "overrated."

Barbara and I would like to have you and your wife come by the U.S. Embassy (42-A Waldorf Towers) for a cocktail on Tuesday, January 11, at 6:30 p.m.

I'll invite the guy who wrote the story plus the editor of New York Magazine—We'll get some of my colleagues at the U.N. to come by so we can have an international judgment as to who is indeed the most "overrated" of them all.

Please come.

> Very truly yours,
> George Bush

———————

The Security Council met in Africa in February 1972 (it was the United States' suggestion to move U.N. meetings to different countries), giving Barbara and me a chance to visit this fascinating but troubled continent. One of my regrets as President was that we were not able to do more in Africa, where I planned to visit during my second term, if elected. Here are some of my observations from 1972.

Zambia—President Kaunda —we met with him for some thirty minutes. He is a warm, amiable man. . . . He looked far older than his 45 years. He was very friendly to me, gave me a fairly long statement in very tolerant and understanding tones. They wished the United States could do more, wished we could be more helpful to the freedom fighters . . . He is not nearly as uptight as many of the ministers we met but he was very concerned. An example—he mentioned going down the river in a canoe on a continuous journey. He and many other African leaders have a question of whether the canoe can continue its journey or whether it will be upset, given its troubled waters of racism. . . .

Wednesday—visit to Botswana . . . They have no means to solve their own problems. They need a $12 million loan to help them with this road that means so much to them. It is something I want to strongly recommend when I get back.

Our Ambassador Nelson was there at the border to meet us. We were observed closely by the Rhodesian and South African troops who stood only 10 yards away from us—taking pictures, looking through spyglasses as we crossed the river, etc. At one time they fired shots at the ferryboat from Botswana to Zambia.

Zambia is a land of contrast. They can eliminate dissent and political freedom of those that oppose them and yet they give us lectures on establishing freedom on racial basis in the south. We don't mention this but maybe we should publicly. It is annoying for the United States to get constantly lectured on what the United States should be doing about guaranteeing freedom by countries thousands of miles away who have yet to perfect their own political processes to guarantee even much less freedom than our country has. It is a great exercise in keeping one's temper, and yet one cannot question as one looks at apartheid and the police methods in South Africa and Rhodesian South Africa that one must be tremendously concerned. But the nasty question lingers on. What should the United States do about it? . . .

The problem of development in Africa is so tremendous, particularly in countries like Somalia and Sudan, as opposed to Zaire which has made some progress, that it is almost like throwing a penny into the ocean to fill it up. I am continually appalled by the difference of standards in Zaire. There are some beautiful living sections, but of course immense poverty. Once one gets out in the countryside in the Sudan, poverty is all around you all the time. . . .

Zaire is easily the most up-to-date. Officially they are very friendly with the United States—they are very leery of China and Russia. President Mobutu runs a tight ship and our ambassador pointed out that this is the only place where the soldiers saluted the American Ambassador's car whether his flag was flying or not. . . .

I had a long, roundtable discussion with the ambassadors from Tanzania, Kenya, Zambia, etc.—a very frank exchange in which I took the offense and criticized them for not criticizing other countries, while they all felt free to blast us on things like Rhodesian sanctions. It is odd how much we agreed and how much they seemed to like one's taking the offense.

I discussed the same thing with the Zairian Foreign Minister. He felt we should indeed use more rhetoric and more name-calling at the U.N. when people chewed us for being the old colonialist, imperialist. I am getting sick of hearing our country so abused. He felt we should respond in kind. He said it would be well received. My own view is that we respond too little to these outrageous charges and thus it was fun to have a very frank discussion with these ambassadors, to take the offense, and to get the feeling that at least they were listening. . . .

Though I readily admit that it is hard to judge without having been to Rhodesia or South Africa, I am convinced that the United States must find ways to help solve these problems. The system of apartheid has got to go, and the United States would be helpful without sending troops or resorting to violence. Many Africans think when I talk about peaceful change, that we are not talking about change at all. I made this point very clear to the President, Kaunda, in Zambia and the foreign ministers in the various countries. We are talking about peaceful <u>and</u> change but sometimes they fail to realize this . . .

Looking ahead to the day when we would return to Houston, Barbara and I had purchased an empty lot (later sold) where we could build a house. Our new neighbor wrote and asked permission to cut some trees down on the property line.

June 26, 1972

Mr. Paul G. Bell, Jr.
Houston, Texas
Dear Gervais:

Thanks for your great letter. Short of chopping down all the trees on our place, please make whatever minor adjustments are required. . . .

We are looking forward to being your neighbors someday. As a matter of fact, it gets kind of exciting thinking about building a house again. My future is kind of undetermined at this point as far as a time frame goes. I still love this job but I must confess I look forward to coming back to Houston someday too. . . .

Yours very truly,
George Bush

September 1972

. . . Mother called to say that Dad is sick, that there is a pain by his heart. I have a deep worry about him. He seems instantly old, unlike his old self in many ways . . .

I was at a dinner last night where the guest of honor didn't get up to leave and finally at 11:15 p.m. I got restless, looked over at him, yawned, stretched, made somewhat of a fool of myself, but it broke up the party.

Memo for the Record—September 18, 1972

Security Officer Joe Glennon, accompanied by Tom Lias,* talked with Ambassador Bush concerning the personal security of the Ambassador and his family. (Glennon had mentioned the evening before to Lias that there was some intelligence coming in which indicated that the Ambassador should take certain additional precautions.)

Glennon advised the Ambassador that intelligence sources indicated that the Black September† organization was planning some new move, possibly in New York, and possibly against Israelis or Americans. Glennon recommended that steps be taken to arrange for Dorothy Bush to be driven to school instead of using public transportation as she has been doing.

There was some discussion of the handling of this proposal and the Ambassador agreed that beginning Friday morning, he and Dorothy would leave the Waldorf together and Jerry would drive the Ambassador to the Mission and Dorothy to school. Because Dorothy has been reluctant to arrive at school in a chauffeured limousine, it was further agreed that the car Jerry would use would be one of the sedans and not one of the black Cadillac limousines.

Glennon further suggested that the Ambassador consider the possibility of utilizing personal security guards for himself throughout the day and possibly to some extent at 42-A.‡ At this point, the Ambassador said he would like to get the advice of his friend, Richard Helms at CIA, and a call was placed to Director Helms. The Ambassador and Helms discussed the situation and Helms advised the Ambassador the intelligence on this matter was not at all "soft" and that he was most concerned about some aspects of this and was following one situation very closely. . . .

Dad's persistent cough was diagnosed as lung cancer.

September 27, 1972

A tough day. Dad had his prostate operation, unconnected with his cancer. It was supposed to be routine, but it became clear that he was

*Tom was my very able assistant. Later, he worked for me at the Republican National Committee.

†Black September was a radical Arab terrorist organization that shocked the world when they assassinated eleven members of Israel's Olympic team at the 1972 Summer Olympics in Munich.

‡The apartment number in the Waldorf Towers.

having complications. There was some infection, constant fever, an irregular heartbeat, blood pressure bad. They stabilized the condition in the afternoon and Pres and I went up to talk to the doctor at length at 4:30. Doctor Beattie made clear that it was very serious. He was a very reassuring, confident and inspiring man. He pointed out that they were concerned about the lesion in the arm which could be an extension of the cancer, that they weren't sure about that. He pointed out that the tumor in the lung could possibly be extending to rub on the heart. . . . He pointed out it could be a question of weeks or months. He said he would watch it very closely. I gave him my home phone number and the number at the Peruvian Embassy where I would be at 8:15 . . .

I got a phone call that they said was a matter of some urgency. I got Beattie who reported that there were quite a few complications. He suggested that we be at the hospital at 11:00 with Mother. She was already in bed, but I woke her up. I told her that I would meet her there and that I loved her. I met Dr. Beattie there, and went up to see [Dad]. He was full of tubes. He was conscious though very sleepy with drugs.

He kept asking what time it was. I told him about the dinner with the Russians. His answer was, "Who picked up the tab?"

[My father, my mentor, my hero, died on October 8.]

October 16, 1972

Dear Mr. President,

Your beautiful tribute to Dad then the lovely flowers, and now your warm letter of Oct. 9th all mean so much to me and to my Mother and to all our family. My Dad was the real inspiration in my life—he was strong and strict, full of decency and integrity; but he was also kind, understanding and full of humor.

He died of fast spreading cancer without too much suffering. So often we talked, even in the hospital, of your Presidency—he was in great admiration of your ability to make the tough decision. My mother is heroic—buoyed up by the kindness of friends. I expect I've concentrated less this last week on our U.N. problems than I should have, but things are getting clearer now and I've got a lot from my Dad to be thankful for.

Thanks for helping us all so much.

George

November 14, 1972

Mr. C. Fred Chambers*
Houston, Texas 77002
Dear Fred:

Dad was a spectacular man and our family was shattered when he died.

I guess you, probably more than any of our friends, knew what he meant to me in terms of inspiration in my own life. Wherever I was, whatever I did, he was the incentive behind everything.

He died fast, in less than a month, from rapidly spreading cancer. But the happy thing is that we now have great memories of this strong man and mom is fantastically unselfish and strong.

And so the Bushes are OK. One of the things that makes us OK is that we have lots of friends who have told us good things about Dad.

. . . Let's try to get together more. Darn it! We have missed you the last two times I have been in Houston. Love to Marion and all the gang.

Yours very truly,
George Bush

President Nixon summoned me to Camp David in November to discuss "the future." I was not overly surprised. Immediately following the President's landslide victory over George McGovern in early November, Nixon called a cabinet meeting. When it was over and he left the room, Haldeman announced that every cabinet member should have his letter of resignation sent over to the White House right away. It was not kind and gentle. He also said the President wanted to visit with each of us individually. I was not ready to leave the United Nations, but I suspected it would not be my choice. I already had heard talk that he might ask me to be number two at the Treasury Department, under George Shultz. Then the call came—President Nixon wanted to see me at Camp David.

November 21, 1972

Honorable Richard M. Nixon
President of the United States
Washington, DC
Dear Mr. President:

. . . I want to thank you for yesterday.

Frankly, your first choice for me came as quite a surprise particularly to Barbara. The rarefied atmosphere of international affairs plus the friendships

---

*Fred and his wife, Marion, were among our best friends in Texas. A few years down the road, Bar would name our next dog in Fred's honor.

in New York and the Cabinet seem threatened to her. She is convinced that all our friends in Congress, in public life, in God knows where—will say, "George screwed it up at the U.N. and the President has loyally found a suitable spot". Candidly, there will be some of this.

But—here's my answer—·

Your first choice was the Republican National Committee. I will do it!

The treasury slot—#2 there—is an interesting job but I wouldn't really be running something—the stamp, the imprint would and should be George Shultz'. I have deep respect for George, but that slot is not for me.

. . . Number 2 at State, which I realize is all but committed, would be different. I have been dealing happily, and I hope effectively, with the top international leadership. I could continue this—arrogantly tucking into the back of my mind the thought that a) if I performed and b) if all the other panting candidates for Secretary of State dropped by the wayside—I might get that—a slot which in my current thinking would be tops.

The under Secretary for Finance at State is like #2 at Treasury—a fascinating job but not really up to the offered Treasury post. My love affair is not with State, it's with high-level policy dealings on international matters—this U.N. job has that—Deputy Secretary has it—the Under Secretary for Economics does not.

As to the Republican National Committee—access to you is all important, trying to gear up for the '74 elections is important, the "imprint" or "image" I can bring to the job is important. You visualize a very different role—getting all politics out of the White House and into the Republican National Committee through its chairman. This I find really challenging. With [John] Ehrlichman's approval I talked to John Mitchell* today, and he was really re-assuring on this.

John Ehrlichman told me he raised a ticklish point with you—I can and will of course take orders, but I'd like to retain options on the style in which to carry them out. I can be plenty tough when needed, but each person has his own style, his own methods, and if I get too far out of character—I'll be unconvincing and incredible and this will not serve you well.

Our Chinese friends here at the United Nations are proud but not vain—maybe I'm the same way—proud but hopefully not to the point of vanity. To the degree you can launch this thing with some "newness", "change", etc. it would help offset the cynic's inevitable charge that we Bushes are going backwards. After talking to you and to Mr. Mitchell and Mr. Ehrlichman I am intrigued with the concept of helping you on a wide spectrum of political matters.

---

*Ehrlichman was a top White House aide; John Mitchell had been attorney general but left that post to head up the Committee for the Re-Election of the President.

I believe we can fully develop this relationship on the "inside" political advisor basis that you spelled out at Camp David. I must have the personal access to you and Bob that we talked about. . . .

My thanks to you for your friendship and loyalty. I will repay it with hard work and loyalty in return.

My wife's initial reaction is understandable, for she is but a mirror of how the real world regrettably views politics. Most people feel it is not the noble calling it should be—not the noble calling like affairs of state. One real challenge lies in enchanting the disenchanted young who view partisan politics with a worrisome cynicism.

But with your help maybe I can be a part of changing some of that. And in the final analysis that's one hell of a challenge.

So my initial "no" has changed after a sleepless night to a happy "yes". The shock has worn off, and Barbara will see that it makes sense. And besides, she's your biggest fan.

So I'm ready.

Respectfully,
George Bush

**Republican
National
Committee.**

George Bush, Chairman

CHAPTER 5

The Eye of the Storm

At 2:30 A.M. on June 17, 1972, police caught five men breaking into the Democratic National Headquarters at the Watergate complex in Washington, D.C. Despite rumors about political espionage with a possible link to the White House itself, it obviously did not affect Nixon's successful bid for a second term. When I took over as chairman of the Republican National Committee (RNC) in January 1973, shortly before the President's second inauguration, I still firmly believed that President Nixon had nothing to do with the unfolding scandal that became known simply as Watergate.

Mail poured into the RNC office, most of it from loyal Republicans. I spent an enormous amount of time as chairman trying to reassure them that our political system was sound, that the Republican National Committee, thus the party, had nothing to do with Watergate, and that our President was innocent. It was not an easy job.

––––––––

April 9, 1973

Mr. H. E. Anderson
Piedmont, California 94611
Dear Mr. Anderson:

Thank you very much for your recent letter. It was good to hear from you.

I recognize that some people may be trying to blow the Watergate incident out of proportion, but at the same time I think that the connotations of Watergate are very serious, and I think they degrade our political system.

I don't believe that politics is a grubby business. I personally gave up a successful business life and a very interesting career in diplomacy to get re-involved in the political process, and incidents of this nature—no matter on what side they occur—downgrade the political process.

I consider myself a very loyal Republican, but I don't consider the bugging of Democrat headquarters to be the kind of thing we should condone or cover up. I know the President feels this way.

I hope this letter does not sound naïve to you. I believe politics to be a noble calling and these kinds of incidents hurt it. I recognize they go on both sides—to a degree—but I'd like to lend a hand in making politics a cleaner business. I'm sure you agree.

Thanks, again, for a good letter.

Yours very truly,
George Bush

On April 30, President Nixon announced the resignations of three of his top aides: H. R. Haldeman, John Ehrlichman, and John Dean. Attorney General Richard Kleindienst also resigned. Nixon named Elliot Richardson the new attorney general, and together they approved the creation of a special prosecutor's office, headed by Archibald Cox, to investigate Watergate.

May 18, 1973

Mr. John Alsop
Hartford, Conn. 06101
Dear John:

Thank you for your thoughtful letter of May 11. These indeed have been troubling times for agony and concern. In the long run, though, I'm not pessimistic. I think out of it will come a stronger and more independent Party, and a more sensitive and compassionate White House.

I also think that in the next few weeks we're going to see more return to civility on all sides, including the press. The press has done a good job in many ways, but they have overlooked some of the basic principles, such as a man is really innocent until proved guilty.

I share your indignation. Putting it on a very personal basis, everything that my Father stood for in life seems from time to time threatened by the arrogant behavior of a handful of people, but we must look ahead. We must accentuate the positive. To the best of my knowledge the Party is clean and though my life has been hell in lots of ways, I see this job much more of a challenge now than when I took it on. . . .

Yours very truly,
George Bush

_____

The Senate's Select Committee on Presidential Campaign Activities, under the chairmanship of Senator Sam Ervin, began their hearings in May. The testimony of John Dean (for whom I had little respect) riveted the nation as he linked Nixon to the cover-up. Haldeman, Ehrlichman, and John Mitchell denied wrongdoing and defended the President. Like the rest of the country, I was confused.

June 27, 1973

MEMORANDUM

TO: General Alexander Haig*
FROM: George Bush
RE: Presidential Press Conference on Watergate

Prior to Dean's testimony I had dictated a letter strongly recommending a Presidential press conference. I had in mind the meeting we had with the Republican leadership, and my own conviction that the more information that could be put out directly by the President on the subject of Watergate the better off we are.

There is a feeling of confusion; there is a feeling of "not knowing"; and there is a feeling of wanting to believe the President which can be totally shored up by yet another Presidential statement. . . . I recognize there are certain complications, but I would strongly urge that the President have another press conference as soon as some of the rebuttal witnesses to Dean have been heard.

I worry about the lack of civility at some of the recent White House press conferences. The President should not be subjected to the shouting, screaming and accusing that have faced some of the White House staff and many of us on the outside. In all likelihood the press corps would be more civil to the President than they have been with others. The hysteria surrounding the revelations on Watergate should be subdued by the fact that this was a Presidential press conference. To avoid any risk, however, thought should be given to an interview type press conference with the three major television network interviewers asking the questions.

SUMMARY:

People want to believe in the President and the Presidency. Basically they do, but particularly in Party circles there is a feeling that they must have more information. This is especially true now in light of Dean's testimony. I therefore recommend:

a) That the President hold a press conference soon selecting the optimum format, and

*Haig had been named chief of staff after Haldeman resigned.

b) The President should move around the country as much as possible speaking on major issues, meeting Party leaders—business leaders, labor leaders, etc. I would think that possibly four trips two weeks apart over widely dispersed geographic areas would be good. I am convinced the President will be warmly received.

[All these years later, I do not remember how the White House reacted to my memo. Apparently, it was not memorable.]

June 28, 1973

Mr. Elias F. Buckley
Colorado Springs, Colo. 80906
Dear Mr. Buckley:

Thank you for your good letter of June 21. I am glad to know of our family connections.

Thank you, also, for your words about Watergate. I believe you have it in proper perspective. It has been ugly and outrageous, but there are things much more important in terms of the ongoing nature of this country, I continue to have confidence in the President and I will until he is proved guilty, which I am confident will not happen.

About the family,* Aunt Margie is Mrs. Stewart Clement. Her husband is ailing and aged but she is full of life and pep and lives in New Haven, Connecticut. Her sister, Mary (Mrs. Frank House) is widowed. She lives in New Haven, also, and she and Aunt Margie remain very close. Uncle Jim Bush is a sad case. He has vanished—literally vanished from the face of the earth. He was married about four times, was living in Italy, left his wife there and has not been heard of since—that was about two years ago. At the time of my own father's death last Fall nobody even heard from Jim and he was very close indeed to my father, Prescott. As for my own family, there are four boys aged from 27 to 16, and one daughter 13. They are all doing great—spread out all over the country—from Texas to California to New England.

Warm regards, Mr. Buckley, and thanks for a good letter.

Yours very truly,
George Bush

---

*He asked about my father's two sisters and brother.

July 9, 1973

MEMORANDUM
TO: Bryce Harlow
FROM: George Bush

Early in June I received the attached letter from Barry Goldwater. I went to see him on the 13th, the day on which I received the letter, and we had a good frank discussion. It all boiled down to the fact that Barry feels the President ought to "sit down with some of the boys"; "drink some of that White House bourbon"; and "do what I did."

From reading the letter I thought he had some deep comments to make about the Republican National Committee, but the only complaint he raised with me was the inaccessibility to the President and the President did not call people in for advice. Barry, of course, was enthusiastic about the rumors that you were coming on board.

Let's discuss what we might do to iron this out. A few informal visits, in my view, would be well worth it, for the President and Senator Goldwater.

August 10, 1973

Mrs. Verta Hardegree
Colorado City, Texas 79512
Dear Verta:

It was great hearing from you. Of course I'm interested in your ideas. There's a lot of speculation now about my coming back to Texas and running [for governor], though I am inclined at this moment not to do that. . . .

The Bush family are all fine. Barbara is up in Maine and the boys will soon be arriving. Dorothy has been there with her all summer. Jebbie is out on the west coast working—one more year in college to go. George is going to go to Harvard Business School for two years, Marvin is at Woodberry Forest, and Neil is just starting at Tulane. Golly, I can hardly believe they're so grown. I hope your family is all well.

Thanks again for a wonderful letter.

Yours very truly,
George Bush

August 10, 1973

MEMORANDUM
TO: Mel Laird*
FROM: George Bush

I don't want to sound like I've got a one-track mind, but it seems to me it would be good for the President to have some contact with the Black Republican leadership in this country. A meeting at the White House of the Black leaders in government or from around the country might be extremely helpful. I, of course, would like to see it Republican, but I think any contact with Black leaders would be good. I'd say the same is true for Mexican-Americans. . . .

Don't bother to acknowledge, but I do think the more of these things the President can do the better it is for him, for the Party, and indeed for the country.

———————

Another Watergate bombshell broke that summer when former White House aide Alexander Butterfield testified before Congress that Nixon taped conversations in the Oval Office. I was deeply offended and amazed. Not only were people shocked to hear this, but it also began a huge legal and constitutional battle on whether the White House had to release the tapes. All these years later, I can still remember the day I learned of the tapes. I encountered Bryce Harlow at the White House, and we both felt it could be the beginning of the end for Nixon.

September 6, 1973

Mr. Paul Sabatino
Huntington Station, N. Y. 11746
Dear Mr. Sabatino:

Thank you for taking the time to share your thoughts with me about the President's stand regarding the tapes. I believe that at first glance releasing them would appear to be a direct and immediate way of resolving questions about Watergate, but in the long run such action would be detrimental both to the Administration and the country. My reasoning for this is twofold:

1. By revealing the conversations which took place, even if only in part, a precedent would be set for betraying the confidentiality which previously had always been respected by Presidents and those with whom they came in contact. As a result of such action those people who dealt with President Nixon or future leaders would always be faced with the possibility of their views being made public and would be very hesitant about expressing anything they wouldn't be willing to read in print.

2. By submitting the tapes the President would also be setting aside the

———————

*Laird, formerly secretary of defense, was now a White House counselor.

principle of balance of powers which is the cornerstone of our democratic process.

I agree these are difficult times and that it is imperative we get back on a forward-moving course, but I do not feel that revealing the contents of the tapes is the answer. From the reaction to the President's press conferences it looks like we are "returning to some normalcy", and I am counting on the fairness of the American people to judge Watergate and those involved in terms of the overall situation and not instantaneous reaction. Our judicial system and our democratic process are slow at times, but they cannot be surpassed—that I am certain of after viewing other governments in action at the United Nations.

Thanks again for writing, and please continue to support the President. It means more than you can imagine.

Yours very truly,
George Bush

October 17, 1973

Mr. Thornton Hardie, Jr.
Midland, Texas 79701
Dear Thornton:

I was deeply touched by your October 12 letter. I am giving serious thought to this matter, but I'm just not sure whether the governor's race is winnable. . . .

Of course, it would be a tremendous honor and challenge to be governor of Texas. I hope it doesn't sound egotistical, but I believe I could do the job, but there are an awful lot of factors that have to be heavily weighed. . . .

Many, many thanks for a letter that "made my day."

Yours very truly,
George Bush

I was flattered by the urging of friends and supporters to come home to Texas and run for governor, but in the end, I felt I had to stay put.

November 1, 1973

Mr. W. V. Ballew, Jr.
3000 One Shell Plaza
Houston, Texas 77002
Dear Cat:

I'd love to come home—I really would. In fact, Bar and I can already picture the house we're going to build right there on Sage Road on our little lot.

There are a lot of reasons I want to come home. One of them is that I long for the normalcy of the life there. The other is that I'd sure like to argue with you from time to time.

But, Bill, this isn't the time to quit, it's not a time to jump sideways, it's not a time for me to wring my hands on the sidelines. I am sure you know how I feel about some of the things that have happened. I also feel deeply about much of the unfair criticism of the President.

God, how we need civility. In any event, we'll be back there one of these days. It was good hearing from you.

> Warmest personal regards,
> George Bush

The administration continued to unravel throughout the fall of 1973. In a completely separate controversy from Watergate, Vice President Agnew resigned October 10 and pleaded guilty to tax evasion in the state of Maryland. Attorney General Elliot Richardson resigned rather than obey Nixon's order to fire the Watergate special prosecutor, Archibald Cox. On October 20, Nixon dismissed both Cox and Deputy Attorney General William Ruckelshaus, which came to be known as the Saturday Night Massacre. Nixon finally agreed to turn his tapes over to Judge John Sirica, who oversaw Watergate's legal battles. The tapes of two subpoenaed conversations could not be found; and one tape contained an eighteen-minute gap. Nixon's secretary, Rose Mary Woods, said she had accidentally erased the tape. I dictated to my diary on November 30:

> I am appalled at the handling of the Watergate tapes matter. . . . I don't know who makes the decisions on how this information oozes out, but the last Rose Mary Woods tape thing stretches my ability to believe enormously. It doesn't have the impact of the missing tapes however. . . . There is something unclear about all this. There is something going on I don't know about, there's something either on the tapes or about the tapes that does not ring true to me. . . .

George Bush End of Year Summary

Dec. 31, 1973

Things I've liked and disliked about '73 . . .

A. Disliked:

- That [Archibald] Cox, whom I respected as a lawyer, but disagreed with on some of his operations, negated much of his work by leaking to [Senator Ted] Kennedy and [Senator Gary] Hart. . . .

- That, on a tiny scale, my little "Support the President" bumper sticker was torn off, showing how high emotions seemed to be running.
- That Republican morale is lower than it should be based on our wins and losses this year, based on that great year-end poll showing Vice President Ford* clobbering the best that the Democrat's have to offer in 1976.
- That I get so much advice from those who will "withhold support", "not register", "be an independent", when the times cry out for more participation, not less.
- That we seemed in '73 to lose perspective. Our blessings far out weigh our shortcomings, yet we seem to be at the hand-wringing stage.
- That both Democrats and Republicans have suffered voter-identification loss, when one needs only look around the world to see that our two-party system, with its stability and its basic fairness, deserves more support.
- That the President has been subject to "piling on". Watergate was bad, the handling certainly less than perfect, but with no proof—a drum-fire of charge and counter-charge against the President.
- Watergate cover-up. The ruined lives of decent men who were guilty. The ruined lives of decent men who were innocent. Cynicism replacing idealism.
- High interest rates.

Things I've liked about '73:
- The end of the Vietnam War and the return of the prisoners.†
- The improved balance of payments situation.
- The move towards peace after a dreadful war in the Middle East.‡
- The President's ability to take the heat, given unbelievable criticism, some of it fair, much of it grossly unfair.
- The loyalty of our Party leaders, their constancy, their faith, their support.
- The fact that we won so many more elections all year long

*President Nixon picked Michigan congressman Gerald Ford to replace Agnew.

†The Paris Peace Accord had been signed January 27; the last U.S. troops left Vietnam March 29; and 590 American POWs were released by April 1.

‡Egypt and Syria had attacked Israel on October 6; Israel counterattacked. A cease-fire took effect October 24 and a U.N. peacekeeping force was sent to the Middle East.

than our political opponents or some of those biased reporters
would have believed possible.
- The basic fairness with which the Party has been treated by
the press. I wish the President had gotten as fair a shake.
- The basic fairness of my Democratic counterpart, Bob Strauss.

---

*On March 1, 1974, seven former Nixon aides were indicted for conspiring to
obstruct justice, including Haldeman, Ehrlichman, Mitchell, and Chuck Colson.
On March 13 I dictated to my diary:*

Alexander Haig called me—about a quarter of four and asked if
we could get together. I said, "When?" He said "Four o'clock." I
went on down there—was a couple of minutes late. The mood was
grim to say the least. [Ron] Ziegler* was standing there. It was chilly.
He said, "Hello" but the secretaries were much less relaxed, no joking, the whole mood was very, very grim. Haig looked grim. We sat
down and chatted for thirty minutes. . . .

He started off by being fairly tough and firm with me, telling me
that it was getting down to the wire, that if the President was going to
survive there had to be an all-out offense, that they were preparing
papers and they wanted me to give it full range support. I asked what
it was. He then went into a discussion about what he could or couldn't
give to the Judiciary Committee. He mentioned Connally and governors and others who were engaged in a big support effort and he
wanted me to say that I would support it. I thought for a minute—low
keyed it and said that in my opinion the President was entitled to
advocacy and that if in conscience I couldn't support what it was that
he was talking about then I would resign. I said I felt I probably could
but I didn't want to say without seeing in advance what it was. Haig
talked a little bit about the President's situation, indicating the Party
wouldn't recover for 10 years if the President had to get out. There was
too much, for my thinking, of the feeling that everyone that wasn't
exactly supportive was totally against, in other words—turning against
the whole Judiciary committee, the House, we don't have any friends
on the Hill—nobody is standing up for us. This went through the
whole theme. He was upset as hell with the Vice President . . . I did get
the feeling that Haig goes through a great deal of turmoil in his own
mind. He must have some difficult times with the President though he

---

*White House press secretary.

would never say this to me. I said, "Al, I wish that you would look at the Agronsky Show that was run last night to see how I have been trying to defend the President." He made one comment, "Don't get me wrong, I'm not critical of you. We just need the support." . . .

After the meeting I thought at length and I felt that they don't understand the relationship of the Party. I told Al that he and I have slightly different constituencies, that most of the time they interact but that sometimes there are differences, that I am concerned with future elections and Party as well as President, and they are not always in agreement. I think he did understand that point. There was no rancor in the meeting. It was philosophical, it was calm. I put my hand on his shoulder when I left and said, "Al, you are doing a magnificent job. I have respect for what you are doing. Hang in there." He seemed very tired, very determined. I hate the criticism of Haig—of the military mind. He does have that discipline, the commander-in-chief order that he is determined to carry out, but I think he also reserves in the corner of his heart some understanding for a person like me whose respect for the system sees that there are differences—Party must have my judgment and if it doesn't then I have failed the Party. And it is the Party that I work for, not the President.

I thought at length after I left about what would happen if I did resign. The Committee might not accept the resignation. In my judgment the White House would not be able to get its own candidate nominated—one who was going to carry out every whim of everybody down there. . . . I went home, discussed the matter mildly with Bar, and went to sleep at 9:45 p.m. I had the best sleep that I have had in the last three months. I am not sure why except I felt an inner contentment. I went down to the White House frankly with some trepidation. I guess one always wants to avoid an ugly scene. But it was pleasant—the friendship I have with Haig prohibited it from being different. I have great respect for him and what he is about. I wouldn't be surprised if he does for me too. But he must not let that show, if he is going to carry out this last ditch stand. It comes far easier to a [Colson]* or a Ziegler than it does to a Haig. Haig does it with more dignity and grace. I am not sure they are all that wrong. At this moment I haven't even seen the papers that Pat Buchanan†is putting together—his talking

---

*I have since changed my mind about Chuck Colson, who totally changed his life around while serving a prison term and today is doing wonderful ministerial work in prisons and elsewhere.

†Buchanan worked for Nixon as a speechwriter.

points. They are talking about an all-out offense—whatever the hell that means. I have called them as I see them so far. . . .

<hr />

March 25, 1974

Mr. Allen L. Lindley*
The Mutual Life Insurance Co.
New York, N.Y. 10019
Dear Pete:

. . . I hope you know how painful Watergate is to me personally, and how betrayed I feel by it and all its connotations. Knowing dad, as you did, I'm sure you can understand when I say that I really am glad he is not around to have to worry about Watergate. His whole sense of morality would have been deeply offended by what went on, and I hope you know that mine has been. Having said all that though, Pete, I feel that there has been unreasonable harassment in some areas. I feel that we have seen double standards in terms of investigation, and I take some comfort from the fact that the Ervin Committee dug deep for a year, and the Special Prosecutor dug deep for a year and neither of them, to my knowledge, has implicated the President. Should this change all bets are off. I, for one, hope it won't though I know some feel that if the President would get out it would make the problems I'm coping with now much, much easier.

In short, these are extremely complicated times—this job is no fun at all. Many of our strongest supporters have lost sight of the forest for the trees. They refuse to support the party, our candidates, and its principles all because of Watergate. This, too, complicates my life and the lives of all Republicans, but, on the other hand, it's a good time to be involved and, in my view, it's a time to hang in there. No one wants to see "this over with" more than I. No one wants to see us get to solving the other problems that confront us more than I, but I just can't accept resignation as the answer.

Sometimes I long for an escape—and an escape in my fantasy usually takes the form of running around in the boat in Maine—no telephone, clean, cool air, lots of relaxation. The exciting thing is that this might take place for a weekend or two this summer, and I look forward to seeing you then. Perhaps we can discuss all of this in a lot more detail.

Thanks for writing. Love to Lucky.

Yours very truly,
George Bush

<hr />

*Pete was a close family friend from Kennebunkport, a good friend of my Walker uncles and of mine.

April 4, 1974

Mr. William K. Marshall
Rochester, Michigan
Dear Mr. Marshall:

I note in your letter of February 22 that you have convicted the President. You call him a "liar and a crook."

I gave up a good business and my private life to get involved in politics because I believe in certain ideals, and I won't take second place to you in any way whatsoever in terms of who is the most offended about Watergate and all the ugly revelations attached thereto. Having said that, I'll be damned if I'm going to convict a man without the facts.

Nobody's feeding you any bull. You go and do exactly what you want, write critical letters to me, which is part of our participatory process. I'm going to stay in here, do the best I can, speak out against Watergate, position our party in the forefront of meaningful reform, but I'm not going to convict the President without evidence.

. . . Your letter was a good one because it made me think, and it was frank. I hope you don't object to my writing back with equal frankness. I may have lost touch with my traditional constituency, as you suggest, but it's not because I haven't been out there where the people are. I have been doing nothing but travel so much so that I'm about to drop in my tracks, and I find many, many Republicans who disagree with your view. Most retain the conviction that a man is innocent until proved guilty, even though they hate Watergate and all there is about it.

Yours very truly,
George Bush

In April, under court order, the White House released the edited transcripts of forty-six taped Oval Office conversations. Although there was still no evidence that the President had engaged in criminal activity, the tawdriness of Watergate continued to be revealed. The language used in the conversations was abusive and offensive, and it became evident that the White House was obsessed with the cover-up.

May 24, 1974

Mr. John Reagan McCrary*
New York, New York
Dear Tex:

What a thoughtful guy. I, too, was sickened by the transcript. There is no point denying it. The whole amoral tone made me ill. I have tried to make

---

*Tex McCrary, a strong Republican and a big Nixon supporter.

this clear in public without quantifying my emotions because it is important that people know that their National Chairman and their Party faithful do not approve of the tone of those tapes. Having said that, fair play must set in terms of the ultimate fate of the President. I will do nothing to interfere with the free working of the system.

Boy, these are rugged times. . . .

Warmest regards,
George Bush

———————

June 4, 1974

To the Concerned Students
East Valley High School
Spokane, Washington 99216
Dear Students:

I was very much interested in the class poll that you sent me. I am not sure that it differs from the national averages, except for the fact that the impeachment and resignation figures are higher than the national samples I have seen. Perhaps it would be useful to you to have my own views.

I was Ambassador at the United Nations for two years and there I had a chance to learn a great deal about 132 other countries. I became reimpressed with the fact that our system is stable and that our system is capable of working. In fact, there are not many other systems in the entire world that can investigate the overwhelmingly elected leader of the country.

Having said that, I think resignation is a "non-answer." It would inject instability into our system for a long, long time. It would not make sense politically since people would feel—rightly or wrongly—that the President had been hounded out of office without proof of guilt. It would not make sense from the system standpoint because it would undermine the basic stability of our constitutional system.

As to impeachment, there is great confusion in the country as to what "should he be impeached" really means. My position is that the Judiciary Committee should do its thing fully and with maximum cooperation from the White House and from all concerned. It should not be a political inquiry—it should be an open, honest inquiry with decisions being made on the facts. I think it is wrong for Members of Congress to prejudge the matter. I think it is worse for people to say the President should be thrown out than to say we don't think he should be thrown out. The reason I say that is that we do have a fundamental premise in this country of "innocent until proved guilty."

When you answer question 4—78% to 22%—that President Nixon should be brought to trial you obviously feel that the evidence means the

House should impeach the President. I respectfully disagree with this, but I am no lawyer and I will abide by the decision of the House Committee.

One last comment and if this sounds like a partisan comment, too bad. The President is taking a lot of heat of Watergate—some of it unfair. I would hope that as you raise questions of Watergate and express your moral indignation, which incidentally I share about Watergate and all its connotations, that you would give credit for the things that have gone right. Not one of you is being drafted. I think it's fair to give the President credit for that. No Americans are getting shot at for the first time in a long, long time. I think it's fair to give the President credit for that. The Middle East is a lot closer to peace now than when it was when I was battling those Middle East resolutions up there at the United Nations just two years ago. I think the President deserves credit for that. I have been troubled that people give the President grief over Watergate and seem unwilling to give him credit for accomplishments that are tremendously fundamental to your lives and to mine.

Thank you for sharing that poll with me.

Yours very truly,
George Bush

———————

July 23, 1974

Dear Lads,*

We are living in "the best of times and the worst of times".

You can sort out our blessings as a family. We have a close family, we have a lot of love around. You guys come home (and this sure is a blessing for Mum and me). We've got enough things. If we get sick we can get well, probably, or at least we can afford to pay the doctor, and the schools.

More blessings—you guys know no prejudice. You judge people on their worth. You give your grandmother and your parents a lot of happiness. You will do well in a world full of opportunity. Our country gives us a whale of a lot, and so we are privileged people in a privileged country. We are in the best of times.

My Dad felt strongly the firm obligation to put something into the system. He felt compelled to give, to be involved and to lead—and that brings me to the worst of times. I mean the part about Watergate and the abysmal amorality it connotes. You must know my inner feelings on this. Because of my job and because of my past associations with the President, it might well be that you don't know how I feel.

———————

*Our four sons, George, Jeb, Neil, and Marvin. (Apparently I thought Doro was too young at the time to receive this letter.) My dad had used the old-fashioned term *lads* a lot, and I have always used it—jokingly—to refer to our four sons.

It's important not from the sense of my interpretation of the facts; but it's important because as Dad helped inculcate into us a sense of public service I'd like you boys to save some time in your lives for cranking something back in. It occurred to me your own idealism might be diminished if you felt your Dad condoned the excesses of men you knew to have been his friends or associates.

Where to begin—The President first. He is enormously complicated. He is capable of great kindness. When Dad was dying of cancer I was leaving the Oval Office one day, having conferred on some UN matter, and I lagged behind to mention this to the President. His response was full of kindness and caring. He tried then to phone and wish Dad well.

Or again at the UN when a hand-written note arrived from the President telling me of a kind word spoken to him about me by the Foreign Minister of Turkey.

I am not that close to him as a warm personal friend—for he holds people off some—but I've been around him enough to see some humor and to feel some kindness.

He gets no credit for these or other nice things. Partly it's because he doesn't do them for public approbation—and it's partly cause when he does do them in public it's kind of stiff. He means it, but it doesn't pour gracefully out.

One Christmas the President entertained his Cabinet and others in the East Wing. That morning he had invited a Korean singing group that he encountered on a White House tour to come and sing. They were thrilled and they did a classy job—little Asian faces radiant in the joy of Christmas and thrilled to be singing for the President. As the kids left the stage they thanked the President and one little one threw her arms around his neck.

He responded properly, and I'm positive inside he felt all warm and pleased, but outside there was the appearance of discomfort. He wasn't relaxed—and the moment just didn't click.

On the professional side he has strong deep convictions. Foreign affairs, as you read, is his abiding interest. His accomplishments are enormous and they are his.

Some say it's Kissinger's magic soaring over the President—but not I.

He calls the shots, he takes the heat, he faces up to the tough ones and he's right an awful lot.

The war brought him, as it did Johnson, enormous abuse but he realized that our credibility as a world power would have been rendered useless for the future if we took the easy path. He stayed in there, took the heat on the bombing, and the heat was enormous (butcher, tyrant, Hitler).

The way in which the war ended guaranteed that our country could once more move on to help in other areas—the Middle East, the prime example.

Kissinger, an extraordinarily able man, got the peace prize. Nixon took the heat.

In the Middle East—"it was Nixon's [way] to offset Watergate"—vicious reporting at its worst—but when the separation of forces was achieved between Israel and Egypt, then Israel and Syria, it wasn't really the President that got the credit.

This must have hurt him personally. Indeed from a conversation I had with him before a dinner Fred Dent* and I gave for the Cabinet I could see that he was concerned on this, but he was not small or bitter about it.

You should know that I continue to respect the President for his enormous accomplishments and for some personal things too.

But you must know that I have been disappointed and disillusioned by much that has been revealed about the man from Watergate tapes and other sources.

He has enormous hang-ups. He is unable to get close to people. It's almost like he's afraid he'll be reamed in some way. People who respect him and want to be friends get only so close—and then it is clear—no more!

He has enormous hang-ups in other things too. He refers often to the Ivy League with total contempt—derision—but with all kinds of unlovely hang-ups coming through; and yet at various times you look around the very Cabinet table where the remarks are made—and there sits a Rog Morton, and Elliot Richardson, a George Shultz, a Fred Dent, and me and more I expect in the Cabinet, in embassies, in Departments—all appointed by him.

His comments are beneath his greatness but they possibly explain Watergate a little.

The President's hang-up on Ivy League is two-fold. The first relates to issues. He sees the Ivy League type as the Kennedy, liberal, Kingman Brewster† on the war, arrogant, self-assured, soft professors moving the country left. Soft on Communism in the past—soft on socialistic programs at home—fighting him at every turn—close to the editors that hate him. In this issue context he equates Ivy League with anti-conservatism and certainly anti-Nixon.

Secondly I believe there is a rather insecure social kind of hang-up. Ivy League connotes privilege and softness in a tea-sipping, martini drinking, tennis playing sense. There's an enormous hang-up here that comes through an awful lot. I feel it personally. It stings but it doesn't bleed because I know if I said, "Mr. President, do you mean me or Rog" he'd say "no". But I must confess that I am convinced that deep in his heart he feels I'm soft, not tough

---

*Fred was secretary of commerce and a close personal friend.

†The president of Yale, and very liberal. He later served as ambassador to Great Britain under Jimmy Carter.

enough, not willing to do the 'gut job' that his political instincts have taught him must be done.

He is inclined to equate privilege with softness or stuffiness.

I use the Ivy League hang-up simply as a point of departure to explain further on Watergate.

(Let me say right here there is an arrogance about some Ivy League connections that is bad. I remember Yale during the [Vietnam] war—its unwillingness to preserve a climate on campus where diversity could flourish. My hang-up with Brewster was not his own honestly held views on the war but his unwillingness to insist that other views could be expressed. He did not lead—he followed the mob. In fairness so did many, many others. Thank God, George, you got the best from Yale but you retained a fundamental conviction that a lot of good happens for America south and west of Woolsey Hall.*)

But back to RN. He surrounded himself on his personal staff with people unwilling to question the unlovely instincts we all have—and that he has in spades.

I had great respect for Haldeman. We liked his family and I saw him as loyal—simply implementing the President's will.

But now, in retrospect and in personal sorrow, I see him as unwilling to say, "This is wrong"—unable to exercise political judgment—condoning things he should have condemned—arrogant to a fault.

I see Ehrlichman with the mean gut memos—ordering the O'Brien tax investigations†—enemy lists, filth gathering, gut-fighting, taping—appealing to the dark side of the Nixon moon.

Colson—no judgment, a mean and vicious streak—so insidious and ugly that it would never seem to him that forging a cable to hurt arch enemy Kennedy was wrong.

Dean—a small, slimy guy—unprincipled—groveling for power.

I could go on and on in my indignation.

Little soft men like [Jeb] Magruder—unwilling to say, "Hell, no, I get off here". Enraptured by the power of his station but so unawed by the political process that he felt "any means to achieve an end".

It galls me now to see him on Today, his book a best seller—his criticism of Nixon bringing him fame and fortune—his morality so sincerely conveyed; but for heaven sakes where was what Dad always called 'conscience'—where was that morality when he walked all over the decency that really does exist in politics.

I remember Magruder when employed at Commerce long after Water-

---

*One of the main student centers on the Yale campus.
†Larry O'Brien, chairman of the Democratic National Committee.

gate—still arrogantly driving a RNC car—or sitting next to your Mother at the Japanese embassy, drawing her even at that late date into the enormity of his lie.*

I hate to sound bitter about these men and others, but I am.

In this job I have seen a common web of arrogance towards the Republican Party by these people.

Haldeman never showed it to me personally nor did the others for that matter, but as soon as I came to the RNC it was clear.

"Have the Chairman sign this and send it out"—arrogant, insensitive orders not requesting any judgment—simply viewing the Party as one more tool to be used. It was apparently unbelievable in 1972.

As 1973 developed, a change took place—but it was less a change of heart than a change forced by circumstance and by my unwillingness to surrender my judgment. . . .

A basic problem is that the President has little regard for the Party as such. There is much to reinforce his position, but what is lacking is any respect for party at all.

This must have been conveyed to these subordinates, and they simply went out and downgraded and insulted party in every way possible.

The relations between the arrogant staffer and elected politicians was more complex.

The President has served in the Congress. He knows practical Hill politics but this was no inhibiting factor on staff arrogance toward elected officials.

I didn't taste the lash of arrogance for as a Congressman the President was always helpful and friendly and the staffers may have sensed this. But when I came to RNC I'd hear junior staffers talking about "rolling" Members of Congress. Arrogant little squirts using the President's name to big shot those outside the White House fence.

Once in my early days a staff guy working for Colson told me the President wanted me to do something. I said, "How do you know?" (I knew he never saw the President.) He told me the President had marked the news summary with instructions. I insisted on seeing the instructions. What was shown was some comment with Haldeman's initials. Not good enough.

To sum up—The President was ill-served. He'd say in frustration— "Damn it, do this" and the word would go down—'the boss wants this done' and echelon upon echelon of people would lay aside their own judgment and do tough or dirty things. The evidence is overwhelming. The staff played to

---

*Magruder, who had been Mitchell's deputy at the Committee for the Re-election of the President, was one of the first Watergate participants to come forward and testify against his colleagues, always downplaying his own involvement (at least in my opinion).

the more unlovely side of the President. They didn't understand politics or politicians and they ill-served the man they wanted desperately to please.

Others did it—it is said. I am sure they did. The press never had the incentive to dig in on others though clearly others did it. The antagonistic relationship between press and White House has made it all uncivil in D.C.

Ron Ziegler is thoroughly discredited but he lacks the stature to see that and to leave. At a time when the President desperately needs Hill support Ziegler antagonizes every single member on the Hill.

I can understand the President's hostility towards press for they despise him. Long before any evidence was on the table many in the press had concluded that RN was evil and no good.

Rowly Evans* told me once "to get out before he drags you into the mud like everyone else he touches". (He later in the same conversation apologized for this—because he is decent—and he saw the comment had upset me.)

But now the Congress will decide. The President's position has eroded, not because of <u>an impeachable offense</u> but because of an accumulation of crud, a pattern of abuse. In my view that's not fair or right, but it appears to be what's happening. After the ugly transcripts the President's support eroded precipitously—then it came back as the evidence appeared flimsy, unfirm—not as sensational as the predictions relating to the locked briefcase would have us believe—and then another shift—the Judiciary transcripts hurt, Ehrlichman's conviction hurt—the constant accumulation of a wide series of unhelpful disclosures weighted people down and good men on our side had increasing doubts.

The White House is now embattled.

The people there have one constituent—the President. As chairman of this Party my constituency, if you can call it that, is broader. Normally a President and Party are not only compatible but quite inseparable—but these are not normal times.

I should not be critical, as a matter of course, of Republicans who vote against the President.

Larry Hogan† spoke out and indicated how he'd vote—issuing a strong statement of condemnation of the President. The White House took him on. I will not. His move was too political—he should have waited until the vote—but he reached his decision after agony and worry and study.

When I heard of the taping in the White House—I felt disturbed and concerned—standing in the Southwest Lobby of the White House. I told Bryce Harlow "I am shocked, the President can't survive this taping of all his conversations"—but I was wrong. The public concern was not with the taping

---

*One half of the Evans and Novak commentary team.

†Republican congressman from Maryland.

but with 'what's on the tapes'. To me it's just plain wrong to tape all those conversations, but I guess that's an old fashioned view.

I have not read all the impeachment evidence, but if I felt after reading it as I feel now—I would vote <u>not</u> to impeach. That would be considered by many as a cop-out. (My close friend Railsback* told me, "George, if you read the evidence I know you'd vote to impeach.")

Censure for permitting tone of arrogance and disrespect for institutions to spring up and fester—yes.

Incidentally the doing of things that now sound bad for reasons of national security do not trouble me for an Ellsberg should be stopped. Don't bug his psychiatrist but stop the flat out stealing of classified documents. That is clearly wrong and yet an Ellsberg enjoys today a respectability because of the methods of those who tried to bring him up short.

I shall stop with this gratuitous advice. Listen to your conscience. Don't be afraid not to join the mob—if you feel inside it's wrong.

Don't confuse being 'soft' with seeing the other guy's point of view.

In judging your President give him the enormous credit he's due for substantive achievements. Try to understand the 'why' of the National Security concern; but understand too that the power accompanied by arrogance is very dangerous. It's particularly dangerous when men with no real experience have it—for they can abuse our great institutions.

Avoid self-righteously turning on a friend, but have your friendship mean enough that you would be willing to share with your friend your judgment.

Don't assign away your judgment to achieve power.

These have been a tough 18 months. I feel battered and disillusioned. I feel betrayed in a sense by those who did wrong and tracked corruption and institutional subversion into that beautiful White House. In trying to build Party, I feel like the guy in charge of the Titanic boiler room—one damn shock after another.

But too I retain a basic confidence in the President's ability. I respect him still—not at all for the tapes nor for some of his employees' past—but for his courage under fire and for his accomplishments.

I will never feel the same around the President after all of this, but I hope he survives and finishes his term. I think that's best for the country in the long run.

Civility will return to Washington eventually. The excesses condoned by the press will give way to reason and fair play. Personalities will change and our system will have proved that it works—more slowly than some would want—less efficiently than some would decree—but it works and gives us—even in adversity—great stability.

*Tom Railsback, Republican congressman from Illinois.

I expect it has not been easy for you to have your Dad be head of the RNC at this time. I know your peers must put you in funny positions at times by little words in jest that don't seem funny or by saying things that hurt you because of your family loyalty.

I can't wait to see you all in August. I'm still family champ in backgammon.

> Devotedly,
> Dad

Nixon had appointed Leon Jaworski—a respected Houston lawyer and longtime friend of ours—to replace Archibald Cox as the special prosecutor. Determined to do a thorough job, Jaworski asked Judge Sirica to subpoena an additional sixty-four tapes and documents. Nixon refused, and Jaworski took his case to the U.S. Supreme Court. On July 24, the court ruled 8–0 that Nixon did not have "absolute authority" to control the material and ordered him to turn over the tapes. The President complied. Many more shocking revelations were on the tapes, but the most damning—the "smoking gun" tape—was a conversation from June 23, 1972, where Nixon could be heard telling Haldeman to block the FBI's investigation of the Watergate break-in, which had occurred just six days earlier. This was proof the President had been involved, at least in the cover-up. This was proof the President had lied. After this, I lost faith in Nixon. I could not forgive him this lie.

None of this had been made public yet when Al Haig called me to the White House on July 31. I dictated to my diary:

July 31, 1974

. . . We talked for close to an hour. He reviewed the entire situation. I spoke to him very frankly about the President's chances. I told him that I thought we were worse off in the House than the White House probably thought—losing votes from people that we should be getting them from and that I thought the Senate would similarly deteriorate. He indicated the following to me:

- That there would be more bad news including a major shock from one of the tapes.
- A sentence that the President had been up the mountain top and down several times meaning considering resignation. Haig's own view tended toward resignation though he certainly told the President he obviously would stick by the decision (the more I see Haig, the more I realize what tremendous pressures he's been under.)

He told me that Ziegler was no longer going to speak out on

Watergate and agreed that the Kangaroo Court wordage that he thought might have come from the President, came from Ziegler. He told me the President denied he had even had anything to do with it. Ziegler is now out of the Watergate statement business but it's too darn late in my view.

The President is holding up pretty well. He is under tremendous pressure. I reminded Haig that nothing we had ever discussed had been leaked in any way. He noted that, and proceeded to be very frank with me. . . .

Haig made some reference to the fact that the decision would be made within the next twenty-four hours and he thought the decision was going to be made all out to go ahead. If it was made the President would have to take the offense, go up and testify himself, work with the Party, work with the Senators, have a very strong offense. I asked how the family was holding up. Haig said fine. Haig was terribly complimentary of Ford and the job he was doing, indicating that that was one of the best things the President had ever done. . . .

I don't know how Haig remains as decent and pleasant as he is under this enormous pressure where I am sure he feels great isolation. . . .

I told him that in my view if the President was going to resign he ought to do it now rather than later. If he resigned after the elections we would probably take a bigger bath in the elections and then the new president would be faced with a Congress far to the left of where the country stood and he would also be denied a honeymoon period because many of the people coming in would have no personal affection for the Vice President such as the present members of Congress both Democrats and Republicans feel. I felt that the honeymoon period now indeed would help the country and clearly would help the country keep from moving left in the elections. I told Haig I didn't feel that political expediency should be a consideration for resignation however. But it was hard to discount politics. We both agreed that what is best for the country counts. We discussed the effect on the President, the humiliation, the economic effects. I suggested that clearly the country would not expect him to be dragged through courts and stuff. . . . I told Haig that in my view that what happened to the President was just an accumulation of the weight of it all. One shock after another. Matters like the Connally indictment,* the

*John Connally was indicted and later acquitted in the famous "milk fund" scandal. Connally was accused of accepting a bribe from a dairy organization that wanted a promise of higher milk-price supports from the federal government in return for campaign contributions.

Ehrlichman conviction, the various White House aides, etc. were the things that all added up and dragged the President down. I told him that I wished the President did not have to have the opinion that these were the two finest servants. Haig indicated to me that he realized that he had been had by the finest top aides. I told him how very strongly I felt on this. Haig stopped short of being critical of me although I will readily concede the White House probably feels I have not done enough to partisanize [the RNC]. He feels the proceedings of the Judiciary Committee have been much less than fair, that there has been a vendetta, that they oozed evidence out to hurt the President, that many of our people bit the bullet and are going to have revenge taken by the voters. I told him I didn't think there would be as much of this as he felt. . . .

———————

August 5, 1974

A calamitous day. Burch called me right after noon and asked me if I could come down to the White House, that he had some news, that he was going to go out and brief Johnny Rhodes and was taking Buzhardt* with him. Wondered if I could come down there and ride out and get clued in. I went down. The news was, of course, the tapes.† . . .

It became clear we were all upset. I even suggested that in order to move things forward I would consider resigning, saying the President was entitled to some kind of defense but I could no longer defend him. Therefore I would resign. I would call a meeting of the national committee and let them select a chairman who could. . . . My feeling being not to run away but simply to highlight the dilemma. Burch and Buzhardt said that somebody needs to be around to pick up the pieces and clearly this wouldn't be a good thing to do.

I felt at the time I should have made clear to them that it was not my intention to run away from a tough situation but rather to lead, because I feel so strongly about what happened. . . .

I talked to Haig at 9:50 in my office. He indicated that he didn't think it was a surprise, he didn't feel the President ought to speak out like Agnew, but of course he was giving a lot of consideration to res-

————————

*My close friend John Rhodes, congressman from Arizona, was House minority leader. Fred Buzhardt was the chief White House lawyer.

†I'm talking about the "smoking gun" tape where we learned Nixon had lied about his knowledge of the cover-up.

ignation. I told him about the erosion on the National Committee, that I thought it was serious. He asked me to be sure of my judgment etc. I told him I was, and he said if we get that kind of erosion then we can be sure the President will do the right thing. He simply is waiting for the right time. He thinks he can survive in the Senate. He realizes there is a tremendous deterioration in the House. But he says "Not so in the Senate. Guys are hanging tough in the Senate." . . . I told him I wondered who he was talking to . . .

Haig said we must think big, think big about the country first. Let's worry about the country first. I tried to indicate to him that that was what we were doing. He did not think the President's survival is the answer, but he does think that we should be moderate and reasonable and be sure of the weight of the thing. They had just called about a Cabinet meeting. I asked him what that was for. He said [Nixon] was going to tell why he did and what he did. He told me I was in a very difficult position, getting whip-sawed and kind of complimented me on the way it was going. Although I told him I felt in a half-assed position—neither fish nor fowl. He told me he had spent an unbelievable week with this guy—meaning the President. Bitter—very tough week. He didn't know how the President keeps going. . . .

He predicted the President would not survive but that we would look back when we were both 80 and say he had been one of the great presidents of our time . . .

As I dictate this memo at 10:10 p.m. on August 5 I do not feel the President can survive. . . . I have decided not to issue a statement. I am torn between wanting to express my own agony and my own emotion, and get out front and cry resignation and this is too much. And at the same time recognizing that this system must work, should be permitted to work fairly, and as Burch says somebody has got to pick up the pieces. I got torn between how to lead and what is leadership at a point like this. Oddly enough at this moment leadership may mean doing nothing. There's an awful lot of noise out there. . . . Maybe by sitting quietly, accurately reporting, trying to hold the party together, one can do the most service. But it means the risk that people won't know how strongly and deeply I feel about this whole grubby Watergate mess. It is beneath the dignity of that oval office, and yes the President's accomplishments are magnificent, but Watergate is a shabby, tawdry business that demeans the Presidency. Am I failing to lead by not stating that?

————

August 6, 1974

A traumatic day. The Cabinet meeting, set back from 10:30 a.m. to 11:00 a.m., proved to be a grueling session. . . . the atmosphere was one of unreality in one sense. The President sat there, strong, determined, announcing his decision to remain in office and yet unreality prevailed. Jerry Ford reiterated his position that because of his peculiar situation he was not going to involve himself in the President's defense. The statement is public. It kind of cast a pall over the meeting. Haig later told me he thought it was wrong, the President was clearly shook up. Ford later told me that he wondered if it had offended the President and how it had gone over. I told him I thought that he had done the right thing and that I had told Haig, which I did, that Ford was simply reiterating a position he expressed the day before, so that the President would be sure to know it. Because the President indeed at that meeting was saying we should all go out, be together, be unified, go forward, etc. The President tried to express his concern about the affairs but it just didn't come through. His explanation of this awful lie was not convincing. It simply was unreal, but everybody just sat there. . . .

The President looked uncomfortable, once he smiled over to me and with his lips said, "George," smiled and looked warm and my heart went totally out to him even though I felt deeply betrayed by his lie of the day before. The man is amoral. He has a different sense than the rest of people. He came up the hard way. He hung tough. He hunkered down, he stone walled. He became President of the United States and a damn good one in many ways, but now it had all caught up with him. All the people he hated—Ivy League, press, establishment, Democrats, privileged—all of this ended up biting him and bringing him down. . . .

The minute the meeting was over I got aside with Al Haig. I told Haig the whole goddamned thing had come undone and there was no way it could be resolved. . . . I said your Senate count is wrong . . . I told him that people were not leveling with the White House. That it was much worse. Haig in his total decency pointed out to me that the President did understand this. I requested a meeting with the President. I told him I felt that if I were going to say something publicly, I should first do it to the President. I didn't want to be dramatic. I didn't want to be the bearer of bad tidings, my heart ached for him and for his family but I felt I had a real obligation to make clear the point. Haig told me to kind of stand by (I told him I was going to have lunch with Dean Burch) and he would then let me know whether the President would see me. . . .

I left the meeting, went to Burch's office—Burch had already gone to lunch. Kind of hung around waiting for Haig to call to see if I would see the President. Nothing happened. I then went down and had a solitary lunch at the conference mess, made a few calls. There were all these messages that the press were calling frantically. My temptation was to blast the President, blast the lie, and then I thought why add to the personal tragedy and the personal grief. Events were moving so fast that it just didn't seem right to kind of "pile on." . . .

I think of that little Julie . . . so sensitive and thoughtful and loyal too, and I wonder, "My God what would that be like for our family." At the end of my luncheon Haig called. I went up to his office and he told me that the President did not want to see me. . . .

I must confess that I was somewhat offended . . . I asked Al, "What was his reaction? Why won't he see me?" He said, "Well, he just wasn't up to it. He said, 'maybe tomorrow.' " . . . The President simply cannot bring himself to talk to people outside of a tiny, tiny circle and this has brought him to his knees. . . .

It is so hard to know what is fair and right. It is so easy to get a headline. It is so difficult to assess how the sublimation of one's views in a position of leadership might be detected as softness. All of this is quite clear to those on the outside but it is never clear to those on the inside. I don't want to pile on. I don't want to add to the woes of the President, I don't want to increase the agony of his family. And yet I want to make damn clear the lie is something we can't support. But this era of tawdry, shabby lack of morality has got to end. . . . I will take Ford's decency over Nixon's toughness because what we need at this juncture in our history is a certain sense of morality and a certain sense of decency. . . .

We have had a lot of press calls about Ford picking me for Vice President. Bill Steiger called and said that he and Martha Griffiths had decided that I was the guy—Martha of all people. Mary Matthews in Barber Conable's office said that Barber had said that's what it should be. Jerry Pettis said that he and many are undertaking it.* The press are hypothecating. And yet I am convinced that it won't happen and almost that it shouldn't because the Vice President needs something separate, apart and clean. And unfairly or not I may have tracked it in and kind of spread it around the living room car-

---

*Bill Steiger and Jerry Pettis, both congressmen, were among my closest friends on the Hill. Martha Griffiths was a Democratic congresswoman from Michigan. She and I had served on the Ways and Means Committee together.

pet—not by design and hopefully not by character, but rather by an association. It's a weird, weird world.

My own views are that the Vice President can make it as President. He needs to surround himself by quality, stature, academicians, brilliance but I am not sure it will happen. I think it will though because he asks for advice and you know he wants to listen. He is a latter-day Eisenhower. He is an Ike without the heroics but he has that decency the country is crying out for right now.

. . . The incivility of the press had been a disturbing and paralyzing kind of thing over the last few months. And now it continues, that blood lust, the talons sharpened and clutched, ready to charge in there and grab the carrion of this President. I am sick at heart. Sick about the President's betrayal and sick about the fact that the major Nixon enemies can now gloat because they have proved he is what they said he is. No credit, no compassion, no healing, simply the meat-grinder at work. I suppose when it is written one can establish that perhaps I should have done more, but I am not made up to walk on the body of a man whom I don't love but whom I respect for his accomplishments.

. . . I was sorely tempted there with the Vice President to talk about immunity. I did tell him about my concern and agony over the family, but I felt like saying, "Jerry, you must, you have to clear this matter from the Nation's conscience by declaring when you become President that Watergate is behind us." The President will not be harassed by every penny ante judge or prosecutor in this country. Surely this nation has that much forgiveness in its heart.

————————

August 7, 1974

Hon. Alexander Haig, Jr.
The White House
Washington, D. C.
Dear Al:

I have no plans to release this letter, but it comes from the heart as I am sure you know. . . .

Respectfully,
George Bush

————————

August 7, 1974

The Honorable Richard M. Nixon
President of the United States
Washington, D. C.
Dear Mr. President:

It is my considered judgment that you should now resign. I expect in your lonely embattled position this would seem to you as an act of disloyalty from one you have supported and helped in so many ways.

My own view is that I would now ill serve a President, whose massive accomplishments I will always respect and whose family I love, if I did not now give you my judgment.

Until this moment resignation has been no answer at all, but given the impact of the latest development, and it will be a lasting one, I now firmly feel resignation is best for this country, best for this President. I believe this view is held by most Republican leaders across the country.

This letter is made much more difficult because of the gratitude I will always have for you.

If you do leave office history will properly record your achievements with a lasting respect.

Very sincerely,
George Bush

The President announced to the nation on August 8 that he was resigning, effective noon the next day.

August 8, 1974

. . . The day was unreal. A pall was over the White House. I met with the Vice President. We discussed [Democratic Congressman] Dan Rostenkowski's offer to be helpful in lining up votes for the Vice President to grant immunity. I talked about the White House staff and my concerns about it. I particularly mentioned the press section, and that Ziegler had to go. I told the Vice President that I had dealt with this situation for a year and a half and would like to have an input based on experience with whomever was going to sort that all out. He indicated that he had seen the President, the President had told him that of the whole Cabinet in his view Kissinger should stay and in the White House Haig should stay.

I then went on to the National Security Council. I told him that in my judgment he should revert to something between what it used to be when Rogers was Secretary of State and what it is now when

Kissinger totally dominates it.* I said that the President must put an imprint of his own on foreign policy, that there must be a mediator in the White House as the head of NSC who would mediate between the Secretary of State and the Defense Department, and represent solely the President or present solely to the President the views of these two departments. . . . The Vice President made little comment on this but seemed to have some appreciation of what I was talking about.

I then went to the National Committee, told him that I should resign from there, that again the Vice President should be looking forward to '76 very soon, that there would be a honeymoon period during which the National Committee would do anything he wanted, that he should get his own man in there and get him in right away.† He indicated that he wanted me to stay for awhile, that he had total confidence in me, that he didn't want it to look like he didn't have confidence in me, nor did he want it to look like I didn't have confidence in him, by doing anything precipitous. . . . During the visit his son called in from way out in Utah. It was really amazing to hear the father talking to the son—down to earth. The son had heard part of what was happening—and Jerry told him matter of factly that the next day at noon he would be sworn in and about how the kid was going to get there. There was a natural quality about it all. . . .

August 9, 1974

There is no way to really describe the emotion of the day. Bar and I went down and had breakfast at the White House. Dean and Pat Burch and the Buchanans were there in the conference Mess. There was an aura of sadness, like somebody died. Grief. Saw Tricia and Eddie Cox in the Rose Garden—talked to them on the way into the ceremony. President Nixon looked just awful. He used glasses—the first time I ever saw them. Close to breaking down—understandably. Everyone in the room in tears. The speech was vintage Nixon—a kick or two at the press—enormous strains. One couldn't help but look at the family and the whole thing and think of his accomplishments and then think of the shame and wonder what kind of a man is this really. No morality—kicking his friends in those tapes—all of them. Gratuitous abuse. Caring for no one and yet doing so much. . . .

*At this point Kissinger was both secretary of state and the NSC adviser.
†I later recommended Mary Louise Smith, whom President Ford did appoint. Mary Louise was the first woman to head up one of the two major political parties.

The Nixon speech was masterful. In spite of his inability to totally resist a dig at the press, that argument about hating—only if you hate do you join the haters. We walked through the bottom lobby to go out. Many of the pictures were changed with a great emphasis on the new President. We went over and hung around waiting for the swearing in of Ford. And then the whole mood changed. It was quiet, respectful, sorrowful in one sense, but upbeat. The music and the band seemed cheerier, the talking and babbling of voices after Ford's fantastic speech, crowds of friends, indeed a new spirit, a new lift. I walked through the line and the President was warm and friendly, kissing the wives, telling Bar he appreciated my job, and on and on. It was much more relaxed. There of course were a lot of people that didn't know what they were going to do. There was great turmoil in that sense.

The rest of the day was swirling around on the vice presidential speculation. We got our telegrams out asking for input from the National Committee. . . . Jerry Pettis working on it, a lot of speculation. Timmons* called to say the President wanted to talk to me about this matter at 3:00 p.m. on Sunday. . . . Quiet evening. Suspense mounting again. Deep down inside I think maybe it should work this time. I have that inner feeling that it will finally abort. I sure hope not. Another defeat in this line is going to be tough but then again it is awful egotistical to think I should be selected.

———————

On August 20, I was in Kennebunkport, watching TV with my family and waiting for the President to enter the East Room of the White House to announce his vice-presidential choice. While the TV announcers were speculating as to why the President was late, our telephone rang. It was President Ford, telling me he had picked Nelson Rockefeller. He did not have to take the time to call and tell me that, but that was typical of Jerry Ford. I wrote Jim Baker.

August 21, 1974

Dear Bake—

Yesterday was an enormous personal disappointment. For valid reasons we made the finals (valid reasons I mean a lot of Hill, RNC, & letter support) and so the defeat was more intense—

But that was yesterday. Today and tomorrow will be different for I see now, clearly, what it means to have really close friends—more clearly than ever

*Bill Timmons was one of Ford's top advisers.

before in my life. I take personal pleasure from the great official support, but I take even more from the way our friends rallied around. None did more than you to help me with a problem that burned my soul and conscience. The sun is about to come out and life looks pretty darn good—

Thanks
George

August 22

Meeting in Oval Office . . . The President indicated that the decision on the VP had been very close. "You should have been very complimented by the support." "What do you want?" Haig had indicated that the President had told him George can have anything he wants. . . .

We discussed my being chief of staff if there was some real substance. I brought it up. Ford seemed very interested in that. Ford just having said however that the chief of staff job was changed—he wanted to see more people than Nixon did. He wanted to deal more with them himself. I told him I could see a role where I would deal with the embassies, special interest groups, etc. but only if there was some stature or substance involved in this deal.

We went back and talked more about England. He wondered if it was substantive enough—so did I. We talked about the money. I told him I had lost a lot of money and didn't know if I could afford it. He indicated there were some outside ways of doing this. I told him I was aware of this from my U.N. days.*

Ford said, "I will mention it to Kissinger. I see no problems there." We also touched on France and China. . . .

We went back to China. I told him the U.N. vote conceivably could be against me although I got along with them once they were there. I told him that I was very interested in foreign affairs. . . . I indicated that way down the line, maybe 1980, if I stayed involved in foreign affairs, I conceivably could qualify for Secretary of State. The President seemed to agree. He was very warm, very grateful, very friendly. I told him that if I was appointed to England the party people would think he was moving me over and out—or kicking me upstairs. I told him this was perfectly OK with me though because I thought it was a great

---

*Being ambassador to the United Kingdom was considered expensive since the ambassador was expected to provide lavish entertainment, only a fraction of which was covered by the government.

challenge. I told him, "You don't owe me a thing. I could very easily go back into private life." Indeed we discussed it. He said, "I don't want you to do that. I don't want to lose your talents."

───────────

After much thought, and after discussing it with Barbara, I decided what I really wanted to do was represent the United States in China. We did not yet have full diplomatic relations, which meant I would not be an ambassador but a "liaison officer." But I felt China was so important to our future, and a bigger diplomatic challenge than even Great Britain or France. I decided I needed to talk to the best China expert I knew—President Nixon.

September 4, 1974

Talked to President Nixon—reserved, very reserved—"How's your family"? "Fine, George. Give my best to your family," he said. He was very formal, very perfunctory. I said it would be nice to come out there.* Hinted twice about being nice to chat—like very much to visit on this, and the President never responded. He sounded very quiet. He chatted a little bit about China—saying that after 25 years—that it would be such a power—that [my job] would be kind of lonely and quiet—things are isolated and separated—you only see people at big diplomatic functions—but it would be a great experience.

He was less than warm personally. I inquired about him and he was reserved. I gave him credit saying "This wouldn't have been possible of course without you" etc., etc., but he never warmed up at that. The conversation was very brief. . . .

───────────

September 16, 1974

Mrs. Estelle Stacy Carrier
Secretary, Republican National Committee
Washington, D. C. 20003
Dear Mrs. Carrier:

I hereby submit my resignation as Chairman of the Republican National Committee.

Sincerely,
George Bush

*Meaning California, where they were then living.

UNITED STATES LIAISON OFFICE
PEKING, PEOPLE'S REPUBLIC OF CHINA

CHAPTER 6

China

Barbara and I began preparing immediately for our move to China. She packed and got the children settled in various schools while I attended endless briefings at the State Department. We both took Chinese lessons. Finally, on October 17, we left. Even before we reached Chinese soil, I began keeping a diary about the adventure and challenge that awaited us.

———

This is the beginning of Peking* Diary. October 21, 1974
. . . My emotions are mixed about this. I read the <u>Japan Times.</u> I begin already to wish I had more details on American politics, the elections. . . .

When we got to Anchorage there was a message for me to call Leon Jaworski.† . . . They were asking me about a conversation on tape in April, 1973. They had not heard the tape but they saw a transcript. In it Richard Moore apparently told President Nixon that I had been approached by Mardian‡ to raise $30,000 for the Water-

———

*When we lived in China, Beijing was still spelled Peking. In 1979, the Chinese government began using a new system of transliteration—in other words, how you represent corresponding letters in different alphabets. This changed the English spelling of the names of people and places—e.g., Peking became Beijing. Names will appear in this chapter as they were spelled when we lived there.

†Jaworski was still investigating Watergate.

‡Robert Mardian was a good friend of Nixon's who worked at the Committee for the Re-election of the President and was among those indicted for wrongdoing. All charges were later dropped.

gate defendants and that Moore told the President that I refused to do this and had urged the whole thing to come out. They were asking me my recollection. I told them that I had absolutely no recollection of this, that I was confident I had not talked to Mardian about this, that I hadn't seen him since I had become National Chairman. Indeed I hadn't seen him since perhaps a year before that and then only in passing. . . . I told them I would look at my notes and try to recall any conversation. . . .

The incident itself is not important except that here I was leaving the United States, last point of land, and a call out of the ugly past wondering about something having to do with Watergate, cover-up and all those matters that I want to leave behind.

In going to China I am asking myself, "Am I running away from something?", "Am I leaving—what with inflation, incivility in the press and Watergate and all the ugliness?" Am I taking the easy way out?" The answer I think is "no" because of the intrigue and fascination that is China.

I think it is an important assignment, it is what I want to do, it is what I told the President I want to do, and all in all, in spite of the great warnings of isolation, I think it is right— at least for now.

General Notes—People at the State Department seem scared to death about our China policy. Kissinger keeps the cards so close to his chest that able officers in EA* seem unwilling to take any kinds of initiative. This troubles me a little bit because I worry that our policy is "plateaued out," and that if we don't do something the policy will come under the microscopic scrutiny the CIA has come under, that the Middle East policy has come under. And indeed the American people are going to be looking for forward motion. And it is my hope that I will be able to meet the next generation of China's leaders—whomever they may prove to be. Yet everyone tells me that that is impossible. I have the feeling that David Bruce† felt it was best to have a small mission, keep a very low profile, do little reporting and to feel his way along on this new relationship. He was revered, properly so and respected, but my hyper-adrenaline, political instincts tell me that the fun of this job is going to be to try to do more, make more contacts. Although everyone all along the line says that you will be frustrated, won't be able to make contacts, won't be able to

*Eastern Asia, a division within the State Department.

†I replaced Ambassador David Bruce, perhaps our most distinguished diplomat, who was the first head of the U.S. Liaison Office in Beijing.

meet people, they will never come see you, etc. etc. I fear this may be true, but the fun will be trying . . .

October 25, 1974

Strauss* you old bastard,

You'll never believe this.

I come to Peking, China to get away from you—I'm doing my thing—out of politics half way around the world . . . trying to bring peace to a troubled world—when I turn on the short wave and 'midst much whistling and woofing I hear—"Robert Strauss called Pres. Ford's statement irresponsible."

. . . How far away do I have to go?

Anyway we're here—fascinating in so many ways—I miss our jousts and our leisure times of pleasantness, but this is right for us for now. We are happy—

Hang in—pleasantly—

Best to all at DNC but damn it lose!! Bar sends love.

Best

GB

October 25, 1974

. . . We went to bed early. They put a board under my bed, making it properly hard but we were confused. The wind was whistling outside and yet the heat inside was enormous. I went around and turned off all the heaters. Bar got snoring again just like West Texas. I turned on the Sears humidifier and she did OK. She'll have that place singing in a day or two. It needs pictures, it needs some warmth, it needs some table-top items, but other than that we have inherited a lot in the Bruce style. It's great. All's well. End first night. No substance. Lot of new sights and sounds and smells. Don't drink the water. The soap is good. The eggs are little. Short-wave makes a lot of whistling sounds—sounds just like 30 years ago . . .

October 27, 1974

. . . People stare at you. Gather around the car. Look at you. Once in a while smile. No hostility but tremendous curiosity. Our driver,

---

*Bob Strauss, chairman of the Democratic National Committee and a great friend to this day. As President, I named him ambassador to the Soviet Union.

Mr. Kuo, is amazing. It looks to me like we are going to crash into bicycles, donkey carts, overloaded buses, trailer-type setups, or get lost in a dust storm but sure enough Mr. Kuo manages. Yesterday a bicyclist almost ran in front of us and Mr. Kuo held up his finger and disciplined the young bike rider with a rather serious reprimand. The kid looked somewhat chastened but continued boldly across the great breadth of highway and was soon blended into a jillion other cyclists, a bunch of buses, and a few pulled donkey carts.

October 27, 1974

Dear Kids,

This is the first chance I've had to write. Excuse my typing but this is the best way to make it readable. Life here is really different—a world of contrast. The society is closed no dissent, no real freedoms; and yet they've made much progress from the bad old days with people dying on the street etc. Our house is nice—plenty of room for all of you. The people helping us (large staff) speak no English at all. We've been having our large meal at noon—always new Chinese dishes—they are sensational but the jelly-like spiked sea slugs that looked like those horrible Sculpins in Maine only smaller. The rest of the dishes are really something—I hope I'm not putting on weight.

Some observations: too few contact with the Chinese officials and people—they just don't want the contacts. Everything gets gray in Peking—it's like west Texas in a lot of ways—lots of dust in the air at times. Fred* is gray inspite of two baths. People stare at Fred in amazement—the young are scared of him, the older heads seems to smile at him—but they don't call him or pat him. We start Chinese lessons next week—We've gotten no mail and we miss you all a lot—Today we went to a little Church service in a run-down Bible Institute. 4 Chinese oldsters singing forth in Chinese as we 14 petitioners equally divided between African and European diplomats sang in English. Mum and I were both choked up—here we were worshipping in a land where this kind of worship is all but forbidden. They permit services but in a very limited way. Yesterday we went to Western Hills for a climb. It is very pretty there. In Chinese a big sign said "Don't pick the red leaves" (bright fall colors) Yep, guessed it—all the kids were walking around with red leaves in their hands. There is no handholding in public—no heing and sheing in sight. Hap and Robin† would have a rough go here if they were Chinese. The weather, except for the

----

*C. Fred Bush, our cocker spaniel. There weren't many dogs in China, so Fred was an oddity.

†Hap Ellis, my sister Nancy's son, and his wife, Robin.

dust, has been beautiful—warmish fall weather. I've played tennis once—The Int'l club has a bunch of poorly surfaced courts, tho they are resurfacing the 2 indoor courts with a red concrete which will be pretty nice to have. The Club for diplomats and some Chinese is very spacious, is a few blocks (easy cycle) from our house. It has billiards, [ping] pong, outdoor basketball etc. A haircut costs 30 cents. Some things here are very expensive—some quite cheap/A lot of things that we take for granted at home you just can't get; but there are no hardships in this direction. I feel cutoff from the day to day news. Our short wave works pretty well so we get a good 7 a.m. news report but it is just the highlights. Very few dogs around here—great bunch of USLO* staff—A pace in my life less hectic than I have known in many many years, but still plenty to do. I haven't gotten a phone call in a week—imagine that! I jog every a.m. at 6:30 with Fred—1 mile—I hate it. I also do sit-ups. Everything gets pretty dirty in the house though it is kept up very well. Soon it will get really really cold. I hear there are two really cheap round trip fares out here— Air France and Air (Pakistan) have trips US-Peking for less than $1000. Mum just called wanting me to go to the Friendship store (hooray my first phone call) . . . I have a nice Chrysler car and a good driver Mr. Kuo who speaks no English but is a great driver in horribly difficult circumstances. The difficulty comes from the cyclists. There are few cars around— lots of Army trucks etc. The People Liberation Army [PLA] guard our gate—nice looking young men. Yes Doro they have women in the PLA too but they don't guard the gate. I have made a lot of calls on other Ambassadors and Chinese officials but the latter calls are formalities pretty much. We are permitted to travel in China and we will do so a lot. The Chinese have been most hospitable in the sense of politeness and trying to provide us with certain courtesies.

. . . Dying to hear how all goes with all of you. I may be homesick for all of you, but really we are very close as I know you know. You will all five enjoy this experience seeing and wondering at different things. The sights to see are fabulous, the dining out a new experience with each place. The difference between our countries immense—and yet a feeling that the people would like to be friends. I just wish we could do more in this regard. I better run now— just wanted you to know that your folks are doing O.K. That we think of you all the time—that we talk about each of you a lot. That we miss you and that we love you very much—our pride in all five of you is even greater here— never thought it would be possible.

Devotedly
Dad

---

*United States Liaison Office.

As part of my plan to socialize with the Chinese as much as possible, I decided to reverse my predecessor's policy of not attending various embassies' National Day receptions (similar to our Fourth of July celebrations.) I decided I better let Washington know via a State Department telegram, our best way of communicating.

TELEGRAM
SUBJECT: NATIONAL DAY RECEPTIONS
ACTION: SECSTATE WASHDC
October 31, 1974

1. We plan to slide into attendance at National Day Receptions unobtrusively. Holdridge* and I will attend Algerian affair November 1, which happens to be the first one to which we have been invited. The Soviets on November 6 are next in line.

2. We will not seek press attention, but all at USLO will simply state if queried that Mr. Bush and others at USLO feel this is a way to widen our contacts in Peking. If pressed, we will tell journalists not to read anything into this shift—just something new USLO Chief wanted to do in effort to expand his contacts and contacts of others at USLO.

                                                              Bush

———————

November 1, 1974

We went to our first National Day reception. It happened to be the Algerian. The Holdridges and ourselves walked in together and the Algerian ambassador looked like he was going to fall over in a dead faint when he saw us arrive. The affair was very formal. After the guests had come in, the Chinese guests and the Algerian host took overstuffed chairs at one end of the room. The ambassadorial corps kind of formed in the room, milling around eating lavish hors d'oeuvres. At the other end of the room were table after table at which the Chinese guests gathered around and ate and ate and ate. The only people that visit with the Chinese officials are the foreign minister and other Algerians. And this was interrupted only by long interpreted speeches that went on too long and bored the hell out of everybody. There was a great deal of comment by other ambassadors

———

*John Holdridge was deputy chief of mission (or the number two man) at the liaison office. He went on to become ambassador to Singapore, assistant secretary of state for the Far East, and ambassador to Indonesia. He and his wife, Martha, became good friends of ours and I considered him a mentor on Chinese affairs.

about our being there. I met many ambassadors there including the Soviet, Polish, Rumanian, several Africans. The Europeans all sought me out and told me they thought the change in policy was a very good one.

I then came home, we formed in a big group and about 14 strong from the US Mission went off to one of the guest houses where Chiao Kuan Hua* gave us a beautiful banquet. We sat in overstuffed chairs in the reception room to start with where we had a chance to discuss some things with substance. He raised the question of oil and we discussed that. He thinks I am a bigger oil expert than I am. We also discussed Kissinger's trip. . . . The atmospherics were great. He opened his tunic at the end of the meal and leaned back. Instead of giving a standing toast, he made the point of giving a sitting toast and I made the point of trying to leave fairly early to try to keep the atmosphere informal. I had the distinct feeling that Huang Chen† might have told him about the way we threw the oysters [shells] in the middle of the table in Washington because they had a lovely mixing pot of all kinds of Chinese delicacy and flavors where people get up and hold their meat or fish or chicken in this common kettle of water cooking all the ingredients and turning in the end into a wonderful soup. The dish had a way of relaxing people and getting them together in an informal way. There was plenty of wine, plenty of Mao Tai, and plenty of frank conversation. I made the point for example that we got attacked an awful lot at these international conferences when we really went there to help. I liked the tone of the meeting. Chiao's wife was charming. She told Bar she had been to the States five times—U.N. She had almost a western style hairdo and was very very pretty. Chiao kidded Bar, telling her not to laugh at me during my Chinese lessons. And once he referred to her as Barbara during his toast. I thanked him as effusively as I could at the end of the meeting and he told me "we would want to have a nice banquet for you anyway, but I wanted to especially repay you for your hospitality to me at your mother's home," referring to the time when he and Huang Hua came out to mother's in Greenwich that informal Sunday.‡ It is won-

*Chiao was then foreign minister, but I had gotten to know him when, as vice foreign minister, he accompanied the first People's Republic mission to New York to take their seat in the United Nations. A brilliant man, Chiao suffered at the hands of the radical Red Guards during the Cultural Revolution.

†Huang was my counterpart in Washington.

‡Soon after the Chinese arrived in New York, I had invited the delegation to my mother's house in Greenwich for an informal Sunday-afternoon get-together.

derful how he remembers. The entrance to the guest house when
we drove in was a real contrast to some of the rest of Peking. Beautiful, well kept, plenty of greenery. It was apparently the old Austria-
Hungary legation where we had the dinner.

The next day Holdridge, Anderson, Brunson and I went to call on
Teng Hsiao-Ping.* He was a very short man. We went to the Great
Hall of the People and met in a room where [Premier] Chou En Lai
apparently meets a lot of the people. As we walked in we were ushered over in the middle of the room for a picture. Holdridge and I
were flanking the very short Teng. We then moved on into the reception room where we had a long good discussion with the Vice Premier. It lasted about an hour and a half. He gave us a lot of
interesting agricultural statistics. We talked about world politics and
a need for continued relationship. I gave him my thesis that there
must be visible manifestations of progress for our China policy so it
will avoid some of the hyper-microscopic analyses that we are getting
on other policies in the States. He touched briefly on Taiwan . . .
Teng seemed very much in control, clicking off minute agricultural
population statistics, concerned about India, thought we hadn't
done enough at the time of the India-Pakistan war.† I was too polite
to ask them what they had done. Nancy Tang did the interpreting.
Chiao Kuan Hua sitting to the left of Teng and Wang Hai Jung‡
down from there. She is a very quiet little girl and it is believed she is
put into this high position so she can be around all functions [for]
Chairman Mao. She lacks the outgoing appeal of either Nancy Tang
or Mrs. Chiao Kuan Hua. As we left, Teng left the door open for
future visits though he indicated I would be seeing "others." . . .

----

*You probably recognize him as Deng Xiaoping, who was then vice premier. The staffers
who went with me, in addition to Holdridge, were Don Anderson, our expert on Chinese
political affairs, and Brunson McKinley, who was an aide.

†This war took place while I was at the United Nations and resulted in the creation of a
new country, Bangladesh. The United States tilted diplomatically toward Pakistan. The Chinese openly sided with Pakistan; the Soviet Union with India, which caused a great deal of
international tension.

‡Nancy Tang, an excellent interpreter, was close to the top Chinese leadership. She was the
daughter of the highest PRC official at the U.N. Secretariat. Wang Hai Jung was Mao's niece.

November 5, 1974

The Honorable William Steiger
House of Representatives
Washington, DC
Dear Bill:

Bar has written Jan all the news and if I started in to give you all my reactions to this fabulous assignment, it would take too much of your time. Suffice it to say the Bushes are alive, well, challenged, interested, excited, and, all in all, finding this land of contrasts a magnificent new experience.

Having said that, I have a favor to ask of you. Would you call a good cross section of our friends in Congress and ask them to put me on the mailing list for their newsletters in Washington. . . . I do find that I am cut off from domestic politics far too much, and though I am an instant diplomat and no longer a consummate politician, I don't want to be out of touch. . . . Fifteen or so would get the job done. I don't think there is any problem regarding postage. I'd like a philosophical cross section. . . .

I hope this isn't an imposition. Suffice it to say, I miss my godson.* I miss my own sons; I miss my daughter; I miss my godson's parents.

Hastily, but with warmest regards,

George Bush

———————

November 17, 1974

Dear Bake [James Baker],

We're here. We have been for almost four fascinating weeks—weeks filled with a variety of emotions. This is a land of contrasts. Great beauty but also a lot of gray dirt and drabness. Clear (almost balmy) skies then fierce penetrating cold, urged on to ferocious heights by a North wind that reminds me of the West Texas winds, carrying a lot of real estate. Enormous beauty of the children with their captivating smiles and robust healthy looks contrasted with a certain dreary sameness as one watches the workers cycling out of Peking to work in the AM and back from work in the PM. It's great and we are very happy here, though both Bar and I miss family, friends, news, even politics. It is funny how fast we get cut off. . . . We have great communications with DC, but the wireless file (USIS)† only comes here in part, the papers and mags are real late, and the Hinshua News put out by the New China News Agency is nice to have but concentrates on international events—usually not the ones I want to read about. I have a great short wave

*I am Bill Steiger Jr.'s godfather.
†United States Information Service.

given by the office—a very good one, but it gets a lot of whoofing, blowing wheezing like all short waves. Ask me anything about radio Moscow—those weiners come in like gangbusters, but I don't want to hear all about the "imperialistic USA exploiting the third world".

The food here is out of this world/ Food is more than a passing meal here—it is an art. In our house we have a good Chinese staff and the cook, a Mr. Sung, is an artist. We have had mainly lunches and the dishes are always new and different. The only thing that was tough to get down was the sea slug—a plateful of gravy covered wiggly purple spiny gelatinous spiked looking things. They say sea slugs are aphrodisiacs so I wolfed one down (N.B.* if that's what it takes I'm ready for a celibacy course)—Anyway I am eating too darned much at home and in the fantastic restaurants in Peking. The restaurants aren't that much to look at inside—all kind of old and run down, but the food is exquisite and fairly reasonable as well.

I have been far busier than I thought I'd be—diplomatic calls, calls on Chinese officials—one trip to Tientsin, 2 hours from Peking.

We are well received here. Kissinger comes in a week or so, and that is great 'cause it will set the course for the next year or so. . . .

Bar comes home very soon—leaving around Dec. 4—maybe leaving with Kissinger. She likes it here but I am glad she'll be with the weiners† for Christmas. She comes back out on the 6th of January. I go to Honolulu for a chief of Mission Conference around Dec. 6th for about 9 days—good duty—then I come back here for Christmas—Mother joining. Let me know if you and Susan ever feel like a trip to Peking. I know we can work it out as far as visas go—just tell em you will stay with us. . . .

Had a haircut, massage—shoulders head, plus shampoo—60 cents US.

The friendship store sells almost everything we need. Bought my whiskey etc. in Hong Kong. Our house [is] plenty roomy—4 bedrooms up, one down, massive downstairs kitchen—small one up for family. Darned nice. Bought a championship pong table—but the Chinese are so good that I just quietly hit in the dining room with limited hot air. . . .

We sure miss the Houstonians. I hope Jeb is getting along O. K. I expect they've all written but we haven't heard from him—oh yes Columba‡ wrote us a nice letter. All's well. Your Pekinese buddy misses you. I'm shipping you a few gallons of sea slugs—do with them what you will.

Happily,
GB

*N.B. is from the Latin *nota bene*, which means "note well."

†I always called the kids "weiner" or "tennie weeny." Today, all the grandkids are weiners.

‡Jeb had married Columba—we call her Colu—Garnica Gallo in February 1974. They were living in Houston, where Jeb worked for Texas Commerce Bank.

Sunday, November 17

. . . On a beautiful, warm sunny day went to the Great Wall in two trucks. A hazardous ride, unbelievable. Going around blind curves. Honking like mad. Pushing pony carts and various forms of decrepit looking vehicles off to the side. We climbed to the top of the left hand side of the Wall. A real workout, tough on the legs, but exhilarating when one gets through. We had been told that it might be windy and very very viciously cold but it was neither, We must have hit a lucky day. It is hard to describe the spectacle of the Wall. I can just hear a whole bunch of coolies sitting around and the foreman coming in and saying to them, "Men, we got a new project. We are going to build a wall, yep—2,000 miles. OK, let's hear it for the engineers. Let's get going on the job." What a fantastic undertaking. We then drove down and had a picnic near one of the Tombs. All by ourselves in a courtyard. The sun was out. I sat in my shirtsleeves and we ate a delicious picnic. A kind of a sweet and sour fish. Excellent fried chicken. Lots of hard boiled eggs. The inevitable tasty soup. The only thing we forgot was ice so the beer was warm but we had worked hard enough walking up to the top so that we devoured about six bottles of it. It's a heavy beer and I find it makes me sleepy but it's awful good. We then went to the Ding Ling tomb and looked around there. Plenty of exercise climbing up and down. When we got home at about 5 o'clock I totally collapsed.

Secretary of State Henry Kissinger arrived for his much awaited visit in late November. I dictated to my diary:

November 26, 1974

I attend, sitting next to the Secretary, meetings in the morning at the Great Hall and in the afternoon at the guest house, meetings with Teng Hsiao Ping. . . . Kissinger is brilliant in these talks. Tremendous sweep of history and a tremendous sweep of the world situation. He is at his best. It is a great contrast to the irritating manner he has of handling people. His staff are scared to death of him. The procession is almost "regal." People quake, "He's coming. He's coming." And don't dare tell him when he's keeping them waiting. In the Wednesday morning meeting, "I want my staff. I want them all in this room. I want them right here now. Where are they?" All kinds of yelling of that nature goes on. I guess it is the way he keeps from getting ulcers at the pace he is working at. I came home and had lunch with Bar . . .

———————

November 28, 1974

Kissinger was anxious to know my plans. He asked how long I planned to stay. This is the second reference he made to it. I had in my mind that he was probing to see what my political plans were. I told him I had no political plans, that I thought the ticket for '76 was locked in with the appointment of Rockefeller, which I do, and that I had no plans at all. Kissinger made some reference to my running for President in 1980. I told him I couldn't see that far ahead but I was very much interested in doing a good job here—learning the substance of our foreign policy and getting an overall view of it. He pointed out that this was a good place to do it because of the kinds of reviews the Chinese get from him and also because from time to time there are substantive items here. I made clear to him that I was not expecting high profile, I knew the limitations of this post and that it didn't bother me. I really think he is still curious as to why I am here, when, as he knows, I could have gone to Paris or London. . . .

———————

December 4 , 1974

Enroute Peking to Tokyo
Dear Gerry [Bemiss],

. . . This won't sound like much, Bemiss, but I wish you could attend the Christian Church service with us (you will I hope). It is in downtown Peking in the old Bible Society Building. There are 5 Chinese who attend. They alternate preaching. The service is in Chinese totally, no sermon, lots of hymns, communion every Sunday.

It is strange and yet very moving. Here we are in a totally controlled atheistic tough society. They permit tokenism. It means a lot of hymns, all the beautiful well known ones, boom out with the strong handful of Chinese voices—it's almost too much. It makes me count my many blessings right there.

Not the least of which is the feeling of love and affection we, Bar & me, have for you two.

I have time to think over here—even read (I know you don't believe it); But here one sorts out his values—freedoms we take for granted come to the fore here as treasures but for us it's family and close friends—ever thus in our lives, but here it's vivid and in perspective.

Come see us—when you are ready—tell me. We can get the visas.
Love to Margaret to the kids.
Just know that your friend in Peking is doing O. K.

> Best
> GB

December 4, 1974

. . . Great talks with Bar on the phone. The kids all doing fine. It is as if each one of these five kids, recognizing that the family was undergoing a different experience, are pulling together much more. There are no longer those juvenile battles and each one comes through strong, vibrant, full of humor and different, full of life and we are awfully lucky. It is right that Bar be there but boy do I miss her. . . .

December 17, 1974

His Excellency Chiao Kuan Hua
Minister of Foreign Affairs
Peoples Republic of China
Dear Mr. Minister:

My mother and an aunt will be here for a couple of weeks. Even though Barbara is with our children in the United States and thus won't be here to greet you, I would love to have you come for a very small, very informal supper next week.

Could you and your wife join us on Thursday, December 26th at 7:00 p.m.? If that day is impossible the 27th would be fine too.

I know how busy you are, so if dinner doesn't seem possible perhaps we could call on you some day during the next couple of weeks. My mother would enjoy seeing you again.

Maybe you would like to bring some others with you. If you want to do that I will invite an equal number from the USLO—otherwise there will be just us.

> Respectfully yours,
> George Bush

December 17, 1974

. . . A lot of our mail is opened when it goes international. Indeed it has been checked through some very sophisticated methods that international mail is read rather regularly. . . . In checking around I find this is not unusual. I write the mail that I send international knowing that it will be checked.

Mother arrives tomorrow. I have that kind of high school excitement—first vacation feeling. Weather still cold, but very clear. Great for bicycling. I hope it holds out for her. Mr. Wong hustling around the house. Three guest bedrooms have been painted and they are pale yellow. Much different and better than the flat water paint. Apparently they started using some kind of a plastic paint.

December 18, 1974

Mother arrived on a beautiful day. Gave her a nice 20 minutes or so to shape up and then we took a long bicycle ride down past the Great Hall of the People. You should have seen the people stare at old momma on the bicycle. They would stand by and watch her. It reminded me of the old joke—about the railroad train crossing at the time zone—it left at five minutes of and arrived 100 miles later at 3 minutes of. The crowd stood around to watch that mother take off. At each traffic light a little group would stand around, nudge each other, look at each other, the kids were openly incredulous, but she cycled majestically off at each stop, doing beautifully in her PLA hat, teenage looking ski outfit and did just great. . . .

December 19, 1974

The big game is trying to figure out whether what they say in public is what they mean or not. Example. Mobutu* is here. He is praised—the toasts of the dinners hit the super powers. Mobutu enters in by saying "For Africa the peril is white rather than yellow." Mobutu I am sure will have a different view when he talks to the United States. But I am increasingly upset at the public blasts at the United States. . . . I am absolutely convinced that American public opinion will turn against this at some point and a relationship which is very important to China will be damaged. Maybe China's rhetoric is more important to them than the relationship, but I don't really think so. . . . Most people in this town feel that this relationship is the most important one they have got. But they have a funny way of showing it. . . .†

---

*President of Zaire.

†Perhaps I overestimated the impact of Chinese propaganda. Much of it was aimed at their own people, not at the outside world.

Christmas Day

. . . We had our first Western meal at the house. Turkey, cranberry sauce, tons of vegetables. Mr. Sun doing a first-class job, Peking dust for dessert.

. . . Called home. Couldn't hear the kids except to get the feeling that they had been broken out of the sack at 7:45 a.m. their time. All was well at home. Neil having racked up good marks. Jeb made Phi Beta Kappa officially. Marvin's starring in basketball. All these little mundane things are of tremendous importance here in China. It was funny to see Peking bustling here on Christmas Day. Worlds apart in some ways and yet most of them wished us a happy holiday etc.

. . . Our USLO kids played hockey down at the Russian embassy, being whipped by the Russian kids. There are hockey games every Sunday for the Russian kids versus an international team. Sports really are marvelous for getting across political lines. It is hard to equate the decency, kindness, humor, gentility of the people of China with some of the rhetoric aimed against the United States. I think back to our own recent experience in World War II. We sought no territory. We were trying to defeat a common enemy. We came to help and yet we are bitterly attacked and lumped in with those who tried to colonialize and pillage. We are the imperialists.

December 27, 1974

In bed, fever about 100.5. Tons of great fresh orange juice. Decision having to be made as to whether to cancel the dinner for Chiao Kuan Hua. I decided to go ahead with it in spite of feeling rotten. Six Chinese, three Bushes counting Aunt Marge, and the Holdridges will be there. Mr. Sun has gone through the darnest orgy of preparations you have ever seen. The menu is something to behold. And the concern has got to be unsurpassed. I did a little reading but most of the time I just slept—tired and aching.

Out of the sack. Fever dropped at four thirty miraculously. Then fantastic dinner prepared by Mr. Sun. Pigeon eggs, swallow nest soup, crisp duck, shark fins, stuffed mushrooms, grilled chicken, mushroom and fresh bamboo shoots, steamed pancakes, rice, sugar and white fungus and a lot of mao tai. It was a great evening. Chiao Kuan Hua was in good form—relaxed. We had a lot of good warm discussion with Chiao Kuan Hua. Chiao tells me at the end that

Rumsfeld* had told him we ought to stay in very close contact. I told him I would like to do more of that and all he had to do was say when. I didn't want to impose on him but I was available. . . .

———————

In January I was called back to the States for consultation. I stopped in Pakistan en route and contracted some terrible bug while there, resulting in a severe intestinal disorder. I was hospitalized several days in Washington and suffered recurrences for months. On the way back to Peking, I wrote our friends Flo and Holt Atherton (Flo was formerly Flo Kampmann):

Dear Flo & Holt,

. . . This bug has had me really weak, but as each day goes by I get stronger. Bar is lonely and I can't wait to get back to our home half way around the world.

Washington depressed me—the mood 'mongst my hill colleagues and at State was one of down, down, down.

I hate to see that for our country's sakes.

I worry lest our friends-foes around the world really begin to wonder if we can keep a commitment in foreign policy.

All you have to do to have real renewed respect for the U.S. is to live in a country where our taken-for-granted freedoms are non-existent. Yet sometimes our press or some of our people want to alter all institutions and tear us down. . . .

Love—
George

———————

February 15, 1975

People universally stare of course everywhere one goes. I am wearing my PLA army hat, my Marlborough country wool jacket, sometimes my Chinese overcoat. The diplomats look askance at this informality or at least some do. But on the other hand I get the feeling that the Chinese like the feeling that the U.S. ambassador is not some stuffy guy above everyone else. In fact I am quite confident of this though not absolutely positive. We prefer not to use our car when we go to the International Club 3 blocks away but I notice our African neighbors all driving up in Mercedes with the flags flying. I like to see the American flag flying here in China both on the flag pole and on the car going around town. But I think it is a little

———

*Donald Rumsfeld, then Ford's chief of staff and later his secretary of defense.

inconsiderate to the driver to have him come all the way in, wait three hours to take us home three blocks.

The staff is doing very well. Mr. Wong* continuing to be the supervisor, a marvelous fellow. I showed him the moon landing, he and Sun and Chen the other day on the VTR.† They were absolutely amazed. They stayed glued to their chairs throughout the whole performance. I asked Mr. Wong if the staff would all like to bring their children to watch cartoons if we ever got them and they said they certainly would like to do that. He is the politest guy and the best fellow . . .

I am amazed when I went back to the States at the malaise, the tearing down of institutions, the broadcasts this far away. I have more confidence in our country than the mood that was prevailing back home would have one believe one should have. . . .

It is a tough situation we are in but I am confident that this country can and will prevail. We just must not lose sight of our own perspective and of our own raison d'etre as a nation. So much of the world depends on the United States, so much depends on our own self-confidence in our own ability to cope. If we project this confusion and failure and discouragement it will show up all around the world. People wonder anyway when they see commitments unkept. I think of Cambodia and I think of Vietnam and I think of what that means to the Chinese government and others as they see us unable to fulfill commitments made. I happen to be concerned about Cambodia and Vietnam and think the American people don't care about them anymore. But that isn't the point. The point is that if we make a commitment we ought to keep it. We must deal straight forward so we can have trust. I hope that the Chinese continue to trust the United States. It is important to our relationship that they believe what we say and that we deal truthfully and openly and honestly with them. In spite of the fact that they in history did not always deal direct, much of their dealings have traditionally been through nuances and in great subtleties. I don't think we must adopt the same method in dealing with them. We must be Americans. We must be what we are. We must be sure they understand what we are. And that we not be devious or be indirect in dealing with them. I think they would appreciate it if we are more frank. End of George Washington's Birthday, Monday, February 17, 1975.

---

*Mr. Wong is still running things at the ambassador's residence in Beijing.
†Today we know VTRs (videotape recorders) as VCRs (videocassette recorders).

February 25, 1975

Driving along the street it is so interesting here. One gets the feeling among other things of strong family ties. One of the misconceptions I had before coming here was that family was no longer important. Yet on the holidays and on any day one gets the strong feeling of family. Grown girls looking after their grandparents. Grown parents looking after their mothers. Children together with parents. . . . Respect for family. Talking about family. Talking about visiting family. All very important. . . . There is this feeling that we are close to the forest but somehow are not seeing the trees. And yet the other side of it is that you do get much more flavor for China by being here. You don't know exactly what's going on in the government. They are secretive. The preparations for the National Peoples Congress were done in total secrecy. They are not outgoing. You can't go into their homes and yet you get a general impression of China that you can't get from outside. You see kids slugging it out on the streets, playing, fighting, just as you do in the States. You see little girls doing that funny jump rope game with kind of elastic looking jump-ropes in parallel, low to the ground where their feet weave almost like weaving on a loom. You see young teenagers kind of hanging in together smoking. Men smoke a lot. You get used to people spitting on the street although I am told that they are working against this.

The grayness is beginning to give way a little bit as warm weather approaches. The padding doesn't look quite as great on the clothes, both women's and men's. I am anxious to see summer and spring here. Interesting lunch today. Chicken, a great soup and one of the ingredients was chicken blood. Fresh blood of chicken made into a jelly, almost like a bean curd which was then cut into squares and served. Barbara told me what it was after we finished. I must say it tasted delicious, but I am glad she didn't let me know ahead of time what I was eating.

New discovery to go with the orange juice (not fresh) that is served absolutely everywhere in China. A lemon juice. I have got to find out where we get it. Pretty good. Marvelous letter from Marvin, saying things are great. Bar sat and cried as she read it. The kid has had a tough go until the last couple of years when he has really done a first-rate job. He was admitted to the University of Texas, still waiting to hear from North Carolina and Colorado.* Basketball going

---

*Marvin underachieved at Andover and changed schools to Woodberry Forest where he did very well. He went to the University of Texas for one year, but then transferred to and graduated from the University of Virginia, which he loved.

great. His great sentence was, "Johnny Bush is coming down to see a
basketball game. You can't help but love a guy that would do a thing
like that." I miss the children a lot every day and yet they seem to be
holding together. They seem to be getting strength from each other.
They spell out their love for their parents. We are very lucky.

I am finding a little more time to study China's history, read about
Chairman Mao. There are great inconsistencies in Mao, what he says
now and what he used to believe. Nothing too fundamental but time
and again one can find them. But come to think of it who shouldn't
"change his mind."

March 2, 1975

. . . Marvin, Neil, George will have a great time hitting with the
Chinese in both ping pong and tennis. The philosophy of the Chinese government is not competition itself, the friendship developed
from those sports is what counts, not the victory.* I believe this
somewhat though I am a little bit more like Bear Bryant†—frankly
the Chinese guys I am playing tennis with are a lot like Bear Bryant.
They are stoic in that they don't show their emotion and they don't
get mad. They don't get sore when they lose but I am absolutely convinced from playing that they like to win. . . . Beginning to feel that
the informal style, riding on the bike, the informal dress, the openness with the diplomats and the Chinese may pay off. At first I wondered but Mr. Lo at the store said, "You are getting to be a legend in
your dress." He wasn't ridiculing me I don't think. In fact I am sure
he was not. And they all talk about our riding our bikes, Barbara and
me. One mission man from Italy told me, "I can't imagine my
ambassador riding a bike."‡ And I am convinced the Chinese like it.
They are not themselves as open and outgoing but they are warm
and friendly, and I remain convinced that we should convince them,
even through the limited contacts we have, that Americans are not
stuffy, rich and formal.

---

*"Friendship first" was an often-repeated slogan.
†Famous football coach of the University of Alabama.
‡When I visited China as President in 1989, Premier Li Peng gave Barbara and me bicycles
as gifts, to remind us of our China days. On my many trips to China since 1992, both in Beijing and in other cities, many people still refer to our bike-riding. Amazing!

March 3, 1975

Mr. Jerry Weintraub*
Management Three, Ltd.
New York, New York
Dear Jerry:

I have a long shot thought. Think about it and tell me if it would have any appeal at all.

This 4th of July here in Peking we are going to have the first 4th of July National Day reception held by the U.S. in Mainland China in a long, long time.

We will invite Chinese friends and we will invite the Diplomatic Corps. Last year the U.S. did not attend diplomatic receptions but we have changed that now, and it is appreciated. Typically we have no budget, but Bar and I are prepared to spend enough personal money to make it a fun event.

We want it to be informal—it will be hot in Peking then. We want it to be typically American—maybe a bring the kids kind of outdoor thing—with beer and hamburgers and hot dogs. And we want it to be patriotic.

Now for my long shot idea. Is there any chance that John Denver will be traveling in this part of the world around that time. He would be the ideal guy to put on a short show of his great American ballads. . . .

. . . I don't believe that at this juncture he would be permitted to sing before any Chinese audiences in a public place in Peking. I can't even offer him plane fare unless we could get the USIS to spring for that.

We can only offer him a week in our home with tender loving care, a chance to see Peking, and one hell of a lot of gratitude for coming to this isolated post to help us celebrate a very special day. His wife, who we met at your house, would be most welcome of course. We couldn't get permission for technical people, lights, cameras, etc. It would be a one man, informal kind of thing.

Does it make any sense at all?

If it has no appeal to John is there anyone that you know of who will be out in this part of the world who might conceivably like to do what I am suggesting. It's a long shot but I am determined to try to do something different—something that will bring a touch of American talent to this land—even in this very confined way.

Bar and I thought of John Denver because we will never forget that night at Carnegie Hall when I was at the U.N. You invited us to hear him sing, and

---

*Jerry, now a Hollywood producer, and I became friends when he married longtime family friend and famous singer Jane Morgan. At this time, Jerry managed tours of many singing stars, including John Denver, Elvis Presley, and Neil Diamond.

his rendition of "America the Beautiful" and other songs as well made a lasting impression on our hearts. The impact of this sincerity and love of country in Peking would be fantastic. . . .

Warm regards.

Yours very truly,
George Bush

[Although he was interested, it did not work out for Denver to come.]

March 8, 1975

. . . I have been reading a fair amount of books: <u>Centennial, Dogs of War,</u> a mystery story, and now <u>Before the Fall</u>* by Safire. On the Chinese side I have read Pearl Buck's <u>Good Earth,</u> I read the story of Empress Tz'u Hsi, <u>The Dowager Empress,</u> Barnett's book <u>After Mao,</u> Teddy White's book <u>Thunder Out of China.</u> I am reading a book by Han Suyin.

March 12, 1975

. . . In Chinese I still feel a certain frustration. When I just sit and chat with Mrs. Tang† I lose my embarrassment factor and I can do it, but my problem is practice, practice, practice. But I love the Chinese lessons and I hate it when I have to miss them. Mrs. Tang has enormous dignity and a kind of serenity and I wish I could find out what is really in her heart. . . .

March 13, 1975

Mr. Jack Valenti
Motion Picture Association
Washington, DC
Dear Jack:

It was good seeing you all too briefly when I was home for the Alfalfa dinner and consultations. . . .

This year we at USLO have started going to the National Days of various countries who have embassies here in Peking. This 4th of July will be the first National Day to which USLO has invited foreign diplomats. Most of the

---

*The full title is *Before the Fall: An Inside View of the Pre-Watergate White House.*
†Mrs. Tang gave Bar and me Chinese lessons one hour a day, five days a week.

diplomatic corps will be invited and so will many of our Chinese friends.

I want to do something American, something fun, something informal. Nothing is final but I am beginning to plan a typical American 4th of July picnic to celebrate our 199th year.

If the logistics all work out we will have red, white and blue bunting; we will have beer, coke, burgers and dogs. (In fact if we can get the crowd quiet I might even give a 45 minute campaign speech.)

But I want to top off this 1½ hour picnic with a first-class U.S. film at the International Club theater just 3 blocks from here.

Can you recommend (not furnish, honest) any great American films depicting either the revolution itself or something unmistakably American. The film should be good entertainment. It needn't be new. It should show our country in its true light—favorable.

It occurred to me that with the 200th year coming up some good films must have already been produced that would serve our purpose.

If there is no film depicting the revolution what might you recommend that would fill the bill? Oklahoma, Carousel, That's Entertainment come to mind; but I'm sure I'm missing something great.

I hate to impose but I'd really like to have your ideas on this.

National Day receptions here are deadly. There are a lot of reasons why I think this year is a good one for us to do something different than the dreary standing-whiskey at the Peking Hotel.

Love to Mary Margaret. . . .

Yours very truly,
George Bush

We had many visitors while we lived in China because we wanted to share our wonderful experience with our friends. Among them were Dillon Ripley, head of the Smithsonian Institution, and Paul Austin, CEO of Coca-Cola.

March 15, 1975

I had to work. Bar went off sightseeing with the guests. Paul Austin and I took a walk to the Friendship Store, Austin not having heard from the three Chinese we requested he see on business. But Friday the 14th we went to the zoo. Dillon Ripley was disappointed in the zoo and he also thought the zoo was well below standards of any other international zoo. He asked about the musk ox.* There

---

*We had given the Chinese two musk ox as presents, just as they had given us the famous panda bears.

were supposed to be two of them and there was only one there. We had requested to see three zoo people. None were available. I mentioned to Mr. Liu I thought it was a little unusual because when the Chinese zoo people had come they had been given the run of Washington, and I thought it was a little peculiar that we had never heard from them. Saturday noon I get a note from Mr. Liu saying that all three zoo people were out of Peking. We are speculating that the main reason for the failure to go to the zoo was either the condition of the zoo or possibly the dead musk ox. Probably the latter . . .

Pouch—we are missing mail all the time, and it is hard to explain to people in the States what this means. I remember in the Navy wondering where is our mail, where is our mail, but it is the same kind of feeling. But here we are thirty years later. You think it could be done better. But it simply reminds me of our isolation here. . . .

Saw the Ripleys and the Austins off at the airport at noon. . . . I believe they had a good time. We discovered the following day that the musk ox, Milton, had died. We were officially notified by the Chinese. The mystery is solved.

Three pouches came in on March 17. We have had hell with these pouches. Some mail was dated February 5, some as late as March 5. We have a small post and a tough area and yet we seem to be on the tail end of things. We get the worn out films, it is hard to keep maintenance on old stuff around here and I get the feeling that because it is a small outfit, this wheel seems to get less grease. . . .

Today in front of USLO on March 18 the whole school down the street was out for drilling—marching to command etc., getting ready, I guess, for the May 1 big day. We keep getting various reports of struggles in provinces around China. There are fewer here apparently. When people are caught, they are publicly humiliated etc., led around with signs around their necks. I have still seen no crime first-hand. I did see a couple of Chinese who looked like they were getting pretty crocked at a reception but good god that can happen any place.

Spent the afternoon getting caught up—digesting the mail from the three pouches. Our children are doing great. The letters from all of them are mature, sensitive—they are doing well in their work, no drugs, no dope, no crime, no troubles. We should knock on wood. I think it would be awful to be way over here and have family problems where you'd want to be home helping out. . . .

Word travels in this city. Nancy Tang mentioned, "You're having many guests." Why would she, a rather high official, know this. Chiao Kuan Hua, the Foreign Minister, mentions, "I hear you won a prize in tennis." Hsu Huang, head of the DSB,* mentioned, "I understand you gave some books to our people on tennis." The zoo logs us in. Barbara spots the same guy watching twice when she's at the Ming Tombs. In a way it is comforting. In a way it is rather eerie.

———————

March 18th

Dear Pete [Roussel],†

John Burns a great guy who writes for the Globe and Mail (and will be leaving soon to work for the Times in NY) is doing a 'Cover' story for People Magazine. He has been running around taking pictures, jumping out from behind trees to shoot us on our bikes, going to the zoo, then he will pose us at the Forbidden City for what he says they want as a cover shot. It is 'lifestyle' in Peking kind of thing . . .

For your info only. If the Texas Gov thing in '78 made any sense at all I'd maybe take a look at it hard—Go back to Houston after the '76 elections, win or lose for Republicans, involve myself in academia and business, move around the state plenty and try one last gasp for '78 keeping in mind that I wouldn't do it unless there was a possibility of taking a shot at something bigger in '80—not necessarily on the latter, but having it way off dimly in the future. Just a reminiscence—not a hard thought, certainly not a plan at this point. As you know well a GOP Gov in our State is tough.

. . . Maine—maybe maybe maybe. Bar, I will insist, goes there for August. She's got to hold this gang of ours together. They are all doing good but Maine for us is like a magnet—we are drawn to it, and I want it to be that way for all our kids, forever. If she goes for August I may try to get up there for two weeks end of August . . . .

Best,
GB

———————

The State Department "slapped my hands" for inviting too many members of Congress to visit us in China, and a few months later, they would do the same when I invited my fellow East Asian ambassadors to visit me in Peking. Everyone wanted to come, but without an invitation to come as our personal guests, it was next to impossible to get a visa. I think the State Department wanted more say on who got invited. My response:

———————

*Domestic Service Bureau, which was responsible for looking after all the embassies.
†Pete was working at the White House for Rumsfeld.

March 20, 1975

Honorable William H. Gleysteen, Jr.*
Department of State
Washington, DC 20520
Dear Bill:

I appreciate very much the spirit of your letter of March 12th.

I served in the Congress for four years and served as Chairman of our Party for two years. Thus many of my closest personal friends happen to be members of the House and Senate—not professional friends, close personal friends. When I left Washington at one of several going away parties I naturally said to these people "come see us" and I meant it. Frankly, I think it would be very useful to have them do just that. I cannot conceive of any member of Congress that I invited doing anything that would embarrass our policy but I can see how some might understand it a little better.

The Roth† visit will be pure sightseeing. He and Jane, his wife, are attending a Tokyo Conference and he asked if he might come to Peking for two or three days to look around. I will try not to set up any appointments with Chinese officials for him. Indeed I don't know at this writing whether they will even give him a visa.

In the future, I will simply advise members of the House and Senate that I am not free to invite them without their first getting approval of the Secretary of State. However, I would strongly urge that this be carefully thought out back there. I do understand congress pretty well, and I do not believe this would be understood very well on the Hill.

Perhaps I am overreacting to the Secretary's expression of "concern". In short if it is a firm decision I will abide by it, but I want to be clearly on record as disagreeing with it. I will do my best to see that it causes no problems but if pressed I will simply tell the truth and say that I am not free to invite members of Congress without prior State Department approval.

Yours very truly,
George Bush

———

March 25, 1975

Mr. John A. Schneider,
President of CBS Broadcast Group,
New York, N. Y. 10019
Dear Mr. Schneider:

*Bill was deputy assistant secretary for East Asian affairs.
†Senator Bill Roth of Delaware. His wife, Jane, is a federal judge.

. . . Peking is "entertainment starved". There is no way to overstate this. Visitors who come here for brief visits have so much to see and absorb, so many fascinating banquets to attend, so much jet lag to overcome that they do not focus on the totality of our isolation from what we Americans consider entertainment.

I am convinced that if we get some up-to-date entertainment that can be shown on our VTR TV set it will serve three main purposes:

It will help morale in our rather isolated post.

It will maximize the effectiveness of our representation with other diplomats.

It will help us find a way to possibly increase our contacts with the Chinese.

The kinds of tapes we would like to have might include:

> Sporting events—for example, a bowl game, tennis matches, a basketball classic
>
> Movies—I think particularly of something like Brian's Song.
> I mention this one because if we had five or six couples
> watching in the relative closeness of TV it would create
> an atmosphere of intimacy that would help particularly
> in our diplomatic contacts.
>
> Specials—those superbly done CBS specials would be just great
>
> Miscellaneous—just pure serial type entertainment shows from time
> to time would be most welcome

. . . I realize that what I have requested is most unusual, and I do not want to abuse my friendship with Mr. Paley* in any way. However, I am convinced some special access to these cassettes will be especially productive given this very different environment. . . .

Very truly yours,
George Bush
Chief, US Liaison Office

TELEGRAM
FOR: OSCAR ARMSTRONG†
SUBJ: GIFT OF MUSK OX TO CHINESE

The more I think on it the more I like the idea of having the Chinese receive another ox from the US. Milty is dead but a young and virile Bullwinkle could do a lot of good for relations (diplomatic relations, that is).

Bush

---

*William Paley, president of CBS, and a good friend of Dad, who served on the CBS board.
†Oscar was head of the China Desk at the State Department.

For the United States, the Vietnam War had ended in 1973, but the war between North and South Vietnam had continued. The fighting came to a disastrous conclusion in April of 1975. As the North Vietnamese forces closed in on Saigon, we evacuated our embassy on April 29; South Vietnam officially surrendered on April 30.

April 29, 1975

Went to the National Day Reception for the Netherlands and there I heard, not through the State Department telegrams but through gossip at a reception, that the big, big men in Vietnam had surrendered. . . . The Viet Cong and the North Vietnamese embassies are bedecked in flags and having understandable celebrations. Firecrackers are heard. It is a rather sad thing and you can sense the hostility and certainly the tension when I walk by certain groups at these receptions. John Small of Canada made an interesting comment. It is important that the U.S. stand firm in Korea, and it is important that this slide and decline be halted. It is important that these people stand for something. Where is our ideology? Where is our principle? What indeed do we stand for? These things must be made clear, and the American people must understand that, as soon as America doesn't stand for something in the world, there is going to be a tremendous erosion of freedom. It is true. It is very true. And yet it is awful hard to convince people of it at home, I am sure. I am a little annoyed about getting nothing from the State Department, hearing about the surrender . . . from a drinking party. . . .

May First today, but April 30 I guess ends up as a gloomy day. A lot of dust in the air. And all in all not a happy time, but we are big enough and strong enough so we can regroup, redefine and move forward. A lot of human tragedy there. A lot of loss of life. . . .

June 4, 1975

. . . There is no credit in this work, but I think it is an accumulative thing and you've got to keep digging. I've tried to give the right impression of America here—not too formal. We have a good organized staff, tried to move around in the diplomatic community, tried to increase our contacts with the Chinese, tried to have interesting people from the States here, and tried to learn and make suggestions to Washington. Beyond this though, it is hard to "do" anything. And yet I wouldn't trade it for England, Paris or any of the other posts. The others get more notoriety, and Elliot's [Richardson] publicity is good I think out of England, but I think this is more substantive in one sense and certainly more interesting. A beautiful letter from Jeb about the problems of Columba adjusting, how much he loves her, how marvelous she is, and what she needs is self-confidence. It was a thoughtful, sensitive piece—an attractive kid who has got it all. I just hope he is fully happy because, knowing him and his sensitivity, he would be deeply hurt if she was ever hurt.

Hurray, George arrives tomorrow . . .

FOR THE PRESIDENT FROM GEORGE BUSH
THRU: GENERAL SCOWCROFT* ONLY

Brent, please pass the following to the President. I hope it will be shared only with SecState and not be passed to NSC staff or Department. It is pure politics, but I feel strongly about it.

Dear Mr. President:

. . . The Taiwan issue is on the back burner right now as it relates to domestic politics. I am very concerned that as your trip to China approaches this will change dramatically. Your own personal interests dictate that serious thought be given to what is possible from a purely political standpoint.

Answers to the Taiwan question that may have been possible before the collapse in Cambodia and Viet Nam may no longer be any answers at all. I would strongly suggest the following:

(a) An in-depth poll be taken to measure public opinion on various solutions to the Taiwan question (the last poll, I believe, was by Gallup late last year). The poll should probe into opinion of conservatives and liberals and should sound out attitudes towards various solutions. Obviously this polling should be done in great confidence and commissioned by outside sources.

(b) An in-depth research job be done on what the conservatives in the US have said and are likely to say on this issue. A similar study should be undertaken on what the leading Democrats have been saying. N.B.: It seems to me that your political problems arising from this issue are quite different pre-GOP convention compared to post-GOP convention.

(c) Thought be given as to how to keep this issue from building into a

---

*Brent Scowcroft was Kissinger's number two man on the National Security Council. Over the years, Brent and I became the best of friends, and as my national security adviser when I was President, he was a most trusted confidant.

major weapon for your opponents be they Republican or Democrat. Some will try to paint a China visit without a final solution to Taiwan as a diplomatic failure, an inability to solve the tough problems. Others, particularly the right wing, will soon start criticizing the visit itself and will be on guard to immediately criticize any concessions as a sell-out of Taiwan.

In this communication I am not attempting to go into the foreign policy merits of China options. I firmly believe, however, that your coming to Peking this year, whatever the concrete results, is the right thing to do. What is done at this stage to assess the politics of the visit should be separate from the foreign policy machinery and not in any way inhibit the thinking and planning which undoubtedly is going forward at the State Department and NSC. I am suggesting that a trusted confidant who would not be involved with this planning be encouraged to think out the domestic political implications of your China visit.

I have already discussed with the State Department my concern that work need be done fairly soon to minimize expectations. Many journalists are saying, "The President can't possibly go to China without solving the Taiwan problem." It is to your advantage to have this talk dampened, so that expectations be realistic not euphoric and that a visit that does not solve the big Taiwan problem will not, post facto, be considered a diplomatic failure.

Pardon my intrusion on your busy schedule, but, based on my own political past, I worry that this issue can build into a political nightmare unless a lot of pure political thought gets into it soon.

Barbara and I are happy out here. We feel we are most fortunate to be in this fascinating job in this fascinating land.

Warmest regards to Betty.

Sincerely,
George

[Twenty-four years later, the Taiwan "problem" is still not solved. I felt back then as I feel now—that this issue will be resolved, but by the Chinese on both sides of the straits—not by outsiders.]

June 12, 1975

Doro, Marvin and Neil arrived along with a small industry delegation. They looked great, giggling, bubbling over with enthusiasm—having enjoyed Honolulu, tired, not seen anything of Tokyo, only one night there and into Peking. They were great. They rushed down and played basketball, rode down to the Great Square. Marvin played tennis with Te and then off we went to the Soup Restaurant where we had eel and they all loved that. Neil Mallon* bought the dinner and it was all pretty good.

———

June 24, 1975

Oscar Armstrong, Esq.,
Department of State,
Washington, D. C. 20520
Dear Oscar:

I am sending you excerpts from a June 10 letter to me from Dillon Ripley of the Smithsonian Institute on the question of finding a replacement Musk Ox for the deceased Milton. I find his arguments against providing a replacement persuasive. As you know, I originally favored a replacement Ox, but now I am not in favor. I frankly don't know where this question stands back there and whether or not people are clamoring to send a replacement Ox. It would not be appropriate for President Ford to bring an Ox with him, and probably not an appropriate gift for the Chinese at all.

. . . If the subject has died down in the U.S., I am perfectly willing to let the subject drop from this end. Why should we flog a dead Musk Ox?

Sincerely,
George Bush
Chief, US Liaison Office

———

DEPARTMENT OF STATE
TELEGRAM
THE GREAT HOTDOG ROLL CRISIS
June 27, 1975
1. There is not a hotdog roll to be found in China. Is there any way you could ship us 700 hotdog rolls for guaranteed delivery prior to July 4?
2. We also need 100 large bags of potato chips in same shipment.
3. Please advise soonest.

Bush

———

June 15, 1975
. . . Church, visit to the tailors to get the kids suited up—about $70.
. . . Tennis was indoors this afternoon because the weather was bad.

*Neil and his wife, Ann, were visiting.

Marvin threw his racquet which really burned me up with the Chinese all watching. Sportsmanship and that kind of thing mean so much more here. We joke about "friendship first" here a little bit, but carefully. But it is an important concept and I ate him out for that display, much like what I might have done when I was his age—but he should be getting over that. Actually he is doing darn well—in his work and from reports from the Congress job he had—the reports were fantastic.

June 29, 1975

. . . Dorothy was baptized at our little Chinese Church.* The ministers were extremely happy and smiling—pleasant, wonderful. It was very special. There were six guardian group people taping and flashing pictures of the ceremony, not knowing what was going on really. But we were very happy that the Chinese agreed, after they consulted in a meeting, to baptize Doro. They wondered why we were doing it. Bar explained that we wanted the family together and hadn't been able to do it. A very special day. . . .

July 4, 1975

. . . It was a tremendous success. We all got out and worked on the roof, on hanging up plastic banners, weighing them down with welding rods, setting tables, cooking hot dogs on charcoal. It is hard to light. But it all fell in place with the rain drizzling a little during the day, but clearing miraculously in time for a well attended, perhaps 500 people, reception. Dogs,† Miller beer, American cigarettes, a raffle, coca cola, lots of loud music—John Denver style—and it was great. The Americans wore red, white and blue. We had American flags around and I am confident it conveyed the right kind of impression about our country. . . .

July 6, 1975

The family left yesterday for Shanghai and now I am a bachelor. I am reading Grey's <u>Hostage in Peking</u> which, along with Ricketts' book

---

*It must seem odd that Doro was baptized in China. Over the years, for a variety of reasons, her baptism had been scheduled and postponed a number of times. Twenty years later, at a well-attended church service in a bigger church, we saw one of the ministers who had baptized Doro.

†The hot dog buns did make it in time.

about their imprisonment back in the early fifties, is interesting reading. The Ricketts come out as great admirers of the system of rehabilitation and are kind of ashamed that they were spies. <u>Hostage in Peking</u> is very different. It shows the horrible and ugly side of the Cultural Revolution . . . stoning embassies, stripping embassy people as they were thrown out of China, spitting on them, plastering posters, vilification, and ugliness that one doesn't see now. And frankly it is kind of hard to imagine. But it is a good lesson to keep in mind.

. . . Today is George's twenty-ninth birthday. He is off to Midland, starting a little later in life than I did, but nevertheless starting out on what I hope will be a challenging new life for him. He is able. If he gets his teeth into something semi-permanent or permanent,* he will do just fine. . . .

July 8, 1975

Long walk with Fred where he spotted the Polish cat again. Practically pulled my arm out of my socket . . . and I tore down the road, past the PLA guards . . . Fred made a dive at the iron gate, sticking his neck all the way through it in quest of the elusive cat. We then had to sniff around the tall grass for five minutes till Fred satisfied himself the cat was gone. What a horrible international incident if he ever caught the cat. Lots of couples out on the hot summer night. People jump away when they see Fred. They shy back. They show their kids Fred—kids in their arms, but then they sidle off as we get near with Fred on his rope.

. . . I wish I could tell what China's real intent is. After reading <u>Hostage in Peking</u> and reliving some of the horrors of the Cultural Revolution I can't be sure. Should Soviet Union and China get together, it would be, in my opinion, a whole new ballgame. And yet there is a latent interest in and respect for the United States. China keeps wanting us to be strong, wanting us to defend Europe, wanting us to increase our defense budget, etc. And yet their rhetoric and propaganda against the imperialist aggressive U.S. is so blatant that it makes me furious. But the question is what is their real heartbeat? What is their real intent? I don't think the United States has anything to fear from China. The talk about how we lost China infuriates the Chinese and now it infuriates me. I can see where it is very clearly wrong. China was not ours to lose and that has been part of the problem. . . .

---

*The day before he had to have a tooth drilled in a Chinese hospital.

*Following are diary notes kept while on a tour of some other cities in China. I was
particularly interested in seeing an oil field near Harbin.*

July 20, 1975

The man in charge of the Revolutionary Committee who greeted
us, named Min, young looking guy, maybe 33 or so, looking bright-
eyed and bushy-tailed. I asked him how they protected the derrick
men in the winter, and he said that they didn't put 'em inside, they
didn't enclose his platform up there, but the spirit of the work kept
him going and also that they protected him with excellent clothing,
work tools, etc. Great pride, obviously, in this oil field. Too early to get
a feel for it, but it made me a little homesick for Midland and made
me think how lucky George is to be going back to the oil business.

July 22, 1975

There seemed to be still the same amount of spitting and coughing and belching as in other parts of China. In reading Barbara Tuch-
man's book, Chiang Kai-shek campaigned for awhile against these
things, but obviously he was not overly successful. Somehow it's not
offensive at all, although the spitting can get you down in Peking.

Taching in the afternoon: we went to the refinery, and then took a
train—we sat in an old-time car, very, very old, which was half dining car and half soft coach. But it was very clean. The toilet, an old
trench-type unit, was spic and span.

. . . We had a long discussion led by Mr. Lin about the difference
between capitalism and their system. I asked him why they needed a
valve factory in Taching—why they didn't use a central one and simply ship the valves in—that it seemed to me that [their system] might
be inefficient. . . . He made some comments that I thought seemed
critical of "the profit" motive. We were motivated for profit. I emphasized competition was the thing that resulted in services being furnished at the lowest possible cost to the consumer, that if you were
going to buy valves in the United States you would go to several manufacturers and get bids and then you would buy the cheapest price.
He kept using the word "profit" as something bad, and I kept using
the word "competition" as something that should result in profit but
that resulted in benefit to the consumer. We had a long discussion. I
asked about firing people. I asked him how a man that was ineffective
could be fired. I said, suppose the man in charge of drilling in Taching, the number one person, is ineffective, and therefore his units

produce less, he completes fewer wells—he's a good guy, people like him, but he's ineffective—what would happen. The answer was that he would be criticized and helped by the masses, but if in the final analysis he didn't produce he could be replaced by the State.

I asked if a worker simply was lazy, if he was transferred up from some other part of China and didn't like it and just decided—I used the example, suppose the girl we saw, instead of being able and energetic, which she obviously was, was lazy, she was homesick, and she just decided to sleep in past six o'clock when everybody else was up looking after the wells—what would happen then. They all laughed enormously at that and said that her colleagues would work with her to overcome that. And then I kept pressing on it and said that suppose she didn't overcome it. Then they conceded there would be disciplinary action taken.

. . . These kinds of discussions with the Chinese—they seemed very interested in them, and its the kind of things I wish we could do every day. It does increase understanding, and it does make us have a better feel for their system. But these visits of that nature are almost impossible in Peking. That's one of my great regrets, that you cannot sit down and, as the kids would say, "rap" with Chinese officials on any substantive matter.

―――――――

Our fall was consumed with preparing for and then hosting two high-profile visits to Peking. Henry Kissinger came first to plan for the visit of President Ford himself. A lot of the following correspondence concerns those two visits.

For [Brent] Scowcroft
From George Bush

Last year when the Secretary's plane rolled up to the ramp I was standing next to Nancy Tang. The door opened and quite a few security people came down the stairs before the Secretary got off the plane.

Nancy Tang rather pointedly commented on this to me, making the point that she felt the number of security personnel was excessive. China does pride itself on the safety of foreign friends here in this country.

Perhaps a way can be found to have the security people be not quite so conspicuous as the Secretary de-planes. This is a small matter of a cosmetic nature but since it was mentioned very directly by Nancy Tang it might be worth some thought. Warm Regards.

―――――――

Oct. 29, 1975

Dear T.L. [Tom Lias],

The Kissinger visit went well. He was much more gracious to me than ever before. Meeting Mao Tse Tung was a thrill of a life time. He is old and has a ghastly speech problem, but still sharp. The adulation on the face of the Chinese in the room was unbelievably worshipful. . . .

I have been very happy here since coming back in Sept.* I wonder if it's the escapist in me. For first time I feel I am accomplishing something. The Chinese seemed to reflect a confidence to HK which was nice. We are excited about our kids coming out here for Christmas . . .

China thinks we are falling apart—a paper tiger (not quite), a country whose principles are hazy and whose discipline and order are in chaos. . . .

Best
GB

————

Our kids never came for Christmas. They didn't have to. Instead, we unexpectedly went home.

NOVEMBER 2, 1975

TO: SECRETARY KISSINGER AND FOR THE PRESIDENT
           THROUGH SECRETARY KISSINGER
FROM: George Bush

Your message came as a total and complete shock. I have followed from afar some of the debate on the agency† but I am totally incapable of assessing the entire situation from way out here.

Here are my heartfelt views.

First, I wish I had some time to talk to one or two close friends about this matter.

Second, I do not have politics out of my system entirely and I see this as the total end of any political future.

Third, I cannot from out here, half way around the world, measure the mood on the Hill as to my nomination for this new job.

Fourth, I sure wish I had time to think and sort things out.

Henry, you did not know my father. The President did. My Dad inculcated into his sons a set of values that have served me well in my own short public life. One of these values quite simply is that one should serve his country and his President.

*I had taken a whirlwind trip back to Washington.
†The CIA.

And so if this is what the President wants me to do the answer is a firm "YES". In all candor I would not have selected this controversial position if the decision had been mine, but I serve at the pleasure of our President and I do not believe in complicating his already enormously difficult job.

There are some matters both professional and personal that I think should be understood or considered:

First, on the professional side: One, I would like the freedom to select my own top deputy and small personal staff in consultation with the President.

This I feel is absolutely essential.

Two, I would want it totally understood that I would have free and direct access to the President in conjunction with my new duties. I would not abuse this access but I would want to know it is there at all times.

Three, I believe, with all my fiber, in a strong CIA. I have been appalled at some of the attacks on the agency just as I have been appalled at some of the Agency's excesses that have become public. I am confident that the President shares these views that the USA must retain a strong, well financed intelligence capability.

I can not tell when I would be expected to come back for hearings, confirmation, etc. My personal views, which are clearly secondary to the President's desires, are that I would like to remain here until the first of the year. I would definitely like to stay here through the President's visit. I realize neither of these things may be possible.

On the diplomatic side there is something to be said for a reasonable period to say farewell to a job I have loved, to a land that I have found totally consuming and fascinating, and to people who, inspite of our enormous differences, have befriended me.

In conclusion the President should know that when President Nixon summoned me from the U.N. to Camp David on but another of those helicopter journeys that shook things up after the '72 elections Bar said to me "George, do anything except one thing—Don't accept if he says he wants you to head the Republican National Committee."

I said I wouldn't and I did.

Today this message came in. We were on our bikes back home when a messenger found us. We cycled back to the house, I whipped open the message. Tears came to her eyes and she said "Remember Camp David, I think I know your answer;" and I do know the answer. It is, with only the conditions expressed, an enthusiastic "I Accept."

For the President—Thank you for this honor. I will work my heart out.

Warm regards
George Bush

CHAPTER 7

Protecting Secrets

Although I would not become director of the CIA until January, it immediately overwhelmed our lives. Everything else became almost secondary, even finishing my job in China. The CIA was awash in controversy, accused of everything from assassination plots to attempts to overthrow governments. And suddenly, I was to be in charge.

———————

NOVEMBER 3, 1975

TO: BRENT SCOWCROFT
FROM: GEORGE BUSH

1. My thanks to you and Henry for your warm words. I think it will be tough but feel it is so important to try to get the CIA off the front pages and take the tough steps necessary to restore that agency to its deserved place of confidence.

2. If indeed all signals are go and those limited conditions I outlined in my cable of acceptance are agreeable I have one very personal request.

3. It occurs to me that my kids and family may have some understandable misgivings about this new direction in our family life.

4. Therefore, prior to the announcement I would ask that you tell Pete Roussel in the White House about this and ask him to convey the following message by phone to our five children and to my mother:

5. "The President has asked us to leave China. He wants me to head the CIA. I said yes. This new job will be full of turmoil and controversy and Mum and I know that it will not make things easy for you. Some of your friends simply won't understand. There is ugliness and turmoil swirling around the agency

obscuring its fundamental importance to our country. I feel I must try to help. I hope you understand. Soon we can talk it over. Love."*

6. Just now a call came in from the US from I believe CBS. I only heard the beginning of the callers words linking me to the CIA and fortunately we got cut off. I will not take any calls.

7. The VOA† just carried a story of Def Sec Schlesinger leaving and secstate giving up the NSC slot. As soon as possible I would appreciate you filling me in on the shifts. I would like to know with whom I will be working.‡

8. Thanks Brent. I look forward to working with you and learning from you.

9. Warm Regards.

George Bush

NOVEMBER 6, 1975

FOR: BRENT SCOWCROFT
FROM: GEORGE BUSH

1. Unless I am required back there for hearings, I am now totally convinced that it would be better to remain here, giving no visible attention to my new job until totally free of my responsibilities here.

2. It is hard to read Chinese reaction to this new appointment. In a sense they should like it, for they at least might feel that I have been exposed more than most to their strongly held view about the Soviet threat.

3. On the other hand in a tiny little incident Tuesday a Chinese guide escorting a British visitor here in Peking, knowing the visitor had been to my house, commented that he was "very shocked" about Mr. Bush's appointment, concluding that I had been associated with the Agency all along and that it was therefore shocking that I had been Ambassador at the UN and Chief in Peking. Other than this very low level isolated incident we have no indication as to how Chinese will feel. We doubt this is the line that PRC will be providing cadres but I report it as the very first Chinese reaction to my appointment of which we are aware.

4. Nevertheless I have now concluded that if I am called back for [congressional] hearings before the President's visit, which I fervently hope will not

---

*George W. wrote us a letter on behalf of all the kids, giving us their full support. "I look forward to the opportunities to hold my head high and declare ever so proudly that yes, George Bush, super spook, is my Dad and that yes I am damn glad for my country that he is head of the agency."

†Voice of America.

‡There were many other changes afoot. Scowcroft was going to replace Kissinger as National Security Council (NSC) adviser; Kissinger, who remained as secretary of state, had been doing double duty. Donald Rumsfeld was replacing James Schlesinger as secretary of defense.

happen, serious thought should be given to my not returning to Peking. The Chinese conceivably might find that embarrassing. . . .

George Bush

I still had a job to do in China, especially since President Ford's long-anticipated trip to Peking was looming.

NOVEMBER 6, 1975

FOR: SECRETARY KISSINGER
FROM: GEORGE BUSH
SUBJECT: THE PRESIDENT'S VISIT

The mood in our recent brief meetings with foreign minister Chiao Kuan-Hua has been noticeably chilly. There has been no small talk and no relaxed opening sentences, only "Let's proceed with the business at hand." On Tuesday, Chiao delivered the PRC reply delaying the advance and the announcement and offered a seemingly gratuitous lecture on the need for airing differences. He rejected our communiqué draft out of hand, said again he would not care if there were no communiqué, and seemed to move away from the "we have time" theme to the hoary "you owe us a debt." (his emphasis in this last point seemed curiously out of step with that of Chairman Mao on the Taiwan question.)*

All this may merely be tactical posturing designed to strengthen the PRC negotiating position prior to the visit. However, I doubt this is the case, and it would be prudent in any case to assume that the Chinese will employ some fairly unpleasant language, both in public and in private, during the President's visit. Given the probable cost at home to the President for having to subject himself to this and the limited likelihood that there will be any forward movement on Sino-US relations, I would incline toward postponing the visit if there were a genuinely legitimate reason to do so. (At this late date, of course, this seems highly unlikely and I do not advocate putting the visit off.)

The question at hand is how to best respond to tough Chinese statements on their view of the world scene, détente, and the Taiwan issue in a way that minimizes the dangers for the President without unduly disturbing our bilateral relationship. I would suggest the President come armed with a general exposition of US support for the Shanghai communiqué† and hopes for the world—peace, freedom, equality, etc. . . . If the Chinese escalate further by

---

*Mao would say, "One, ten, one hundred years" to solve the Taiwan problem.

†The Shanghai Communiqué was the statement issued by President Nixon and Premier Chou En-lai during Nixon's historic visit to China in 1972. Much of it dealt with Taiwan, and the United States carefully agreed with the view of Chinese on both the mainland and on Taiwan that there was but "one China" and the issue should be settled by the Chinese themselves.

openly suggesting they may use military force to "liberate" Taiwan, it seems to me there is no alternative to the President's insisting that any settlement will have to be by peaceful means. The President can hardly afford to subject himself to public or private Chinese tirades on these critical issues without replying in some way, but we see no reason to spend our time merely responding to their statements. . . .

Given the current Chinese frostiness, I think the President in both his private and public statements should strive to leave the Chinese leaders and the world audience with the unmistakable impression that Gerald Ford is a straight-talking man, contemptuous of overblown rhetoric, and a man who sets policy based on our own view of what is right and of our interests. All should know that the President is a good decent man, but one who can be tough as nails with the Soviets, the Chinese, or others when necessary. Needless to say, he (and other members of the party) should avoid effusive praise of the Chinese and their system or too many diplomatic niceties during banquet speeches which may be in answer to or followed by Chinese lectures on the poor state of the world and American impotence.

Warm Regards,
George Bush

November 6, 1975

Tom Lias
Department of Health, Education & Welfare
Washington, D.C.
Dear Tom:

. . . I wish I had been able to talk to you before making the tough decision I had to make recently. I think this probably spells the end to all politics. Certainly I will not approach the new job with any politics in mind. I think it is a political graveyard, and perhaps that's the way it should be. In any event, I have a strange contentment about it, even though it means a lot of unpleasantness and turmoil.

See you soon.

Warmest regards,
George Bush

A note to my three brothers and sister:

Dear Pres, Buck, Nancy, John,

Pardon the joint message. It occurs to me that my controversial new job may cause concern—if not to you, to some of your kids. No I can't see (5-year old) Billy* bitching about the CIA to his peers, but for the older ones, it might not be easy.

It's a graveyard for politics, and it is perhaps the toughest job in government right now due to abuses of the past on the one hand, and an effort to weaken our capability on the other. Besides, it's not always a clean and lovely business.

I am convinced it is important.

I know we will be thrust into ugly controversy—my intentions and character will be questioned.

But overriding all this is what I perceive to be a fundamental need for an intelligence capability second to none. It's a tough, mean world and we must stay strong. My year here has given me a chance to think and to observe. . . .

When the cable came in I thought of "Big Dad"—what would he do, what would he tell his kids— I think he would have said, "it's your duty."

It is my duty and I'll do it.

I love you all.

Pop

NOVEMBER 7, 1975

FOR: JACK MARSH†
FROM: GEORGE BUSH

I would appreciate your evaluation of the situation on the Hill.

I have noted some comments by Frank Church.‡ Perhaps you could ask him to withhold his fire until we have the hearings. I will leave that to you. Maybe it's better to let him pop off.

In talking to the Senators you can emphasize for me my total commitment to laying politics totally aside. I have done it at the UN, I have done it in China, and I recognize that it is essential to do that in the new job.

It would also be fair to mention, if necessary, that in my two diplomatic jobs I have dealt extensively with the product of the CIA and have a feel for its mission.

As for cooperating with Congress I will follow the President's guidelines as spelled out in his press conference. I do believe in the absolute essentiality of a strong agency. . . .

Thanks,
George Bush

*My brother Jonathan's son.

†Jack was a counselor to the President and helped shepherd me through the confirmation process. He later became secretary of the army.

‡Senator Frank Church, chairman of the Senate Select Committee on Intelligence Activities, was being vocal about his opposition to my CIA appointment, saying it was too political. Newspaper columnists were hammering away on the same point.

_____

We heard from a lot of friends who were worried about what lay ahead. I wasn't sure myself. I wrote this note to Bill Steiger:

Nov. 9, 1975

Dear Bill,

I wish I had been free to talk, really free, when your typically considerate call came in.

Of course I have mixed emotions—I think it is and perhaps should be, the political end. I was <u>not</u> told when I was asked to decide on the CIA that Rocky was going to step out.* I was given no options. I was asked to take on the CIA—I agreed. I agreed because of a fundamental sense of duty . . . It's just that uncomplicated.

It will be tough on our kids, I am afraid. But, Bill, in this job and at the UN I saw first hand—clearly—the need for an intelligence capability second to none.

How you stay strong while ridding the system of outrageous excesses is the tough one—but trying, though tough on the lower duodenum, will be worthwhile.

I honestly feel my political future is behind me—but hell, I'm 51, and this new one gives me a chance to really contribute.

I have a gut feeling there were some behind the scenes politics—but now all that doesn't matter. I will give this my all—I'll tell our fair weather friends who will be embarrassed by all of this—hell with you. To our close friends like you-Jan, I'll be grateful always for your support. So will Bar. She's shed a few tears . . . But she now sees, that in spite of the ugliness around the CIA, there's a job to be done.

I can tell you, as my friend, it would have been nice if it had been something else but it wasn't, it's this, and I'm ready.

Look at it this way—you are guaranteed a few free Sunday burgers. See, it's not all bad. . . .

GB

_____

November 18, 1975

Dear Gerry [Bemiss],

God your letter was kind. The new job, controversy and all, will be tough but a good one. I can't assess the columnist 'flak' and what that means in the

_____

*Vice President Rockefeller would not be on the GOP ticket in 1976.

Senate, but I am at peace. I'll go up there—lay it out from the heart and I think they'll want me.

If not—well I won't take it personally.

We have loved our life here—so different from the stormy future, so we are clinging to each day and moment before we leave.

I have firm convictions about our own country's cynicism. I'd love to have a small part in righting that—

Gratefully
GB

———

The following Message is from Ambassador George Bush and is to be passed to Director William Colby:*

Dear Bill:

I have the utmost respect for the job you have been doing.

I have not yet been fully advised on matters of timing, but needless to say, if you are agreeable, I would appreciate enormously the chance to have some good long chats with you. I am coming into this post at a time that could be less difficult, but I realize full well that without your endless months of selfless service the job I am about to enter would be one hell of a lot rougher.

I will try and to live up to the high standard of decency and excellence you have set for this job and for the agency.

Good luck in the future, Hope to see you soon.

———

November 20, 1975

FOR: EYES ONLY JACK MARSH
FROM: GEORGE BUSH

. . . The thing that must be stressed in talking to the Senators is character and integrity, thus the ability to lay partisanship aside in a non-partisan job. The UN experience can be stressed here plus my role in China.

. . . There are several incidents of my having to resist White House pressure during Watergate times that Tom Lias . . . can give you if you need them without giving details to Senators, which I will do if necessary. The theme should be emphasized that Bush did withstand WH pressure, but did not do it glamorously on the front pages. I will approach my CIA job in the same way.

Further point should be made that someone with some feel for public opinion might better keep Agency out of illegal activities.

As the argument of rubber stamp for President, some might make the

*The man I would be replacing at the CIA.

point that being "close to the President" is asset rather than liability. The views of the Agency might get a better Presidential hearing this way. But in the final analysis it comes back to character and integrity as to whether one knuckles under or not on matters of deep conviction. I will continue to avoid discussions along these lines with press or others, but perhaps this general thinking may be useful in quieting some of the critics.

One absurdity that you might like to squelch is the idea that the President rethought the nomination and thus asked Colby to stay on. I could not possibly have left before the President's visit. It would have been gratuitously insulting to the PRC in my opinion.

Frankly I'd love to have been there to tackle the problem and I think the delay has permitted the columnists all to 'pile on' but perhaps that point can be made that at times one must do what is proper and right. . . .

> Warm Regards.
> George Bush

Perhaps the best advice I received came from President Nixon. "What you have been through before will look like a cakewalk compared to what you will now be confronted with," he wrote. He told me not to "give away the store" by promising too much during my hearings. He told me to stand up for the CIA and its important work.

> Dec. 4, 1975

Dear Mr. President,

Your letter about the CIA job was delivered here yesterday.

I couldn't agree more. We must not see the Agency compromised further by reckless disclosure.

I can't tell you how much I appreciate your taking the time to give me your views on the job that lies ahead.

The President's trip has gone well. He leaves tomorrow morning.

The Chinese leadership always speaks respectfully of you.

I am sorry to miss Julie and David in Peking.

We have been <u>extremely</u> happy here but now we must move on. Thanks so much.

> Sincerely,
> George

President Ford did a terrific job during his visit to China. Although there were no major pronouncements (and none were expected), he managed to smooth out some rough edges and put the U.S.-China relationship back on track. Almost as soon as President Ford headed back to the States, so did we. I wrote the staff we left behind:

December 7, 1975

40,000' between Tokyo and Honolulu

Dear Friends,

We are relaxing now. Fred wolfed down his dinner at Tokyo and now, I hope, he's having pleasant dreams of harassing David, Robert, John & Evan.* He will miss USLO—and that brings me to the point.

To all the entire USLO family, American and Chinese, our heartfelt thanks for an unforgettable year of happiness. We shall miss you all. I will always be grateful for your service to this great country of ours and I will treasure the friendship you have given all the Bushes.

Good luck, God speed, and thanks for so much—

George Bush
ex-chief

Oh yes the party and our presents—the airport send off complete with great kids—do you think Mr. Lin Ping† thinks it's OK if my eyes got a little wet as I climbed up the ramp? Maybe it was the cold—GB

I typed this draft of my opening remarks before the Senate confirmation hearings, which we squeezed in before Christmas:

> The Charge: Will not be able to stand up against White House Pressure because a politician— former Chairman of GOP.
>
> This charge has been levied and has been enlarged to include the 'politicization' of the CIA.
>
> First, I think it is wrong to suggest that a person who has participated in purely partisan politics cannot set that aside and be fair and independent of partisan politics when he or she embarks on a new undertaking.
>
> I have served in two responsible jobs dealing with Foreign Affairs—Ambassador at the U.N. and Chief of USLO in Peking. In neither of these jobs did I 'politicize' the mission. I laid politics aside.

---

*David Bocskor, Robert Booth, John Chornyak, and Evan Dewire, the State Department security officers assigned to the liaison office.

†A Chinese national who worked at the USLO.

I will do the same in this new job. To set the record straight let me set out my intention to keep the Agency totally free from domestic politics. I will not attend political meetings. I will not discuss domestic politics as it relates to myself.

I view being head of the CIA as negative factor in terms of one's own political future.

I will not agree that I will never, ever again, participate in politics. I don't think any American should be asked to state that he won't participate in the political process ever in the future.

I will say that I am not a candidate for Vice President. I will not discuss this matter with my political friends. I will not encourage any such talk directly or indirectly and I state here and now I am not seeking the Vice Presidency and to the degree there has been public speculation about it, that speculation should end. I am not available. When confirmed for this job I will give it my all, without any thought of trying to make political mileage.

Second, the charge has been made or the worry expressed that I might not be independent enough to withstand White House pressure or to strongly go to bat for a point of view which the Agency is totally agreed upon but that is known to be out of favor by the President.

I have worked closely with the President in the past—both when I was a member of Congress and when I was Chairman of the Party. To me this should not be a liability as far as the Agency goes, but a plus. I will have access to the President. He knows that I can forcefully present matters that I believe in and I know that he will be fair in giving our views proper consideration.

When I was Chairman of the GOP I was asked to do certain things at the Committee that I didn't think were correct. I resisted White House pressure then, and in the highly unlikely event, the Agency was asked to do something that I viewed as against the laws of this Country or something that would weaken or cheapen the agency, I would resist again . . .

The Charge—Has had no experience in this field.

I might have to plead part guilty to this charge. I am not schooled in espionage. I am not intimately familiar with all the workings of the CIA. Nor have I had much personal contact with other intelligence agencies that would have given me a total insight as to how they work.

On the other hand I have served in two important diplomatic assignments. In both of these I have had access to analysis done by the CIA. I think I have a clear picture of what good intelligence can do and should do.

As to the charge itself. The Rockefeller Commission made the suggestion that "Persons appointed to the position of Director of Central Intelligence should be individuals of stature, independence, and integrity. In making this appointment, consideration should be given to individuals from outside the career services of the CIA, although promotion from within should not be barred."

Having had serious responsibilities in foreign affairs, having sat in on Cabinet meetings for four years running, I feel that I have a proper sense of the role of the agency. I appreciate its fundamental importance.

I also feel that with a rather broad background in public life which includes four years in Congress I am sensitive to the proper demands in this country that the Agency in the future not engage in the excesses of the past.

I have had enough management experience in business and in public life that I believe I know how to run an organization.

I must earn the confidence of my peers at the Agency and I am well aware of that. I am not, however, overawed at the prospect.

I intend to provide leadership, strong leadership both to the Agency and to the coordinating efforts for all intelligence which is a vital part of my job; but I believe this can be done while accomplishing an equally important task. That is the restoration of confidence in the CIA from without, and the restoration of morale within.

January 3, 1976

MEMORANDUM
FOR: The President
FROM: George Bush
SUBJECT: Suggestions for Presidential Directive to the new Director-CIA

Since our last conversation I have had many intelligence briefings and I have read the various reform proposals that have been submitted to you, along with some that weren't submitted.

I have not felt free to attend official coordinating meetings, not wanting to put any pressure on Bill Colby who has been extraordinarily thoughtful to me. I do want, however, to give you some of my personal views, before any final decisions are made—decisions that clearly affect the conduct of my new job.

I have prepared twelve recommendations that you might want to include in a "letter of instruction" to the new Director of Intelligence. These recommendations do not require legislation. The list is not intended to be all-inclusive. . . .

A personal note: I am told that the Senate is going to act on my nomination soon after it comes back. Barbara and I plan to go to the Bahamas for one week commencing January 7th. Before that and after I will be in my EOB* office. I hope you and I will have a chance to visit in person before any final decisions are made. Hopefully, this could be done immediately upon my confirmation.

GENERAL OBSERVATIONS:

A. I hope whatever is done will not be too defensive. In my view the general theme should be:

Intelligence is vital to our country. We are making proposals to strengthen it and improve it. The President will see that abuses are eliminated and he will guarantee that we will maintain and strengthen our vital foreign intelligence capability.

B. I think you should move immediately to take certain steps that do not require legislation. This can best be done by a letter to the new Director along the lines of your previous letter to Bill Colby. It can be done at the same time as you propose legislative changes, but in any event it should be done shortly after I take office.

C. My specific twelve points follow.

Point 1.

The DCI will have access to all intelligence information. None shall be withheld from him, and when he asks for any information from any department it will be granted to him. The Director will take the appropriate steps to guarantee that information provided him is kept secret. . . .

Point 2.

The Director will have direct access to the President. The President instructs the Director to give him objective and independent intelligence without regard to any foreign policy considerations. The President expects the Director to work closely with the NSC, but the President wants it understood that the Director will have direct access to the President when he feels such access is necessary. . . .

Point 3.

The Director will be given Cabinet rank, but he will <u>not</u> attend Cabinet meetings unless they relate to foreign affairs.† . . .

Point 4.

The President reiterates his support for the Director as his top intelligence offi-

---

*An office in the Old Executive Office Building, in the White House complex.

†President Ford disagreed with this point and did not give me cabinet rank. He was absolutely right. I attended only those cabinet meetings where I was needed. On the other hand, President Reagan did give his CIA director, William Casey, cabinet rank, and Casey often annoyed the other cabinet members by interfering with domestic affairs. I did not give either of my very able CIA directors—William Webster and Robert Gates—cabinet rank.

cer and instructs him to meet from time to time with the Secretaries of State and Defense as well as the head of the NSC in order to insure the President of maximum cooperation between the producers and the users of intelligence.*
Point 5.
The President plans to appoint an additional Deputy for CIA. He instructs the Director to have one Deputy concern himself with managing the agency under the direction of the Director. The other Deputy would concern himself primarily with coordination of the Intelligence Community for the Director. . . .
Point 6.
The President instructs the Director to renew his efforts in the resource field for the entire community. The President will look to the Director for maximum effort to eliminate waste and unnecessary duplication regarding resources of both money and manpower. The Department of Defense is instructed to provide the Director with maximum cooperation in this regard. . . .
Point 7.
The Director will not have as priority the tactical intelligence field. Tactical intelligence has been and should continue to be the priority concern of defense intelligence. The Director shall be alert to eliminate wasteful duplication in the entire Intelligence Community, however. . . .
Point 8.
The Director should give immediate attention to housing his Intelligence Community Staff in a location separate from CIA Headquarters at Langley . . .
Point 9.
The Director is instructed to give maximum attention to cooperating with Congress. Where there undoubtedly will be some matters of difference between the Executive and the Legislative Branches and the Director is expected to follow Presidential directives to the letter when disputes arise, the Director is instructed to work closely with the appropriate authorities in Congress on matters relating to national intelligence.
Point 10.
The Director is instructed to make a thorough review of all CIA instructions that have been issued over the years regarding guidelines for proper conduct of intelligence matters. He should take any additional reform steps that he deems necessary. Many reforms have already been implemented by Director Colby, but the President wants direct assurance from the new Director that he has done everything in his power to guard against the abuses that have damaged the Intelligence Community. . . .

*The director of the CIA (DCI) not only is the head of that particular agency, but also coordinates intelligence activities of other government agencies, such as the Department of State, Department of Defense, FBI, etc. They all come under an umbrella organization called the Intelligence Community, which had a separate staff that reported to the DCI.

Point 11.

The Director, working closely with the NSC, is instructed to take the initiative in finding more satisfactory "cover" arrangements for CIA personnel operating abroad. Appropriate departments of government are instructed to give full cooperation to the Director. . . .

Point 12.

Covert Action. The President instructs the Director that no covert action be initiated without signed formal approval of the 40 Committee* and direct Presidential instruction. . . .

[For the most part, except for giving me cabinet status, President Ford agreed with these suggestions and they were enacted.]

March 6, 1976

Dear Henrietta,†

. . . Bar and I were homesick for USLO when we got your letter. I'm a little jealous—Mr. Guo driving for Thayer,‡ Mr. Wong sitting there waiting for someone new when we consider him a part of our family, and Mrs. Tang as well.

My life is hectic and full, but when things get really rushed or when I get really tired, I get enormous restful pleasure from thinking of our happy days in Peking.

I have been disturbed over the furor of the Nixon visit, mainly because I don't think the Chinese intended anything bad by it. It played so badly over here in the papers that I'm afraid they will think we don't value our relationship with them.§

. . . Bar shed a tear over your description of the ministers. We miss them too. I don't know how you could convey that to them, but please do it.

C. Fred has stopped fighting; at least he no longer gets into losing situations by challenging every big dog in sight. All in all, he is a happy guy. He's forgetting his Chinese pretty fast and taken up Spanish again, so he can get along well

---

*The 40 Committee operated within the framework of the National Security Council and was made up of a group of undersecretaries from the various departments.

†Henrietta Morris, a dedicated career Foreign Service secretary, who served with us in China.

‡Harry Thayer, who was my number two, was acting chief at the liaison office.

§President and Mrs. Nixon were in China, which was controversial at home. It came during the primary season when former California governor Ronald Reagan was challenging President Ford for the GOP presidential nomination. At that time, Reagan felt both Ford and Nixon had been too accommodating to China.

with Paula.* He's still a bit of a "sellout" whenever a brother or sister returns home. He deserts his place at the bottom of our bed and promptly moves in with whomever descends upon our house. It's not your basic infidelity, but it does show a lack of concern for his mother who gets highly upset over this.

Now, Henrietta, when you come to Washington, remember a big steak awaits you at the Bushes along with a cozy evening so that we can hear all about China—firsthand. Indeed, if you need a sack, there are plenty at our house. . . .

Warm regards,

> Sincerely,
> George Bush

––––––––––

(Note: For the purposes of writing this book, the CIA graciously let us go through my DCI files that are still classified. Most of the documents we requested were declassified, but portions of some documents had to be redacted in order to protect what we call in the intelligence business "sources and methods." In the interest of authenticity, those sections that were blacked out are reflected in the relevant documents.)

MEMORANDUM FOR: THE RECORD
SUBJECT: Meeting with the President,
            Thursday, 11 March 1976
            8:15 to 8:50 a.m.

I talked to him about my European trip and told him that I would like to report to him when I get back on the state of play with our foreign intelligence services. I was somewhat worried about cooperation, not by the services, but by people abroad generally, and by the effect that the hearings† may have had on our relationships, and though, officially, things were in good shape, there were some indications that some of those who have cooperated with us have been genuinely concerned. . . .

China: We talked about the need to get the information from Nixon. The matter was still rather dicey and tense. I showed him the cable xxxxxxxxx xxxxxxxxxxxxxxxxxx The President read the entire cable. I gave it to him to show that China was indeed trying to send a signal to us that they wanted good relations, etc. Following the meeting I had a discussion with Scowcroft . . . on Freedom of Information problems that relate to the release of the Pres-

––––––––––

*Paula Rendon, our longtime housekeeper, who came to us right after Doro was born.

†I am referring here to the congressional hearings during the last several years that had examined and for the most part greatly criticized the CIA; hearings that had also disclosed sensitive information, thus making getting cooperation from abroad much more difficult.

ident's written report from Nixon. The report of the conversations can be classified, but there is some question as to Nixon's observations being classified. To all concerned I keep insisting that we get access to the information. The problem apparently is that Nixon will only talk to either Scowcroft, Kissinger, or me. . . .

I mentioned possible coups in Thailand, Argentina and Peru. . . .

The President asked how I liked my job. I told him that I liked it very much, was getting good support, and that I felt the whole matter "would work." I told him that this might come as a surprise to him and that though I was obviously interested in the elections, that I found I was picking up the paper and looking at items of much more direct concern and only glancing at the political content of the paper. I'm not sure he believed this, but it is certainly true.

I told him these meetings were very, very important to the entire Intelligence Community. The President is relaxed and is always most gracious with his time, and interested.

George Bush
Director

———

March 12, 1976

MEMORANDUM FOR ALL CIA EMPLOYEES

As Director of Central Intelligence I am determined that the Central Intelligence Agency conduct its activities in strict adherence to its legislative charter, to applicable laws, Executive Orders, and appropriate National Security Council Directives. Only by such adherence both to the spirit and letter of the law can the Agency continue to serve the People of the United States by properly carrying out its mission to contribute to the national security.

A CIA regulation requires that any employee who has knowledge of past, current, or proposed CIA activities that might be construed to be illegal, improper, questionable, or outside CIA's legislative charter, inform the Director or Inspector General immediately.

I expect each employee to comply with the regulation. You may report any information relating to these matters directly to me or to the Inspector General at any time.

George Bush

———

I want to share with you excerpts from a speech I wrote (the occasion was the Commemoration of the Revolutionary Battle of Guilford Courthouse in North Carolina) in which I said plainly how I felt about the Agency:

March 14, 1976

Intelligence is a demanding craft. I have not been in this business for very long, but already I can tell you a few things I have learned. One is that the quality of the people I have met—at the Central Intelligence Agency and in the other parts of the Intelligence community—gives me great confidence. I am impressed with the competence and dedication of the people in our intelligence community. They are professionals in the finest sense of the word. I might add that the spread of academic skills is remarkable. The CIA alone has enough PhDs to stock a university faculty with everything from historians and economists to mathematicians and aeronautical engineers.

Another thing you should know: I am convinced that the CIA and the intelligence community are under control and doing their jobs. The agency indeed made some mistakes in the past. I am not here to defend them. But I am here to tell you that the agency itself rooted out those errors and put an end to them well before they were publicly revealed.

. . . Let me tell you another thing I have learned about the CIA. Its employees have very deeply ingrained pride and loyalty. They also have an extraordinary sense of duty. It is my belief that the guidelines laid down by the President will be followed to the letter. I have made a personal commitment to see that this is so.

. . . There is no substitute for honesty. There is no substitute for conscience. There is no substitute for common sense.

It is not fashionable in these days of tearing down our institutions to say, "trust me." Yet Americans have to have faith and trust in some degree or none of our governmental systems will work. I do believe that oversight of the intelligence community is necessary, and I strongly support the new measures set out by the President. I welcome the responsible exercise of oversight by the congress as well.

But it still comes down to a basic fact. You cannot conduct an intelligence agency out in the open. There must be secrecy. Much of what we do can and should be shared with the public and all branches of the government.

In this job I will cooperate as fully as possible with the congress, but there are certain pieces of information that must not be divulged—and they won't be. I don't think that the American people really want reckless disclosure. Sometimes we lose sight of the fact that secrets are respected in many areas of our lives. Americans expect confidentiality at the ballot box. They expect it with their doctors and lawyers and clergymen. We have laws to protect certain business secrets and even to protect Department of Agriculture crop estimates. I am sure that no one in this audience thinks it is in our national interest to make public the war plans of the Department of Defense, or the in-chambers conversations of our Supreme Court.

I am confident that the vast majority of the American people support the need for protecting real intelligence secrets. I am completely committed to working for such protection. And I do not intend to use the over-worked words "secrecy" and "national security" to hide abuses or cover up mistakes. . . .

There is great misunderstanding about our work. As a result of the past year's revelations, both true and false, our intelligence failures—and there have been some—have been widely publicized. But the nature of our work is such that we can seldom talk of our many successes without revealing our "sources and methods." We do battle with kidnappers abroad; we struggle against a network of narcotics peddlers who try to spread their poisons in our country; we get information on the plans of other countries to inflate artificially the prices or control the supplies of vital raw materials; we resist the evils of communist intelligence services abroad. Every one of those things could affect you personally as well as our greater national interests. And it is the real mission of intelligence to see that our policy makers have solid information so they can move to frustrate the plans of those who would harm us.

. . . Our intelligence people have suffered a vicious battering. Their families have been under great pressure. Many of the charges have not been true. . . . I wish you could all have the chance to feel the spirit and pride I feel in the intelligence community. There is a dedication that is fully compatible with the spirit of Guilford Courthouse.

. . . In closing let me tell you about an incident that occurred shortly before I became the Director of Central Intelligence. A correspondent I know made the remark on a talk show that anyone dumb enough to take this job was too dumb to do it. He got a good laugh out of it among his fellow panelists—but to me it was a little sick. It displayed an appalling insensitivity to our legitimate national security needs.

We at the CIA are trying to conduct foreign intelligence, not to weaken our country, but to strengthen it. It's those who would disclose the names of our agents abroad; it's those who believe they can recklessly reveal classified documents; it's those who would dismantle the CIA, that in reality are damaging our country.

I wish you could talk to some of our employees whose heads are high after a couple of years of enormous attack. They are as vigorously opposed to the mistakes of the past as our strongest critics, but they have retained a perspective, they know the need for strong intelligence, and they are prepared to withstand the attacks, if that is necessary, to work for a cause they believe in.

I wish you could have met the son of Richard Welch, our station chief in Greece who was gunned down following disclosure of his name by people bent on destroying CIA. This young man knew well that his father had died for a cause in which he deeply believed.

If you could do these things, you would understand much about the fiber of our country in 1976 and you would understand much about the fiber of the patriots at Guilford Courthouse 195 years ago.

They are one. They are the same.

Despite the seriousness of my new job, I tried hard not to lose sight of what was important in life. This was for an article in Texas Monthly *about hamburgers.*

March 29, 1976

Mr. William Broyles, Editor
Texas Monthly
Austin, Texas 78767
Dear Bill,

Now about the hamburger!

We serve a pretty mean hamburger every Sunday at our house. I do the cooking, but when the going gets tough, I can press some of our kids into service if they're home.

Ingredients— just hamburger, a good grade beef. I base this on the theory, "let the meat do the talking."

Bread—I'm sorry but I go for the basic hamburger roll, toasted on the grill, but not too much.

I prefer a glass of ale with my hamburger. I've been going with the basic green can of Ballantine but I'm open for further suggestions.

Side dish— our lunches are usually very informal, paper plate style, but there is room for a frito or the potato chip.

We make our own burgers, and darn it I haven't been to Texas enough lately to check the burger out. It's not that I don't love burgers, but when I get to Texas I like a plate of barbecue at Otto's in Houston, postponing my love for the burger "til I get back to our house. . . .

Sincerely,
George Bush
Director

March 30, 1976

Mr. Robert W. Blake
Lubbock, Texas 79408
Dear Bob,

Great hearing from you on March 25th. I was delighted to get the word on George.* He's a hardworking guy with a lot of ambition and a fair degree of restlessness. Barbara and I just can't tell you how grateful we are for the interest you have taken in this kid. It means an awful lot. He respects you and respects your advice.

I'm delighted you're involved in politics again, but don't let it interfere with your fishing.

You and I keep talking about getting in a little hunting or fishing out there in West Texas. I have it very much on my mind, but I have never been so swamped in my life as I am in this job. I like it though—there's plenty to do and the work is fundamental to the security of our country, something that gives me great reassurance, even when I'm dog tired.

Love to all Blakes,

Sincerely,
George Bush

TO: xxxxxxxxx
REF: xxxxxxxxx
FROM: DCI

I wish to express my appreciation to you and your colleagues for the excellent intelligence you provided giving forewarning of the potentially very dangerous demonstration planned against the Embassy on 12 April. Through your efforts Ambassador Crawford† and the Department of State (as well as other members of the Intelligence Community) were alerted to the threat in time for them to be able to make representations to the Cypriot and Greek Governments to control the demonstration. The success of these efforts was a graphic illustration of the use to which good intelligence can be put. Good work.

Director

*George had been in Lubbock the day before on behalf of President Ford's campaign.
†William Crawford Jr., ambassador to Cyprus.

May 4, 1976

Mr. Jack Mohler*
Denver, Colorado 80202
Dear Jack,
    . . . I've never worked so hard in my life, and after three months here I con-
clude this is the most interesting job I've ever had. That includes [Congress],
the UN, Peking, and the RNC. There are great people, fascinating subjects to
get into, but just not enough time. Glad things are going well—stay in touch.
    Hastily, but with warmest regards,

                                        Sincerely,
                                        George Bush

————————

*I wrote this letter to my friend Tom Devine after my disastrous appearance before
the Overseas Press Club. They literally heckled me about the CIA, including
reports that some overseas journalists had been used as spies (which was true).*

May 12, 1976

Mr. Thomas Devine
New York, New York 10036
Dear T.,
    You're too kind. I really bombed at the Overseas Press Club. My excuse—
it's tough to talk to a group of press people after two hours of cocktails. The
only consolation was that they told me I did better than Schlesinger, who
talked 45 minutes the year before, and [Senator Henry] Jackson, who mono-
toned on for about 30 minutes the year before that. I still felt the evening was
a failure, and the only bright spot was getting an all too short glimpse of you
and Alex. Anyway, thanks for your kindness. Live and learn.
    We miss you, darn it!

                                        Sincerely,
                                        George Bush

————————

TO: xxxxxx
FROM: George Bush
    I had an inquiry from Dillon Ripley of the Smithsonian Institution saying
he had heard that Matilda the Musk Ox had joined Milton in heaven. Could
this possibly be true?
    Warm regards to all at USLO.

*An old friend, an ex-newspaperman who had worked on my 1970 Senate campaign.

_____

Ethel Kennedy had kindly asked me several times to play in the Robert F. Kennedy Pro-Celebrity Tennis Tournament at Forest Hills. "Rummy" is Defense Secretary Donald Rumsfeld.

June 21, 1976

Mrs. Ethel Kennedy
Hickory Hill
McLean, Virginia 22101
Dear Ethel,

It's not that I hoped I'd never hear from you again—not at all! In fact, riding a fairly impressive victory streak on the courts, I was hoping, for ego purposes, that I <u>would</u> hear from you again about the big Forest Hills event.

But, here's the dilemma. Each year you ask me and I end up saying "no" only because the date conflicts with the major event of the Tennis Year—the five-team Kennebunkport Open. Last year, two of my kids reached the finals. The "arrogance factor" subsequently has been so high that I must get in there and bring reason to those proceedings.

Besides, this event is the forerunner of the Father-Daughter event at Doro's school next fall and our team must hone its doubles play to a fine edge.

I'd love to be at Forest Hills—I am confident we could crush Rummy and partner; but, Ethel, I just can't do it.

All of our kids hope to be there in Maine that weekend and in these funny times we've got to hold it all together—real close.

Love and thanks.

Sincerely,
George Bush

_____

June 28, 1976

The Honorable W. Averell Harriman*
Washington, DC 20007
Dear Governor Harriman,

I just want to thank you for taking the time to come out here and have lunch. . . .

_____

*Harriman had a distinguished career in public service, including as the Democratic governor of New York and ambassador to the Soviet Union during World War II. He and his brother Roland were partners in my dad's Wall Street firm, Brown Brothers Harriman & Co., although Averell was not an active partner. Averell was a supporter of the CIA.

I know I speak for the entire Intelligence Community when I express my appreciation for your support for the mission of the CIA. I am totally dedicated to the concept that we must have a strong intelligence community—second to none in the world. I am equally dedicated to the fact that it must be run with total objectivity and with sensitivity to the changed times in which we are living. By the latter, I don't mean that we should be weak or afraid to move, but we must rethink carefully all facets of our operations.

Lastly, it was mighty magnanimous of you to mention the conversation you had with my Mother. I do have a "darling Mother." There has never been any doubt in the minds of the Bushes that the Harrimans are our close, warm friends. It meant a lot to my Dad and it means an awful lot to me.

Warmest Personal regards,

Sincerely,
George Bush

————

August 3, 1976

The President
The White House
Washington, D. C. 20500
Dear Mr. President:

I have been in my job as DCI exactly six months. Herewith a brief report on certain highlights, which is short enough to read but not long enough to be all inclusive.

A. CONGRESSIONAL APPEARANCES

I have made 30 official appearances before Committees on the Hill. This does not include 33 other meetings with Members of Congress or Congressional Staff.

The appearances before Congressional Committees require a good deal of pre-briefing time. We are trying to cooperate fully with Congress but I now report to seven Congressional committees. This is too much. I am pressing to implement your stated objective of more consolidated oversight, but neither House nor Senate is really striving to achieve this goal.

B. IMPLEMENTATION OF YOUR EXECUTIVE ORDER

We have implemented the Order. The Committee on Foreign Intelligence (CFI) has met 16 times. It is doing what you intended it do; namely, making budget decisions and setting priorities. . . . The system is working. . . .

C. AREAS OF PROGRESS

1. I believe CIA's relationship with the State Department is improving. At some echelons in State there is a lot of foot dragging, but thanks to great

cooperation from Dr. Kissinger and Larry Eagleburger,* we are getting better access to State xxxxxx and I am less concerned about our diminishing State xxxxxxxx than I was—though overall xxxxxx still plague us. I have had individual meetings with xxxxxx.

2. Morale at CIA is improving. As the excesses of the past investigations fade, things on the morale front improve. Our recruitment is up. Our people are willing to serve abroad and take the risks involved. The CIA is a disciplined organization—trained to support the director. During this 6 month period, I have made 12 changes in our top 16 slots at CIA. These personnel changes have helped revitalize our various Directorates. They have, I believe, been accomplished with a minimum of personal and institutional heartburn.

3. I feel I am getting first-class support at CIA and, for that matter, from the Intelligence Community.

4. We have an excellent relationship with the NSC staff. On the personnel side, I get total cooperation from Brent Scowcroft, for whom I have the highest personal regard.

5. To help morale as well as my own education, I try to meet with as many of our Station Chiefs as possible on an individual basis (33 such meetings to date); to appear before CIA groups at Langley (16 such meetings); and to visit Intelligence Community installations and contractor sites (21).

D. <u>AREAS OF MAJOR CONCERN</u>

1. There is too much disclosure. We are continually pressed by Congress, by the courts, by the Freedom of Information Act, to give up sensitive material. We are trying to hold the line but there is a continuous erosion which gives away classified information at home and complicates our liaison relationships abroad. I am frustrated by our inability to deal with the leaking of classified information.

2. The press continues to berate us, though I sense a slight improvement. xxxxxxxx said, "George, your problem is that our profession thinks you are all lying bastards." As long as this attitude prevails, there will be frivolous stories in print about CIA. I have made 21 public appearances but have turned down many more. I want to get the CIA off the front pages and at some point out of the papers altogether; thus, I have turned down many national media opportunities while accepting only a few. It is still almost impossible to have a speech containing positive things about CIA given prominent coverage.

3. The Congressional mood towards CIA is improving, but there is still a staff-driven desire to "expose" and to "micro-manage." Staffers demand more

---

*Larry was deputy undersecretary for management. During my administration, he was number two at the State Department under Jim Baker. After Jim resigned in 1992 to be White House chief of staff, Larry became the secretary of state and did a great job during the final months of my presidency.

and more. Our relationship with the new Senate Intelligence Committee is promising, though their many subcommittees give the appearance of many more investigations. The Staff of the House Appropriations Committee, on the other hand, gives appearances of wanting to run CIA.

E. <u>SUMMARY</u>

Things are moving in the right direction. There are an infinite number of problems stemming, some from the excesses of the investigations and some from the abuses of the past—real and alleged. Somehow the problems, however, seem more manageable. Our organization is good, our product is sound though it can always be improved. Some of our assets have been diminished, but the CIA is intact, and functioning pretty darn well.

> Respectfully,
> George Bush
> Director

> August 4, 1976

Mr. J. C. Mohler
Denver, Colorado 80202
Dear Jack,

I don't want you to think I was dead, but things have been hectic and I have been bad about personal correspondence.

That outrageous joke you sent me was opened by somebody else, much to my embarrassment. I have been bawled out by everyone and am just now getting over it. Plus Mohler, it wasn't that funny!

Here's one for you:

> The answer is, "Eddy Nelson."
> OK. What is the question?
> The question is, "How does Nelson Eddy
> list his name in the phone book?"

See, it's clean. (It occurs to me you might not get it!) But in any event, it won't get me in trouble with your secretary if she reads it.

Things are rocking along. I am staying the hell out of politics, but it isn't easy. . . .

> Sincerely,
> George Bush

As his party's candidate for President, Jimmy Carter was given the courtesy of national security briefings. The day of my second briefing with him, a newspaper article came out that said Carter had sort of a "hit list" of Ford appointees, accusing the President of using federal agencies as a "dumping ground" for washed-up

Republicans. Yes, I was on the list. Carter was furious and publicly said there was no such list (apparently a member of his staff had drawn up and leaked such a list), and he especially went out of his way to say nice things about the job I was doing at the CIA. I wrote him this note:

8-16-76

Dear Governor,

I appreciate the way you handled the little incident regarding me and the "list".

I just want you to know that as far as I'm concerned, you walked the 'extra mile', and in this screwy climate we're living in, that meant a lot to me— Everyone's got a certain pride factor and you helped keep mine intact—

These things do happen—

Thanks—

George

Thanks, too, for the hospitality at Plains—lunch etc. GB

August 16, 1976

Dear Neil [Mallon],

. . . I dictate this as the Republican Convention gets under way. I must confess to a certain nostalgia. When I see all my political friends charging around Kansas City, I have a twinge of regret—but only a twinge, for this work is fundamentally important and I comfort myself with the fact that I am very lucky to be here and to be surrounded by so much excellence.

Our briefings with Jimmy Carter have gone pretty well. The Agency intelligence officers that I had with me have done a first-class job. The briefings have been in his living room. Miss Lillian sticks her weathered face in (well preserved) and Rosalynn, the Governor's wife, fixes sandwiches for us. Amy runs around playing with the cat. It's all very homey, but there is no nonsense about the Governor. I am having some difficulty trying to figure out what the heartbeat really is there.

The family is in Maine; Mother never looked better, nor has she ever been more full of life. Neil is there for another week before going back to Tulane. He keeps singing your praise, and Ann's also. You have been so nice to him. Marvin goes to the University of Virginia the 28th, but those two will be replaced by Jebby and family and also George. Doro will stay there through Labor Day.

Hope all goes well.

Sincerely,

George

_____

August 17, 1976

Mr. John Fonteno*
Houston, Texas 77004
Dear John,

I got your letter. I'm sorry people don't understand my going to brief Jimmy Carter. The President has instructed me to do this so that Governor Carter will be as well informed as possible on all the happenings around the world. I am strongly in favor of this Presidential decision.

We are living in tough times and any candidate for President must be up to speed on where things actually stand in the world. If we don't have these kinds of briefings, Governor Carter would have to rely on the papers and other sources and he simply wouldn't be getting the most factual and up to date information on the terrible problems he would have to face should he become President.

. . . You are a good friend, John, and I am sorry our paths haven't crossed lately. I am glad you do understand the rigors of this job.

Love to your family.

Warm personal regards,

Sincerely,
George Bush

_____

August 19, 1976

Mr. Hugh Sidey
Time
Washington, D. C. 20006
Dear Hugh,

Maybe it is of little consequence, but I read your piece in the August 23rd edition of Time and I wanted to make a quick comment.

My position on Nixon was not that I "had to support" Nixon's contention of innocence, but rather that the system was working, and under the system a man was innocent until proven guilty.

I continued on through those two ghastly years of being chairman to try to separate the Party from Watergate. I am confident the record will reveal I spoke out over and over again against Watergate. I did, however, stop short of condemning the President until the final tape proved to me that he had been lying. At that point I urged him to resign.

*A loyal Republican.

I guess at this late date all of this matters little to anyone else, but the distinction is quite important to me.

I am writing this letter, not for publication, but rather as a personal letter from a friend who wants a guy he respects to know his feelings.

I hope our paths cross soon,

> Sincerely,
> George Bush

MEMORANDUM FOR THE RECORD
SUBJECT: Meeting with the President
                    8:00 a.m., 10 September 1976
ATTENDING: The President
                      General Scowcroft
                      George Bush
      The following subjects were discussed:

a. xxxxxxxxxxxxxxxxxxxxxxxxxxxxxxxxxxxxxxxxxxxxxxxxxxxxxxxxxxxxxxxxxxxxxxx

b. xxxxxxxxxxxxxxxxxxxxxxxxxxxxxxxxxxxxxxxxxxxxxxxxxxxxxxxxxxxxxxxxxxxxxxx

c. Warsaw Pact Intelligence. I briefed him on the xxxxxxxxxx item, showed him the plan and explained to him the intelligence benefits that could come from that. He thumbed through the plan and showed interest.

d. We discussed the BACKFIRE Bomber. I told him exactly what we planned to do and told him that there would not be a full community position soon. Briefed on Sandy McDonnell's visit to General Jones. Told him that, in my opinion, we would not get Community agreement. Went over the figures with him on BACKFIRE—differences between Air Force and CIA. He asked exactly what figures Brezhnev was using.*

e. China, the death of Mao. I showed the President the last page of the CIA June report on Mao's health. He read the paragraph about Mao's health and I made the point that CIA was on record predicting that he would not live through the year. . . .

f. Egypt/Libya. I went through the briefing paper on Egypt/Libya, explaining

---

*The Soviet's Backfire bomber was one of most controversial issues I had to deal with while DCI. There was huge disagreement in the intelligence community on the Backfire's capabilities—especially whether it had the range to reach the United States. Needless to say, it was important to know the truth, not only for national security but also for arms controls negotiation purposes. The CIA was accused of downplaying the Backfire's capabilities, which was ridiculous. I refer in this memo to Sandy McDonnell, president of McDonnell Douglas, who was advising us on the issue. General Jones is David Jones, head of the Air Force.

that there was less buildup and explaining Sadat's problems of having to do something. xxxxxxxxxxxxxxxxxxxxxxxxxxxxxx

g. Discussed the fact that Carlos* appeared to be in Yugoslavia.

h. xxxxxxxxxxxxxxxxxxxxxxxxxxxxxxxxxxxxxxxxxxxxxxxxxxxxxxxxxxxxxxxxxxxxx

i. xxxxxxxxxxxxxxxxxxxxxxxxxxxxxxxxxxxxxxxxxxxxxxxxxxxxxxxxxxxxxxxxxxxxx

George Bush

This letter appeared in the "Letters to the Editor" column of the September 27 issue of Aviation Week & Space Technology. *The topic again was the Backfire bomber, and whether the CIA had misrepresented its capabilities:*

The <u>Aviation Week & Space Technology</u> for Sept. 13th in the Washington Roundup section made reference to alleged manipulation of intelligence produced by the Central Intelligence Agency. It is regrettable that you had made no attempt to give us an opportunity to comment on the relevant portion of your report which impugns the integrity of the national foreign intelligence production process, of Secretary Kissinger, of myself as the President's chief intelligence adviser, and most important, of all the intelligence professionals who serve this country.

Specifically I have never received nor would I ever entertain a suggestion, from whatever source and for whatever reason, to slant the intelligence product. I would never consider abusing my authority as Director of Central Intelligence for the purpose of manipulating results of professional analysis of intelligence data. I have complete confidence that CIA and intelligence community analysts working on this type study would resign before they would do what your article suggests.

In one short article, Secretary Kissinger, CIA analysts and, by inference, myself, have been maliciously slandered. I hope you will try to partially correct the damage by printing this letter.

George Bush
Director
Central Intelligence Agency

Despite a last-minute surge in the polls, President Ford lost to Jimmy Carter. That meant even more detailed briefings for the new President-elect.

---

*It would be another twenty years before Carlos the Jackal, perhaps the most famous terrorist ever, would finally be apprehended.

MEMORANDUM FOR THE RECORD
SUBJECT: Meeting in Plains, Georgia
           19 November 1976, 1:00 to 2:00 p.m.
PRESENT: President-Elect Carter
           Vice President-Elect Mondale
           George Bush
           xxxxxxxxxxx

The following subjects were covered:

1. Personal. I discussed the DCI situation, expressing my strong view that the DCI should have direct access to the President; that the President should have confidence in the DCI; and that the organization at CIA and the Community would be strongly supportive of the President . . .

2. I briefed him generally on Agee* . . . although I did not go into all of that detail. I did make clear that he was being thrown out of England by the British, that I was concerned what would happen if he came back to this country and tried to get across to the President-Elect that Agee was not simply a disenchanted former CIA employee who wanted to clean up the Agency. Rather he was something much more sinister.

General Comments

As I look back on it, there is one strange thing. There was no comment and almost no questions during the entirety of the briefing above. The briefing lasted almost an hour, covered a list of highly sensitive subjects and the President-Elect never indicated that he thought these operations were good or bad, that he was surprised or unsurprised. He registered no emotion of any kind, asked for little follow-up and frankly seemed a little impatient at the end of my presentation of these items. Perhaps it was because he knew that there was a full plate waiting for him in the next room of several more hours of briefings. I am unable to give an opinion at this juncture as to whether the President-Elect plans major reorganization of the Intelligence Community, whether he supports human intelligence or not, whether he was pleased that we have these special arrangements and that we have such excellent sourcing. I frankly just don't know.

Addendum to Carter Briefing.

I emphasized the need to be very careful using the telephone. I gave him some indication of the Soviet capabilities to read phone calls, to copy thermofax transmissions and to penetrate in many ways. . . .

                                          George Bush
                                          Director

---

*Philip Agee was a former CIA agent who had violated his secrecy obligations after leaving the Agency and contributed to the "outing" of undercover agents. Based on these activities, I viewed Agee as a traitor and still do. I believe he was morally responsible for several agents' deaths.

December 5, 1976

Dear Mr. President [Nixon],

I just can't tell you how much I appreciate your Thanksgiving Day letter. Both Barbara and I are very grateful.

I have loved my work at CIA. The people are unselfish, dedicated, able, and patriotic. They have given me full support from the very beginning.

I told our President Elect that I felt he should have someone here who has his total confidence and who will have total access to him. In this troubled climate in which CIA is a target for irresponsible criticism in the press and on the Hill, the Director cannot lead forcefully without full Presidential support.

I have a feeling of work unfinished, a fascinating job, in a sense just beginning, but because of the "access" and "confidence" factors it is the time to go.

I will always be grateful to you for the assignments you gave me—the UN and the RNC—both complicated, each rewarding.

Now, we will most probably head back to Texas—by mid February. I want to keep up my interests in foreign affairs and national politics. I also must work for a living; so the future like the past will be a challenge.

One of these days, if agreeable to you, I will come by to call.

In the meantime my thanks to you for your letter and for the opportunities you gave me to serve my country. Love to Mrs. Nixon.

Sincerely,
George

December 8, 1976

H.E. Ambassador Yakov Malik
USSR Mission to the U. N.
New York City, N. Y. 10021

Dear Yakov,

I see that you are leaving New York. I just want to wish you the very best as you return to your home.

It was for me a pleasure serving with you at the U. N.

. . . I will leave government soon (Jan 20th) and we will probably go back to Texas.

Some day maybe I will get a chance to visit Moscow—If I do maybe I can get you to buy me a glass of vodka.

So long, my friend, good luck.

George

I enlisted the help of an old friend to come lift the spirits of everyone at the CIA as they prepared for yet another transition.

December 10, 1976

Mr. Lionel Hampton
New York, New York 11220
Dear Lionel,

You and your entire band were a tremendous hit! I have gotten an unbelievable amount of favorable "vibes" on your appearance. Your appearance was, in my view, great for morale here at CIA.

All of us want to thank you for donating your time and the band's time. What a wonderful Christmas present. It was most generous of you.

. . . From a grateful Agency and a grateful Director, thanks for coming our way. . . .

Your friend,
George Bush

———

January 19, 1977

TO MY FELLOW EMPLOYEES:

It's time to go now, and yet it seems as if I have just begun.

First, I want to say Thank You to all. I have never been associated with any institution that gives its leadership more cooperation and more support. I wish I could thank each of you personally.

As I leave the Agency and the Intelligence Community there are a few personal observations I would like to make.

First, I believe it is essential that the American people give this Agency its full and unqualified support. The world we live in demands no less. The support for the Agency was shaken during the height of the public hearings in 1975. It was shaken even more by the endless stream of allegations which were untrue but which were given great attention.

This is changing now, and it is changing for the better. We are still slugged at times with unfair criticism, but the sensationalism is giving way now to legitimate inquiry; the adversary relationship with Congress has given way to thorough and constructive oversight; the frantic search for reorganization and dismantlement has given way to a legitimate search for ways to improve things.

It is essential that CIA continue to work with the Congress, with the rest of the Executive Branch, and to some degree with the public, to demonstrate that CIA the Reality is very different from CIA the Myth. We are cooperating fully with all concerned; and this is bound to result in the Truth. We honor the Truth; we do not fear it.

Secondly, we should continue to strive for fair and better legislation to protect sources and methods of obtaining intelligence. We should do all we possibly can to guard against unauthorized leaks, and I strongly urge that we have a reawakening of the need for present and past employees to honor their security commitments. No foreign intelligence organization can be run without careful adherence to security, and we should be ever mindful of the fact that security is everyone's job.

Thirdly, I am pleased with the way the President's Executive Order has been faithfully implemented. All components have cooperated fully. As a result we are operating within the guidelines—guidelines designed to safeguard the rights of private citizens. To deserve the confidence of the American people, we must continue to operate, as we are now, within the law, responsive to Congressional and Executive oversight. I congratulate all for working to make the Executive Order effective.

Lastly, a word about the dedication here. I have been privileged to serve in many fascinating assignments in public and private life, but nowhere else have I ever encountered the same degree of unselfish dedication to country as I have encountered here at CIA. I thank each and every one of you for the cooperation you have given me over the past year. I know you will give our new Director the same support you have given me.

I am leaving CIA now, but I take with me many happy memories. Even the tough, unsolved problems don't seem so awesome; for they are overshadowed by our successes and by the fact that we do provide the best foreign intelligence in the world. I am leaving, but I am not forgetting. I hope I can find some ways in the years ahead to make the American people understand more fully the greatness that is CIA.

Sincerely,
George Bush

George Bush
for President.
710 North Post Oak Road, Suite 320
Houston, Texas 77024

CHAPTER 8

"Fire in the Belly"

After being gone for ten years, Barbara and I moved home to Houston. I was sad to leave the CIA, a job that I loved. But it was great to get back to Texas. Now my main challenge was to figure out what came next in my life. Suggestions came from everywhere.

———

January 24, 1977

Mr. George Champion*
Economic Development Council of New York City, Inc.
New York, New York 10016
Dear George,

I don't know if I can write a book or not and I have not been overly enthusiastic about the "kiss and tell" post-Watergate trend.

On the other hand, as you point out, I have had a fascinating series of assignments and maybe there is a story there. In any event, the CIA has been the greatest of them all and I wouldn't mind letting the world know what the institution really is like—a vast contrast from the gore and lies that I read in the press. . . .

Sincerely,
George Bush

———

*George had also been chairman of Chase Bank.

January 29, 1977

Mr. James S. McDonnell
McDonnell Douglas Corporation
St. Louis, Missouri 63166
Dear Mr. Mac,

I was deeply touched by your phone call. That you would consider me for membership on the Board of McDonnell Douglas is a high compliment and honor.

Mr. Mac, I have been thinking about it and it is with great reluctance that I have decided I should not be considered further. Frankly, I worry about conflict of interest. Your firm has done fantastic work for CIA and, given the extraordinary climate that we are living in, I am afraid my joining your Board would work against the good relationship that now exists. It would be unfairly alleged that I had capitalized on CIA business in order to get on your Board. Normally I wouldn't worry about the critics, but I just don't want to do anything that would bring more notoriety to CIA, nor would I want to do anything that would work to your detriment. . . .

Sincerely,
George Bush

––––––––

February 14, 1977

Mr. Bayless Manning
Council on Foreign Relations
New York, New York 11220
Dear Bay,

How does a guy who is: (a) blessed by having had fascinating government assignments, (b) now going back to Houston as a private citizen, (c) has not lost his interest in national politics, and (d) has been spoiled as DCI with the totality of the information available to him—how, from Houston, does he informationally on foreign affairs, stay alive?

I am going home. I have made enough broad contacts to make a living, but I would welcome any suggestions from you as to how to stay informed. I hope this is not an imposition on our friendship.

Yours very truly,
George Bush

––––––––

March 9, 1977

Dear Gerry [Bemiss],

. . . I thought I would be returning to boredom and quietude—not so.

There have been a lot of little speaking requests before small associations of one kind or another—I'm doing a few.

There has been getting settled in this little office—one at the 1st Int. Bank in Houston where I will spend 1 day or so a week.

There have been offers of Boards which require sorting and contemplation. I will do 4 or 5 so I can a) pay our bills b) move around the US and to some degree abroad.

There has been some politics—a meeting with among others Simon, Connally, Baker, Mosbacher, Brock . . .*

There has been moving—selling a house . . . and moving into our new neat house.

There has been withdrawal symptoms. I've been tense as a coiled spring hopefully not a shit about it, but up tight.

There has been the joy of seeing old friends here but the pain of leaving old friends there.

Today I went back to CIA. I saw our President swear in Stan Turner as DCI. The President, who I think is doing darn well, dwelled too much I thought on past abuses—and I found myself thinking Mr. President, these are great people, they have been through all this bad stuff, now lift them up and lead them.

There is a missing of stimulating talk. I just get bored silly about whose daughter is a Pi Phi or even bored about whose banging old Joe's wife. I don't want to slip into that 3 or 4 martini late late dinner rich social thing. There is too much to learn still.

I think I want to run or at least be in a position to run in '80—but it seems so overwhelmingly presumptuous and egotistical; yet I'll think some on that.

I am going on the Trilateral Commission† and will attend the fall meeting in Bonn.

We will go to Maine for most of August. I may even try to write there.

I write this on the plane heading home.

---

*Bill Simon, treasury secretary under Nixon and Ford; John Connally; Jim Baker; Bob Mosbacher, a close Houston friend and successful oilman whom I would name secretary of commerce; and Senator Bill Brock of Tennessee.

†The Trilateral Commission was formed in 1973 by private citizens in Japan, Europe, Canada, and the United States. The idea was to draw together leaders from all sectors to discuss common problems facing those countries. My short-lived membership (I didn't have time to be a member) would cause me some heartburn down the road, since some people thought the Commission conspired to rule the world.

I feel warm inside—my return to CIA made me feel this way. The future, though uncertain looks OK . . .

There's a lot I've left out. Bar's great job on our house—The joy of our grandson,* the normalcy of things.

But, somehow I will churn until I can find the formula to be involved, to be <u>doing.</u> It's not the need for the head table or the Washington protocol. It's a funny feeling that we're running out of time and I don't want to spend what's left of it learning to putt—

Poppy

_____

March 25, 1977

Mr. H. Ross Perot
Electronic Data Systems Corp.
Dallas, Texas 75235
Dear Ross,

. . . I went on Bobby Stewart's Board† and the Board of two of his subsidiaries. This is a part-time commitment. They pay me as a consultant and I give about two days a week. I am also on the Board of Eli Lilly and Texasgulf. I have decided not to get back in the oil business; though I may participate in a deal or two from time to time.

I do want to keep up my foreign affairs interest as best I can and also my interest in the national political scene. I will be doing some speaking for the national Party from time to time. I do not have politics out of my system (I guess I never will); but I do not want to make a run for governor here in Texas in 1978. . . .

Thanks, Ross, for your interest in me. You called when I was kind of down. Though things didn't work out, I will always be grateful for your interest. Needless to say, if I can ever be helpful to you or your people down here in any way, please don't hesitate to call.‡

Love to Margot, in which Bar joins me.

Sincerely,
George Bush

_____

George W., who was living in Midland working in the oil business, decided to run for Congress. I wrote this note to GOP political consultant Eddie Mahe Jr.

---

*George Prescott Bush, son of Jeb and Columba, had been born April 24, 1976, in Houston.
†First International Bancshares in Dallas.
‡Perot had asked me to run his oil business in Houston.

7-25-77

Eddie,

George is off and running in Midland. The Party poohbahs are not thrilled,* but the guy is energetic, attractive, he grew up in Midland and has lots of friends. I'd say he's an underdog now, but he'll acquit himself well I'm sure. I'm tickled pink about this.

Other political churning going on— nothing definitive yet.

Stay in touch.

> Best ever,
> George

———————

November 8, 1977

Mr. Richard A. Moore
Washington, D.C. 20036

Dear Dick:

I saw that Yale story and I've told them on several occasions that I am not interested. I must confess such consideration is flattering.†

Mother is here as I dictate this letter and she keeps telling me that she wishes I would take this. I think she thinks that my other plans for politics in '80 will be backbreaking and killing.

We've got lots to talk about. I will be up soon. In fact, we are going to be there on the 8th but you probably won't have gotten this letter by then. It's just for a quick dinner. . . .

Let's stay in touch. Thanks for your great letter.

> Warmest regards,
> George Bush

———————

A man named Michael Randall Hewitt wrote and asked if I could write his one-year-old nephew, David Robey, a letter. He planned to give David a scrapbook of letters from "leaders" on his twenty-first birthday, in 1997.

Dec. 11, 1977

Dear David,

Your uncle asked me to send you this note—what a guy he must be to think in these terms.

---

*A very conservative Republican activist was already running, so now there would be a primary.

†Several people had approached me about possibly becoming president of Yale University. I asked that my name be taken out of consideration.

Anyway, what does the future hold. I can't see too far down the road, but I have been Ambassador in China, I have headed the CIA and the Republican Party, and I've been in Congress and Ambassador at the U.N. I also built a business. So, you can see I've had lots of exciting things to do.

All of them lead me to the conclusion that our Country is unique. We care about ourselves and about the rest of the World. I'm convinced that when you get to be 21 we'll still be going strong.

I'd like to think that we'd reach agreement with the Communist Powers under which they would not try to impose their system on the free world. I doubt that will happen. We must stay strong, David, so they will not attempt to impose their values on us by force. Right now they are moving, predominantly the Soviet Union, to achieve military superiority over the U.S. We must not let that happen.

The future holds in store for you great treasures, the greatest of which is freedom. Before you get to be 21 we must do all we can to preserve our freedom, to guarantee that you can live in a country unequaled in its fairness, its greatness, its measure of freedom.

I am optimistic. I see enormous problems at home and abroad but they can be solved by 1997. I wish I were a little guy 1 year old. There is so much to do, so far to travel, so much happiness to live and to give.

Good Luck, kid.

George Bush

Jeb, Columba, George P., and the newest Bush—our first granddaughter, Noelle— had moved to Venezuela where Jeb worked for Texas Commerce Bank.

April 24, 1978

Mr. Jeb Bush
Caracas 107 Venezuela
Dear Jeb:

. . . I am dictating this prior to leaving on our around-the-world trip. Attached are some copies of my schedule and some recent articles from the columnists . . . We are not doing any of the things that one should be doing if he wanted to attract columnists' attention; but, nevertheless, there seems to be a credibility to my effort that is reassuring.

We get back to Houston the day before George's primary; and we'll all be keeping our fingers crossed. Reports from out there are pretty darn good.

We really miss you, Columba and those two kids. We miss you an awful lot.

Hang in. Just know that we think of you with pride, all the time.

Devotedly,
Dad

Among my and Barbara's many stops on our business/speaking tour was Iran, where I had a long visit with the Shah. He was a fascinating man who had a good grasp of the international scene. Ironically, in January of 1979, he fled his own country as supporters of the Ayatollah Khomeini seized power. I typed this memo:

Audience with the Shah

April 29th, 1978

I met with his Imperial Majesty at 10:30 a.m. Meeting lasted about 40 minutes. Just two of us were in room. There was brief interruption when TV camera and photographers were ushered in and out for shots—no sound. . . .

The Shah was most gracious and immediately put me at ease.

Subjects covered were:

1. Afghanistan. His Majesty is most concerned about recent developments, citing coup as one more example of the Soviets' grand design. He had warned Presidents Nixon, Ford and Carter about Afghanistan.*

He cited his concern about Gulf States—run by "bunch of bedouins." They have no plan; they are no match for forces determined to overthrow them.

He sees Iraq and Syria as real menace. He is unsure of Pakistan now.

2. He questions will of USA to stand up against USSR's long-stated plan to conquer world. "I will fight". "No matter what happens, I will fight and the Soviets will know this." He gave distinct impression that we are not properly concerned about Soviet intentions. He is clearly concerned about increased KGB activity around the world.

3. The Shah repeated his oft-stated concern about what the U.S. is doing to itself—continued attacks by the left plus such media as <u>N. Y. Times, Washington Post,</u> TV notoriety on our intelligence agencies and on Iran and himself concerns him enormously.

4. Though discreet about it, his concern about our human rights policy came through. (I must confess at this point that I told him of my own concern about our human rights policy and further that I had been speaking out in the USA expressing my concern on certain aspects of this policy, namely our selectivity and my further concern that some of the results were weakening or straining traditional U.S. Friendships. End of confession.)

5. China. Relations are good with China. The Shah may go to Peking. I encouraged him to go, suggesting that in wake of Afghanistan's apparent fate, visit would have special significance. He felt we had an opportunity to do much more with China now.

*Pro-Soviet leftists had overthrown the government in a bloody coup. The Shah of course was right about Afghanistan; by 1979, the Soviet Union was involved in a full-scale guerrilla war.

6. The Shah suggested that, given U.S. dependence on imported oil and Russia's designs on Gulf States, that Europe and Japan could eventually be compelled to make deals with Soviets if their grand design materialized.

7. He expressed his concerns about Europe, citing his fears that threats would materialize through underbelly—Italy, Spain and Yugoslavia. He expressed his concern about Algeria and Libya and his fear that Soviets would quietly move back into Egypt if "you let Sadat* down."

8. Continuing theme was concern about what the West was doing to itself by attacking its own national security agencies; by failing to keep commitments; by underestimating determination of USSR to vanquish West by whatever means necessary.

———————

I asked some close friends to come to Kennebunkport that summer to talk politics, issues, and my future. This letter went to Congressman Bill Roth of Delaware:

July 12, 1978

Dear Bill,

On August 18-19, I am inviting a handful of people to come to Kennebunkport, Maine to chat informally about the economy and some domestic issues.

The group will consist of a few economists, several Members of Congress, some business people and a liberal representation from the Bush family. . . .

The idea is to chat on Friday afternoon on the big issues. It won't be high structured with formal presentations, et cetera. I'd rather have a lively, informal discussion.

Friday evening, I'll talk my family into having a good seafood dinner for everyone. On Saturday, we'll chat again in the morning or afternoon, taking some time off to get out on the water. . . .

We will not seek any press coverage. The Fund for Limited Government will pay for travel and living expenses. The Fund is a political action committee with which I am associated (James A. Baker, III is the fund's chairman). We may print up some general conclusions from the meeting which can be shared with various candidates for the U.S. Congress or which can be supplied to spokesmen who are out speaking for candidates. I am doing speaking like this under the Fund's sponsorship.

Please <u>let me know if you can come.</u> I will send along more details as the day approaches. Try to do it! I'd love to have a chance for a good visit with you.

Most sincerely,
George

———

*Anwar Sadat, the respected leader of Egypt.

George W. won the GOP primary in his congressional race but it was a tough election. A friend and editor of the Lubbock newspaper wrote and said I should be proud of George, that he had showed "a lot of class."

July 14, 1978

Mr. Charles A. Guy
Lubbock, Texas 79413
Dear Charles:

I just can't tell you how much your letter meant to me (and to Barbara). It was typical of you—a thoughtful, constructive, helpful letter—written from the heart.

You know how close our family is; and therefore, you know of the pride I have in my own son.

He kept his head high in the face of some tough, bitter, mean little ultra-right attacks during the primary. I think his opponent got slightly desperate. Reagan endorsed Reese, which obviously didn't make me happy;* and then this nutty Clarence Warner from Oklahoma came in assailing George, because I am a member of the Trilateral Commission. I was proud of my boy. No one likes his father to be attacked; George did not overreact nor did he panic. He beat a good vote-getter and beat him rather soundly.

Your observations about the need for balance in the Congress and the need for independence from good ole Tip† was very sound.

I hope our paths cross before long, Charlie. In the meantime, though, let me tell you again, you have my gratitude.

As I get older, I realize that friendships are what it's all about.

When I do see you, I want to tell you of my ambitious plans for '80. I honestly believe I can do it. . . .

Sincerely yours,
George Bush

---

*Obviously Reagan and I had not yet formed a personal friendship; I was disappointed only that he had endorsed anyone in the primary at all.
†Tip O'Neill, Speaker of the House.

August 8, 1978

Mr. Charles Bartlett
Washington, D.C.
Dear Charley:

. . . The "tough enough" theme is getting fed by some of the adversaries. It does not bother me; I've had tough jobs, made tough decisions, and emerged with the respect of people whom I worked for and whom I led.

We're putting together some material for interested feature writers, based on interviews with people I work with in various jobs. This material will be emphasizing tough decisions, leadership, etc. Down the line I think it can be extraordinarily helpful. . . .

I continue to travel. Here is a copy of our fall schedule. Please keep it confidential. There's a helluva lot happening. I am not discouraged. Indeed, I believe I can pull it off, Charley; we'll see.

Sincerely yours,
George Bush

———————

October 3, 1978

Mr. Alan Greenspan*
One New York Plaza
New York, NY 10004
Dear Alan:

. . . The big question I have is how does one, short of major revision, cut back on the built-in increases in payments to individuals. Will any congress go back and cut down on future payments of Social Security, Medicare, etc.? In my view programs should be reviewed and we should not be afraid to reduce the benefits in the future. But I am wondering if it is practical. I would sure appreciate any advice you could give me on this point. I talk about spending cuts. People keep saying, "Where do you cut?" My answer is simply to inhibit, hold the growth to 7 percent, or some such figure, and the dynamic growth in the economy will put the budget in balance down the line. Or, I have resorted to some discussion of the 2 percent across the board cut. If you have written anything on <u>where</u> to cut spending or <u>how</u> to cut spending or in what manner to cut personal payments in the future, I sure would welcome it. It is a tough subject but it is so darn important.

*Alan was not yet head of the Federal Reserve Board. (Reagan would appoint him in 1987 and I would reappoint him in 1992.) At this time he was president of Townsend-Greenspan & Co. and had been chairman of the President's Council of Economic Advisers under President Ford.

Let me tell you again how much I appreciate your coming by to see me.

Sincerely Yours,

George Bush

12-5-78

Mr. Toby Hilliard
Woodside, Calif 94062
Dear Toby,

You left a few hours ago.

Now I'm home, and I got to thinking— How many guys would come all that way to sit down and help a friend by taking the tough road and bringing up the "not so easy things."*

I am really grateful. I need help. I need advice. I need criticism. For me this goal is the end all-be all. I feel driven. Hopefully for altruistic reasons. But I do want to succeed, and I can't do that by hearing only the soft and easy stuff.

Thanks, pal. Keep the cards and letters coming. I want you involved. Sometimes I wake up and wonder what's a little guy like me doing taking on a project of this magnitude— then I think—I can do it

I have been blessed by birth, by experience, by training. And I have friends. Loyal close friends, men of quality. Thanks for being a part of all this.

Best Ever,

George

January 31, 1979

The Honorable Richard M. Nixon
La Casa Pacifica
San Clemente, California
Dear Mr. President,

That was a very thoughtful note you wrote me on January 9. I am determined to make an all-out effort for 1980. I start with no name identification and I realize that. I will, however, continue to keep a "low-profile." I am traveling with no press secretary, no advance text and no fanfare. I am determined to organize, and organize well, before escalating the candidacy to high levels of public attention.

---

*Both Toby and his sister Elsie Hillman were good friends and members of my national steering committee. Toby pointed out I had low name recognition nationally, despite my already long career in public service. He also reminded me I was not known as a charismatic speaker, a problem I never quite overcame.

I couldn't agree more about avoiding a massive blood-letting. I know I can campaign so as not to tear down somebody else.

Again, my sincere thanks to you for this helpful advice and my warm regards to Mrs. Nixon, in which Barbara joins me.

Sincerely,
George Bush

———

April 6, 1979

Dr. James L. Jablonowski
Milwaukee, WI 53222
Dear Dr. Jablonowski,

. . . As to the Mideast, I am terribly concerned. I give Carter credit for getting Begin and Sadat* together, but I am convinced that peace is not at hand. There are some enormously complicated times ahead. We failed to shape events in Iran, and now we are failing to keep the Russians from mucking around in some of the Gulf countries. Our problem is that our leadership is not generating any confidence abroad, and thus we are seeing a decline in U.S. credibility, and certainly a mounting perception of weakness. The situation is serious. Thank you for your supportive letter.

Yours very truly,
George Bush

———

A note to my wife, Barbara, on her birthday, June 8:

Happy happy 54th
love you—I love you very much. Nothing—campaign separations, people, nothing will ever change that—
I can't ever really tell you how much I love you.
Your 55 yr. old husband.

Pop

———

*Carter brought together Israel's Prime Minister Menachem Begin and Egypt's President Anwar Sadat for peace talks at Camp David, which resulted in the Camp David Peace Accord.

June 16, 1979

Mr. L. W. Bankston
Decatur, AL 35601
Dear Mr. Bankston,

Many thanks for your letter and for the sharp comments.

I do not believe in the "trickle down" way of doing anything. I do believe in deregulating industry since small businessmen are hit the worst by excessive Federal regulation. Our country was built on individual initiative and I want to bring that "can do spirit" back into emphasis. . . .

Sincerely,
George Bush

July 13, 1979

Mr. Roy E. Hardman
Nixon, TX 78140
Dear Dr. Hardman,

. . . I oppose the national health insurance plans of President Carter and Sen. Kennedy. The financial costs of such programs would necessitate higher taxes which I adamantly oppose. . . .

Sincerely,
George Bush

September 18, 1979

Miss Ruthie Stephenson
Houston, TX 77055
Dear Ruthie,

. . . Ruthie, we live in a regulated, complex society and to comply with the law, it is impossible for me to accept your generous contribution. You see, I can not accept money from anyone under 18 years of age.

I have enclosed a check for $1.79, which is the combined total of your two contributions. I am sending you a George Bush for President T-shirt to let you know how grateful I am that you are one of my best supporters.

When I get back to Houston, I hope I can meet you in person.

Most sincerely,
George Bush

September 18, 1979

Mr. Gary Hanauer
Oakland, CA 94602
Dear Gary,

Sorry for the delay in responding to your letter, but I've been on the road constantly. The answers to your questions are as follows:

1. Handshaking—Yes, it is possible to tell things by a handshake. I like the "looking in the eye" syndrome. It conveys interest. I like the firm, though not bone crushing shake. The bone crusher is trying too hard to "macho it." The clammy or diffident handshake—fairly or unfairly—get me off to a bad start with a person.

2. Kissing babies—I love kissing babies, but I don't like the "full court-press-mandatory" baby kiss—you know, where the baby, screaming and kicking, is thrust forward simply to fulfill a time honored tradition. In addition, babies get a lot of colds this way.

3. Non-political identity—I have always participated in athletics. I love fishing, tennis, jogging and baseball. I enjoy fast boats. I don't know which one will emerge as my identifying activity, but all will be prominent

I hope this information is useful.

Sincerely,
George Bush

———

Toward the end of 1979 I began to keep a campaign diary (although I dictated only sporadically), which I mainly used to talk about the rigors of being on the road.

September 29, 1979
. . . I think I'm putting on a little weight. I got to run only once this week, and that was in Iowa. The food varies. . . . What I like are the barbecues. The chopped beefs or chopped pork in Alabama or Georgia; the ribs we had in Iowa and ribs we have in Texas; these kinds of food are much better—chicken once in a while can be all right, but often it is pale or liquid or hard or dreary and I push it away.

. . . I saw Barbara twice this week: once in the middle of the night at Des Moines, Iowa and once briefly in Indianapolis. She's working hard and getting good press. I am awfully proud of the children and what they are doing . . .

———

October 10, 1979
I'm so digging in, so tense . . . I have no time to think about relaxation. Just this one goal . . . no time to think at all. That troubles me

a little bit. Drive, drive forward. I'm surprised my body can take it. The mind is still clear, although I totally lose track of where I've been and whom I'm with. I've given up on names. . . . David Bates* got so tired that he really had to go home. He was just dropping and drooping. I felt the same way but I was just determined not to show it— determined to push on. . . . I don't want to look back and find that I've left something undone.

October 14, 1979

Mrs. Robert Wells Carton
Winnetka, IL 60093
Dear Mrs. Carton,

. . . It is a treat in this strenuous campaign to read something humorous. Your ideas are creative and delightful.

The major problem is cost. We have to spend our resources on our great professional staff and on TV ads which will start running soon in the early primary states.

So, though I love "Secretly, I'm For Bush," and "Plant a Bush Over a Peanut"† I'm afraid we don't have the means to distribute any significant number of these. . . .

Sincerely,
George Bush

November 26, 1979

Mrs. Ormond T. Johnson
Lakewood, California 90712
Dear Mrs. Johnson,

. . . I must respectfully disagree with your support of SALT II. I, too, have studied the Treaty and don't believe that it is verifiable or equitable. I firmly believe that the Russians do not seek parity with the United States but superiority. We must have a treaty that insures parity; and then, we can move toward a real strategic arms limitation agreement in SALT III. That would be my objective as President.

Best Wishes,
George Bush

---

*David, now a successful attorney and businessman in San Antonio, was my traveling companion—the "bag carrier." I came to think of him almost like a son.

†Campaign songs sent in by Mrs. Carton.

December 1, 1979

No Christmas shopping. I look at Bar's schedule and I think it is too intense, too tough. She doesn't get home enough. We've overdone it. . . . Marvin wants to go back to school and Jebby bawls him out, but he should go back to school. We cannot disrupt our lives. On Jeb's case, [Jim] Baker wants him to go to Puerto Rico and yet, I'm not sure that is right. Georgie is just learning to speak and he is in school and he has his routine. I want to be careful that we don't disrupt the lives of all of them. . . . God, Jeb is doing so fantastic though. Has such good judgment, good with people, great grasp of the issues* . . .

We haven't given proper attention to Neil. He's engaged, and we've really said nothing about that, done nothing about it. The girl must wonder, what kind of family are we. . . .†

Doro has a boyfriend, the first time. Yet, we haven't taken them out to dinner together—done any of the things that normally we do. Yet, the family is in close, in tight, doing well. George and Laura‡ getting along fine on their own. . . .

December 2, 1979

Mr. Ray Zauber
OAK CLIFF TRIBUNE
Dallas, TX 75237
Dear Ray,

. . . My record is sound and strong and these really extreme types will never like me. I want the vote of all. I will get the vote of sound conservatives—not the conspiratorial ones. We are on the move Ray—I think I will beat Connally in some of the early states. If I do, he will be on the ropes if not KO'd. Baker§ must fall early too. Reagan is still tough out there. I respect his strength. You are right that the people want strong leadership. They want principled leadership and integrity and experience. I know I can fill the bill. . . .

This schedule is a real back breaker—96 hours at home in Houston since Sept 30th til Thanksgiving.

I am going to win this thing.

Best Ever,
George

---

*Jeb had moved back to Texas to work full-time on the campaign.
†Neil met his wife, Sharon Smith, while campaigning for me in New Hampshire.
‡George had married Laura Welch from Midland.
§Senator Howard Baker of Tennessee.

December 23, 1979

   Winging from Puerto Rico to Miami sitting next to a boring guy
that recognized me. . . . he's concerned about things—and I couldn't
be less interested; and yet, I've got to smile and sit here as I'm about
to eat. "Okay fellow, let's have your say—you solve all the problems."
Maybe that's bad, but on the other hand, maybe it's good. (It's) bad
in the sense that I should have some privacy, but good in the sense of
what's the point of turning off a fellow who says, "Boy, I'll never get
a chance to talk to a Presidential candidate."

   . . . That's what our system is about; so why shouldn't I be pleasant
to this guy? I'll drop off to sleep in awhile, and let him do his own
number; but I think I'll have to hear him out and who knows, I may
learn something. . . .

———————

12-29-79

relaxed—flying home
Dear Flo & Holt—

   . . . I think of all you've both done for me over the years and my heart is
full. I know this project is tough—but as the year ends I have a quiet confidence that it will work. When it does it will be because of the "asterisk" club.
Those who were at my side while I was still an asterisk on the polls*—Consider yourselves "charter members".

   Bushes love Athertons

                              Gratefully,
                              George

———————

*On November 4, 1979, sixty-three Americans were taken hostage at the Ameri-
can embassy in Tehran, Iran. The crisis gripped the nation all of 1980.*

January 12, 1980

Mr. James W. Beasley, Jr.
Beasley & Olle
Miami, Florida 33131
Dear Mr. Beasley,

   . . . On the situation in Iran, I firmly believe that all of us, citizens and presidential candidates alike, should stand behind the President in the handling

———————

*When your poll numbers are so low, you are not even listed by name, but instead only by
asterisk, under the group heading "All Others."

of this extremely sensitive matter. I say this with the conviction of having worked in two presidential administrations in a foreign policy role and seeing the United States weakened in the eyes of the world because potshots were taken at the President for political reasons. To do so in this present crisis might help me as a candidate but would be wrong for our country.

After all our hostage fellow Americans are returned safely from Teheran, we can then examine the decisions which caused the crisis to occur, and I expect to make my voice heard at that time.

Sincerely,
George Bush

January 12, 1980

Mr. R. W. Lundreen
Midland, Michigan 48640
Dear Bob,

. . . Your recommendation on reaching out to the so-called disadvantaged, letting them know that their hopes for a future, free of handouts, lies with the free enterprise system as defended by the Republican Party, is excellent. Too often we Republicans just say the words "free enterprise" and assume everyone knows what we mean; [that we] feel it's a good thing for all citizens rather than an evil plot to help Big Business. I feel that, having built my own business, I can help articulate this message to precisely these groups. It's already well received among Hispanic-Americans, who from their personal experience know how much opportunity and hard work can give worth and meaning to human lives, something that being a welfare recipient simply cannot provide. . . .

Sincerely,
George Bush

My campaign peaked on January 21 when I upset the front-runner, Ronald Reagan, in the Iowa caucuses. Of course we didn't realize then we were peaking; we thought we were on our way to the White House.

January 28, 1980

Mr. Robert J. Arnold
Northeast Chemical Company, Inc.
Amherst, NY 14150
Dear Bob,

Thanks for your note. The "Sixty Minutes" appearance did not go badly at all, especially since those guys are given to pulling out a piece of paper and asking, "What color necktie did you wear on July 16, 1954?"

The Iowa results were tremendously heartening, but there's a long way to go yet before the convention. Still, I'm getting more and more confident of winning both the nomination and the election. . . .

Sincerely,

George Bush

February 2, 1980

Mr. Ethan Allen*
Chapel Hill, NC 27514
Dear Curly,

We're still elated over Iowa but the road to the nomination is still long and difficult. The national publicity has been great, including Mary McGrory† (her comments about my clothes notwithstanding.)

Sorry you missed seeing Georgie. All the kids are helping us all over the map. Neil is working New Hampshire and is engaged to a girl he met there. Talk about winning the hearts and minds of the people!

Sincerely,

George Bush

February 10, 1980

Mr. Ray G. Goodman
Boston, MA 02109
Dear Mr. Goodman,

Thank you for your advice about emphasizing the word "statesman" rather than "politician" in my speeches and publications.

I want to be—and, as President, I believe I would be—a true statesman. The only reason I shrink from using the word very often is that to many ears it sounds pretentious. But you're right: "politician" hits other ears as badly, or worse.

Then again there's the famous definition given by the 19th century Speaker of the U. S. House of Representatives, Tom Reed. He said a statesman is a politician who has died. . . .

Sincerely,

George Bush

---

*My baseball coach at Yale.

†A columnist from the *Washington Post*. She was always very tough on me, but apparently she hadn't gotten tough yet, except about my clothes.

February 10, 1980

Mrs. Eleanor Langley Fletcher
New York, NY 10021
Dear Mrs. Fletcher,

. . . As for my view on gay rights, I believe that the government should not harrass or allow discrimination against anyone on the grounds of their sexual preference. But this principle is rooted firmly enough in law and court decisions that I believe no further legislation is required. . . .

Sincerely,
George Bush

———

February 10, 1980

Mr. Robert L. Dixon
Rockport, Massachusetts 01966
Dear Mr. Dixon:

. . . One of the ways we can contain inflation is to balance the federal budget, something that I have pledged to do and will do if elected President. . . .

Sincerely,
George Bush

———

The low point of my campaign was February 23 in Nashua, New Hampshire. The Nashua Telegraph *newspaper had invited Governor Reagan and myself to debate one-on-one, without any of the other GOP candidates. Both of us accepted these terms. Angry at being left out, the other candidates still in the race—John Anderson, Howard Baker, Bob Dole, and Phil Crane—showed up and insisted on being included. The Reagan camp reversed course and sided with them. I will be the first to admit I looked like a fool, rigidly playing by the rules. I also was angry. I wrote all the candidates this letter. Eventually, I lost the New Hampshire primary.*

February 25, 1980

The Honorable John B. Anderson
1101 Longworth House Office Building
Washington, D. C. 20515
Dear John:

I want to express to you my regrets about the misunderstandings relating to Saturday's debate. The Nashua Telegraph has issued a strong statement that has clarified some points that you may not have been familiar with. Please let me quote in part from The Telegraph statement.

"There have been suggestions by some candidates—particularly some of those who were not invited to participate in The Telegraph-sponsored meeting—that George Bush was a party to The Telegraph's insistence that the agreed upon format be observed. That suggestion and/or implication is totally without foundation. At no time did Ambassador Bush or any of his representatives take an intransigent or intractable position on the question of the meeting format. Mr. Bush's representatives, in fact, made a point of informing The Telegraph that if we chose to change the format their candidate would have no objection whatsoever; that he was there at the invitation of the newspaper and would abide by whatever the paper decided. The Telegraph—the only sponsor of last night's meeting—insisted that both candidates meet their commitment to participate under the terms of prior agreement."

It now occurs to me that you might not have been informed of this position held by the newspaper or of the position taken by the campaign. If you did not know of my willingness to have you join the forum should The Telegraph have decided to alter its plans, that is partially my fault, and I express my regrets. I am sorry that in the course of the last couple of days we didn't have an opportunity to discuss this matter. I wish I had called you and I hope you know that if you at any time had personally asked to see me or speak with me I would have come to see you, or returned your call. You should know that Governor Reagan never contacted me on any of this even though he had been in contact with most of the other campaigns. The first we heard that Governor Reagan might not debate as planned was when the newspaper contacted my New Hampshire manager Saturday afternoon. Confusion reigned until debate time. . . .

Unlike Governor Reagan, I have not ducked joint debates, having joined you on many occasions in joint events in many states. For this one particular occasion I was challenged by Governor Reagan. I accepted his challenge for a one-on-one debate. I was anxious to have that debate in addition to the other debates, past and future, we have scheduled. But the record should show that, as The Telegraph clearly stated, our campaign advised them we were prepared to enlarge the field should the sponsor have determined that was the thing to do.

One last point, twenty-five minutes after the program was to have started I received word to be on the stage. The Nashua Telegraph was anxious to commence the program. On the way to the stage, after this long delay, I was stopped by a prominent Reagan supporter who has been attacking me all across the State of New Hampshire. He asked me to have a joint meeting with you and the others and lectured me on the Republican Party. Now that I realize you might not have known that I was not blocking your participation, I wish in retrospect that I had met with you. A lot of misunderstanding might have been avoided. The producer was signaling me to the stage, the commitment that I had made was on my mind, and the emissary was not exactly the ideal choice. In addition, I felt that Governor Reagan had definitely not played fair with me. I wish we had been in personal touch. I'm certain that much of this unpleasantness could have been avoided.

Sincerely,
George Bush

————————

February 27, 1980

Dr. Bernard M. Barrett, Jr.
Houston, Texas 77030
Dear Barney,
   . . . The New Hampshire results were disappointing and I know the road to the nomination will be long and tough. But we'll pull out of this temporary slump and win the nomination as surely as if the figures Tuesday night had been reversed. . . .

Sincerely,
George Bush

————————

March 9, 1980

Pastor D. D. Peterson
Faith Baptist Church
Tulsa, OK 74112
Dear Pastor Peterson:
   . . . I am a strong believer in the separation of church and state. Government must stay out of the area of religion except to guarantee religious freedom under the First Amendment.

Sincerely,
George Bush

————————

March 10, 1980

Olga Jonasson, MD
Cook County Hospital
Chicago, Illinois 60612
Dear Doctor Jonasson:
   I am grateful for your letter on the sort of gunshot cases with which you and your colleagues deal every day.
   . . . I have the deepest admiration and respect for the tough job that you perform so well. I wish it were in my power as either a citizen or potentially as

President to halt the senseless killing which stalks our land. But after many years' thought on this question, I have concluded that no law will stop someone from taking a pistol and shooting another human being. We have had laws on this general subject since the greatest of them all was brought down from Mount Sinai, and they have had scant effect.

A law controlling firearms would be no different. What we in this country have is a human problem, infinitely complex in composition and certainly in solution. If the problem were simply one of weaponry, then legislators might well consider steps to control it. But when, for whatever twisted reason, a person intends to kill another, he or she will proceed to do so with whatever tool is at hand. It does not have to be a Saturday night special. It can be a knife, a shovel, or a firepoker. Without even visiting your highly-reputed emergency room I can predict you get a large number of patients who have been stabbed or bludgeoned, perhaps even more of these than you have gunshot victims. Yet no one seriously proposes outlawing every sharp or blunt instrument within the reach of a possible murderer.

I hope you understand, Doctor Jonasson, that I do not oppose gun control because I am insensitive to the sort of brutality you and your staff see every day. I do so because I believe gun control does not work. The actual solution lies far beyond the power of lawmakers and magistrates, in the vast territory of the human mind. There it is either adopted by rational man or woman in moments of anger or thrust aside in the impulse to kill.

Thank you for writing me, and I hope someday we have a chance to meet so I can visit the Trauma Unit.

Sincerely,
George Bush

―――――――

March 10, 1980

Mr. Edward E. Joiner
St. Petersburg, FL 33706
Dear Mr. Joiner,

Many thanks for your constructive criticism of my speaking style.

I know I'm not a Churchillian orator and that definite improvements can be made in my delivery. It is hard to do a 100% effective job making speeches in a presidential campaign simply because a candidate gets so tired and must think of several things at once. And I suppose we both wish that voters (and, more importantly, political journalists) paid more attention to <u>what</u> a candidate says than to <u>how</u> he says it.

Sincerely,
George Bush

March 14, 1980

Mrs. Mia Grasich
Chicago, Illinois
Dear Mrs. Grasich:

. . . You asked my views on labor unions. I believe in every person's right to organize into a union and work together for improved conditions on the job. The problem comes when unions begin to wield political and economic power far beyond the workplace. Our American system works best when all elements within it are balanced: government, industry and labor. When any one sector gains too much power, we all lose. . . .

Sincerely,
George Bush

After New Hampshire, I won a few primaries but lost many more. I wrote my friend Noel Gayler, former chief of naval operations:

March 14, 1980

Admiral Noel Gayler, U.S.N. (Ret.)
Steamboat Village, Colorado, 80499
Dear Noel,

Many thanks for your kind, cheering note.

The past few weeks have not been the happiest of the campaign, but at least they have sorted out the crowd and given us a better idea of how things might go between now and the convention.

Despite New Hampshire and the southern primaries, my campaign remains strong, with the finances, organization, and top-level support (from people like you) to last through the final ballot. I'm in for the long haul, regardless of what President Ford* decides to do.

Thanks again for your encouragement. Hope to see you soon.

Sincerely,
George Bush

March 31

Superior, Wisconsin and yet another Holiday [Inn] . . . Holidays are all right. The soap is not as thin as they are in some of the other

---

*There were rumors that President Ford might enter the race at this late date. He did not.

places. When you take a shower, the toilet doesn't bubble, or you don't get scalded by that guy next door. The food isn't bad. The Secret Service* spoil you. Great Guys! We're lucky to have them, but they do add to such a 'big show.' . . .

———————

April 1, 1980

Mr. A. Reed Aiden
Buckhannon, West Virginia 26201
Dear Mr. Aiden:

I appreciate your frank letter wanting to find out why you should vote for me. I'll be just as frank.

You should vote for me because of my qualifications for the job: starting and running my own small business, serving in the Congress, representing our country in difficult diplomatic jobs, holding our party together during the Watergate period, and heading our nation's foreign intelligence arm during a time it was coming under great attack. These jobs give me the breadth of experience needed in a President for the 1980s.

Another reason, Mr. Aiden, is that I've been all over this country of ours, meeting people in their living rooms and neighborhood cafes, so I have a strong idea of what the people want. They want an end to inflation, to unnecessary government spending, and to America's weakness in the world. These are things I would correct as President.

I hope you will decide to support me for the Republican presidential nomination. Thanks again for writing me.

Sincerely,
George Bush

———————

April 1, 1980

Honorable John A. Berman
State House
Hartford, Connecticut 06101
Dear John:

Many thanks for your letter of March 18th and for your great work on my behalf in the Connecticut primary a week later. It was just what the campaign needed at just the right moment.† I'm glad it provided the chance for us to see each other.

*Like all of the candidates, I had Secret Service protection.
†I won the Connecticut primary.

The problem you addressed in your letter—that 'people cannot figure out what (I am) for'—is one that frankly puzzles me. I have not been deliberately vague on the issues and indeed have published specific statements on all the major ones (foreign affairs, defense, the economy, energy, etc.) as well as on the extremely controversial ones . . .

What is happening is that the press, operating under the 'pack journalism' ethic that is particularly virulent during a presidential campaign, has simply decided I am not specific on the issues. The Reagan and Anderson people have, of course, picked up on this with relish and do their part to spread it. Thus, the fact that I have been specific on the issues is unimportant; what is important is what conventional wisdom says is true, not what actually is true. . . .

Sincerely,
George Bush

————

April 23, 1980

Ms. Bessie Z. Aldrich
Dallas, Texas 75217
Dear Ms. Aldrich:

. . . I think you are quite right in condemning the foolish talk this year about my being an 'elitist'. For one thing, the word itself is wrong. It's undeniable that by God's will I was born to a family of comfortable means and given many opportunities. I suppose this makes me one of the elite. But an 'elitist' is a person who wants to associate only with other elites; in other words, a snob. I assure you I would never have moved to the oil fields of West Texas if I were an 'elitist'. . . .

Sincerely,
George Bush

P.S. I hope you've recovered fully from your back injury.

————

April 28, 1980

Mr. and Mrs. Robert L. Cannon
San Antonio, TX 78217
Dear Mr. and Mrs. Cannon:

. . . The victory in the Pennsylvania Primary gave my campaign a terrific boost and caused the political "experts" to rethink their weeks-old conclusion that Governor Reagan is a shoo-in for the Republican nomination. I'm in this fight through the final ballot of the national convention, and I am optimistic of winning. Poll after poll shows that the American people do not want a choice this November between Reagan and President Carter.

So, don't get discouraged. I'm not! . . .

Sincerely,
George Bush

―――――――

April 28, 1980

Mr. John P. Hoyt
Lancaster, PA 17603
Dear John:

. . . I have supported the admission of refugees from communist tyrannies into our country. This is in the richest tradition of our country, the United States, to be a beacon of freedom and opportunity to the world. But we have been rewarded for this hospitality because the Cubans, Hungarians and Indochinese—to name the major groups—have become some of our finest, hardest working and most productive citizens, building business, raising patriotic American families and paying taxes. Yes, they may use social services when they first arrive, but the record shows they quickly get off welfare and onto their own feet. The rebirth of Miami under Cuban entrepreneurship is the best proof of this. . . .

Sincerely,
George Bush

―――――――

May 8, 1980

Mrs. Sara K. Kerr
Cheverly, Maryland 20785
Dear Mrs. Kerr:

. . . It will please me to have your first registered male boxer named for me. May I suggest you stay in the business and when you come to the "P" litter— the male will hopefully be President Bush.

I liked the spirit of your letter and appreciate your good humor. Thanks for writing and for your support.

Sincerely,
George Bush

―――――――

May 15, 1980

Mr. William F. Gorog
McLean, VA 22101
Dear Bill,

Thanks for your cheering note after the Texas primary. Although we missed a victory in the popular vote, it was a sizable moral triumph, for Texas was long considered an impregnable Reagan bastion.

. . . Yes, a "break" would be useful right now, but throughout my life I've been a believer that luck come to him who makes sure he's in the right place when the right time comes. That's what I've been working my heart out all year to do.

Sincerely,
George Bush

———————

May 19, 1980

Mr. Richard C. Murphy, Jr.
Napa, California 94558
Dear Dick:

Thanks for your recent letter and candid advice.

I am in this race to win the nomination, but I don't want to say anything that would cripple our party's ability to win the November election.

That is why I have very carefully campaigned by emphasizing the differences between Governor Reagan and me on the issues, rather than on sensitive subjects such as his age. I have made the distinction between us on that too by jogging three miles every day, but the voters have been uninterested in the so-called age issue. . . .

Sincerely,
George Bush

———————

On the day I won the Michigan primary—a big upset—Ronald Reagan won the much smaller Nebraska primary. But it gave him the number of delegates he needed to win the nomination. Given advice from Jim Baker and other trusted advisers, I decided the best thing to do for the party and for my friends and supporters was to get out.

May 22, 1980
    I can't think toward '84* . . . I have got to go back to work for a living. But, I'm lucky to be able to take the time, to spend money to

———

*Some friends were already encouraging me to try again in 1984!

come out right personally, to do my best. And, that is about where we stand on the 22nd, having come close, close, close to where I wanted to get, not in terms of total delegates, but in finishing with style. . . .

What is it going to be like? Driving a car, having C. Fred, being lonely around the house? It's kind of fun thinking about all of that— back to the real world. . . .

Here are excerpts from the statement I issued on May 26:

. . . I have never quit a fight in my life. But throughout my political career—as a precinct worker, a county chairman and national chairman—I have always worked to unite and strengthen the Republican party.

. . . In that spirit, earlier today, I sent the following message to Governor Reagan:

CONGRATULATIONS ON YOUR SUPERB CAMPAIGN FOR OUR PARTY'S 1980 PRESIDENTIAL NOMINATION. I PLEDGE MY WHOLEHEARTED SUPPORT IN A UNITED PARTY EFFORT THIS FALL TO DEFEAT JIMMY CARTER AND ELECT NOT ONLY A REPUBLICAN PRESIDENT BUT REPUBLICAN SENATORS, CONGRESSMEN AND STATE AND LOCAL OFFICIALS WHO WILL WORK TOWARD OUR COMMON GOAL OF RESTORING THE AMERICAN PEOPLE'S CONFIDENCE IN THEIR GOVERNMENT AND OUR NATION'S FUTURE.

. . . Am I disappointed in not achieving what I set out to achieve on entering this race?

Of course I am, not simply for myself but for Barbara and my entire family and friends and the thousands of workers—especially those dedicated volunteer workers—who made personal commitments on my behalf and whom I'll never be able to fully repay for all they've done.

Was it worth it? Did we achieve anything?

Yes, we did. I entered this race because I have a vision of America as a strong, purposeful, compassionate nation in need of new leadership for the decade of the Eighties. I have addressed the issues facing our country as I saw them and as a result I believe our political process has been strengthened. . . .

Barbara and I will see you in Detroit in July.*

*The site of the Republican convention.

May 30, 1980

Dear Hank,*
    No one died but it feels like it.
    Your letter and your loyal support makes it all O.K. Barbara and I are so grateful.
    We're going to Maine soon—then to Detroit—then regroup.
    We're OK.

Love to all,
George

June 14, 1980

Mr. Nicolas Biddle, Jr.
Narberth, Pennsylvania 19072
Dear Nicolas:
    . . . I am complimented that you want me to be the vice-presidential nominee, but I hope you understand that I am not interested in seeking that position. I will work hard to unite the party and to help defeat Jimmy Carter in November.
    Barbara and I and our entire family thank you for your faith and loyalty. We will never forget it.

Sincerely,
George Bush

June 30, 1980

Mr. G. David Kelly, Jr.
Mt. Berry, Georgia 30149
Dear Dave,
    Your terrific letter just caught up with me in Maine where Barbara and I are getting some rest in between fund raising events to pay off the campaign debt. The loyalty and support of people like you and Kay mean so much.
    The Vice Presidential speculation is flattering, and of course I'll do what's asked of me, if anything. I really feel it should be Reagan's call, though, uninhibited by pressure. . . .

Sincerely,
George Bush

*Hank Knoche, one of my top deputies at the CIA.

_____

I went to the Republican convention in Detroit knowing the vice presidency was a possibility, but I did not expect it. Rumors were flying that Reagan would ask President Ford to join the ticket, and in fact the two did discuss it in Detroit but could not reach an agreement. No one was more surprised than I was when I answered the phone in my hotel suite and Ronald Reagan was on the other end of the line. One of my first congratulatory calls came from the man I wanted to defeat, Vice President Walter Mondale, for whom I have great respect.

July 19, 1980

Vice President Walter F. Mondale
United States Senate
Washington, D. C. 20510
Dear Fritz,

Thank you for your courteous call. It was most thoughtful of you to call all the way from Africa.

I do believe a debate such as you suggest would be useful and I heartily accept.

Barbara joins me in sending both you and Joan our best regards.

Sincerely,
George Bush

_____

July 22, 1980

Mr. Ray Zauber, Editor
OAK CLIFF TRIBUNE
Dallas, Texas 75237
Dear Ray:

Thanks for your note and the copy of your fantastic open letter to Governor Reagan.

All I can say is that he must have read it, banged his fist into his palm, and said, "By George, it's George!"

Seriously, I appreciate all the help and friendship you've shown me over the years. I know Governor Reagan and I can count on you in the months ahead, too.

Sincerely,
GEORGE BUSH
(Dictated but not signed)

_____

7-29-80

Dear Mr. President [Nixon],

That was a most thoughtful note you sent me on July 19. I am pleased to be on this ticket. We can win, but I'm one who feels it will be a very tough race—Pr. Carter is a no-holds-barred guy—

... My love to Mrs. N and the girls—

Most sincerely,
George

———

One of the first things Reagan asked me to do was travel to Japan and China and meet with leaders there to discuss our views. I wrote this letter upon my return:

September 15, 1980

To: Republicans Abroad

I took a week of precious time early in the campaign and went to Japan and China because of the great importance a Reagan-Bush administration would attach to the entire Pacific Basin, and the vital role U.S. relations with Japan and China would play in establishing peace, stability and economic growth in the area. I went there in order to meet directly with the leaders of these two great countries, to talk with them freely and candidly, and just to learn more. . . .

In Japan I had the extraordinary opportunity to be the first candidate in the campaign to meet Key leaders in the new government . . . We exchanged views on a wide range of international and bilateral issues and I found this personal exposure invaluable in terms of getting a first-hand account of how Japanese viewed such crucial issues as trade, Soviet expansionism and defense. At the same time I was able to explain Reagan-Bush policies to the people that mattered. I left Japan sensing there was a strong enduring relationship between our two countries but that a great deal still needed to be done—to increase Japanese confidence in the U.S. credibility and to develop a more fruitful and equitable trade relationship.

In China I saw at length the men I came to see and I explained directly to them our world view, our constructive approach to U.S.-Chinese relations and our position on Taiwan. I was not seeking agreement or approval. I have known these men for years—we are old friends and we can therefore talk frankly to each other. My relations with Vice Premier DENG Xiaoping and with Foreign Minister HUANG Hua (Just promoted to Vice Premier) go back a long way—in HUANG's case almost ten years. I am sure that a Reagan-Bush administration will have strengthened relations with China, built on a solid base of shared objectives and interests, but not at the expense of our old friends. Integrity is not divisible.

. . . Clearing the air does not necessarily result in a love-fest. Relations with Japan and China will improve during a Reagan-Bush Administration because we in America will be perceived by them as strong, credible and honest. This, I hope, saw its beginning in my brief trip.

Sincerely,
George Bush

9-26-80

George Thompson Corp
Monterey Park, California
Gentlemen:

I am a coarse ground pepper lover. Tonight, on the campaign trail, I used a Thompson pepper mill. The pepper came out in large chunks (coarse ground).

Will you please send me an Olde Thompson pepper grinder that grinds the pepper coarse. Send it to the above address and I'll pay promptly.

George Bush

I made the big mistake of telling a reporter that the vice-presidential debate was minor league stuff. "It's the Toledo Mud Hens. It's not the big league," was my exact quote. I received a reprimand from our good friend Lud Ashley, whose congressional district included the home of the Mud Hens, Toledo, Ohio. My reply:

10-5-80

Dear Rep. Ashley,

Surely your baseball career—no field, no hit—fast yes, but no field, no hit—should make you wise enough to understand that my reference to the Mud Hens was adulatory. Yes I know the hens lost to Columbus, but gosh, gee, let's face it—the Astros they're not. Mondale may be bigger than the Hens . . . but me— I'm a Mud Hen at heart—comfortably slipping into the role. If I offended any Mud Hen fans please straighten them out—go out there, dance around second base and tell em' "I, Lud Ashley, was wrong. I maligned G/Bush. I recall him as a .345 hitter, a man of class with the glove as well! Unlike my leader Jimmy Earl* when I make a mistake I will apologize—-so now right here near first base, the very base that Bush immortalized, I want to say I am sorry. . . . I wronged this great <u>heavy hitting</u> first baseman."

Lud, this will win for you—maybe not for Jimmy but you.

We miss you, darn it.

George

*I'm referring to President Carter. Lud was a Democrat.

10-5-80

Alan Wolfe
Potomac, MD 20884
Wolfgang—

Your note received and digested. Life is now hectic—pushed here & there. I think we're going to win it.

But underneath everything—the balloons, the cheers, the good stories & the bad—underneath it all is friendship. Thanks for your vote.

GB

October 25, 1980

Mr. Albert Showfety
Joe Mill Hosiery Company
Hickory, NC 28601
Dear Mr. Showfety,

Thank you so much for the socks with REAGAN/BUSH on them. They are very nice and I'm quite sure few people have a pair just like them. . . .

Sincerely,
George Bush

Ronald Reagan defeated President Carter on November 4 in a sweeping victory. After a tumultuous two years, I suddenly was Vice President–elect of the United States. One of the first notes I wrote after the election was to Vice President Mondale:

11-8-80

Dear Fritz—

You & Joan have been most thoughtful & courteous. Bar looks forward to her visit with Joan in 10 days or so. I'd love to sit down with you. Thank you for your wire, your call, your just plain decency. I've lost—plenty— I know it's no fun—

My best to you—

George

November 10, 1980

President-elect and Mrs. Ronald Reagan
Los Angeles, California 90045
Dear Ron and Nancy,

Barbara and I are unwinding in Houston—off to the Florida Keys tomorrow for 4 days—then to D. C. on the 17th.

This is just a quick thank you—thanks for making us feel so welcome, thanks for the joy of working with you, thanks for those little touches of grace and humor and affection that make life sing.

Please know that we both want to help in every way possible. I will never do anything to embarrass you politically. I have strong views on issues and people, but once you decide a matter that's it for me, and you'll see no leaks in Evans and Novak bitching about life—at least you'll see none out of me.

I will make some suggestions (attached are 2 memos) but again I will respect your final judgment. Call me if I can lighten the burden. If you need someone to meet people on your behalf, or to turn off overly-eager office seekers, or simply someone to bounce ideas off of—please holler.

Thanks for the great opportunity to serve and to help make things a little better here and abroad.

Respectfully and with friendship.

Sincerely,
George Bush

CHAPTER 9

A Heartbeat Away

Even in the beginning, when we were really just getting to know each other, President Reagan always made it clear to me that I would have direct access to him and that he would welcome my advice and suggestions. I didn't waste a lot of time. Here are the first two memos I wrote him:

———

November 10, 1980

Memorandum for President-elect Reagan
From: George Bush
Subject: Intelligence Community

I feel strongly that the Director of Central Intelligence should be a professional—preferably a person coming up through the ranks of CIA. This will do much to restore the confidence in the Agency and in the intelligence community that has been lacking. It will help with our Liaison Services abroad such as the British, French, Israelis, etc. It will be a signal to all that you plan to have a thorough going professional service.

I am confident such a move would be very well received abroad and inside the Intelligence Community—on the Hill as well.

I have no person in mind but I would be glad to assist Ed [Meese] in searching for such a person if the idea has your approval.

There are several people who have been working for us in this campaign, who if appointed, would demoralize the intelligence community. I will communicate my views on this to Ed Meese*—no need to bother you.

———

*Ed, one of Reagan's top aides, was instrumental in staffing the administration.

I also favor reinstituting the President's Foreign Intelligence Advisory Board. I would recommend a smaller board than before. This move would be particularly appropriate if you go with my suggestion above—appointing a "pro" to head CIA.*

———

November 10, 1980

Memorandum for President-elect Reagan
From: George Bush
Subject: Texas Appointments

I understand that it is traditional that the Vice President be consulted on all appointments from his home state. I would like very much to have this same understanding with you. Needless to say, if you feel strongly about <u>any</u> appointment that would of course override any objection that I might have and I would strongly support your decision.

I can assure you there will be no problems between you and me on this if you instruct your staff to consult me on all Texas appointments. In fact, in some sensitive cases, I can see a good "out" for you.

P. S. When I mention home state, I am not talking about Connecticut, Maine, Ohio or Massachusetts—just little old Texas.†

———

The transition period was intense. We needed to hire a staff, get ready for the inauguration, and answer the literally thousands of letters that poured into our office from people seeking jobs, airing their opinions, or voicing their concerns. I took some time out in December to do some hunting—and to write a friend:

12-21-80

Dear Gerry [Bemiss],

I'm heading back to the home after 2 relaxing nights in So. Tex.‡—reminiscing in the back of this long black car. Alone—except for State Police—2 S Service guys in front—Back-up car following but alone with my thoughts. So

---

*President Reagan clearly overrode my advice and appointed William Casey. (Casey had been a member of the CIA's forerunner, the OSS, during World War II.) Given that I was appointed DCI without prior intelligence experience, I could not say too much.

†President Reagan used to joke about all my "home" states. I had grown up in Connecticut, had a home in Maine, my father was from Ohio, I was born in Massachusetts, and I lived in Texas. I actually left one out: my mother was from Missouri.

‡I almost always went hunting around Christmastime (usually between Christmas and New Year's) near Beeville, Texas, with my good friend Will Farish.

much has already happened. So much new, and challenging exciting & frustrating lies ahead. And yet I'm sure of one thing—I am lucky to have friends who really count—who have been at my side to help with advice and criticism and the willingness to do tough thankless things—That all counts. Thanks & love at Christmas.

GB

On January 20, 1981, President Reagan and I took our oaths of office. Our entire family—children, grandchildren, my mother, brothers, and sister—everyone came to help us celebrate. I wrote my aunt Mary, Uncle Herbie's widow.

2-8-81

Dear Mary,

Life has been too darned hectic lately, but it is full and fascinating and Bar and I have never been busier in our lives.

My only regret over the whole inauguration was that we didn't have a second to really visit with family and friends. I have had so many letters from friends saying they were here—people we never laid eyes on in the crowds.

The house* is warm and livable and Bar has put in many little family touches. My public life is almost out of control, in terms of complex scheduling but the President is a joy to work with and for; and he and Nancy have both shown us so many courtesies you wouldn't believe it.

The Point is coming along well,† we are told. Longley Philbrick is the contractor. We have no written contract—just mutual trust; but that's just fine because he is conscientious.

I don't know how much of the big House will be ready for summer, but "worry not" is my motto.

The garage will be the Secret Service Command Post. They are fixing up the gates, wiring the House for fire and break in alarms and will be covering the place year round as the law provides.

We want the Point to be as Herby [sic] would want it to be—open to all family to come and go and love it as we all always have. I am grateful to you for your patience and understanding on all the details of transfer. . . .

---

*The vice president's official residence, which is on the grounds of the Naval Observatory in Washington.

†Bar and I had just bought Walker's Point, which had been put up for sale after Uncle Herbie's death. When it was about ready to be sold out of the family, we decided to step in and buy it, mainly so Mum could keep her house on the Point. It of course turned out to be one of the best decisions we ever made. We were in the middle of major renovations since little had been done to the house after it had been clobbered by a storm several years earlier.

Our house is your house. Walker's Point is your Walker's Point and your kids' too.

The Secret Service will be there but they will not obstruct family coming and going.

Thanks, Mary, for working all this out. I hope we can give the place the same love Herby did. We want it to keep its character. We want it to be the anchor for all the family.

Much Love,
Poppy

———————

One of the first things President Reagan asked me to do was to head up a special Task Force on Regulatory Relief. Our goal was to eliminate or at least revise unnecessary federal rules and regulations. In other words, get rid of red tape. I sent a copy of this letter to all cabinet members:

February 10, 1981

The Honorable Terrell Bell
Secretary of Education
Washington, D. C.
Dear Ted:

As I indicated at last Wednesday's Cabinet meeting, it would be very helpful to our Task Force on Regulatory Relief if you could designate a representative from your Department who can speak for you in dealing with our Task Force staff. . . . I think this will expedite our joint efforts to reduce the burdens of regulation and facilitate the workings of the Task Force.

I think we are going to produce solid results, and I look forward to working with you and your staffs on these important regulatory issues.

Sincerely,
George Bush

———————

February 23, 1981

Miss Irene Cassert
Starpoint Central School
Lockport, New York
Dear Miss Cassert and Children:

How thoughtful of you to send me one of the folders you made for your parents in honor of the release of the hostages.* I wish you could have shared

---

*The remaining fifty-two American hostages still being held in Iran were released on January 20.

with me the wonderful experience I had when I greeted the hostages at Andrews Air Force Base, and felt the outpouring of faith and affection from those thousands of Americans who were there to greet them and also from those millions of people across the country who were there in spirit. It was a moment I shall never forget.

It is young people like you who will be the backbone of our country in the future, who will keep the American dream alive. You must work hard and stay involved. I'm sure your parents are very proud of you.

Warm wishes.

Sincerely,
George Bush

March 9, 1981

Mrs. H. Webster Smith
Hart House
Tenants Harbor, Maine 04860
Dear Mrs. Smith:

I am writing this note sitting in front of a beautiful mahogany secretary bookcase in my office four doors down from the President. As you know, thanks to your enormous generosity this [case] has been used in the White House since 1973. I find it extraordinarily beautiful, and urged the curator, my friend Clem Conger to permit me to have it in my office where many visiting dignitaries would see it.

It just occurred to me that having lent this beautiful piece to the government, you might have a personal interest in where it is. I am attaching a picture. I am the one standing next to your beautiful mahogany piece. . . .

Sincerely yours,
George Bush

On March 30, John W. Hinckley Jr., shot and seriously wounded President Reagan as he left the Washington Hilton Hotel. Three other men were wounded as well: Press Secretary Jim Brady, Secret Service agent Tim McCarthy, and police officer Tom Delahanty. I was about to land in Austin, Texas, when we received word, and I immediately headed back to Washington. Like the entire nation, I was stunned. I jotted down these notes on my Air Force II *flight information card. "Murphy" was my chief of staff, Dan Murphy; Ed Pollard was head of my Secret Service detail. You will see at the time I wrote this, we thought Jim Brady was dead.*

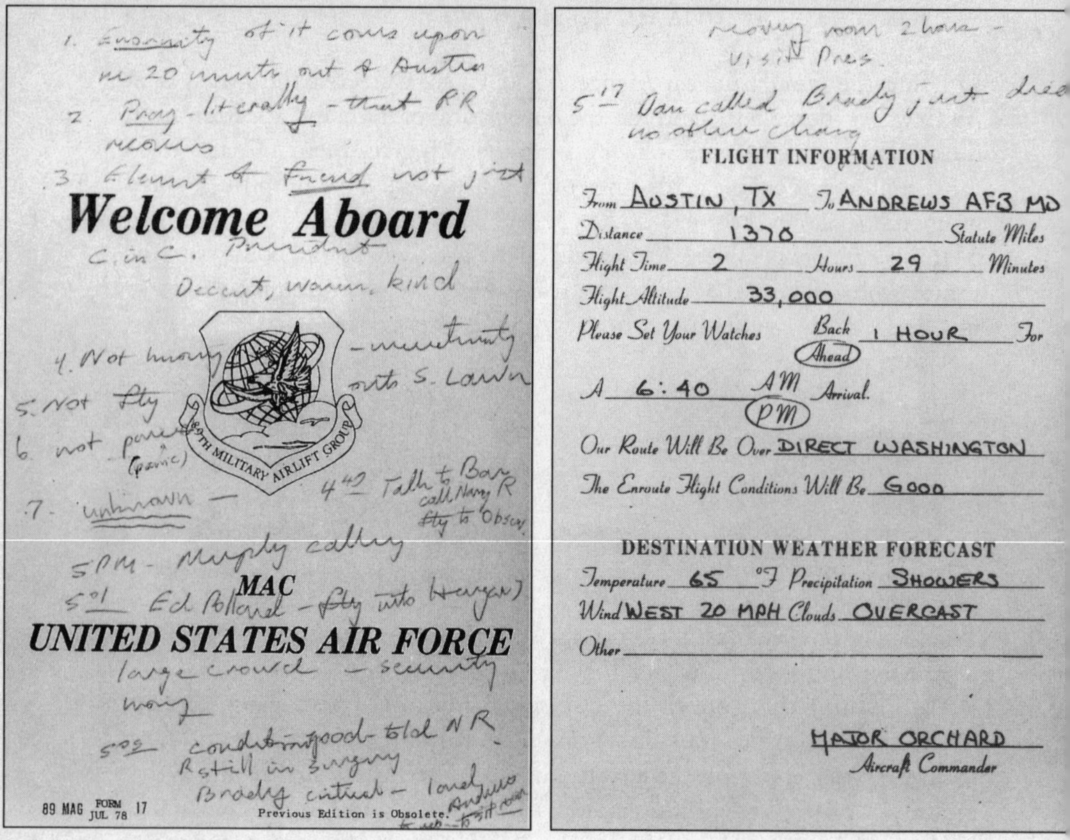

Welcome Aboard

89TH MILITARY AIRLIFT GROUP

MAC
UNITED STATES AIR FORCE

89 MAG FORM 17
JUL 78
Previous Edition is Obsolete.

Handwritten notes (left card):
1. Enormity of it came upon us 20 minutes out of Austin
2. Pray - literally - that RR recovers
3. Element of friend not just — C in C, President. Decent, warm, kind
4. Not many — uncertainty onto S. Lawn
5. Not fly
6. not panic
7. unknown — 4:42 Talk to Barr call Nancy R fly to Obscur
5 PM - Murphy calling
5:01 Ed Pollard - fly into (Hangar)
large crowd — security wrong
5:?? condition good - told NR R still in surgery Brady critical - lonely...

Handwritten notes (right card top):
recovery room 2 hours - visit Pres.
5:17 Dan called Brady just died no other change

FLIGHT INFORMATION

From AUSTIN, TX To ANDREWS AFB MD
Distance _____ 1370 _____ Statute Miles
Flight Time _____ 2 _____ Hours _____ 29 _____ Minutes
Flight Altitude _____ 33,000
Please Set Your Watches Back 1 HOUR For Ahead
At 6:40 AM PM Arrival.
Our Route Will Be Over DIRECT WASHINGTON
The Enroute Flight Conditions Will Be GOOD

DESTINATION WEATHER FORECAST
Temperature 65 °F Precipitation SHOWERS
Wind WEST 20 MPH Clouds OVERCAST
Other _____

MAJOR ORCHARD
Aircraft Commander

April 10, 1981

Mr. Frank Osanka
Naperville, Ill. 60540
Dear Mr. Osanka:

Thanks so much for your thoughtful letter of March 31. We were all shocked by the terrible events of last week, but are grateful that the President is now well on the way to recovery.

I understand your feelings entirely concerning the protection the President is receiving, but I am sure you will agree that in a democracy such as ours it is almost impossible to have a 100% success record unless we stopped him from going out in public at all, which I don't think any of us would want to see happen. You can be sure that all possible measures will be taken in the future to ensure that something like this does not happen again.

Sincerely,
George Bush

Secretary of State Alexander Haig came under terrible criticism the day of the shooting when he announced during a White House press conference he was "in control." Haig made the comment to reassure both the country and our allies, especially since I was still in the air rushing back to Washington. I wrote this letter to a first cousin:

April 13, 1981

Mr. George Walker
Iuka, Ms. 38852
Dear George:

Thanks so much for your thoughtful letter of March 31. Fortunately, we all came through the tragic events of last week very well. It certainly proved that our system of government really works, and that we can survive a crisis of this kind. We feel that Secretary Haig acted just as he should, and he has the full support of both President Reagan and myself.

The President returned to the White House today, and I'm happy to say he is in very good shape. He is truly a remarkable man.

I'm glad to hear that all is well with you and the family. Life is very hectic for me—more than ever before—but I am enjoying the challenge.

Love to you and Connie from both of us.

[copy unsigned]

————

April 18, 1981

Mr. Ralph P. Davidson, Chairman of the Board
TIME Incorporated
New York, New York 10020
Dear Ralph:

I have now read the major TIME essay on "American Renewal" . . .

First, let me congratulate TIME Incorporated on its bold project to spark such a renewal. I was impressed that many of the changes for which you called would have been attacked by the liberal establishment (maybe even by TIME) only a short while back as endorsing the Imperial Presidency, a Cold War Strategy, a Powerful Speaker, and Laissez-Faire Capitalism, to use a few epithets. I believe a new national consensus is forming that says, okay, we tried the sackcloth and ashes routine and we're worse off than before. America is a great country and should act like it. This was the clear message I got on the campaign trail for two years, and it's certainly the message with which President Reagan won the 1980 election.

A couple more comments: Otto Friedrich's "To Reform the System" despaired over the vice presidency but made no clear proposal to alter it. He was correct in saying that the most important thing any Vice President can become is "senior adviser with portfolio". Indeed, to saddle the Vice President with the job of White House Chief of Staff would serve to weaken rather than strengthen him, diluting his prestige as the only nationally-elected official other than the President with decisions over who gets the parking spaces right next to the West Wing. My predecessor, Fritz Mondale, forged an agreement with President Carter which was wholly adopted by President Reagan and me. By this, the Vice President has total access to the President and all his meetings, where his voice can be heard in the highest councils on matters of national policy. Further, the much derided role of being President of the Senate gives a Vice President a unique opportunity to work for the Administration's programs on Capitol Hill without being considered a crass lobbyist.

As for the changes in the political process listed in Friedrich's article, I agree that campaigns are too long. Yet, I cannot forget that without hard, steady work at the grassroots, I would probably not be sitting where I am today. Because there are as many minuses as pluses to the question of changing the rules of American politics, the best course is to let matters evolve on their own without some new edict out of Congress. . . .

I really didn't mean to write a counter-essay. But the "American Renewal" . . . proved quite thought-provoking.

Sincerely,
George Bush

———

6-1-81

Frederick J. Harrigan
Colebrook, New Hampshire 03576
Dear Fred,

I was delighted to get your letter. My only regret is that you don't look like me—I could use a surrogate around here.

I do appreciate your offer for the President. Security is such that it would be hard to do what you suggest, but the offer is what counts.*

Also, it was very thoughtful of your dog George to remember Fred, Fred. Lest George forgets what it is Fred looks like, here is a relatively recent shot. Incidentally Fred is writing a book, immodestly titled preliminarily "Famous People who know Fred".† It is mainly pictures. Fred has forsaken us at night,

---

*Fred was a distinguished newspaper editor and perhaps one of the most respected citizens of New Hampshire's North Country. He thought he resembled President Reagan and offered to stand in for the President at times if it would help improve his security. His offer was serious and sincere.

†It was eventually published as *C. Fred's Story* and raised a lot of money for literacy. Barbara was Fred's ghostwriter.

finding he likes the raccoon action at the security post near our gate. Besides the midnight shift must be feeding Fred for he has more than his normal amount of stomach gas which regrettably he vents a lot.

I am getting a bum rap on being a preppy, but other than that things are going very well here. It would be nice to get to the North Country—to see you, to run with your fleet footed son, to hear your latest jokes, and to relax. We were in Kennebunkport, Maine for two nights last weekend and I came alive. We are fixing up a house my grandfather built near the sea at the turn of the century.

President Reagan is a great man to work for and with. He gives me plenty of things to do, and he is a guy you can discuss things with without getting your head bitten off. We know the problems are immense, but I believe we can turn things around.

Again, thanks for your offer, and my warm best wishes to you—joined in all of this by Barbara and Fred am I.

Most Sincerely,
George Bush

7-20-81

Martin Allday
1600 lst Nat'l Bank Bldg.
Midland, Texas 79701
Dear Martin,

I loved your newsy letter about Midland. It was just great. I will try to work something out for Midland C of C [Chamber of Commerce] but not sure if it will fit. I have asked Jennifer Fitzgerald in my office to call you on this. It would indeed be great to see booming Midland, to see friends, and hopefully to see our new grandchild* out there. We still miss Midland, you, our other friends.

Life is full and hectic. I am typing this at home—Bar in Maine moving into new house up there—well rather, an old house that we are doing completely over. It will be winterized and summerized so we can spend a good deal of time there when we retire. Someday you've got to see it.

My job is full and fascinating. Not enough hours in the day. Pres. R is great to work with. He is quite a guy—marvelous sense of humor, unthreatened by people or events, a superb person. The top staff are good people too—of course Jim Baker being here is great.†

----

*George and Laura were expecting a baby. It turned out to be two babies—Jenna and Barbara, born November 25.

†Jim was Reagan's chief of staff.

Better run, but thanks for your great letter. Warmest Regards. Love to all.

George

After Labor Day I finally began keeping a diary again, having quit when the campaign ended in 1980. Despite my best efforts to make note of something every single day, I would sometimes let the diary lapse for weeks, even months—something I profoundly regret today. Most days, the schedule was too busy to reflect on what had been. It was all I could do to keep up with what was ahead. Anyway, I have scattered some diary entries throughout the vice-presidential and White House chapters.

September 7, 1981

My first day back in Washington after a fantastic time in Maine. . . . It's a great joy being there with the sea pounding into the rocks, the boat, the new [tennis] court, being with Mother, seeing the Walkers and the kids, and our own grandchildren running around the place. It was supreme joy, a physical lift. I ran comfortable and fast, played reasonable tennis, took up golf again, learned to putt, and had two birdies on the front nine against Ed Muskie* and the pro from Kennebunk Beach, only to clutch on the back nine—minor interest.

. . . The job is still totally fulfilling, and I must say I got that feeling tonight having gotten home after a light run—I'm ready to get back to work again.

October 6, 1980

Today was the day that Sadat was shot and killed. Two days ago, Mubarak, the new President of Egypt, was in our house sitting in the corner of our living room looking out on the porch, wanting to go for a walk, but chatting about Egypt. It was my second meeting with him, and today, he is wearing the crown, and heaven knows how easily or uneasily in Egypt, the turmoil, the killing and the plotting—it gets you down. At the NSC planning group meeting, I made some joke about . . . I hated to leave the room because somebody would vote to send me to [a] funeral;† and then I realized later that maybe

---

*Former Democratic senator from Maine, secretary of state, and presidential candidate.
†I had already attended one state funeral that year.

the President would take it seriously. So I called him up in the Residence—he had gone home around 6 p.m.—and said, "I hope you understand," and he said, "No, I don't think either of us should go. We have three former Presidents going, and I think you should be treated the same as me in this regard." I told him that I wasn't worried about it, and if things mounted and the pressures mounted, that I would be glad to go.*

October 14, 1981

Mrs. Sidney W. Davidson, Jr.
Milwaukee, Wisconsin 53202
Dear Mrs. Davidson:

I was, of course, pleased to hear from you but I must confess I was disappointed in what you wrote about. Thank God we have a President who is trying to get this economy under control after decades of reckless deficits and inflation driven higher taxes.

On foreign affairs we do adhere to human rights. We are not propping up authoritarian governments all over the world, but we are determined to help those who are trying to resist the insidious onslaught of Castro-backed revolution or Soviet inspired mischief. We had better wake up in this country to what the Soviets and its friends are doing. Take a look at Poland; take a look at the Caribbean; take a look at Qaddafi.† Don't you think we should resist this kind of tyranny.

I hate to disagree with you but I think the President is doing a first class job, and I have no difficulty in supporting him fully.

Sincerely,
George Bush

January 12, 1982

The Honorable Richard Nixon
26 Federal Plaza
New York, N. Y.
Dear Mr. President:

I received your warm letter of January 7 and I am very appreciative. A lot of people simply don't understand the advice you gave me.

---

*There was tremendous concern about security at the funeral. President Reagan thought he should go, then decided neither of us should. Instead, Presidents Nixon, Ford, and Carter went.
†Muammar el-Qaddafi of Libya.

A couple of months ago I had a letter from a very prominent Republican Senator, saying "separate yourself from the President". This was written at the time of some tough budget vote. I have had lots of writers hone in on differences that I may have had with President Reagan during the primaries, trying to get me to highlight these differences now.

I don't believe a President should have to be looking over his shoulder wondering if the Vice President was out there carving him up or undermining his programs in one way or another. I guess every Vice President has had to endure the annual rounds of "whatever happened to V.P._____ stories". They don't bother me a bit. I like my job, I have plenty to do, and I believe I can be helpful to the President. So what else is there?

Thank you so very much for that insightful letter. Barbara joins me in sending our best to Mrs. Nixon.

Respectfully,
George Bush

January 13, 1982

Mr. Stephen Offerman
Amsterdam Color Works Inc.
New York, N. Y. 10461
Dear Mr. Offerman:

. . . The President of the United States, together with Secretary of State Haig and others in this Administration, felt that the sale of AWACS* to Saudi Arabia was not a threat to Israel but a calculated move to help advance permanent peace in the Middle East.

The question is not simply one of Israeli versus Arab. There are exterior forces at play in the region, supported and financed by the Soviet Union or surrogate states such as Qaddafi's Libya, who would like nothing better than to destabilize nations such as Saudi Arabia, Egypt or Jordan. We are confident of Israel's strength. We are also committed to Israel's right to exist within safe and secure borders and in peace.

Honest men approach solutions differently. Our efforts towards peace in the region are as honorable as yours or any other American. I strongly challenge your assertion that the President is a "bully". There is nothing in his make up that even the most critical observer would charge along the lines you suggest. I respect and support your right to fight for those principles in which you deeply believe. The President of the United States has the same right. . . .

----

*Airborne Warning and Control Systems, an electronic surveillance aircraft. Israel was strongly opposed to the sale.

I have been in public life a long time. I have encountered great passions in the arena, and sometimes men of integrity, myself included I hope, realize they have made mistakes and say so. Think about it and write me back, for in spite of my first flush of anger at reading your letter, I have respect for a man who fights for his strongly held beliefs.

Sincerely,
George Bush

March 15, 1982

Mr. and Mrs. William McKenzie
Dallas, Texas 75205
Dear Billy Mac and Sally:

You won't know me. I look like the guy on channel 4—every hair in place, the natural dry look to perfection. Why? Why you ask—because of my new redkin (?) hair spray. It's me after all these years—natural yet aggressive— quasi militant but not offensively so. I am very excited about all of this, and am entering the Senior Body contest relying heavily on the judges to 'think hair'. Many many thanks. And much Love.

George

3-30-82

Dear Miss Hepburn,

We so enjoyed our meeting—too brief of course; but for Barbara and me, a highlight not soon forgotten. We respect you so—and I guess as a little kid I thought you were the meowest of the cat's meows—Anyway now we've met.

But this is about last night's Oscar too.* Hooray for you—3 cheers for excellence and style and class and honor and warmth. 3 cheers for your decency—

Affectionate regards from yet another Hepburn fan—

George Bush

Given that I had recently visited China during a trip abroad, and given some recent statements from President Reagan about China, Barry Goldwater wrote me an angry letter, accusing the administration of forsaking Taiwan for China. I had great respect for Senator Goldwater but wholeheartedly disagreed with him.

---

*Katharine Hepburn had won best actress for *On Golden Pond*.

May 28, 1982

The Honorable Barry Goldwater
United States Senate
Washington, D. C. 20510
Dear Barry:

Your letter about Taiwan and the PRC was, as they say in diplomatic circles, frank and candid, I'm not surprised. I long have known your views on this subject.

I don't expect you to change your mind, Barry, but I do think I should make a few points.

You think the U.S. stands on two different policies—one for the PRC and one for Taiwan. But in fact, we have one policy—there is one China and we acknowledge the PRC view that Taiwan is part of China, a view that is shared by Taiwan. We respect the sovereignty of that one China. We believe it is best to let the PRC and Taiwan work out their differences peacefully, without outside pressure or interference. We stress a peaceful solution. We remain a loyal friend to Taiwan while we simultaneously try to advance our relationship with the PRC. We believe that good relations between the U.S. and the PRC advance the cause of peace worldwide and that we would be irresponsible to let the opportunity for improved relations pass us by without a principled effort on our part. Note, I say principled. We will not turn our back on an old friend, Taiwan. We will uphold the law of the land. President Reagan and I took an oath on this.

I spent hours telling the PRC leaders that President Reagan is a man of principle. He is a friend of Taiwan. He will uphold the laws of the U.S.A. He wants to improve relations with the PRC but within his principles, commitments, promises, and oath of office. We seek some formula that allows the U.S. to have good relations with the PRC while at the same time maintaining our historic friendship with Taiwan. We know that's not easy. And it will not be made any easier if you say the things you hint at in your letter.

One last point—every friend and ally we have in Asia . . . all urge that we strengthen our relationship with the PRC. They see it as in their strategic self-interest, and ours as well. The same is true for our European allies.

Barry, you are a highly respected U.S. leader. What you say is very important to the people of America, Taiwan and the PRC. As we search for a way to insure peace in the world—a way to influence and control a very dangerous Soviet Union—we need your help.

Sincerely, and with warm
personal regards,
George

June 2, '82

Dear Hugh,*

Thanks for the clipping which Don Rhodes† handed me along with your note when I arrived home tonight from Colorado.

I keep hearing rumors of early activity up there . . . Majority Leader of the US Senate‡ was getting active; then this clip about Jack Kemp.§

. . . My problem is that I will do nothing at all of any kind that could even marginally be considered as moving around for '84. I am too devoted to the Prez to do this and it would be wrong. Others may have different plans—quite obviously they do. I'd love to get the Gregg advice on this.

Life continues full blast, exciting, frustrating at times—the latter because of the persistent economic problems.

I have learned a great deal and am doing some fascinating things. This week flew in an AWACS to Colorado from Oklahoma—a fantastic learning experience. Doing a lot of travel and speechifying—a lot on pure politics already, but also much civic stuff.

Dying to chat soon—Maine maybe??? Love to Cay.

[UNSIGNED]

I had been exchanging letters with my friend Bart Giamatti, the president of Yale University and later the commissioner of baseball, about the religious right. Here is one in the series:

July 29, 1982

Mr. A. Bartlett Giamatti
Yale University
New Haven, Connecticut 06520

Dear Bart:

But what is the difference between the Religious Right and the Religious Left? If I felt that the Religious Right or Left could impose their views on me by use of political power I would be upset; I don't feel that way. But given your concern, why do you feel a threat from the Religious Right but not the Left?

I'm not sure what God wants of us; but that others think they know what God wants is okay with me. Why is it all right for Coffin** to urge defiance

---

*Hugh Gregg, former governor of New Hampshire and chairman of my 1980 campaign in that state.

†Don has been my loyal assistant since I was elected to Congress in 1966 and is still with me.

‡Howard Baker of Tennessee.

§Former quarterback for the Buffalo Bills and at this time a congressman from New York.

**The Reverend William Sloane Coffin, a liberal activist.

on Viet Nam, tolerance on Khomeni, or advocate "gay marriages" but it's not okay for the Right to get together and work against abortion or for prayer in school.

My problem Bart is that until the Religious Right got involved because of their concerns on drugs, decline in family, shifting views on homosexuals or divorce, no one gave much of a damn. We might not have agreed with the more liberal activists when they were (are) up in arms: but we said okay, let them do their thing.

Now the Religious Right is up in arms. Most of them (while believing deeply) are not totally intolerant of the views of others. Most get lumped in with some few that do what you say—namely, refuse to tolerate any difference.

Your letter was great. You say things better than I do—much better; but like you I have been across the country a lot and met with lots of people. We must be careful not to lump all the Religious Right in together. We must understand that in our post-Viet Nam post-Watergate guilt, we have condoned things we should have condemned. Now a decade later a lot of people are concerned. Some of them are totally intolerant, but in my view most are not.

They have seen those espousing different views asked to speak at prestigious schools, or had the Mary McGrory's do well written editorials about their conscience. They have been deeply troubled as they see religious men of the Left deliberately break laws (Thoreau might say "okay", but a lot of people worry about that).

Now, clumsily at times, vindictively at others (ask me, some of them took a big bite out of my behind during the campaign), they are trying to stand up for things that fundamentally I believe in. I differentiate between the "extremists" and the Religious Right in general.

I love Billy Graham, I really do; some of the flamboyant money-mad, teary temple builders worry me.

Okay, friend, now where am I wrong?

Best.

Sincerely,
George Bush

P.S.: I think you're wrong on prayer in schools. It is not just ideologues who want the voluntary prayer in school. Believe me Bart it is much deeper than that. And then there's the Pledge of Allegiance. The journalists slouch through it, the cynics might look down on Middle America, but Bart it feels good to go to some Rotary meetings in Iowa and say the Pledge—it really does—especially that part "one nation under God". It's all winners and no losers. I have a funny feeling it keeps us a little more together. Is it okay to say the Pledge in schools but not to have voluntary prayers [?]

I sent this photo to our daughter-in-law Laura Bush in 1983 with this note: "30 years ago your husband looked like this—so did your father-in-law; and so did Robin who might well today be your best friend had she lived."
(Bush Library photo.)

To Rep. Jack Fields
With best wishes from two Georges
G Bush

I sent this photo to Texas congressman Jack Fields in 1989. However, it was taken in March 1956 at commissioning ceremonies for one of our offshore drilling rigs, the SCORPION. That's the governor of Texas with me.
(Bush Library photo.)

Taylor — No one worked harder. Our Sincerest Thanks
G Bush

Sent to our friend and campaign volunteer Taylor Blanton on election night, 1964. I lost. (Photo courtesy of Taylor Blanton.)

To Pete Roussel —
good fields, good hit
Best GB
'74

The RNC co-ed softball team. I'm way in the back, with a woman sitting on my shoulders.
Pete Roussel, my press secretary at the RNC, is the guy lying on the ground in front.
(Photo courtesy of Peter Roussel.)

Photo taken by Pete Roussel
sometime in 1973 or '74.
That's C. Fred, one of
our literary dogs.
(Photo courtesy of Peter Roussel.)

To Pete c Fred's
from c Bar's
father c Bar's
husband !!
GB

Pete — such love
from your # 2 Ma.
Bar

Playing golf with President Reagan and Donald Regan in 1983. I sent this photo to my mother with this note: "Do you think Dad would approve of the swing on the guy farthest away? Much, much love, Pop." (Photo courtesy of Reagan Library.)

"Dear Geraldine [Ferraro]— Here's a couple of lunch shots. I enjoyed it. Merry Christmas to you and yours—George Bush." December 6, 1984.

(Bush Library photo.)

"Dear Aunt Marge [Clement], Here's our family picture from the inauguration. (Green Room in the White House) I love you—George." January 20, 1985.

(Photo courtesy of Reagan Library.)

George P— Nice Running. Devotedly, George

Jogging in Houston, October 9, 1986.

(Bush Library photo.)

Will Lots of birds (Dec. '86) Lots of friendship —

Hunting in Beeville, Texas,
with Will Farish, December 30, 1986.
(Bush Library photo.)

"Mum—I love this shot of Jenna and Barbara, taken on Air Force II
as we flew to the Amer. Legion Convention in San Antonio." August 25, 1987.
(Bush Library photo.)

"Dear Mum, I love this picture of you and me . . .
Devotedly, George." September 2, 1987. (Bush Library photo.)

Now, Bjorn, try to do this — bend your elbow
but keep arm stiff, see?? Glad to help, fella!
Geo Bush

Showing off to Swedish tennis star Bjorn Borg, September 10, 1987. (Bush Library photo.)

John Brotherhood! *(signature)*

Jonathan Bush, June 24, 1988. (Bush Library photo.)

To Neil • Sharon
You give us great joy! Devotedly, Dad!

Republican National Convention, August 18, 1988.
(Bush Library photo.)

"Doro—Happy memories of a good parade day. Sam's a ham—(get it—poetry)—Devotedly, Dad." At the state fair in Detroit, August 31, 1988. (Bush Library photo.)

With New York mayor Ed Koch at the annual Al Smith Dinner in New York, October 20, 1988. (Bush Library photo.)

Governor Michael Dukakis, December 2, 1988. (Bush Library photo.)

To General Secretary Mikhail Gorbachev With Warm Best Wishes from our family to your family. May the young ones know a world at Peace. Respectfully G. Bush

Sent to Gorbachev on December 10, 1988, when I was president-elect. The shot was taken in Maine on August 7, 1988. (Bush Library photo.)

To Pam- If you could serve like the Secretary of State and hit a back-hand like I do you'd be not in tennis but in politics Affectionately — G. Bush

Tennis star Pam Shriver and Jim Baker, December 12, 1988. (Bush Library photo.)

Dan. Here we go!! G. 1-20-89

Sent to Dan Quayle. (Bush Library photo.)

Dear John — We're looking for you!
Geo Bush, Millie, and the kids.

Sent to John Sansing at the *Washingtonian Magazine* after they named Millie the ugliest dog in Washington. April 20, 1989. (Bush Library photo.)

To the First Place winner of the first annual Scowcroft award; clearly, sir in a highly competitive field you have excelled. *Geo Bush*

Brent Scowcroft caught sleeping on Air Force I, May 12, 1989. (I should add that no one worked harder than Brent.) (Bush Library photo.)

Buck – Watch and Learn – !!.
G Bush

Playing golf with brother Bucky, professional golfer Doug Sanders, and golf pro Ken Raynor at Cape Arundel Gold Course, July 3, 1989. (Bush Library photo.)

To Dick Sternberg – The day I broke the jinx – Sept. 3, 1989. Best Wishes. Keep on fishing
G Bush

Dick was head of the Hunting and Fishing Library in Minnetonka, Minnesota. That's my boy Marvin helping me out. (Bush Library photo.)

To Kate and Sadri With the Hope that this handshake will lead to a more peaceful world. Love from all Bushes – G

This was taken at Malta, December 2, 1989. I sent it to my friends Catherine and Sadruddin Aga Khan. (Bush Library photo.)

Jogging with Nancy Ellis, January 7, 1990.
(Bush Library photo.)

To my sister — some special sister — with love — GB

Fishing with Senator Alan Simpson in Islamorada, Florida, April 21, 1990.
(Bush Library photo.)

Al — My idea of heaven — What ever would we do without friends   G Bush

The Joy and the Agony of a "Six Pack" —

Facing off against White House residence staffer Ron Jones in the Horseshoe Tournament Finals, June 24, 1990. (Bush Library photo.)

SPC Jeffery Buono
Good Luck on this Special Turkey Day '90
George Bush

Thanksgiving Day in Saudi Arabia, November 22, 1990. (Bush Library photo.)

A gift from Mexico President Carlos Salinas. I sent him the photo with this note: "If you see a slightly overweight, 6′2″ gringo in an enormous sombrero in black with silver on the legs <u>smiling</u> happily, that'll be me. George." November 28, 1990. (Bush Library photo.)

Dear Mikhail — Here We Are In Maine Talking to You in the Crimea. Thank God You and Raisa Were Safe & Sound Sincerely, G Bush

This was taken the day we found out Gorbachev had survived the attempted coup against him in the Soviet Union, August 21, 1991. I sent the photo to him several months later with this note: "Everything in this picture, except for Barbara, is now gone. This is our bedroom and the wave knocked down a wall and sent all these things out to sea." The storm occurred on Halloween 1991.

(Bush Library photo.)

With my brother Prescott
in Maine, June 30, 1991.
(Bush Library photo.)

Pres — Happy Memories! G

Colin: Congratulations on this well deserved honor (Medal of Freedom) Your Leadership made our entire Country proud. G. Bush

To Norm — Congratulations on this well deserved honor Medal of Freedom You made our Nation proud. G. Bush

Giving two great Americans the Medal of Freedom, July 3, 1991. (Bush Library photos.)

I sent this photo to my Yale baseball coach. "Dear Ethan . . . Here's a picture, taken on opening at Camden Yards, the new magnificent ball park of the Orioles. '3 Georges'—George 'P,' the newest ball player threw a perfect strike on his opening pitch. Mine, clocked at 39 mph, ran out of gas at the plate. Geo W., the Ranger's man, didn't throw. Poppy." April 6, 1992. (Bush Library photo.)

I sent this photo to the mayor of Shanghai, after he sent me a note of congratulations on my parachute jump in March 1997. Holding on to me are my jumpmasters, Glenn Bangs (left) and Andy Cerrano of the United States Parachute Association. I jumped again, with the same team, on June 9, 1999 to celebrate my seventy-fifth birthday. (Tom Sanders, Aerial Focus)

September 19, 1982

Rabbi Hyman Judah Schachtel*
Congregation Beth Israel
Houston, Texas 77096
Dear Hyman:

You are a thoughtful guy. How kind of you to write me about Doro's wedding.† You must have known that it was a very special day for the Bush family and maybe you knew, too, how much I love my daughter and how close to her I feel. I must make a slight confession, I shed a few tears as she and I drove to the Church, but don't worry! The Secret Service didn't see them.

Warm regards.

Sincerely,
George Bush

In 1982 I undertook an increasing number of foreign trips on President Reagan's behalf, representing him and the country in talks with leaders around the world. In the spring, I had taken a huge trip to Asia; in June, I represented the United States at the funeral of Saudi king Khalid; in August, I attended the inauguration of President Betancur of Colombia; and in November, Barbara and I went to Africa. However, the trip was interrupted by the death of the Soviet Union's longtime iron-willed leader, Leonid Brezhnev. (It could have been about this time that my dear friend Jim Baker penned the saying "You die, I'll fly.") Truthfully, these funerals often resulted in many useful bilateral meetings with the incoming leaders. I sent this cable to President Reagan after I met the new Soviet leader, Yuri Andropov.

Nov. 15, 82

FM Vice President Bush Aboard Air Force Two
TO White House for The President
Subject: My visit to Moscow

. . . I am glad you sent us. The Soviets clearly appreciated the gesture and shared their appreciation in several ways.

. . . By way of example: George Shultz‡ and I walked to the receiving hall, took off our coats, and went to the rear of the line, when we were halfway up the stairs walking along with the likes of [Pakistani] President Zia, [Japanese]

---

*A respected civic leader and perhaps the leading rabbi in Houston.
†Doro had gotten married earlier that month, to Billy LeBlond.
‡George had replaced Al Haig as secretary of state.

Prime Minister Suzuki and many more. A Soviet protocol officer pushed through the crowd on the stairs and told us to come forward. Reluctantly we obliged, being led obtrusively past all the waiting dignitaries. . . .

There were other little gestures, but the major event was our meeting at 4:30 p.m. with Andropov and Gromyko.* Soviet watchers were amazed that Andropov received us.

I will not report here on the conversation. A verbatim report is being prepared, but since this was the first known visit with Andropov by Americans, let me convey some impressions.

He seemed sure of himself. He read his three page brief but with ease and self-assurance.

He conveyed strength, but not in a bellicose way.

He dished it out, but did not flinch as I mentioned Poland, Afghanistan, and Human Rights.

He smiled and seemed genuinely warm when I made joking reference to his having been KGB Chief while I was head of CIA.

It is of course too early to predict how things will evolve in Moscow, but for some reason I feel up-beat, opportunity may well lie ahead, though much of the rhetoric was predictable and accusatory.

I am writing this cable as we fly Moscow to Frankfurt—A Soviet navigator up front in the cockpit. The impressions of Red Square and the pageantry of Brezhnev's funeral fresh in my mind.

We were very close to the front. When the goose-stepping, arm-swinging, Elite Guard marched in I at first saw only hostile troops and hostile power. We had a little wait and I watched the changing of the Guard and looked at the faces and then I saw my sons and yours: George, Jeb, Neil, Marvin, Mike and Ron.

I saw a funeral without tears, save for the immediate family, I saw a funeral without God and thought "How sad—how lonely."

I can't speak for George Shultz with whom it was a total joy sharing these responsibilities, but let me say two things now: First, thanks for sending us on an unforgettable mission. Second: we must succeed in our quest for peace.

Now back to Africa.

> Warm regards,
> George

Barbara and I then returned to Africa to resume our trip. Here are excerpts from a memo I wrote President Reagan about my impressions:

*Andrei Gromyko was the Soviet foreign minister.

. . . I have been deeply struck by the gravity and extent of Africa's economic crisis. Many of our best friends are in serious trouble and face a difficult political future unless the world economy turns around. I stressed the vital importance of each getting his economic house in order and discouraged them from expecting increases in assistance from us. They were impressed by what we are going through at home and have a better understanding of the tough decisions we have had to make. . . .

I return confident that we have strong relationships in Africa. Our diplomatic and aid missions are ably staffed and lean; the Peace Corps is making an outstanding contribution. Each of the leaders I visited was impressed by your interest and sympathy. The policies we are pursuing are sound, and we gained increased trust in our purposes. . . . Africa needs us, and all those I visited make it clear the Soviets have little to offer. We will have to be imaginative in finding ways to meet the continent's many needs.

―――――――

The day after Christmas, our church in Houston, St. Martin's, asked me to speak to the congregation. Here are excerpts from my remarks:

It's great to be back at St. Martin's. The happy memories come flooding back. I remember teaching Sunday School here, so does Barbara. I remember the sixth or seventh pew from the back, how it wiggled and shook as our four boys and, sometimes, Doro got the giggles or got mad or couldn't see during the Christmas Pageant. . . .

I don't want to hold it over the rest of you, but how many of you can say of the Christmas Pageant, "My grandson was a shepherd in 1980 and Noelle, his sister, was an angel." Imagine both in the <u>same</u> year! Barbara said, "Did it ever occur to you they both may have made it because you had just been elected Vice President of the United States a month before?" No, it didn't. I still carry the picture in my wallet. I am <u>convinced</u> they made it because, with all respect to you other grandfathers of potential angels, our angel <u>looked</u> like an angel and our shepherd—he was four then—had that dark nomadic look of a real shepherd who knew how to tend his flock by both day and night. . . .

We have done many interesting things. None was more interesting than our recent trip to seven African countries with a detour to Red Square, Moscow. I wish I could share with you my inner feelings about Africa, about their struggle after years of colonialism to find democracy, to build new nations—the handicaps they start with are immense. In Zimbabwe, in the entire country, when independence came, there were one hundred college graduates—only 100.

The thing that gave me hope about Africa, in the face of enormous economic problems, was their adherence to Christian values and to Christianity. The most moving grace I have ever heard was given by an African chief of state. If ever faith offered hope, almost the only hope, it is in Africa. . . .

But it was in Moscow that I was most deeply struck, but in quite a different way. . . .

It is hard to describe emotions or even scenes. Barbara is good at that. I am not. The flowers were spectacular. The setting awesome. The music Chopin, superb. We spoke to the grieving Mrs. Brezhnev and her family. She said, "We must all work hard for peace."

The next day we stood in Red Square. The funeral procession arrived right on time in front of Lenin's tomb, just as the clock struck twelve. Impressive timing. Right in front of us young soldiers strutted onto the cobblestones. The elite guard changed every fifteen minutes. We arrived early so we saw several shift changes. At first I saw only the goose-stepping-arm-swinging precision-trained young soldiers. I felt a tinge, not of fear, but of amazement at the power and the discipline. After a shift or two changed, I began to study the faces. They were young and healthy looking. One of them smiled as he almost missed his 90 degree turn. I thought not of hostile soldiers but of my own sons and the joy of being young and strong. I thought of our soldiers lost, and then I thought of young kids like this that died defending their Russian homeland in World War II.

As I stood there near our European allied friends, our African friends, our Latin-American friends—and a little down from Castro and Arafat and Jaruzelski of Poland, my mind thought not of the fallen Soviet leader but of peace, the crying need for world peace.

The eulogies were impressive. Yuri Andropov, with whom I met later, was firmly in control. A marshal spoke, a labor leader, a party boss. They all spoke of Leonid Brezhnev's role as leader.

He was buried behind Lenin's tomb in the Kremlin. Then the leaders re-mounted the viewing place atop the Lenin monument. The 300 strings that played so beautifully gave way to a military march. The troops marched by and the proceedings ended.

But you know what. It suddenly dawned on me and on Barbara and on George Shultz throughout all of this, the night before, the ceremony itself—something was missing. There was no mention of

God. There was no hope, no joy, no life ever after, no mention of Christ and what His death has meant to so many. It was very different. So discouraging in a sense, so hopeless, so lonely in a way.

I thought of St. Martin's Church, of our joy all year long, but especially at Christmas. If only their country was one nation <u>under God,</u> If only the kids there had grown up with a Christmas angel and maybe a shepherd in the family . . . peace would be so much easier to achieve.

Blessed are the peacemakers for they shall inherit the earth!

———

One of Washington's big social events is the annual Alfalfa Club dinner, held every January in Washington. For years it was stag only until just recently when Alfalfa saw the light and admitted women. The club has only one purpose: to have this dinner once a year where we put aside all our political and other differences and rib each other. In 1983, I took as my guests our four sons.

Dear George, Jeb, Neil, and Marv,

Before the dust settles, I want to tell you how much this past weekend meant to me. I have had many truly happy moments in my life. Having you guys here this weekend was one of those.

My heart was full of pride when I got to introduce you to my friends at Alfalfa. I was proud—very proud with the way you looked and acted, and responded. You give Bar and me great happiness all the time.

I'm getting a little older. I'm not sure what the future holds. I don't worry about that.

Win or lose, older or younger, we have our family. When all the politics are behind me, and they will be one day, I'll be the happy guy around Golden Pond who knows what it is to be surrounded by kids—and grandchildren, too. I may have my racket slightly unused and my running shoes gathering dust, and they may make me go slow in Fidelity,* but I'll be surrounded by love—so what else counts!

Devotedly,
Dad

———

I took a swing through Europe in early February, touching base with most of our major allies. Here are just some of my notes from the trip:

———

*My Cigarette boat that I kept in Maine.

Feb. 2, 1983

. . . The starkest memory so far is seeing the wall in Berlin with the dogs and the watch tower and the human component of all of that. What an impact it makes to stand up and see the tanks, the guards and the wire and the soldiers looking at you. I wonder how in God's name anybody could think that the Soviet Union wanted normal relations or share any values on human rights when you see the barb- wire, and the stark brutality of it all. . . .

February 10, 1983

. . . The highlight of Rome was the visit to the Pope . . . At one point in the conversation, I was almost in tears—and I hope it didn't show, though maybe it did—as I tried to explain to him how strongly we felt about peace. It was like a confession in a sense, but all I felt was good- ness and strength coming from the Pope. It was wonderful, uplifting feeling . . . there was this strength of the church, the strength of Christ, the strength of his dominating faith, and that made a tremendous impact. I told him about the impact that the Wall had made on me . . . I expect he, having come from Poland, must have wondered of my naiveté; but somehow it felt right to tell him the emotional feeling I had as I saw that closely knit barbwire, so closely knitted, that a per- son looking for freedom couldn't put his fingers through it. . . .

March 16, 1983

I love country music, I know the names of some of the big stars, but I couldn't go through and give you list of all the records and, yet, when I hear them, I know them, and I love them. . . .

I don't know why country music sticks with me. I like listening to symphonies, and I don't know the names of them, but I know what I like in it, and I can relax and go to sleep with that music. I love the lyrics of country, and I love the patriotism of the people. One of the Gatlin Brothers is from Odessa, Texas, and he came up to me and said he knew George and it made me feel great. The Oak Ridge Boys—weird look- ing beards—but they are such warm, wonderful guys, and they sent us two little pink shirts for our twins. They are just terrific—just terrific people. I don't know what their politics are, and I don't really care; but they really gave us a thrill, and every time I met one of them or saw one at some reception or something, they were just terrific. . . . I would rather see this country western show, Hee Haw, or the Grand Ole Opry, than go to a ball game—I really would. It's a great mix of music, lyrics, barrooms, Mother, the flag and good-looking large women. There is something earthy and strong about it all. . . .

———————

4-5-83

Mr. Marvin P. Bush
Alexandria, Virginia 22302
Dear Marv.

I wore this tie for 2 hours today. The reviews, frankly, were not good.

It is an expensive Italian cravate, given to me by Lionel Hampton. Even that impressive pedigree did not dissuade the critics. They remained militantly opposed.

Perhaps, on a younger man the results would be different,

Accept this new (all but 2 hours of its life lay before it) tie. May you wear it with more success than I had. If not, sell it.

Devotedly
Dad

———————

April 13, 1983

I hurt my tailbone. I've got a bruise and nobody is sympathetic. I carried the rubber ring into the Oval Office for lunch on Thursday* and asked the President if I could blow it up and sit on it; and then he told me a story of how he and Eddie Bracken† crashed into each other and he hit his tailbone. He's a great story teller, a great joke teller, and the most understanding human being. It never occurred to me that he would be uncomfortable about my using that silly thing, and he wasn't—he was just great about it. I do feel close, and he makes you feel totally relaxed. He's hard to read; he doesn't ask for advice; he doesn't say, "what do you think about this," very much—but the other side of that is, I feel uninhibited in bringing things up to him. When I do bring up something controversial, he might not comment; he might not say anything right there; and he might not look particularly enthralled about it or say, "tell me more;" but I never get the feeling that he doesn't want me to tell him, so I do and I try not to overdo it. . . .

———————

*President Reagan and I had lunch every Thursday. It was just the two of us, no agenda, with the understanding that what we talked about would stay between us.

†One of Reagan's many Hollywood friends.

5-5-83

Mrs. Prescott S. Bush, Sr.
Pheasant Lane
Greenwich, Connecticut 06830
Dear Mum—

It's <u>mother's</u> day on Sunday. But everyday is Mother's day. I love you—then, now, always.

Middle-size

On April 18, a bomb exploded in the American embassy in Beirut, killing forty-six people, including the entire CIA staff based at the embassy. It was a horrible tragedy. After I attended a memorial service for those who had been killed, I was shocked to get a letter from a family member who felt my "performance" at the service was insincere. It really hurt and shows just how tough it can be to be a "public" person.

6-13-83

Miss Catherine Votaw
Philadelphia, Pennsylvania 19146
Dear Ms. Votaw,

I was deeply disturbed to receive your letter. First, I want you to know how sorry I am that you felt this way. I was deeply moved by the tragedy. I had personally called many families. I received many expressions of appreciation from others for coming there; but that matters not. If I seemed casual and unconcerned and thus insensitive to your feelings—that <u>is</u> what matters. I came there to help not to hurt; obviously in your case I failed miserably when I told your Grandmother "I wouldn't have missed it"—that did not mean I was enjoying some festivity. It meant the least I could do was to be there to express the <u>sincere</u> condolences of a grateful country. It wasn't easy for anyone—I know that. One of my good friends lay dead.

I know my own emotions—I know my own convictions—that you don't though, is clearly not your fault but mine.

I have been raised in the Episcopal Church. It is customary in our Church when one <u>enters</u> a pew—to pray briefly—on one's knees—This was not done, as you suggest, for some TV appearance.

I am deeply sorry that you are hurt and that I added to this hurt. Please forgive me. I went to honor your Dad and others for their dedication and sacrifice—

Thank you for writing from the heart, as you did; please accept this expression of apology and concern. It comes from my heart.

Sincerely,
George Bush

_____

I went back to Europe the end of June to meet with European leaders. One of my chief tasks was to reassure the Germans about the deployment of intermediate-range nuclear forces (INF), the Pershing II missiles, in West Germany where they were controversial. There was a strong antinuclear movement in Germany and elsewhere in Europe, but INF deployment was essential to offset the Soviets' SS-20s, already aimed at Europe. I ran into heavy protests in Germany.

Jun 27 83

TO THE PRESIDENT
FROM THE VICE PRESIDENT
SUBJECT: MEETINGS WITH CHANCELLOR KOHL
. . . All in all, the visits to Krefeld and Bottrop were useful. The Germans were deeply embarrassed by the fact that our motorcade had suffered a few dents and broken windows. I downplayed the issue . . .

The violent demonstrators were ugly—their hand gestures, though not new, had real vigor—and their appearance made them likely candidates in case central casting ever had a call for "Radical Left Demonstrators." The sad part is they ruined the day not for us but for our Krefeld hosts . . .

Kohl is a true friend, who faces real domestic problems as deployment approaches. While keeping absolutely firm on our schedule, we must be sympathetic to Kohl's problems and do all we can to ease his way through them.

With solid support from us Kohl and the Germans can, I believe, be counted on. But difficult days lie ahead—Krefeld might prove to be the Iceberg's tip.

_____

5 Jul 83

FOR THE PRESIDENT
FROM THE VICE PRESIDENT
President Koivisto of Finland was pleased to receive your invitation and accepts.* The September time frame is agreeable. He is particularly pleased since he has met Soviet leaders four times in last year.

He took me aside to tell me of Andropov's health. He thought it was better

*To visit the United States.

than the original report out of Finland but still Andropov had to be carried down the stairs to greet Koivisto.

. . . The high point was a genuine Finnish Sauna at the finest Sauna Association. I felt a little self-conscious at first sitting around stark naked with four Finnish guys I'd never laid eyes on before. We all did the whole treatment including jumping in the ice cold ocean. We saw less of each other after the jumping in that ice cold water. . . .

Warm regards.

On October 23, 1983, 241 Marines, sailors, and other members of a multinational peacekeeping force in Lebanon were killed when a suicide bomber blew up Marine headquarters near the Beirut airport. President Reagan asked me to go quietly to Beirut to bolster the morale of our remaining troops and to observe firsthand what had happened. It was one of my most difficult and emotional assignments.

26 Oct 83

PLEASE PASS TO THE PRESIDENT, SECSTATE, DCI & SECDEF
FROM THE VICE PRESIDENT
SUBJECT: VISIT TO GEMAYEL IN LEBANON

1. After an emotion packed visit to the carrier, Iwo Jima, where I had the privilege of pinning the Purple Heart on two wounded Marines, and a visit ashore to the pile of rubble that was once our BLT Headquarters and a chat with our Marines and Sailors on duty at the airport, I flew by chopper to the Presidential Palace to see [Amin] Gemayel.

2. Gemayel's analysis of things in Lebanon was disturbing and disappointing. Here are some of his points:

   A. When I asked him how he saw the upcoming reconciliation talks in Geneva all he would say was he would try to make them successful—but he showed no enthusiasm and certainly no optimism.

   B. Pointed out he controlled as President only 15 percent of the land and the people and said he was performing miracles accomplishing the things he was for Lebanon.

   C. Noted that as fast as the U.S. trained the LAF some would leave the Army under pressure from Syria. . . . He added that these same forces might some day turn and fight him.

   D. He described four Armies fighting in Lebanon. Namely, Syrian, Iranian, Libyan and Israeli. Combined they control over 80 percent of his country.

   E. He sees the U.S. Marine presence as essential to his survival. Without the Marines he suggested the Soviet backed Syrians would be sitting in his office.

F. Suggested that the answer was more pressure on Syria and Israel by the U.S. to get out of Lebanon. He could not say how.

G. Said he realized the MNF* would not stay forever but saw no way to let them go home. And he expected more, similar terrorist acts in the future.

In short he painted us into a quagmire with little hope for the future.

I'm not in a position to explain his feelings today. Maybe he was on a downer. But his analysis, following on the heels of my visit to our brave dedicated troops, is very disconcerting. I was particularly disturbed by his talk about possibly more defections from the LAF along religious lines. I'll bring you more on our great Marines and Sailors when I get back. They support you 100 percent.

Another grandchild, John Ellis Bush Jr., was born December 13th.

December 14th 1983

Dear Jeb and Colu,

Last night's phone call brought us true happiness. Nothing else matters. The birth of JB Jr. put everything that is important into perspective. The birth of our boy, family, love, whatever.

That kid has a running start. He has two great parents. He has a wonderful brother (even though the guy does give me grief on the football teams).

He has a beautiful sister who will hold him and play with him and love him.

. . . Hug the little guy and tell him that even though he is a tiny little fella, he has already enriched our lives.

Devotedly
Dad

Andropov died February 9, and I returned again to Moscow for a funeral and to meet the next Soviet leader.

15 Feb 84

FM: THE VICE PRESIDENT
TO: THE WHITE HOUSE, THE PRESIDENT

I'm sending you this message from the plane following my meeting with [Konstantin] Chernenko. We will be sending a detailed report shortly, but I

---

*The multinational force.

want to give you my first impressions of the new Russian leader. Impressions shared by Howard Baker who was great to have along.

Despite reports that he might be ill and lacks the intellect and authority of Andropov, Chernenko seemed in command of the situation. He seemed alert, in good health, with a sparkle in his eye, and somewhat younger than his years. He did almost all of the talking on the Soviet side and what he had to say was, in my view, encouraging. He asked me to tell you that we can have better relations. That he believes it is possible to do so. He said that it is by no means certain we will have a fatal confrontation; that we are not inherently enemies. I told him that we, too, were ready for dialogue and progress.

Chernenko is no pushover but he does seem open and treated us graciously. He gave the clear impression that there is somebody at home in the Kremlin with whom we can do business. . . .

I'll have the small Mexican plate if lunch is on Thursday.

George

2-16-84

Dear Jenna,

. . . We love you so very much. I just wish your Mum and Dad would let you come stay with us here in Washington. I would come home early from the office and we three could play and do fun stuff.

We love you both and we love your Mother and Dad.

Devotedly,
Gampy

And another grandchild was on the way:

3-26-84

Mrs. Dorothy LeBlond
New Canaan, CT 06840
Dear Doro,

. . . Names are important. If I were you I would not go for "Herby"—that's a nickname normally and though I would of course be pleased personally, it isn't right to put the emphasis there.

Walker—well maybe. I was called that when they first shipped me off to Country Day at age 5. Mum thought it was better than Poppy. It lasted about 10 days—then it shifted over to Poppy— a burden I bore heroically until, thank God, we went to war with the Japanese and I went to the Navy and I left Poppy pretty far behind. No, Walker Leblond* is a little formal some-how—though don't rule it out entirely.

George. I see your point. George W is one of a kind and it wouldn't do at all to have George L be under the undue influence of Uncle "W".

Wait a second—is it worth another try—have you thought of Poppy Leblond only this time have it be his real name. Poppy Richard Leblond—nice ring somehow.

Oh well I'll keep working, firing the ideas in for better or for worse. I've just begun to think.

Hey, Doro, we're going to love the kid no matter what you call him/her. I for one can't wait.

Devotedly—with love to Bill,

Dad

In April I went to Geneva to represent the United States at the disarmament conference. I went specifically to ask for a treaty banning chemical weapons, an issue I spent a great deal of time on as Vice President and President.

April 17, 1984

MEMORANDUM OF CONVERSATION
Conversation with Ambassador Viktor Israelyan
USSR Ambassador to Committee on Disarmament in Geneva
Attendees: The Vice President
His Excellency Prince Sadruddin Khan†
Ambasador Viktor Israelyan

The meeting lasted about an hour and a half. Prince Sadruddin Khan joined us. It was very informal and very relaxed. Viktor's main theme is that to eliminate the lack of trust the USA should take some specific action. It wouldn't have to be a big action—it could be on bilateral relations, but there should be something visible.

He referred several times to the fact that the Soviets had come a step forward on verification in terms of destruction of chemical weapons. He made the point that this was his initiative and that he had talked them into it back in Moscow. He further alluded to my speech of tomorrow saying, I don't

*Although Doro eventually named her first child Sam, we do now have a grandchild named Walker Bush, as fine a name as they come.

†His official title is His Highness Prince Sadruddin Aga Khan. Barbara and I became great friends with Katie and Sadri while we were at the United Nations. Sadri was then the U.N. high commissioner for refugees. The son of the late Aga Khan, he was vitally interested in and well informed about international affairs.

know what's in it, but if it is not forth coming, I could be in trouble for recommending the above step.

I made a strong pitch to him about our President's desire for progress and arms reduction telling him I could understand from public statements and other ways that a lot of people wouldn't believe this. Speaking to him as an old friend, I knew President Reagan better than most now and I knew what his heartbeat was on all this. . . .

All in all, it was just a very frank, very friendly discussion in which we both agreed that relations weren't good and should be improved. . . .

I told him . . . there had to be a bold step forward in terms of openness. Viktor told me that their objection to openness was not hiding but was based on decades of concern from foreigners coming into their country, 20 million lives lost, etc., etc.*

I said that that was fine, but that now we were in a nuclear age and we had to think all these positions anew and as we reached out for more verification, we ourselves would have to be opening facilities that had heretofore not been opened and that they would.

He did not jump on the proposal though I had an idea that he already had his instructions.

Not much else. He inquired warmly about Barbara. Talked to me about my former UN colleague Jacob Malik at the time of Malik's having lost two of his sons and his wife dying. Malik came to Israelyan in tears saying what could I have done that God punishes me in this way. Interesting from a hard line Russian Communist.

In May I traveled again to Asia where I had a fascinating visit with Indian prime minister Indira Gandhi. Tragically, she was assassinated that October by two of her bodyguards, one of whom I know was there the day of our meeting.

18 May 84

TO: THE WHITE HOUSE, EYES ONLY FOR BUD MC FARLANE†
SUBJECT: VP'S PRIVATE MEETING WITH MRS. GANDHI
 . . . We talked about the elections, both in the US and India. I asked her if she had any feeling that we were trying to intervene in her election in any way. She said that I know you and President Reagan would never do this, of course, but yours is a large Government. Sometimes people do things that others don't know about. I asked her if that meant that she felt the intelli-

---

*A reference to the two world wars.
†The national security adviser.

gence community was involved. She was not clear in her denial. My gut feeling is that she thinks that there had been some monkeying about with support for opposition parties. I told her that if she ever had the feeling that we were working against her in her own elections, I hoped in frankness she would contact me so that I could convey this to the President. I referred to the fact that there were various politicians in India who used "The Foreign Hand" argument during the campaigns in India; that we in the United States knew that "Foreign Hand" meant the US.

I told her that I was a politician and that if being anti-American was good politics, I might not like it, but I would understand. However, if the people who used that expression really meant that the US was intervening in the election process, then we would be very much concerned about that.

She said she appreciated that and there was no direct evidence. . . .

I would say that if the visit accomplished anything, it was establishing a very good personal rapport with Mrs. Gandhi. The conversation was totally relaxed, totally frank—no tensions, no bristlings, no sticky points—nothing purposefully avoided that I could detect. I was determined to make her understand the heartbeat of the President and frankly, I hope and feel that she may have a better knowledge of what makes the President tick at this point.

---

20 May 1984

FM: THE VICE PRESIDENT ABOARD AIR FORCE TWO
TO: THE PRESIDENT WHITE HOUSE WASH DC

Dear Mr. President,

We have just left Oman heading home.

Our ranks have been severely weakened by the usual gut problems, but the trip has been worthwhile with the top leaders of Japan, Indonesia, India, Pakistan and Oman all giving the visit first-class attention. I will share some observations when we meet, but because of its potential for real trouble I wanted to comment on The Persian Gulf. Sultan Qaboos, a wise man and a good friend of the U.S., strongly urges that we stay cool.*

Incendiary statements about what we might do, or what we are planning militarily, would be especially provocative he feels.

He clearly appreciates our commitment to keep the straits open, but he points out the straits are open, and that a lot of public speculation about U. S. military cover for tankers and stepped up U.S. Military pressure is genuinely counter-productive. . . .

---

*Tensions were particularly high in the Gulf region because Iran—embroiled in the Iran-Iraq War—kept attacking neutral shipping in the Persian Gulf.

In summary, I feel we should generate support for what we do both with the Gulf Cooperation Council States and with the Japanese and Europeans. We may well have to act militarily at some point, but it should not be the USA sweeping in alone, dictating to the Gulf States and without the key Europeans and Japan on board.

Flamboyant statements from our bureaucracy really have an unsettling impact on our friends in the Gulf area. They are grateful for our interest but they don't want to be smothered or crowded by us.

Except when the goat was slaughtered before our eyes to welcome us in Lahore, I conducted myself with decorum and dignity on the entire trip. Barbara did too, but we're glad to be heading home.

Best,
GB

It was the year for grandbabies. I wrote this letter to Neil and Sharon's first child shortly after she was born:

6-28-84

Dear Lauren,

You're just a few days old. Already you have made your old grandparents very very happy. We saw that picture of you in the Daily News and in the N.Y. Post. That's pretty good coverage for a 3-day old. You were smiling right out there in front of all the world, just like your wonderful Dad has done all his life—even when it hurt.

You are a lucky girl. You have a loving Mother who is always thoughtful and nice; and you have a Dad who his brothers and sister named "Mr. Perfect". (Even when he bet your Uncle Jeb that Jeb couldn't survive 30 minutes in the steam bath, only to chicken out on payment when Jeb did it—even when Jeb was chasing him about to exact either payment or flesh your Dad was smiling—running fast, but smiling.)

Anyway, Lauren, we can't wait to see you. We want to see you smile, to hold you, to love you.

It's a funny thing—when you get older, even if you have an exciting life surrounded by interesting people and having a chance to meet all the world's leaders—even with all of that—what counts is family and love.

We love you already, more than tongue can tell.

Devotedly,
Gampy

Nineteen eighty-four was of course an election year. Since President Reagan had no primary opponents, politics did not really start dominating our schedule until that summer. Walter Mondale, the Democrats' nominee, picked New York congresswoman Geraldine Ferraro as his running mate, the first woman picked by either major party. I will confess that I was a little apprehensive to be the first man to run against the first woman. It was uncharted territory. But I sent her a note of "welcome."

July 12, 1984

Dear Geraldine,

It is a good job.

Congratulations on your selection. Good luck—up to a point.

Sincerely,

George Bush

July 15, 1984

I get sick of Vice Presidential jokes, but everyone really does want this job if they can't have the number #1 slot; and, yet, the political satirists and commentators continue to downgrade the job even though it's taken on vast new dimensions like the funeral going, and all of that. But what they overlook is the substance of attending funerals and inaugurations, and the diplomacy that goes with it, the showing of the flag, and the meetings with the Chiefs of State.

There are frustrations at 3½ years. You're not making a lot of a decisions, and you have to hold back more than I would be used to if I were running a company or something of that nature; but it's the best place in the world from which to have access to information, and to be able to be in direct daily touch with the President, to confer, and to be able to give your opinion, particularly the way this President operates. . . .

I'm beginning to think a little in my heart of hearts of the Presidency. Working with Ronald Reagan these years has made it much clearer to me to stay with some fundamental principles; keep the United States of America strong; resist pressures to compromise all the time; be willing to talk, but do it from strength; and now we're getting in a good position on that. Then at home, the economy, prosperity, and do what is necessary to keep this economic machine going. . . . I do believe that we've got to keep trying to get government spending under control, and I'm much more concerned than some about the size of these deficits. The President remains concerned, and I think he's right not to want to dramatically raise revenues; but only through a compromise in '85 are we going to get the restructuring of the entitlements that is necessary for the future solvency of this country. There will have to be more revenues raised, and it's going to be a bloody, gory year.*

The publication of C. Fred's Story *not only made our dog famous, but helped highlight Barbara's fabulous work with literacy. She had been working hard for years, but it wasn't always easy to get the word out. A friend of my uncle's not only sent a fan letter to C. Fred, but a check for $25,000 for Literacy Volunteers of America.*

July 20, 1984

Joseph Uihlein, Jr.
Milwaukee, Wis.
Dear Joe,

O.K. consider me demoted!

C. Fred has already taken over and he has given up chasing cars. He is now chasing Geraldine Ferraro.

As for me, my ego has accepted my new status, but I don't like Ken-L-Ration twice a day.

Joe, Bar & I were deeply touched by that most generous support for Literacy Volunteers. Barbara is devoting a lot of her life to helping wipe out illiteracy. She just couldn't believe this fantastic generosity.

We Bushes are so grateful and a lot of other Americans will be as well.

I accept the nomination (oops that's next month)—I mean, the demotion.

Thanks, Joe, from 2 friends who are very very appreciative—

Sincerely,
George

For me, the 1984 election was tough and sometimes bitter. I wrote my sister Nancy:

10-25-84

9 campaigning days to go not counting today.

Mrs. Alexander Ellis
Lincoln Center, Mass 01773
Dear Nan:

Tensions are very very high. I am totally convinced (I hope not conspiratorially so) that we are up against many in the press who hate to see the demise

---

*Although he was strongly against tax increases, President Reagan did raise taxes in 1982, 1983, and 1987.

of Ferraro and the defeat of [Mondale]. In any event it has been very rough going, tons of nits to pick—not that I haven't made mistakes; but when we get lumped into the tax question in the same way as Gerry there's something wrong.*

. . . Anyway not long to go and then I have some serious thinking. I am not sure I could, in my sixties, undergo this ordeal again—however—not make a decision when one is bone tired.

. . . Soon this madness will be over. In a way it has been good for me. We have really felt the pulse of the country—from the groves in the San Joaquin Valley, to the bottom of the mines in Kentucky, to the yards on both the West and East coast—to the campuses, to the factories and farms. It has been exhilarating in lots of ways; but the press part has been ugly. I mentioned this to a close friend and he helped put it in perspective by saying 'true GB but what about the bashing the Prez gets every single day—much worse than you get.' . . .

We are going to win. Then let's sit and chat.

Love
GB

———————

Geraldine and I had one debate, which I thought went well. The day after the debate, I was visiting with some longshoremen in New Jersey, and they were congratulating me on the debate. One guy followed me with a sign that said, "George, you kicked a little ass last night." As I was getting in the car to leave, I repeated his statement back to him. Big mistake. Unfortunately, a TV boom mike, which I did not see, picked it up.

October 26, 1984

Mr. Alex Burton
c/o KRLD Radio
Dallas, Texas 75247
Dear Alex:

. . . You editorialized about a comment that I made in private—at least I thought so—to a person on the docks in New Jersey. I have been in politics a long time, and I guess I should have learned that if someone can eavesdrop electronically or otherwise, you are fair game.

I never used the words that offended you in a public way—and no matter

*Ferraro and her husband, John Zaccaro, had come under fire from the media on their personal finances and income tax questions. As a result, the media tried (unsuccessfully) to find something wrong with my tax returns.

how hard the press has goaded me to state the words in public, I have not done so.

I have not become cynical, but neither, I hope, have I become the prime hypocrite. I do use that expression in competition. It is not sexist and in sporting vernacular at least, it is not offensive.

I expect each of us, maybe even you, has said things in private that he doesn't regret but that he would not say in public. Such is the case with my remark.

I do appreciate your very kind words about Barbara. She too has come under unconscionable fire.*

I just want you to know I had read your commentary, have taken your comments to heart, but cannot be hypocritical by trying to weasel out of what happened. I have not changed, believe me.

Sincerely,
George Bush

We won the election, but I was exhausted. I wrote my friend and former House colleague:

11-8-84

Barber Conable
Member of Congress
Dear Barber,

The dust is setting. Time now to say thanks for being at my side. . . .

I'm glad it's over. It got ugly—you saw vestiges of that ugliness.

But, worth it?

You bet—

All the best, with heartfelt thanks,

George

---

*Much to her dismay, Barbara became famous that campaign when in a moment of extreme frustration (the Mondale campaign kept referring to me as a rich elitist), she called Ferraro that "four-million-dollar—I can't say it but it rhymes with *rich.*" She felt horrible and called Geraldine to apologize. Gerry could not have been more gracious.

CHAPTER 10

The Rough-and-Tumble

After the bruising election of 1984, I was most interested in going back to being Vice President of the United States. Unfortunately, what seemed to me the far-off campaign of 1988 almost immediately invaded our lives. For the next four years, I juggled politics and my job. I wrote my friend Bob Mosbacher, who was organizing a political action committee on my behalf.

February 14, 1985

Dear Bob:

George and Jeb both want to help on the PAC. George feels that he can bring in a lot of young business people from the West coast . . . Jeb, as you know, is the County Chairman for the Republican Party in Dade County, Florida.

. . . I have not talked to Neil in Colorado, Marvin here in Washington, or Doro LeBlond in Connecticut. Maybe it would make sense to have all 4 boys and Doro on the masthead in order to get the Bush name identified with the PAC—your call.

From this point on, I will keep Craig Fuller, my new Chief of Staff, apprised by copy of everything we do. In the event I am not around, feel free to talk to him on any of this.

Warm regards,
George

In March I went back to Africa—specifically the Sudan, Niger, and Mali—to see firsthand the devastation brought on by a terrible drought. The plan was for me to

341

go from Africa to Geneva, to address the United Nation's emergency conference on African famine relief. I wrote the President:

7 Mar 85

FM THE VICE PRESIDENT ABOARD AIR FORCE TWO
TO: THE PRESIDENT

Until you hold in your arms a one year old baby weighing 5 pounds or a seven year old kid weighing 14 pounds it is hard to really feel the ravages of the famine.

Our food is helping a lot. The private sector is doing an excellent job.

I leave Sudan with mixed emotions. We have done a lot, there is so much left to do.

The Sudanese leadership in Khartoum and in the rural areas are truly grateful for our help.

Our food aid has literally made the difference as to whether a kid lives or dies. That is impressive. As Lee Greenwood put it: "God Bless the USA!" On to Niger. Warm regards.

George

While in Geneva, we received word that Chernenko had died, the third Soviet leader to do so in less than three years. Once again, I flew to Moscow to attend a funeral and to meet the new Soviet leadership.

March 13, 1985

For the President:

I have had about 8 hours to think about our 1 hour and 25 minute meeting with Gorbachev. . . .

Gorbachev will package the Soviet line for Western consumption much more effectively than any (I repeat any) of his predecessors. He has a disarming smile, warm eyes, and an engaging way of making an unpleasant point and then bouncing back to establish real communication with his interlocutors.

He can be very firm. Example: When I raised the human rights question with specificity, he interrupted my presentation to come back with the same rhetorical excess we have heard before. Quote: "Within the borders of the US you don't respect human rights" or "you brutally suppress their rights." But along with this the following, "We will be prepared to think it over" and "Let's appoint rapporteurs and discuss it." The gist being as follows—"don't lecture us on human rights, don't attack socialism but let's each take our case to discussion!"

. . . George Shultz made a superb presentation at the very end of our meeting in which he told Gorbachev that you wanted to be personally engaged etc. He did it with great sincerity and warmth and even though it went through translation, I had the feeling Gorbachev responded with the same kind of man to man sincerity—

. . . In his conclusion, though, he came back to human rights but in a way that made his summation positive. The following is almost an exact quote. "It is a good thing we have spoken not in diplomatic but political language. Leave aside, in brackets, human rights, the subject matter was important. If what I heard from the V.P. and Secretary of State quoting the President reflects wanting a 'normal road' and if all this reflects a 'serious side' we cannot but welcome this!!"

. . . I didn't get the feeling he had to prove how tough he is.

He seemed self confident turning to [Foreign Minister] Gromyko and chatting from time to time but not being worried that Gromyko might differ or not afraid to show lack of total knowledge in front of Gromyko.

This Gucci Comrade brings the General Secretariat a quantum leap forward in overall appearance. His tailor does not rival Deaver's* man at Adler's but he beats the hell out of the Penney's basement look that some of his predecessors projected.

He has a large very prominent birth mark across his balding head, but because of his attractive manner of presentation it is not something you notice all the time.

I feel he will want to meet you. He will handle his end well—so well I'd predict that it will help him at home and show the West a much more reasonable face. Having said that the big question will be—will this "new look man" merely be a more effective spokesman for tired, failed policies or will he have enough self assurance and foresight to "start anew"—a term he himself used in expressing hope for U.S.-Soviet relations.

I don't know the answer to this question but I strongly urge that we try to find out.

I personally would like to see you set up a true back channel totally apart from the wide array of experts upon whom we must depend, but the channel should have a tiny handful of key players whom Gorbachev knew were truly your personal confidants and in whom he would gradually get confidence as he saw there were no leaks.

If one of these key players had to go public in a rhetorical way, Gorbachev should be told as in the early days of our Chinese relationship when one side or the other publicly attacked: "These are empty cannons of rhetoric".

All normal channels would remain open, but this would be something

---

*Mike Deaver, a good friend of Reagan's and a former White House staffer.

very special that you could use, in confidence, to establish a truly personal rapport with this new and different leader.

One has got to be optimistic that Gorbachev will be better to work with, a more permanent addition to the scene and hopefully one who truly will "start anew"; but, after 8 hours of contemplation, there is also the possibility that his attractive personality will be used to divide us from our allies and to attract more support for old views and themes. I can just see some of our M.C.'s* eating out of his hand in wishful anticipation of achieving détente but giving away too much in the process as we try to figure out who this man really is. It will be an interesting trip but as the monkey said when he was shot into outer space "It beats the hell out of the cancer research lab."

> Warm regards,
> George

4-4-85

Dear Noelle,

I got a wonderful invitation from you to come to Gulliver for Grandparent's day on April 21; but I can't make it and I am very sad about that.

You see if I could come I would, but I have to work. Please tell your classmates that if I didn't have to go to the White House, I would come to Gulliver.

Do you think they will understand?

Last week Ganny and I went to Maine. It is still cold there, but everything looks ready for you, for "P"† and for Jebbie. When can you come up there?

I love you very much. A lot of grandfathers don't have a granddaughter that sends them valentines and invitations. I do, though, and I am lucky.

> Much Love,
> Gampy,

One of the perks of being Vice President is you sometimes get to throw the ball out on opening day of baseball. In 1985, I did the honors for the New York Mets. I wrote my friend and one of the owners:

---

*Members of Congress.
†Some people called George P., "P," just as they later would call George W., "W."

4-27-85

Mr. and Mrs. Nelson Doubleday
Doubleday and Company, Inc.
New York, NY 10167
Opening day
Dear Nelson & Sandy,

Somewhere down there Gary Carter* is putting liniment on his hand, but up here there is joy on Air Force II.

It has nothing to do with my 'fast' ball that, thank heavens, did not go into the dirt; Rather it has to do with friendship. Who but you two would have given over the big opening to jillions of agents, tons of politicians, a South American President cum entourage,† Lionel Hampton and us.

The only thing missing was the dog act and the 3 aristocrats; but come to think of it there were a couple of narc dogs . . .

Bushes all have that Walter Mitty streak—but mine really knows no bounds today. Striding through the dug-outs "Hi Whitey [Herzog]", "Yeah, Dave [Johnson],‡ it's your year"; "Daryl [Strawberry], you're looking A-OK"; or "Ed [Mayor Koch] you old bastard why don't you fill the pot-holes, ha, ha, ha" or "Mr. President, isn't this a great way to conduct diplomacy?" Then to the mound—all the way—<u>my</u> shoe on the Mets real toe plate—The fans not booing, the sun breaking out—then Gary giving me a break—10 feet worth, then the release—the catch—the thrill of having thrown out the first pitch.

Thanks for welcoming us so warmly and giving me a thrill that will rank right up there with seeing Joan Williams naked when I was 8;§ coming back from the war alive; and looking at half grown Sam LeBlond the day after he was born.

Being V.P. is great. Being a friend with Nelson and Sandy is what life's about.

Love
George

---

*The Mets catcher.
†I took President Leon Febres-Cordero of Ecuador.
‡Whitey Herzog managed the St. Louis Cardinals, whom the Mets were playing that day. Johnson was the Mets' manager.
§My brother Pres and I paid her ten cents to run across the room naked. She did, then went home and tattled. I'm not sure we had ever seen our dad so angry, and he made us go apologize.

6-19-85

Dear "P",

. . . I understand you are at baseball camp. May all your swings turn into line drives, and may all your pitches be over the plate; and if you get a bad bounce in life, shake it off and grab the next one.

I love you, you little wiener, and I can't wait to see you Noelle and Jebby in Maine. I just can't wait.

Love,
Gampy

_____

September 3, 1985

Mr. Jim Hataway
Pepe's Barber Shop
Miami, Florida 33156
Dear Jim:

My son, Jeb, passed along your outstanding petition about those Americans still being held in Lebanon.*

We are leaving no stone unturned to gain their freedom, and we will not knuckle under to the demands of the terrorists. To do that would be to jeopardize the lives of many Americans living abroad.

We will continue to work for the release of the "Beirut 7".

Please thank all your co-petitioners. Your support and understanding mean a great deal to President Reagan and me.

Sincerely,
George Bush

_____

In October we traveled to Asia. My visit to the Philippines was my first since I flew over Manila Bay in 1944, and it was impossible not to look back. I dictated to my diary:

October 12, 1985
. . . My mind races back to forty-one years ago when we covered the landings here in Saipan. I can't see the exact spot, but I'm high on this hill and you can just picture the carriers, the battleships, the destroyers and all the landing craft laying off-shore shelling the high ground which is off to my left not very far from here. It all comes

_____

*Americans living in or traveling to Beirut were routinely taken hostage by Arab extremist groups during this time. It was a horrible situation that the government could do little about.

back . . . as I came across in my torpedo bomber, we had total control of the skies, and I kept thanking my lucky stars that I wasn't involved in slogging through the dense jungle which now surrounds us. The beauty of the place, the flowers and the kindness of the people were all obscured then by total war.

. . . I remember a little incident where we were all sent out to attack Palau. I remember seeing a small boat, going right down, right next to the water, and strafing it, and actually seeing someone jump over. Our instructions were to wipe out all shipping, but this was a fairly small boat, and last night, as I was enjoying the wonderful hospitality of the people here, some from Palau, I wondered to myself, I wonder if I might have killed this guy's dad, or one of his family. . . .

———

Oct. 20, '85

The Honorable Geraldine Ferraro
Forest Hills Gardens, New York 11375
Dear Geraldine,

We got back at 1:30 AM today from China—and here at home was your signed book. How thoughtful of you.

I'll read it with avid interest. . . .

George

———

Neil wrote me a letter, upset about a negative magazine article. That is one of the toughest things about public life—helping your family deal with the inevitable nasty articles that will be written. It was about this time when George Will wrote his famous column calling me Reagan's "lapdog" because of my loyalty to the President.

3-25-86

Whit*—

I got the article from the Economist—more pack journalism, more piling on; in spite of George Will which attracted the pack like a gorilla in heat, things look pretty good. It is way early, but the figures look good and the vibes outside the belt way are encouraging.

None of this matters though, compared to the joy that Pierce† brings to our lives.

---

*My nickname for Neil was Whitney; it started out as Whitey, because of his blond hair, and somehow it evolved into Whitney.

†Neil and Sharon had just had their second child.

We can't wait to see the lad. If he's as loving as his Ma, and as kind and as thoughtful and as decent as his Dad, then life will be great for him and he will give only happiness to his parents and his friends.

That's all that <u>really</u> matters, Whit—not politics—not public life but family, kids and now grand-kids.

Love to Sharon.

Love to Pierce.

Devotedly

Dad

The presiding bishop of my own church, for whom I had great respect, wrote me a letter objecting to the administration's support of the contra "freedom fighters" in Nicaragua, as opposed to the communist-supported Sandinistas, who were in power.

April 3, 1986

The Most Reverend Edmond L. Browning

The Episcopal Church Center

New York, New York 10017

Dear Bishop Browning:

. . . The Freedom Fighters have always made it clear that they will lay down their arms when genuine democracy is permitted again in Nicaragua, as the Sandinistas promised nearly six years ago. The United States Government has supported the struggle of the Freedom Fighters as we support efforts to establish democracy elsewhere. . . .

We have asked the Sandinistas to stop exporting subversion to their neighbors; that they reduce their bloated military apparatus to restore regional military balance; that they sever their military ties to Cuba and the Soviet bloc; that they begin to honor their promises to the Organization of American States to establish a democratic, pluralistic political system; and, that they begin a genuine dialogue covering the entire political spectrum in Nicaragua. . . .

Someday I would like so discuss this with you. I am totally convinced that the <u>moral</u> ground is on our side. I respect the Diocesan views but I disagree profoundly. I hope my Episcopalian credentials are not diminished because I disagree with my Bishop on this.

I hope Democracy will come to Nicaragua with all that means—free elections, free press and yes a free church.

I hate to differ with you on this key question but my view is not simply <u>official</u> it is profoundly personal, stemming largely from what my Episcopal faith has taught me.

Sincerely,

George Bush

None of this mattered much a few weeks later when Marvin fell seriously ill and underwent a colostomy. He became so weak at one point that his mother and I feared for his life. The entire family was overwhelmed by the number of people who reached out a helping hand to Marvin.

May 21, 1986

Mr. Arthur Richman*
New York Mets
New York, NY
Dear Arthur:

There is no way that Barbara and I, or any of Marvin's brothers or his sister, can possibly thank you enough for caring about Marv and for your friendship.

About ten days ago Marvin literally was at death's door. He was in great pain, and all of us who love him so very much were scared. And then along you came with your thoughtfulness and your words of cheer. I honestly believe, Arthur, that your kindness and love for Marvin played a major part in bringing him through.

It's like he was in a tough slump—0 for 6 and hurting. And then came those phone calls. They got him mentally ready for the ordeal of a most serious operation and a painful recovery. All your caring was symbolized by that wonderful picture you sent Marv. Please thank all those involved in that and in the phone calls.†

Arthur, being Vice President means a lot to me, but it is zero—zilch—compared to family. Marvin is doing fine now, physically and mentally. He's hitting about .485, better than my friend Gary [Carter]; and his ERA threatens Gooden's. He'll make it, because when he was down a good friend named Arthur Richman lifted him up. With lasting thanks,

Sincerely,
George Bush

June 3, 1986

Dr. Peter Petrucci
Washington, D. C. 20016
Dear Dr. Petrucci—

A lot of time has gone by since you took our boy Marv from serious worrisome illness and put him back in the sunshine. He went to work yesterday.

---

*Arthur was the longtime road secretary for the Mets and now works for the Yankees.
†Arthur had arranged for a number of players to call Marvin and cheer him up.

Thanks so very much for all you did for our son surgically—it was great; but it was a lot more. Marvin was down and you really showed him the way— His mental outlook, I think, is A-1.

Thanks from a very grateful Dad,

George Bush

––––––––––

In August I took a trip to the Middle East where I had interesting discussions with the leadership there. Here are excerpts from my memo back to President Reagan:

August 3, 1986

I am writing this as I leave Luxor on my way to visit the Sinai Peace Keeping Force. We have sent back lots of cables and phone calls: but before meeting Mubarak later today, I wanted to share a few observations on Israel and Jordan.

I am convinced that [Shimon] Peres really wants peace. He has grown enormously during his time as Prime Minister.

Though I touched on Pollard,* we both agreed the fundamental relationship was too strong to be diminished by these events. I did tell him there was no "vendetta" against Israel but that we had to follow our laws. . . .

Peres asked that I tell Mubarak they are seriously ready to cooperate on "tourism, high tech, and energy".

I had several contacts with a much more cheerful, outgoing Vice Premier Shamir. In a lovely pleasant private chat he made some interesting comments.

On Pollard—"Let's put an end to this, past is past". He hopes the fall-out will be over—"no duration". "Let me assure you we respect your laws and will cooperate." . . .

Shamir said that he has "no doubt Hussein wants peace with us". "If we can't solve the peace problem, let's solve others", citing water, communications, Dead Sea . . .

In Jordan we were received with great warmth. I had a lot of private time with King Hussein . . . though Crown Prince Hassan did not go to Aquaba with the rest, he did brief us on the economic situation and on a grand plan to computerize Jerusalem's multi-faceted history. (Oh yes, Prince Hassan suggested a 6:00 p.m. tennis game. He is a little guy in height but he weighs a <u>ton</u> as a tennis partner.) . . .

Hussein spent a lot of time telling me about the Iran/Iraq war, even urging me to meet with Saddam Hussein of Iraq, stating that I would find him much more reasonable than his reputation. Hussein clearly is deeply concerned

*Jonathan Pollard, the CIA employee who was given a life sentence for spying on the United States for Israel.

about an Iran victory—an enormous worry to all the GCC* states and to Jordan, Egypt etc. . . .

All in all the visits with all the principals have been long, upbeat and fruitful. A visit with a general rather than specific purpose can be helpful. I know the Israeli and Jordanian leaders feel this way. . . .

Though I can't point to any specific actions to prove it, I do feel the climate is better now for peace between Jordan and Israel. . . .

I have eaten too much and too well in service to country. On the other hand, I have not drunk enough nor slept enough to serve my country well.

I have not missed the "leaks", the political gossip, the "style section", nor Congressional intransigence.

I have missed the United States of America and our 9:00 a.m. meetings.

See you Wednesday morning. By the way, I'll have the full Mexican plate at lunch on Thursday.

> Warm personal regards,
> George

I asked my good friend and great writer Vic Gold to ghostwrite sort of a "political" autobiography, the kind of book that comes out about the candidate during an election year. Since I was traveling so much, we exchanged a lot of notes as I tried to answer some of his questions. Here is one I wrote on leadership and vision:

Vic:

Leadership is listening then acting. Leadership means respect for the other person's point of view, weighing it, then driven by one's own convictions acting according to those convictions.

If you can't listen, you can't lead.

Humor brings joy and helps make life sing; but if that humor is mean spirited or hurtful of another the lightness and the laugh give way to embarrassment and resentment.

<u>Vision</u>

On the domestic side jobs, but jobs in an America that is free of drugs, that is literate, that is tolerant. On the foreign policy side—peace, but peace in a world that offers more freedom, more democracy to the people of the world.

We were big fans of columnist Georgie Anne Geyer, who had written a nice column about me.

*Gulf Cooperation Council.

October 6, 1986

Dear Georgie Anne,

Having just read your column in today's <u>Washington Times,</u> I'm sitting here trying to figure out how to do this. I don't write letters to those who write nasty stuff, and frankly there hasn't been too much of an opportunity to write regarding the other kind of columns—then along comes this column and without being gratuitous, I really want to say "Thanks".

The Harrington* piece in my view was, on balance very good. I got to like the guy; but I did argue with him, more than the story tells, about "class", "privilege", etc. I told Walt—"Look, yes I was lucky enough in the depression to have three square meals and a Dad that could pay the hospital bills when I got sick; but, Walt, I never felt the world owed me anything—'class' in that sense. I never felt superior to some other guy who had less." I said, "You sound like Soc. 10 or even Soc. 22." He allowed as how he had studied Sociology. On balance, I have no complaints about Walt's piece. The "class" stuff said more about him than it did about me, me thinks. But your story told me that some do understand what makes our family tick. It's funny how some sharp criticism does really sting then along comes a rainbow.

This is a personal letter. Your column meant so very much to both Barbara and me and we are grateful

Sincerely,
George Bush

––––––

November 4, 1986

The great question "WHY DO YOU WANT TO BE PRESIDENT?" And, I've tried to write it down. Believe me, even though I know it is not easy. I know I've got the leadership ability. I know I've got the experience. I want to see an educated America. I want to see a literate America. I want to see a drug-free America. I want to see America with opportunity and jobs. I want to see the emphasis remain on the family values. I want to use our abilities to bring peace, to continue the discussions with the Soviet Union, to reduce the fear of the kids of nuclear weapons, and also to be a beacon for freedom and democracy. I feel strongly on the Sandinistas for example.

But, how do you say all these things and get it into a slogan or a formula—a catch-all. I don't know. But, this is what I feel very com-

*Walt Harrington of the *Washington Post* had just written a cover story about me for their magazine. I thought he did a fair, balanced job, although he focused too much on the so-called class issue.

fortable with—the philosophy. I want to see us do better in terms of opportunity for Blacks, for Hispanics, but again with the emphasis on the private side—private opportunity and education rather than vast government spending programs.

So it is putting these themes together. Getting good people. We are going to have to get into the nitty gritty—like, what we'll do about the deficits, what we'll do about the competitiveness and international trade. But I have had enough experience to feel comfortable with the issues. Eight years—six years ago, much less comfortable, much less experience. But, now—knowing the world leaders and seeing first-hand the President's decision making process and frankly, learning from him a lot about keeping my cool and turning the other cheek and being pleasant and not getting bogged down in a lot of meaningless detail. All of these are good lessons about how one should go about being President. . . .

About this time George and Laura and the twins moved to Washington so George could work full-time on my presidential campaign. Jeb was also very involved in Florida. I dictated to my diary:

Nov. 12, 1986

I think George Bush coming up here will be very helpful and I think he will be a good insight to me. He is very level-headed, and so is Jebby. I think some of our political people are thinking, "Oh, God, here come the Bush boys." But, you know where their loyalty is and they both have excellent judgment and they are both spending a bunch of time on this project. Neil gets rave reviews out in New Hampshire—both he and Doro going there. I would love to see Neil full-time in New Hampshire, but I don't think it can work* . . . they love him there and he does an outstanding job there and elsewhere. Big Marv is not involved in politics at this juncture, but he is a great comfort, having him and Margaret and Marshall here.† It adds a joyous family dimension to our lives. It puts it in bright colors. It makes me feel that I haven't lost all sense of priority here. . . .

---

*Neil and Sharon were living in Denver where Neil had just started a business. Therefore, it was not possible for him to campaign full-time in New Hampshire, as he had in 1980.

†Marvin had married Margaret Molster from Richmond, Virginia. They had just adopted a beautiful little girl, Marshall Lloyd Bush.

On November 3, the news broke that the Reagan administration had secretly been selling weapons to Iran. Critics immediately charged it was an "arms for hostages" deal, although President Reagan steadfastly insisted it was part of an overall plan to improve relations with Iran, which would in turn hopefully bring the hostages home. The controversy turned into a crisis a few weeks later when it was further revealed that several NSC staff members had decided on their own to funnel the money from the arms sales to the contras in Nicaragua. This was in direct violation of Congress's decision that the United States should no longer provide funds for the contra movement. When I dictated this entry into my diary, it was still unclear who knew what and when.

    Nov. 13th 1986

    The President showing great tension for the first time. . . . The NSC seems to be wanting to hold the line, trying to get the hostages back. There's tension between the various players . . . a tendency to say everybody knew it when Shultz himself has felt clued out. I am urging being very careful of what is said—not trying to say the whole Cabinet was involved, when they weren't. Not trying to put the facts beyond where they are. I remember Watergate. I remember the way things oozed out. It is important to level, to be honest, to be direct. We are not to say anything, but the damn gates are open. Everybody is making judgments based on erroneous information and it is a flood of wrong facts coming out. . . .

———————

As the news continued to unfold, there was growing speculation about my involvement. I had known about the sale of arms to Iran. I had not known about the diversion of funds to the contras. Friends began urging me to back away from the controversy and even criticize the administration. I wrote my good friend Norm Brinker:

Nov. 23, 1986

Mr. Norman Brinker
Dallas, Texas 75248
Dear Norm, my friend.

    If you were in deep and serious trouble, caught up in a fire storm of some truth and some distortion you wouldn't want a friend to go out and be on record as 'known to feel this way or that' or to even appear to be second guessing.

    There's a lot at stake here—some of it relates to the President's very ability to govern for two years. Yes, I have a lot at stake politically for my own future, but I have a lot at stake in terms of my own self respect. Thus I must resist any temptation to look good or bright by jumping into the public fray.

I have such great respect and friendship, too, for you; that I hope you understand where I am coming from on all this. I may be wrong, and I may get weakened but I cannot treat this President any differently. I, of course, will not tell an untruth or shade the truth in any way, but having said that I cannot turn on a friend either.

Love to all the family,
George

———————

Dec. 1, 1986

The Honorable Henry E. Catto*
Washington, D. C. 20007
Henry, my friend,

I just saw yours of Nov. 21—postal reform dammit, but then you are two blocks away. (I hope it's not my vast bureaucracy.)

. . . These are tough times. Tonight we had call from NY Times saying they had it on good authority that Bud [McFarlane] had told the Senate Comm. that he had told me about arms money from Iran going to the Contras. "Explosive" the Times man said. We told him 'not true'; checked to find that no such testimony had been given. Later found that same NY Times guy had called Regan's† office saying he had been named by Bud etc. Regan checked with Committee staff, told "No" this never happened, called Times man back. We'll see if Times goes with it. I cite this so that you will know what you already know, things are tough out there.

There is a frenzy. My mode, having been through history's greatest frenzy, albeit as a spear carrier—Be calm. Tell the whole truth, not panic when one's political opponents spread lies or plant little negatives. Push for prompt revelation of all facts. Get the truth to the American public, suffer indulgently the arrows let fly by a hungry press—do your best and don't worry about things you can't do anything about. Give sane advice to the President but don't talk about it. Do all this and you'll live to be 100. Maybe your colon will have a kink or two in it from concern, but life'll go on.

GB

———————

*Henry and Jessica Catto were good friends from Texas. He had a long, distinguished diplomatic career, including representing the United States in the Organization of American States and serving as ambassador to El Salvador. I named Henry my first ambassador to Great Britain.

†Don Regan, former secretary of the treasury and now chief of staff. After the 1984 election, he and Jim Baker literally switched jobs.

December 16, 1986

Mrs. Prescott S. Bush, Sr.
Jupiter Island
Hobe Sound, Florida 33455
Dearest mum,

... These are not easy times here, but they are times that the things you and Dad taught me come to the fore. Tell the Truth. Don't blame people. Be strong. Do your Best. Try hard. Forgive. Stay the Course. All that kind of thing.

The President is embattled. Some of our political friends worry about me and what all this will do to me; but you see, I don't worry—really. I know the President is telling the whole truth. I know I have, too. And I also know that the American people are fair and forgiving.

So don't worry about middle-size—And besides if all goes wrong (and it won't) look at all the blessings I have in life. Bar, kids, 10 grandkids. And besides I have the neatest Mum in the whole wide world; and I love her very very much.

Poppy

December 21, 1986

... Nobody had any dream that these kinds of things were going on, and it should have been coordinated and reported. . . . The President can't give advice in private—can't get advice in private without reading about it in the newspapers. I'll probably be pressed now on advising him—what I told the President, but I simply can't do that. One thing I might do is put out a chronology of what meetings I attended and let that serve as a record, cause on these key meetings that they are talking about, the key meetings that are disputed, it appears I was not there. I can not possibly reconstruct events. I can not remember details and nobody can. But, I can only do my best to recall these matters. There is a mood and the White House is totally down. . . .

The hardest thing of all this is to have your honor and your integrity questioned. The kind of doubt and meanness that gets into the faces of the reporters when they simply don't think you are telling the truth. . . . It is disappointing, but goes with the territory. This is the biggest political test—or test of any kind—that I've ever been through. I suppose that one could say that it would end—if it continues like this—it would make it extremely difficult to get the nomination. But, it is far too early to make judgments of that nature.

A note to my wife on our anniversary:

January 6th, 1987

Let's see Bar—42 years ago this minute I was a nervous wreck—you, too, maybe. Anyway, here we are 42 years later, and I am a very happy guy—the luckiest in the world actually. I have a skinny, miles walking wife; I have a lot of grandkids (so do you) and they all, each and everyone, bring me happiness just thinking about them. Our own kids are great; our dog is in tough shape, but he's given us joy; our house wasn't even nicked by the seas or the snow; we aren't rich, but we are awful lucky. We don't owe any money and if either of us get sick the other guy can pay the bills. We have a lot of friends—no real enemies tho there are some who aren't exactly rooting hard for us; we have quiet faith that gives us strength; so—when we count our blessings we've got to count on a long long time.

How do I love you? Let me count the ways—one, er, ah, lets' see—I'm not good at that. But I love you very much. Have for more than 42 years and will for the next howmsoever many lie ahead. I can't ever say it too well, but you know that, don't ya?

Love,
Pop

———————

January 11, 1987

Mrs. Prescott Bush
Links Road
Hobe Sound, Florida 33455
Dear Mum,

Loved your post-visit letter; but let me clear up one point. The President did NOT know about the diversion of funds to the Contras. He has stated what his policy was on a limited amount of arms to Iran,* but he has stated he did not know about the diversion of funds. As a matter of fact there is some reasonable doubt that no funds may have ever reached the contras. More on this after North† testifies.

Don't worry about all this stuff, please. I don't like the constant drum beat on the news, but the total truth will be out soon, and the people will see that

---

*The arms sent to Iran were spare parts and defense weapons.

†Marine colonel Oliver North, who was a member of the NSC staff, was in the middle of the Iran-contra controversy and ended up taking most of the blame, along with National Security Adviser John Poindexter. They had both resigned from the NSC in November, shortly after the news broke.

the President has told the truth. That's the main thing. Of course there will be differences about arms to Iran etc., but so be it.

Loved seeing you—all too brief though. . . .

Much Much Love,
George

———————

Feb. 25, 1987

Dear Noelle,

Here is a picture of our new dog.* Her formal name is Mildred K but we call her Millie. She was named after Mrs. Baine Kerr whose first name is Mildred.

You know what she does?—well when I am asleep she cuddles up right next to me, I mean really close, then she puts her nose in between my cheek and my neck. I mean she is a cuddly warm little pup. She is good on retrieving tennis balls and she follows Ganny everywhere she goes—I mean everywhere, get it?

We miss you. You are my very favorite second oldest grandchild.

Devotedly,
Gampy

———————

March 17, 1987

This being President and running for it—sometimes I pinch myself when I see polls showing me as the leading contender. Of course, it is vitally important, but family, faith, and friends—that is the priority—in politics, do your best, do it with honor, do it with dignity. . . .

It is a terrible climate—awful ugliness of the business. The press—cynicism, shouting and yelling and snide and yet you know you've got to do what you've got to do. The country is so great, I've got to make a contribution. We'll know soon—in just about a year. Tired, dead bone tired the night of March 17.

———————

March 18th '87

Dear Sister,

. . . It's going to be a long ghastly year, but mentally and physically I am up for it. Look at it this way, in less than a year I think we'll know the full story. I am

---

*C. Fred had suffered a stroke and died. The household was forlorn so I wasted no time in getting Barbara a new dog, an English springer spaniel who was destined to become even more famous than Fred.

going to go the extra mile, take the extra shot of flak, smile, work hard, not bleed too much, all with the certain knowledge that I can win it and go all the way, but knowing that IF that doesn't work a great life out there is holding out its arms.

Just being with George P. and watching him face life's wonders would count for 3 months a year, and that doesn't leave enough time for the other nine or Bar or Millie (new dog) . . . Anyway life is pretty good.

Poppy

March 31, 1987

MEMORANDUM FROM THE VICE PRESIDENT
FOR:　　　Howard Baker
　　　　　　Frank Carlucci*

I received two calls today, one from Mr. Richard Stethem and one from his wife. I did talk to Dick Stethem, the father of the kid that was killed by Hamadei.† I told him that the U.S. Government's policy remains the same in favor of extradition. I said I had seen that same story, but that we were still determined to see this man brought to full justice in the United States in accord with the terms of our anti-terrorism policy.

I guess we can all understand the anxiety that the Stethem family feels on this matter. Should the Germans do anything but bring this man to full justice in lieu of extradition, it would be very, very bad.

George Bush

April 8, 1987

Went out to the National Institute of Health for a very impressive AIDS briefing. Dr. [Samuel] Broder, Dr. [Tony] Fauci‡, the head of the hospital, Dr. [James] Wyngaarden and others. Blood supply is being screened and is safe. They are encouraged by some of the vaccines . . . They can keep people alive quite a bit longer. It sounds like the early research on leukemia to me. I sat and talked with a gay man who has AIDS—no visible signs. . . .

---

*Baker had replaced Don Regan as chief of staff; Carlucci had replaced Poindexter as NSC adviser.

†Their son, Navy SEAL Robert Dean Stethem, had been killed in 1985 during the hijacking of the TWA plane to Beirut. Lebanese Mohammad Ali Hamadei had been arrested for the murder.

‡About a year later, I would be asked in one of the presidential debates to name some of my personal heroes. I named Dr. Fauci because I was so impressed with his unselfish dedication to AIDS research.

Education is important, but I'm troubled by teaching every little kid how to use a condom. Monogamous sex and sex with love is very important. I think that the values should be at the family level, the local school level, the local community level, the church and religious-centered level. I did come out for mandatory testing at the time a marriage license is issued. The papers played it up as being very cautious on this question. Certainly, intravenous dirty needle or infections should be strongly and roundly condemned. . . .

April 12, 1987

. . . Flew late Saturday night to Maine. Had a total non-political day in Maine. Doro came down and left Ellie* and Sam in my charge when she and Bar went downtown. Ellie woke up, Doro predicting that she wouldn't. I picked her up, changed her diaper, putting the new fangled kind of diaper on backward and using Sam's diaper and not hers. Warmed up her bottle in the quick heating deal there and tested it on my wrist, just like the old days and fed her—three enormous burps. Ken Raynor the golf pro was over and he knew less about it than I did. He said, "No, no you don't have to burp them anymore," but after she showed a little discomfort about one third of the way through, I put her on my shoulder and up came—right from her toes—the most enormous burp, with some kind of after-wave of formula. It just about knocked me out. She is such a beautiful girl—big eyes and I just love that quiet time with her in my arms. Sam came in, after he got up— his mother had gotten home by then. He's so sweet. He loves Ellie— no longer jealous. All in all, it is just heaven. . . .

I headed up several task forces for President Reagan, including the one on deregulation, one on terrorism, and the National Narcotics Border Interdiction System. We worked with the Pentagon, the Coast Guard, and local law enforcement agencies in trying to cut down on the amount of illegal drugs flowing into the country. It was interesting but often grueling and depressing work. I dictated to my diary:

May 5, 1987

Big day in Houston. Flew down yesterday on the 4th for drug coordinating meeting in Houston. A lot of flap on drugs, a lot of concern. . . . Customs and other people telling me that Mexico was

----

*Doro and Billy's baby girl.

giving us better cooperation on drugs. The enormity of the problem—It won't be solved by interdiction. It will only be solved by education, though we're interdicting enormous amounts. In another year, we'll have in place balloons that will go all the way across the long border of the Pacific to Brownsville, Texas. It is a tough job. . . .

It was about this time that my friendship with Ross Perot began to sour. I had always been supportive of his efforts to solve the POW/MIA issue in Vietnam. But when he began accusing the Pentagon of lying about whether there were live Americans in Vietnam, I could no longer support him. Also, President Reagan had tasked General John Vessey, the former chairman of the Joint Chiefs of Staff, to deal with the POW/MIA and other Vietnam-related issues. General Vessey told President Reagan that Perot's trips to Vietnam were interfering with his work, and I had to tell Perot the trips had to stop. He was furious and insisted on seeing President Reagan.

May 7, 1987

. . . Ross Perot had been in—flamboyant guy—acting like the President and I had twisted his arm; he was trying to change our whole foreign policy toward Vietnam . . . [He has] no knowledge of the balance involved or what it all means to the surrounding countries. The President was firm, trying to get him out of the mix and Ross blowing up as he walked down the hall with Howard Baker, and then calling Colin Powell again.* Ross is acting strange. He makes it that we twisted his arm to get in to all of this, and it is simply not true. He's smeared the character of some good people and I am very concerned about him. There is a certain arrogance that goes with wealth, but in our political system, now with the limits at $1,000,† his thousand spends like anybody else's thousand. I'm disappointed in him. I've always had him on a high plane, high regard; but, he has acted badly and has not kept his word. For example, he said he would not go to Vietnam unless he saw live prisoners. He said that over and over again, and then he went. He sent an advance team, went, sent people back, and he's trying to conduct an independent foreign policy. . . . In any event, I think that he now maybe is out as he should be. There's no question about his intention, but he is just too much . . .

---

*Colin Powell was deputy national security adviser at this time; in a few months, he would become the top man at the NSC, when Carlucci became secretary of defense.

†The maximum amount of money an individual can contribute to a presidential campaign.

May 24, 1987

Mr. FitzGerald Bemiss
Richmond, Virginia 23209
Gerry,

Today the newly painted Fidelity flew out of the water, conquered the sea,
and brought me total R&R. . . .

I am tired, but in spite of an ugly atmosphere out there in the press, I feel
good—at peace.

The lessons we learned from our folks still count. Do your best, keep your
chin up, work hard, be tolerant—good sense.

Love to all Bemi,
GB

5-27-87

The Honorable Hugh Gregg
Nashua, New Hampshire 03062
Hugh:

Right about the applause lines. Maybe I need to wait longer hoping that
someone will get the urge to clap—I am doing a little better on this. . . .

Hectic travel schedule but I am pleased with the way things are going. Our
man Felix Rodriguez, the mystery man of the Contras, testified today, totally
exonerating me, but I'll be damned if it got much coverage on the tube. . . .
c'est la guerre. Hang in with love to Cay.

George

June 16, 1987

Mr. James A. Thomas, Jr.
New Northern Group
New York, New York 10022
Dear Jim:

Pardon my delay in answering your good letter of May 21. I'm on the road
all the time.

I am encouraged about the way things are moving politically and appreciate your interest and suggestions. On Iran-Contra, I have told the full truth
to the FBI, and we have turned over all relevant data to the various [Congres-
sional] committees. . . .

On "distancing," I will remain loyal to the President, but I will be saying,

"Here is what we have done, here is the unfulfilled agenda, and here is what I, George Bush, will do in the future."

On speaking style, I appreciate those constructive suggestions. God knows, there's plenty of room for improvement.

I hope you will keep the suggestions coming from time to time. I welcome your support and your constructive suggestions.

Sincerely,
George Bush

6-18-87

Dear Jack (and les girls, too)*

Someone from our office down there sent me a couple of vulgar birthday cards, thus making my pristine celebration into something slightly off-color. I know you know how vulgarity offends.

Oh actually there was a nice one or two. That sweet Dot Burghard† cleaned up her act enough to send me a clean one with a rural theme. Marilyn Gibbons passed muster with her delightful attack on the Pentagon; but oh those ugly ones—bathroom habits etc.

Jack, knowing how you feel on this, please tell those girls down there, those volunteers, that their pay will be sliced if they don't go the way of the righteous.

Hang in all. Thanks from this 63 year old.

George

July 12, 1987

Dear "P"

Here are some stamps. People love getting your letters from camp.

Camp sounds terrific. I have never heard of so many wonderful activities.

. . . The campaign is going pretty well, but I am a little tired of travel. Today it's very hot in DC but at high noon we are going to have a pitch off in the horseshoe pit. George W, a pretty fair ringer man, is going head on head with Don [Rhodes] as his partner against me and Senator McClure.‡ I think we'll take 'em. Yesterday George W and some California teen-ager did us in.

---

*Our friend Jack Steel, who ran my office in Houston, and all the wonderful volunteers who staffed it, many of whom still work in my office today. For years we've had many running jokes, including about "vulgarity."

†Now ninety-one years old and still opening mail in my office.

‡Jim McClure of Idaho.

Soon you'll be in Maine, and then a little later I'll be there. . . .

Ganny and Millie send their love. Millie brought in another bird and one possum. The possum played dead and when Millie left the possum waddled off.

I miss you but will see you soon.

Devotedly,
Gampy

————————

August 13, '87

Mrs. James A. Baker, III
Washington, D. C. 20007
Dear Susan,

I loved your letter.

. . . We're in Maine—Grandchildren are churning twisting, jumping, laughing, singing, crying—growing bigger—discovering life

I watch, Bar too, we smile & love. Love to all Bakers.

GB

————————

September 9, 1987

Mr. William F. Buckley, Jr.
NATIONAL REVIEW
New York, New York 10016
Dear Bill,

Your August 26 letter caught up with us in Maine. We had a good rest there.

I am glad the debate matter has been resolved.* I would much prefer to have had the debate later on, as you know, but I'll be damned if I wanted to have what will probably be a pin cushion—have been a real punching bag.

I'm living by the Eleventh Commandment,† and it's a great character builder. I hope that I prove to be the "rightwardmost viable candidate." I do feel confident about the outcome of the primaries. I've taken an enormous number of shots for refusing to jump away from the President. I don't have that luxury, and I don't want that luxury. But now, things seem to be on track. Reagan did not lie about the diversion of funds, and those who were a little

————

*I had agreed to participate in a debate, moderated by Bill Buckley, with the other GOP candidates.

†In politics that means not attacking your opponent.

cautious about accepting his word are not going to look very strong, in my view.

All the best, and thanks for your good letter.

Sincerely,
George

_____

Barbara and I headed for Europe the end of September, parts of which trip were very emotional, especially our visit to Poland. I met Lech Walesa for the first time, at a time when his Solidarity movement could still go either way, success or failure. It was an exciting, nail-biting time.

September 29, 1987

Flying out of Poland on our way to Germany. The Poland visit is a blur of excitement, emotion, and sometimes wonder.

. . . Walesa was very interesting. He had several of his people there. Some that had been in jail, some that had gone underground. . . . they talked very openly. Their whole pitch is for pluralism and obviously, for freedom of the elections. They hate the Communists and talk openly about it. If the houses are bugged over there, it doesn't seem to bother the Solidarity people. . . .

The Church is stronger than I ever would have thought—freer, more able to do its thing. The people are overflowing in their enthusiasm for the U.S. Flags, crying out "long live Reagan," "long live Bush."

Other impressions . . .

It's the meeting with the intellectuals at the Ambassador's house, talking openly against their government, and yet, are drawn up short because of their inability to really do anything about it.

It is the pleasant nature of the Communist rulers—Jaruzelski,*at first shy and then relaxing and pleasant, bright. . . .

It is a hospital in Krakow, where you see the little children. We went into the leukemia ward and we saw the kids, stripped of hair, all because of radiation. But it never occurred to me that was leukemia. Then, we saw a sick little guy, sitting in his bed—7 or 8 years old— the nurse saying that this is the one that specially wanted to meet you. I greeted him and I said what does he have wrong. And, they said "leukemia." My eyes flooded with tears, and behind me was a bank of television cameras—a reporter from TIME, an awful nice

_____

*General Wojciech Jaruzelski, head of Poland. Over the years I would get to know him well, and although he was a communist, he also was a patriot and a military hero.

guy named Beckwith,* I think, standing as a pool reporter. And, I thought to myself, I can't turn around, I can't dissolve because of personal tragedy in the face of a host of reporters and our hosts and the nurses that give of themselves everyday. As I stood there looking at this little guy, tears running down my cheek, but able to talk to him pleasantly, hoping he didn't see but, if he did, hoping he'd feel that I loved him. . . .

I get the distinct feeling as I leave Poland that the state is very careful. They know the people are not with them. They know the people have faith in God and are Catholics. They know their history, and yet they control. The police are omnipotent. The union has been beaten to its knees. The leaders tell me Solidarity is nothing, it is dead, it doesn't exist, and yet, you stand at the cathedral of Father Popieluszko's Church, the Father, the slain leader, the man who was murdered by the secret police, and thousands, literally thousands of people calling out 'Solidarnos, Solidarnos' and cheering Walesa. And, asserting their affection for the Union. It is powerful. . . .

We went to Auschwitz today, on the 29th, and it was moving. The thing that struck me the most was the naked women, trying to cover their bodies as they were led—to the graves dug for them—to be shot. There is something so demeaning, so undignified, and the same was true as men—one hopeless looking, terrified man—covering his privates in a lost gesture of decency, in a world that knew no decency. Murdered, slaughtered by the hundreds, the gas chambers, the pictures of the children . . . How in God's name could anyone ever be so brutal? Could any people be so sick? God spare the world from this kind of brutality. . . .

I sent this letter to all our Texas friends and supporters, the people who had stood beside me for so many years.

October 6, 1987

Mr. Trammell Crow
Dallas, TX 75021 2997
Dear Trammell,

Next Monday, October 12, I will officially announce my intention to run for the Republican nomination for President of the United States.

Barbara and I have just returned from a very successful 9 days in Europe,

*Dave Beckwith, who went on to work for Dan Quayle when he was Vice President.

and I wanted to write you immediately and ask you to join me and my family as I take this important step toward the Presidency.

All of us have worked hard and waited a long time for this day. I want you to know that you have helped to make it possible. Barbara and I could not have come this far without you.

Together, with your help, we can make America's future every bit as proud and prosperous as her past.

I hope you will be able to join us at the Houston Hyatt Regency on October 12th.

Sincerely,
George Bush

October 10, 1987

I'm dead tired. We've been out every night this week. But I leave to go to Maine and N.H. . . . We fly to Fryeburg, Maine, where, we're greeted by Doro, Sam, Billy and Ellie, along with Gov. McKernan and Congresswoman Snowe.* A marvelous day at the fair. The leaves were breath-takingly beautiful. The yellows and the bright reds are my favorites, but all of them blended in for a sweeping sea of color. When the sun hit the leaves, it was particularly brilliant.

We walked around the racetrack there at Fryeburg and then had a marvelous Norman Rockwell-like parade with balky goats being hauled by young kids—great big horses—the inevitable old car—the Boy Scouts—the float—the older ladies—great big drawing teams of horses endlessly marching by and crapping all over the things right in front of the reviewing stand—people giggling nervously about that. I said a few words—the band boomed out and the girls chorus singing . . . I shook a thousand hands and my tendon on my right arm began to hurt.

We had a great day there. Little Sam walking along and waving, holding my hand, and then suddenly he decided he didn't want to do that at all anymore, so he kind of sulked and went through his difficult phase.

We fly to Greenfield, N.H. to the Judd Gregg† house and there is a crowd in excess of 2,000 people. One of the biggest political crowds, if not the biggest, that I've ever seen in N.H. It was fantastic.

---

*Now Senator Olympia Snowe and wife of the former governor Jock McKernan.

†Judd is the son of Hugh Gregg, the former governor who ran my campaign in New Hampshire. Judd was then a congressman, went on to be governor, and is now Senator Gregg.

Judd Gregg, John Sununu* and I spoke. They were very brief and I was informal. Sununu told me that I had the fire in my belly and it was the best he'd ever heard me give. I'm confused, cause I keep thinking "I've been giving that speech day in and day out" but I shook every one of those hands, and it took two hours, walking up and down the rope line, endless pictures, autographs, and literally, by the time that I got finished, just before I spoke, my tendon and arm really hurt. . . .

October 12, 1987—THE BIG DAY

. . . Beautiful clear day in Houston. Margaret Warner of *Newsweek* is on the plane. George giving her grief about the story we haven't seen. He asked if on the *Newsweek* cover, is the word 'wimp' on it? Margaret seems a little uncomfortable.†

. . . Supposed to be a good welcoming crowd. Bar looks beautiful. Thirty-four years ago today, Robin died.

. . . The events were terrific. In the Hyatt Regency Ballroom, a crowd of about 2,000 for the speech . . . The press generally received it well. Seeing differences from Reagan, but not in a very negative fashion . . .

Mickey Gilley‡ was good. Milo Hamilton of the Astros was good. They had astronauts and ball players and many, many old friends and kids. Neil was there. Marvin wasn't. George was there, Jeb wasn't. Doro was there. Pierce and Lauren were there, but Pierce didn't make it on stage—tired and irritable. Colu was there with Noelle and George P. Johnny Bush came down on the plane and Lionel Hampton, loyal to the end. Loyal, loyal, loyal.

Paul Boesch, the wrestler, was there. Our great office people from Houston were there. They'd done an awful lot of the work.

The balloon drop that started at the top of the Regency was marvelous. For a frightening moment, it looked like a condom drop—raw rubber appearing from the ceiling—balloons that had popped during the night. But, then down came the array of balloons after a short rah-rah speech following my main speech in the ballroom. Loyal friends

---

*Then the governor of New Hampshire.

†Margaret Warner, pledging that the story would be a good one, was given full access to our family for a *Newsweek* cover story. Then we were tipped off that the cover headline was "Fighting the Wimp Factor."

‡Country-western singer whose Houston-based place, Gilley's, was made famous in the movie *Urban Cowboy.*

were there. Baine and Mildred Kerr but I didn't see the Chambers. I didn't see the Ashmuns and I didn't get to shake hands with so many of the thousand (2000) people that were in the ballroom itself . . . The press don't understand that there is strength in all of this. . . .

October 22, 1987

The handlers want me to be tough now, pick a fight with somebody . . . boy, we live in a world of reaction. That Newsweek story was the cheapest shot I've seen in my political life. The 'wimp' cover, and then everybody reacts—pick a fight—be tough—stand for something controversial, etc., etc. Maybe they're right, but this is a hell of a time in life to start being something I'm not. Let's just hope the inner strength, conviction and hopefully, honor can come through. . . .

November 5, 1987

Dr. Charles LeMaistre, President
M.D. Anderson Hospital
Houston, Texas 77030
Dear Dr. LeMaistre:

This is to notify you that I have chosen the M. D. Anderson Hospital and Tumor Institute,* along with the United Negro College Fund, to be the co-recipients of the proceeds of my autobiography, Looking Forward. These are two causes that are very important to Barbara and me and I hope that the book sells well enough to make a meaningful impact on your activities.

Sincerely,
George Bush

November 6, 1987

Mr. Harold R. DeMoss, Jr.†
Houston, Texas 77002
Dear Hal,

. . . On "English First," I cannot change my position. I strongly favor every child learning to speak English, but I don't think we need a federal law. I worry about prejudice against Hispanics, particularly, and I am afraid that the "English First" debate could stir up prejudice and curtail linguistic education

---

*I am now on the Board of Visitors at M.D. Anderson and will be chairman in 2001.
†A good friend from Houston who is now a federal judge.

programs that I think are absolutely essential in order to teach all Americans to speak English <u>properly.</u> Please keep me informed on the issue. I do not want to be blind-sided. I know public opinion is on the other side, but this is how I feel.

Warm best wishes,
George

———————

November 7, 1987

    Brandon, Iowa. A tiny little town. More people in the middle of the little town than lived in the town. They came in from every-where. The firemen, dressed in yellow coats, holding the crowd back. Young kids, banners, homemade signs welcoming the Vice Presi-dent. I go into the Brandon Feedstore, and just before walking in I was shaking hands with all the people and an older woman said to me, "You look younger than I thought." I said, "A lot of people say, taller." She said, "No, I say a lot younger." I said, "Well, I'm 63." She said, "No shit?" Everybody heard her. All of the people standing next to her looked shocked, looked kind of held back. I laughed and then they laughed like mad. It was absolutely fantastic. One of the great moments in my life politically. . . .

———————

I took time out from politics to help host the Gorbachevs during their state visit to Washington. It was fascinating getting to know them better. Here are some of my diary notes:

December 9, 1987

    Gorbachev is amazing in style. In our meeting he'd grab his pen-cil, write furiously and then put it down and then look with amuse-ment at some statement as it was translated. A couple of times, he'd flare up, but not really like he did when I talked to him about human rights in Moscow. But, he clearly was in command: He would turn to Shevardnadze* and let him participate, but, he does it differently than the President. The President will make a broad statement and then Shultz will fill in the details. But, Gorbachev was in on all of it, including a lot of details. He has a ready smile, and a clear wit. You feel he wants to communicate when you first see him across a crowded room, he'd wink or smile. No question, he's tough. I'm

———

*Eduard Shevardnadze, the foreign minister, for whom I have great respect.

impressed with the man, cause it is so different than Malik or so different than Gromyko. . . .

Dinner at the Soviet Embassy. I sat at the Head table with Dobrynin, Obie Shultz, me, Raisa Gorbachev, the President, Gorbachev, Nancy Reagan, Shevardnadze, Bar, Yakovlev,* and George Shultz. It was an interesting evening. . . . I talked to [Raisa] at length about who she really was; where her family were from, etc. She told me that her mother was from Siberia; her father was a railroad man from the Ukraine; they met as he was coming through Siberia. She told me that she, her husband, their daughter's husband, grandchild, her mother, his mother all lived in the same house. She is very domineering, self-assured— telling me about her teaching. I asked her, "Who are you really? What are you really like? What are your main interests?" She couldn't separate them from her duties in the State. I asked if it was difficult [for their daughter] to have a father who is the General Secretary. She didn't rise to the bait on that, even though I told her that Jaruzelski told me that it was difficult for his daughter. But she was quite a talker and quite good fun. . . . She told me all about the opera singer who was really very good. Kiddingly, I said to her, through the interpreter, "I think I'm falling in love." There was a long silence, and then she said, "This is an election year, you shouldn't do that. You might be like Gary Hart."† Pretty interesting, pretty up-to-date.

. . . I talked to her about the Jewish question. She gave me the standard line. I said, "Look, I'm not criticizing you. I just want you to understand that this is a matter of great seriousness to all Americans. And to understand the future of relations, what's required for good future relations, you have to understand that point."

We had nine courses. Damned good caviar, tons of vodka, white wine, red wine, champagne, and all in all, it was too much. But, a nice, relaxed evening. . . .

———————

Everyone who loved Malcolm Baldrige—and that's everyone who knew him—was devastated when he was killed in a rodeo accident in July. He was then serving as secretary of commerce. I wrote his wife, Midge:

———————

*Anatoly Dobrynin was the Soviet ambassador to the United States for twenty years. At this time he was a special assistant to Gorbachev. Alexander Yakovlev was Central Committee secretary.

†This was in reference to the Gary Hart–Donna Rice controversy, which forced Hart to suspend his presidential race for a few months.

Dec. 20, 1987

Dear Midge,

. . . Christmas won't be easy for you—Bar & I know that. But that special strong sweet guy somehow seems here at my side. . . .

Often in this rugged ugly world of campaign politics—I find myself thinking what would Mac do? How should I react—I wish he could tell me—should I smile? Or should I fight back?

It's more than the advice department, Midge—it's the trust, the unquestioned friendship, the humor the joy, the caring. This strong guy more than once picked me up, dusted me off, gave me a touch of his wisdom and sent me back into the fray.

The last time I saw Mac, Jim Baker, Mac & I were sitting in my West Wing Office. Something was up. Some problem facing the Prez. Down the hall beyond the closed door we thought about it, agreed what we'd do or say or recommend—then we reminisced and relaxed. The last time I saw Mac his friendship gave me strength and I'm saying to myself—I love this guy; decency and honor really count.

Bar & I send our love at Christmas. . . .

George

———————

Through the years our great friend Fred Zeder from California was the champion giver of weird gifts. 1987 was no exception.

Dec. 24th '87

Dear Fred,

How did you know—how could you have known—that what I wanted was a desk top bow and arrow set. I have been firing random shots at daughter-in-law's behinds—lots of fun at this time of year. Sip a little "Zeder red" or taste a hint of that saucy white, fire your arrow at a passing rump and you have one heck of a Merry Christmas—

Many thanks—Love to all Zeders, Always,

George

———————

December 27, 1987

We drove to Camp David* in a big motorcade on the morning of the 24th, for a glorious Christmas weekend. We spent the night of the 24th and the 25th there. The first day was warm. We ran out-

———————

*President and Mrs. Reagan generously offered us the use of Camp David for the holidays.

doors on both the 24 and the 25th. Saw the deer, went bowling, played horseshoes, saw movies, went to the gym and worked out and had a sauna, all three days in a row

. . . The kids were in good spirits. The little ones behaved well. Little Jeb wins the most improvement award. Ellie was smiling and wins the smilingest award—pressed closely by Jenna, who is on stage a lot and is just a joy. Barbara is the serious one. Sam is as cute as he can be, takes an occasional sock at the dog or even a passing cousin here and there. Great little guy. Barbara and Jenna are all excited about going to West Texas. George P. is still very special. He's got the great form in bowling—loses his temper—but not as much as he used to. Full of competitive zeal. Noelle is very beautiful. Neil's little family is fine. Pierce, the screamer, adjusted nicely, and ended up winning the short-term improvement award, the 48-hour award. The new guy that came in screaming and went out smiling. It's tough to jump around and move around that much. Lauren, still beautiful and cozy, and they're off to N.H. They moved the whole family up there the day after Christmas to work for me. Marvin and Margaret and Marshall are special, unflappable. Little Marshall climbed on her wooden hobby horse and rode and rode and rode. I don't know what the stewards* thought at Camp David, seeing the whole gang together—all 22 of them and a couple of screamers in the high-chairs from time to time, but generally compatible. Millie loved it. She ran and ran and ran. Did not chase the deer, but came bounding over falling logs, the leaves—it was great. . . .

December 30, 1987

Grateful for friends . . . Grateful for the peace of mind I get from Kennebunkport. Just seeing a picture of it, as I am now on Air Force II, brings me great relaxation.

Grateful for my health. Grateful that Marvin seems to have come through with flying colors from his operation.

Concerned about the "insiders" in Washington. Recognizing the need for total change, total shaking up of things. The insiders always have a way of ending up on their feet. Insiders in foreign affairs, insiders in staff, insiders in personnel, insiders in whatever it is. . . .

Grateful for the relative peace of mind I have; not fearing the

*The fabulous Navy stewards who staff Camp David, the White House, and the Vice President's house.

future; not all hyped up with ulcers or sweating what would happen if things don't go the way I want them to go. I'm confident that I could do the job, recognizing that nobody has the answers to all the problems. Nobody possibly could.

These are just some year end observations as the new year approaches.

CHAPTER 11

The Long Home Stretch

We began 1988 feeling confident that we could finish what we had started such a long time ago: winning the presidency. But we knew lots of obstacles were still ahead, and like many of my friends and supporters, state senator Roy Goodman of New York wrote me a note of encouragement and concern:

January 13, 1988

Dear Roy,

Thanks for your letter and your advice. I think once in awhile you have to stand up and defend yourself, but I am going to try to stay above the fray and not slug it out with any candidate on a personal basis. I'm going to win this nomination and election, and I want to do it in an honorable way. Thanks, my friend, for continuing to keep me so well informed.

Hastily,
George

After that note of reassurance to my friend, the year really did start off with a bang. Dan Rather asked if he could do a profile for his CBS Evening News *broadcast. We were told it would be a biography-type piece, just like the ones CBS was airing on the other candidates. What we got was something else. I dictated to my diary:*

January 24th

We've been invited to do a CBS "profile." They wanted me to tape for 40 minutes and [Craig] Fuller wisely said "no, we'll do it live."* We didn't think they'd do it live, which will be for 4 minutes, but they came back and said they would do it live. But, then we get to New Hampshire and we find the promo on the CBS show for tomorrow is "Dan Rather talks to George Bush about Iran-contra," or something of that nature. I wonder if it is a straight up deal, or what they're doing.

I called Teeley† and told him this and he was going to talk to the producer. They've done profiles on every candidate, but the way they are advertising it on this candidate, they want to talk just about Iran-contra.

Nice Sunday, other than that. . . .

_____

January 25th

. . . When I returned from New Hampshire in a big-flake snow-storm, we decided to go right to the Capitol. I was doing the Rather live program from my office right in the Capitol, and I figured if I tried to go home, I wouldn't have time to get back. Barbara met me and brought some clothes. . . .

We came on the air. There were four minutes of clips—all questioning my word. It was a mean, tough interview. Dan came on, and he and I got right with it. I tried to keep my cool. In fact, I think I did. But, I'd be damned if I was going to let this guy walk all over me. "Your judging my whole career by Iran would be like somebody judging your whole career by the 7-minute walkout when the air time went blank,"‡ I said to him.

The interview is now history. When it was over, I felt like I had been through a couple of rounds in the ring. The adrenaline was pumping. The mike was still on, against all custom I might add, and CBS taped me laying in to the producer telling her this is the last time you can deal with me. "Your network can deal with me at press

_____

*I much prefer to do my interviews live or to tape them to length. That way you avoid your forty-minute interview being cut and pasted down to four minutes, the result being that some-times your words can be taken out of context.

†Pete Teeley, who had been my press secretary but by now had gone back to the private sec-tor. I still depended on him for advice—and still do today.

‡This refers to an incident in 1987 when Dan Rather was upset by his network's decision to finish airing a tennis match at the U.S. Open instead of starting the news as scheduled. He stormed off the set to call the president of CBS News, and when the tennis match ended ear-lier than expected and the network switched to the news, they had six minutes of dead air-time.

conferences by holding their hand up and I'll treat reporters with respect, but no more inside stuff." . . .

The minute the program ended, switchboards lit up all over the country—telegrams poured in, calls flowed to New York—500 calls to CBS—two CBS affiliates called in to apologize. The White House phones were jammed, and all and all, people were glad to see me do what I did. . . . When I climbed on to the helicopter, the pilot says the boys sure salute you for what you did. The firemen gave me a thumb's up at the helipad. People calling in from Des Moines and all over.

A lively debate as to whether Rather should be fired. I expect there will be back lash, but the initial reaction has been absolutely fantastic and far stronger than I would possibly have imagined.

People don't like television stars being rude, and a lot of the telegrams cite "rude to the Vice President." There was a certain respect for the office and they felt that Rather walked across the line. I don't want to fight with Dan. I've liked Dan, but he apparently told somebody that the newspaper people are free to get all of the information and that Rather would go for the knockout. You could sense it the minute I was there.* . . .

———————

We were focusing most of our attention on Iowa, whose caucus on February 8 would be the first major test of the election. We were not doing well in the polls. My toughest opponent was Bob Dole, then minority leader of the Senate. But television evangelist Pat Robertson was running strong in Iowa. I dictated to my diary:

Feb. 7th, a clear, crisp, Iowa Sunday.
. . . We all went to Church and after church, the question came to me, "Are you trying to lower expectations?" Here we are 15 points back in the poll and someone says "Are you trying to lower expectations?" I said, "Expectations are already lowered, but we're fighting it." It's my hope that if we get wiped out here that it just doesn't bounce back too much in other states. Also, I'd hate to come in third, with Dole first. I wouldn't mind being third if Robertson beats out Dole. But, I don't want to be third in any sense. . . .

Having the kids around and Bar makes me relax a great deal. It makes me feel much, much better. We're going to have another big day tomorrow, on Monday the 8th, and then fly into N.H. The press

———————

*I won the battle with Dan Rather that night, but he won the war. His coverage of my campaign and presidency was consistently negative.

asked me why I was doing that and I said, "I want to hit the ground running, win or lose. The action starts in N.H. the minute the people go to the caucuses in Iowa." I also remember last time talking too much about big momentum and all of that.*

Out in the country, driving in a long motorcade across Iowa, crystal clear, farm houses stand out etched against the sky; Farm machinery around, a light dusting of snow along the cornfields and the abundance of Iowa's lifeline lies frozen and snow-dusted. What a magnificent country we have.

———

February 8th

Nervous. Gloom and doom amongst the campaign people. There is a feeling that we are going to get beat. The question is how bad. . . .

We get to New Hampshire, have dinner with Hugh Gregg, and then the first returns come in and they are horrible. I'm running a poor third, and it's clear that we've lost and that it's Dole and Robertson, and me a distant third, and Kemp back, then Du Pont and Haig.† I just know how the press will play it. There were already columns about Bush being a hemophiliac, and if he finishes third, he's through, etc., etc. But, that hasn't always been the case. It feels like you've been hit in the stomach.

It's really gloomy.

———

February 12th

I do have peace of mind now. If I don't make it, I have no excuses. Just go on about my life, which will be an exciting one. I would have no politics, no head table, no Republican Party, a total hiatus, shifting directions of my life. And if I win, and I still think I will, my hands will be full. The biggest job in the world. . . .

———

February 15th

We have a lot of events in the day. I'm getting awful tired. I'm dictating this on Monday noon. We've been to Dunkin' Donuts. We've

———

*I am credited, or discredited, for coining the phrase "the Big Mo" when I beat Reagan in Iowa in 1980. Reagan proved then that the Big Mo can be terribly overrated. If I lost in Iowa, I was hoping to prove the same thing in 1988.

†Congressman Jack Kemp, former Delaware governor Pete DuPont, and former secretary of state General Alexander Haig.

been to McDonald's for an Egg McMuffin. We've been to the pancake house for pancakes. I'm bloated and very tired.

Ted Williams has been at my side and he keeps pointing out how exhausting it all is. They love seeing him in these shopping centers and malls. Sununu is indefatigable, traveling with me all of the time.

Feb. 16th

. . . . Our people feel good and we think things are moving in the right direction. I know I'm going to be faced with an awful downer if we lose here, but I'll pick myself up and go South* and recoup. But, if I win here, then we go South with a lot more confidence and conviction. I desperately want to win. The kids have worked hard, and Bar has worked hard. Everybody has killed themselves. Sununu, Judd Gregg, our friends and supporters and all of them feel genuinely upbeat. There is such a thing as a "feel" in a campaign and this one feels a lot better.

I'm dictating this on the morning of the election day. We've been to two polling places and the spirits are up. . . . As I left one of the polling places, [the press] were yelling, "How much do you have to win by? What happens in the South if you lose? Will you be dead? "Are you going to be able to go forward if you lose in New Hampshire?" These were the inevitable questions and the inevitable answer is a thumbs up and a cheerful look, exude confidence, and again, as Mum would say, "Do your best."

With John Sununu's hands-on management, we won a huge victory in New Hampshire, which more than made up for the Iowa defeat and gave our campaign a renewed vigor as we headed South. I took some time out to write our friends and supporters.

February 17, 1988

Mrs. Sally Novetzke
Cedar Rapids, Iowa 52403
Dear Sally,

I am back in Washington for one day, about to head out for another 20 days. But now that the dust has settled in both New Hampshire and Iowa, I want to send you and a handful of others this letter.

---

*After the New Hampshire primary, the next big hurdle was Super Tuesday, when most of the Southern states would hold their primary on the same day.

There is no way I can properly express my gratitude—Barbara's, too. You worked hard, you stood at my side when the going got tough, and you were with me, your hand on my shoulder, when things looked very gloomy indeed. There is nothing more you could have done; there is probably a lot more I could have done. But in any event, that's history, and yesterday's result in New Hampshire has given us an enormous lift.

When I win the nomination, I will be grateful to you not just for your support, but for your friendship.

Barbara sends her love; so do all the Bush kids. We are going to make it!

Love,
George

2-24-88

Mr. Bob Boilard*
Biddeford, Maine 04005
Dear Bob,

Articles on both Blues and Mackerels made me think of you.

It was great seeing you in New Hampshire.

Bob, I'm going to win, but I'll promise you one thing—it won't affect our fishing together.

Life is about friends and values.

You are my friend.

Keep your fingers crossed.

George

February 29th

On Monday I have lunch with the President. He does not want to get involved in the politics, but he's very interested. . . . Ken Duberstein† told me after he reported to him that I had won New Hampshire, that the President said, "I'll sleep better tonight." . . .

On the night of the 29th, Monday, alone in a Charleston hotel, I'm recognizing that I won't be back in my own bed now—having been there for one night—for another fifteen days; wishing the sand was running through the clock faster; and seeing the polling numbers holding up. Each day that they hold up, the better it is. . . .

---

*One of my Maine fishing buddies.

†Duberstein was then deputy chief of staff. In a few months he would take over the chief of staff's position when Howard Baker decided to retire.

March 3rd

We give the regular speech, and Fuller hands me a prepared speech to attack Dole on taxes. I said, "Why do we want to attack Dole." We need one news bite, so I went ahead and hit him on the taxes against my better judgment, and the press went ballistic. David Hoffman* started yelling at me, "Is this a fair attack?" They were screaming, jumping up and down—literally swarming—and wondering why the attack. Was it fair?

I think [my staff] are a little sobered by the fact that the media swarms like this, and I think they now understand that my instincts are correct; but I shouldn't have done it and not gone with the flow. This pressure that you're under when they hand you a statement at the last minute is too much, and I've got to resist it better. . . .

March 6th

In Kansas City, we went to a shopping center and it was good, though weird T-shirts. There was one woman who had the most unusual T-shirt on I had ever seen—it was pink with light blue writing, and it said something on it like, "What would happen if everyone in the world farted at once?" She was a nice woman, and she had her child with her; but she and her husband seemed totally oblivious to the fact that she had that sign painted on the front of her shirt. . . .

March 9th

Super Tuesday came and went. The results were very, very clear, and the best that we could have possibly expected. It was unbelievable, and there is no way to measure the impact. . . . The enthusiasm is high, and the bottom line is, it was the best political night of my life and couldn't possibly have been better.†

---

*A reporter from the *Washington Post* who covered my campaign.

†I swept all sixteen GOP primaries held on Super Tuesday, giving me more than half the delegates I needed for the nomination.

March 19, 1988

Mr. Larry McMurtry
Washington, D. C. 20007
Dear Mr. McMurtry,

Having read and thoroughly enjoyed "Lonesome Dove," I have now just finished "Cadillac Jack." Having lived in West Texas for 12 years or so, I got a tremendous kick out of Jack.

Now for the favor—do you sign bookplates? If you have a couple of your own I'd love to have them signed to stick in the front of these two books for our library. If you don't have your own, perhaps you'd sign the two book plates attached.

As a peace offering I am sending along my non-best seller.

Sincerely,
George Bush

Mario Cuomo and I got into a letter exchange about economic policy. Here's just one in the series.

April 11, 1988

The Honorable Mario Cuomo
Governor of the State of New York
Albany, New York 12224
Dear Mario:

Good letter, yours of March 16; but let me comment on one or two specifics. . . .

You cite your own record for cutting taxes and balancing 6 consecutive budgets up there. That is good—outstanding. Please join me in getting the Congress to give the President the tool that you and 42 other Governors have—the line-item veto. I'll bet it would help work wonders at the Federal level.

You seem to indicate the new Commission* may not endorse a tax hike. Please join me in urging the Commission to reject any increase in taxes. This Commission was your idea and the Commission will undoubtedly listen if you encourage them to resist all tax increases.

The election in 1988 will be about a lot of issues, a principal one being how do we get the deficit down. The Congress appropriates and tells us how to spend every dime. Let's get more people in Congress who will hold the line on taxes and help us do a better job on constraining the growth of spending.

My specific proposal is a four year flexible freeze. Total spending, except

---

*President Reagan had just created the bipartisan National Economic Commission, something Cuomo had suggested.

for social security and interest, could grow at no more than the inflation rate. I call for a line-item veto for the President and for passage of the balanced budget amendment, something the American people overwhelmingly support. "Flexible" means the President could add in areas he felt needed more funding but then he'd have to recommend less spending in other areas. . . .

The existing election process is a real grind, but it is really the best way to take one's case to the American people. The best way to make a point about . . . anything facing this nation, is first to fight it out for one's own primary nomination, than having been seasoned and tested by the grueling primary process, to move into an equally grueling general election campaign. . . .

One of your fellow Democrats running for President talked about "Midnight in America." Cheer him up. This is a great, powerful and dynamic country. Let's work together to keep it that way.

Thanks so much for writing.

Sincerely,
George Bush

_____

April 16, 1988

Prof. Samuel Hynes
Woodrow Wilson Professor of Literature
Princeton, N. J.
Dear Prof. Hynes,

Recently you sent me your new book <u>Flights of Passage,</u> and I wrote you back a rather perfunctory thank you note.

Now I have read every word in <u>Flights</u>; and even though the book is closed I am still enjoying it all. You see, I was at Ulithi and Guam. I had clean laundry, but I flew the same steady old Turkeys you did. I sang the same songs, told the same lies, censored the same letters, and felt the same way when I released the bombs.

. . . Your Dad underexpressed stuff just like my Dad did, but I sure wish my Dad were here now giving me that same kind of understanding and love.

I expect if I had studied Literature at Yale (sorry) instead of History of Art 34 I could more eloquently tell you what I thought about your book; but we'll just have to settle for "thanks for helping me relive some of my most formative and enjoyable and sad and maturing days. I loved the book!"

P.S. If I had studied under Princeton's Woodrow Wilson Prof, I might have learned to type better, too—forgive!

Sincerely,
George Bush

_____

April 28, 1988

The Honorable Richard Nixon
New York, New York 10278
Dear Dick, (I am taking you at your word)*

Thank you for that very good letter of April 19. I totally agree with you on the need for change. Here is [a] quote that shows my state of mind:

"You asked earlier on about change. I want new people. If they've got some new approaches, fine. There's going to be wholesale change—you have to do that—If you had two people who think exactly alike, one of them sitting outside, one of them in, it's better to bring the new guy in because of revitalization." (Interview with U.S. News and World Report, April 21, 1988.)

Needless to say, I enjoyed our chat very, very much, and so did Barbara. I would welcome further suggestions at anytime on any subject.

Respectfully and sincerely,
George

———

May 1, 1988

Dear George "P",

This jacket and shirt have your name on them. They both may be a little large now, but not forever.

You sounded a little tired today when I called, but I was glad to hear that your marks are good and the baseball is great.

I threw out the first ball at the Mets game. That was good fun. It would have been more fun if you had been along.

I am now locked in the struggle of my life, but in just a little over 6 months I will know whether I will be President of the United States or whether I will be through with public life altogether. Whatever happens I will work very hard, and the future is exciting. If I win you will come stay with me from time to time in the White House. If I lose we can do a lot of good fun things together—no one watching, no one but us caring. If I win, I want you to cheer me up when I get tired or when the problems get very tough. If I lose, I'll do the same for you, and I'll live a new life watching you compete and grow up and love and have a family. I'd like to be a Great Grandfather. And somebody will say: "Hey you old man, who is that great looking little kid with you?" And I'll say with pride—that's my first Great Grandson. His Dad is that guy over there—the one that has been so nice to his Gampy".

Devotedly,
Gampy

———

*President Nixon had insisted I start calling him by his first name.

Our friend Anne Phelps from Kennebunkport wrote to say a rumor was going around town that if I became President, I would not spend too much time at Walker's Point for fear it would be too disruptive to our tiny town. She wrote to say that she and everyone else thought that was ridiculous.

May 4, 1988

To California

Ms. Anne Phelps
Kennebunkport, Maine 04046
Dear Anne—

Your letter really gave me a lift. Barbara & I have been very worried about adversity affecting the peace & tranquillity of K'port. This year there will be more attention to us; and heaven knows what if I win in the Fall.

K'port is our anchor to windward. It's where I totally relax. I get more pure joy out of watching our grandkids discover the wonders of nature in our tidal pools than I do in meeting the Kings & Queens of the world.

We hate to think that we might cause others who feel the same way we do to have less enjoyment in this special place.

What a very kind and loving letter you sent me.

Sincerely,
George

––––––––––

I sent this letter to my siblings and our children:

May 9, 1988

Mrs. Alexander E. Ellis
Lincoln Center, Massachusetts 01773
Dear Nan,

We are about to sail into uncharted waters, in terms of family scrutiny. We've all been through a lot of inquiry and microscopic probing; however, it'll get worse, not just for our family, but for Dukakis,* too. Hence this letter to family.

. . . As we move closer to November, you'll find you've got a lot of new friends. They may become real friends. Or if the polls show Dukakis kicking us—there might be some friendships that will vaporize. They'll ask for things—"Do you know anyone at Commerce? Can you call Joe Doakes at State?"

My plea is this: Please do not contact any federal agency or department on anything. A call from a "Bush" will get returned, but there is a great likelihood that it will be leaked; maybe deliberately misrepresented.

*By this time it had been determined that Massachusetts governor Michael Dukakis would be my Democratic opponent.

If there is a legitimate inquiry, call my office. It is certainly appropriate to contact your own government, but let's do it through my office so no one can accuse any of the family of trying to use influence.

I know I must sound very defensive, but—believe me—every effort will be made to find some phone call, some inquiry, some letter that can be made to <u>appear</u> improper.

Soon the election will be at hand, and then you will not have to put up with preachy letters from your brother, as in this case, maybe.

Devotedly,
GB

P.S. Please keep me advised of any press calls. It is important that our communications people know who is working what story.

———

May 15th

Sunday, Medford, Oregon—driving from Medford to the Rogue River. It's a beautiful day, and we're driving through beautiful timbered hills. The sun is out, and it makes me feel even more strongly that I don't "fear the future." There is so much to see and so much to do in this beautiful country of ours, and somehow on a day like this, it makes me cope better with the political pressures.

I talked to Mother at 7:00 am our time and she was so sweet and said, "Oh George, I always feel much better after talking to you, because I worry about all those nasty things they say about you. Today, it is the fact that you have four names," she said, "and I will take the full blame for that." She is so sweet and so loving and so protective as a mother. I keep explaining to her not to worry. Today I told her there are only five and a half months to go, and it's going to get worse. There will be uglier things said—meaner, nastier things and even from friends—so let's just do our best and don't worry about it. . . .

———

May 18th

. . . I've become more convinced than ever that the Noriega deal is terrible.* It will go down bad; it's wrong for our country; it sends the wrong signals to the drug pushers; and it's almost an Iran situation—

———

*In February, a federal grand jury in Florida had indicted Manuel Noriega of Panama on drug-trafficking and other related charges. The Reagan administration was trying to work a deal with Noriega that if he would leave Panama until after democratic elections could be held, the charges would be dropped.

doing that which we said we wouldn't do.* I make some comment in a speech that I wouldn't deal with drug dealers—domestic or foreign—and people take it as a break with Reagan on Noriega which to some degree it is. I hate doing this, and I don't feel comfortable with it! I like the President so much, and yet, he's wrong on this one.

I gave a good drug speech at the L. A. police department, and we had good talks with the Chief of Police, Daryl Gates. We went to the crack house and see the ugly slum surroundings, and yet meet [people] with guts and courage and toughness to fight . . . It's depressing and discouraging but it's heroic. I go to the police department and see close to a billion dollars worth of crack and heroin picked up by the cops and lying on a shelf attended by a sergeant. Thank God for those who turn in the cash and fight the drugs. And yet, here we are in Washington about to make a deal with a drug dealer. I think it stinks.

On Thursday, I'm back in Washington, and I get the word that . . . Noriega decides for the deal. My heart sinks, and I can just see it as a major catastrophe. Howard [Baker] says I ought to go down and see the President so I did, and I strongly urged that he call our [negotiator] home. I gave him encouragement to call the damn thing off, but he doesn't see any other way to get this job done. I keep telling him, "You just don't know what this is going to do to law enforcement."

Leon Kelner, the U.S. Attorney from Miami, was in my office at that very moment, waiting to tell me about the deal. I told the President that, and he said, "I wonder if Kelner realizes that we can't enforce the indictment, and that there is no other way to get the job done."

The President's mind is firmly made up, but I go down and see Kelner and he makes a dramatic pitch that this will be seen as a total cop-out, and that these are the people who put poison into the kids. Noriega is a murderer and drug dealer, and how can you believe him when he says he'll leave after we drop the indictment on August 10th. He says it will demoralize the department. I said, "What do the people in the office think?" He said, "Can I be honest with you? "They think the President is covering up for you, and that Noriega has something on you." I said, "They have nothing," and this makes it worse.† . . .

May 22nd

I have made the case as strongly as I can based on policy and politics, and the President has been adamant. In fact, he got sore a time or two, and I cannot present it more forcefully than making the point that dropping the indictment would be terrible . . . I point out—not just at this meeting but to the others—that Noriega claims to have the goods on me, and that in itself puts me in a terrible position. But that much more importantly, we're going to devastate our law enforcement community; we're going to send the wrong signal to the U.S. Attorneys all around; we're going to say that you can drop indictments even without plea bargaining.

. . . The President looked at me three times and said, "George, I'll make this up to you; I'll go out and make people understand," etc. I don't think he can on this one, and I will not go out and argue vociferously against it. Once the deal is made, I can't start doing now that which I haven't been willing to do . . .

This is the most difficult decision process I've seen since I've been here and much more so than Iran—not expo facto, but at the time. The meeting lasted for an hour and fifteen minutes upstairs at the White House, the President in his White House tennis suit. He was very sweet and nice, and it's a tough decision for him; but he's determined, and my protestations were to no avail.*

––––––––––

I answered some questions about my wife for a reporter working on a profile of Barbara:

5-23-88

Re: Your questions—

Nothing irritates me about BPB. When you have been married 43 years there isn't any irritation. We seldom even argue, and when we do it's over in a hurry.

Yes, best friend—I can talk to her about what bothers me. When the kids are down or the grandchildren have problems we can talk about these things share our views with one another. Family is the key to an awful lot. She is very close to my mother. Bar is seen as the strong woman of our family. My mother, older now (87 almost), is still the anchor to windward for all family members of whatever generation—she is their idol; but Barbara will be the next generation's idol.

–––––––––––––––

*In the end Noriega called our bluff and turned down the deal, staying in power illegally. Unfortunately, it made the United States look rather foolish.

Secret successful marriage—give and take. Respect for the other guys opinions. Give each other some elbow room in terms of not insisting on doing what you want to do.

She has enhanced my life and career by caring, by loving, by supporting. She has her own array of interests—garden, literacy, grandkids, her love of our house in Maine, needle point, reading herself, reading to the children, now grandchildren. She likes to exercise. She does all these things but remains interested in what I am doing. She is on the Board of Morehouse [School of Medicine] in Atlanta—she does heartfelt work for leukemia and other causes. But she never loses interest in family or in how I am feeling about things. If I am down she cares a lot.

Nothing annoys me about her—nothing at all. There is no single thing I like most about her. It all comes together, her laugh, her beauty, her caring, her love, her being with me through thick or through thin. In the early days we moved a lot. In the Navy, base to base, then to New Haven for 2½ years then out to West Texas, then to Whittier Cal., then Ventura, Bakersfield, Compton, then back to Midland, then 8-10 years later to Houston, then to Washington, but never a complaint, never a selfish word.

What has she meant to me—everything!!!!

George Bush

June 5, 1988

The Most Reverend John Allin*
23rd Presiding Bishop, ECUSA
Sewanee, Tennessee 37375
Dear Jack,

. . . Thank you for your helpful advice on the campaign. It is rough. There is a tendency to tear down—to destroy. The press loves to see blood on the floor and there is an ugliness about all of this that keeps some good people from being in the arena. Having said that, I would not trade. I know where I want to lead this country and I think I'd be a good President. There is an awful lot I don't know, but I feel strongly about our ability to solve problems and to lead in this troubled world.

The problems are immense. The choice between Bush and Dukakis will be very clear. He is the consummate traditional McGovern-type liberal. People don't see that yet. Indeed, on a national poll, two-thirds of the respondents

----

*Jack Allin, at one time the presiding bishop of the Episcopal Church, was one of the pastors at our summer church, St. Ann's in Kennebunkport. He became a close friend and spiritual adviser, and we felt a great loss when he died in 1998.

that favored Dukakis think he is more conservative than I am. My job will be to get things in focus.

My job, also will be to do that which you suggest—establish my own clear identity. I will do that without insulting or tearing down the President.

Thanks for your most thoughtful and insightful letter. I am grateful. Barbara joins me in sending our love.

George Bush

June 26, 1988

Hawaii Islands Cockroach Racing Association
245 North Kukui Street
Suite 204
Honolulu, Hawaii 96817

Best wishes to the Hawaii Heart Association for a successful Cockroach Racing Classic. I understand that my previous entry, Yellow Roach of Texas, while retired at stud, has sired the awesome Oval Officeroach. He sounds like a sure winner.

Aloha.

Sincerely,
George Bush

July 11th

Home from Maine. Jenna and Barbara are our house guests, and the three of us have dinner. That was fun, and rather cute, the girls showing off claiming they should be in bed at 9:30 p.m. Well it was earlier, and then I got George on the phone, and he said 8:30 p.m. You should've seen their faces caught in the act, both of them. They are so cute, and Millie is glad to have company.

July 12, 1988

The Honorable Gerald R. Ford
Dear Mr. President,

Bar and I send our family love as you reach the ¾ century mark—a day for great celebration. If I am successful in my quest, I only hope I can conduct myself in office with the same sense of decency, honor and integrity that you displayed.

To you and Betty, our warm personal regards.

Many happy returns,
George

———————

Speechwriter Peggy Noonan was working on my acceptance speech at the Repub-
lican convention, to be held in August in New Orleans. I sent her some thoughts
to work with:

7-15-88

TO: Peggy Noonan
FROM: The Vice President
I'm just me!
Know where I want to go—Have the experience to get there:
Jobs, peace, education
I know what drives me-comforts me : <u>family,</u> faith, friends.
• strengthen families
• invest in our kids
• everyone matters
the handicapped
the kid in that Harlem (????) hospital "thrown away" by drug addicted AIDS
ridden parents—Good God we must help that child.
From child care to education in fighting drugs we need American helping
American
Offended by those who deprive others of human rights, of freedom, racism,
fascism, communism—whatever denies people <u>liberty</u>
My background is one thing I'm proud of —
I've worked
I've fought for my country
I've served
I've built
I want to lead—
When mistake is made admit & never apologize for U.S.—
Let others propose turning our decisions and our leadership over to a multi-
lateral body—We have a special obligation to lead. We must not forget our
responsibility.
As the strongest, freest nation in the world we owe it to the free nations of the
world to lead, to stay strong, to care
We are just plain the kindest nation in the world so when a baby is starving in
Ethiopia we reach out
Freest, most decent, I will never tear down this country
Strive for a truly bipartisan foreign policy—and never give up on liberty.
Need a reference to sanctity of human life
Yes, I do feel kids should say the Pledge of Allegiance
Words I like: family, loyalty, kids, freedom, grandkids, caring, love, heart,

decency, faith, honor, service to country, pride, fair (fair play), tolerance, strength, hope, healing, kindness, excellence

I don't fear the future

Opportunity, Experience, Jobs, Private lives, Faith in God

Don't mention Dukakis—

Pledge of Allegiance—reference perhaps to 'pride' I felt when my grandson stood here leading the Pledge" (if "P" does it)

No unilateral cuts in the essential military strength of this country

Pride in staying firm until we accomplished what had <u>never</u> been done in nuclear age—ban an entire generation of weapons chemical-biological

The image of mother shielding her child from invisible death—horror—I want to lead world to find way to ban chemical, biological weapons

Education

Give a kid an education and just watch what that kid can do

Change—It is time for full equity Women—equal pay—whatever we do keep our families strong (child care)

What hurts? An abused child; a scared child; an unloved child

Others may speak better, look better, be smoother, more creative but I must be myself. I want you to know my heart beat—thus where I'd lead

I like people; I'm proud of USA; I like sports; I'm experienced; I love kids; I know good honest people when I see 'em; Highest Ethical standards in terms of conflict of Interests; serve not profit

Now Peggy—I have done to myself, as I fly to Wyoming's serenity, that which Gail Sheehy* (that_____) tried to do—

Can't wait to chat.

Let's aim for the right or left field seats—just inside the foul line—top deck though.

––––––––––

Jim Baker, who had left his job at Treasury to head up my campaign, suggested that during the Democratic convention, he and I leave it all behind and go fishing in Wyoming. It was a brilliant idea.

    July 19th

       It's now the 19th, Tuesday, outside of Cody, Wyoming. I came up here with Jim Baker. We flew in a Gulf Stream III with a minimum staff out of Andrews into Cody. We changed into a helicopter; flew up to the park; and then we completely escaped. . . .

––––––––––

*Writer Gail Sheehy had written one of those touchy-feely "get inside my head" profiles of me for *Vanity Fair*. I hated it.

Baker and I share a tent. We go to sleep every night by 9:00 p.m. or 9:15 p.m., and dawn comes early; but this morning, Tuesday, I managed to sleep until 7:15 after getting up once at the crack of dawn, and then back to bed.

I'm dictating this lying on my bedroll outside of my tent looking at the most beautiful ridge of pines in the mountains, a crystal clear blue sky, and there is not a cloud in the sky today. Fly casting that I learned years ago at the Adirondacks come back to me, and I haven't done it since, but I love it—throwing the fly where you see a rock, or under a log, or behind a tree. It's a real skill. You stand out alone and think, and it's beautiful. I'm getting better with the fly casting. The little fly floats, and you see these little fish come up. There are tiny fish in the river, cut throats, brook, rainbow, and they are delicious. We had some for breakfast . . .

I took a bath under an ice cold waterfall. I didn't get totally in, but I took the crystal water to clean myself off and to wash, and I felt like a million dollars. Today I plan to bathe in the river when the sun is at its height.

We woke up with ice in our pail this morning, a pail of cold clear water outside our tent to brush our teeth and wash our faces, and now, three hours later, I'm lying with no shirt on a bedroll out in front of the tent. Things seems far away. . . .

I have concluded from this trip that I can be very happy in what follows on. If I lose, I don't know what I'll do, but I know I'll be happy. But the main thing is, I'd like to do something to help others, though I don't know what it will prove to be. I still feel confident that I will win, but the polls are tough. Bentsen is seen as a stroke of genius* even though he's way, way apart on the issues, but we've got to get it in focus. We've got to make people understand how far left Dukakis is. . . .

But as I dictate this, Saturday night blends into Sunday, then into Monday, and now Tuesday, it doesn't seem to matter—I feel rested, and my mind is clearer. We'll go back to the rat races; the copies of memos; who has the action on this letter and that; the stacks of paper; the endless criticism; great pressures; and the ugliness; but this little jaunt has proved to me that you can get your soul refurbished.

---

*Dukakis had picked Texas senator Lloyd Bentsen as his running mate.

July 27th

What a funny lull of a period. After the Dukakis triumph at the convention, we're getting all kinds of cosmetic advice: wear dark suits, stand up straighter, wear Cary Grant glasses—those are the ones with the dark frames—hold hands with Barbara more, be politer to her, didn't you see the way the Dukakises were hugging there in public; and I'm thinking, come on, this stuff about them dancing with no music in the holding room, and the press finding out about it—that's crazy; or that arm around his shoulder looking like they're madly in love—it just doesn't seem real. And yet, I'm being advised to do that, reach out, hold Bar's hand, and she and I laugh about it and think how ridiculous it's gotten in this country; but that's the way things go, and that's probably why I'm 18 points back. . . .

———————

Kitty and Michael Dukakis were getting lots of great publicity, especially during the Democratic convention, for being romantic and affectionate. My nervous campaign staff immediately began fretting that Barbara and I needed to do the same. So I wrote Barbara a note:

8-8-88

Sweetsie:

Please look at how Mike and Kitty do it.

Try to be closer in, more—well er romantic—on camera.

I am practicing the loving look, and the creeping hand.

Yours for better TV and more demonstrable affection.

Your sweetie-pie coo-coo.

Love 'ya

GB

———————

August 21st

Sunday, and the convention has come and gone. I'll just make a few general observations.

Having the family there was great. The kids and the grandchildren were front and center, and they did well. Doro speaking so beautifully for her Mother and also on the convention floor. The boys, all of them, on the television and speaking at the convention, all were terrific. Our family got much more focus. They took the heat well, and they showed great presence and great warmth.

. . . I worried some about the speech and worked on it over and over again—first with Peggy [Noonan] and then with Roger[Ailes]* alone. We changed it, and in the final analysis, we shortened it a little though it ran over 50 minutes in all. It was less than Dukakis', but more than we originally planned. There was nothing to say on the speech except that it worked far better than I thought. I remember sitting there when the family had all gone to the convention hall . . . I felt calm; I knew what I had to do. I can't say that I was absolutely positive that it would be a "home run," but I was determined to do my best. I knew, having rehearsed the speech, I felt very, very comfortable with the humor, with the punch-lines and with the challenge. The press was building it up and up and up—had to do this, had to do that—and it was the biggest moment in my life, which it was; and almost setting expectations so high, that they couldn't be matched and, yet, they were.

Immediately after the speech, I knew it was good. . . . all the people on the platform vigorously giving me an up-signal. At conventions, you can't tell because of the mandatory "spontaneous" demonstration; but there was something different, and there was something pretty special about it all, and I felt that it had worked.

The kids came out on the stage. I loved standing next to the Oak Ridge Boys and hearing them sing the closing number. Shirley Jones with her great big voice gave a marvelous close, and all in all, it worked very, very well, indeed.

Of course, we're plagued by the Quayle-National Guard Service, and they've been pounding the poor guy.†

. . . I think the press understands that there has been a feeding frenzy over Quayle, but they haven't proved anything wrong. A few demonstrators are cropping up yelling about Quayle being a draft dodger, but there is going to be an awful lot of people out there that understand that the Guard is honorable; that he played by the rules; and that's the point.

. . . There is a definite sea change since the speech—you can feel it in the crowds, and it's something fantastic. We're here in Cleveland on the 21st; but first to Indiana, then Dayton, Columbus, Cleveland, Ohio, then on into Springfield, Illinois at the State Fair, and then into Chicago. All along the way, it's amazing—it's a different change, and things have changed dramatically. . . .

---

*Roger had joined the campaign as a media consultant. He is now head of Fox News.

†I had picked Indiana senator Dan Quayle as my running mate. The press were hard on him from the beginning, first by unfairly accusing him of avoiding the draft by joining the National Guard. He kept his head high and was loyal to me, and I never regretted my choice.

September 2nd

 Forty-four years ago this very day, I was shot down in combat, and I think how my life has changed. That was one of the most formative experiences, obviously, and here I am now 44 years later, one of two people to be the next President of the United States of America. And yet, I think today about life and death: The life of Delaney and Ted White, and the life of Davis Patrick Murphy, a young police officer. Delaney and White died in service to their country; 44 years later to the day, Murphy is lying in a funeral home, having given his life for his country yesterday or the day before.* . . .

 Life goes on with all its mystery and wonder. I think of when I was a little tiny boy how I feared death, and now I don't fear it at all. I want to live to do good things and partly to meet the challenges that lie ahead, but I don't fear death. Oh, how I love life—how I love my life with my family and my kids and my grandchildren. I love them!

9-4-88

Mrs. Ann Redington France
Kennebunk Beach, Maine 04043
Dear Ann:

 Here's a shot at my views on being a Grandfather. Pardon typing. I'm rushing to the West coast early in the morning.

 The most important things grandchildren contribute to us? They make me feel young. They hug me, and they pull at my hand getting me to do all those fun things—you know—putting up the tent, reading to them, going on the boat and suddenly I feel young, very young, again.

 Some of the grandkids are aware of my position—some are not. All of them are relaxed unspoiled and couldn't care about all the publicity etc. They are so natural.

 They call us Ganny and Gampy (same as I called my grandparents)

 I have all the fun of the grandkids without having to discipline them.

 Once in awhile I get a little tired—when the minnows keep churning and when I've seen ["Karate Kid"] for the <u>third</u> time in one day, or when a tear just won't dry up—yes sometimes a little tired but not often.

 I hope my public position will never encroach on the quiet time with them

---

*Murphy was a young sergeant on the Prince George's police force in Maryland. Married just three weeks, he had been killed in a drug raid.

and that it will never distort their values. Family love is our anchor and it must never be weakened or strained by public attention.

And, yes, we treat them as we did our own but without the responsibility of making them mind.

In sum these 10 grandkids brighten my life and give me great joy. I love them all very much.

Best Wishes,
George Bush

———————

I received a distressful letter from Tom DeFrank of Newsweek, *a reporter whom I respected.* Newsweek *was seeking special access during the campaign to facilitate the writing of a book when the election was over: I felt strongly* Newsweek *should be treated fairly, but given the "wimp" cover, I couldn't see why they should be given special treatment.*

September 6, 1988

Mr. Thomas M. DeFrank
Newsweek
Washington, D. C. 20006
Dear Tom:

I was distressed to get your letter of September 4th, handed to me yesterday here in California.

I am afraid I have not made my position clear. Indeed, you do have many friends working in my campaign. Certainly you are not "forbidden from doing business" with them. The last thing that I want or would condone would be taking a person for whom we all have <u>real</u> respect and making that person a "journalistic leper."

On the book project itself—I thought, when you and I talked long ago, that you understood my position. I even felt, perhaps wrongly, that you personally were somewhat sympathetic. I have made very clear to all concerned that NEWSWEEK is to be treated with total fairness. NEWSWEEK reporters are to be granted the same access and shown the same courtesy as others. I have no reason to believe this is not the case.

When it comes to going beyond these guidelines into giving NEWSWEEK special consideration, giving them access to internal memoranda, indeed, giving them special treatment, I just can't do that. In my view, I would be proving NEWSWEEK'S point—that controversial editorial conclusion they reached and chose to express the very day I announced for the Presidency.*

*That I was a wimp.

Some day I would be glad to discuss this further. As a matter of fact, Kay Graham* mentioned this to me and I gave her a "burst transmission" telling her I would be glad to discuss it in further detail.

You and I both know and appreciate the fact that some journalists are more respected than others. Some build confidence where others build disdain. All should, in my view, be treated fairly.

In your case, Tom, every single one of us involved in this campaign has great respect for you and great confidence in your fairness. You have earned this and, quite properly, friendships have developed.

The line in your letter that really hit home was the one where you expressed your view that you personally were being "singled out for retribution." This cannot be—must not be.

When I got your letter yesterday, I called Jim Baker and reviewed this matter with him.

My suggestions is that you call him, sit down with him, and work out whatever it takes to be sure you personally are treated with total fairness and given unfettered journalistic access.

I know they didn't teach "retribution" at A&M† for I know and respect the real values taught there.

My position is not based on "retribution." Getting even is not a part of my make-up. I also know there is a personal risk to me in all this. But I do not want your editors to totally misjudge my character once again.

I know, Tom, just as sure as you know, that your editors made a cool, calculated decision. They took a reporter's story and drastically changed it by inserting time and again a most prejudicial word—one that dramatically changed the reporter's view of my character. No one can argue about their right to do so. When a reporter's story is radically changed in a way that is demeaning and in a way that attacks character, surely you do not want me to <u>reward</u> such a decision by giving that publication favored treatment. Surely you don't want me to prove them right all along by rolling over and singling them out granting them access and special inside, off-the-record handling not granted to others.

Fair access, unfailing courtesy, benefit of the doubt—yes; but proving their "Big W" point—never.

But back to my respected friend—Tom DeFrank. I'll be damned if I'll diminish a friendship over this sorry matter; and I'll be damned if you'll be diminished professionally.

---

*Owner of the *Washington Post,* which owned *Newsweek.*

†Texas A&M University, Tom's alma mater and a school that I loved. Eventually I would decide to locate my presidential library on the A&M campus.

Work something out with Jim, but don't prove those nameless editors right all along.

I'll give him a copy of this letter which I trust you will consider personal—

Con Afecto
George B.

————————

In addition to the nonstop travel, we also began to prepare for two debates against Dukakis. I am not a big fan of debates—they are more show business than anything else. Nevertheless, they have become a part of our political process.

9-18-88

Sunday Evening 9 PM
TO: JAB III* EYES ONLY
RE: PHONE CALLS WITH NIXON AND FORD
FROM: THE VICE PRESIDENT

I called both former Pres's tonight to check in and get 'advice.'

Both very friendly. Both send best to you.

Both say—Don't get over prepared for debates—take time off.

RN: It isn't the substance it's the appearance. Stay cool etc look rested take at least two days off without briefings and staff pounding away at you.

Ford: Take deep breath before answering question—Think carefully before each answer. Take time/Do not try to overprepare on statistics etc.

Just FYI.

GB

————————

Ray Siller was one of Johnny Carson's talented joke writers. He occasionally would send me lines to use. I sent him this SOS:

Sept. 19, 1988

Wisconsin
Dear Ray,

On the road constantly.

I need an opening joke or two about: "speaking before the meal—then leaving".

I am doing a lot of that now. People then go on to eat their meals and the Senator/Congressman/Governor speaks <u>after</u> the meal.

————————

*James Baker.

It can tie in to being "mercifully brief—know you're hungry" or "first course before even the olives".

But it is a little awkward this speaking & leaving while everyone else stays for dinner.

Any thoughts?

Things look pretty good. I'll stay on the trail then catch my breath after Nov. 6th.

> Thanks
> George

[It wasn't until I became President that Ray helped me solve this problem. He then sent me this line: "The food taster is facedown in the salad." It always got a good laugh.]

———

September 23rd

All the news coverage on the major networks is about the debates, and here I sit one of two people to be involved in this before an entire nation. The pressure is mounting, but I feel fairly relaxed. I'm dictating this Friday night, and I'm tired because we got in at 1:30 a.m. from Texas and I was up for an early breakfast; but I don't feel terrified about the issues. . . . Bar has been off in Connecticut, and the little girls are staying here. It's fun, but I'm very tired.

[The first debate, held in Winston-Salem, North Carolina, came and went without incident and I felt I did pretty well.]

———

> Sept. 26, 1988

enroute to Tenn. From N.C.

President Jimmy Carter
Plains, Georgia 31780
Dear Mr. President,

Barbara and I send to you and all your close family our sincere condolences. I am very close to my three brothers. Billy's death must hurt a lot—I sense that. I feel it.

Our respects and family love to you.

I expect your grief is tempered by your certain knowledge that with the battle over, Billy is indeed in God's loving arms—

> Respectfully,
> George

_____

Oct. 8th

I'm not looking forward to the debate* too much, at least today, but that's because I'm tired and I have a cold. Some time off tomorrow, though I do have to go and be in a parade in Chicago.

The polling is looking pretty good—about even, ours says—but one or two of them have us slightly ahead. The electoral states are looking pretty good, and I should be more optimistic; but I'm not—nervous, fingers crossed.

Dinner at our house with just the [Dick] Moores and the Simpsons. Al Simpson† and Anne are two down-to-earth, decent, wonderful people and, of course, Dick and Esther are dear friends. It's funny with friends, close friends—you shift gears, you relax, and you forget the tensions. I played the tape of Marvin's speech to the Crohn's & Colitis Foundation in Cleveland, and tears came to my eyes; in fact, they streamed down my cheeks. . . . I heard our son talk about love, strength and courage. It wasn't in an ostentatious way, but in a caring, loving way, and here I am 31 days short of knowing whether I will be the next President of the United States, but that was gone.

What mattered was, in this case, Marvin Bush and what he had been through; his confessional and his trying to help others after experiencing a trauma in his life; and confessing to a group of 2,000 people what mattered; what really was important; and I'm sitting there after a wonderful dinner listening to my son, and all these issues are swirling around, but in my mind I'm saying, "This is what matters—this boy's strength, his love of his wife, of his little daughter, and of his mother and dad—that's what really matters in life." So if it works in a month from this very day, fine; but if it doesn't, I can say flip the page and move on into the future, and know you're a very lucky guy. . . .

_____

October 13th

The debate is over, and I do feel much more relaxed. The panelists came across with strong questions but no hostility, and that made a difference. I felt better prepared for the subjects . . . once I got out there, I relaxed, smiled and looked at the audience, and I felt much more comfortable than before.

*The final debate was in Los Angeles.
†A great friend and senator from Wyoming.

October 14th

The speechwriters hand me a couple of red meat speeches—one for an environmental thing with several more subtle digs at Dukakis, and then a rally speech that was too negative, negative, negative; but I sent it back and said, "Please don't hand me this crap." It was totally out of sync with what we want to be doing.

Oct. 18, 1988

flying Missouri to Detroit
Mr. Craig Stapleton
Greenwich, Connecticut 06830
Dear Debbie, Craig, Walker, and Wendy*—

. . . I am glad that debate is over. I am glad the polls look better; but I wish the election were now—today this minute.

I am getting a little tired and I'd like it to be a summer day in Maine with a hot "shoes" match on at the Stapleton Memorial pit—

With tennis action—

With the pool full of bodies—old saggy bodies then sylphs like Wendy, too.

Even with that wretched little short haired dog that barks and turns circles near the diving board.†

You see when the day ends out here on this seemingly endless trail—it's family and friends that matter—

Love
GB

October 25th

. . . I went down to the gym and worked out. I saw this guy kind of watching me. I said to someone after I finished my workout, "Do we know who that guy is?" They said, no, and I said, "He might be with the press so I think I'll go into the steam room." He then came into the steam room . . . so then I finished and went in to take my shower, and he confronted me. There we were naked as jay birds, and

---

*Debbie was my first cousin. She had married Craig Stapleton and they had two children, Walker and Wendy.

†This would be Uncle Lou Walker's dog Caper. He was Debbie's father.

he said, "I don't want to impose on your privacy, but I'm a member of the press, and I would like to ask a question." I said, "Please don't" but he went on and asked the question, "When is the next press conference?" I said, "Look, we've had 207 press conferences; we've averaged one every ten days since the convention; and I think that may be about it." He went away, but I was furious. The guy should've at least worn his credentials around his neck even though he was bare-assed. I don't know, it just didn't seem fair—no privacy in that sense at all.

———————

Nov. 4, 1988

Ms. Loretta Lynn
Nashville, Tennessee 37203
Dear Loretta,

In about 72 hours I end my campaigning.

Before the polls open I just want to say <u>thanks</u> from me, from Barbara and from all the kids & grandkids.

You were magnificent out on the road.

Fingers crossed.

Love & thanks

George

———————

Mr. Arnold Schwarzenegger
Venice, California 90291
Dear Arnold,

What a great boost you gave my campaign. With only 72 Hours of campaigning left, I just want to say "Thanks, thanks, thanks". Doro joins me in this—Barbara and the rest of our family too.

You really helped me and I am grateful.

Hope I'll see you before the election; but in any event many thanks.

George Bush

———————

November 7th

The day before the election, I wake up and do the four network interviews. Then the rally in Michigan; rally in Ohio; rally in Missouri; and now we're off to the rally in Houston, Texas. . . .

I sat with Jim and talked to him about the future: about announcing him [as Secretary of State]; announcing John Sununu as Chief of Staff; but that will come a little later. . . .

I called Claude Payne at St. Martin's and told him we would like to have a church service on Wednesday morning at 8:00 a.m. I do want to ask for the Lord's help, encourage our staff and friends to go, thank God for our blessings; and quietly with some attention to our family faith, give thanks to God and ask for his support.

The election feels good to me and, yet, there is a nervousness. Dukakis is frantically going around the country, flying all night two nights in a row, and the poor guy will be dead. . . .

There is an apprehension and a nervous waiting, anxiety and recognition, but Wednesday it will be all or nothing, and the desire to do what's right, do my best, and the recognition that it's going to be extraordinarily difficult.

It's fitting that we come back to Texas where I voted first 40 years ago almost to the day in West Texas. Then it was Dewey and Truman, and I remember the upset result, and I'm just hoping against hope that that same thing doesn't happen again. I don't know what we could do differently. The polls are strong, although there has been shrinkage in one or two of them; but the polls today are strong, and there hasn't ever been a modern race where all of them have been that wrong. So we should win it, and then the real problems will begin. I can't believe it's almost over—I simply find it incredible and almost impossible to believe.

And just like that, it was over. We won a decisive victory, and as promised, I began my first day as President-elect by going to church.

Nov. 9, 1988

The Right Reverend Maurice M. Benitez
Episcopal Diocese of Texas
Houston, Texas 77002
Dear Ben,

Your being there today made our special service—<u>extra</u> special. Thanks for that. The awesome nature of what lies ahead is just beginning to sink in . . .

Sincerely,
George

Then, it was immediately to work. I was determined to have a good working relationship with Congress, which really was essential if I was to accomplish what I wanted to do.

November 10, 1988

TO: CRAIG FULLER
FROM: THE VICE PRESIDENT

I would like to meet with Bob Michel* next week or the following week. Meeting location makes no difference. I think Michel leaves for a short vacation the day I get back—but work this out for a convenient time.

Also, I would like to meet with Jim Wright† next week. Wright offered to come down to the White House. I said "no" that I would go to see him.

We talked about lunch but if that doesn't fit, let's just work out a meeting at the Speaker's office at a convenient time.

November 21, 1988

The Honorable Zbigniew Brzezinski‡
The Federalist Society for Law and Public Policy Studies
Washington, D. C. 20006

Dear Zbig:

I have now had a chance to think more about your memo of November 9.

I had not given a lot of thought to institutionalizing our Trans-Pacific Partnership. We have been looking at this area almost exclusively in a bilateral context. The importance of China is very clear to me. I'd love to return to China before Deng leaves office entirely. I feel I have a special relationship there.

I like your idea of a Pacific Rim summit and will ask Jim Baker to give this some serious consideration. Frankly, I think such a summit would help with Europe in a perverse sort of way.

Eastern Europe has a real chance now for more liberty if we handle their Soviet relationship properly.

On consultation with Congress, I meant what I said in the campaign about "bipartisanship," and I have already written several Senators suggesting the very meetings that you suggest.

We are considering an early bilateral [meeting] with Japan; and as you have now seen, a meeting with Mexico's new President§ is set for tomorrow.

I will not neglect Canada.

Since your memo, Gorbachev has asked for and we have agreed to a meeting in New York.

I just want you to know I read your memo carefully and appreciate it.

Sincerely.
George Bush

*House minority leader.
†Speaker of the House.
‡Jimmy Carter's NSC adviser.
§Carlos Salinas had just been elected president of Mexico.

Dec. 1, 1988

The Honorable Geraldine A. Ferraro
Forest Hills, New York 11375
Dear Gerry,

I mean—talk about a thousand points of light—your letter was the 1001st point. It brightened my day!* It made me want to go out and kick _____ no, no, never again—

Love to all your family—We ached for you awhile back but I hope all's well now—your family love came through strong and proud.†

Barbara sends her best, too—

George

Dec. 12, 1988

The Honorable Guy Molinari
House of Representatives
Washington, D. C. 20515
Dear Guy,

After thinking seriously about the situation for days I have concluded that I should not go to Congress for my Cabinet Offices. You are superbly qualified and I'd love to have had you at my side; but I just can't bring myself to deplete our ranks. You made the point, quite properly about working the Hill from the Cabinet as former Members; but I just feel I need our good people up there on the Hill—full time. In a way I hate to go this route; but overall I think it's best—stay with me, pal.

George

[This was a tough decision for me as I had some great friends in Congress who would have been terrific cabinet members. However, with the Democrats controlling both houses of Congress, I really needed them to stay on the Hill. However, it wouldn't be long before I would have to change my mind on this.]

---

*She had sent me a wonderful note of congratulations, taking credit for teaching me everything I knew about debates. Another note: I first used the term *a thousand points of light* in my convention speech, referring to the importance of volunteerism.

†One of their sons had been in some legal trouble.

December 17, 1988

Frito-Lay Inc.
Nazareth, Pennsylvania 18064
To all at Frito-Lay-Nazareth:
My sincere thanks for those pork rinds and for the 17-signature card.
Merry Christmas to all of you.

George Bush

———

Dec. 25, 1988

Mrs. Henry L. Hillman
Pittsburgh, Pennsylvania 15213
Dear Elsie,*
The Westminster Choir is on in the background, their lovely music of Christmas putting into focus for me what a lucky guy I am. A lot of it is family, a lot of it is friends. Thanks dear friend for your steadfast loyalty, your valued advice, your leadership—most of all for your friendship. Next year won't be easy; but even when it's real tough I'll know there's a hand full of close friends who really care.
Love to all your gang—

George

———

Dec. 29, 1988

F & M†—
The combination of wine cum bullhorn really hit the target for classic Xmas gift of '88—you should see Bar come running when, wine in hand, I give her a command call through the bullhorn. It works—it's miraculous—

Love and thanks
George

———

December 30, 1988

Mr. George G. Harris, Sr.
Houston, Texas 77001
Dear George,
Barbara and I appreciate very much your generous offer to help with our move next month. Fortunately, one of the advantages of being President is

*Elsie is a great friend and one of my strongest supporters.
†Martha and Fred Zeder.

that the move is taken care of by the Government. You are thoughtful to offer, though, and we are grateful.

Warmest best wishes to you and yours for a great year ahead.

Sincerely,
George Bush

January 7, 1989

Mr. Willie Morris*
Oxford, Mississippi 38655
Dear Willie,

. . . Tough days ahead, but I am now getting excited about moving down the hall and getting to work. If it weren't for the damned deficit I'd be kicking up my heels and feeling like a Spring colt. I do feel that the potential out there for a more peaceful world is pretty good. I'll work hard, after proper review, to move our relations with the Soviets along on a prudent course. I am very impressed with Mr. Gorbachev. I will not neglect our own hemisphere, but an easy answer for Nicaragua and Panama is not on the radar screen.

At home I'll push for a "kinder gentler" nation, but for those who measure a commitment to that solely in terms of federal money there may be disappointment (deficit deficit deficit).

See, what I want to do is confound my old friend Ronnie Dugger† by doing a good job, by caring, by reaching out. Having said that, Ronnie may have to wait for the full impact because there ain't no dough around for the Feds to do all some would like—as a matter of fact to do all I would like to get done.

Why unload all this on you, when I simply write to say "Thanks and Good luck".

Sincerely,
George Bush

January 16th [1989]

People say, "What does it feel like? Are you ready, can you handle it? What do you do?" The answer, "Family, faith, friends, do your best, try your hardest, rely on your innate good sense, kindness, and understanding of the American people." That is where a President gets

------

*Famous Mississippi author whose works include *North Toward Home*. Although he was a liberal, we were friends.

†The founder of the very liberal *Texas Observer* newspaper.

his strength, I'm sure of it. No one can have instant success, no one can make this nation kinder and gentler overnight, but we can try.

January 17, 1988

The last day in [the vice president's] house—the longest we've been in any dwelling since we've been married . . .

Now the reality settles in that I'll be President of the United States. Today at noon—72 hours away.

January 18th, 1989

An Open Letter to the Clergy:

Barbara and I believe it is most fitting that the events of my Inauguration as President conclude in an ecumenical service of prayer and thanksgiving. In the Nation's Capital, this Service will be part of the regular morning worship on Sunday, January 22, at the Washington Cathedral. We are grateful to the Right Reverend John T. Walker, Episcopal Bishop of Washington, who has invited us to share in this time of praise and renewal.

Dan Quayle and I very much hope that this Service will be part of similar observances of prayer and thanksgiving throughout our Country. We ask you to join us through your service of worship on Inaugural weekend by using elements of the National Service. We will be united in praise to God for the blessings which have endowed our Nation and in asking for leadership as we face the challenges of the future.

Worship is basic to my own life. Our family has endeavored to uphold our faith by participation in the life of our Church. I am particularly pleased that the American Bicentennial Presidential Inaugural will end on a note of asking God's guidance on the new beginning which opens before us.

As the bells ring across our land on January 22, may their joyous sound express our gladness for the blessings the Lord has given and equally express our renewed commitment to seeking goodwill and peace among all peoples.

Sincerely,
George Bush

CHAPTER 12

"Mr. President"

On January 20, I was sworn in as the forty-first President of the United States. The next day, I dictated to my diary:

_____

January 21st

The big day came and went. . . . The day was cold, not as pretty as the day before, but as we were riding up to the Hill, the President said, "When I became the Governor of California, just as I placed my hand on the Bible, the sun came through and warmed it." And sure enough, while we were on the platform, the sun started through. . . .

We were a couple of minutes late taking the Oath, but no one noticed. The speech went about 20 minutes, and it was well received. Congress liked it. We've got to find ways to do this compromise, "kinder nation, gentler world." . . .

The balls—going around to 14 different events, I think 10 hotels or 11 hotels—it was too much. We were just exhausted when we got home. When we got back, I had that almost so tired you couldn't sleep feeling and I knew that at 8:00 this morning, we had to greet the first group of people who stayed out all night to get to be one of a handful of several thousand people to go through the White House.

I loved that part. Young people and old, so grateful that they had a chance to go through the White House. Even though they had to stay out all night, they get to do it. It's interesting in that regard how people view their country—it's wonderful indeed. . . .

I feel comfortable in the job. I'm not quite used to being called,

"Mr. President." Beautiful winter day, January 21st—clear, sunny, cold. The People's House, the Family's House—it is great.

Then it was down to business. One of my first and biggest challenges was the huge federal deficit ($170 billion when I took office), brought on by years of uncontrolled spending by the government. I was convinced the well-being of our country depended on getting it under control. However, I knew it would not be an easy task, especially since I would have to work closely with the Democrat-controlled Congress. Unfortunately, I had the great honor of being the first President in years to have the opposition party control both houses of Congress during his entire presidency.

January 21, 1989

The Honorable Jim Wright
Speaker of the House of Representatives
Washington, D. C. 20515
Dear Jim:

Yesterday, in my Inaugural Address, I suggested that together we should begin the process of working to achieve a deficit reduction plan—and that we should do so soon. I had previously stated that I would lead such an effort on behalf of the Executive branch and that I would begin the process promptly upon taking office.

In accord with that commitment and our discussions, I extend to you today an invitation to join me in a meeting at the White House on Tuesday, January 24. At that meeting, I would hope we could discuss how best to proceed toward deficit reduction. I would also like to take the opportunity to follow up on suggestions made by you and your colleagues on ways we can move towards effective bipartisan support for our foreign policy.

In addition, I would like to confirm my request, which you indicated could be honored, for the opportunity to address a joint session of the Congress on Thursday, February 9.

Again, let me say how much I look forward to our working together on these critical issues. I am sure the American people expect that concerns of such national import should be tackled in a spirit of bipartisan cooperation, and am hopeful that we may prove worthy of the confidence they have placed in us.

Sincerely,
George Bush

On February 7 our family grew once again, when Ashley Walker Bush—grandchild number eleven—was born to Neil and Sharon.

Feb. 7, 1989

Miss Ashley Walker Bush
c/o Mr. and Mrs. Neil M. Bush
Denver, Colorado 80218
Dear Ashley,

On this the first day of your life, your old grandfather sends you his love. Today was the day after my Savings & Loan proposal;* the day of my visit to Capitol Hill to see a lot of Congress Members; 2 days before my speech to the nation—but on this day of your birth, I'm thinking of you. You have 2 great parents, an older sister who will teach you and a brother who will protect you. You have grandparents who love you a lot already. Welcome, welcome to this big loving family—I am a happy Gampy because you're here.

Devotedly,
George Bush (formal!!)

On February 9 I did address a joint session of Congress, outlining my plan for the country, "Building a Better America." Even the President worries about getting the jitters.

February 9th

. . . I wasn't nervous at all. I could communicate with different people in the audience once I got started. I caught Rosty's† eye; I caught the eye of Jesse Helms‡ and some of our guys; caught the eyes of Sonny Montgomery;§ and I felt relaxed once I got started. . . .

Interrupted by applause a lot—speech went well. My voice held out,** although I had to drink some water; but I felt in command and in control, no nervousness—it was almost like coming home. I recognize there's going to be a lot of criticism of the budget, but that is nothing to be surprised about.

Went home and drank a beer with Marv and Doro. . . .

---

*After years of abuse, the savings and loan industry was reeling from bad debt and bankruptcy. My goal was to protect the depositors—not the owners—and to put into place tough new rules to get the industry back on track and protect Americans' investments. It was an expensive and ugly task but an accomplishment I am proud of.

†Dan Rostenkowski, Democratic congressman from Illinois.

‡Republican senator from North Carolina.

§Sonny, a Democrat from Mississippi, and one of my best friends. We entered Congress together in 1967.

**I was suffering from laryngitis.

All left-handed people immediately considered the new left-handed President a friend. After all, we left-handers have to stick together. A writer asked me to jot down a few words that she could include in a musical she had written, called Left Out.

February 13, 1989

Ms. Narcissa Campion
Brookline, Massachusetts 02146
Dear Narcissa,

I'm sorry this quote is probably too late for your play, but maybe you can find a way to use it later.

Being left-handed is no different than being short or tall, young or old, blond or brunette. Things can have more advantages or disadvantages, depending more on your outlook. Left-handed is <u>great</u> if you're a first baseman. Of course, you've got to be careful not to smear things when you write. I don't think anyone's ever held it against me to be left-handed, though. Besides, sometimes the seat at the end of the dinner table is a better place to be! . . .

Sincerely,
George Bush

I had nominated Senator John Tower to be secretary of defense. Not only did I think he would do an outstanding job, I also assumed his nomination would glide through the Hill for two good reasons: he was more than qualified for the job, and Congress is usually kind to its own. I could not have been more wrong. He was getting hammered, mainly as a result of rumors about his personal life. I wrote my friend Charley Bartlett:

February 21, 1989

Honorable Charles L. Bartlett
Washington, D. C. 20036
Dear Charley,

Thanks for your most encouraging and supportive letter of February 11. I am going to stand with Tower all the way, and I am confident he will make it. I have never seen such a campaign of innuendo, vicious rumor and gossip in my entire life. . . . I am not considering alternatives.

Warm regards,
George

On February 23, Barbara and I attended the funeral of Emperor Hirohito. It was a controversial decision, especially among veterans' groups, given the emperor's role in World War II. But Japan now is one of our strongest allies, and I was convinced it was the right thing to do. I dictated to my diary:

February 24th

A big day at the funeral. It was ice cold. The Chairman of Ghana (Rawlings), sitting a row behind me, gave me his cashmere scarf. I said, "I can't accept that." He said, "You must." It saved my life. People were coughing and drippy. The funeral service was run to perfection—every footprint raked every so often. Great long curtains covering the official mourners; short speeches; endless procession of priests presenting the late Emperor's worldly goods to the altar, and then taking them all away again. Weird costumes out of history—majestic and somber. The new Empress, dignified—she looked like a black swan. Her neck bent forward; dress reached all the way to the ground, and a long full veil following behind.

My mind raced back to the Pacific. I did think of my fallen comrades . . . here I was, President of the United States, paying respects to the man who was the symbol of everything that we hated. A man whose picture was always shown to keep us all together, fighting hard. Endless pictures of Japanese soldiers cutting off the heads of prisoners or firing the coup de grace against thousands as they were dumped into the graves alive, all in the name of Hirohito. And here we were, paying tribute to him, a gentle man indeed. A man who decided to come see MacArthur and whom MacArthur properly did not try as a war criminal—amazing. . . .

After leaving Japan, we flew to China for an emotional two-day visit. In addition to meeting with the Chinese leaders, Barbara and I saw many old friends and even got a chance to visit our old church. However, we got caught up in a terrible controversy when the American embassy invited one of the leading dissidents in China, Fang Lizhi, to attend a Texas barbecue we were hosting. I dictated to my diary:

February 27th

. . . We had a good Texas barbecue; big Texas flag; the Navy country music gang played; checkered tablecloths; bandannas around the necks of the waiters; White House China for the head table, including the [Woodrow] Wilson plates; and it was a very relaxing, friendly evening. I leaned over and thanked [Premier] Li Peng for his understanding and he said, "We may need your help later on." I took this to mean that they may get a great deal of flack for attending the same banquet with dissident Fang. The room was crowded, several hundred people. I didn't ask which one was Fang, because I was sitting next to the Chinese [leaders] and didn't have any opportunity to do so. All of our people assumed he was at the banquet. It was this morning, Monday, that we find out the Chinese stopped his car; detained him from taking a taxi; kept the buses from picking him up; and all in all, made sure he wasn't going to be at the banquet. We end up with the worst of worlds out of this. Newspapers are all over the story, "human rights abuse." They won't point out that two of the dissidents were there, and that China has come a long way. China overplayed their hand and I expressed my regret to Deputy (Vice) Premier Wu at the airport. And now we're scurrying around trying to figure out how to handle it with our press. In the long run, it will not obscure the substance of the visit with the Chinese; but it is not a good thing, and the press will have a field day—"don't know how to handle things," on top of "being dogged by Tower"—this incident mars the visit.

March 13, 1989

His Royal Highness Sadruddin Aga Khan
Chateau de Bellerive
Switzerland
Dear Sadri:

. . . Things have been a little hectic lately with the Tower matter dominating the news coverage,* but I am very pleased with the overall progress. The problems are enormous but we've made some sound proposals; and when we finish our foreign policy and defense reviews, we'll have some more solid proposals to make. I'll be darned if Mr. Gorbachev should dominate world public opinion forever.† His system has failed and it's democracy that's on the march. . . .

Sincerely,
George

---

*Tower lost in the Senate, a terrible blow to a man who had served his country with distinction. I quickly nominated Dick Cheney, then minority whip in the House. I hated to steal from our congressional ranks, but I knew Dick would be accepted on the Hill and would do a great job. I was right on both counts.

†At this point Gorbachev was beating us at the public relations game through high-profile visits in Europe calling for peace and change.

March 14, 1989

The Honorable Lee Atwater*
Republican National Committee
Washington D. C.
Dear Lee:

Today your character will be ridiculed. Your taste will be assaulted. Your shortcomings will be exaggerated and laughed at. And your self-respect is going to be violated. And that's just from your friends! In other words, they will do to you what you did to Governor Dukakis for five months. So don't count on any help when the Democrats have their turn. They've been waiting for this opportunity for a <u>long</u> time.

But, Lee, I've known you for a long time too. You know how to take the heat, and you know how to take the humor. So when the comic characterizations get fierce today, don't get angry, don't lose your temper—just remember: Kinder, gentler.

> Sincerely,
> George Bush

We had sent Millie back to her original owner, our good friend Will Farish, to have her bred. We were amazed at the attention paid to the blessed event: the birth of her six puppies.

March 20th

Millie had her puppies, and it was a beautiful moment Friday night. I saw one born, and it was very, very moving. Before all this, Millie looked confused and I kind of felt she was wondering what was happening to her, but then the babies started coming. I saw number four being born. She cleaned them off, tucked them in comfortably next to her, looked over at each one, and now on this Monday, she's a caring, loving, and experienced Mother. If one goes too far away, she nudges him over; she rolls him over; and cleans him up. She's feeding them, and the milk has come in, so she's looking baggier. She looks at us with soulful eyes. When she goes out to run, she does just like the old Millie—though not quite as fast—but then gets restless and wants to be back next to her puppies. . . .

*Lee was sort of the "chief operating officer" of my 1988 presidential campaign. He was young, aggressive (some people would say ruthless), and brilliant at politics. After the election, I appointed him chairman of the RNC. I wrote this note before he was to be roasted at a charity event.

March 22nd

. . . I just want to get progress on the budget, Savings and Loan, the ethics bill, the education bill, and the re-evaluation so we can move out in front of Gorbachev.* We cannot let him continue to erode our standing in Europe. Eastern Europe offers an opportunity and it's all a tremendous challenge and I'm loving every minute of it.

Newt Gingrich† is elected Whip. The question is—will he be confrontational; will he raise hell with the establishment; and will he be difficult for me to work with? I don't think so. I called him and congratulated him. He's going to have to get along to some degree, and moderate his flamboyance. He will be a tough competitor for the Democrats, but I'm convinced I can work with him and I want to work with him. He's a very bright guy, an idea a minute, but he hasn't been elected President and I have. . . .

March 27, 1989

The Honorable William F. Buckley
National Review
New York, New York 10016
Dear Bill:

Now that the dust has settled, I want to thank you for all you did over the last month or so in behalf of my nomination of John Tower to be Secretary of Defense. I am convinced we did the right thing by standing behind this nomination. We were fighting to protect a President's right to have his own team, and we were fighting for the honor of a decent man and a friend of all of ours.

Although I am disappointed about the Senate's vote on John Tower, I am thrilled about our new Secretary of Defense, Dick Cheney.

Again, thank you for your diligent efforts. It's nice to know you were there when we needed your support. I look forward to working with you in the future.

Sincerely,
George Bush

---

*I had asked the foreign policy team to do a thorough reevaluation of our foreign policy and where we should go from here. The press was accusing me of dragging my heels, especially since it was a tumultuous time in Eastern Europe where the cries for democracy were growing louder. However, I felt strongly it was important to know where we wanted to go before we started going there.

†A young, aggressive, bright congressman from Georgia.

March 28, 1989

Mrs. Sarah Brady*
Washington, D. C. 20005
Dear Sarah,

Thanks so much for filling me in on your future plans regarding the prevention of gun violence in America. I respect your dedication and hard work in this area. I know the difficult road you, Jim, and your family have had to travel, and your courage has been truly inspiring.

I can certainly understand your feelings about assault weapons. Our problem has been that, while fully automatic AK47s are banned in this country, semiautomatic ones present another whole set of issues. As you know, I asked Bill Bennett† to take a look at this matter to see how we might resolve it. At his suggestion, the Bureau of Alcohol, Tobacco, and Firearms has decided to ban temporarily the importation of more than 110,000 semiautomatic rifles, pending a ruling on whether such guns are suited to sporting purposes.

Although my commitment to the rights of sportsmen and others who own guns legitimately remains firm, I'm eager to do anything within reason to keep these weapons out of the hands of criminals.

Barbara and I enjoyed having you both at the residence the night of Millie's big event. We remember you in our prayers with the hope that each day brings you happiness and success. May God bless and keep you. Our warm regards to you and Jim.

Sincerely,
George Bush

One of the most difficult issues I dealt with as President was abortion. It is personal, it is divisive, and unfortunately, the debate is often ugly. George Pfau, a good friend from Yale days, wrote and asked me to meet with Planned Parenthood.

*Sarah Brady had been active in the antigun lobby since her husband, Jim, was shot the same day as Reagan. I had great respect for them, but we did not agree on gun-control issues. She and Jim eventually supported Governor Bill Clinton in 1992.

†I had just appointed Bill Bennett head of the Office of National Drug Control Policy, a newly created position that still exists today. As "drug czar," his job was to coordinate our efforts on the war on drugs.

March 29, 1989

Mr. George Harold Pfau, Jr.
San Francisco, California 94111
Dear George:

I have received your letter of March 21 and I have read the telegram initi-ated by Planned Parenthood and signed by some of my closest friends and strong supporters.

If there was an issue in the campaign that was clear, it was the abortion question. As you know, my opponent strongly supported the "choice" position, and I strongly supported the "life" position. I am not "imposing" my views, because, you see, I clearly stated them in running for office, and I am not about to change.

I strongly support family planning and have always favored disseminating information on birth control. I do not favor advocating abortion in any way, shape, or form.

Planned Parenthood, to my regret, has chosen to be in the forefront of the pro-choice or pro-abortion position. The lines are so clear that I do not see that any useful purpose could come from the meeting. I will say Mr. Hamilton of Planned Parenthood did a wonderful job of identifying close friends of mine. They all remain close friends, though we do differ on the abortion question.

I will continue to welcome your views on this important subject, but the meeting Mr. Hamilton seeks is not possible at this time.

I will welcome any suggestion you care to send on how we might do a bet-ter job of education on family planning, but my mind is made up on the abortion question.

Thanks, old friend.

Sincerely,
George

March 30th

. . . The days are long and full. Today, Thursday, we had a budget meeting up in the office with a handful of our top people—Darman* conducting a good briefing. His message: we can get by this year and perhaps get a deal with no revenue increase, but after that, we're going to have to raise revenues—there's no way to get around it given the sharp cut in the Gramm-Rudman.† I tell him that I can't raise

*Richard Darman, head of the Office of Management and Budget.

†The Gramm-Rudman bill was passed in 1985 and set maximum budget-deficit levels for each year. When those levels were met, the legislation provided for automatic cuts across the board, although some programs such as Social Security were off limits.

taxes this go round, and it will be very hard in the future, but I want to see the options, and I'm not going to be held up by campaign rhetoric* . . . If the facts change, I hope I'm smart enough to change, too. If we can get by this first one, then I'll take a hard look; but I'll be damned if I'm going to let the muscle be cut from our defenses. It really would be great to make a deal on social security, taxes, spending cuts and strength for defense. . . .

On December 21, 1988, terrorists had blown up Pan Am Flight 103 over Lockerbie, Scotland, killing all 259 on board and 11 people on the ground. We had received thousands of letters from the families and the general public wanting us to do more to bring the perpetrators to justice. One widow especially wrote me a bitter letter, accusing me of not caring. After I met with some of the families, I wrote her back:

April 3, 1989

Mrs. Wendy Giebler
Hasbrouck Heights, NJ 07604
Dear Wendy,

Now that we have met and now that I have seen your letter of March 18th let me try to reply.

First, I truly understood your frustration and the agony that comes from feeling no one cares. I hope today's visit will help change things; so that others will not be needlessly hurt—will not have insensitivity by government add to their hurt.

On a more personal side I <u>really</u> ached for you in your loss. You see long ago we lost a child. She was almost four and we watched her fight a losing battle to leukemia. True, I had Barbara, but maybe there is <u>some</u> common ground. At least I want to understand. I remember crying 'til my body literally ached—

. . . Now can I give you a word from the heart of this 64 year old husband. Time and faith heal. Be strong. Have faith in God for he does work in mysterious ways. Someday the <u>happy</u> memories of your loving husband will crowd out the grief and that terrible agony of his loss.

Maybe it's of a little comfort to know that your letter (I've still seen only the 3-18 one) and your visit might help spare others some of the hurt that's been yours. I'll try hard to do my part. When a sparrow falls, or a hostage is

---

*By this I meant when I said, "Read my lips, no new taxes." If I could take back that one statement, I certainly would.

held, or a beautiful girl from Hasbrouck Heights loses part of her soul and has her heart broken, we must care.

Most sincerely,
George Bush

P. S. Please let me know now or in the months ahead how you're doing. Just write Walker* on the envelope corner—the zip 20500.

[Ten years later, in April 1999, Libyan leader Muammar el-Qaddafi finally turned over the two suspects in the bombing. At this writing, trial is pending in the Netherlands.]

————————

April 18th

. . . When we came back from the building trades meeting, the puppies were in a pen in the front yard, and there were lines of people inside by the family theater waiting to go on a tour. I walked in and took a little girl in the front of the line, and said, "You're going to come out and see the puppies, and then come back and report to everybody in the line." Out she came, and the next thing I knew, her mother was there with her two brothers and a sister. The kids leaned down and played with the puppies, and the mother couldn't believe it. They were a family from Maine. They went back in when I had to go back to the Oval Office, and I asked them to report on the puppies. We also had the puppies in a pen on the first floor of the main State Floor of the White House. I told the building trade people that they could see the puppies, and we planned to have them outdoors but a terrible storm came along, so there they were—in a pen right near where the Marine band plays—and the labor guys loved it. Millie didn't seem too nervous. She came in dripping wet, and I think a lot of the guys were saying, "You know, this reminds me of our house: wet dog, puppies, etc."

. . . Interesting meeting with Burt Lee† on the succession of the Presidency. It is not easy. We're trying to get the procedures down so if something happens to me in some kind of accident, the doctor—seeing that I'm incapacitated—will get a hold of John Sununu who will immediately contact Quayle. On the more difficult case, when I go gaga, or get some horrible degenerating disease, we'll work on some procedures for that, too. It is no fun talking about it, and nobody likes

————————

*This was a secret code for family and friends to put on personal mail, to make sure it ended up on our desk.

†I had appointed Dr. Burton Lee to be White House physician.

to discuss it, but I said, "Now we've got to be very frank." I had fun, as we discussed this. Barbara was in the Oval Office with Susan Porter Rose,* Sununu, Burt Lee, and Dan Quayle. I started twitching, and then acted like a flasher as they were talking about abnormality. Susan Porter Rose, who I like very much, seemed a little uncomfortable with the flashing shot. It wasn't a real one, but just the thought of it. In any event, one has to prepare for even the worse contingencies, even though nobody likes talking about those things. . . .

April 24th

. . . I get home at night very tired. I try to work in my office, as much as I did in the V. P. office, but at times, I'm overwhelmed with the reading, and yet, it's essential I keep up. I'm still plugging away on finishing Teddy Roosevelt's memoirs, which I've enjoyed immensely, but it takes forever, because when I get into bed at 10:00 p.m. to read, I fall sound asleep. Camp David is good, but I end up with a lot of work up here.

For example, on Saturday, the 22nd, we had the economists up there . . . a very fascinating discussion. I listened carefully to see how these supply-siders would go on taxes, and the bold positioners wanted me to handle entitlements, revenues, and spending freezes all on one bold sweep. . . . I think some of these [proposals] could mean a one term Presidency, but it's that important for the country. But I listened to the discussions and learned. . . .

On April 19th an explosion in the USS Iowa's *gun turret killed forty-seven sailors while the ship was participating in naval exercises near Puerto Rico. Barbara and I flew down to the Navy base in Norfolk, Virginia, to attend memorial services. I dictated to my diary:*

April 26th

. . . I kept rehearsing and reading my speech aloud. I did pray for strength, because I cry too easily, so I read it over and over again. I tried not to personalize it when I gave it. I tried not to focus on a grieving parent or a grieving spouse; I tried to comfort individually in the speech; but then I got to the end, I choked and had to stop. I then turned, and in somewhat of a fumbling fashion away from the podium, I shook hands with one of the chaplains, and went back to my seat. But going through three lines to see relatives, it was easier

*Barbara's very able chief of staff for both the vice-presidential and presidential years.

than I thought, though tough. I put my arm around some of them, and Barbara was magnificent at this. The tough ones were when they said, "Here's a picture of my son," or "Look at this picture of my husband"—fine looking young men, oh so young kids living their lives in service. It was extraordinarily moving . . .

———————

April 26, 1989

Admiral Carlisle A. H. Trost, USN
Chief of Naval Operations
Washington, D. C. 20350-2000
Dear Carl:

Since leaving Norfolk on Monday, I have been thinking a lot about the *Iowa,* about her lost crewmen, their families, and about the Navy.

I am writing to you with the express desire that you convey the following thoughts to all involved in Monday's Memorial.

First, the Chaplains—thank you all for your loving attention to the concerns of the families, and to the concerns of the surviving crewmen.

Second, to all involved in notifying the next of kin, my thanks to you for the caring way in which you handled the most difficult assignment.

Third, my thanks to all at Norfolk involved in Monday's fitting tribute to those 47 who gave their lives.

And fourth, will you please express my high regards to Captain Moosally, and to the officers and men of U.S.S. *Iowa.* It hurts to lose a shipmate—it hurts a lot. But even as you showed your concern about your lost shipmates, you have held your heads high and conveyed to the nation a wonderful pride in the Navy, and a pride in serving this country of ours. You have my gratitude and respect.

> Sincerely,
> George Bush

———————

May 1, 1989

Reverend Robert M. Howes*
Kennebunkport, Maine 04046
Dear Bob,

I have a special request.

Would it be possible to have an early service on Sunday May 21. We will

———

*Pastor of the First Congregational Church in Kennebunkport, which we attend in the winter, spring, and fall months. Our other church in Maine, St. Ann's, is open only in the summer.

have the President of France at Walkers Point and we must leave the Point at 9:45 on Sunday to go to Boston.*

Though the French President would not attend church there will be many many people up there. I was thinking of a special service at 8 or 8:15 to finish before your regular 9 AM service starts? A 30 minute prayer and hymn service perhaps.

I know this is a horrible imposition on you, but I am trying hard not to miss Sunday service as President.

Warm regards,
George

May 1st

The puppies are about to fly the nest. Yesterday when we got back from New York, we had them out on the lawn rolling and playing just like old times in Texas with no cameras and no people, but then there were people outside of the White House fence yelling, "Barbara, George—bring the puppies over." Marvin had three friends there who were playing fantastic tennis; and then we went to the horseshoe pit, Don [Rhodes] and I, and Marvin and his friend whipped us each round. Barbara was in the swimming pool. First she had to flush out two ducks—a Mallard hen and a Mallard drake—and then when she was swimming, a rat got in there somehow and was swimming along the edge of the pool. She jumped out in horror, and we had to get the damn thing, drown it, and it was terrible. . . .

Several ugly, gossipy articles appeared during the first few months of my presidency saying there was a rift between President Reagan and me. Nothing could be further from the truth. I wrote my friend and mentor this note:

May 9, 1989

Dear Ron—

I got your message . . . many thanks—There is much mischief in the air. . . . The main thing is let's us vow not to let it come between us.

There was a horrible George Will piece recently which said I called Carter

---

*I had invited François Mitterrand to visit us at Walker's Point since we were both scheduled to speak at Boston University's commencement. That visit was a turning point in our relationship personally and helped improve the relationship between the two countries.

but not you upon my return from Japan. Marlin read Will the phone logs,* but no retraction from the little _____. Anyhow I am determined that none of these mischief makers will diminish a friendship that is so important to me.

Sincerely,
George

Joke: Beautiful girl with fantastic figure toweling off after a bath. Knock on the door—She: "Who's there?" He: "Blind man"! "Oh well," she says, "Come on in." He: "My you have a beautiful body—where do you want me to put the blinds?"

———————

A meeting of the NATO nations at the end of May in Brussels was my first major test in foreign policy. There was major disagreement within the alliance on where to go on arms control negotiations. I will spare you the details, but we went to Brussels uncertain that we could get everyone to sign on to our plan, which I felt called Gorbachev's bluff on arms control. While the heads of state tried to eat dinner, our emissaries were arguing behind closed doors. I dictated to my diary:

. . . The Chiefs of State Dinner was a little tense. Margaret Thatcher kept telling me not to negotiate . . . "We must not give on this, and you're not going to give, are you?" she asked me plaintively over and over again. Why does she have any doubt that we feel this way on this issue? . . .

During the dinner, Manfred Woerner† kept reporting that they're making some progress, so when I got home—Barbara didn't get in until 11:30 p.m.—I was chomping around at the bit because I didn't know if the foreign ministers, then meeting, were going to get a deal . . . and if they were going to get a deal, whether it would be one that Margaret Thatcher could buy. About midnight, Jim Baker called with a formulation.‡ . . . I wasn't sure if Margaret would buy this, but Jim predicted she would. I asked him to check with Brent Scowcroft§ and he did. He called back and said that Brent was for it, and I said, "Well, let's go forward with it and be enthusiastic and hope they sell it to the Brits." I've got to admit, ex post facto, that I didn't think

---

*Marlin Fitzwater, my press secretary and also a good friend and key adviser. I had of course called President Reagan, along with all the other presidents. Will's information was wrong.

†NATO secretary general.

‡The "formulation" was a detailed plan on how to negotiate with the Soviet Union on both nuclear and nonnuclear weapons.

§My national security adviser. I always suspected Brent would have preferred to have been secretary of defense, but I needed him at my side in the White House.

Margaret would go along—that she would rather stand alone—but the next morning, Jim told me that they were on board. When we got to the Hall, Margaret waved very enthusiastically. She did not want to be separated from the United States, and her own people were telling her that the language was okay.

The agreement was announced, and there was almost a euphoric atmosphere . . . The press, who had been cynical and skeptical, were just wondering how we pulled it off without their knowing about it. How could we have made the deal without having it leaked?

———————

June 2, 1989

enroute to K'port

Dear Brent—

. . . As we fly home I'm looking over my shoulder, not just to NATO and the US key role there; but back further to Jan 20th.

You told me what we needed to do. I agreed. Then you did it. And a few arrows did come our way. But I have never questioned your advice. Oh, I might disagree when you take a cheap shot at Domingo's* coffee—but on other important matters like missiles and Nato and Kohl and Margaret you've steadily showed me the way.

After the euphoria of this trip wears off—and it will as the Monday morning quarterbacks start second guessing the plays—I will remember the sound advice you have given me. . . .

Thanks for your key role. Thanks for being at my side. Thanks for being my trusted friend. Get some rest now—a lot of battles lie ahead.

Most sincerely,

George

———————

June 2, 1989

Dear Jim—

As I fly home I just want to tell you, my close and trusted friend, how grateful I am for your absolutely key role in what transpired on this trip. That midnight phone call which followed your hours of painful negotiation was the key; and, once again your advice was sound.

There is something very reassuring to me (comforting—if that's not too wimpish) to have you running our Foreign Policy—

Neil Mallon gave us a little welcome mat many years ago. "What would we

———

*Domingo Quicho was the faithful Oval Office steward.

do without friends?" it said. I don't believe I could do this job without trusted close friends nearby. That's you. I'm glad; grateful too.

George

———————

June 15th

On Thursday morning, I had a long phone call from Helmut Kohl—very personal, very friendly—and a debriefing on Gorbachev. "Gorbachev has respect for you intellectually; Gorbachev wants better relations; and Raisa said wonderful things about Barbara." Kohl made clear that Gorbachev could not split him away from the West, and away from the United States. Gorbachev said he doesn't want to do this, so, all in all, he was upbeat.

On a personal side, Helmut mentioned a special sausage he was going to send me three or four different times, so I've got to talk to the Secret Service about getting it. They will be uncomfortable, but here's one where we need to bend the rules a little simply because it means so much to Kohl, and, besides that, I like wurst.

———————

That spring, the desire for democracy spread from Eastern Europe all the way to China. In April, thousands of Chinese students poured into Tiananmen Square, demanding more freedom. Despite the government's attempts to break up the demonstrations, the crowds kept getting larger and more defiant. Finally, on June 3, tanks and troops put an end to the protest, resulting in much bloodshed. Publicly, we immediately condemned China for its action and called for sanctions. Privately, I wrote this anguished letter to an old friend:

June 20, 1989

His Excellency Deng Xiaoping
People's Republic of China
Beijing
Dear Chairman Deng:

I write this letter to you with a heavy heart. I wish there was a way to discuss this matter in person, but regrettably that is not the case. First, I write in a spirit of genuine friendship, this letter coming as I'm sure you know from one who believes with a passion that good relations between the United States and China are in the fundamental interests of both countries. I have felt that way for many years. I feel more strongly that way today, in spite of the difficult circumstances.

Secondly, I write as one who has great respect for what you personally have done for the people of China and to help your great country move forward. There is enormous irony in the fact that you who yourself has suffered several reversals in your quest to bring reform and openness to China are now facing a situation fraught with so much danger and so much anxiety.

I recall your telling me the last time we met that you were in essence phasing out of the day-to-day management of your great country. But I also recall your unforgettable words about the need for good relations with the West, your concerns about "encirclement" and those who had done great harm to China, and your commitment to keeping China moving forward. By writing you I am not trying to bypass any individual leader of China. I am simply writing as a friend, a genuine "lao pengyou".

It is with this in mind that I write you asking for your help in preserving this relationship that we both think is very important. I have tried very hard not to inject myself into China's internal affairs. I have tried very hard not to appear to be dictating in any way to China about how it should manage its internal crisis. I am respectful of the differences in our two societies and in our two systems.

I have great reverence for Chinese history, culture and tradition. You have given much to the development of world civilization. But I ask you as well to remember the principles on which my young country was founded. Those principles are democracy and freedom—freedom of speech, freedom of assemblage, freedom from arbitrary authority. It is reverence for those principles which inevitably affects the way Americans view and react to events in other countries. It is not a reaction of arrogance or of a desire to force others to our beliefs but of a simple faith in the enduring value of those principles and their universal applicability.

And that leads directly to the fundamental problem. The early days of the student demonstrations, and indeed, the early treatment of the students by the Chinese Army, captured the imagination of the entire world. The wonder of TV brought the details of the events in Tiananmen Square into the homes of people not just in "Western" countries but world-wide. The early tolerance that was shown, the restraint and the generous handling of the demonstrations won worldwide respect for China's leadership. Thoughtful people all over the world tried to understand and sympathize with the enormous problems being faced by those required to keep order; and, indeed, they saw with admiration the manifestation of policy which reflected the leaders' words: "The Army loves the people." The world cheered when the Chinese leaders were seen patiently meeting with students, even though there were "sit-ins" and even though disorder did interfere with normal functions.

I will leave what followed to the history books, but again, with their own eyes the people of the world saw the turmoil and the bloodshed with which the demonstrations were ended. Various countries reacted in various ways. Based on the principles I described above, the actions that I took as President of the United States could not be avoided. As you know, the clamor for stronger action remains intense. I have resisted that clamor, making clear that I did not want to see destroyed this relationship that you and I have worked hard to build. I explained to the American people that I did not want to unfairly burden the Chinese people through economic sanctions.

There is also the matter of Fang Lizhi.* The minute I heard Fang was in our Embassy, I knew there would be a high profiled wedge driven between us. Fang was not encouraged to come to our Embassy, but under our widely accepted interpretation of international law we could not refuse him admittance.

In today's climate I know this matter is of grave importance to you and I know it presents you with an enormous problem; a problem that adversely affects my determination and, hopefully, yours to get our relationship back on track.

We cannot now put Fang out of the Embassy without some assurance that he will not be in physical danger. Similar cases elsewhere in the world have been resolved over long periods of time or through the government quietly permitting departure or through expulsion. I simply want to assure you that we want this difficult matter resolved in a way which is both satisfactory to you and does not violate our commitment to our basic principles. When there are difficulties between friends, as now, we must find a way to talk them out.

Your able Ambassador here represents your country firmly and faithfully. I feel that Jim Lilley does the same for us; but if there is some special channel that you would favor, please let me know.

I have thought of asking you to receive a special emissary who could speak with total candor to you representing my heartfelt convictions on these matters. If you feel such an emissary could be helpful, please let me know and we will work cooperatively to see that his mission is kept in total confidence. I have insisted that all departments of the U.S. Government be guided in their statements and actions from my guidance in the White House. Sometimes in an open system such as ours it is impossible to control all leaks, but on this particular letter there are no copies, not one, outside of my own personal file. . . .

I send you this letter with great respect and deep concern. We must not let this important relationship suffer further. Please help me to keep it strong. Any statement that could be made from China that drew upon the earlier

---

*The dissident Fang had taken refuge in the American embassy in Beijing. Eventually China expelled him and he came to this country.

statements about peacefully resolving further disputes with protesters would be very well received here. Any clemency that could be shown the student demonstrators would be applauded worldwide. We must not let the aftermath of the tragic recent events undermine a vital relationship patiently built up over the past seventeen years. I would, of course, welcome a personal reply to this letter. This matter is too important to be left to our bureaucracies.

As I said above, I write with a heavy heart; but I also write with a frankness reserved for respected friends.

Sincerely,
George Bush

[Within twenty-four hours I had a personal reply from Deng, who accepted my idea of a personal emissary. I sent Brent Scowcroft, who asked Larry Eagleburger to go with him. Their mission was so secret that their plane was almost shot down when it entered Chinese airspace unannounced. Their trip was successful in that it conveyed to the Chinese how serious the divide was between us but also how much we respected our friendship. It kept the door open.]

―――――――

On June 26 Barbara and I decided to go see the Marine Parade held every Sunday evening at the Marine Barracks. The Marines were famous for their precision and for not making mistakes. Of course the one night we were in attendance, one of the Marines dropped his rifle. I was hoping a note from his commander in chief might help:

6-27-89

CPL Cullen Plousha
Marine Barracks
Washington, D. C. 20390-5000
Dear Cpl. Plousha,

Last night's drill was very special. I want to thank you and the others in the platoon for a super performance.

Col. Pace told me that you were the guy selected by his peers for that key inspection role—quite an honor, well deserved.

Please thank all involved in the drill—

Sincerely,
George Bush

P. S. Don't worry about anything—you did A-OK.

―――――――

June 28, 1989

Mrs. Antonin Scalia
Chamber of Justice Scalia
Washington, D. C. 20543

Dear Maureen,

As we shook hands last night, in frankness and in jest, you made a comment, a passing nice comment, about the flag decision. When I got upstairs, I got to thinking about that in the light of the Court decision.*

I'll bet a lot of agony goes into "calling 'em as they see 'em"; but the point of this note is to say—my respect for <u>your</u> Judge's scholarship, integrity, and honor knows no bounds. Don't show this to Nino, but just tuck it away in your heart because it comes from mine.

George Bush

———

In July we headed to Paris for the annual G-7 Economic Summit meeting, which included the United States, Canada, Great Britain, France, Germany, Italy, and Japan. En route, we stopped in Poland and Hungary, where democracy was "busting out all over." Our visit to Poland was emotional and came at a crucial time as Solidarity had just won a huge victory in the National Assembly elections. I dictated to my diary:

> July 11
>
> [Our security] has warned us about surveillance and electronics, and yet typically there is no evidence of such; but what I have to say, I would like for them to hear anyway, so I don't worry about that.
>
> I have an upbeat feeling about the politicians coming together,† but I have a down feeling on the economic reform, and on the magnitude of the problems facing Poland. Their agriculture is chopped into small blocks; they're inefficient; and yet, their agriculture contingent is very powerful. What I really felt the most about was the warmth of all the interlocutors, be they from Solidarity or from the government, and about the way the government and solidarity were talking to each other—dramatic progress. . . .

---

*Much to my disappointment, the Supreme Court had just ruled 5–4 that the Constitution did not protect the flag from being burned. Justice Scalia was in the majority opinion. His wife feared I might be holding it against him, which of course I did not. However, I did immediately call for a constitutional amendment banning flag burning.

†I had long talks with both Lech Walesa and General Jaruzelski during my visit about the importance of their working together as they tried to navigate these exciting but still potentially dangerous times. Freedom was most important, but so was stability.

There's no way to properly describe the excitement at Gdansk.* There were thousands of people lining the street going into town, and then estimates of up to 250,000 people in the square in front of the shipyard. It was an emotional moment with grown men and women crying. There were all kinds of signs of affection for the United States all along the way, and there were flags; handwritten signs welcoming me; and friendship between the United States and Poland . . .

July 21, 1989

His Excellency Mikhail Gorbachev
Chairman of the Presidium of the Supreme Soviet
of the Union of Soviet Socialist Republics
Moscow
Dear Mr. Chairman:

I am writing this letter to you on my way back from Europe to the United States. My mind is full of the fascinating conversations that I had with people in Hungary and Poland and with the many world leaders gathered in Paris for France's bicentennial.

Let me get quickly to the point of this letter. I would like very much to sit down soon and talk to you, if you are agreeable to the idea. I want to do it without thousands of assistants hovering over our shoulders, without the ever-present briefing papers and certainly without the press yelling at us every 5 minutes about "who's winning," "what agreements have been reached," or "has our meeting succeeded or failed."

Up until now I have felt that a meeting would have to produce major agreements so as not to disappoint the watching world. Now my thinking is changing.

Perhaps it was my visit to Poland and Hungary or perhaps it is what I heard about your recent visits to France and Germany—whatever the cause—I just want to reduce the chances there could be misunderstandings between us. I want to get our relationship on a more personal basis. If you agree that an unstructured meeting would be productive, I would make the following suggestion.

My suggestion is that you decide, on your own, to come to speak at the U.N. early in the General Assembly session—perhaps around the end of September (the 27th and 28th of September would be perfect for me, but so

---

*Walesa took us to the shipbuilding town of Gdansk, where Solidarity was born. We first had lunch at their modest home, then went to the town square.

would other dates). Immediately following your public announcement that you were coming to the United Nations, I would invite you to come to meet with me for an informal, "no agenda" visit. In my view, it would be preferable to avoid the word "summit" which is, at best, overworked and, at worst, a word whose connotation is one of a momentous happening.

I would propose inviting you to visit me for a day or two of private chats.

There are two alternative ways I would suggest to do this. One way would be for you to fly from New York to Washington where I would meet you at Andrews Air Force Base. We could then go by helicopter to Camp David. There, in a relaxed setting with neckties off, we could talk about any and all subjects. The very nature of the invitation would guard against the danger of "overpromise." I would propose no more than a handful of advisers on each side. I would visualize long chats between you and me alone and, also, good discussions with my Secretary of State, NSC Adviser, and Chief of Staff present, along with their counterparts, of course.

Another option would be for you to visit Barbara and me at our seaside house in Maine. Late September can be very nice there. You could fly to Pease Air Force Base in New Hampshire, about 40 minutes from New York and helicopter another 15 minutes to our home, for the same kind of talks.

Camp David perhaps would offer the most privacy, but Maine would offer you a glimpse of our Atlantic seacoast. It would also give me a chance to take you for a ride in my speed boat and maybe catch a fish.

Perhaps there is some entirely different way more convenient for you, and I would welcome a suggestion. The General Assembly seems to me to provide the ideal cover needed for a "spontaneous" invitation to an unstructured, informal meeting. I do not intend in any way to put you in an awkward position and I will understand completely if, for whatever reason, you do not feel you can respond positively to my suggestion.

General Brent Scowcroft and Secretary Jim Baker, plus my Chief of Staff John Sununu, are the <u>only</u> ones who know of this letter, which I have personally written. I hope I can demonstrate to you that some things need not "leak."

My respects and sincere regards,

Sincerely,
George Bush

[Gorbachev agreed to meet, but we had great trouble settling on a time or place. Eventually we would meet at Malta, off the coast of Italy, in December.]

Obviously I was in the mood on July 21 to write world leaders:

July 21, 1989

His Excellency Deng Xiaoping
People's Republic of China
Beijing
Dear Chairman Deng, Dear Friend:

I use this unique form of salutation because General Scowcroft told me that if I would continue to treat you as a friend, you would welcome that—no matter the outcome of the difficulties now between us.

Of course, I, too, want it to be that way.

First, let me thank you and Li Peng for receiving General Scowcroft and Larry Eagleburger. The minute General Scowcroft returned to the USA, he came to Maine to brief me on your talks.

I have waited to send you this letter. I wanted first to go to Eastern Europe and the Economic Summit Conference at Paris, because I wanted to listen carefully to their views on their relations with China.

Also, in waiting, I was hoping against hope that some new development would take place that would enable us both to move towards improved relations. Unfortunately, no such development has occurred.

The G-7 Communiqué in Paris made reference to events in China. I can tell you in total confidence that the U.S. and the Japanese removed some rather inflammatory language from the Communiqué. It was still a Communiqué which I'm sure you'd rather not have had at all, but in the final form it did not urge new action affecting China.

Brent Scowcroft told me of your reference to the Chinese proverb: "It is up to the person who tied the knot to untie the knot."

Herein lies our major dilemma. You feel we "tied the knot" by our actions, especially regarding military sales.*

We feel that those actions taken against peacefully demonstrating (non-violent) students and the nationwide crackdown against those simply speaking for reform "tied the knot."

Please understand, my friend, that when I use the word "we" in the preceding sentence, I am not simply referring to the United States. Rather, I am referring to many, many countries from North and South, East and West.

Let me emphasize, if there is anyone on the World Stage who understands how China views interference in its internal affairs, it is I. Likewise, I could indeed identify with the problems China's government faced when, as Li Peng told General Scowcroft, it felt that Zhongnanhai itself might be invaded

*After Tiananmen Square, I had suspended all military sales and contracts between our countries.

or overrun. Li Peng pointedly asked General Scowcroft how we would feel if the White House were threatened by a mob out of control.

But here's the big problem. Given the all-penetrating (but not comprehensive) nature of television, people all around the world first saw massive but peaceful demonstrations, peacefully contained. With approval and respect, they saw Chinese leaders meeting with the students. They heard authoritative voices saying, "The Army loves the People;" and they saw soldiers showing amazing restraint. And people around the world saluted China and its leaders.

It is what happened next that we believe "tied the knot." You and Li Peng frankly described what you thought happened to the character of the demonstrations and what you felt you had to do. But people all around the world, with their own eyes, saw other happenings, too; and China, which had been praised for restraint, was widely criticized.

I have great respect for China's long-standing position about nonintervention in its internal affairs.

Because of that, I also understand that I risk straining our friendship when I make suggestions as to what might be done now. But the U.S.-China relationship, which we have both worked so hard to strengthen, demands the candor with which only a friend can speak.

If some way can be found to close the chapter on the students whose actions were those of peaceful demonstrators, that would help enormously.

General Scowcroft reported to me that many of those arrested were common criminals, repeat offenders. I am not talking about these people.

If forgiveness could be granted to the students and, yes, to their teachers, this would go a long way to restoring worldwide confidence. Such a move could well lead to improved relations with many countries. For example, it would give me the opportunity to make a statement supporting your decision. Also, if it would be helpful to China, I could then publicly dispatch a high-level emissary to Beijing thus signaling to the world that our country was prepared to work our way back towards more normal relations.

You see, rightly or wrongly, it was the students who captured the imagination of so many people around the world. They are young and, like students everywhere, they are idealistic.

In our country, as Li Peng pointed out, there was, not long ago, much student unrest. There was some force used to quell the unrest and much criticism came our way. Many countries criticized us. Perhaps China did. But the unrest disappeared in time and the students here were leniently treated, even though some of our laws were deliberately broken. We never doubted that the students, even in dissent, truly loved our country.

Perhaps the differences in our systems are so great that you will find the above analogy irrelevant. I hope not. But of this I feel certain: the Chinese students who have spoken out truly love China. . . .

Please understand that this letter has been personally written, and is coming to you from one who wants to see us go forward together.

Please do not be angry with me if I have crossed the invisible threshold lying between constructive suggestion and "internal interference."

When we last met, you told me you had turned more day-to-day matters over to others; but I turn to you now out of respect, a feeling of closeness and, yes, friendship.

You have seen it all—you've been up and down. Now I ask you to look with me into the future. This future is one of dramatic change. The U. S. and China each has much to contribute to this exciting future. We can both do more for world peace and for the welfare of our own people if we can get our relationship back on track. I have given you my unsolicited advice. Now I earnestly solicit your advice. If there is to be a period of darkness, so be it; but let us try to light some candles.

> Respectfully,
> George Bush

[Deng's reply was respectful, but he held steadfastly to their position that this was their internal affair. Eventually, our relationship and friendship would recover, but it took a while to work through these problems.]

———

On July 31 we received word that Marine colonel Robert Higgins, who was being held hostage in Lebanon, had been murdered because of Israel's refusal to release prisoners being held for terrorist activities. Higgins had been kidnapped a year earlier, ironically while serving as part of a UN peacekeeping force.

July 31st

We were in Chicago when we heard that Higgins had been executed, murdered, and I made the decision to turn around and come home back to Washington . . . They released a videotape showing his execution, and all in all, it's a sick situation. On the way back to Washington, I called De Cuellar* at the U.N., and he told me he doesn't want to believe that this is real. They're liars, he said, they'd done this thing before. I told him that we felt that they should make a demand that the body be returned . . .

This is cowardly, horrible terrorism. A very complicated and diffi-

---

*Javier Perez de Cuellar, the secretary general of the United Nations.

cult situation right now, but we will get our best intelligence; get our best involvement with everyone; and see what we can do. . . .

—————

August 1, 1989

Mr. Merle Haggard
Palo Cedro, California 96073
Dear Merle,

"Me and Crippled Soldiers"* said a lot.

I read that a comrade in the U. N. Peacekeeping Force told Col. Higgins that if he removed the stars and stripes patch the radicals would not bother him. He was a great Marine and, of course, he said "No".

He's dead now. He sure gave a damn. And he loved the flag.

I am going to keep on about our flag. Your song was great. Good luck,

George Bush

—————

August 7th

The Congress has gone home—thank God! We had a relatively quiet day. I went to salute the Department of War's 200th anniversary, and I addressed the end of my remarks to Colonel Higgins. My voice cracked, because I feel so emotionally involved in this matter. The FBI came out today and said that Higgins was most likely killed earlier, and I think of his courageous little wife, who later in the day, I called† It is so brutal and so cruel what's going on. The diplomacy is still going forward. . . .

Bar went back to Maine, and the house, though bright, cheery and museum-like, is lonely. But I'm tired and I'll go to bed real early. . . .

The approval ratings stay high, and yet, I feel like we're on a kind of uneasy precarious perch. We're not getting the legislation through to support me on clean air, on anti-drugs, education, or any of these things—it's in the Congress. We were attacked tonight on our political appointees, and that irks me, too. The end of a grumpy Monday, August 7th.

—————

*Merle sent me a song about patriotism and the flag.

†Robin Higgins, also a Marine, and a courageous woman. I saw her again in April 1999, when I attended the commissioning of the USS *Higgins,* a fitting tribute to a fallen hero.

For years my cousin Betty Holden and I, as the only two members of our exclusive Poetry Club, have exchanged poetry with each other.

August 12, 1989

Dear Beldy Girl:

    . . . I strongly oppose expanding the Club. . . . I just don't want to see our standards lowered. Incidentally, I thought your recent offerings held high our standards. "Monsieur Curley, Un peu surley"—a genuine classic—and then the classic rhyme that brought life to truly new height "jog, fog"—oh yes— and the truly memorable one "horse shoe-leaner, demeanor—" No, let us not lower our standards just cause there is clamor for outsiders wanting to be insiders. Why risk excellence when it is so hard to come by.

    Of course within the next 12 months I shall serve up another contribution or 2. I may well make my next offering a poetic insight into world leaders— or should I stay with family, or a domestic policy theme? The joy of figuring out how best to contribute is upon me.

    On Wednesday next I head to K'port for a rest. Bar is there now—only 9 grandchildren on the point, but worry not, the other 2 soon arrive. Rest? Oh well.

Love to all,
GB

[I will not be brave and share any of my poetry. But I will share one of the above mentioned poems from Betty:

> *they say it makes the secret service unduly nervous*
> *trying to jog in Maine fog*
> *to locate their president*
> *and not confuse him with another resident.]*

September 4th

    . . . I feel comfortable in the job—not overwhelmed—and confi-dent that I can hold my own for the United States in the interna-tional forum. But on the domestic side—it troubles me the most. I worry long run about the 1991 budget and how to get it in shape. Sununu is doing a very good job, and got some good press over the summer. He's doing a superb job. . . .

    Dog note: Ranger is now almost part of our family—a big lovable guy who bounds in. Both dogs sleep on our bed—Ranger and Millie— and they get along fine, although every once in awhile, Millie has to dis-cipline her son. It's a joy watching them, particularly running through the woods at Camp David sniffing and sniffing, and turning, and dramatically running after a deer here and there. I really love them. . . .*

September 10th

The question came up whether to see Boris Yeltsin.† The Ambassador recommends that he be received in the White House, but not necessarily by me. I think it's a good thing to do. Yeltsin is over here and seems to be blasting Gorbachev . . . State is goosey about my seeing him, but I don't quite see why we shouldn't see him. . . . The Soviets receive all kinds of people running for President who are against me and trying to get my job, so they've got to be understanding about our willingness to see their people, especially those who want to see perestroika succeed. It's not like we're seeing some curmudgeon who was trying to throw Gorbachev totally out of office. . . .

Although Dan Rostenkowski and I were on opposite sides of the political aisle, I had enormous respect for this powerful congressman from Illinois and chairman of the Ways and Means Committee. I knew he always had the country's best interests in mind. An article came out in the Wall Street Journal *saying that our friendship sometimes clouded the issues, to Dan's detriment. I wrote him this note:*

Sept. 19th Spokane to D. C.

Dear Dan,

Sometimes Washington D. C. can be pretty mean and ugly—People write vicious stuff. Small minded politicos and gossipy pundits want winners and losers.

I saw an ugly piece in the WSJ today: and I hated it. My heart hurt.

Dan, you got your views on taxes and I've got mine. You've got your big job to do and I've got mine; but for me—more important than this issue is a friendship.

I do not want the battle up there to affect a friendship that means a lot to me. Don't let's let the carpers on either side diminish something that matters—at least to me.

That my friendship with you now appears to some to be a burden to you troubles the hell out of me.

I called you Friday but given today's WSJ piece I felt it better to scribble

*Ranger was really Marvin's dog but eventually he became mine.
†He was then Gorbachev's most outspoken critic and a leader of the opposition.

this personal note. Long after the dust has settled on tax bills, reconciliations, amendments and all the rest—Long after all of this, we will be friends.

Right now I am sorry if our closeness has hurt my pal, but there's tomorrow out there. I care, Barbara too—

Call me, come see me, or leave me be; but I'm your friend. I hope you know that—

George

October 7, 1989

FROM THE PRESIDENT
TO: Brent.

Reading this, I am convinced more than ever that we should try to extricate Noriega.* Let's go back to the drawing board now.

I think recent events make a grab of Noriega more acceptable certainly at home, maybe abroad. If he carries out the threats contained in the [intelligence] reports the climate both at home and internationally will be even better.

Please discuss.

gb

By that fall, democracy and freedom were no longer marching through Eastern Europe—they were racing. Hungary had opened its Austrian borders earlier in the year, and a flood of "vacationing" East Germans were using this as an exit to the West. As a result, even East Germany—the jewel in the crown of the Soviet's Warsaw Pact—was teetering on the verge of collapse. It all came crashing down on November 9 when the Berlin Wall was opened. It was the beginning of the end for not only East Germany, but the entire Warsaw Pact. However, despite the euphoria, it was still a fragile and even frightening time. The Soviet Union still had troops and tanks stationed in East Germany, and we knew it was not entirely impossible for Gorbachev to clamp down. We were all haunted by the crushing of the uprisings in Hungary in 1956 and in Prague in 1968. We did not want to provoke a similar disaster. I dictated to my diary:

November 8th
    I keep hearing the critics saying we're not doing enough on Eastern Europe; here the changes are dramatically coming our way and,

---

*My daily classified intelligence report contained reports of Noriega's continuing bullying of people in Panama, including Americans who were stationed in the Canal Zone. His continued narco-trafficking and his aborting of the results of the last election in Panama made me more determined than ever to bring him to justice.

if any one event—Poland, Hungary or East Germany—had taken place, people would say, "This is great." But it's all moving fast—moving our way—and you've got a bunch of critics jumping around saying we ought to be doing more. What they mean is, double spending. It doesn't matter what, just send money; I think it's crazy. And if we mishandle this and get way out [in front] looking like [the rebellions are] an American project—you would invite crackdown, and invite negative reaction that could result in bloodshed. The longer I'm in this job, the more I think prudence is a value and experience matters. . . .

November 10th

We get a message from Gorbachev yesterday urging that we not overreact. He worries about demonstrators in Germany that might get out of control, and he asked for understanding. I think Kohl and the other leaders know we're being restrained, but Kohl's only suggestion is that we get the IMF* to move before the end of November to help Poland. He thinks the Polish leaders are naïve. They are good people, and they really want to succeed. Moscow warns me in the same letter about letting this talk of reunification get out of hand. It causes them real problems, but what I've been saying is, this is a matter for self-determination, and a matter for the German people, and I don't think he could object to that.†

November 13th

Lech Walesa came to town, and we had a very moving ceremony.‡ . . . We presented him with the "empty chair," symbolic of the honorary degrees that he once could not receive at various universities but where they placed an empty chair on the stage to honor him. So we did the same thing.

The labor group is in town for the AFL-CIO convention; and from Lane Kirkland on down the heads of all the unions were there.

---

*The International Monetary Fund, which we had asked to help Poland with its financial crises.

†Now that East Germany appeared to be collapsing, Moscow was worried about a unified Germany again. Actually, it wasn't only Moscow, but almost all of Europe, whose memories of World War II were still rather raw.

‡I gave Lech the Medal of Freedom.

We surprised Lane Kirkland with the Citizens Medal*—just a notch below the Medal of Freedom—and he was totally surprised and very, very moved. In the receiving line, the labor union leaders one after another told me how nice it was. They were deeply moved and deeply touched by this.

. . . Now I'm under fire from George Mitchell† saying I ought to go to Berlin, and the posturers are all over the place. Mary McGrory hits me on lack of emotion, but I think it's coming out just about right.

———

Meanwhile, with all this whirling around, one of my best friends died, C. Fred Chambers. I attended the funeral but could not bring myself to speak. I asked Marvin to deliver my eulogy instead. I wrote Marion Chambers:

Nov. 16th, 1989

Dear Marion,

I hope I haven't let you down by not speaking in tribute to C. Fred. We've got a good pinch hitter lined up—my boy Marv. It's the same because all of us Bushes loved Fred. Oh, I loved him the most—I laughed with him and played and giggled like best friends are supposed to do; but the point is Bar and the kids—all of us loved your man.

There are so many funny wonderful things that will lift me up if I ever get down.

Remember when we caught the red-fish, Fred & I. We brought 'em over to Bar to clean & cook (unfair I know but Fred & I just had to go off for some steam.) Anyway we had the steam [bath] and a beer or two—came back and the whole house smelled. Regrettably, I said to Bar "You don't expect me to eat this s—t, do you?" She cried—Fred & I laughed. I'll bet she never forgives us. I blamed Fred, but that's what friends are for. There was the golf, business together—bar b que together.

And the politics—I'd lose but he was at my side to pick me up and dust me off. He made me understand that defeat is not the end—there's a tomorrow and sure enough he was right—tomorrow is today—and I still feel his arm around my shoulder.

God Bless you and Yours. I'll never ever forget C. Fred. I will always love him—my true, ever true, best friend—

George Bush

*Lane, president of the AFL-CIO, and other union leaders had been supportive of the Solidarity movement and deserved a great deal of credit for its success.

†Senator from Maine and Senate majority leader. He and I tangled a lot, and although I respected George, I found him partisan and therefore sometimes difficult to work with.

Preparations were under way for my meeting with Gorbachev on Malta in early December. I had told Gorbachev we should have a "no agenda" meeting, but of course I already had a long list of things I wanted to discuss with him. I decided maybe I should give him a heads-up. This is my first handwritten draft of the letter I eventually sent him:

Nov. 22, 1989

Dear Mr. President,

After talking with Anatoly Dobrynin* yesterday it occurred to me that even though we have a "no agenda" meeting, you might be interested in <u>some</u> of the topics I would like to discuss—

Here is a <u>non</u>-inclusive list:

    A. Eastern Europe

    B. Regional Differences

          Central America

          Angola

          Afghanistan

          Middle East

          Asia (Cambodia)

    C. The Defense Spending of both our Countries and how changing times will affect these numbers.

    D. Your vision and mine of the world at the start of the next Century (2000)

    E. Human Rights

    F. Arms control—philosophy & objectives in a broad, general sense

Of course, you will have your own priorities—

I want the meeting to be seen as a success.

Success does not mean deals signed in my view. It means that you & I are frank enough with each other, in a confidential setting, so that our two great countries will not have tensions that arise simply because we don't know each others innermost thinking.

I will be working with our top people for the next week to flesh out our side's thinking. I will not try to bring off a "December surprise" but if there is some proposal not covered by the list above I will feel free to make it.

I am writing this on the eve of our special Thanksgiving Day—a Day in which all Americans thank God for our blessings.

I will give thanks for the fact that we are living in times of enormous

---

*One of Gorbachev's advisers.

promise—that our 11 grandchildren might have a real chance to grow up in a less scary more peaceful world.

I will give thanks that you are pressing forward with glasnost-perestroika,* for you see, the fate of my own precious grandkids and yours is dependent on perestroika's success—

With respect,
George Bush

My brother Bucky wrote and said that Carol Walker, married to our first cousin Bert, was concerned because her name had shown up in the newspaper as being pro-choice.

Nov. 28, 1989

Dear Buck,

Yes, I knew that Carol was to be put down as 'doubtful' on my abortion position; but so is the rest of the garden club, the social register, and, ironically, most of my close friends. If Carol seems concerned please tell her "no problem"!

People do feel strongly over this very divisive issue; and she will cause me no concern at all, even if she beats on the White House gate—I really mean that. My problem is the longer I think about this very difficult issue the more strongly I feel about the human life side of the question. When I have real doubts, and I do, I look at Marshall.† I wish the whole bloody issue would go away. It won't so family members should all do their own thing without fear of embarrassing me. They should know that because they are related they'll get 'ink' that otherwise they wouldn't get; but that is life. As they say in Malta "gracek erg talket, sodak!"

Your concerned brother,
George

This is a personal letter not to be shared with Planned Parenthood or Save the Whales.

December 1st
    Friday night aboard the USS *Belknap,* the flagship of the Sixth Fleet anchored off Malta. Ahead of us is the *Slava,* the Soviet cruiser

---

*These were the key words of Gorbachev's reform movement. *Glasnost* stood for more "openness"; *perestroika* simply meant "reform," in this case, economic reform.

†Marvin and Margaret's daughter who was adopted.

that is bigger and more resplendent, though not nearly as effective of a fighting vessel as this one. It's been some day.

We left last night, and I was awakened in the middle of the night on Air Force One, having taken a Halcyon sleeping pill, by John Sununu telling me that things were tough in the Philippines, and that Aquino had requested our help—no troops, but the use of our air force to keep the rebel forces from coming into the air and bombing the palace, etc. I gave permission, and Dan Quayle, Bob Gates* are working the problem on the U.S. end.† . . .

I dictate this as I go to bed the night before the Summit that has now taken on worldwide proportions. How do I feel? I feel confident. Our brief is good, and we're going to offer him certain things on the economy. I will convince him that we want to move forward on defense; I will convince him that I can lead the alliance; but I will impress on him that he must stop screwing around with El Salvador‡ and Cuba. If he really wants help, and he really wants progress to go forward, then we've got to move—not only on the economic front— but on the political side. He's come a long way. I'm criticized for not doing enough, but things are coming our way, so why do we have to jump up and down, risk those things turning around and going in the wrong direction.

There are some gales out there, apparently, but as I dictate this just before going to sleep, there is a very gentle lull, and I think of my days aboard *San Jacinto.* I love the Navy, and I felt 31 years old walking around the decks of the *Forrestal*§ and the *Belknap.* I even went out and fished off the fantail. No fish, obviously, but did get one nibble. It must have been some tiny little thing.

―――――――

December 2nd

It's the damnedest weather you've ever seen. . . . the highest seas that they've ever had, and it screwed everything up. In the first place, we could not go to the *Slava* because Gorbachev did not want to go out to *Slava*—the seas were plenty rough—so we went to the *Maxim Gorky,* a great big beautiful cruise liner laying against a berth in the harbor. Getting on the boat was a little bit of a challenge, but noth-

―――――――

*Brent's deputy at the NSC. I would later make Bob director of Central Intelligence.
†The uprising ended without major incident.
‡Leftist rebels had been engaged in civil war in El Salvador for ten years.
§One of our aircraft carriers, the USS *Forrestal,* was also in the waters off Malta.

ing like coming back onto the *Belknap.** Anyway, we made it into the *Gorky,* and the meetings, I'd say, went reasonably well. I tabled a series of proposals. It seemed to disarm him but, sure enough, we did have some progress on arms control; on what we can do for MFN,† etc.

Gorbachev looked tired. He wore a dark blue pinstriped suit, a cream colored white shirt (like the ones I like), a red tie (almost like the one out of the London firm with a sword), and he was graying at the temples. The spot is prominent on his head, but you don't notice it all the time, and a nice smile, though there was something different. He seemed laid back and reserved but, of course he was dead tired; he had gotten in late that night. . . .

I strongly raised Nicaragua and Cuba, but he resisted. . . . He made a strong pitch for me to talk to Castro. I hit him hard on arms to Nicaragua, and I accepted his denial that they weren't his; but I did point out that [Soviet-made] helicopters were on their way, and this was very damaging. He seemed laid-back, or not as aggressive as I thought he might be, on these points on Cuba and Nicaragua. I explained our position about Noriega, and he did not defend Noriega, but he said that Ortega‡ in Nicaragua was not a Marxist, and that he [was allowing] elections. It was a weak defense, but I tried to make the point that this was a real sticking point in our relationship and he ought to do something about clearing it up. He said, "I want to talk to you about Afghanistan; I noticed that you didn't mention that in the other meeting." And I said, "Well, that's true, I didn't, but I'm prepared to talk to you, and sure enough, we will."

We had a good meeting . . . about four hours, or four and a half hours, and then we came back to *Belknap.* But then the weather really broke for the worst. We barely got aboard *Belknap* with the Admiral's barge charging up and down, but once we got on, the landing platforms had to be pulled up. The Maltese said this storm was one of the worst they had seen, and they didn't expect it to

---

*Everybody was a little excited, especially the Secret Service, watching the President of the United States transferring from one boat to another with swells almost overtaking our launch boats. It didn't bother me a bit, but I felt bad it caused such a furor.

†Most Favored Nation, a term used to describe the status given to our best trading partners. Congress had enacted legislation making it available to the USSR and other communist countries, but only under special conditions.

‡Daniel Ortega, the dictator who ruled Nicaragua and head of the Sandinistas, a communist.

clear. There was some talk that it would clear in time for dinner, but I'm dictating this at 10:00 p.m., and the ship is rolling like mad. I've got a patch behind my ear—the things really work—but I'm blessed by not getting seasick. I can't say I don't feel the ship's motion.

I walked after a marvelous dinner that was supposed to be for Gorbachev—swordfish, fresh lobster, etc. I walked the deck; spoke to the enlisted men, with the spray and rain driving down way up on the bow; then on the walkway back to the stern; and then through the enlisted men's mess where they were about to have a movie. It was wonderful. What fine looking kids, and they were all very friendly, taking pictures, my standing with them for the pictures with their own camera, and making it much more fun.

The best laid plans of men: Here we are, the two super power leaders several hundred yards apart, and we can't talk because of the weather. . . .

Despite the weather the meeting was seen as enormously successful. Gorbachev and I talked about everything and established a good working relationship, which would be important in the days to come. After the meeting was over, I personally briefed our NATO allies and sent Brent to China to brief the leaders there. I did it out of courtesy, and to extend a hand.

December 10th

Congress jumps all over me, and the press is in a frenzy on the China trip. It's as if we totally normalized relations. It looks like it's going to be hell but I'm confident we did the right thing. . . .

I like this fight, because I'm convinced it's the right thing to do, and there's not a hell of a lot that Congress can do about it. Bob Strauss checks in and says it was a statesman-like thing to do. He said, "You're strong as President, and you can afford to do this kind of thing." I was very pleased by that. . . .

A personal cloud was developing over our family that Christmas. Neil was being dragged into the savings and loan mess, only because he was an outside director of a S&L called Silverado. He was one of thousands of Americans who sat on S&L boards, but because his name was Bush, he was being singled out. As President, I could not step in and help him, which killed me. But once again, our good friend Lud Ashley—now out of Congress—offered support.

December 13, 1989

The Honorable Thomas Ludlow Ashley
Association of Bank Holding Companies
Washington, DC 20005
Dear Lud:

Thank you for your good memo December 8th.

I would appreciate any help you could give Neil. He tells me he never had any insider dealings. He got off the Board early—long before I was elected President. The Denver paper apparently ran a very nice editorial about him on that. He is an outside Director, and thus I guess has liability, but I can't believe that his name would appear in the paper if it was Jones not Bush. In any event, I know that the guy is totally honest. I saw him in Denver and I think he is worried about the publicity and the "shame." I tell him not to worry about that but any advice that you can give as this matter unfolds would be greatly appreciated by me. If it turns out there has been some marginal call, or he has done something wrong, needless to say there will be no intervention from his dad. But I'm quite confident that this is not true. . . .

Warm regards,
George

December 16th

Ellie* walked in about 4:00 a.m.—she was sleeping in Bar's little office off our bedroom—and I was aware of her presence. I held out the blanket (we didn't say anything), pulled her in, and then rolled her over into the middle. Millie was already there, so in went Bar, Millie, Ellie and me. I said, "Be quiet, and go to sleep," but we really never did go back to sleep, but she didn't say anything. She was a wiggly little thing, but she hugged me and it reminded me exactly of when Robin was sick. It was frightening it was much the same—her little figure standing there, roughly the same age, equally as beautiful, just walking towards my bed, and standing there, just looking at me . . .

December 17th

Last night a young Marine was killed in Panama. Hectored by blockade guards, the Marine and his three companions tried to get away from a road block, but they had gotten lost, and they were shot

*Doro's daughter.

at. The Panamanians claim that the Marines fired on them, which was bull because none of them had any ammunition or guns.

Shortly after that a Navy lieutenant and his wife were taken in by the same check point people and harassed for 30 minutes. He was kicked and brutalized, kicked in the groin. A day or so before that, the Panamanians declared war on the United States, and they installed Manuel Noriega as the maximum leader. . . .

So this Sunday afternoon, I put into forward motion a major use of force to get Noriega out. It's a major gamble. We do not want to be an occupying power in Panama. World opinion will be difficult, but I decided to send a cable to the OAS* states saying that what happened was unacceptable . . . the Soviet reaction will probably be negative . . . Certainly some of the Central Americans will be very wary . . .

Things that are on my mind: Loss of American life; what if we don't get Noriega and bring him to justice—that he escapes our net. We'll go after him in every way possible.

––––––––––

December 20th

I'm thinking about the kids . . . those young 19 year olds who will be dropped in tonight . . . The operation has been rehearsed, and I'm thinking about the brutality of Noriega and what he's apt to do. I'm thinking about what happens if he gets away or flees into some Embassy—hostile or friendly. And I'm wondering if Endara and Ford† will accept their responsibility to stand up, be declared the democratically elected leaders, be sworn in and govern.‡ It is a major decision. . . .

So the tension mounts. They asked whether I would sleep; but there's no way I will be able to sleep; during an operation of this nature where the lives of American kids are at risk. . . .

––––––––––

Our military performed brilliantly during the nighttime invasion, but 23 Americans were killed and 323 were injured. Noriega did flee and could not be found

<hr>

*Organization of American States.

†Guillermo Endara had been elected president and Guillermo Ford had been elected vice president back in May, but Noriega had overturned the election results.

‡The plan was for the democratically elected leaders to immediately be sworn in and take power.

for a few days, but Endara and his team were sworn in and took over immediately, and the people of Panama were relieved and grateful.

December 24th

The phone rang and it's Brent saying Noriega has turned himself in to the Vatican Embassy in Panama. . . .

So what are my feelings when I hear that Noriega has given himself up? Great relief, and then my mind starts ticking—what are the complications? Will they try and give him asylum somewhere else? Will they try and arrange for him to be shipped to some third country? What about the indictments? It had been said that we'd pass the word that if he went to a third country on his own, we wouldn't pursue him . . . but that was before we lost American lives. . . .

It's got to be good news for Christmas Eve—very good news— because I think that with Noriega coming along into custody, even to the Vatican, that resistance will melt. He has no real following— he's a thug, crook, witch craft drug dealer, everything evil, and his time is up. This could be a great Christmas Eve . . .*

———————

December 31st

It's been some year—a fascinating year of change. I end the year with more confidence, and end the year with real gratitude to our team. They've pulled together. They had very little individual grandstanding. . . .

I'm certainly not seen as a visionary, but I hope I'm seen as steady and prudent and able.

The tough thing was going down early in my Presidency to speak at the ceremony for the *Iowa* sailors. I've gotten a little better at that at year's end, but not very good. When something close and personal happens, I break up and I know it. I couldn't speak at Fred Chamber's funeral. . . .

Bar's been sick this year,† but she's as strong as she can be, though her eyes bother her. She's captured the imagination of the country, and it's wonderful. My worries are about her eyes—they hurt her.

———————

*Noriega gave himself up to American authorities shortly after the New Year and was brought here to stand trial. He was found guilty on drug-trafficking charges and is serving a 120-year sentence.

†Bar was diagnosed with Graves' disease, which affects the thyroid, but she was doing better on medicine.

They're changing the medication, etc., but she'll do fine. I'm sure of that—she's got to. . . .

One of the greatest highlights was the day after Christmas. I was getting ready to go to the office, and Ellie—beautiful Ellie, who lights up any room she's in—said, "Gampy, come here," so I went into the bathroom. She pointed into the toilet, and said, "Did you leave that poo-poo?" Not many people would talk to the President of the United States like that.

THE WHITE HOUSE
WASHINGTON

CHAPTER 13

On the Front Line

On New Year's Eve, Barbara and I went to San Antonio to visit some of the injured troops coming back from Panama. It was an emotional day for both of us. This was one of several thank-you notes that I wrote:

Jan. 1, 1990

Brigadier Gen'l William L. Moore, Jr.
Brooke Army Medical Center
Fort Sam Houston, TX 78150-6189
Dear B Gen Moore,

I wiped away a tear or two as we drove back to the plane—a tear of sadness that those young kids are hurting—a tear of joy that your loving care and the care of all involved with our wounded men knows no bounds when it comes to excellence and concern.

I am grateful to you and yours; and I am thankful that your love and your medicine will give our heroic young men the chance to lead normal productive lives. May God Bless you, your family, and your critically important work—

George Bush

1-3-90

FROM THE PRESIDENT

TO: Marvin*

The two boys, squad mates, who were blasted in Panama and are lying there in Brooke Army Medical Center with colostomies are:

PFC Patrick Kilgallen

Bravo Company 3/75th Rangers—21 years old, single—spirits <u>fair.</u> His folks were there and he seemed a little confused and scared about what lies ahead, Mom mentioned your colostomy and Kilgallen's mother, at bedside, thanked her.

PFC Darron Murphy. Same exact outfit. 20 years old, married w/ daughter—spirits good. They told him when he came out of the operation that the Pres' son Marv had had the same operation.

The boys are lying there side by side in a room. Their squad leader was killed.

A phone call, like only you can do, would make a difference. We can set it up if you'd like or you can call the hospital, speak to General Moore who showed Mum and me around. Ask him what would be best way to talk to both kids. It will mean an awful lot.

———

Maureen Dowd of the New York Times *wanted to do an article about Marlin Fitzwater. I agreed to jot down some thoughts:*

January 7, 1990

Dear Maureen,

Yes I am a note answerer, and a note writer, and a self typer because my handwriting is pretty awful. You ask about Marlin:

He is a serious contender for the coveted Scowcroft Award.† Marlin, though it is early in 1990, has already demonstrated an amazing ability to fall asleep at the drop of a hat. He needs to improve his record on sleeping in important meetings. The Scowcroft award gives extra points for he/she who totally craters, eyes tightly closed, in the midst of meetings; but in fairness a lot of credit is given for sleeping soundly while all about you are doing their thing.

---

*I also sent notes to George and Jeb, asking them to visit wounded soldiers in their areas.

†The Scowcroft Award was a highly coveted recognition that I handed out upon occasion to cabinet members and White House staffers. It went to the person who could fall asleep in a meeting but make a good recovery and act as if he or she had not been sleeping. It was named for Brent, who was the champion at this. (I should add here, Brent fell asleep only because he worked impossible hours and cared for his invalid wife.)

Here Marlin does very well. As I say, it is early in January, but already, Marlin Fitzwater is building on last year's record. It was on a short hop from Texas to Alabama, early in the A.M. when most were just getting 'hyped' up for the day, that Marlin, mouth open, head back, set a new high standard. It is said that 2 people were talking to him when he clonked out—an amazing performance.

Marlin is a hat man. Most men, at least younger men Marlin's age (younger by my gauge) are careful about hats—not Marlin. Unafraid of what his peers might think, he'll try any hat. You might think this is trivial. I don't. I respect him for this—a trait some would consider eccentric.

You ask about tennis—Yes. For awhile when he was carrying excess tonnage the ranking committee* felt his claims of prowess in Kansas were a bit exaggerated—the committee watched, saw some potential but couldn't picture the gazelle like qualities he claims he once had. Now, however, Slim Fast having hammered his body into hard rock muscle, those critics can see what he meant about himself when he said "I used to run like a deer and have the finesse, on the court, of a fox-owl combined." Yes. Tennis. He's into it.

Humorist you ask? Of Course. For the most part Marlin's jokes could be told over there at the DAR HQ†—well not all of them but many. He laughs well and others laugh with him. He better though, how could he survive in that briefing room if he couldn't laugh it up from time to time.

What else?—Let's see.

He's a classy guy and I depend on him, not just when we land but when we take off, too. He's my guy and I am proud to have him at my side.

George Bush

I sent a copy of this letter to our entire family.

January 17, 1990

Mr. George W. Bush
Dallas, Texas 75225
Dear George:

On Friday, January 12th, in Cincinnati, I met with a Mrs. Sandra Rouse. Her son, PFC James Markwell, was a paratrooper and a medic trained, as he said in his own words . . . "to kill and to save."

---

*Members of the ranking committee, whose sole job is to judge the tennis-playing ability of friends and family, are secret. Their meetings are closed to the public. The ranking-committee chairman, also a secret, is all-powerful.

†Daughters of the American Revolution, located just down the street from the White House.

Markwell wrote the attached letter on December 18th.* He was killed on the first day of battle.

At our meeting, Mrs. Rouse was courageous and strong; her faith in God sustaining her. She cried. I put my arm around her shoulder.

I thought—I sent her son into this battle and here she is telling me with love about her son and what he stood for. She said, "You did the right thing."

PFC Markwell died, I'm told, as he attended to a wounded man. Yes, he was taught to kill and to save.

Markwell's letter will give you a glimpse into the thinking of a special, courageous, patriotic young man.

But there are others like him. Bar and I saw this in the wards of two San Antonio military hospitals.

On my desk, as I write, is a flag given to me by a Ranger severely wounded in Panama. One leg had been amputated. He is paralyzed. He handed me a little American flag and said he wished he were back there, in Panama, with his unit.

Each member of the Joint Chiefs and our able Chairman, Colin Powell, says these are the finest, best trained kids we ever had. They have all volunteered.

Back to Markwell. His mom told me he had a chance to go to West Point, a chance to go to college, but he wanted to be a Ranger. He desperately wanted to serve his country.

I just wanted to share all this with family. Please do not let this get out of your own hands.

When I mourn our dead and wounded, when I think of their families and loved ones, I also think of the courage of our troops.

I expect I'll remember PFC James W. Markwell as long as I live. I'll remember a loving mother's grief but also her pride in one young, courageous, and patriotic soldier.

Devotedly,
Dad

I had gotten to know the president of Finland, Mauno Koivisto, quite well during the vice presidency. He was especially helpful on giving us insight into Soviet affairs.

*He had written his mother telling her, "I have never been afraid of death but I know he is waiting at the corner . . . do not mourn for me . . . revel in the life that I have died to give you . . . remember I joined the army to serve my country and insure that you are free to do what you want and live your lives freely."

January 23, 1990

His Excellency Mauno Koivisto
President of Finland
Helsinki
Dear Mr. President:

I have read and re-read your good letter of January 9. First, let me thank you so much for sending it along. As you know by now, I truly value your advice, your insights, and your judgment.

I, too, have a feeling of "uneasiness." Recent events inside the Soviet Union have been very difficult for Mr. Gorbachev. In my view, he is handling things well, but the recent use of force will, undoubtedly, cause ongoing problems. I don't know what he could have done differently, however, given the tremendous ethnic violence.*

At Malta I was amazed at how little Gorbachev really knows about Free Market economics. The Soviets have enormous economic problems, far greater than most of the world realizes. . . .

Yes, we will push forward on arms control talks. I think Gorbachev wants to see both START and CFE† treaties signed at our summit which comes up this summer. We may have a chance to get even further reductions in both Soviet and U.S. forces deployed in Europe.

I am not sure I agree with you that "the West must be prepared to give more and quicker assistance." I think some more serious reforms are needed before financial assistance will really help. I do think we can do much more in helping with suggested basic reforms in the Soviet Union, just as we are trying to do with Poland. Shevardnadze, himself, said, "we don't want to be bailed out" (a paraphrase).

I was interested in your thoughts on the Soviet Union "turning inwards." There is evidence of this—particularly when one considers recent comments by Gorbachev about Lithuania. Who would have dreamed there would be even talk about autonomy or independence of the Baltic States, without drawing Soviet threats of force.‡

I will continue to signal to Gorbachev that we want to see him succeed. I really have great respect for what he has done—great understanding for the enormous problems he faces. Yeltsin is now giving him some grief and those old guard types like Ligachev still fire a few salvos, but Gor-

*Gorbachev had sent in troops to end ethnic violence between the Soviet republics of Azerbaijan and Armenia.

†Strategic Arms Reduction Treaty and Conventional Forces (nonnuclear weapons) in Europe.

‡All of the Baltic states, but especially Lithuania, were clamoring for independence.

bachev keeps on trying to keep perestroika moving and to keep glasnost alive.

Thanks again for that fine letter.

Most sincerely,
George Bush

I wrote this note to Mexican president Carlos Salinas:

Feb. 3, 1990

Sat. A cold rainy day
My Dear Friend,

. . . I'm told that there was a recent TV Program here that offended many in Mexico.* I have not seen it. As for me, I will continue to say that Mexico, under President Salinas, is giving us great cooperation in the anti-drug fight.

I realize that Panama has caused some heartburn in Mexico. I hope that has lessened now; and I hope you personally know that I had to protect American life. I am gratified that the Panamanian people supported our action by over 92% at one point. I'm also pleased that Democracy has a chance now—a real chance there in Panama. In any event I do understand Mexico's predictable response just as I hope you understand I have not lost my determination to work closely with you and other democratic leaders to our South.

My respects to your family and with high esteem my warmest, friendliest personal best wishes to you—

George Bush

February 13th

Ranger was up in the middle of the night outside. I heard him barking, and I had to go out and bring him in at 2:00 am with my pajamas on and overcoat, much to the giggling and not consternation but enjoyment of the Secret Service . . . I heard their [radio] message—"Timberwolfe is on the White House lawn; Timberwolfe is out."† . . . The agents tell me that he was on the tennis courts, so we go off looking for him. . . . Out of the ivy toward the tennis courts charges Ranger, happy to see me, and wagging his tail. I take him up to the third floor where Marvin is asleep with Marshall in two twin

---

*The program focused on drug problems and poverty in Mexico.
†Timberwolfe was my Secret Service code name.

beds, and Margaret is off in another room with Walker.* Fortunately, I stuck him in with Marvin and said, "He's your dog."

What a fantastic dog he is, and what a great lovable dog Millie is. She no longer sleeps on the foot of the bed—say nothing of her in her basket—it's right up between Bar and me on the head. We have two kinds of round pillows, very hard, and I stick them about half way across the bed as a "barrier". She has to stay on her side of the "barrier" and now she knows, but her head comes across and she'll nudge me. She'll turn over in the middle of the night, and while my hand is reaching over for Bar, I'll find Millie's legs in the air and I'll give her a scratch under her arms, and she falls asleep. . . .

On February 15 I went to Cartagena, Colombia, to attend a drug summit. The drug lords were waging a guerrilla-like war against the Colombian government and there were huge concerns about security at the summit.

February 14th

It's 9:30 on Wednesday night. I decide to come out to Air Force One and climb on the plane now rather than wake up in the middle of the night [to leave]. We first go out to dinner with George, Marvin, Laura, Margaret and Bar, who's just had a cancer removed from her lip. She's obviously worried about her stitches and the way she looks, but we have a wonderful Peking Duck dinner joined by the Burt Lees.

I feel a certain tension about our trip to South America, a certain anxiety, but nobody wants to talk about it. I go into the restaurant, and people clap, and when we walk out, they say, "Go safely, we're praying for you." And at the end of the line going out, I found myself choking up. I don't think it was the martini or the white wine or the Peking Duck—it was the genuine warmth and affection of the people.

. . . I can tell John Simpson† is nervous, and I wonder, "Why don't I feel nervous," and I think maybe it's because of World War II when every day you got up, you went into combat, saw your friends going into combat, or knowing your assignment was to go into combat. I'm convinced we can hold the line. . . .

---

*Marvin and Margaret had adopted their second child, Walker, who was born in November 1989.

†Director of the Secret Service.

We go back to the White House after this marvelous dinner at Peking Duck, and then we hear the helicopter. I can tell Bar is nervous. It worries me a little, but I give her a hug and she worries about my going. I hate to leave her when she needs somebody to have their arms around her and lift her up . . .

In any event, it's 9:40 PM, the night of the 14th, and in another six hours, they will be pulling this plane out of this great big hangar; and in another seven hours we'll be on our way to Cartagena [Colombia]. I know it's the right thing to do, and I'm not afraid; and yet, I worry that some journalist might get zapped or somebody else (not us) might get hit. We'll get the blame, so then we'll wonder— why did they do this? . . . And then I think Barco* is risking his life for the kids in Chicago and Texas every single day, so we've got to do it. Sometimes you've got to do what you think is right.

They say I live by the polls and want to be popular . . . well, Panama might not have gone down well, and certainly this isn't the popular decision, and clearly China wasn't popular, so you've got to do what you think is right, take the heat, and that's what I'm trying to do.

[The summit was successful in that it renewed our determination to cooperate on the drug problem. Everyone got home safe and sound without incident.]

———

February 24th

. . . The concern about a unified Germany has intensified . . . Thatcher now has much more concern about a unified Germany than about a Soviet threat. We're in this fascinating time of change and flux. . . .

[Brian] Mulroney† points out, "You're the only one to lead this alliance—you must do it." Kohl, I think, recognizes the key role of the United States, and I think we have a disproportionate role for stability. We've got strong willed players—large and small in Europe—but only the United States can do this . . .

I told Jim and Brent yesterday that I don't want to move to isolation, but I don't want to see us fettered by a lot of multi-lateral decisions. We've got to stand, and sometimes we'll be together with

---

*Colombian president Virgilio Barco, who was fighting a courageous battle against the drug lords.

†Brian Mulroney was prime minister of Canada from 1984 to 1993. He was a close friend and wonderful ally and I depended a great deal on him for advice.

them; but sometimes we'll say we differ, and we've got to lead, so we should not be just kind of watered down, picking up the bill, and acquiescing in a lot of decisions that might hurt us . . . I've got to look after the U.S. interest in all of this without reverting to a kind of isolationistic or stupid peace-nik view on where we stand in the world.

Who's the enemy? I keep getting asked that. It's apathy; it's the inability to predict accurately; it's dramatic change that can't be foreseen; and its events that can't be predicted like the Iran-Iraq war. . . . There are all kinds of events that we can't foresee that require a strong NATO, and there's all kinds of potential instability that requires a strong U.S. presence.

March 9, 1990

Mr. Dan Jenkins*
Ponte Vedra Beach, Florida 32983
Dear Dan,

Your article came in two days after I decided to take up golf again. It all happened when I got 3 fairway short irons off the turf without sticking my pick in the turf. The long putter paved the way. I don't sink putts now but the long one has given me confidence to follow through, thus avoiding the automatic 4 putt greens. Now there is light at the end of the short-game tunnel. I'm not ready for a guy that shoots 77 or <u>ever</u> shot 77. Here's my sports game plan—Keep throwing 'shoes'—try to improve. Tennis—keep playing doubles but recognize that the kids of mine, by tying their shoes when I say "let's hit," are sending me a clear message that I better think "phase out". Golf—more of it. Fishing—bitch more at the schedulers around here demanding more fishing time. quote Isaac Walton a lot "Time a man spends fishing should not be deducted from the time a guy spends on earth" (something like that). Baseball—watch it as much as possible pointing out to the scheduling dynasty that The National Past-time demands A President's respect.

Skeet and Quail Hunting—beg for time. Jogging—stay with my current 3 times a week, 2 miles at about 9 minutes per. Hips and knees hurt more now so keep phasing in with cycles, stairmasters, fast walk up hill, tread mills etc. So there it is—My life its ownself. . . .

George Bush

---

*Dan is a great friend and a great author of books such as *Semi-Tough, Life Its Ownself,* and *Bubba Talks.*

March 10, 1990

Marlin—

Having bitched about Day-in-Life-of by Brokaw* as it was being born; and having now a week or so to look back on it—

I now salute your decision—Reviews good—all clicked—your staff did good work.

What's next—

Roseanne Barr & me going tummy to tummy?

George Bush

———————

March 15, 1990

Mrs. Peggy Say†
Cadiz, Kentucky
Dear Mrs. Say:

Barbara and I were deeply moved by your eloquent and profoundly sad letter to us.

We share your great sorrow at the approach of the fifth anniversary of Terry's abduction. As you so poignantly expressed in your letter, the tragedy of your brother's merciless imprisonment exists in his missing the simple enjoyments of watching children born and growing up. So much has changed in the lives of his family and indeed, in the world as he knew it five long, lonely years ago. Yet so little has really changed for your brother.

Let me assure you, your family and all the hostage families that securing the freedom of your brother and the other American hostages is a matter of great importance to me. We continue to call for the immediate, unconditional, safe release of the hostages. As a further signal of commitment to resolving this tragedy, I intend to keep open lines of communications with all parties, including Iran, who have influence over hostage takers. Please be assured that your government will take advantage of all legitimate opportunities to obtain the safe release of all of our hostages.

Although I regret that I will be unable to be with you and the other families as you remember the tragic day five years ago when Terry was abducted,

———

*We had agreed to give NBC special access for one day so they could do a "Day in the Life of the President" with Tom Brokaw. I was not thrilled with the idea but then enjoyed the program.

†Peggy Say is the sister of Terry Anderson, the AP reporter being held hostage at that time in Lebanon. She wrote us a heartbreaking letter about their ordeal. Terry, along with all the other hostages, was released in 1991.

please be assured that Barbara and I think often of the hostages and their families. We pray for the speedy return of your loved one.

Sincerely,
George Bush

P. S. I found the story in today's [Washington] Post very heart warming, a tribute to your dedication.

————————

Without really meaning to, I announced to the world about this time that I did not like broccoli, that I had never liked broccoli, and now that I was President of the United States, I was never eating it again. It caused a huge stir, and I still hear about it today.

March 23rd
. . . The broccoli war is heating up. On March 21st, the Broccoli Association announces they're sending a couple of tons of the stuff, but I'm sticking with my position that I hate broccoli. I think I'll get Barbara, who likes broccoli, to go out and greet the broccoli caravan. I refuse to give an inch on this, and I so advised the press. I can't stand the stuff; it smells up everything; and I'm against it. . . .

————————

March 22, 1990

Mrs. Jane C. Schultz
Ridgefield, Connecticut 06877
Dear Mrs. Schultz:

Your letter has touched me deeply. Thank you for telling me about the thoughts and feelings that you have had since hearing my State of the Union Address. While I knew that your Thomas was among those killed aboard Pan AM Flight 103, I was not aware that you had also lost your only other child, Andrew, in a terrible accident. You and your husband have suffered great pain.

I want to assure you that not a day goes by that I am not mindful that we have an obligation to the victims of the Pan Am 103 bombing to see that those responsible for their deaths are brought to justice. Our investigation into the destruction of Pan Am 103 is ongoing and is by no means completed. New and important information continues to be found. But the point here is, we have not forgotten and we will not forget. International investigations take a lot of time, but our various agencies are determined to get to the bottom of this horrible tragedy.

Your letter was a cry from the heart and I have heard this cry. Perhaps I truly <u>can</u> understand your deep hurt, because as you point out, we did lose a child.

When our beloved daughter was about to die another little child in the next room lost her life. The grieving parents, heartbroken by their loss, turned on the doctors and nurses who had requested permission to perform an autopsy. They said, "Haven't you done enough to our child?" The doctors and nurses who had labored to keep that child alive were deeply hurt; and yet they tried to understand the parents' grief and they forgave the parents.

We will continue to try to get to the bottom of this matter; and I will continue to care about your loss, and about those hostages you mention, and about those courageous soldiers who died in Panama, and about those victims of AIDS who feel that no one cares.

Your letter helped me, in a sense, for it made me focus yet again on another's sorrow. Perhaps I will be a better President. . . .

Sincerely,
George Bush

––––––––––

March 23, 1990

Mr. Dick Sternberg
The Hunting and Fishing Library
Minnetonka, Minnesota 55343
Dear Dick:

I love those marvelous fishing books. They are now in my personal office at Camp David. The place I use to "think" fishing after my homework is done.

My tip is a simple one, "If at first you don't succeed, hang in there!"

Last summer I had a run of ten days getting skunked looking for bluefish in Maine waters. Other boats were catching them, but I kept striking out. The Portland paper raised the stakes by printing a "no fish" sticker everyday.

Finally . . . I broke the jinx—I kept the hook in the water. I refused to get too tense. Tense yes, "too tense," no. I cast into every swirl I saw; I trolled 'til the sun had sunk. I changed lures and rods for luck; and finally on the second to last day as I began to troll, a good bluefish hit my diving Rebel (mackerel color).

The press boats honked their horns, same for the Coast Guard and Secret Service boats. I knew great happiness.

My fishing tips—"Keep the hook in the water. Never give up. Enjoy the contest even when the pressure mounts. But best of all, go fishing when there is no pressure, and relax."

Sincerely,
George Bush

March 27, 1990

Mr. Raymond J. Mitchell
Miami Township, Ohio 45439-3124
Dear Mr. Mitchell:

Barbara was touched by your letter telling her of your wife's rebellion against peas, caused by my rebellion against broccoli.

Tell Janice Ann to "hang in there;" however, Ray, I cannot accept your check even though the cause for which you sent it in is a noble one. I love Baby Ruth's and Heath bars too, but I just can't spend your fiver on that. "Eat it today, wear it tomorrow."

Barbara, broccoli lover that she is, joins me in sending our warm best wishes.

Sincerely,
George Bush

The wonderful cockroach racers from Hawaii surfaced again.

March 27, 1990

Mr. Kimo Wilder McVay
Chairman, Roach Bowl III
Honolulu, Hawaii 96814
Dear Kimo:

I was very pleased to get your letter and to learn that Kinder Gentleroach has indeed been officially received as an entry for this year's big race.

I know a lot of thoroughbred roach lovers were disappointed that Oval Office Roach did so badly back in 1988, but lots has happened since then.

Commissioner Conrad, through his own success, has brought great lustre to this event. (I am told that his own entry this year has little chance, however, given the fact that his roach is overweight—sad to say.)*

I am a great believer in the Thousand Points of Light concept, and I salute you and all the others for what you are doing to help battle Multiple Sclerosis.

Please consider this your official permission to permit Kinder Gentleroach to enter not only the Roach Bowl classic, but also to run in the Iolani Derby. Kinder Gentleroach is willing to submit to an anti-steroid test, saliva test,

*This would be actor William Conrad, who had moved to Hawaii during his TV series *Jake and the Fatman.* He had agreed to be commissioner of Roach Bowl III.

etc., and I challenge all other roach owners to compel their entries to do the same.

Sincerely,
George Bush

P.S. I still feel both <u>Yellow Roach</u> of Texas and <u>Oval Officeroach</u> were robbed because Fred Zeder . . . had an illegal bet on other roaches. All we ask for is fair play.*

————————

On March 11, Lithuania declared its independence from the Soviet Union and declared that Vytautas Landsbergis was president. Gorbachev condemned the action as "illegitimate and invalid" and threatened military action. Again, I was frustrated by the difference between what I would have liked to have done and what was the right thing to do.

March 28th
Everyone wants us to "do more," though nobody is quite clear on what that means. Congress has a free shot because they can exhort and urge without being specific except that they want immediate recognition of Lithuania, which I think would be quite dangerous. So they're hitting me as the wimp unwilling to move, but the big thing is to get through this so the Soviets and the Lithuanians get into negotiations, and handle it without bloodshed and force. If there is bloodshed, there is not a damn thing the United States can do about it and you'd have blood on your hands for encouraging her and enciting the Lithuanians to bite off more than they can chew at this point. We are continuing to talk about self-determination and freedom, but this is a fine line for walking here. . . It's funny how these things aren't quite as simple as they seem from the outside.

The NEA† for example. When I see Jesus Christ shooting up heroin or floating in a bottle of urine, I figure that there ought not to be one dime of federal funds going into this. And then you think of the alternative which comes to mind— federal censorship—and you worry, "Where will this lead?" . . .

Margaret [Bush] came over with Ranger, and the two kids, and I

————————

*Our friend Fred Zeder, who has a home in Hawaii, knew these charity cockroachers and was responsible for my involvement with their causes.

†National Endowment for the Arts. They were under fire for underwriting an art exhibit that featured a controversial painting of Jesus.

had a quiet supper with her. She is so sweet to me. When Marv's gone and Bar's gone, she's always considerate thinking I might be lonely. She's a lovely girl, and I'm very lucky to have her as one of our wonderful daughters-in-law. I love holding Walker. He's more alert now, and his little face looks up, and if you talk to him just right, he'll give you a tremendous broad smile. Marshall doesn't seem jealous. She doesn't eat much, though. We told her that her eggplant was pizza, but that didn't work, so we gave her a couple of scoops of ice cream, and she managed to get some of that down.

April 16th

Barbara Bush is annoyed and I don't blame her about the students at Wellesley protesting her visit.* They're protesting because she hasn't made it on her own—she's where she is because she's her husband's wife. What's wrong with the fact that she's a good mother, a good wife, great volunteer, great leader for literacy and other fine causes? Nothing, but to listen to these elitist kids there is. . . .

April 17th

Bar is gone. . . . I sit here at the White House rundown by health problems† and a little gloomy given the magnitude of the problems. It might be the first day I've really felt an accumulation of problems: the Middle East, the deficit, environment, and Lithuania . . . but that's what I get paid to do.

April 29, 1990

His Excellency Mikhail Sergeyevich Gorbachev
President of the Union of Soviet Socialist Republics
Moscow

Dear Mr. President:

These are trying times. I have tried very hard to understand the problems you face at home. Indeed as Jim Baker has told Foreign Minister Shevardnadze, not only have we tried to understand, but we have acted with restraint and prudence.

---

*Barbara had been asked to be the commencement speaker for Wellesley College in Massachusetts. A group of seniors objected loudly because she wasn't a "career woman."

†I can't even remember now what they were, so they must not have been too serious.

I understand your view that the Baltic States are part of the Soviet Union; and I expect you know our view that we have never recognized their incorporation into the Soviet Union.* I have given a lot of weight to your stated view that force would not be used and that eventual separation or self determination is in the cards for Lithuania.

The problem is we can no longer sit idly by, giving the impression that we are unconcerned about the aspirations to freedom of the people of Lithuania.

I have often stated publicly, not only my desire to see perestroika succeed, but also to see you personally prevail. I still feel very strongly about that. Last Monday, the Minister from your Embassy came to the State Department and once again asked that we show restraint. On Tuesday I met with key leaders in our Congress and explained that I was not prepared to take action on this matter, though there is a growing feeling in this country that my inaction delivers a serious blow to the aspirations of freedom loving people in Lithuania, and indeed everywhere. This growing feeling, which I share, leads me to believe that there is no way we will be able to conclude our Trade Agreement, and thus MFN, unless dialogue with the Lithuanians begins.

We realize there is no easy answer; but, as you know, we felt that a "suspension" by Lithuania of its resolution,† as suggested by President Mitterrand and Chancellor Kohl, coupled with your willingness to meet with the Lithuanians outside the federation concept, would be the best way to break the ice. We have, as you probably know, urged this course upon Mr. Landsbergis.

Here is the basic reality—there is no way Congress will approve MFN under existing circumstances—no way at all. Further, under existing circumstances, I will not be able to recommend approval. I have felt that these negotiations should continue and, indeed, have taken some "flak" for not cutting off trade talks from our end. I assume that you have seen some of the statements on this critical subject.

I recognize, with respect, the restraint that you have shown, indeed, the encouragement you have given, to the new democracies in Eastern Europe. I recognize that this restraint and understanding has cost you support at home. You have a large stock of goodwill here and in other western countries for what you have done. But now we have Lithuania and the other Baltic States, which, to us, to repeat, have special standing.

I wish I could think of a more positive role that I could play to help ameliorate matters. In this regard, I would welcome any suggestions you might care to make. . . . It would be very useful if we could talk this out in a reason-

---

*Lithuania had been annexed by the Soviet Union in 1940 against its will.

†Many world leaders were urging Lithuania to go a little slower, including suspending their declaration-of-independence resolution.

able way, trying to work together to solve what at this moment is a terrible problem between us.

I may be forced very soon to state publicly that under existing conditions there can be no trade agreement. This is simply a statement of reality. It is not intended to be provocative. It is not intended to complicate matters for you. I will accompany this "marker" with the fervent hope that dialogue will begin between Lithuania and the Soviet Union. I regret that the latest Lithuanian attempt at dialogue, with Supreme Soviet Chairman Lukyanov, failed to produce positive results. We must clear the path so that the era of improved relations between our two great countries will continue to flourish.

You have done too much, and we have come too far to see matters between us revert to tension and anxiety.

I would welcome any suggestions. Please know that this was not an easy letter to write. I have tried very hard to keep relations on track, recognizing the dramatic changes that you have brought to much of this world.

I have no choice now but to identify with our strongly held convictions about Lithuania's self determination and the right to control its own destiny.

I look forward to seeing you at our upcoming meeting. I am determined to keep that meeting on track in spite of existing tensions. There is a lot at stake there.

> My sincere best wishes.
> George Bush

[Gorbachev, obviously annoyed by the letter, sent me a strong reply, saying the situation in the Baltics was an internal affair.]

May 2nd

Mum was here—she came yesterday and she looked very tired. Her cheeks were hollow and I was absolutely shocked as I walked across from the Oval Office to the Diplomatic entrance, and she said, "Who's that? Who's that?" I said, "Mum, it's George." Here she was on the White House grounds surrounded by the White House presence, and she didn't know. But then I hugged her, and she knew . . .

While walking the White House grounds, my mind is not on tomorrow's press conference; it's not on Lithuania and the problem there; it's not on the leak on the budget committee meeting . . . it's on Mother and our family, and our love for her. She won the Mother's race when I was in the fourth grade, and she was the captain of the Mother's baseball team when I was in the 6th, 7th, or 8th grade—but it matters not. At Andover, she was the most vivacious when she came, and I know all my friends looked at her and said how wonderful she was. As the years went by, she was the leader for the Walkers, the Stapletons, the Bushes, the Jansings, and whoever—but now, she is a tired old lady. She stares a lot when she focuses, and it's that focus of love. I said, "Did you see your newest little great-grandson, Walker?" And she knew and she lit up, and she said, he's the most beautiful little boy she'd ever seen . . .

Tomorrow she leaves, and maybe I'll never see her again, but I love her very much and that's what counts. All the criticism, all the fighting, all the ups-and-downs, all the right-wings, the left-wings, the press, and controversy—they all mean nothing. It's Mum's words: do your best; try your hardest; be kind; share; go to Church—and I think that's what really matters on this evening of May 2nd, 1990. . . .

May 4th

It was a very full day, and I had to cope with the leaks on my proposed talks about the budget. I had asked Mitchell, Michel, Foley* and Dole to come to a Sunday meeting. We all pledged to secrecy, but then the night before the press conference on the 3rd, we got a call, and the word from the Hill is—there is a budget meeting. So there is a lot of preliminary jockeying, but if we handle it wrong, our troops will rebel on taxes—everybody will rebel on social security benefits—and there will be no deal at all, and we need a deal. I'm willing to eat crow, but the others are going to have to eat crow. I'll have to yield on "Read My Lips," and they're going to have to yield on some of their rhetoric on taxes and on entitlements—

In any event, as I dictate this now on the 4th of May, Friday night, heading for Camp David, I'm tired, relaxed though—maybe it's the martini—but convinced we're on the right track in the big picture, and wondering how long the public will support me because I must say, as I drive around the country in the car, there seems to be a warmth of feeling to me and Bar, and that's good for the country, I think. By that I mean, respect for the institution—respect for the Presidency. . . .

Gorbachev arrived May 31 for our first official summit meeting. We had many difficult issues to discuss, including German unification, the Baltics, arms control, and a trade agreement.

*Tom Foley from the state of Washington was now Speaker of the House.

May 31st

I'm dictating this in-between meetings with Mr. Gorbachev. We spent a couple of hours together this morning. He asked me to outline for him how I saw the Soviet Union for the future, and where we place the United States and how he looked at the United States. I told him I stressed equality. We weren't trying to complicate things for him, but that we wanted perestroika to succeed . . .

I told him we understood the loss of 27 million lives [in World War II.] He had referred to the arrogance of some countries, meaning mainly Japan and Germany. I told him that we no longer looked at them as arrogant, and that we fought in the war against them, but that in my view, they should be constructive partners of the Soviet Union in the future—both of them.

I told him the threat would come from "singularization," meaning if you caused Germany to be treated differently and set aside and made to be neutral or made to have no weapons, you would risk a repeat of history. He alluded to the enormous problems.

I talked to him about Lithuania; I talked to him about how it caused difficulties for me politically; I mentioned Cuba; I talked to him about cooperation and lack of suspicion, saying that if they thought we wanted to install a regime hostile to them in Afghanistan, that would be bad; and similarly that we didn't like support for a regime that is inhospitable to us 90 miles off our borders.

. . . We did not talk about the internal affairs much, though he did talk about their commitment to economic reform; their commitment to markets; and their commitment to reform in the provinces. I told him that as you approach market economics, you've got to go all the way or it won't be effective. I said it's just like being pregnant—you can't be a little bit pregnant. He replied, and I thought cleverly, "Well, you can't have a baby in the first month either—it takes nine months, and you want to be careful that you don't have an abortion along the way."

. . . In talking about Lithuania, he made clear to me that the constitution must be followed. He said if this was in the United States, George Bush would take care of the problem in twenty minutes.

June 1st

On the 31st, the dinner went well. Gorbachev was in a good mood . . . After the dinner, Gorby got me in the hall and said if we didn't have a trade agreement, it would be a disaster—it would be terrible—repeated: a disaster. He was very agitated, and almost acted like he had not received the letter I wrote, which we've kept confidential—a letter in which I told him that we could not go forward with MFN unless there was some solution to the Lithuania problem. As I dictate this on the morning of June 1st, we have not talked in detail about Lithuania or trade or MFN, although he did touch on his need for support and not being isolated—don't embarrass us, don't humiliate us.

. . . Bar is very nervous about Wellesley this morning. She read me her speech. I called her about 7:30 and told her to be sure and put in there that reading to a child is self-rewarding, etc. She said, "Well, you didn't listen to my speech when I read it to you" and I'm afraid she was somewhat right, although I did think the speech was very good. Now all three networks are carrying the speech live . . .*

Here we sit with all of these problems, and yet, when a bird flies by or two ducks land in the swimming pool, or I see the fountain down near the tennis court, I get a restful feeling. There is a bearded gardening man from the park service. He's a great big guy, a giant— a tough looking guy—and I watch him from the Oval Office as he tends the flowers with the loving care that just shines through. I go out and talk to him for sometime, and he gives me great detail as to what it is he's doing, and what flowers will bloom next.

On Saturday we took the Gorbachevs to Camp David. We had serious talks in the morning and afternoon but we had some fun, too.

June 2nd

. . . The toast [at dinner] was marvelous. Gorbachev had picked up a horseshoe when I was taking a little nap. He had gone for a walk, thrown it and hit a ringer on the first shoe. So Tim† had gotten the other shoe, had it put on a plaque with a little etching on there about his visit, and I handed it to him with a very informal toast at the end of dinner that included our top people and their top people—about 30 at dinner. He was very emotional and choked up when he described what he felt was this relationship. . . .

---

*Barbara was a smash and the speech is still quoted today: "What happens in your house is more important than what happens in the White House." She took Raisa with her, which was also a hit.

†Tim McBride, who was my wonderful personal aide.

It's funny how in dealing with the Soviets we think we know a lot, but we know so little. We heard that Gorbachev didn't like to fly in a helicopter, yet he seemed very comfortable in the helicopter—totally relaxed, looking out the window, and asking a lot of questions—and if he was nervous, he damn sure didn't show it.

June 3rd

Sunday afternoon. I brought Gorbachev into Lincoln's bedroom and showed him the room in which Lincoln signed the Emancipation Proclamation. I showed him the Gettysburg Address, and explained what it was about. I showed him the pictures of the slaves waiting to be freed, and then I brought him into the office and showed him my five screen television set, and the computers. I showed him my schedule for Monday, and he said, "I've got to get my office modernized. I don't have this kind of thing." Then I showed him the block schedule and he seemed positively amazed, so I just handed it to him for the month of May and for Monday, June 4th. He said he'd like to send his Chief of Staff over to work with my Chief of Staff, and I mentioned that in front of John Sununu, and I said Sununu would be glad to go to Moscow or he would be glad to have his chief come to us. He also asked me to be sure to come to the Soviet Union, and I told him, yes, I'd be glad to do it. . . .

[The summit was a big success. We made headway on arms control and got a surprising concession from Gorbachev that German unification and German membership in NATO were really up to the Germans, which was a huge step forward. Publicly, we gave Gorbachev his trade agreement, but the secret deal we made with him was that I would not send it up to Congress for approval until progress had been made on Lithuania.]

In March, a young and energetic Lee Atwater passed out while giving a speech. It was discovered that he had a nonmalignant brain tumor, which would eventually claim his life. I wrote him this note after he sent me a wonderful letter about our friendship:

6-14-90

Dear Lee,

I was touched—deeply moved—by your letter.

I am so proud of you and Sally, too

We need you badly, but take all the time you need to fight and win.

I'm at your side with <u>all</u> our family love coming your way.

Life is values—and one of those is "class"—not in a elitist sense but in a life its ownself sense. You've got it—

Love from all Bushes,

GB

June 15th

On Flag Day, I went to the Vietnam Memorial at 6:30 a.m. I presented a flag that's been flown over the White House, and then gave the one flying at the park to a boy scout, a young black kid named Wilson, who presented his father, a fine looking guy, and gave his father credit for what "I am today"—a 13 year old straight arrow Boy Scout. Helen Thomas* kept yelling at me—"What are you here for? What are you doing?" I did not answer. It was a solemn occasion and when I do go to the Vietnam Memorial, and this is about the third time, I feel tears welling up in my eyes especially when you look at the little cards, flowers, crosses laid up against the memorial, and the little messages of "we love you." There were some 55,000 lives lost. . . .

It was a beautiful morning. The flag looked spectacular, and I hope we're not going to be accused of demagoguing this day which is Flag Day, USA. But in any event, I think the American people do understand. . . .

My big moment in horseshoes—"I'm back."† I beat Ron 21 to nothing in a little exhibition match . . . Ron couldn't believe it, and frankly, he didn't have a chance to warm up. I think he was nervous with the little crowd that was gathered. At dinner, Buddy and George‡ both mentioned to me, "You didn't tell us you beat Ron." I told them that the ranking committee had already agreed that Ron gets another shot at me. Anyway, Walter Mitty is back. I couldn't miss. I was as good as I was bad the horrible day Marvin and I lost to the engineers. . . .

---

*Helen is dean of the White House press corps. I respect her professionally, and like her personally but I don't miss her yelling at me during events.

†We had a biannual horseshoe tournament at the White House that included teams from the household staff, the medical unit, the uniform division of the Secret Service, groundskeepers, *Marine I* and *Air Force I* staffs, and of course my team—Marvin and me.

‡Ron Jones, Buddy Carter, and George Haney, all members of the residence staff.

Democratic Congressman Dante Fascell of Florida, chairman of the House Foreign Affairs Committee, wrote me a supportive note about Neil and the testimony he gave on the Hill about his involvement with Silverado:

July 12, 1990

Dear Dante,

I can't begin to tell you how much your comment to me about our son meant to me.

I have a Dad's understandable instinct of wanting to defend his son. I believe in my boy's integrity and in his honor. I feel that in staying out of the fray I am letting down my kid who is very very close to me. I see him twisting and I see him worried that he is hurting me—and, yet, I know I must stay out of it in every way except to say "I believe in my son"—

This, too, will pass, but what will remain is that a kind friend, sensing the concern of a proud father, held out his hand of comfort. That really counts.

Your friend,

George

————

July 24th

If I didn't have this budget deficit problem hanging over my head, I would be loving this job . . .

————

On July 26, I signed the Americans with Disabilities Act, which was really the world's first comprehensive declaration of equality for people with disabilities. I wrote this note to Mike Deland, head of the Council on Environmental Quality and a leader in the disabilities movement. Mike has never let his own disability diminish his outlook on life.

7-27-90

Friday—off to K'port
Michael Deland
Washington, D. C. 20005
Dear Mike,

Your note touched my heart. As I looked out at the audience yesterday, I was saying to myself "don't choke up"—hang in there. As I walked out saying "hi" to you—I felt the Bush tears (we do cry a lot) coming on—tears of gratitude for your example, for your cheerful way and for your being at my side.

Yes, yesterday was special for so many—including me—your friend—

George Bush

————————

August 2nd

6:00 a.m. I am in the Oval Office den. Brent came over at 5 confirming that Iraq had moved into Kuwait . . . they're trying to overthrow the Emir. Yesterday evening about 9 I met with Scowcroft and there were scattered reports that Iraq had moved. There is little the U.S. can do in a situation like this, but this morning at 5:00 I sign an Executive Order freezing the assets of Kuwait and Iraq. Worry being that the Kuwait puppet government set up by Iraq would try to move billions of dollars out of Western banks and out of U.S. banks illegally. The Kuwaiti Ambassador agreed with this move.

I'm moving the fleet up early from [the Indian Ocean]. Saudis are concerned, and my view, all the GCC* countries must be quaking in their boots. This is radical Saddam Hussein moving. . . .

————————

August 5th

It has been the most hectic 48 hours since I have been President . . . the enormity of Iraq is upon me now. I have been on the phone incessantly . . . the bottom line is that the West is together. Japan's Kaifu called me early Sunday morning to tell me that his Cabinet had acted on four major points. It boils down to cutting off everything economically with Iraq. . . .

On Saturday at Camp David we have a long briefing and we go over the military options—what can be done with augmented air power; what can be done and how long will it take to put the proper number of ground forces on the ground to repudiate any Iraqi attack.

————————

August 6th

One of the most traumatic days of my Presidency.

I went to see Lee Atwater and he looked terrible. He has the courage to fight on. Brain swelling tumor may be under control, but who knows. . . . I am convinced they think he has very, very short time to live. I am very, very worried about our friend who is fighting with such conviction.

Big day regarding Iran and Iraq. Dick Cheney goes to see [Saudi Arabia's] King Fahd and calls back. Fahd accepts [our offer] and

*Gulf Cooperation Council.

invites our troops to come. I give him the order on the telephone this afternoon to alert and send the 82nd Airborne and to do the same with two tactical fighter squadrons, and then we start in with much more massive dispatch of troops. All kinds of questions abound. Margaret Thatcher was sitting in the office when Cheney called. I confided in her and asked her to tell no one. . . .

I have lunch with Tom Foley. I tell Tom that I am going to have to go forward and get out from behind the rock.* I said the Democrats are laughing all the way to the bank. Ron Brown† is being outrageous and I am looking like a sucker criticized by my own people and criticized by the Democrats. Foley cautioned me against going public saying it would undermine my leadership in this important Iraq crisis. I told him I didn't think that was the case. He said Democrats and Republicans alike are giving me strong support on Iraq. I said, "I know, but they are also out carving me up in their various town meetings, selling out on taxes," etc. . . .

I feel tension in the stomach and the neck. I feel great pressure, but I also feel a certain calmness when we talk about these matters. I know I am doing the right thing. . . .

———

8/10/90

FROM THE PRESIDENT
TO: MARLIN FITZWATER
CNN uses a picture of me that is printed backwards (hair parted on right).
Can you get them to use another. It's the little one up in the right corner of the screen when my name is used.
(It's weird—weirder than I really am!)
Thanks.

———

August 17th
. . . Bob Gates calls me and said the speaker of the Iraq Parliament said they were going to "detain foreigners" . . . They would place them in various facilities— he mentioned near oil dumps or chemi-

---

*Up until this point I had tried hard not to criticize the Democrats on the budget negotiations. I truly wanted to work together in a bipartisan spirit. However, they were pounding me in the media, and I had had it.

†Chairman of the Democratic National Committee. He was secretary of commerce under Clinton until his tragic death in a plane crash while visiting Bosnia.

cal plants—whatever. Clearly putting them there so [the buildings] could not be bombed. Blatant hostage holding. Another blatant disregard of international law by a cruel and ruthless dictator. I cannot tolerate, nor will I, another Tehran. I am determined in that. It may cost American lives, but we cannot sacrifice American principle and American leadership. . . .

––––––––––

On September 12, I addressed the people of Iraq—or at least we tried to pipe my translated remarks into the country using the Voice of America and other venues. I jotted down these notes on September 6, getting ready for the speech:

Some scribblings on my speech to Iraq
American people have no argument with the people or indeed Gov't officials. Our argument is with one man S. Hussein.
Your beloved country violated International Law
S.H. took over a neighboring country.
An Arab country
A country that is a member of UN
This causes world outcry
Iraq was condemned by UN
Iraq's strongest friends condemned its aggression.
Arab Countries condemned Iraq
SH is trying to make this Iraq vs US
Regrettably to the people of Iraq I tell you it is not Iraq vs. U.S. It is Iraq vs the entire United Nations.
Iraq hospitably is well known, but when your President holds thousands of innocent people, you are fundamentally violating Intl. Law. It is sad and sorrowful. You the people of Iraq are decent kind people but your country has now been condemned by the entire world.
Policies will not be changed by barbarian tactics.

––––––––––

September 7th
I do have a confident feeling here—maybe it's the support from the American people—maybe it's the fact that I have been intimately involved in the personal diplomacy with the leaders. Certainly it is the trust that I have in Brent Scowcroft, and Jim Baker, and Dick Cheney and Colin Powell and all our team that are intimately involved in this very dicey problem. . . .
Got a call at 7:30 this morning from Margaret Thatcher. She's

staunch and strong and stays in there and worries that there will be an erosion on force. She does not want to go back to the UN on use of force; nor do I. She does not want to compromise on the Kuwait government; nor do I.*

In essence, she has not "gone wobbly" as she cautioned me a couple of a weeks ago . . . I love that expression.

The importance of the United States leadership is brought home to me clearly. It's only the United States that can lead. All countries in the West clearly have to turn to us. But it is my theory that the more they are included on the take-off, the more we get their opinion, the more we reach out no matter what is involved, in terms of time involved, the better it is. Everyone is proud. Everyone has his place in the sun—large country or small, they should be consulted, their opinions considered. Then when the United States make a move and I make a decision, we are more apt to have solid support. . . .

Saddam Hussein declared that I was a criminal and should stand trial in Iraq. The charges against me were (1) sending American troops to the Gulf region and occupying Moslem shrines; (2) threatening to attack Iraq; (3) imposing economic measures against Iraq; (4) issuing orders to the CIA to conspire against Saddam. I sent this tongue-in-cheek note to my friend and head of the White House Counsel's Office, Boyden Gray:

9-9-90

FROM THE PRESIDENT
TO: Boyden Gray

Please get a visa and be ready to go to Baghdad to defend me on these 4 charges.

I can beat the third 'rap' by citing the UN.

The same would apply to sending troops but be sure you are ready to present my case on the "Shrines". I am innocent.

They can never make rap #4 stick.

I am not worried, but please call me after the first day of the tribunal.

Should they not permit you to leave, wire home; and we will have someone temporarily hold down your job here.

Many thanks.

---

*Saddam Hussein was calling for "elections" in Kuwait. His plan, of course, was to install a puppet government.

9-14-90

Boyden—

Get going. Time is running out! We must beat the rap. May Camels not violate your Mercedes!!

GB

———————

September 25th

Budget is getting down to the crunch.* . . . Republicans are nervous about it—everybody is nervous about it. But we simply have got to get a deal. We are being accused of being too rigid. But we've given on taxes, generally. And now, we've worked out a compromise on capital gains so it is not called capital gains but there is some incentive for growth. I make a strong, personal appeal to Rostenkowski, saying, "Look we've got to get this thing put to bed, now let's go." But they haven't done their part on spending cuts either. They damn sure haven't got what we want on budget reform. Tough go round. Tough, tough, tough.

But now we are getting into enormous game of who blinks first?

My problem is I don't know whether our Republicans will stay with me. Some of them want to paint their asses white and run with the antelope, as Lyndon Johnson said. They want to do it right now. Isn't that a marvelous image? From a very tired George Bush.

———————

October 6th

I think this week has been the most unpleasant, or tension filled of the Presidency. More so than when we're together going into Panama, or when we're together moving on Iraq. Here we are divided. There's name calling, and accusations—and I don't like it. There's a story in one of the papers saying that I am more comfortable with foreign affairs, and that is absolutely true. Because I don't like the deficiencies of the domestic, political scene. I hate the posturing on both sides . . . [people] putting their own selves ahead of the overall good.

. . . It's the damnedest pounding I've ever seen, but I will just have to hang in there and do my best. I feel a little more tranquil than I

———

*The federal fiscal year ends September 30. Without a new budget, we would be forced to shut down all nonessential federal offices on October 1, which we did end up doing for a few days.

thought I would feel—a little more relaxed. It's tough when you don't control the Congress. . . .

If you want a friend in Washington, get a dog, and I sure have a good one.

_____

We did get a budget deal, one that included a tax increase but also accomplished my number one goal of getting spending under control. On October 5, the House voted it down.

October 15, 1990

The Honorable Jim Lightfoot
U.S. House of Representatives
Washington, D. C. 20515
Dear Jim,

I am off to do what you suggested I do. Take my case out across the country—5 states (including yours*) in 2 days. My case will be Congress must act now. I respectfully suggest I am not in the Beltway Mentality, as you call it. The pundits and the critics love all this battling—they love it best when Republicans FIGHT A Republican President . . . The real news—man bites dog—is when the leaders in the President's party stand against the President.† I understand this. It is essential we get a good budget deal. It will not be as good a budget deal as I want or as good as what we have proposed; but it is essential that we get a deal. . . . One sees today the pounding I am taking and the White House is taking, but I will not take the advice now being given by many who wish us ill—namely that I attack other Republicans. Candidly, I have resented some of the attacks on the White House by some Republicans; but I learned long ago this goes with the territory.

I will now head off to "get on with the business of making Congress responsive to the American People."

Thanks, old friend. I trust you will treat this letter as a confidential personal letter from one who respects you and values your friendship.

All Best,
George

_____

*Jim was a Republican congressman from Iowa.

†This is in reference to Newt Gingrich, who led us to believe he would support the budget deal, then revolted against us in the eleventh hour and convinced other Republicans to join him in voting against it.

I wrote this letter to Kathleen Darman. Dick was getting pounded by the press and by Congress, and I thought she might need a little moral support.

10-17-90

It's 10AM Do you know where your Congress is?

Dear Kath,

I'm back from a 2 day 5 state swing—and oh how true it is that happiness is being outside the Beltway. Anyway, as I was 'roughing it' on AF-I last night (Grand Rapids to D. C.) I got to thinking that inspite of the flak, I'm a very lucky guy.

That brings me to one Dick Darman—and that brings me to you, because I know you've been hurt by some unkind, unfair arrows aimed at Dick's back.

First—Dick has done a superb job on the budget. He came up with a deal, after months of labor, that would have been good for our country. He negotiated superbly—When you're out gunned you better have more brainpower and ingenuity than the opposition—and with Dick, Nick [Brady], John [Sununu] we sure did.

Washington loves to kick people. The press thrives on <u>blame</u> or on who's up, who's down!!

The politicians want to be sure they emerge blameless, unscathed, untouched by compromises. But Dick and the others were trying to do something for our country & to help me <u>govern</u>—to make something happen. And the reward?—a few crappy little barbs from "friends" and opponents.

OK, why this note?

1. I don't like friends and family to get bruised

2. My confidence in and my respect for Dick is higher than ever. You see he simply knows more about this than anyone else, and he has always kept my interest in the forefront.

So don't let the bastards get you down. The CW song says it best: "If we're gonna see a rainbow we'll have to stand a little rain".

You're a caring loving person and Barbara & I don't like it when you feel the pain that too often goes with public service.

Dick Darman is A 1!! So there!!

Con Afecto—
George Bush

———

October 17th

. . . Had dinner with Brent Scowcroft. Talked about how we get things off center in the Middle East. I feel that these two problems, the budget deficit and the Middle East are large—overwhelming in a sense—and yet I feel I can handle it. Because I go back to "do your best." Nobody is particularly happy with me. Our support is eroding in the Middle East, and the budget is a loser. But some way I have got to convey to the American people that I will try my hardest, and doing my best. Don't want a terrible deal to take place, but don't want to be off in some ideological corner falling on my sword and keeping the country from moving forward.

I think this is the biggest challenge of my life—by far.

[We eventually did get a budget deal, and although it was not as good as our original one, it was a major step in the direction of getting our deficit under control. Through a combination of tax increases and spending cuts, it slashed the accumulated deficit by $500 billion over five years. We also set strict limits on discretionary spending. I will confess to feeling a little vindicated in 1998 when the federal budget deficit was finally erased and a number of economists, journalists, and government officials cited "Bush's 1990 budget compromise" as the beginning of the end of our deficit problem.]

We were disappointed and surprised that an old friend and ally, King Hussein of Jordan, was not supporting the international coalition that was forming against Iraq. I wrote him this letter from my heart:

10-20-90

His Majesty Hussein I
King of the Hashemite Kingdom of Jordan
Amman
Your Majesty:

One of the most agonizing by-products of this terrible situation in the Gulf has been the strains now placed on the relationship between Jordan and the U. S. I hope I need not tell you that I have always tried to demonstrate the respect I feel for your country, your countrymen and especially for you personally.

As you know, in spite of these strains and difficulties, all caused by Saddam Hussein's brutal aggression against Kuwait, we have been trying to encourage economic support for Jordan. We have been doing this in spite of some concerns that I would now like to call to your personal attention.

The Conference in Amman hurt—so many known terrorists convening to blast the U.S. joined, I hate to say, by some of your own officials. I tried to understand the pressures that you and the government are under from the more radical left; but you must know that blatant attacks on my country, attacks that assign to us outlandish motives, only make things very difficult. Had a Cabinet member in my government attacked Jordan the way your Prime Minister attacked us, he would have been dismissed. I refer to his public remarks on our motivations in putting forces into Saudi Arabia.

I am determined to keep relations from totally disintegrating. I say this as one who wants our friendship to be strong and intact when all this ends. Thus may I comment on your recent interview with the <u>New York Times.</u> I make the following comments based on the premise that if I don't level with you and you don't level with me it will be more difficult for both countries.

In your recent interview with the <u>New York Times,</u> Your Majesty, it is simply incorrect that the United States decided to send, let alone dispatched, troops to Saudi Arabia before receiving a request from King Fahd. Our only motivation was to deter Iraq and, if necessary, defend a friend; we went when asked and we will leave the same way. It is also deeply troubling to read that an old and close friend "honestly can't tell" if Iraq's invasion was justified, when the entire world is united in condemning this action.

I was also troubled by your apparent acceptance of Saddam the Invader's claim that Saudi Arabia was not threatened by him. The irrefutable evidence, which I thought we had presented to you, shows that the very day he announced he was moving his forces out of Kuwait, vast Iraqi armor was heading south toward the Saudi border.

Now, let me tell you what concerns me a lot. In that entire interview there was no mention of concern about the brutal treatment of the people of Kuwait, and no mention about Saddam Hussein's barbaric policy of detaining innocent foreigners—holding them as hostages and staking them out near plants and installations so as to avoid retaliation for his brutality. The reports coming out of Kuwait are horrible.

I know how you personally feel about young people—surely you must be shocked and offended by the documented reports of rape, of shooting children for passing out leaflets (and making their parents watch), of the systematic dismantling of Kuwait from the hospitals to the factories and stores. It is tragic. It is indeed reminiscent of how Hitler behaved in Poland before the rest of the world came to its senses and stood up against him. As I write this I know you, too, care deeply about these atrocities.

Having written the above right from the heart, I simply want to add that I hate it that you and Jordan are in this very difficult situation. I would be no friend at all if I didn't understand the enormous problems all of this has inflicted upon your wonderful country.

The other day I saw a picture of you and some of your associates receiving yet another delegation. I recognized several of your associates. All of them friends, all of them not historically opposed to the U. S. All of them having worked with us in difficult situations before. I still remain hopeful that it will be that way in the future.

I have a personal feeling that perhaps you don't like it when those wild demonstrators in Baghdad and regrettably Amman attack me in very personal terms.

I know you have tried hard to find peace through dialogue; but the longer this matter goes on, the more I am convinced that there can be no compromise that stops short of the United Nations' demands and universal condemnation.

I have warned Saddam Hussein that any terrorist act against us or our allies will be his responsibility. Further containment and continued brutality against "hostages" (he still refers to them as "guests") will hasten the day of other than a peaceful settlement.

This letter is being conveyed to you in this special channel. I did not want it ricocheting around the corridors at State or anywhere else. It comes from a man who is your friend. It comes from a heart ladened with grief and sadness; but it also comes from one who is determined to see the total failure of Saddam's unwarranted aggression.

Barbara enjoyed her visit with Queen Noor and Brent Scowcroft filled me in on every nuance of your distinguished brother's recent visit. I ask you to convey my respects to him.

I pray we will find a way out of this terrible situation; but the longer I think about this it can only come from Saddam Hussein's turning 180 degrees and his trying to undo the horrible offense he has committed against the rule of law.

My sincere best wishes to you and your family.

With respect,

Sincerely,
George Bush

[As soon as the war ended, we repaired our friendship, and we began to assist Jordan in every way possible. I felt the loss of a true friend when King Hussein died in 1999 and was glad to be given the opportunity to attend his funeral.]

Another brewing controversy was the pending civil rights legislation. I desperately wanted to sign a civil rights bill but refused to sign one that included quotas. I do not believe in quotas and feel they do more harm than good. But despite my pleas, Congress passed a quotalike bill, and I promptly vetoed it. My position created a difficult situation for the African-Americans serving in my administration. I wrote Fred McClure, who headed up the legislative affairs office:

10-20-90

Dear Fred,

You & I have not discussed the Civil Rights Bill. Let me just say I am certain this has not been easy for you. I can guarantee you it's a tough one for me; but I have been thinking about you and Lou Sullivan, Connie & Art.* I hate to see friends troubled and hurt—

Fred, you are doing an outstanding job, and I hate to see your life complicated by something of this nature, as I assume it is.

Hang in—

Warm regards,
GB

_____

Democratic congressman John Lewis wrote me a passionate letter asking me to sign the bill.

10-22-90

The Honorable John Lewis
U.S. House of Representatives
Washington, D. C. 20515
Dear John,

I was moved by your letter—written from the heart. I do understand how strongly you feel. I have said all along I want to sign a bill. If the current bill fails to override [my veto] I hope you will take a look at the bill I've sent up there. It accomplishes many if not all of the same things you advocate. And it does guarantee against the possibilities that quotas might be resorted to.

John, I hate it when, in this country, we cannot disagree without challenging the other person's motives. I've tried to have a good civil rights record because I believe we should "stand up for what's right". I shall continue to do so.

Sincerely with best
Wishes—
George Bush

_____

The tabloid newspaper National Examiner *came out with the shocking news that Saddam Hussein, Queen Elizabeth, and I were all blood relatives. I moved quickly to reassure the team:*

*Lou was secretary of Health and Human Services; Connie Newman, director of the Office of Personnel Management; and my old friend Art Fletcher, chairman of the U.S. Civil Rights Commission.

10-25-90

FROM THE PRESIDENT
TO: The Vice President
               SecState
               Sec Def
               NSC Adviser
               Chief of Staff
               Director of Central Intelligence.
   Disclaimer—
No decisions I make will be affected by relationship with Saddam Hussein.
The Queen and I would have it no other way.

George Bush

———

John Sununu received a letter from an American soldier in Saudi Arabia complaining that whenever he saw me on television, my tie was askew. I sent him a presidential tie clip and promised to do better.

11-1-90

Mr. Bill Winter
FPO San Francisco, CA
Dear Bill—
   The Chief of Staff gave me your letter. I will remember to straighten my tie. I will use this kind of tie clip.
   Now—all best wishes to you and the Seabees.
   We will not fail in our moral mission. There can be no compromise with Saddam's aggression.

Good luck—
George Bush

———

November 16th
   On Thursday, I signed the Clean Air Act. Lot of Congressmen there. What got me was the emotion of it. You could sense in the East Room a strong emotional commitment to this legislation. In fact, it was somewhat overwhelming. After I walked out, it was genuine expression of appreciation and thanks from many, many people, including George Mitchell and a lot of people from the business community and the environmental community. It took me by surprise and I realize more fully now how important this legislation was. . . .

On November 16 we left for Paris to attend the Conference on Security and Cooperation in Europe—which included the heads of state of all European countries—where we signed a historic arms control agreement greatly reducing NATO and Warsaw Pact troops in Europe. However, the first stop was Prague.

November 19th

We've been to Czechoslovakia in a very moving and historic visit—the first visit of an American President to Czechoslovakia and obviously the first since the Czechoslovakian revolution. I spoke in Wenceslas Square, one year after the Communists went out. Estimate was 750,000 people. It was wall to wall. I regretted we had to be in a Plexiglas cocoon—dictated by the security people. But even that did not detract from the moment . . .

I felt a sense of awe standing with [President] Vaclev Havel . . . Havel is a very modest, close to shy man. Unpretentious to the T. He took great pleasure in introducing me to his playwright and his artistic friends. This man was in jail a year ago. This man was beaten and driven to his knees but refused to give up.

. . . We can never take our democracy for granted.

November 20th

I am feeling out of shape, overeating, clothes tight, not enough exercise and tired—not a good position from which to make tough decisions.

Our speech [at the CSCE conference] was the shortest yesterday except for Jacques Delors.*

We were supposed to speak for fifteen minutes, total. I was eight minutes. Said as much as the others and set an example. . . . The smaller the country, the longer the speeches—that's the old UN adage. . . .

Had dinner with Gorbachev. . . .

It was a warm friendly conversation in the den, just Brent and one other, his man as an observer, and two interpreters. He still is charismatic and everyone at the Embassy wanted to meet him.

At dinner, we were totally relaxed, and we told jokes.† They told

---

*Head of the European Community.

†We had started telling each other jokes at Camp David, but to avoid a R rating on the book I can't share them. Joke-telling is a great icebreaker and I really think it helped our friendship.

stories about Stalin, all of them having seen him when they were younger. Stalin had gone down on a vacation and he asked for somebody to come have a drink with him. His Minister came, drank about a half bottle of vodka, Stalin drinking wine. Stalin offered him more vodka and he said "No, I know my limit." Later on they sent a team to Stalin with a list to be chosen for some [high position.] This man was on the bottom. They told him he was the least distinguished, and Stalin chose him, saying "I chose this man cause he knows he knows his limits." An interesting story. . . .

We then flew to Saudi Arabia to have Thanksgiving Day with our troops.

November 22nd

There is no way to adequately describe the moving time in the desert. We went first to greet the Air Force, then up to an Army base in the sand,* then over by chopper to the USS *Nassau* in international waters where we had a nice prayer service for Thanksgiving on the deck: and finishing with the first Marines back in the desert.

. . . The kids were fantastic; it was an emotional day. I wasn't sure I could get through the speeches, and I did choke up in the hangar, on the flight deck of *Nassau* at the Church service. The kids look so young and yet they are gung-ho. I had a long briefing on AF-I with Schwarzkopf,† and I am convinced more than ever that we can knock Saddam Hussein out early. I'm worried that the American people might think this will be another Vietnam and it isn't and it won't be.

November 22, 1990

Fahd bin Abd al-Aziz Al Saud
Custodian of the Two Holy Mosques
King of the Kingdom of Saudi Arabia
Your Majesty,

We are 30 minutes out of Dhahran, heading for Cairo. But before any of the vivid memories that are now in my head and heart diminish, I want to send you this note of thanks.

First, thank you for the lovely evening at the Palace in Jeddah. The dinner

---

*The Air Force visit was to a military airlift-command base in Dhahran; the Army base was miles and miles into the desert.

†General Norman Schwarzkopf was in charge of the allied troops.

was special, the hospitality superb, and I found our conversations to be extraordinarily useful and encouraging. I am proud that we are standing shoulder against Iraq's evil dictator, Saddam Hussein.

My Thanksgiving today with our troops in the desert was very moving and very encouraging. Our troops are motivated and ready to do whatever is required. I hope this, plus the additional troops we are sending to the Kingdom, convince Saddam Hussein to give up, but personally I am inclined to doubt that.

In any event, General Schwarzkopf tells me of the superb cooperation he is receiving from your various officials, and I want to thank you for that, too.

Will you please convey my thanks and my respects to Crown Prince Abdallah, a man of strength whom I consider a friend.

To you, Your Majesty, my additional thanks for that beautiful present you gave me. The camels with the flags flying symbolize, for me, the United States of America and Saudi Arabia standing together.

My respects to you, Sir. Barbara joins me in thanking you from the bottom of our grateful hearts for a wonderful, but all too brief, visit.

> Respectfully yours,
> George Bush

[Before returning home, we visited Mubarak in Cairo and then had an unprecedented meeting with President Haffez al-Assad of Syria in Geneva. We had never been close, but on the issue of Saddam Hussein, we stood together.]

11-25-90 (at Camp David)

To: Brent
Subject: Questions re: Gulf Crisis
1. Exact Status of Iraqi Nuclear Capability
2. Best estimate now from Cheney and Powell as to how long it will take, once all forces there, to conquer Saddam.
3. The Embassy in Kuwait.
   How to relieve it
   How to call its plight to US public opinion.
4. How the scenario plays out in detail after UN Resolution*
   What do we ask Congress to do if anything
   When go to Congress if we decide to do that.

*We were asking the U.N. Security Council to pass a resolution approving the use of force to get Saddam Hussein out of Kuwait. On November 29, with Jim Baker chairing the meeting, the council approved the resolution by a vote of 12–2—Cuba and Yemen voting against; China abstaining. The resolution gave Hussein a deadline of January 15.

5. Getting the final word to Saddam.
   Visit for General Scowcroft, other emissary . . .
6. Yemen—be careful on promising them AID
7. When and How to assure people This Is No Viet Nam very important.
8. If force is decided upon—
   How notify innocents inside Iraq
   How notify partners in Gulf
   How notify Congress
9. A better 'public diplomacy' program.

———————

November 29th
    I've spent an hour writing out some comments for tomorrow when we are going to announce that I would see Aziz* here and then I'll send Jim Baker to Baghdad to see Saddam Hussein. This will be big news. There is some danger that the coalition will think we're going "wobbly," as Margaret would say, but we can do whatever diplomacy is required to see that that doesn't happen. It will be the last extra step for peace. . . .

———————

I believed strongly that the Constitution gave me the authority to send our troops into battle without Congress officially declaring war. However, I wanted to cover all the bases:

December 5, 1990

MEMORANDUM FOR BOYDEN GRAY
THROUGH: BRENT SCOWCROFT
FROM: THE PRESIDENT
Boyden—
Please prepare for me a short analysis of the War Powers Resolution. . . . Without recognizing the constitutional validity of the War Powers Resolution, is there a way for the President to fulfill <u>all</u> his responsibilities to Congress by saying, a few days before any fighting was to begin, "hostilities are imminent—period!!
I am several thousand miles south,† but these questions stay on my mind:

———

*Iraqi foreign minister Tariq Aziz.
†Shortly after getting back from the Middle East, I visited Mexico, then went to South America. The timing was terrible, but when I became president, I had promised not to neglect our southern neighbors and the trip had already been postponed once.

1. How do we fully involve Congress?
2. If we have to attack from a cold start how does the latest UN
Resolution impact on congress?
   1. Is there something short of "declaring" war that satisfies Congress yet
      doesn't risk tying the President's hands?
   2. As the clock on the UN resolution keeps running toward the time when
      force has international authority, what possible official requests
      can/should a President make of Congress?

If you reply to this memorandum before I return, please hand carry your reply to Brent for "Eyes Only" transmission to me.

Please share a copy of this memorandum with John Sununu and Brent only.

Warm regards.

———

Dec. 11, 1990

Mr. Dan Jenkins
Ponte Vedra Beach, FL 32082
Dear Dan,

Your letter came in just in time. Dan Rather or some other expert on the Gulf had just taken a pot shot, and two soldiers had been found out in the desert who wanted to go home—surprise. Anyway I was sitting here, po'd at the world, not because of the Gulf but because I've had the gut flu, over-working every orifice. In fact I almost ricocheted some food off of Nurse Major Mary Jackson—she moved a bit slowly. Good sport though, Mary—Anyway your letter came in. I promptly had it copied and sent over to Powell and Cheney. I agree with you on the job they did in those hearings.* In fact I saw only bits of their testimony, but I cabled them from Uruguay. (incidentally the South American trip went well. Overshadowed by the Gulf Crisis it was, but really it was terrific. Very few hand gestures, no serious demonstrations. There was one small demo in one country. The President apologized; and I said 'this is a cake walk—Come with me whenever I visit San Francisco.")

I've all but given up Golf except for hitting at Camp David. . . . I just don't want to risk sending the wrong signal right now to the troops. I even had to cancel my Beeville quail shooting. First time I will have missed in 25 years. I love it, but now I will stay here or at [Camp David]—no hardship however.

*They had testified on the Hill about the situation in the Gulf and had indeed done an outstanding job.

Thanks, Dan, for your great letter. When Saddam gets his out of Kuwait please get yours back on up here . . .

I accept my copy of YOU GOTTA PLAY HURT—I won't run it by the ethics office, not because it exceeds the cash limit,* but if it's like semi tough the ladies over there may wear it out before I get the copy back over here.

Thanks, Dan. Hope you have a great Christmas. We will, cause even though the economy is batting .199 and the Gulf is hitting .178, life is treating the Bush family with a WILLIAMS like .401. Thank God for kids and Bar and two dogs and 14 grandkids† and the great people around here with whom I work—for Friends too. Hang in.

George Bush

Dec. 13, 1990

THE FOLLOWING IS THE TEXT OF A LETTER FROM PRESIDENT BUSH FOR THE AMIR OF KUWAIT. PLEASE DELIVER ASAP TO HIS HIGHNESS SHEIKH JABIR AL-AHMAD AL-SABAH, AMIR OF THE STATE OF KUWAIT.

Your Highness: Now that I am back from my visit to South America, I just want to take a moment to give you my sense of where we stand in the Gulf. I am pleased that all American citizens in Kuwait and Iraq wanting to leave are so doing.‡ You know we had kept our Embassy open in Kuwait to administer to our people there. We decided to withdraw our remaining diplomatic staff from Kuwait while leaving the Embassy itself open since with the American community gone, there is no official business for us to conduct there until your government is restored. Your Highness, let me reassure you that for our part, the hostage release has changed nothing and done nothing to diminish either our opposition to negotiation or our determination to see all the relevant security council resolutions implemented in all their parts.

On our upcoming talks with Iraq, we still have not resolved the dates for Tariq Aziz's visit here and Jim Baker's there. It is obvious that Saddam's desire to put off the Baghdad meeting until January twelfth is only the latest example of his desire to manipulate diplomacy to weaken the coalition against him and to make the potential use of force more distant and hence less likely. We will continue to resist this and other such attempts, just as we will resist attempts to link Iraqi aggression against Kuwait with other issues, like the Palestinian issue.

---

*Government officials cannot accept gifts valued at more than $100.

†I must have been psychic. We had only twelve grandchildren then; we have fourteen now.

‡Hussein had decided to let the foreign "guests" leave Kuwait and Iraq.

Your Highness, I want to personally underscore to you that our talks will include no compromises, nor partial solutions, no deals and no face-saving gimmicks. We also are stressing to other governments that intend to communicate with Iraqi officials over the coming weeks the need to reinforce this. Saddam must understand that the choice to comply with the UN resolutions is his, or he will risk the consequences of his inaction. I believe we are all in for a great deal of testing of this sort between now and the middle of January as Saddam and his officials will try to do everything to split the coalition and enhance their public posture. Needless to say, we just continue to hold firm and hold together. This is not the time for compromises or for suggestions, public or private, of what Iraq might expect should it withdraw from Kuwait. I know that we can count on you and your Government to stand with us until we succeed in realizing all our objectives without condition or concession. I will stay in close touch with you on my thinking as we proceed, and as always, I would value hearing from you at any time.

With my warm regards

Sincerely,
George Bush.

––––––––––

12-14-90

FROM THE PRESIDENT
TO: Brent/Bob Gates
    1. Pan AM 103—reminder:
       I'd like to get something on this a.s.a.p.—also need to get it to Assad whenever we can.*
    2. Bob—we owe Mrs. Noriega an answer on her request for a visit—conjugal or otherwise.

GB

[I believe the answer to Mrs. Noriega was yes.]

––––––––––

I managed to get on Dan Rostenkowski's bad side again, this time by calling for term limits, which he took personally.

––––––––––

*I had discussed Pan Am 103 with Assad during our meeting and suggested he could be helpful in bringing the perpetrators to justice.

December 21, 1990

The Honorable Dan Rostenkowski
House of Representatives
Washington, D. C. 20515

Dear Rosty

Hey, nothing's gone wrong. You look at limitations one way, I look at it another. The President has a term limitation and the Republic hasn't screeched to a halt.

Our national platform calls for some type of limitation, so this is not something brand-spanking-new with us.

In your case, yes, you're like that old wine you talk about—better with age; but let's face it, some old wines get corked.

I can't believe the term limitation issue is, as you say, "partisan". Look at the votes in the various states.

In any event, this issue is not going to divide you and me. Go on out to the 8th* and get some rest so we can slay some dragons in the months ahead.

Oh, yes, real friendships survive these little bumps in the road.

Your <u>friend,</u>
George

———————

Democratic senator Robert Byrd of West Virginia wrote me a letter urging me to get congressional approval before going into battle and urging me to give sanctions longer to work.

Dec. 22, 1990

Dear Robert,

My typing is better than my handwriting so here goes. I simply wanted to thank you for that thoughtful letter re: the Gulf and what to do about it.

I differ with you on a couple of counts. I don't think we have six months to wait. The economies of Eastern Europe and the Third World and, indeed, our own are being devastated by what Saddam has wrought. The U.N. Resolution must be fully complied with or else the new promise of the U.N. that we helped bring about will be ground into dust. Kuwait is still being brutalized. That Amnesty Int'l report is devastating. I want Congress on board—fully.

Saddam will only unconditionally pull out when he is convinced on two points about which he now has doubts:

1. That the united world will use force against him. And
2. That if that force is used he will lose.

*His congressional district in Chicago.

I had not intended to do other here than to say thanks. And, yes, Merry Christmas to you and your family. It is a time, especially this year, to give thanks for our many blessings and to pray for peace on earth.

Most Sincerely,
George

December 24th

Up at Camp David with the family. It's funny—I tossed around last night, and I had a very interesting dream about Dad. We were driving into some hotel near a golf course, and there was another golf course way over across the fence, though not a very good one. I heard Dad was there, so I went to see him, and he was in a hotel room. We embraced, and I told him I missed him very much. Aren't dreams funny? I could see him very clearly: big, strong, and highly respected. . . .

I make the call to Norm Schwarzkopf; try to get Max Thurmond;* call nine kids scattered around the world—enlisted people—several in Saudi Arabia, Alaska, Korea, Panama, and other places as well. They seemed kind of bewildered by the phone call, but nice, very friendly, all appreciative, and no gripes, though it would be pretty hard to do that. Colin Powell reinforced for me the morale of the troops is excellent.

It's Christmas Eve, and you think of the families and loved ones apart. I read ten or fifteen letters, all of them saying, "Take care of my kid." Some saying, "Please don't shoot." Some saying, "It's not worth dying for gasoline," and on and on it goes. But the cry is, "Save my boy—save my boy." Then I sit here knowing that if there is no movement on Saddam's part, we have to go to war.

But we're in a war—little Kuwaiti families being devastated and scared, and even killed this very night. The principle has been set, and we cannot fail. . . .

Dec 31, 1990

Dear George, Jeb, Neil, Marvin, Doro,

I am writing this letter on the last day of 1991.

First, I can't begin to tell you how great it was to have you here at Camp David. I loved the games (the Marines are still smarting over their 1 and 2

---

*Four-star-general Max Thurmond was the commander of the Panama forces. At this time he was dying of leukemia and I called him in the hospital.

record*), I loved Christmas Day, marred only by the absence of Sam and Ellie.† I loved the movies—some of 'em—I loved the laughs. Most of all, I loved seeing you together. We are a family blessed; and this Christmas simply reinforced all that.

I hope I didn't seem moody. I tried not to.

When I came into this job I vowed that I would never ring my hands and talk about "the loneliest job in the world" or ring my hands about the "pressures or the trials".

Having said that I <u>have</u> been concerned about what lies ahead. There is no 'loneliness' though because I am backed by a first rate team of knowledgeable and committed people. No President has been more blessed in this regards.

I have thought long and hard about what might have to be done. As I write this letter at Year's end, there is still some hope that Iraq's dictator will pull out of Kuwait. I vary on this. Sometimes I think he might, at others I think he simply is too unrealistic—too ignorant of what he might face. I have the peace of mind that comes from knowing that we have tried hard for peace. We have gone to the UN; we have formed an historic coalition; there have been diplomatic initiatives from country after country.

And so here we are a scant 16 days from a very important date—the date set by the UN for his total compliance with all UN resolutions including getting out of Kuwait—totally.

I guess what I want you to know as a father is this: Every Human life is precious. When the question is asked "How many lives are you willing to sacrifice"—it tears at my heart. The answer, of course, is none—none at all.

We have waited to give sanctions a chance, we have moved a tremendous force so as to reduce the risk to every American soldier if force has to be used; but the question of loss of life still lingers and plagues the heart.

My mind goes back to history:

How many lives might have been saved if appeasement had given way to force earlier on in the late '30's or earliest '40's? How many Jews might have been spared the gas chambers, or how many Polish patriots might be alive today? I look at today's crisis as "good" vs. "evil"— Yes, it is that clear.

I know my stance must cause you a little grief from time to time and this hurts me; but here at 'years-end' I just wanted you to know that I feel:

—every human life is precious— the little Iraqi kids' too.

—Principle must be adhered to—Saddam cannot profit in any way at all from his aggression and from his brutalizing the people of Kuwait.

---

*In wallyball, which is volleyball played in a racquetball court. The walls are "in play."

†They had spent Christmas with their father. Doro and Billy had divorced earlier in the year.

—and sometimes in life you have to act as you think best—you can't compromise, you can't give in—even if your critics are loud and numerous.

So, dear kids—batten down the hatches.

Senator Inouye of Hawaii told me "Mr. President, do what you have to do. If it is quick and successful everyone can take the credit. If it is drawn out, then be prepared for some in Congress to file impeachment papers against you"—that's what he said, and he's 100% correct.

And so I shall say a few more prayers, mainly for our kids in the Gulf. And I shall do what must be done, and I shall be strengthened every day by our family love which lifts me up; every single day of my life.

I am the luckiest Dad in the whole wide world.

I love you, Happy New Year and May God Bless every one of you and all those in your family.

> Devotedly,
> Dad

CHAPTER 14

Peaks and Valleys

January 5, 1991

His Excellency Saddam Hussein
President of the Republic of Iraq
Baghdad
Mr. President:

   We stand at the brink of war between Iraq and the world. This is a war that began with your invasion of Kuwait; this is a war that can be ended only by Iraq's full and unconditional compliance with UN Security Council Resolution 678.

   I am writing you now, directly, because what is at stake demands that no opportunity be lost to avoid what would be a certain calamity for the people of Iraq. I am writing, as well, because it is said by some that you do not understand just how isolated Iraq is and what Iraq faces as a result. I am not in a position to judge whether this impression is correct; what I can do, though, is try in this letter to reinforce what Secretary of State Baker told your Foreign Minister and eliminate any uncertainty or ambiguity that might exist in your mind about where we stand and what we are prepared to do.

   The international community is united in its call for Iraq to leave all of Kuwait without condition and without further delay. This is not simply the policy of the United States; it is the position of the world community as expressed in no less than twelve Security Council resolutions.

   We prefer a peaceful outcome. However, anything less than full compliance with UN Security Council Resolution 678 and its predecessors is unacceptable. There can be no reward for aggression. Nor will there be any negotiation. Principle cannot be compromised. However, by its full compliance, Iraq will gain the opportunity to rejoin the international community. More immediately, the Iraqi military establishment will escape destruction. But unless you withdraw from Kuwait completely and without condition, you will lose more than Kuwait. What is at issue here is not the future of Kuwait—it will be free, its government will be restored—but rather the future of Iraq. This choice is yours to make.

The United States will not be separated from its coalition partners. Twelve Security Council resolutions, 28 countries providing military units to enforce them, more than one hundred governments complying with sanctions—all highlight the fact that it is not Iraq against the United States, but Iraq against the world. That most Arab and Muslim countries are arrayed against you as well should reinforce what I am saying. Iraq cannot and will not be able to hold on to Kuwait or exact a price for leaving.

You may be tempted to find solace in the diversity of opinion that is American democracy. You should resist any such temptation. Diversity ought not to be confused with division. Nor should you underestimate, as others have before you, America's will.

Iraq is already feeling the effects of the sanctions mandated by the United Nations. Should war come, it will be a far greater tragedy for you and your country. Let me state, too, that the United States will not tolerate the use of chemical or biological weapons or the destruction of Kuwait's oil fields and installations. Further, you will be held directly responsible for terrorist actions against any member of the coalition. The American people would demand the strongest possible response. You and your country will pay a terrible price if you order unconscionable acts of this sort.

I write this letter not to threaten, but to inform. I do so with no sense of satisfaction, for the people of the United States have no quarrel with the people of Iraq. Mr. President, UN Security Council Resolution 678 establishes the period before January 15 of this year as a "pause of good will" so that this crisis may end without further violence. Whether this pause is used as intended, or merely becomes a prelude to further violence, is in your hands, and yours alone. I hope you weigh your choice carefully and choose wisely, for much will depend upon it.

George Bush

[Jim Baker hand-carried this letter to Geneva, where he and Aziz met on January 9. This meeting took the place of my suggestion that Jim go to Baghdad and Aziz come to Washington. The seven-hour meeting ended without an agreement, and Aziz, refusing to take the letter to Baghdad, left it on the table.]

January 6th

It's our anniversary date—46th anniversary. Not special, like 25th, 10th, 50th, but a wonderful, warm feeling. A feeling of great comfort. I think Bar and I take each other's love for granted. I guess I do that more than she does. I haven't really told her often enough how deeply I really feel. She is remarkable, and boy, does she ever stand by her man. . . .

A very supportive phone call from Billy Graham. He quotes from James Russell Lowell's poem, "The Present Crisis." "Once to every man and nation comes the moment to decide and the choice goes by forever twixt that darkness and that light." It does hit me pretty hard—That moment's upon us.

Prayer is important. . . . Billy Graham offers his help and talks about Saddam Hussein being the anti-Christ itself. This is the most momentous decision facing a President in modern times. [Billy] wants to speak out in any way he can, and that would indeed be helpful.

I sent this letter to the House and Senate leaders:

January 8, 1991

The Honorable Thomas S. Foley
Speaker of the House
Washington, D.C. 20515
Dear Mr. Speaker:

The current situation in the Persian Gulf, brought about by Iraq's unprovoked invasion and subsequent brutal occupation of Kuwait, threatens vital U.S. interests. The situation also threatens the peace. It would, however, greatly enhance the chance for peace if Congress were now to go on record supporting the position adopted by the UN Security Council on twelve separate occasions. Such an action would underline that the United States stands with the international community and on the side of law and decency; it also would help dispel any belief that may exist in the minds of Iraq's leaders that the United States lacks the necessary unity to act decisively in response to Iraq's continued aggression against Kuwait.

Secretary of State Baker is meeting with Iraq's Foreign Minister on January 9. It would have been most constructive if he could have presented the Iraqi government a Resolution passed by both houses of Congress supporting the UN position and in particular the Security Council Resolution 678. As you know, I have frequently stated my desire for such a Resolution. Nevertheless, there is still opportunity for Congress to act to strengthen the prospects for peace and safeguard this country's vital interests.

I therefore request that the House of Representatives and the Senate adopt a Resolution stating that Congress supports the use of all necessary means to implement UN Security Council Resolution 678. Such action would send the clearest possible message to Saddam Hussein that he must withdraw without condition or delay from Kuwait. Anything less would only encourage Iraqi intransigence; anything else would risk detracting from the international coalition arrayed against Iraq's aggression.

Mr. Speaker, I am determined to do whatever is necessary to protect America's security. I ask Congress to join with me in this task. I can think of no better way than for Congress to express its support for the President at this critical time. This truly is the last best chance for peace.

Sincerely,
George Bush

January 12th

Jim Baker points out that Fahd tells him we ought not to go on the 15th; wait for a couple of days, because Iraq would be at the highest state of alert on the 15th. I worry about the networks. Both CNN and NBC in the papers today say they're going to keep people in there after the 15th. I worry about the loss of innocent Iraqi life. I worry about the protection of the Soviets who are finishing their contracts. I worry most of all about our own kids that are going into battle.

Some of the debate has frightened the American people. Some of the editorial and commentaries are frightening the American people into believing this will be a long, drawn-out war. I'm still convinced it won't be, that we have made the proper preparations to guarantee that it will be short. I can at least say to myself when the trigger is pulled that I will have done everything possible to guarantee the life of every American kid over there. . . .

I go down from Camp David to make a press statement following the successful vote in the House and Senate.* . . . The debate was soul-

---

*They voted on January 12 to authorize the use of force. Although a number of Democrats supported us, I was disappointed that the entire Democratic leadership in both the House and Senate opposed the resolution. It is ironic that many of those who opposed use of force then are now among the strongest advocates of President Clinton's policy of using force in the Balkans.

searching. There was a lot of anguish out there. It went better than we thought. We had 53 votes in the Senate, and 250 odd in the House.

. . . The big burden, lifted from my shoulders, is this constitutional burden and the threat of impeachment. All of that cleared now by this very sound vote of the Congress.

———————

January 13th

. . . The debate has become simplified. You are for war, or you are against it. Who is for War? I am against it.

We meet Sunday night in the Residence. Once again, Colin Powell, Cheney, Sununu, Scowcroft, Gates, and Quayle. You could feel the difference. We are getting close. . . . The media are full of it— demonstrations, etc. The Church services, and the big news specials—are we ready for war? The battle plans all laid out . . . the flurry, and the crisis mentality. And I sit here with this decision ahead.

. . . We talk about power grids, electricity. We talk about bridges. We talk about refineries. We talk about letting our allies know certain things about overflight. We talk about getting rid of nuclear and biological weapons. How we notify our friends. How we put innocents on notice and how we safeguard American Embassies. About 1 hour and 10 minutes. Somber mood in the meeting room. . . .

It is my decision—my decision to send these kids into battle, my decision that may affect the lives of innocence. It is my decision to step back and let sanctions work. Or to move forward. And in my view, help establish the New World Order. It is my decision to stand, and take the heat, or fall back and wait and hope. It is my decision that affects husband, the girlfriend, or the wife that is waiting, or the mother that writes, "Take care of my son." And yet I know what I have to do this Sunday night. This man is evil, and let him win and we rise again to fight tomorrow. . . .

———————

January 15th

. . . There is no way to describe the pressure. It's 9:45 the night of the 15th. Deadline runs out in two hours, 15 minutes. The United Nations deadline. [The deadline] is already out in Baghdad. The reports from Baghdad are defiant. People marching in the streets. Their faces smile and they chant. And I think, "Oh God, save their lives." There's a kid that comes on television and I pray to God that [the bombs] will be accurate and we will not hit that child.

The Pope wires in and we read his cable . . . It is a beautiful, beautiful piece. Cardinal Law calls me, Bishop Browning calls me. . . . And of course, Billy Graham. Lafayette Square, in front of the White House, is full of candles and praying. I hope to God that they know we are praying.

———————

January 16th

I have never felt a day like this in my life. I am very tired. I didn't sleep well and this troubles me because I must go to the nation at 9 o'clock. My lower gut hurts, nothing like when I had the bleeding ulcer. But I am aware of it, and I take a couple of Mylantas.

People keep coming up, and saying, "God Bless you."

4:15—I come over to the house about twenty of four to lie down. Before I make my calls at 5, the old shoulders tighten up. My mind is a thousand miles away. I simply can't sleep. I think of what other Presidents went through. The agony of war. I think of our able pilots, their training, their gung-ho spirit. And also what it is they are being asked to do.

———————

We began bombing Baghdad at exactly 7 P.M. Operation Desert Storm was finally under way. Like most people in America, I watched it on CNN, with Barbara and Billy Graham.

. . . Well it is now 10:45 at night. I am about to go to bed. I did my speech to the nation at 9 o'clock. I didn't feel nervous about it at all. I wrote it myself. I knew what I wanted to say, and I said it. And I hope it resonates. Just before going to bed, Cheney calls. 56 Navy planes went out, 56 came back. Some two hundred Air Force planes out, and so far, no sign of any of them missing. They just haven't all checked back in yet.

———————

January 19th

Peter Arnett* has an interview with Saddam Hussein. Arnett of course has to echo line from Baghdad. . . . I think he's being used— he was particularly used when the Iraqis claimed we blew up that food plant. Now someone told me he showed damage and there was grass growing in the bomb crater, meaning it was done a long time

———————

*A CNN reporter who stayed in Baghdad.

ago. But he did not point that out. Indeed if he had, he wouldn't have gotten his interviews.

[Arnett's reporting continued to annoy me throughout the war. For example, we blew up a plant that our intelligence indicated was a factory for the manufacture of biological weapons. The next day, Arnett reported on CNN that it was a "baby milk" plant. That the sign outside the factory was in English should have tipped him off that the Iraqis' claim was suspicious. Also, although CNN occasionally did insert the word "censored" on the screen during Arnett's reports, I felt CNN should have done a better job of warning its viewers that everything that came out of Iraq was censored.]

January 21st

I must say I get tired of hearing the whining reporters saying that they are not getting enough information. I am sitting here watching ABC, and there have been some comments about that they are being "spoon fed" and then they are trying to show that we are in disarray in terms of bomb damage, or what our objectives are. Press, God Bless them, are a menace that we can't live with, and we can't live without.

January 22, 1991

His Eminence Bernard Cardinal Law
Brighton, Massachusetts 02135
Your Eminence, my friend,

I want to reply to your letter of January 16 because I have thought long and hard about the question, "War or no war?"

You say, "war is at best a lesser evil." But war started back on August 2. The Kuwaitis don't believe the war ever stopped. Wait until we hear the real story of the brutality to Kuwait.

Before ordering our troops into battle, I thought long and hard about casualties, or, as our severest critics would put it—"body bags." But as I pondered that horrible question, I also thought of unchecked aggression, of what would happen if the butcher of Baghdad could emerge the hero. What would that have meant for tomorrow?

Now he has launched his people-killing, city-busting Scuds against Israel.* The world sees more clearly now what this man is. And, I must confess my

---

*Saddam had launched SCUD missiles at Israel, hoping to draw them into the conflict, which would put the Arab members of the coalition in a difficult position. Anticipating such a move by Saddam, we had sent Israel Patriot defense missiles, which were helping. But I sent Larry Eagleburger to Israel as well to convince them not to retaliate. Prime Minister Shamir did not, which took a great deal of courage on his part, since it was an unpopular decision at home.

mind always went back to the questions: "What if Hitler's aggression had been checked earlier on? How many lives would have been saved? How many fewer Jews would have been exterminated? How many more Polish patriots would be alive today?"

You state that "recourse to war" could make Saddam a hero and a martyr. Yes, there may be such a risk, but the risk of having him prevail is far worse. He has been the bully in the neighborhood for a long time. He stepped back from that posture when he needed help from the Gulf States during the Iran-Iraq war, but everyone out there knows he is brutal, unforgiving, and determined to dominate the entire Gulf area. Obviously, Saddam tried to make the Palestine question the rallying cry, tried to use it to cover up his brutal takeover of Kuwait. The Aziz press conference in Geneva that followed Jim Baker's meeting with Aziz made this so clear that everyone in the world understood it.

I remain determined that he not link the Palestine question, which urgently needs a solution, to the rape of Kuwait. His recent reckless use of Scud city-busting missiles is a blatant attempt to rally all Arabs who hate Israel to draw them into the war. I am determined that he fail in this.

In conclusion, my friend, I must disagree with your conclusions that a quick war from a strategic standpoint would be a "major blunder," and that use of "lethal force which a quick military victory would demand could well render the judgment that the war was fought immorally." What you are telling me is that all war is wrong—morally, unforgivably wrong. I do not agree. This war started back in August. Saddam Hussein showed no signs at all of doing that which the whole world called on him to do. After exhausting all diplomatic initiatives, after the UN's call for withdrawal on a date certain, it is my view that to have done nothing would be the immoral path, for it would have condemned the UN's revitalized peacekeeping effort and it would have convinced our coalition that standing up against evil does not work.

As to the use of lethal force, we have been very careful in the planning of this liberation effort. I think you will agree that up until now, the performance of the Allied Air Forces has been magnificent in the accuracy of its attack and in achieving our goal of limiting casualties to innocent civilians.

Of course, war is hell, but I must conclude that you and I have an irreparable difference over this war. For me this is good versus evil. It is right versus wrong. It is the world versus Iraq's brutal dictator, with his cruelty, his international arrogance, his thumbing his nose at the rest of the world. I thought I was through being appalled by Saddam Hussein, but this recent "parading" of our POW pilots is the last straw.*

---

*Unfortunately several allied pilots had been shot down and were being held captive. Eventually, they all returned safely.

You have given me "frank and respectful counsel." I welcome that. I hope you are not offended, my friend, when I tell you that I clearly disagree with you. I respect enormously where you are coming from. I respect your view that every human life is precious, but I find myself in all of this opposed by some whom I respect the most, particularly in the clergy. I do not enjoy being on the opposite side of this from you, from Bishop Browning, and from many others I respect. I, too, have prayed over this matter. I pray that God will spare the loss of the innocent. I pray that this war will end soon. I pray that Kuwait will no longer have to suffer the brutal torture wreaked upon it by Saddam Hussein. And I pray that out of this turmoil there then will come a peace, not only to the Gulf, but eventually to the entire Middle East. The United States, its credibility restored by its leadership in the Gulf Crisis, can play a significant role in this.

I guess the bottom line is that I do feel that in certain situations, failing to use force is an immoral position, and in certain situations, using force is not immoral, not against God's will.

Thanks for your caring, your friendship, and your loving attention to me and my family.

Sincerely,
George Bush

As the nightly air raids continued over Baghdad, tension mounted in the Baltics, and we increasingly worried that Gorbachev might resort to force to keep the republics in the Soviet Union. Already on January 13, Soviet troops had opened fire and killed fourteen Lithuanians at a TV station in Vilnius.

1-23-91

His Excellency Mikhail Sergeyevich Gorbachev
President of the Union of Soviet Socialist Republics
Moscow
Dear Mikhail:

I am writing to you to express my deep concern about the recent turn of events in the Baltic states. I think that you know how much I value the unprecedented level of cooperation that we have achieved in U.S.-Soviet relations over the last two years. I have also said repeatedly that our successes have been due in large part to your efforts to reform the Soviet Union. As such, the response of my Administration to events in the Baltic states over the last year has been restrained. You, yourself, know that I have faced pressures from many quarters to take stronger measures and that I have resisted doing so.

Last June, during the Washington Summit, we talked about the effect of

Soviet actions in the Baltic states at great length. I explained that I appreciated the constraints under which you were operating but that I too faced certain pressures. Nonetheless, I honored your personal request and signed the Trade Agreement in spite of the economic blockade that the Soviet Union had imposed on Lithuania. You gave me assurances that you would take steps to settle peacefully all differences with the Baltic leaders. Several weeks later, you lifted that blockade and began a dialogue with Lithuanian and other Baltic leaders. From that time on, our cooperation in the economic sphere has expanded, culminating in the steps that I took on December 12 in response to the difficult circumstances that your country faced as winter approached. I said then that I wanted to do something to help the Soviet Union stay on the course of political and economic reform.

Unfortunately, in view of the events of the last two weeks—resulting in the deaths of at least twenty people in the Baltic states—I cannot, in good conscience, and indeed will not continue along this path. I believe that the leaders of the Baltic states have acted with restraint, particularly in the last two weeks, and did not deserve to have their quest for negotiations met with force. The unrelenting intimidation, pressure, and armed force to which these democratically elected leaders have been subjected is something that I frankly cannot understand.

I had hoped to see positive steps toward the peaceful resolution of this conflict with the elected leaders of the Baltic states. But in the absence of that and in the absence of a positive change in the situation, I would have no choice but to respond. Thus, unless you can take these positive steps very soon, I will freeze many elements of our economic relationship including Export-Import credit guarantees; Commodity Credit Corporation credit guarantees; support for "Special Associate Status" for the Soviet Union in the International Monetary Fund and World Bank; and most of our technical assistance programs. Further, I would not submit the Bilateral Investment Treaty or Tax Treaty to the United States Senate for consent to ratification when and if they are completed.

I would not take these steps to, in any sense, punish the Soviet Union. I viewed the expansion of our economic and commercial relationship not as a reward but rather as a natural response to Soviet political and economic reform. Sadly, events in the Baltic states call into question the Soviet government's commitment to the very reforms that provide the basis for much of what we are trying to do in the economic sphere. I remain hopeful that conditions in the Baltic states will soon permit the renewal of our efforts.

In the meantime, I intend to do everything in my power to preserve our relationship throughout this difficult period and to work toward progress in areas of mutual advantage. We have come too far in U.S.-Soviet relations to return to a confrontational course—a turn of events that would serve no one's interests. We have both talked of our desire for a new world order, and we both understand the importance of U.S.-Soviet cooperation to the achievement of that goal. I remain committed to that objective.

In closing, let me say that I do not underestimate the difficulties that you face: I understand that the path to fundamental economic and political reform is neither straight nor easy. No one wishes to see the disintegration of the Soviet Union. But Mikhail, I cannot help but recall that you, yourself, told me that you personally could not sanction the use of force in the Baltic states because it would mean the end of perestroika. You said that only political means in the settlement of political disputes were consistent with your vision of a society based on the rule of law. I urge you to turn back now to a course of negotiation and dialogue and to take concrete steps to prevent the further use of force and intimidation against the Baltic peoples and their elected leaders.

Sincerely,

George

I received a remarkable letter from the widow of the first American pilot killed in Desert Storm, Lieutenant Commander Scott Speicher. She sent me a note saying, "I want you to know that I feel the same way now that my husband and I felt when he was deployed last August. We supported you then and I support you now with all my heart."

January 24th, 1991

Dear Mrs. Speicher, Dear Joanne,

You sent me a very moving telegram. Barbara and I read it together, and we shed a tear for your noble husband. And we said a prayer that God give you the continued strength and courage that you have now.

I have read about Scott. He must have been "Mr. Perfect" for he was loved by all.

Sometimes God acts in strange ways—ways we do not understand right away.

The fact is your husband gave his life not simply so a small country could once again be free, but so that those kids of yours will have a better chance to grow up in a world more peaceful, more just. Give your kids a big hug from both Barbara and me. We know what family and faith can do to lift you up when you are hurt. And clearly those kids have a mother who loves them and whose courage will lead them.

I am proud of your wonderful husband and I will never forget him.

George Bush

Unfortunately, over the next few weeks, I would send out a number of letters similar to this one. The final casualty count for Desert Storm was 148 Americans killed; 467 wounded.

Mr. and Mrs. James T. Stephenson
West Bountiful, Utah 84010
Dear Mr. and Mrs. Stephenson:

Barbara and I were deeply saddened by the news of the loss of your son, Private First Class Dion J. Stephenson, USMC. Our hearts—indeed, the hearts of all Americans—go out to you at this very difficult time.

I understand the enormity of your grief and know that words alone cannot adequately convey our sympathy. Although the days ahead will not be easy for you and your family, I hope you will take comfort in knowing that Dion served his country with courage, honor, and pride. You and your family can always be proud of him.

Though it may be of little comfort to you and your family now, history will show that Dion gave his life for his country in an important and noble cause.

He served his country as a valued member of our Armed Forces, participating in Operation Desert Storm, not only to help liberate the innocent people of Kuwait, but also to ensure that world peace has a better chance after this naked aggression has been checked. He has earned our lasting respect and gratitude, and he will be remembered for his selflessness and sacrifice.

The entire Bush family is keeping you in its thoughts and prayers. God bless you.

Sincerely,
George Bush

P. S. I am glad we talked today. I am so grateful to you for your words of support. You have given me strength, even in your hour of grief.

On February 1, I traveled to three bases to support our military and their families: Cherry Point Marine Corps Air Station, North Carolina; Seymour Johnson Air Force Base at Goldsboro, North Carolina; and then Fort Stewart, Georgia, home of the Twenty-fourth Infantry Division. The emotion was almost overwhelming.

February 1st
The first stop was Cherry Point—some of the Marines [based there] were KIA.* I think I saw tears in Al Gray's eyes. Al, the com-

---

*Killed in action.

mandant of the Marine Corps., looked to me a little down right after the State of the Union, so I stopped and said—"Al, I know you had a tough night. I'm thinking of you and I know you lost some Marines." Yesterday he had the same emotional look, and I could see why. Because when I got up to speak, there were a lot of teary faces of wives in the audience. None of the wives who lost their husbands were there but there were a lot of nervous, worried Marines and families—they have some 70,000 deployed to the Gulf. I decided when I was speaking that I had to get through my text without crying. It's hard to do when they play the Marine Hymn or the Star Spangled Banner or when they salute you and hold up signs of total support, or when you see the kid mouthing words "Bring my dad home safe." I decided to look past the first row where there were a lot of crying faces and look at the press or way back in the back of the room and that helped and I got stronger.

February 14th

K-Day is approaching,* and I feel quite content. I wish it were tomorrow. I have no qualms now about ordering a ground war—none at all. I don't have the aching that I felt the night before the bombing started and we went to war. The reason is that the military are unanimous in recommending the course of action that Colin and Cheney outlined to me the other day. I have not second-guessed; I have not told them what targets to hit; I have not told them how much ordinance to use or how much not to use, or what weapons to use and not to use. I have learned from Vietnam,† and I think the Army and the other services are doing a superb job. . . .

February 20, 1991

Mr. William C. Liedtke, Jr.
Houston, TX 77024
Dear Bill,

I am going to type this—please excuse the errors, but believe me the typing though bad, is far better than my hand. We called Bessie last night—you having hit the sack. She sounded great and brought us up to date on you and the kids.

----

*Our code word for the start of the ground war.
†Civilian leaders micromanaged the Vietnam War and second-guessed the military leaders.

I am writing this as a friend who feels he has not been too good a friend.* Bar and I both wish that we had come by to see you, or get you up here to Camp David. I fear I have been focusing on the War, but after our talk with Bessie I got to thinking "it's friends that matter—good close loyal wonderful friends—that's where you come in". I hope this little note finds you comfortable. I'm sure your sense of humor is intact—anyone that could try slaying Moths with a croquet mallet—on the ceiling no less—has got to be set in the humor department forever. I wish we had Cruise missiles and smart weapons in those early Midland days—all moths would have been done in. I got to thinking of our touch football. Yes I still maintain Terry Moore was not only sexy but highly intellectual—why else would Glenn Davis† have embraced her on the sidelines like he did? What fun we had in those 'good old days'— there was enough stress as we all struggled to make something of ourselves, but there was the wonderful closeness of true friends—rejoicing in the other guy's success or watching with wonder as all our families grew.

I guess what I am saying Bill is that I miss you, that I am thinking of you, and yes, that I love you and I love your family. And though I have different responsibilities now, they will not crowd out the importance Bar and I place on "friends" and "friendship". We are thinking of you a lot—always with joy, always with appreciation for the fact that you and Bessie have enriched our lives.

George

———

February 20th

I've been plagued with the image of body bags. Everybody who opposed this war—good people like Dave Boren and Lee Hamilton,‡ and Foley and others all raised body bags, body bags, and it gets to my heart. Each kid is precious—each soldier, each Marine, each person who gives his life is precious. But I've got to push forward.

We did a lot of diplomacy again yesterday—Mitterrand, Mulroney, Ozal§— keeping the coalition solid. . . . So far, American public opinion is solid, and the New York Times even editorialized that we shouldn't jump at a bad deal.

———

*My friend and former partner was dying of cancer.

†Terry Moore was a glamorous movie star, a native of Lubbock, Texas. She used to play on the Lubbock team when she was around. Glenn Davis was an all-American football hero at West Point who was also from West Texas.

‡David Boren was a Democratic senator from Oklahoma, and Lee Hamilton was a Democratic congressman from Indiana.

§Turgut Ozal, president of Turkey and a wonderful friend and ally. His support before and during Desert Storm was crucial.

The truth of the matter is that we're going to have to capture his army, and we're going to have to get rid of a lot of that armor. Otherwise, we will have diminished his military, but we will not have accomplished our real goals. I would add to that if Saddam's military would take matters into their own hands and get rid of this tyrant, we then would have a real chance. I don't quite see how Iraq with Saddam Hussein at the helm will be able to live peacefully in this family of nations.

It's a tough testing time. The pressure is constant; but oddly enough, with Brent, Baker, Cheney and Powell at my side on these matters, I still feel content.

But the dilemma is, "What is victory—what is a complete victory?" Our goal is not the elimination of Saddam Hussein, and yet in many ways it's the only answer in order to get a new start for Iraq in the family of nations.

. . . Scowcroft comes over yesterday. I love the guy dearly. He is the best. His personal life is hell because his wife is an invalid. . . . Flo* tipped us off that she might be going to the hospital, so I casually said to Brent, "Look, how about going over and we have a debrief over a martini and dinner." Barbara then made a very general inquiry over dinner about his wife, and he did tell us about it. But he did say, "I just don't want to burden you. The President has enough burdens on his shoulders and I just don't want to add to them." This thoughtful quiet, unselfish man is a source of tremendous strength to me. Never a game player, always direct. . . .

The ground war began on Saturday evening, February 23. My right-hand assistant Patty Presock called some administration people on Saturday and asked them to join Barbara and me at church on Sunday morning.

February 24th

It's Sunday morning, and there is no way that I can possibly describe here the emotional feeling I had when I heard that things were going well. I got the word from Cheney,† and then in a briefing after church. I sat down in the flowered room with Barbara and got the briefing from Schwarzkopf from the field, and I felt myself choking up just as I did in church.

---

*Florence Gantt, Brent's loyal secretary.
†Dick literally handed me a note during church saying things were going well.

We had the little church service. It was well attended by the Cabinet and others. The sermon was beautiful—very short and to the point—but all in all, I was very pleased we had it. . . .

But my emotions are in the pride of our troops, and sorrow. I don't have elation in my heart. . . .

———————

By February 27, it was over. Saddam's army—what was left of it—was fleeing up what became known as the Highway of Death—the road between Kuwait City and Basra, just over the border in Iraq. Cheney and Powell came over to the Oval Office and told me we had achieved our objectives. We called Schwarzkopf from the Oval Office and asked him if he agreed it was time to end the fighting. After checking with his commanders, he said yes. One hundred hours after the ground war had begun, I announced to the nation that the war was over.

February 28th

Still no feeling of euphoria. I think I know why it is. After my speech last night, Baghdad radio started broadcasting that we've been forced to capitulate. I see on the television that the public opinion in Jordan and in the streets of Baghdad is that they have won. It is such a canard . . .

The headlines [here] are great—"We win." The television we see accurately reflects the humiliation of Saddam Hussein and it drives the point home to the American people. But internationally, it's not there yet, at least in the Arab world that has been lined up with Saddam. He's got to go, and I hope those two airplanes that reported to the Baghdad airport carry him away. Obviously when the troops straggle home with no armor, beaten up, 50,000 casualties and maybe more dead, the people of Iraq will know. Their brothers and their sons will be missing never to return. . . .

[I was convinced, as were all our Arab friends and allies, that Hussein would be overthrown once the war ended. That did not and has still not happened. We underestimated his brutality and cruelty to his own people and the stranglehold he has on his country. We were disappointed, but I still do not regret my decision to end the war when we did. I do not believe in what I call "mission creep." Our mission, as mandated by the United Nations, was clear: end the aggression. We did that. We liberated Kuwait and destroyed Hussein's military machine so that he could no longer threaten his neighbors.]

———————

This letter went to my nephew John Ellis, who was then at the John F. Kennedy School of Government at Harvard. The Ivy League establishment had been critical of the war, calling it Vietnam—the Sequel. John refers to Harvard as a "boutique" in his letter.

March 18, 1991

Dear John,

I'm sitting here in my residence office—you know, one door down from Abe's bedroom, better known as the room in which Millie hides those rawhide bones. Anyway, along comes your letter reporting that the boutique has been shaken. This letter brought great joy to my tired soul. I am avoiding the 'told ya' so' syndrome, but I must say when constant critics have to digest some crow there is a nice feeling of equity.

There are plenty of problems to go 'round; but the critics can never take away this wonderful feeling of pride and patriotism that has swept the U.S. of A. My problem is I shed tears too much. Yesterday at Sumter*—a three-ish year old girl pointed at a grinning camouflaged soldier who had a tear in his eye—"That's my Daddy—He came home!"

That did it. Thanks John. Hang in there.

Your Ma comes here tomorrow—hooray for our side.

Bar sends her love, too.

GB

March 29th

Lee Atwater died early this morning. He fought the good fight, and he made his peace with those he offended. A good little guy and we'll miss him, but it's a blessing now. He suffered a lot at the end—too much—and off he goes to God's loving arms. . . .

April 15th

Dreary weather over the weekend. I rode down to see Doro's house† and it was fun. The kids and I played animals, and the guy who sees the most animals, etc., wins. Sam spoke up and said, "I have three—a cow, birds and a kitty cat." I said, "Come on, neither of you saw anything," and then both of them immediately came up with a tremendous count. I, who was looking very hard, had one group of

*Fort Sumter, in South Carolina.
†She had just bought a house in Washington.

black cows, but I didn't even dare claim them because nobody else came close to seeing them. Then we played tic-tac-toe. I defeated Ellie, but she beat me once, and then we listened to the golf and the ball game where the Rangers were winning big. It was fun, but at the end of the ride down from Camp David, about an hour and half in the rain, I was exhausted. It's like being in a minnow pond with a whole bunch of minnows pushing you and jumping around all the time. . . .

————————

On April 30, I began personally to keep an important file in my drawer. The name of the file was BRENT, and it was the first official documentation of the Scowcroft Award. My BRENT file entries will be scattered throughout the rest of this chapter.

April 30, 1991

The challenge today mounted by Dick Cheney is worthy of total approval. He slept soundly. Everyone applauded when he woke up. A Sterling performance as far as sleeping goes. The only weakness was in the "recovery." In this category he slept so soundly that when he awoke to laughter he had no comeback at all.

For awhile it looked like Admiral Dave Jeremiah* was mounting a serious challenge. I noted this on my pad, only to find, after more serious observation, that Dave has a way of letting his eyelids close way down when he takes notes. His performance today does not rate him as challenger.

Andy Card† mounted a minor challenge—no real winner here, however.

————————

On Saturday, May 4, I gave a commencement speech at the University of Michigan, and then Barbara and I met our friends Bob and Betsy Teeter (Bob was a well-known political pollster and was chairman of my 1992 campaign) and Craig and Karen Fuller at Camp David. I dictated to my diary:

May 4th

. . . It was the most beautiful day we've ever had. I slept soundly— I was tired, and slept soundly for forty minutes—but then I got

————————

*Dave was vice chairman of the Joint Chiefs of Staff and an important member of our team.

†Andy was a longtime supporter and friend who was deputy chief of staff. In a few months I would name him secretary of transportation.

up and Rich Miller of the Secret Service and I went for a run. I started and then got tired right away, or got out of breath, so I stopped and walked. Then I ran a little, but couldn't run more than a hundred yards, so again, I stopped. I did this for about 30 or 40 minutes, and I told Rich to get the doctor and have him at the medical unit at Camp David. And then just before we got near the chapel, I started to run again—to run into the medical unit—and the same tired feeling came. They plopped me down and gave me an EKG, and I had a fibrillation or irregularity of the heart. So they told me, "Well, you're going to have to go down to Bethesda [Naval Hospital]—we really have to check to see what's causing this"—and my whole mind goes, "Oh no, here we go—here comes a bunch of Democrats charging out of the woodwork to run." There will be a scare scene sent all around the world and a wild speculation will begin about my health and fitness, and it's too darn bad.

They immediately started up the helicopter, so I'm now on the helicopter flying down to Bethesda from Camp David. Bar is with me and she looks a little worried, but I keep telling her I feel good.

I keep thinking, "Oh my God, they've got to tell the press; they've got to notify staff; and there will be all kinds of wild speculation; but there is not a damn thing we can do about it." So off we go, and we'll find out what my fate is in another 20 minutes; but I feel like a million bucks.

May 5th

The heart is still not back into rhythm. Bar went home and then came back out, but it's been quite a day. I've made about 20 phone calls and lying here quite comfortable, though I'm a little weak when I get up, but not a lot. The damn thing is just not snapping back into its normal rhythm. Now they're telling me that they've got to give me some new medicine tonight; and if that doesn't work, to the operating room I go where I swallow some tube. They then give it a shock, which should automatically get the thing back into a normal rhythm, and in which case, I'm free to go, after watching me for a few hours. But it's a pain. I lie here very restless.

I got up and went to the bathroom and ABC carried a picture of me standing there. I'm not sure they can pick up all the detail, but they did say they got a glimpse; so later on, I went back and looked out the window and it was fun. I opened the window and called out to Norm Schwarzkopf and others. I put on my yellow sweater, gave them a wave, and I just wanted to keep things out there as normal as possible. . . .

I sit here on Sunday night and Barbara is just leaving to go on home to the White House for the night. She'll come back in the morning . . . I must confess now that I have a little concern about tomorrow—I just wonder what it's like. I don't worry about the transfer of power, because this is something we ought to do anyway. Bar kisses me goodnight about 8:00 p.m. and heads on home; and I must say through my mind I'm thinking, "Will it be okay." She's a little more worried than she indicates, and I'll probably be thinking tomorrow, "Have I really told her how much I love her, and it's going to be okay?" I just can't believe anything will go wrong and it won't. But this diary is a confession of sorts, and I have no fear of this procedure—but I've left undone a lot of things I should've done. . . .

_____

I was diagnosed with Graves' disease—just like Bar had in 1989—except mine affected the sinus rhythm of my heart. Once they figured out what was wrong, they got me on the right medicine and sent me home, and I have felt great ever since.

May 7, 1991

Dear Ray [Siller],

You are the first to receive a computer-letter from me. It is Tuesday a.m. and I am back at work on the regular schedule (7:20 a.m.).

Thanks for the jokes which were on my desk when I walked into my office. All is well here. I am feeling fine after a good night's sleep—not quite ready for the 10K but getting there.

Since having my LITTLE problem I have met many fibrulators, a fine group generally, all with different ways of staying normal and free to give advice.

It was great hearing from you. Barbara Bush sends love as do I.

Sincerely,

George

_____

BRENT entries:

May 8, 1991

A fine challenge by John Sununu.

His recovery was very good, not too much embarrassment. After returning from Bethesda with me, we had our regular 8 am meeting. At about 8:16 am, JS dropped off into a very sound sleep, but admittedly one of short duration. John dropped off a little in the Cabinet room with some Fast Track* legislators—a very modest challenge, however.

Yesterday a visiting Italian made a move on the couch in the Oval Office, but his sleep was not worthy of even recording his name.

————————

May 9, 1991

A fantastic challenge by Ed Derwinski:†

very firm eye closure and a remarkable recovery gambit. Ed with eyes tightly closed used the seldom used nod technique. He nodded vigorously whenever in his slumber he heard the end of a sentence. This nomination was seconded by Larry Eagleburger who gave me a note just as I was recording Ed's performance on my note pad.

Demarest‡ also challenged, but regrettably he was behind me so I didn't get to see him. Thus, I have to accept Brady's§ word. He said it was star quality.

————————

About this time an old rumor surfaced claiming that Ronald Reagan had secretly worked out a deal with Iran in the fall of 1980 for the release of the hostages, but after the election. Now they were saying that I was the one who flew to Paris to conduct the negotiations. I was disappointed to read that a former hostage, Moorhead Kennedy, was calling for an investigation.

May 9, 1991

Mr. Moorhead Kennedy
Moorhead Kennedy Institute
New York, NY 10038
Dear Mr. Kennedy:

I read with distress your comments reported in the attached clip . . .

I can categorically assure you that I never was in Paris as claimed by the rumormongers. I can also categorically assure you that I have no information direct or indirect of any contact with Iranians relating to this hostage question.

————————————————

*We were working hard on Fast Track legislation, which would give me the authority to negotiate international trade agreements and send them to Congress for approval as is. Congress would not be allowed to tack on any amendments.

†Secretary of the Department of Veterans Affairs.

‡David Demarest, director of communications.

§Secretary of the Treasury Nick Brady.

I am disappointed that you would feel I might have been a participant in a scheme to keep any American held hostage. I emphatically deny any such complicity.

One of the sad things about public life is you have to suffer attacks on your character, on your honor.

I can readily understand your concern when allegations are made like those made by Mr. Sick.* A proposition so fundamentally immoral would certainly concern anyone. Please accept my word that I know nothing about anyone else's involvement in such an insidious plot, and I know for a fact that I had no contact such as those being alleged by Mr. Sick.

I wish you all the best and I hope this has laid to rest some of your understandable concerns.

Sincerely,
George Bush

Queen Elizabeth and Prince Philip arrived for a wonderful, stress-free state visit on May 14. Following are several notes I wrote after the state dinner.

May 16, 1991

Honorable Leonore Annenberg†
Randor, Pennsylvania 19088
Dear Table 8:

It was a pleasure having you at the Queen's State Dinner. Taken as a whole, your table behaved fairly well. All the silver was accounted for!

But then, horrors! I received a note from Table 8 begging for the chocolate wheels off the dessert cart. Appalling!

I tried to be sure that Her Majesty did not see me reading this appeal you sent me. Down, Table 8, down!

Next time, though you all seemed united, it is better you sit apart.

Sincerely,
George Bush

----

*Gary Sick, a NSC staff person from the Carter administration, had just written a book speculating that a hostage deal had been made. Congress investigated and Sick was proven wrong.

†Lee was the former chief of protocol and the wife of our good friend and former ambassador to Great Britain Walter Annenberg. She was one of eight people at Table 8.

May 17, 1991

Ms. Andrea Mitchell*
Washington, D.C. 20016
Dear Andrea,

It was the 'excitement' of the Queen's evening; it was my "heart:, it was the "medicine", it was that I'm "almost 67", it was that you 'looked great'; alas it was that I screwed up.

A thousand sorries.

Here's a peace offering!†

Am I forgiven?

Con Afecto
George Bush

———————

BRENT entry:

Following the Queen's State dinner, Jessye Norman, a fantastic singer with a great voice [sang] . . . She was superb.

The next morning, May 15th, Brent and John Sununu jointly announced that I had made a serious challenge to the Scowcroft Award. Aware of my innocence, I discussed this important matter with Bar who confirmed I was never out of it. Eyes open at all times . . . Brent's witness was Doro, but when she was contacted, Doro defended her father against this ludicrous charge. Though this entry is now part of the SCOWCROFT FILE, it really is so fallacious a charge that it shouldn't have been brought up.

Her Majesty mounted a minor challenge on the way back from the Orioles game on May 16th,‡ but it was night, she was jet lagged and it was about 4 am in London—no entry here.

———————

May 31, 1991

Dear Michael;§

I just finished a very good lunch with your able representative Mr. Primakov.**

---

*NBC's White House correspondent. I called her "Barbara," as in Walters, by mistake.
†A White House key chain.
‡I shocked everyone—even the Queen, I think—when I took her to a Baltimore Orioles baseball game. I thought she would enjoy the national pastime.
§A historic typo. This note is to Mikhail Gorbachev.
**Yevgeny Primakov, a senior Soviet official.

I want you to have this first message that I have ever sent to a foreign leader on my new computer.

Good Luck and Warmest Personal Regards,

George Bush

BRENT entries:

May 31, 1991

At a private lunch with Primakov and the interpreter in my private dining room, Scowcroft himself showed promise. After a chocolate chip cookie—make that 2—his eyes began to glaze over. It can not be fairly said that he slept, but Primakov noted the challenge and smiled at me. I knew he knew.

But that's not all. At a follow up meeting with our delegation that went to the Soviet Union, Brent mounted a serious challenge. A sterling performance, but regrettably not a winner. It's 2 p.m. in the Cabinet Room—about 12 people there. Brent is three down from me (maybe 2).

He drops off.

He recovers nicely, nodding vigorously in assent when his seatmate to his left made a telling point.

Several times the eyes were totally closed—several earned points here. Several recoveries were carried off with aplomb.

It was only near the end of the meeting (2:48pm) that he leaned forward, his head then moving onto his arm, the elbow of which was on the table.

Zoellick* speaks again. Scowcroft [makes] yet another great recovery and nods vigorously as Zoellick spoke of some complicated facet of the [agricultural] credit situation.

At 2:51 pm, the head was all the way down, elbow gone, now, head 4½ inches from table—criticism: The eyes were not <u>tightly</u> closed.

On June 3, I was scheduled to address the National Federation of Independent Businesses. I wanted to include in my remarks a statement about my efforts to get a civil rights bill passed that did not mandate quotas. I sent these notes to Dave Demarest, to include in the speech:

---

*Robert Zoellick from the State Department.

June 1, 1991

I have been accused by liberal democrats of 'playing politics' with this issue. Frankly it's the other way around. We have a good record on Civil Rights and fair play.

My opponents are not even willing to consider my civil rights bill. They keep changing theirs to attract votes. Their obvious move to shift this to a 'women's issue' was pure politics.

Our Bill would properly protect women's rights.

The BELTWAY GROUPS AND THEIR SPOKESMEN want to force me to either accept a Quota bill or to veto their Bill. The fact is we have tried to compromise but not to accept quotas. At one point last year Senator Kennedy agreed to language that could have brought us all together. He went back to the Groups and they said "No". They want a political win.

I want a fair strong anti discrimination Bill that will guarantee workers rights, women's rights but will not result in Quotas and that won't be a bonanza to avaricious lawyers.

Whatever happens to the Bill I will continue to work for racial harmony and fair play.

GB

————————

June 1, 1991

<u>SECRET</u>

His Excellency Haffez al-Assad
President of the Syrian Arab Republic
Damascus
Dear Mr. President:

I am writing you . . . to share my thoughts about the Arab-Israeli peace process. Secretary Baker has reported to me on his many hours of conversation in Damascus. I have heard too from both President Mubarak and King Hussein about their recent meetings with you. I continue to believe that there is a real chance for making progress toward a comprehensive peace in the region. I believe just as firmly that it is in your interest as well as ours to seize that opportunity.

In this regard, I think we have reached a critical juncture in our efforts to put together a peace conference to make negotiations possible. We have tried to structure this process so the needs of all parties are taken into account in a fair and reasonable way. . . .

We intend our engagement throughout the negotiations to be significant. We and the Soviet Union will be a driving force behind the negotiations, taking on a special responsibility for making them succeed and cajoling and pressing the parties forward.

I want to make clear that we will be doing so on the only basis possible for a comprehensive peace: Territory for peace applied to all fronts, including the Golan Heights. We will not change this fundamental policy position of ours; nor will we change our non-recognition of Israel's purported "Annexation" of the Golan Heights.* While Secretary Baker tells me he made these points to you, we both feel they deserve added emphasis and greater consideration by you.

In this regard to increase the probability of a successful outcome on the Golan, I have even been willing to make the offer of a United States Security guarantee of the border that Israel and Syria mutually agree upon. This would go beyond the assurances that the co-sponsors would give (as you requested) that the parties would carry out their agreements. This security guarantee— which is unprecedented and far-reaching—will affect the negotiations and their outcome far more than any symbols relating to the UN or a conference. My decision in favor of such a security guarantee was not an easy one to make. But I did so because I believe it offers the best chance for a peaceful resolution of the problems between Syria and Israel.

At this point, while I am not yet certain, I do believe that Israel is prepared to say "yes" to a conference based on the terms and modalities I have described. It is difficult for me to see how your interest could be served by saying "No" to this process.

The fact is we want Syria to participate because we seek a comprehensive peace. At the same time, we cannot agree that a process not proceed even if you choose not to come. Our bilateral relationship is dependent on many things; but as with other states in the region a critical part of that relationship depends on Syria's position on peace.

Mr. President, I want you to know that I remain personally committed to the principles I enunciated in my March 6 address to the U.S. Congress. Similarly, I cannot over-emphasize that the successful prosecution of the war in the Gulf has created new opportunities for progress in the peace process. These new opportunities may not come again and they ought to be seized.

As you can see, I think it is very important that Syria participate. . . . such a position on your part would, in my view, open historic possibilities for bringing peace to a part of the world that has too often known war. I hope the Middle East and indeed the world, can count on your leadership and your commitment to peace.

Sincerely,
George Bush

---

*The Golan Heights was a major sticking point in the Middle East. Once Syrian territory, it was now held by Israel.

BRENT entry:

June 4, 1991

. . . At Cabinet meeting today, Lamar Alexander* mounted a good challenge. John Sununu reported Lamar was out of it for some nine minutes. This has not been authenticated though the Committee is looking into this for more details.

At same Cabinet meeting, Lynn Martin† made a challenge. Again, we are lacking detail—leave this file open.

———————

Almost the minute you become President you are pestered to put into writing your funeral arrangements. I wrote this note to Patty Presock to add to my funeral file:

June 10, 1991

Patty:

Re: My Burial instructions

Addenda:

I want the song "Last full Measure of Devotion" sung by a good male soloist at any church or memorial service.

Gravestone—the plain stones we see at Arlington. I would like my navy number on it on the back of it. I believe it is 0173464 (ask Don Rhodes)

Also on the stone in addition to what I already requested:

"He loved Barbara very much"

gb

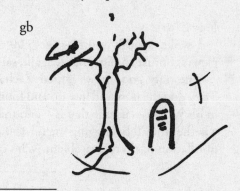

———————

June 16th

We went to Blue Heaven‡ for the name dropping party to end all name dropping parties. A lot of the liberal actors were there and actresses. Goldie Hawn, my dinner partner, was cute, full of fun and

*Secretary of education.

†Secretary of labor.

‡The Malibu home of Jane and Jerry Weintraub.

very nice to sit next to. Johnny Carson, who has had me on his joke list for a long time, was very friendly. . . . Clint Eastwood was at our table, and Sally Field was charming. Bar said she is very liberal, but she couldn't have been more pleasant—She's Goldie's great friend. Barbara was over there with Warren Beatty and Richard Dreyfuss who was wearing a button that said, "How about a Domestic Desert Storm" . . .

June 18, 1991

Ms. Goldie Hawn
Pacific Palisades, CA 90272
Dear Goldie,

Am I enchanted? You bet. Thanks for giving me such a relaxed good time at dinner.

When Jane Weintraub told me where I was sitting, I was a little worried only because sometimes I'm not too hot of a dinner partner. (I didn't ask you to dance—on that one, look at it this way—you've still got 2 good feet)

Anyway you were a fantastic dinner partner. You made me feel welcome and totally at ease. I didn't even have to unveil my 12-point plan for dealing with Gorbachev. Thanks for being so darn nice!! Good Luck—

George Bush

June 27th

I woke up this morning at 5:00 a.m. and started reading the papers, I must confess that I, again, said, "Well, is it worth it?"

The only good news is that Zachary Taylor was not poisoned. They dug the poor old guy up and found out there wasn't any poison in his system—arsenic that is—and that he has good teeth. I wonder whether they'll be digging me up 150 years from now analyzing my fibrillation or thyroid problem. Who cares. . . .

July 1st

We had a nice letter from Chevy Chase—four pages—in which he said he learned something from sitting next to Barbara. He will always be a liberal Democrat; he'll always be on the liberal cause; but he's learned in essence that being nice people, people who are good and kind and who have decent values, can more than offset one's position on issues. He said, "Even if I do get out for the "Dems" in '92, it wouldn't hurt me a bit to know you were still there."

July 1, 1991

Mr. Chevy Chase
Beverly Hills, California 90212
Dear Chevy,

After I sent you a note on that wonderful briefcase that you and Dan [Aykroyd] gave me, in comes your kind letter of June 17. I was deeply moved and touched by it, and Barbara had a tear in her eyes.

I hate the issues that divide, and I hope you and I will always be able to see the other guy's point of view. The fact that you understand that there are values that transcend issues shows both Barbara and me a lot about the Chevy Chase whose name we are now freely "dropping" (even though he is a damned Democrat!)

Sincerely,
George Bush

July 2nd

The Clarence Thomas announcement went well.* . . . It was a hot sunny day, and I took Clarence back into our bedroom and talked to him briefly. I told him that I did not want to talk about issues; told him he must call 'em as he sees 'em—as an umpire would; and asked him if he was ready for the bruising fight that laid ahead. We had a nice pleasant chat. I told him that I'd called him the night before, and stopped short of a full commitment just because I wanted to be sure he felt ready for the bench itself. He said that all was fine. . . .

Yugoslavia is poised on the brink of civil war . . . This is one where I've told our top people, "We don't want to put a dog in this fight."† It's not one that we have to mastermind . . . This concept that we have to work out every problem, everywhere in the world, is crazy. I think the American people understand it. I don't want to look isolationistic; I don't want to turn my back on the desires of many ethnic

---

*While on vacation in Kennebunkport, I announced that Clarence Thomas was my nominee for the Supreme Court. My first had been David Souter, in 1990, who was quickly approved and already doing a good job.

†We are painfully aware today just how complicated the situation in Yugoslavia is. As of this writing in July 1999, the NATO military operations designed to end ethnic cleansing in Kosovo have ceased, though the problems are not solved. It's a troubled part of the world, with ethnic hatred dating back centuries.

Americans that come from that part of the world; but I don't think that we can be looked to for solving every problem every place in the world. . . .

———

July 7th

I am so spoiled by attention. Everywhere you go somebody wants to do something for you— hand you the glass of water, give you the dry tee-shirt, reach out and help in some way or another—the clothes, the service at the White House, the stewards wherever they may be—there's always somebody there and they all want to help and they all do a fantastic job.

And yet I've got to admit that sometimes I crave the quiet. We can get some of that at Camp David and once in a while in our house in Kennebunkport, particularly when the stewards leave, we can do it like it used to be—cooking our own Sunday supper, fixing coffee early in the morning or whatever. . . .

Politics: Democrats still haven't come up with a horse. Cuomo is silent, he's got big state problems and he's now trying to talk conservative on economic matters. He's fast on his feet and a lot of people think it will be Cuomo and Gore.*

Gore [they say] is "wooden" or something like that. An attractive guy, but he says he is a worse speaker than I. Poor guy's in real trouble if he's worse than I. That's the Sunday, July 7th run down—I'm philosophizing.

———

July 25th

Have you ever had one of those days when it just isn't too good?

Ranger wakes you up early.

It rains.

The budget deficit estimates get hit because they're too low. Nick Brady is upset because Dick Darman pointed out that the re-estimate by the Treasury makes it low and he comes over to see me tonight shaking mad.

Before that the Soviets press their case for full membership in the IMF and the World Bank in spite of the agreement by the G-7 telling them they ought to apply for associate member. . . .

---

*Then Senator Al Gore of Tennessee and now Vice President of the United States and running for President.

Jack Danforth* comes down and we can't work out a final agreement on civil rights, although it's a very civil conversation.

And, the Democrats want to press for extended unemployment benefits and we simply can't afford to do it and we don't think it's necessary with the economic situation. . . .

My medicine is making me tired on top of all of that.

Just one of those days when you want to say forget it. Oh, yes, the President of Paramount that owns one of the big book companies called in to say that Kitty Kelley wants to write a book either about the Bushes or the Royals and he turned it down. That's nice—a book by Kitty Kelley† with everything else I've got on my mind . . . I can't see her ever writing anything nice. In any event, maybe she'll settle on the royal family and do her number on them.

And then a discussion early this afternoon about a political meeting at Camp David and the big question about who goes, who gets left out, whose feelings are hurt if we don't do it. I'm trying to postpone organization of the politics until much later, feeling if we get it organized now, it'll press the Democrats into action.

And oh, yes, another vicious assault by a Democrat. This time Jay Rockefeller‡ really going after me and slamming me—and also Gephardt§. They've got a new game plan: Knock the hell out of the President, but I've got to stay above their fray—be pleasant. I think it's a little out of character for a nice guy like Jay Rockefeller . . . anyway, it all goes with the territory of being President.

Not a good day—tiring day. Getting briefed for the Soviet Union and getting criticized for going abroad a lot.** I think I've been abroad less this year than in previous years—I'm going to have that looked up. So long July 25—I won't miss you!

———

August 1st

The Moscow Summit went well. [Signing] START was more than ceremonial—it offers hope to young people all around the world. Idealism is not dead and this significant reduction in these damn intercontinental ballistic missiles is a good thing. I really did

*Republican senator John Danforth of Missouri.

†Kitty Kelley was famous for writing scathing books about people, including Frank Sinatra, Nancy Reagan, and Jacqueline Kennedy.

‡Senator from West Virginia.

§Dick Gephardt, Democratic congressman from Missouri and majority whip.

**I was leaving for Moscow in just a few days.

feel emotionally involved at the signing ceremony and I felt a sense of real gratitude to the people who worked tirelessly on the treaty. I ad-libbed in Ronald Reagan's name, but there was Rick Burt [US Ambassador to Germany] and so many others who were extraordinarily helpful in all of this. The talks with Gorbachev were warm and friendly. . . .

Vice President Yanayev greeted me at the airport, took me back to the airport, and is flying with us as I dictate this on Air Force One on the way to Kiev. He's a friendly man. He came out of labor. Apparently, he has some legal background too. Good sense of humor; and nobody talks about his importance in all of this. He didn't sit in on any of the meetings, but I think it's nice that he and some of his associates are flying with us on this magnificent airplane. . . .

August 1, 1991
(enroute Andrews Air Force Base)

Dear Mikhail:

We are now about 35,000 feet, flying from Kiev to Washington. I am relaxed and happy, because I feel the visits to Moscow and Kiev went well. You and Raisa could not have been more hospitable, so let me start by thanking you both for that.

I think the substantive talks were productive. I know that on our side, at least, there is a much clearer picture of where things stand between us, and of the problems we face. I am going home determined to find ways to assist the economic recovery that is so essential for your people.

The visit to Kiev was a good one, and I hope I did not inadvertently cause any problems. Your Vice President Yanayev, who, incidentally, was extraordinarily hospitable to me at every turn, felt that the speech had gone well. Perhaps some Ukranians were disappointed, because they wanted to hear a clarion call for "independence now." My speech, instead, called for the Republics working matters out with the Center, stating that it is not for us to dictate regarding the internal affairs of the Soviet Union.

So, in sum, it was a great visit, and I am extraordinarily grateful to you for its pageantry. We had a lot of substance, and we had a few laughs along the way. And thanks for sharing those lovely dachas with us*—a magnificent setting, and some good talks.

These sincere best wishes come from your friend,

GB

*We visited the Gorbachevs in their country dacha.

August 5, 1991

Mr. Michael Jacobs
Viking Penguin Books
New York, New York 10014
Dear Mr. Jacobs:

I recently saw a copy of "Charles and Diana: The 10th Anniversary" by Mr. Brian Hoey. On page 63 of this book there is a picture of Princess Diana seated next to an unnamed man. That man is our son, Marvin.

Now for the special favor. I would love to get a copy of that photo. I would, of course, be delighted to pay any expense involved. The photo would be given to Marvin and would not be used in any way for any other purpose.

Can you help me on this family project? Having seen the Princess recently, and recalling that Marvin, on the night the photo was taken, was not in a dancing mood,* I thought I might even ask the Princess to sign this for him.

Thank you in advance for your help.

Sincerely,
George Bush

I wrote this note to Senator Jack Danforth. I liked Jack a great deal but we could not agree on a civil rights bill.

August 6, 1991

Dear Jack,

Thanks for your most recent letter. I am now heading off for Maine. Before leaving I wanted to say a couple of things. . . .

Needless to say we don't feel we are 'turning back the clock on civil rights". Indeed I have stated that I want to sign a civil rights bill. I've also said that it is important that we get a bill, and rather than haggle over what some have called tiny differences why not take a gigantic step forward by going with a bill where we have total agreement, leaving a handful of the knotty unresolved questions to later on.

In any event I will take the suggestions made in your letters of August 2 and go back to the legal drawing board. . . .

Isn't it more important to take a 90% step forward than to take no step at

---

*Marvin had sat next to Princess Diana at a big Washington charity fund-raiser. He refused to dance with her, and we'll never stop teasing him about it. Diana did sign the photo and referred to the fact Marvin refused to dance.

all. . . . anyway, let's keep plugging away not letting the extremes on either side of this debate carry the day.

I'm told you're getting a little much deserved rest. I, too, will be doing that in just 4 hours, 17 minutes, and 32 seconds.

Love to Janet,
GB

PS: Thanks for the super job you are doing side by side with Judge Thomas*— He's such a good man and you have made that so very clear.

[I signed the Civil Rights Act of 1991 on November 21. It did not include quotas. It did promote the goals of ridding the workplace of discrimination based on race, color, sex, religion, national origin, and disability.]

August 12th

The stories keep saying that I will be very hard to beat. The more we hear of this, the more worried I become. "The bigger they are, the harder they fall." That sticks in my mind. The only good thing is the Democrats seem to be feeling a little bit of disarray.

Bill Clinton, a very nice man, may get into the race. Jay Rockefeller is out. Cuomo keeps saying he's not—dancing coyly on the sidelines, being anointed by the press as the best and the toughest of them all—and maybe he is. Tsongas† wanting someone to come in to debate him. . . .

The fishing has been good. I love trolling when the big blues hit. They come in strong—we've gotten them almost every time we've been out. I still use a light tackle. Sometimes the most fun is when you use the surface plugs and the blues explode hitting the plugs and then our friends try to push each other away as they go after the plug and that's a really good sport. Your mind gets totally taken away from the problems at hand as you try to get back through the school or cast into it.

And then on that boat, I count my blessings as I look and listen to the sea. Two or three days ago, we had a big storm come through. The waves were booming. Bar and I went out on the rocks and we watched in wonder as the sea pounded in. And there are other times

---

*Jack Danforth knew Clarence Thomas well. Clarence had worked for Jack when Jack was attorney general of Missouri.

†Senator Paul Tsongas of Massachusetts was the first to enter the race.

I simply sit on the porch and watch the kids playing on the rocks. I wish Neil's kids were here too. . . .

August 19th

At midnight on Sunday or maybe it was 5 minutes after midnight Monday morning the 19th, Scowcroft called me, woke me up, and said there was a report that Gorbachev had resigned for health reasons. I flip on the TV and I call the Situation Room around 5:30 a.m. and they give me the update that Gorbachev has been put out. Some of the news is that we were taken by surprise and I mention this to Brent this morning and he said, "Yes, so was Gorbachev!" And that's about right. They don't know. How the hell could we know! We'll talk to Prime Minister Major, Kohl and probably Mitterrand. . . .

The new president is Yanayev. . . . He was the guy that met me at the Moscow airport. He was the guy that drove in with me. He was the guy that flew down on our plane to Ukraine. He was the guy that congratulated me after our speech in Ukraine about the respect for the Union and the people choosing. I liked the guy. I sent him fishing lures. And, he was rather pleasant. Now it appears from these early reports that he's but a figurehead which we knew all along. It will be interesting to see how all this develops. The press, knowing as little as we do, are going around in circles. We'll now go out and have a press conference at 7:30 this morning and then figure out what to do from here. There's little we can do—in fact, nothing I'd say. . . .

I think of Gorbachev, now on a Crimean "vacation." I think of his sense of humor, his courage. I'm wondering what condition he's in, where he is, how he's being treated. I think of the old guard military, Yazov particularly, who was grumbling all the time at the meetings that we had in the Soviet Union, drinking a lot, complaining at the table with John Sununu and others about how bad things were.*

. . . If I were to comment tonight, I would say: "Mikhail, I hope you are well. I hope we have not mistreated you. You have led your country in a fantastically constructive way even with attacks from the right and from the left—but you deserve enormous credit. Now, we don't know what the hell has happened to you, where you are, what condition you are in, but we were right to support you. I'm proud we have supported you and there will be a lot of talking heads on television telling us what's been wrong, but you have done what's

---

*Dmitri Yazov, the defense minister, and one of the coup plotters.

right and strong and good for your country and I am proud that we have been supportive. I like you and I hope that you return to power, skeptical though I am of that. . . .

––––––––––

August 20th

I place a call to Boris Yeltsin. Much to my surprise, I get him.* We talk for 25 minutes. His building is surrounded. He's worried. He thinks they might storm the building. He says there are a hundred thousand people outside and, all-in-all, this courageous man is standing by his principles.

. . . The complexities of all of this are absolutely phenomenal and, yet, I am determined to handle it without getting us involved in a war and, yet, standing by our principles of democracy and reform. Brent is absolutely convinced that the way we've handled the Gorbachev matter in the past is now totally vindicated, though we'll be hit from the far right a little bit and on the left. People will be saying: "Well, you should have helped Gorbachev more with money to avoid this." There will be a lot of second-guessing, but I'm not worried about all that.

––––––––––

August 20, 1991

Matters to address today.
1. Change vacation to rest <u>and</u> work, formalize briefings daily
     invite key players to KB
     invite outside experts to KB
2. Get Marlin Back to KB
3. Active telephone diplomacy depending on events— not frantic but keep other countries informed including those not on 'front lines"—e.g. South America.
4. Message . . . steady as she goes, not acceptance of 'coup'—perhaps more personal attention to Yeltsin as he calls for return of Gorb and maintaining democratic changes etc.
5. Avoid getting caught up in '92 as it relates to Soviet crisis. Be sure our defenders are fully informed.

––––––––––

*By this time Boris was president of the Republic of Russia. He was defending Gorbachev and trying to keep the coup plotters from taking control.

I wrote some notes to some key senators who were being supportive of how we were handling the crises:

Aug. 20th '91

The Day after

The Honorable Richard G. Lugar
United States Senate
Washington, DC 20510
Dear Dick—

Once again "thanks". When the going gets rough the extremists weigh in. Political opportunists, no matter the gravity of the situation, try to make instant political hay. The extremes on both sides, be they "talking heads" (yes that cottage industry has been revived) or ultra right warriors or hand wringing second guessers on the left want to instantly pile on; but now is the time for steady, prudent leadership from Capitol Hill and from the White House. You've already contributed to the former.

Many thanks,
George

_____

8-20-91

The Honorable John H. Chafee
United States Senate
Washington, DC 20510
Dear Chafee,

Thanks for your words of confidence and support at this important time.

We must not let either the predictable political critics, the talking heads, or the coldest of the warriors prevail.

I will try to prudently manage all this with strength and conviction; but support such as you stated yesterday is vital—

Get some rest—

Gratefully,
George

_____

August 21st

Talk about being in the middle of history—at 8:30 this morning, an hour and half ahead of the scheduled time that Yeltsin and I had agreed on, he called me from his federation building—from his building where he's been for many hours. His tone was somewhat optimistic. He was not declaring victory.

. . . Four of his people [are] racing to the Crimea, but regrettably five coup leaders had left to go see Gorbachev hoping to get there before Yeltsin's people got there. Yeltsin is trying to have them them intercepted . . . the Ukraine leader will try to have them intercepted and keep the five from landing at the Gorbachev villa, making them divert to another airport.

Yeltsin is very grateful for our support. We talked for 30 minutes or more and he still is quite obviously committed to the restoration of Gorbachev. . . .

I got to the house, into the bedroom, to take a call and it was Gorbachev. He sounded jubilant and he sounded upbeat. He was very, very grateful to me, more so than I wanted to say at the press conference, for the way we've conducted ourselves. The same exact statement that Yeltsin had made.

All this brings home to me the importance of how the United States reacts. We could have overreacted and moved troops and scared the hell out of people. We could have under-reacted by saying, "Well, we'll deal with whoever is there." But, I think the advice I got was good. I think we found the proper balance, certainly in this case—we are getting enormous credit from the key players in the Soviet Union.

September 2nd

. . . Sitting alone on our terrace, the last day of what has been a fantastic vacation inspite of the turmoil in the Soviet Union. I'm alone out here. Finished a clam chowder luncheon, a little ham sandwich, glass of sherry. . . .

It's perhaps the clearest September day I have ever seen here. My mind goes back to September 2, 1944—47 years ago, this very day, I was shot down over the Bonin Islands. So much has happened—so very much in my life and in the world.

Today I had a press conference. I recognized the Baltics. I talked to the Presidents of Estonia and Latvia today, having talked to Landsbergis of Lithuania a couple of days ago. I told them what we've got to do. I told them why we waited a few days more. What I tried to do was to use the power and the prestige of the United States, not to posture, not to be the first on board, but to encourage Gorbachev* to move faster on "freeing the Baltics." Yesterday, he did make a statement to this effect and today there is an agreement where the various

---

*By this time the coup had failed and he was temporarily back in power.

republics would be entitled to determine their own relationship with the Center [the union] . . .

The pace will change now. Pressures will mount now, but I've got enough of this sea air, ocean and rocks and pools in my soul that it will give me the strength to get on through a long, cold winter, cold politically—who knows about meteorologically wise. But, it doesn't matter, we'll do O.K. and so, at the end of the vacation, I give thanks to God for my many blessings and for this special place and the special perspective that it gives this aging, but very grateful President of the United States. . . .

———————

October 3, 1991

David S. Broder
The Washington Post
Washington, D.C. 20071
Dear Dave:

Thanks for your September 27 letter. Having read about your approach on the article about the Vice President, I am hopeful the portrait will present a positive view of a good man.

. . . The Vice President does an outstanding job for this Administration directing the Space and Competitiveness Councils. He's extraordinarily effective working with Congress; and, as I am sure you've witnessed, he's well received by audiences all across the country. When he travels overseas, he does first rate work, too.

I guess whoever is Vice President will always take some pounding in the press. So, put down some of what's Dan's been through to just plain cynicism about the Vice Presidency.

I have great confidence in the Vice President and will continue to do so.

Sincerely,
George Bush

———————

October 10, 1991

Mr. Robert W. Blake
Lubbock, TX 79408
Dear Bob,

I am writing this to you on my computer. Incidentally I now use this regularly though I have lots to learn.

Anyway thanks for your supportive card written on Sept 30th. Aren't these amazing times?

The Libs charge that I am not interested in Domestic Policy. Wrong!! The problem is I am not interested in their spend spend spend agenda. I have had to veto a lot of bad stuff, and I will continue to do that in an effort to get good legislation.

What is happening to Clarence Thomas is just plain horrible.* All the groups that tried to beat him on abortion or privacy or affirmative action have now come out of the woodwork. They are trying to destroy this decent man. I do not think they will succeed but they are in a frenzy around here. The most liberal of the women's groups are really outrageous; and then you have the smug liberal staffers who leak FBI reports to achieve their ignoble ends. It is sinister and evil, but I doubt the Senate under the control of the one party will do a damn thing about it.

I know nothing of Ms. Hill who makes a nice appearance, but I know a lot about Clarence Thomas, with whom I visited again yesterday; and I continue to have total confidence in his honor and decency. This is an ugly process and one can see clearly why so many good people elect to stay out of public life.

Bar sends her love. Treat this letter in confidence; but I just felt like telling an old friend how I feel.

Sincerely,
GB

_____

October 10, 1991

Your Majesty,†

I can't tell you how much I appreciate that letter of friendship, written from your heart. Time heals a lot of wounds.

I appreciate your cooperation as we try to be genuine catalysts for peace in the Mid East. And I am certain that, whatever happens, the personal relationship that I, too, value will be strong—is strong.

My Respects & Best Wishes,
George
GB

_____

*Toward the end of Clarence Thomas's confirmation hearings, a former colleague of his, Anita Hill, came forward to accuse Clarence of sexual harassment. He vigorously denied the charges. Eventually, Clarence was confirmed and he now sits on the Supreme Court. I am proud that he had enough courage to take the confirmation heat. I have never regretted selecting and standing by him.

†King Hussein of Jordan.

October 21, 1991

Brent:

Please discuss:

Does Mil Aide need to carry that black case now every little place I go?

Let's discuss.

GB

[The President's military aide always carries the "football," a black briefcase that holds the necessary codes for the President to launch a nuclear strike. With the Cold War over, I did not think it was necessary for the "football" to go everywhere with me. However, Brent and others disagreed, given the uncertainty of who had nuclear capability.]

One of Clarence Thomas's biggest defenders was Senator Al Simpson, who took on the press, the women's groups, and the Democrats.

Oct. 21, 1991

Dear Al,

After you left today I got to worrying. I don't like to see my friend burdened down by anything at all. You seemed a little low. . . .

You were right on all this. You helped a decent man turn the tide.

You walked where angels feared to tread by zapping some groups and some press; and, in the process, they climbed all over your ass—but dammit you were right.

Besides even though some are sore at you, they won't stay sore. They like you, they respect you and they know you to be fair.

Having said all this I'll confess—there are days when I just hate this job—not many, but some.

The articles that demean one's character sometimes get to me, too. The ugly columns don't set very well when we're trying our hardest on some project or another—but then, always, the sun comes up.

Yesterday at Camp David I was a little down. I picked up 2 bright red leaves, and I did something I haven't done in the last 60 years. I put the leaves pressed into a heavy book in my little quiet office.

I felt better—strange but I really did.

Don't let the bastards wear you down.

Your friends love you.

This President depends on you and believes in you and is grateful to you. Nothing you can do can change that. . . .

Abortion, Immigration, Deficits, Judiciary Hearings, all these together pale in importance when up against friendship—

George

Mikhail Gorbachev and I opened the historic Middle East Peace Conference,
cohosted by the United States and the Soviet Union, in Madrid on October 30. It
began the peace process that led to the historic handshake between Israeli prime
minster Yitzhak Rabin and PLO leader Yassir Arafat on the White House lawn in
September 1993. The night before the conference opening, Spain's King Juan
Carlos hosted a private dinner for Spanish prime minister Felipe Gonzalez, Gor-
bachev, and me.

October 30, 1991

His Majesty Juan Carlos I
King of Spain
Madrid
Your Majesty,

I landed in Washington about 30 minutes ago.

Last night's dinner was very very special. . . . They, your family, really made
me feel at home—the very minute I walked in I felt that way.

Then the dinner—so terrific. Yes, I over ate but with gusto, not by accident.

Wasn't the conversation with Mikhail stimulating?

Every time I think "Wow, I've got problems", I think of what he faces every
day he climbs out of bed.

Thanks for a very rare treat of an evening; and special thanks, too, for all
your wonderful country did hosting this historic conference. We sure appreciate it—so does the whole world.

With Respect and thanks to you and her Majesty from your new <u>friend</u>
(and I mean it)

George

On Halloween, a terrible storm pounded our beloved Walker's Point and
destroyed much of the downstairs of our house. I wrote Gerry Bemiss:

11-9-91

Hague to DC

Mr. FitzGerald Bemiss
P.O. Box 1156
Richmond, VA 23209
Dear Gerry,

W. Point-K'Port had its body bent and broken but its soul is OK. Our
ground floor is <u>shot</u>—books, pictures—so many treasures like that gone; but

it will bounce back inspite of its truly historic pounding. Thanks for caring old friend

George

_____

The country had been in a recession despite our many attempts to jump-start the economy. It was beginning to dominate the headlines and influence 1992 politics.

Nov. 26, 1991

The Right Honorable Brian Mulroney, P.C., M.P.
Prime Minister of Canada
Ottawa
Dear Brian—

You sensed that I might be concerned about all the piling-on, and you called me. Thanks so very very much for that.

We are in a tough period. There are no easy "fixes" to this economy and, yes, things are slow and lack of confidence abounds; but there's a lot of fundamental strength out there, too.

Every day I am grateful for true friends (That's you!!)

George

_____

For several months John Sununu had been under fire from the media, who accused him of using government planes for personal use. John had been a great chief of staff, but the clamoring and discontent got to the point where we all knew it was probably time for him to go.

December 3, 1991

Governor John H. Sununu
Chief of Staff
The White House
Dear John,

I now have your letter resigning as Chief of Staff effective December 15. It is with reluctance, regret and a sense of personal loss that I accept your resignation as Chief of Staff.

I am very pleased, however, that you have agreed to remain as a Counselor to the President, with Cabinet rank, through March 1, 1992.

During the period, December 15th to March 1, you will be an official member of my administration and I will continue to seek your counsel on the important issues facing our country.

John, I find it very difficult to write this letter both for professional reasons and for personal reasons.

On the professional side, thanks to your leadership we have made significant accomplishments for which you deserve great credit.

Working with others here in the White House, throughout the administration, and on Capitol Hill, you have played a major role in achieving some of our significant goals.

And, yes, from my vantage point and our families as well, the friendship we treasure is stronger than ever.

I hope you and Nancy, free of the enormous pressures of the office you have served so well, will enjoy life to its fullest. You deserve the best.

Most sincerely from this grateful President,

George Bush

———————

12-6-91

The Honorable Sherwood L. Boehlert
U. S. House of Representatives
Washington, D. C. 20515
Dear Sherry,

I won't reply to every point in your good letter, but I really appreciated it.

. . . I know that this economy will turn. I know our staff changes will help quell the attacks John was under. And I darn sure am not down. I'm used to the heat and I plan to be in the kitchen for 5 more years.

With friends like you—I will be. All Best from a grateful

George Bush

———————

Ironically, the attempted overthrow of Gorbachev by hard-line communists had the exact opposite effect of what they planned. After the coup was squelched, more and more republics announced they wanted independence from Moscow. Led by Yeltsin, the republic leaders began systematically dismantling the old Soviet Union. On Christmas Day, 1991, Mikhail Gorbachev resigned as president of the Soviet Union. Our onetime greatest enemy no longer existed. The Cold War was officially over. I received a message that Gorbachev would like to talk to me. It was an emotional conversation—the last one between a president of the Soviet Union and a president of the United States. I assured him he would be my friend always and that history would treat him kindly. I recorded the conversation in my diary. This is how we ended:

GB: "At this special time of year and at this historic time, we salute you and thank you for what you have done for world peace. Thank you very much."

MG: "Thank you, George. I was glad to hear all of this today. I am saying goodbye and shaking your hands. You have said to me many important things and I appreciate it."

GB: "All the best to you, Mikhail."

MG: "Goodbye."

It was the voice of a good friend; it was the voice of a man to whom history will give enormous credit.

There was something very moving about this phone call—a real historic note. I mentioned to him Camp David and wanting him back up here—the place where he threw the "ringer"—and I think he would like that; but this is the way I feel. I didn't want to get too emotional, but I literally felt like I was caught up in real history with a phone call like this. It was something important, some enormous turning point. God, we're lucky in this country—we have so many blessings.

CHAPTER 15

The Worst of Times

We began 1992 with an important trip to Asia, visiting Australia, Singapore, South Korea, and Japan. The main purpose of the trip was trade, and we took with us a large contingent of American businessmen and CEOs. We considered the trip successful and felt a lot of progress had been made on opening up Asian markets to American products.

However, I'm afraid that is not what most people remember about this trip.

January 9th

I'm dictating this on Thursday in the Akasaka Palace [in Tokyo.] Last night, I went to the dinner given by [Prime Minister Kiichi] Miyazawa, and half way through the receiving line, I began to feel very faint and broke out in a big sweat. I knew I was going to throw up. I asked to be excused from the receiving line, and this caused a lot of consternation, so I went into the bathroom, threw up in there, came back, finished the line, and I felt very, very weak.

I should have gone home but I didn't. I could not eat anything at the dinner—a beautiful dinner, beautiful music—and I couldn't even carry on a conversation. I remember breaking out into a cold sweat, water just pouring out of me, and then the next thing I knew, literally, I was on the floor. I woke up, and I had this euphoric feeling. It's hard to describe it, but it was a light, out of body feeling, 100 percent strange. I looked up and there staring at me were the faces of nurses, the doctors, and the Secret Service guys. I realized I was lying flat on the floor, having thrown up all over Miyazawa.

Barbara saved the day by injecting a little humor, and she stayed at the dinner. They brought in an ambulance, and I decided, no, I would walk out. I put my tie back on, rebuttoned my collar and walked out. I didn't feel all that bad.

The press is dominated by the news of my illness and apparently it was all over the television—my collapsing.

Frankly, we think the visit has been very important, and I think it has gone well. We've re-established our position as a Pacific power, talking about security as well as trade. But the carpers and critics are bitching away at home.

[Miyazawa] was so understanding about my humiliating illness. That was the damnedest experience. Not the best for him either. He is a decent man, older man, has a good perspective and knows the importance of the United States to Japan.

[I have great respect for Kiichi, and he and I remain good friends. Since I've left office, we have met in both Tokyo and Houston.]

January 11, 1992

Dear Ron [Reagan],

I am writing this to you on my new computer at Camp David.

When I got back from throwing up on our friend P.M. Miyazawa, I found that large, lovely picture of the 5 of us.* It will go into that beautiful frame that you gave us. Thanks so very much for such a special present.

The trip to Asia, in spite of the carping and whining from the Democrat protectionists, aided and abetted by the Washington Post, was a success. We made progress getting into the glass, computer and, yes, auto markets. Much left to be done but at least we tried and did it without reverting to Protectionism.

Again my sincere thanks for that present.

I hope you are well and enjoying life to the fullest. Warmest Regards,

George

---

*A photo of the five living Presidents—Nixon, Ford, Carter, Reagan, and me—taken a few months earlier at the dedication of the Reagan Library.

1-12-92

Mr. John P. Ellis*
Harvard University Institute of Politics
Cambridge, Massachusetts 02138
Dear John,

Just back from barfing on Miyazawa (bad news) to find your good letter of Dec. 26th (good news)

Thanks for the coffee machine. Yes, it will be a key item this summer. The house is well down the comeback trail according to Danny Philbrick.†

. . . I'm convinced the economy will bounce back—if it does, I think we'll be OK. Clinton, absent Mario [Cuomo], is getting a good ride; but he hasn't been through the big time meat grinder yet. . . .

Love to all,
GB

IMPORTANT ANNOUNCEMENT
February 6, 1992
THIS IS AN ALL POINTS BULLETIN FROM THE PRESIDENT
SUBJECT: MY DOG "RANGER"

Recently Ranger was put on a weight reduction program. Either that program succeeds or we enter Ranger in the Houston Fat Stock Show as a Prime Hereford.

All offices should take a formal 'pledge' that reads as follows:

"WE AGREE NOT TO FEED RANGER. WE WILL NOT GIVE HIM BISCUITS. WE WILL NOT GIVE HIM FOOD OF ANY KIND"

In addition Ranger's "access" is hereby restricted. He has been told not to wander the corridors without an escort. This applies to the East and West Wings, to the Residence from the 3rd floor to the very, very bottom basement.

Although Ranger will still be permitted to roam at Camp David, the Camp David staff including Marines, Naval Personnel, All Civilians and Kids are specifically instructed to 'rat' on anyone seen feeding Ranger.

Ranger has been asked to wear a "Do not feed me" badge in addition to his ID.

I will, of course, report on Ranger's fight against obesity. Right now he looks like a blimp, a nice friendly appealing blimp, but a blimp.

We need Your Help—All hands, please, help.

* My nephew, Nan's son.

†Danny Philbrick was rebuilding our home in Maine. For Christmas, all of the family had sent us "something that plugs in," a brilliant idea organized by my cousin Susue Robinson. The idea was to help us restock the house in Maine.

February 16th

We've left New Hampshire after an upbeat final day and I'm now back in Washington. So many thoughts go through my head. This will be my last campaign in New Hampshire. I went through the fields of New Hampshire in the summer of '78, and then of course, '79, '80, and '88, and now this. It's hard to tell what's happening.

Right now, some of the polls have us 58 to 30—a couple of them there—but then there is this Bennett poll which has it much, much closer. Buchanan* is attacking and he's mean and ugly. The five Democrats continue to attack. My pitch is enough ugliness, enough campaign rhetoric, enough highfalutin plans with no detail to them. I've got to govern, and we've got our plan before the Congress. . . .

February 25, 1992

(Aboard Air Force One)
(Enroute San Francisco, California)

The Honorable Paul Cellucci
Lieutenant Governor,† State of Massachusetts
Boston, Massachusetts 02133
Dear Paul:

As I head west, my mind flashes back to my final campaign in New Hampshire. In '80, '88, and '92 you were right there by my side, and I just wanted you to know that I am very grateful for your steadfast support.

Despite the spin the press put on last Tuesday's outcome, the win was substantial.‡ We are all pleased with Sunday's great showing in Maine, and I look forward to the upcoming Southern Primaries.

All the best to you, Paul, and my sincere thanks again.

Warmest regards,
George Bush

March 2nd

Monday morning and it's a very beautiful, crisp and cool day, 45, it will probably get up into the 60's, and it's fantastic. It's almost like

---

*Pat Buchanan was the only GOP challenger in the primaries.

†My longtime friend and supporter is now the governor of Massachusetts.

‡Buchanan received 37 percent of the vote in New Hampshire, and some pundits said his "strong" showing was a "win." New Hampshire was his high-water mark, although he hung in until the last primary.

Spring has sprung on the 2nd day of March. There is something about the outdoors—and then I would add the grandchildren—that makes all of this ugly period seem less bad. There is a tomorrow and there is something over the horizon. I'm a fighter, I'll do my best, I'll keep on slugging. But I have that security of having tucked back— way back inside my mindset—the knowledge great happiness lies out there if indeed the voters just say "no."

I don't think they will. I have a quiet confidence that I will win. Some of it is because of the opposition; some of it is because I think things like World Peace and experienced leadership will make a difference; and some of it is because I think the economy is going to turn around. . . .

March 5, 1992

(En route Memphis, Tennessee)

The Honorable Richard M. Nixon
Woodcliff Lake, New Jersey 07675
Dear Dick,

I read your paper "How to lose the Cold War." I certainly agree with the major principle of this paper, namely, that we have an enormous stake with the democratic Russia. . . .

As you know, we are moving on the humanitarian food and medical aid front. Many American technologists are working with the newly energized private sector in Russia. More needs to be done. We are talking with the states of the former Soviet Union on a range of issues.

I am not sure what Russian goods are denied access to our markets. We are working with them on MFN. In my view, it is the EC that must open their markets more.

We are working on the prospects for a stabilization fund—though, we're talking megabucks here. We are also helping some on debt and perhaps can do more, along with the Europeans. . . .

I will be discussing much of this with Yeltsin when he comes over here. Incidentally, the more I see Yeltsin, the more I agree with your assessment of him. He seems to be bearing up well under an enormous amount of pressure.

I look forward to seeing you at the Library dinner next week.

Warm Regards,
George

March 9, 1992

Mr. Heinz Prechter*
ASC Incorporated
Southgate, Michigan 48195
Dear Heinz:

Thank you for your thoughtful and constructive letter. I appreciate, as always, your commitment to our success as a nation and to helping my Administration provide the necessary leadership.

I particularly like your emphasis on the positive. Our industries are becoming more competitive. The specific instances you mention of plants that have dramatically increased their productivity and of workers who have been successfully retrained illuminate this reality. We need to shine the spotlight on such places.

It not only provides genuine encouragement, but it also helps portray a more balanced picture of what is happening in this country. I agree with you that these success stories are all too infrequently reported in the diet of negative stories that fill the press these days.

As you point out, we are going through a period of necessary restructuring. Adjustment is never easy or painless. But we are doing those things that are crucial to competing successfully in a global economy over the long term.

I will make sure that our scheduling people are made aware of your suggestions of places to visit in Michigan. Finally, I take seriously and share your conviction that we need to be proactive rather than reactive. We will do everything we can here and, with the support of friends like you, I am confident we will prevail.

Sincerely,
George Bush

———————

I sent this letter to the entire cabinet:

March 10, 1992

The Honorable James Addison Baker
Secretary of State
Washington, DC 20520
Dear Jim,

It has been a grueling period, and spring is about to spring. Barbara and I would like to offer you and your immediate family 48 hours away from

---

*A good friend and supporter from Detroit. Heinz, who came here from Germany, is a great entrepreneur and gained fame by inventing the sunroof.

the Washington grind—a couple of days at Camp David. This could be scheduled during the week or on a weekend when we are not there. (Inasmuch as we go there most weekends, I would encourage you to go during the week.)

It is a great place to relax, to think, to write, or just plain be with the kids. To guarantee privacy and maximum R&R, only one family will be scheduled at a time. Should you desire to go up there with another Cabinet member however, that can be arranged.

My assistant, Patty Presock, will handle scheduling and coordinating all arrangements with Camp David. You can reach her at 456-7400.

Barbara and I hope you and your family will have an opportunity to enjoy Camp David sometime before this fall.

Sincerely,
George Bush

―――――――

I typed up these notes for the speechwriters on a Saturday at Camp David:

March 14, 1992

The Vision Thing

World Leadership to guarantee that our children live in peace, free from the fear of nuclear war in a world where all people know the blessings of democracy and freedom.

Leadership at Home to guarantee a better America. That means strengthening the American Family (family values). It means being the best in Education. It means winning the war on drugs and crime.

It means striving for a society free of bigotry and hate.

To achieve this 'vision' we must remain as the active leader of the entire world. We must be sure our word is credible—that means we must not only have the convictions about democracy and freedom, but we must have a strong National Defense posture. Our security comes first but the security of other friends around the world is vital too.

To achieve the domestic 'vision' we must fully implement America 2000 in education. That program, with its emphasis on Math and Science etc., will guarantee our leadership in the highly competitive evolving world.

To reassure Americans about their standard of living and their own prosperity we must expand, not shrink, our involvement and leadership in international trade.

We must find every way possible to strengthen the American family. Parental involvement in schools; community action programs that build on our "Points of Light" concept.

To address family concerns on health care we must press for prompt enactment of a new health care plan.

And to guarantee our prosperity we must make a major effort to control the ever spiraling debt of this country.

"Family, Jobs, Peace" can be expanded to :

World Peace and Freedom Abroad led and guaranteed by a strong America. At home, domestic tranquillity where family is strengthened, educational excellence achieved, the threat of drugs and crime eliminated, and the spirit of America is renewed by government being close to the people and by a 'points of light' concept enhanced, a concept which appeals to the better nature of man, a concept of neighbor helping neighbor.

———————

It was a sensitive time in our relationship with Israel. They were asking for $10 billion in loan guarantees, mainly to help them with the huge influx of Soviet immigrants. However, their insistence on continuing the settlement of the West Bank—a key issue in peace negotiations with the Arabs—was putting the United States in a difficult position and hindering the peace process. Israel was an old friend and ally, but I made the tough decision to delay the loan guarantees until they agreed to stop building settlements in the disputed territories because the money, either directly or indirectly, would support those settlements. All hell broke out. I wrote this letter to George Klein, a successful New York City real estate man and a Republican activist in the Jewish community:

March 19, 1992

Mr. George Klein
New York, New York 10022
Dear George:

I have now had the chance to read your letter with the care it deserves. I want you to know that I appreciate your sending it to me; one should never assume that Presidents get the benefit of what people are truly thinking. What you have to say pains me, but I thank you for being a true friend and saying it.

I, too, am anguished over the loan guarantee issue. Having helped bring about the massive immigration,* I would like nothing more than to help see it through, but Israeli settlement activity leaves me little choice. I could not alter long-standing U.S. policy and still be a force for peace. We say that settlements are an obstacle to peace, and they are. I do not exaggerate when I tell you that more than anything else Israel is saying or doing, settlements are undermining

———————

*Our administration had worked hard, and successfully, at getting permission for Soviet Jews to emigrate to Israel.

those forces in the Arab world that at long last are ready to reach out and live in peace with Israel.

Some people here and in Israel suggest that the loan guarantees are solely humanitarian and that we ought not to make them political. But I would argue that it is the settlements that have made this issue political and that in any event peace is also a humanitarian goal. The new immigrants and indeed all Israelis deserve and need peace—real peace along the lines I described in Madrid—if Israel and its people are to thrive. What makes this all so critical is the fact that we finally have a peace process worthy of the name. Nothing should be allowed to jeopardize its prospects; and let me add that we do now have a peace process that was put together in very large part on Israel's terms. For over 40 years Israel has wanted to sit in face-to-face negotiations with its Arab neighbors. We have produced just that. The Arabs know full well that we cannot and will not impose our preferences on Israel. Nor will we link aid vital to Israel's security to policy questions. Our fundamental commitment to Israel is just that—fundamental. Please know this, for it comes from the heart as well as the head.

I hope the guarantee question can still be worked out. I recently proposed a compromise that would enable Israel to receive the full $10 billion. The only part reported in the press was $300 million up front. This proposal was rejected by certain key senators. I still would like this matter resolved. Quite frankly, it will depend upon the priorities of those in Israel's government. But whatever happens, it is essential that this issue not be allowed to weaken, much less cast doubt upon, the core relationship between the United States and Israel. No one should permit disagreement over this or some other policy to affect the foundation of a relationship that has served both countries well for nearly half a century. I for one will do my part to make sure it does not.

George, it is in all candor that I tell you I write this response to your letter with more than a little frustration. I know there is a tendency to add up all the areas where we and Israel have disagreed over the past three years and assume that it represents a trend and a departure from the past. I do not want to raise up all the disputes from previous decades, although I would point out that the past was not always quite the golden age that some remember it to be. Rather, I would prefer to remind people of what we did on Ethiopian and Soviet Jewry, on repealing Zionism is Racism, on defeating aggression during the Gulf War, on convening Madrid and Moscow and the bilateral and multilateral talks to follow. My guess is that historians will look at today's controversy and wonder what much of the fuss was about. There have been and are important differences between our two countries, but no less important are the many examples of cooperation. With so much at stake, we cannot afford to lose perspective.

I have come to believe that the measure of a good relationship is not the ability to agree, but rather the ability to disagree on specifics without placing fundamentals at risk. We do this all the time with Britain: we should manage to do it with Israel. Without assigning responsibility or blame, let me simply say that I am certain that we in the Administration can and need to do better at making this relationship succeed. I will do all that I can to see that the current strains do not grow worse but to the contrary are put behind us, so we can begin to restore with Israel the sort of relationship that you and I both seek.

Thank you again for writing. As always, I appreciate your counsel and value our friendship.

Sincerely,
George Bush

[When Yitzhak Rabin became prime minister, we worked out our differences and Israel received the loan.]

March 30, 1992

Dear Trammell,*

In Lord Tennyson's work that you sent me—excerpted from Ulysses, the bottom line says it all:

To strive, to seek, to find, and not to yield.

These are not the easiest of times, but I am more determined than ever to strive, to seek, to find, and not to yield.

We have much to be grateful for in America; and yet all we hear in the news media is gloom, doom, and dreary pessimism. This will change as the economy comes out of the doldrums.

It is a crazy political year. And it is ugly, too; but this will pass when the election is over if not sooner.

I cannot read the opposition, nor do I spend much time trying. I am trying to move Congress to pass my education, crime, tort reform legislation and more; and I will keep on trying.

One thing, Trammell, that remains very, very clear in my mind is that I am fortunate to have a great strong family and many friends—what a difference that makes.

Love to Margaret.

Most Sincerely,
George

---

*Trammell Crow, a good friend and successful businessman from Dallas.

March 31st

I had an interesting lunch with Howard Baker and McClure.* They are both very concerned about Ross Perot,† but I told them that in three months, he will not be a worry anymore. Perot will be defined, seen as a weirdo, and we shouldn't be concerned with him. They both said, "Well, we hope you're right but we don't agree with you." My view is that when he begins to get defined, either by his opponents or by the press, people are going to see him as strange. Yes, they want change, but they don't want to turn the country over to an eccentric billionaire. Their view is that the move for change is so much outside, that outsiders are in and insiders are out; and that Perot can take his money and parlay himself into victory or into a serious threat. We need to be very wary of this, but time will tell.

————————

April 1st

The economic news for the first time seems universally upbeat. The confidence reports come out and they show major increases in confidence, which is something we've been waiting for a long, long time. I think it's a little early to say our woes are over—way too early—but this turn in the economy, plus a decision on the Democratic side,‡ makes me feel that we might be seeing a real light at the end of this tunnel. . . .

April 8th

It's a good day. Fed drops the [interest] rates one quarter, and Noriega goes to prison for 120 years. . . . It's big, big news and sends a strong message to indicted drug dealers.

Panama is doing much better. They are growing at 9%; Democracy is there; American lives were protected; and one of the results was that this drug warlord was brought to trial and is going to pay a price. . . .

————————

*Republican senator Jim McClure of Idaho.

†Perot had decided he wanted to be President. They were right and I was wrong. In the final analysis, Perot cost me the election.

‡By this time it was obvious Governor Bill Clinton of Arkansas would be the nominee. I was convinced I could beat him.

April 10, 1992

The Honorable Bill Goodling
U.S. House of Representatives
Washington, D.C. 20515
Dear Bill,

Thanks for your letter. It is not my intention to recklessly "bash" the Congress. . . . I hope you agree that real reform is needed—not "perk" reform but real reform. Harry Truman did a pretty good job of running against the entrenched leadership in Congress when things were far less fundamentally fouled up.

I think just one two-year period of Republican control would shake up the ingrained bureaucracy and effect real change.

Thanks, my friend, for checking in.

Sincerely,
George Bush

———————

We were in the middle of trying to decide whether I should attend the United Nations Conference on Environment and Development, to be held in Rio de Janeiro in June. Even though we knew the agenda would be liberal, I felt I should go and eventually did. I received a taped message, "Go to Brazil," from Olivia Newton-John and a group of other Hollywood celebrities.

April 16, 1992

Ms. Olivia Newton-John
Malibu, California 90265
Dear Olivia,

That tape was super. The voices compelling, the message clear.

A final decision will be made very soon. This is a very rough and ugly year as I am sure you know. I hope you will look over the attached pamphlet. I hope it conveys to you my fundamental and total commitment to sound environmental policy.

I think everyone understands that there is a lot of economic hurt in our country today. People without jobs are hurting and those with jobs often wonder if they will have those jobs tomorrow. We must consider not only the critical environmental needs, but also the economic needs of so many American families. I am confident that both needs can be met—they must be met.

Thanks for that tape, made obviously with caring and love.

Now—will you please thank John Forsythe, Jane Seymour and Dennis Weaver, Cher, the Ekharts, those little kids—Tracy, Katlin, Chloe and the rest, my admired friends Joel Grey and Tony Danza, John Ritter, Rita Coolidge, all the rest and of course your sister Rona, whom I so enjoyed meeting.

We will have that personal meeting—soon I hope. In the meantime, your Taped Message made an impact—honest!

> Most Sincerely
> George Bush

———

April 23, 1992

Sam [Skinner]:*

Given the latest **Devroyism**† please ask that our fundraising techniques be reviewed. This article read like 'influence peddling' and I am disturbed by that. I hope the campaign is not going the **hard ball** route and are not resorting to gimmicks that cheapen the Presidency.

> GB

PS Her story related to NRCC‡ but let's check anyway

———

April 26, 1992

Sunday (The 26th day of a nice month but in an ugly year)

Dear Peggy [Noonan],

I agree on Clinton he's got more facts—he's better at facts-figures than I am. I'm better at life. He's a nice guy; and I've always gotten along fine with him.

Glad you're coming here.

We need you—

> Con Afecto (that's Spanish),
> GB

———

I wrote this note to my good friend Dick Jackman, who for years worked for Sun Oil in Philadelphia. He's a great public speaker, especially well known for his humor.

April 27, 92

Dear Dick,

. . . The last 5-6 months have been trying and downright ugly. The press have been awful and the campaigns have all gone after me with a vengeance. That's the bad news.

The good news is the economy is turning around and that will help a lot. I

---

*Previously secretary of transportation, Sam was now my chief of staff.

†Ann Devroy was a reporter for the *Washington Post*.

‡National Republican Congressional Committee.

will continue to focus on doing my job. I will stay out of the junk-yard dog attack business.

After the process is further along I will have to take on Clinton and who knows, even Ross Perot. I've known Ross a long time—a kind of take-my-marbles-and-go home kind of guy if it doesn't go his way.

Thanks, Dick for that wonderful letter of friendship & support

> Your friend,
> George Bush

May 11, 1992

Mr. John F. Welch, Jr., Chairman & CEO
General Electric Company
Fairfield, Connecticut
Dear Jack,

Bob Mosbacher told me that you had agreed to help with the coalition of business people—great!! So many thanks. These are weird and ugly political times; but I do have the feeling the heretofore sluggish economy is beginning to stir. That will help. I will concentrate on this job, then be ready to fight the political wars. It's no fun, but having you at my side makes it one hell of a lot better.

> Warm Regards,
> George

May 17th

It's Sunday, and I'm flying back from South Bend, Indiana to Washington. The weekends are wiped out and I get tired. In Houston I got to run on Friday, Saturday and this morning at 6:30 a.m., running a little over two miles each time on the outdoor track at the Houstonian. That really helps. Running in that hot weather loosens up the old joints and I feel pretty good. . . .

We had a lovely dinner at the Kerrs. It was really fun with the Liedtkes, Brucie Ashman, Daphne Murray, Bessie Liedtke and the Nebletts right in our old neighborhood. It seemed so quiet, so normal and so nice. The kids and their kids, and their neighborhood kids with their little kids were out to greet us. The Vanderhofs even came over, which was nice. My mind went back to the wonderful games that we had in the area and the time that Jeb hit a home run through the Vanderhof girls' window. Barbara was furious and I was thrilled because it was a second story window. It was a powerful, towering hit by our little left-hander, so it was nostalgic. We talked about the old days. Nobody got too far into the problems we face in Washington these days. . . .

In my speech at Notre Dame today, I talked about family values. I followed the Valedictorian, who was a rather skinny and plain girl who made a pitch for more understanding about gays and lesbians. She got booed a little and, frankly, she talked longer than I did. She is a 4.0 student but one of those people that felt since the President is present, here's a chance to give him a little lecture. She got some cheering from the crowd. I thought she went on too darn long and should have resisted getting her own social agenda out there, like "Stop bragging about victory in the Cold War," she says. If Jerry Brown fails, they ought to get this girl right into the act—or maybe she can help out Patricia Ireland.* It was sad and predictable. Some of it you can explain by youthful zealousness, but she came on awfully strong and awfully long—too bad.

Anyway, nobody seemed to give a damn, and I got a very warm reception from the students when I walked in, which made me feel good . . .

———

May 18th

I can hardly believe the television coverage on Notre Dame. Barbara asked me if I was badly received—she having watched CNN last night. I said, no, everybody thought I was well received. Then I watched the morning news and the networks all picked up on it. . . . The skinny valedictorian got all the coverage on the television and it barely touched on what I had to say . . . No mention of the standing ovation and the general warmth of the crowd. Now I'm wondering what we are up against. . . .

———

George Bell, who was from Philadelphia, was one of my oldest friends given that our parents were good friends. He was dying of cancer.

May 18, 1992

Dear George,

Ever since I talked to Bertie and then you last week my thoughts have strayed from our nation's business. I'll be working on some problem, and sud-

———

*Jerry Brown, the former governor of California, was running for President. He had the reputation of being a child of the sixties. Patricia Ireland was head of the National Organization of Women.

denly my mind will shift; and I'll find myself wondering if you're hurting, how all the tests are going, who's there with you, and on it goes.

I wish I could be there—better still I wish I could help. I wish I knew just exactly what to do to make you feel better.

I know you are very sick; and I also know you are a tough courageous guy. If there's a way to whip it, you'll find that way.

I am President of the United States and at 67 (oops almost 68) I've seen a lot, experienced a lot; but one thing is very very clear to me—Friendships really count. They really matter. I treasure ours. I always have, I always will. It's not just that you were a good sport when we did in you and Shepley for $100 way back then on the Prout's* tennis court. Nor is it that we go so far back that I can clearly remember your Dad and mine teasing and kidding each other when we were little kids. No it's just plain—we're friends; and when all is said and done that is very important to me. And there's one other thing. I want you to know it.

I love you very much—my friend

George Bush

———

May 19th

The lawn looks greener than ever. The tragedy is that my three little ducklings were killed by the crows. On the first day, they got one of them; and then yesterday, the mother and the father flew away to get food and when they came back, the ducklings had been killed by the crows. I now see the male Mallard down there on the pond. It's funny how one can't get a little incident like this out of one's mind. But it's nature. The crows are mean. They start yelling at the dogs all the time and my feeling is to blast them, but I guess we can't do that. The dogs love bouncing through the ivy—that's where the dead birds fall. They come out dragging dead birds—horrible looking carcasses—but they love to hunt in there. They even go to the bathroom right in the middle of the ivy—no problem.

I keep thinking of George Bell, my dear friend who is dying of liver and pancreatic cancer, and it's just too much. It makes you very fatalistic.

There is a crow sitting on top of a lonely pine—a small pine right out on the knoll leading down to the road, leading down to the pond. The crow is sitting all alone up there—an easy shot . . .

———

*Prout's Neck, Maine, where the Bells had a house. Ethan Shepley was a friend of ours from St. Louis.

June 1, 1992

Mr. Earle M. Craig, Jr.
Midland, Texas 79702-1351
Dear Earle:

I received your fax, written from the heart.

These are very difficult days. Ross Perot is on a rocket, saying nothing, criticizing me and tapping into the anti-incumbent, anti-Washington theme.

I do not share your view about the campaign; though I do think we have to tighten up the coordination between the staff here and the campaign. Steps have already been taken to do that.*

The Economy is recovering and eventually that will help a lot.

A statistic—the economy grew at 2.4 percent in the first quarter and, yet, according to polls, 70 percent of the people still think it is getting worse. There is a lag that will be corrected and the correction will help us.

Keep the suggestions coming, old friend. Love to you and Dottie.

Sincerely
George

June 6, 1992

To: Bob Teeter/ Sam Skinner
A reminder:

We must figure out how to get out in front of the **DEBATE** question. The debate commission is moving. The nets are moving. Every goo-goo group is moving; and I just want to be sure I'm not put in a losing position. I am not sure what we should be doing.

Maybe we should say. "Yes, I'll debate Clinton once on domestic and once on Foreign" and we'll [deal] with Perot after he becomes a candidate.

Maybe we should say "If Clinton and Perot decide to do a lot of debates, fine let 'em go forward without me."

There are many other formulations.

All Yours!
George

---

*Many of my friends and supporters felt my campaign was in disarray. Part of the problem was I was too darn busy trying to be President.

June 9th

A big debate in the campaign is, how many television shows to do. I want to respect the office of the President, keep its dignity; but the networks are blocking out our television press conference. We may have no other choice but to do the new fad, which is the call-in shows or the network morning news. On Larry King—I told Larry I'd like to do his show, but we've got to do it all with a certain sense of dignity, a certain sense of propriety. I don't want to get caught up, obviously, with Phil Donahue and these sensationalistic, left-handed Mary's-lost-her-cousin kind of shows. . . .*

June 10th

Our new ducks are here and we put a cage in the pond to keep the crows from attacking them. They are doing very well today. The mother had the ducks over by the swimming pool and they walked down, leading a little procession all the way down to the pond. Then they jumped in. I went down and looked at them in the morning and then asked the groundskeeper to do something to make sure the crows don't get them. They are very special. . . .

I read a wonderful column in the Times *of London where the writer said America is still the country where everyone else wants to live. "From recent headlines one would imagine a country teetering towards the apocalypse," he wrote in bewilderment.*

June 11, 1992

Mr. Charles Bremner
c/o Times of London
ENGLAND
Dear Charles,

As I fly to Rio [de Janeiro] in controversy, I am going through a huge stack of papers. Now, this minute, I've stopped; because in that stack was your column about the USA.

I commend you for putting our great country into proper perspective.

I hope that soon the nonsense—writers, the political pundits, and, yes, the candidates will understand that you have the right feel for the USA—"not sinking backwards" "forging ahead" "taking the good with the bad".

---

*In retrospect, Phil Donahue was mild compared to today's Jerry Springer types.

Obviously, after your time here, you understand us. I hope your life over there is full of new challenges and happiness, too.

Sincerely,
George Bush

———————

Doro and Bobby Koch were married at our little chapel at Camp David on June 27. It was a happy family celebration.

June 28th

I pick Doro up in a golf cart with flowers on it and it looked real cute. She looked beautiful. She stopped, as we walked into the church, and cried and turned around and said, "I'll be all right." And then she got up to the altar and Ellie was on her left and Bobby was on her right—and then Sam. The kids got a little reckless, but it was a wonderful service. Sam and Ellie turned and whispered, "Mother is crying"—but it all worked out well, and they went off. Bobby called in thoughtfully from the hotel at Dulles just to be sure we had their place and their schedule.* . . .

———————

July 8th

We're heading for Finland.† It's 9:30 and bright daylight. There are tons of lakes, and we're about to land. We've got some transportation: the phones work; everything is on time; helicopters; great big 747's; beautiful room in front; I'm President of the United States and am treated with great deference.

And yet, I have this marvelous feeling that no matter what lies over the horizon, it will be good. I think I'll win—I'm convinced I'll win. But this little creeping thought comes to mind—if I don't win, I'll be a very happy guy. I'll be opening the beans and the franks—the beans and the brown bread Sunday nights. I'll be washing the dishes with Bar. I'll be going to bed early every once in awhile; do something to help someone else; hold my grandchildren in my arms; look for the shellfish; take them fishing. If I make any money, I might say to Noelle, "Let's fly to Helsinki. Let me show you what it's like half way around the world."

I'll watch Ellie grow up. I'll hold Pierce and Lauren and Ashley.

*We were baby-sitting the kids while they were on their honeymoon.
†For a CSCE conference on arms control.

I'll make it up to Neil. I'll spend time up at Texas A&M* teaching, maybe; but just blending in; growing old with grace and kindness; and truly count my blessings. And then every once in awhile, some big shot will come in—some officeholder, some King, some Prince, some Prime Minister, and some President, and they'll say, "I'd like to see old George Bush."

I'll invite them to our little house and we'll have no press corps, no following, no frantic statements, and we'll look back together and say these were interesting times. And then at night, I'll say that I did my very best, tried my hardest, kept it honest; and put something back into the system.

———————

July 21, 1992

The Honorable Hugh Gregg
Nashua, New Hampshire 03062
Dear Hugh,

No, no your 'impertinence' is not boundless, you're checking in is helpful—a reality check, if you will.

I don't agree on all points. We must make the American people understand why the good proposals I have made have not been passed. Read [David] McCullough's new book on Truman, and read how Harry put it in perspective.

Since your memo was written, Clinton-Gore† have gone into orbit. They have been hyper critical of me. I have been relatively silent. This has got to change. I recognize the danger of the "Blame Syndrome", however.

Hugh, I'm rushing off to yet another event, but I have digested your letter and, believe me, it did not offend.

Love to all Greggs,
George

———————

My friend Bill Clark, former head of the NSC and deputy secretary of state in the Reagan administration, wrote a note saying he did not think we were doing enough to solve the growing ethnic violence in the Balkans. As a result, he said he could no longer support me.

———————

*I had decided my presidential library would be built at Texas A&M.
†Al Gore was now Clinton's running mate.

July 21, 1992

The Honorable William P. Clark
Paso Robles, California 93446
Dear Bill,

I received your personal letter of July 15 and needless to say I'm terribly disappointed. We're trying very hard to have a constructive policy in that troubled area of the world. Neither the Serbs nor the Croatians are without blame when it comes to the killing. Although clearly we put the major share of the blame on Milosevic.*

When I was abroad I had a brief meeting with Tudjman† and a meeting with the Bosnian President. We're terribly troubled by all of this and without throwing a lot of American troops into the fray, we're trying to bring about peace in the area. It is not easy and I would welcome your suggestions as to how the policy should be changed.

I do understand the depth of your feeling and Bill, you've got to know that I respect not only your frankness but the warm, personal words.‡ I am engaged in a very tough battle for re-election. At this moment, we are way behind in the polls, but I have a quiet confidence that I will win. Obviously, I regret your decision and some day I hope you will be back at my side in the political wars.

My warmest best wishes to Joan. You have indeed been my friend and I hope that that will continue.

Most sincerely,
George

———————

As we headed toward the fall campaign, I became concerned that we needed to shore up the White House staff for the tough battle ahead. I turned to an old friend. Jim Baker took a leave of absence as secretary of state and became White House chief of staff and senior counselor to the President.

8-13-92

Jim—

As I listened to that thunderous applause at State just now,§ I realized just how much you are giving up to come here. I am so very grateful.

Get some rest. I'm glad we will be side by side in the battle ahead—

Your Friend,
George

*At that time Slobodan Milosevic was president of the Yugoslav republic of Serbia.
†Franjo Tudjman, leader of the ruling party in the newly independent Croatia.
‡He said he would always be my friend.
§I was watching his "good-bye" statement at the State Department.

August 22nd

The Convention has come and gone. It's been the darndest roller-coaster ride I've ever seen, but we apparently got a good bounce out of the Convention. I checked the morning paper and it says we're 2 points back which is statistically an even race. I don't believe it at all, but everyone thinks things have turned. . . .

The Gulfport, Mississippi, rally was magnificently upbeat. People were waiting for two to three hours in the hot, hot sun and it was entirely different, and a more upbeat spirit then before the Convention. They all talked about it, and the signs reflected it. . . .

There was a tremendous rally in Branson, Missouri: Mo Bandy and Loretta Lynn and others. There were literally 15,000 people out there and I would have said even more. There were signs as far as you could see. The chant that is catching on is: "Clean the House."* The crowd has been doing it—not me. . . .

September 3rd

Tonight Bar came home. She had been down in Florida and she had been campaigning with Gerald McRaney, Major Dad of television fame. She said he was absolutely fantastic. He stepped right in and defended me and doing this out of his own kindness and his own belief. She said he was wonderful.

I went for a run on the White House grounds, analyzing the Teeter poll results which were most discouraging, and then called Bar up and she came down and we walked around the front grounds. Our ducks were all gone, so we came up, sat on the porch, and had a nice drink before dinner, hoping the ducks would come back in. But nothing happened other than a little softball action across the fence towards the monument. It's peaceful, quiet, and the weather was perfect . . .

I found my mind drifting off—what happens if we should not make it? . . . I guess I'd have to say that I would have failed. Then I said to myself, it's not going to happen. I'm a better person, better qualified, and better character to be President, despite some short-comings that I may have and there are plenty of them . . .

Everything is ugly and everything is nasty. But we are a family,

*Meaning House of Representatives.

and I have a certain inner quiet peace, which I'm not sure I've ever had in a situation like this. . . .

———————

September 12, 1992

To: JAB III

I note that we are to do some 'filming' at Camp David.

I have been very careful about using Camp David in any way for publicity. I have done a broadcast from up here. If, indeed, we need to do some family shooting here we must be sure that we don't shoot in any way to call attention to Camp David itself.

Also please see that no one comes up here unless absolutely essential to the project. It is our oasis and I really want to keep it that way.

Thanks

GB

———————

September 13th

I feel much more of a frustration. I guess I'm a little tired, but I'm also frustrated by the press treatment about the distortion of who I am. The record is one thing, but when they distort your character and try to make you ugly—that's a little too much. But you can't feel sorry, you just have to take the message out, keep plugging away, keep working, working hard, and that's what I'm doing and that's what I'll continue to do. Sunday the 13th—52 more days? I can make it; I can out hustle Clinton; out work him; out jog him; out think him; out campaign him; and we'll win. But it's an ugly spot in the road right now. . . .

———————

Sept 16. 1992

Rep. Solarz*

Dear Steve—

I've lost a couple of elections in the past and it hurts. I know that. I just want you to know that I will never forget and always be grateful for your leadership on Desert Storm.

Perhaps, as the voters went to the polls up there, they've forgotten your courage on all that. I never will.

Good luck in what I'm sure will be a bright & challenging future.

Most sincerely,

George Bush

*Democratic congressman from New York who had lost his primary election.

9-18-92

Sen. Robert Byrd
Dear Robert,

These are ugly, confrontational times; but I'm darned if I'm going to let them ruin relationships. I want to thank you for sitting down so constructively with Dick Darman. I look forward to post-election days when we can all really try to cooperate and get things done.

These ugly times have not diminished my respect for you nor Barbara's and my friendship for you and Erma.

Sincerely,
George

October 12th

The day after the first debate. The bottom line is that after the debate our team, I think, genuinely felt we had won or certainly had not lost, and that Perot would emerge as the big winner with his homilies and that Clinton had lost.

And then I pick up the papers in the morning and they say that I had come in third. . . .

The only joy is that if we should lose, there's great happiness over the horizon, but it will be a very painful process—not for losing but letting people down and being vilified for three more months. The big thing is to conduct myself with decency and with honor. So now we go back to the drawing board dictating this at 5:45 a.m. in St. Louis. I start off now to Pennsylvania and then to Michigan and the hill out there is steep to climb. You've got to keep the spirits up for the people around us, got to keep working extra hard, and damn sure can't let this news get everyone down. But what was joy last night is now a somber assessment this morning. . . .

This is all extraordinarily tough on Barbara. She is still wildly popular and gets a wonderful response, but I can tell she is hurting for me. She refuses to watch the television; refuses to read the papers; and she tells me to turn it off when I turn it on because it is always hammering away at me.

The White House staff are wonderful, so sympathetic, so encouraging, so smiling, and so are the boys on Air Force One. I think they really ache for us during this difficult period. I still have this sense of confidence that we're going to win, but I must say it has been bruised and jarred. . . .

_____

October 16th

Colin Powell calls. I mentioned him last night as a possible candidate for President of the United States when they asked me about black leaders, and I saluted him. So he called and thanked me for that and said his relatives were calling from all over. . . .

He said he knew it was the ugliest period for us and didn't know how we could get through it, etc.; but I said, "Well, let's have a drink afterward."

_____

October 20th

Musings from the train: the beauty of this part of South Carolina as we go into North Carolina is something to behold. The leaves are muted with tans and yellows but still plenty of greens. There are no bright reds like up in New England but there are copper tones, muted soft beautiful tones.

We stopped at the Waffle House this morning, symbolic perhaps, and sit next to two guys one of whom is working hard—a tree pruner, a bearded fellow—and he asks me about health care. He's got a 2 year old that has cystic fibrosis and he said, "I'm going to vote for you because I like your faith in God." He said I noticed that you called on God at the end of your speech last night. I thanked him for that. The guy on my left was kind of a small slight looking fellow who works the night shift at Piggly Wiggly, and his girlfriend, Vickie, works the night shift at the Waffle House. His dad has cirrhosis and they help him out as best they can. He's working hard and feels that life is not particularly fair; but he could not have been more pleasant. I loved his grassroots homilies, and after we were about to leave, some little girl came up with a bunch of funny jokes. Her mother was a waitress at the Waffle House, a tired looking aging blonde waitress—very nice—and she says, "What's your name? I said, "George Bush," and she says, "Spell it." So I said "B-U-S-H," and she says, "no, no it's wrong. . . . I told you to spell it I-T."

She had about six other knee slappers like that and it was a relaxed fun few minutes.

_____

October 22nd

Betty Liedtke died. It's now Thursday and I'm in yet another hotel—this one next to the Meadowlands—finishing three rallies today in New Jersey and waiting for a "Ask George Bush" session. And I called Hugh and he sounded composed and said the service is on Saturday. There goes another close friend—one that we love very, very much. I'd love to go to the service, drop everything and do it, but it's pretty hard to do. Barbara may go. My mind goes back to the wonderful times we had—her fantastic humor, her teasing us . . .

There was the time I got mad at Christmas time and broke one of the children's toys—one of the things you blow, the roller goes out like the birthday blower thing—anyway, I got mad at George and told him to stop doing it—no, it was one of those flutes that you pull the handle in and out and it makes a lot of noise. So I broke his flute and then for about three days at the office I'd pick up the telephone and there would be that flute sound and I'd hang up and it would be Betty Liedtke. She had a wonderful sense of humor. She was a great and loving mother, a true and loyal friend, and Hugh is going to be desperately lonely. And here I am caught up in this race and I just hope I can be there at this funeral . . .

_____

October 23rd

We're still trying to work it out to go to Betty Liedtke's funeral. Jim Baker was saying, "Well, can't Barbara do it?" And I'm saying, "No, this is our friend and it matters and it counts," so we're moving the whole schedule around. . . .

[I attended the funeral.]

_____

October 29th

It's now Thursday morning and we're in Detroit, I think. Yesterday was an exciting day. We got the report that two polls had closed—CNN and I believe an ABC poll—to 2 points. People were running back and forth on the plane. The rallies had a new zip and life to them. Bruce Willis was with us and he is amazed at the progress. He's very popular—a little earring in his left ear—an attractive guy that called me out of the clear blue sky and wants to help and here he is.

_____

November 2nd

This is the last day of campaigning in my entire life—the last full day of campaigning for myself for my entire life—and I think back to the days in East Texas with 2 or 3 people in the crowd and Bar and I pressed on across that enormous state back in 1964 with the polls showing us decimated and sure enough we were wiped out. . . .

I gave the same stump speech. My voice beginning to show signs of strain at the end. We have 4 or 5 more rallies to go. It's a joy having George with us—feisty fighter and campaigner if there ever was one—and he and Jim Baker sit up with me in my office on Air Force One and we talk about the pollsters and we talk about baseball commissioner, and how the job has changed, and we talk about the last hurrah, the last campaign forever. We told jokes: "Scrub it with a stiff brush and keep it clean." We even talked about who should be Chief of Staff in the White house after Jim Baker finishes his job, a job that I think will take 120 days.

. . . Marlin is fantastic and so is Brent. Brent is getting a little militant, thinking I ought to attack the press more. He knows this Iran stuff is an outrage, after all, he was on the Tower Commission [that investigated Iran-Contra] and he knows we're getting screwed on Iran-Contra. He knows the truth and the facts and he sees it as just an outrageous political ploy driven by the press.* . . .

The Oak Ridge Boys came into my little office on the plane and sang some gospel songs and just a handful of us were there. I sat on the chair opposite my desk and Mary Matalin† sat on the window sill and the Oaks were on the couch. Almost all of us had tears in our eyes when they sang "Amazing Grace"—so moving, so close, so warm, so strong—and I thought of Dad and I told George, "Boy, would my father ever have loved to have been here hearing these guys sing."

. . . I've given it my best shot, I've run the extra course, and George and Jeb say, "Dad, you've run a great campaign—there's nothing more you can do." And I'm grateful to them. They are the ones who have done so much work, taken so much flak on behalf of their

---

*In the final days of the campaign, Iran-contra reared its ugly head again. The special prosecutor Lawrence Walsh brought a politically charged indictment against former defense secretary Caspar Weinberger just five days before the election. That in turn raised old questions about my involvement. There is no doubt in my mind that this indictment—written by Walsh's deputy, who was a large contributor to Democratic campaigns—stopped our forward momentum.

†Mary was deputy campaign manager and one of my most loyal campaign workers and friends. After the campaign, she married James Carville, who ran Clinton's campaign.

father. They are the ones, all of them, who have lifted me and given me strength.

Barbara, of course, is slamming away out on the trail right now—I'm sure the hero of the hour wherever she goes—magnificent. . . .

November 4th

It's 12:15 in the morning, November 4th. The election is over—it's come and gone. It's hard to describe the emotions of something like this.

. . . But it's hurt, hurt, hurt and I guess it's the pride, too. . . . On a competitive basis, I don't like to see the pollsters right at the end; I don't like to see the pundits right; I don't like to see all of those who have written me off right. I was absolutely convinced we would prove them wrong but I was wrong and they were right and that hurts a lot.

I think of our country and the people who are hurting and there is so much we didn't do. There are so many places we tried, and yes, we made progress. But no, the job is not finished and that kills me. . . .

Now into bed, prepared to face tomorrow: Be strong, be kind, be generous of spirit, be understanding and let people know how grateful you are. Don't get even. Comfort the ones I've hurt and let down. Say your prayers and ask for God's understanding and strength. Finish with a smile and some gusto, and do what's right and finish strong.

Of course it is impossible not to wonder why. Part of that was answered by an unusual letter from Nestle Frobish, who said my comment "Being called dishonest by Bill Clinton is like being called ugly by a frog" was my undoing.

Nov. 4, 1992

Mr. Nestle J. Frobish
Worldwide Fairplay for Frogs Committee
Lyndonville, Vermont 05851
Dear Chairman Frobish,

You were right. It was the frog lover vote that did me in.

I'm the kind of guy who admits his mistakes. I apologize to all members of the Worldwide Fairplay for Frogs Committee. From now on as a private citizen I will croak out this message "Frogs are beautiful"! Keep on hopping—
George Bush

November 7, 1992

Dear Dick [Nixon],

The dust has begun to settle. It hurts still, but we Bushes will do fine.

I just want to thank you for the Tom Dewey letter and, of course, for your kind words.

I want to finish the course with no rancor, not blaming of others. Then Barbara and I will go back to Houston. We will try to be helpful and constructive citizens in our great community there.

As I contemplate private life the way in which one Richard Nixon has conducted himself in his post President private life will serve as a fine example of how to do it.

My respects always to you and Pat.

> Most Sincerely,
> George

November 10, 1992

Ms. Anne Fisher Williams
Thomasville, North Carolina 27360

Dear Ms. Williams:

Thank you for your letter and the news article that you enclosed, which just reached my desk. I was saddened to learn of your loss and extend my sincere condolences to you and your family.

I regret that our train trip last month interrupted your father's funeral procession. However, I was heartened to read that the incident helped to ease somewhat the tension of that solemn occasion. You're right; the Lord does work in mysterious ways. I know that He will keep you and your family strong in the days and weeks ahead.

Barbara joins me in sending warm wishes to you and yours. You are in our thoughts and prayers.

> Sincerely,
> George Bush

11-10-92

Dear Deke*—

I loved your letter.

Don't worry about me; for you see I learned a lot about life's ups and downs from <u>you</u>—years ago!

---

*Deke DeClementi, my old basketball coach at Andover. He went on to become the athletic director. He was a great influence on my life and I still keep in touch with him.

I hate not to finish the job; but we've done some good things.

Thanks for giving a damn about this old friend of yours who will always be grateful to you—

George

November 10th

Bob Dole had called and asked me to come to a Senate Dinner. It's an annual event and the President goes with all the Republican Senators. . . .

I dreaded going but then Bob made it fantastic. He choked up, he showed a warm side that many didn't feel he ever had. He was so generous in his comments and so thoughtful, and I thought to myself, "Here we are, a guy who I fought bitterly with in the New Hampshire primary, and now I salute him as a true leader, a wonderful leader, a guy who bent over backwards to do what the President wanted." I tried to say that in my remarks. They were unscripted, from the heart and I'm not sure they came through.

. . . I want to go to the Vietnam Memorial and read some names, but it would appear as show business, it would be seen as sticking it in Clinton's ear.* But maybe we can do it. Maybe I can get the agents up, go read a handful of names to participate, tell who's ever doing it on the around-the-clock basis that we don't want to be show business but we wanted to participate, do it without the media.

I'm thinking of it as I'm walking past the fountain. Maybe I should wake up Barbara and we should do it. There's not much time left to say what is in my heart but one thing I care about is Vietnam.

The fountain is beautiful and the light on the middle spout makes it stand out in a spectacular way. The other eight little fountains supplement the beauty of the middle one and I think of our ducks. I look out across at the Jefferson, at its stoic beauty. There is the tennis court where we've had so much fun, so many challenges, so many dog-eat-dog matches, and around the corner is the obscured horseshoe pit. The joy I've gotten from seeing the groundskeepers and the ushers and the electricians battling in the tournaments knows no bounds.

I walk around the [circle drive] and I decide to go to the Vietnam Memorial. I don't want any press but the Secret Service sends a guy

---

*I am referring to the controversy surrounding Clinton and the Vietnam War and how he got out of the draft.

over and there are about 20 or 30 people there. It's the 10th Anniversary [of the wall] and tomorrow's Veteran's Day and I want to read some names. It's going to be emotional, I think. Barbara has indicated that she wants to go so I wake her up although she was sound asleep. It's now 11:35 and the agents call and say, "There are only a handful of people there," so off we go.

November 18, 1992

Dear Trammell [Crow],

Now, for sure, I feel **welcome back to the world.** It was your wonderful letter that did the trick.

Thank you so very much for your most generous offer.* It is something that Barbara and I would very much like to do at some time. It is a little early to pin down details, though. The main thing is that your offer has been a wonderful tonic. Just thinking about what you have suggested does the job.

Yesterday we decided to build a small town house on our little lot in Houston. We plan to spend 50% of our time there and 50% in Maine. I haven't even begun to sort out what I will do, but the future looks exciting. The disappointment about not finishing the job here is beginning to subside.

I certainly will not be actively involved in any more politics; but one thing is for sure—I will always be grateful to you and yours who have been at my side for so long.

My Love to Margaret and, again, my profound thanks to you.

George

November 18th

It's now the evening of the 18th and my visit with Clinton has come and gone.

It went well. He's very friendly, very respectful and asked my advice on certain things. . . .

We talked about Yugoslavia, Kosovo, Serbia, Bosnia, etc., and the difficulties he might anticipate there. I told him that I thought that was most likely to be the prime trouble spot. . . .

He was grateful and I took him to see the White House second and third floors, and Barbara coming out with her hair almost in curlers, to say hi. His reaction to the White House was "wow" . . .

*He offered us his yacht, to use whenever we wanted to get away. We took him up on his offer in the summer of 1993.

Gary Walters* was there and went on the tour with us. I introduced him to some of the people that were there in the house, some of the maids, etc. . . .

I told him walking out, "Bill, I want to tell you something. When I leave here, you're going to have no trouble from me. The campaign is over, it was tough and I'm out of here. I will do nothing to complicate your work and I just want you to know that." And he was quite appreciative and I've got to try to do just that.†

Nov. 19, 1992

The Right Honorable John Major, M.P.
Prime Minister
London
Dear John,

I saw your kind comments made at the Lord Mayor's Banquet on Nov. 16th.

You are a loyal friend—a true and generous friend—

Yesterday Bill Clinton told me of his talk with you on the phone. He said, "You know I already have great respect for John Major, for in our phone conversation he told me up front of his wonderful personal relationship with you—I respect that".

Nice words by our new President. Now many thanks again from our old President.

Love to Norma.

George

November 19th

I go up to see Mother this morning, Doro and I. There is no way to really describe the emotions I felt. Her breathing was difficult. She lay on a pillow, tiny, fighting hard for every breath . . . Doro and I sat next to her bed sobbing. Her little frayed Bible, her old one was there, and I looked in it and there were some notes that I had written her from Andover . . .

The memories of her teaching me about life, memories of her sweetness and her leading by example, the strength of her faith, her great capacity for love and kindness . . .

---

*The efficient head usher at the White House, in charge of the residence staff.
†With few mild exceptions, I feel I've stuck to this pledge.

I feel drained even now hours later . . . I'm so glad I didn't take Marvin—he wanted to go but couldn't—because the bawl patrol* would have consisted of three and then we might not have been able to recover. . . .

Mother died tonight at 5:05. . . .

"Mum, I hope you know how much we all love you and care." Tonight she is at rest in God's loving arms and with Dad.

Sig Rogich, who had worked with me in the White House as special assistant to the President for public events and initiatives before I named him ambassador to Iceland, had a reputation around the White House for being a natty dresser.

November 22, 1992

Dear Sig,

I am sitting up here at Camp David looking to the future and counting my many blessings.

I am dressed in fall colors. I have on a brown sweater, a subtly checked shirting of muted greens and rusty reds and amber, too.

Bar said when I left Aspen Cottage just now "You look like Sig dressed you". Then I thought, he did. But not just in amber and mauve. He dressed me by making me a better person—not just looking into the lens and not just making me a touch more real to others, but by watching and learning as he unfailingly supported me, by showing how humor can help in tough times— and by being just plain caring and being kind.

So, Sig, this is a thank you for all you've done for me; and it is a hope that our paths will cross in less troubled times away from the lens, surrounded only by love.

Many thanks, Sig. I'll never forget.

George Bush

November 25th

I called Dana Carvey of Saturday Night Live† a couple of nights ago and asked him to come to the White House for a farewell—he couldn't believe it. He told me I've tried not to cross the line of fairness. I told him I didn't think he had crossed the line although our boys are saying the guy is all out for Clinton and they asked, "Why

---

*We tease each other in our family about how easily we cry. It's called the bawl patrol.
†He did a rather whacky impression of me on the show.

are you thinking of doing this?" Anyway, I think it'll be fun to get him to come to a meeting and say the President will be there and then have Dana Carvey walk in. It's the kind of thing I like to do and I think everybody will get a kick out of it. . . .

———————

Nov. 30, 1992

Dear John [Bush],

I have read and re-read your letter to me.

Since that letter came in, Mum left us. It's kind of like our compass is spinning a little. Even when she was tired and failing she was our guide. I walked by the Bungalow* a lot this long Thanksgiving weekend. I found myself choking up. Then I found myself smiling. The agents probably said to each other "The old guy's finally lost it". But I couldn't help think of the happy things and the sad things, but always at the center was Mum, stable, loving, kind, generous, thinking of the other guy, interested, unfailingly kind, always kind. What an example she set for us all. What you wrote about her for her service was very special, and in a sense, said it all. Now we'll spread out. We'll go our ways more, but we should not fly apart like a centrifuge. I don't think we will.

You and Jody did a lot of the loving care side of things for Mum. You were unfailing in seeing her, in calling her, in loving her. We never failed in that last category; but now I think I was pretty selfish in the "seeing" and even in the calling department. Bottom line—you both were terrific.

. . . I will always be grateful for your loyal advocacy. I am adjusting to the realities. We are building a little house. We are planning for the future. I am beginning to see the bright side of things. I will always regret not finishing the course. I recall the Kenyan runner in the Olympics who limped across the finish line 45 minutes behind the leaders. He was hurting bad. "My country didn't send me all this way to start the race. They sent me here to finish it". I didn't finish the course, and I will always regret that.

Today, though, I was having lunch with Speaker Foley, a decent man, and with my pal Sonny Montgomery and a couple of other Congressmen. In walks Tip O'Neill, a respected friend—a guy I really like. After saying "You ran a lousy campaign" (for which I thanked him) he said, "Don't worry, you'll leave this place with a lot of people loving you. You're a good man. You've been a good President". I'm used to political BS after all these years, but Tip meant it and that gave me some better perspective. I don't know how history will treat us. Your letter carried a very generous assessment of that; but I do know I tried my hardest (Mum, are you listening). I also know I had more loyal support than anyone

———

*Her cottage at Walker's Point.

could ever dream about—and John you're up there at the top of the list on that category. I also know the press were more hateful than I can ever recall in modern political times. I have to get over my "hating". I also know it's been worth the effort. We've done some things that will last and that are good for our great Country. I am rambling here, but I am, as I write, still trying to sort things out. I guess what I hate the most is the charge by the liberals in the media that I never stood for anything, that I didn't care about people, that I was out of touch. I stood for a lot of things on issues (education, home ownership, points of light, less regulation, less taxes etc.—you generously cited many such things), but what I want to have people know I stood for were "Duty, Honor, Country" and yes, as Dad taught us, "service". That's not all bad.

Thanks my brother for lifting the spirits of this bowed but not beaten brother-president. I will always, ever more, be grateful for your loyalty and love.

Devotedly,
George

Although to some extent we had switched to a lower gear, the job of being President never stops. On December 4, I announced to the nation that the United States would lead a coalition to relieve starvation in war-torn Somalia. We sent in American troops, this time on a mission of peace and hope.

December 4, 1992

His Excellency Boutros Boutros-Ghali
Secretary General of the United Nations
New York
Dear Mr. Secretary General:

I want you to know how immensely pleased I am at the news of the passage of the UN resolution on Somalia. I also want to thank you for your tremendous hard work to achieve this unprecedented outcome. A dramatic step has been taken to address the appalling suffering of the Somali people. I want to assure you that the U.S. in accordance with the resolution will discharge the responsibilities which fall to it in a full and comprehensive manner. We will build a coalition and work closely with you under UN auspices.

As the United States prepares to deploy its own forces to Somalia to carry out yesterday's UNSC resolution, I want to emphasize that the mission of the coalition is limited and specific: to create security conditions which will permit the feeding of the starving Somali people and allow the transfer of this security function to the UN peacekeeping force. The military objectives to accomplish this mission derive from the immediate obstacles to the relief effort: the need to secure ports, airports, and delivery routes, and to protect storage and distribution of humanitarian supplies and relief workers. I believe these objectives can, and should, be met in the near term. As soon as they are, the coalition force will depart from Somalia, transferring its security function to your UN peacekeeping force.

I want to conclude by expressing my continuing admiration for your leadership in this crisis and reiterating the U.S. commitment to working closely with the UN to build a secure and stable world.

Sincerely,
George Bush

December 7th

Dana Carvey is here and the young guy wonders why he is here. He and his wife are very nice and I told him I think it's fun to poke fun at yourself, to accept that kind of good natured criticism with good humor, and besides that, our people will like it. I've arranged a little get together for a bunch of them this morning. We're billing it as "the President wants to say a few words as the Christmas season begins." But it's really going to be Dana . . .*

December 8th

8:55 p.m. Our troops were suppose to land at 8:30 and sure enough there is a lot of television coverage in Somalia as they are landing. We'll come in fine, we'll do our job and we'll leave. . . .

I told Bar at dinner tonight, "We've got to see these kids, we've got to go over there," and I think I will.

[We did help end starvation in Somalia, but regrettably, after I left office, the mission changed into trying to bring the Somalian warlords to justice. It was classic mission creep. Several Army Rangers were killed and we saw two helicopter pilots dragged through the streets of Mogadishu. When the starvation was ended, we should have brought our troops home and let the U.N. peacekeeping force take over.]

---

*A rumor was sweeping the White House that I was so despondent from losing the election that I was going to resign. That made the surprise even more fun, which definitely did help lift staff morale. A year or so later, I tried to help Dana in return by doing a guest spot for him on *Saturday Night Live.*

December 15th

Clinton has an economic summit, 300 some people in a big auditorium and they do a call-in show. . . . They are confused because the economy seems to be recovering pretty well. Clinton insists on calling it a recession or quote, "coming out of a recession." . . .*

———————

December 29th

We get a deal with Yeltsin on START II . . . I call Bill Clinton today to tell him we've got a deal and he's very nice about it. He seems very pleased and also seemed pleased that I'm going to Somalia. I told him I might take some shots at the end of the Presidency for doing this, and he said, no, I think you're doing the right thing. He couldn't have been more accommodating. . . .

———————

There was the inevitable finger-pointing when the campaign was over about "Whose fault was it?"—Ross Perot? The media? The campaign? I will always feel it was mine because I was unable to communicate to the American people that the economy was improving. My good and loyal friend Nick Brady felt many people were pointing the finger at him. I wrote him this note after receiving a letter from him:

12-30-92

The Honorable Nicholas F. Brady
Secretary of the Treasury
U.S. Department of the Treasury
Washington, DC 20220
Dear Nick,

Your letter of Dec. 22 is with me here. I've read it carefully.

I agree that Treasury had a key role in some very worthwhile initiatives and in some rock solid accomplishments.

I am sure that you agree when I say we never got any credit in the media for any of the good things. . . . All good news was pooh-poohed and written down—bad economic news dominated the TV networks. It was the most vicious reporting I've ever seen.

I think we failed on some important things. You mention our fine financial

———————

*Ironically, the economy grew by 3.9 percent during the third quarter and 5.8 percent in the fourth quarter. We were well on our way to economic recovery, heading straight to robust. That is probably the greatest gift an outgoing President can give the incoming one. I must confess to certain angst when I heard President Clinton take 100 percent credit for a healthy economy.

reform proposals—for the most part (DOA) Dead on arrival—killed by a partisan congress.

Our Japan trip was productive but "throwing up" was the whole story.

The Budget compromise—that now infamous agreement would have been digested if the economy had vigorously recovered. It didn't and I was the "Read my lips" liar—over & over & over again. I heard it—it killed us.

These are just a <u>few</u> observations stimulated by that good letter of yours—But Nick, we must not let friendship get tied up with Fed Funds Rates, credit crunches, Greenspan, Budget Deals, winners, losers, White House Vs Treasury—All of that is transient—all of it, as far as you & I go, is history.

Friendships don't depend on policy agreement or disagreement. Good strong friendships, like ours, don't depend on those things.

You were my friend before you got here—you still are. Everyone knows that. I sure do.

You have served with great distinction.

The economy was slow and lousy. I got the blame, so did you; but our friendship can't whither because of that—

There's too much life ahead, too much to do and to enjoy free from the pressures of the ugly press and the conniving politicians.

> Let's go!!
> I am your friend—
> George

I took one last trip abroad, to visit the troops in Somalia, and to sign the START II treaty in Moscow.

January 3rd

The Russian visit goes well. . . . The centerpiece of the visit was, of course, the signing of the START II Agreement. I think one of the crowning achievements of my Presidency will be the elimination of all these SS18 missiles*—getting rid of them entirely. I had long frank talks with Yeltsin at dinner and then riding out to the airport. He vows to stay with us on Bosnia. I told him I recognize there were so many big differences there, but I think it's most important that America and Russia not drift apart on this. . . .†

---

*Probably the most destabilizing weapons in the superpower arsenals.

†Unfortunately at this writing there is a lot of tension between Russia and the United States concerning the Balkans.

January 7, 1993

Big Al [Simpson],

. . . We're getting there. The damned special prosecutor went ballistic after I did the right thing on Cap,* but other than that cloud it looks like we can get out of town in about 13 days with flags flying, heads high and over the horizon, a pretty nice looking future. No head table, no fundraisers, no press conferences, lots of grand kids and lots of fishing— not a bad formula, not bad at all.

But I'll not forget my friends. That's where you and Ann come in.

George

January 20th

My last walk around the grounds. It's clear, blue, crisp, cold, and I think of the many walks I've had around here and what a joy it's been. Ranger is in an unusually frisky mood. He's off by the Oval Office when I come out with Millie from the diplomatic entrance, and he sprints. He starts barking at Millie and jumping like he does—He's barking "let's go." He finally calms down and we walk around the whole circle, memories flooding back in. . . .

The worst will be saying good-bye to the staff today, but if I lose it, too bad, they've been a part of our lives and they know we care. . . .

And so time goes on and I'm sitting here now alone, the desk is clear and the pictures are gone. I leave a note on the desk for Bill Clinton. It looks a little lonely sitting there. I don't want it to be overly dramatic, but I did want him to know that I would be rooting for him.

I think of the happiness we've had here. Somebody points out, "Well, the polls look good today—you're leaving with people liking you." And I'm saying, "Well that's nice, that's very nice, but I didn't finish the job." They may be pleasant in that way, but I don't think they know my heartbeat . . .

As I told Bill Clinton, I feel the same sense of wonder and majesty about this office today as I did when I first walked in here. I've tried to serve here with no taint or dishonor; no conflict of interest; nothing to sully this beautiful place and this job I've been privileged to hold. . . .

Barbara is wonderful. She's strong and what a First Lady she's been—popular and wonderful. And suddenly she is eclipsed by the new wave, the lawyer, the wife with an office in the White House;

---

*I pardoned Caspar Weinberger before leaving office.

but time will tell and history will show that she was beloved because she was real and she cared and she gave of herself. She has been fantastic in every way, and my, how the people around here love her, and my, how that staff rejoices in the fact that she came their way.

But we'll make it in Houston—I know we will. We kid about her cooking. We kid about no staff, no valets, no shined shoes and no pressed suits. We did that before and we can do it again. It's my last day as President of the United States of America.

CHAPTER 16

Looking Forward

After Bill Clinton was sworn in as the forty-second President of the United States, Barbara and I and our two dogs left Washington and flew to Houston. Our first challenge was figuring out "What next?"

January 28, 1993

Dear Walter [Annenberg]:

. . . January 20th was, indeed, a very emotional day in our lives; but now we are back here, just plain private citizens, staying out of the public limelight and doing exciting things. By way of example:

Barbara is a good cook.

I AM A GOOD DISH WASHER.

Barbara bought a Sable station wagon and she has driven it for two days with no accidents. Not bad after 12 years.

Barbara has a big book contract and is working away already on her computer.*

I have a wonderful office, modestly staffed with very good people. Rose Zamaria is my chief of staff.†

I will probably do some writing and a little speaking; but for now, it is readjustment time.

A Memoir by Barbara Bush came out in the fall of 1994 and was an instant best-seller.

†Rose ran my congressional office back in 1967–70 and was with me at the RNC. I asked her to come to the White House where she was director of White House Operations and for the last year was also in charge of the Oval Office staff.

Walter, more than ever, I feel that it's family and friends that really matter. Your letter eloquently touched on this, and it is so true. We will spend two-thirds of our time here, and one-third in Maine—always with family in the forefront.

I am sure I will miss certain aspects of public life and will always be grateful for the opportunity to have served. I will now try to conduct myself with dignity and in a way not to dishonor the office I was so proud to hold.

Our love to you and Lee. What would we do without friends.

Sincerely, from this private citizen of Houston, Texas USA—a citizen who respects you and is proud to be your friend,

George

A columnist named Philip Terzian with the Providence Journal *sent me a copy of a nice column he had written about me and my presidency.*

February 4, 1993

Dear Philip,

. . . Thank you for that editorial.

I am now back in private life keeping my pledge to get active in the grandchild business. I am staying away from the head table, for the most part, and I am out of the interview business. Let history be the judge without my pushing and pulling.

I have no bitterness in my heart about the "invective and abuse" that you pointed out came my way. I can't say it didn't hurt, but now it's different. Barbara is way out ahead of me. She is writing away and even though she dropped a $3.00 jar of [Ragu] sauce and splattered it all across our tiny kitchenette she is proving once again to be a fine cook. It's far better than microwaving it. I am the dish man. I rinse the plates and put them in the washer. Almost simultaneously I load our coffee machine, and then we walk the dogs. And along the way we count our blessings.

We have much to be grateful for. And every once in awhile someone says something very pleasant and nice and reassuring; and it all seems like the whole journey was worth every single minute of it. Thank you for "getting it"—for understanding.

My respects, sir, and many thanks. Now back to walking "Ranger."

Sincerely,
George Bush

February 24, 1993

Mr. Robert C. Macauley*
AmeriCares
New Canaan, Connecticut 06840
Dear Bob:

I talked to Barbara about your wonderful letter of February 10. Right now, she is up to her eyeballs writing a book. In fact, every morning, before 5:30, she is sitting next to me in bed, her little computer on her lap, hammering away.

She did express a real interest in AmeriCares. You said you would be glad to fly down to Houston for a few hours to describe your thoughts more fully. That would be fine with us. We will be in Kennebunkport starting the first week in May. Maybe that would be more convenient.

In any event, it might be worthwhile if you and she did have a good talk, and I would sit in and kibitz. We both have great respect for all you have done and, of course, we want to help in any way we can.

You are nice to equate Barbara's concerns with those of the late Audrey Hepburn, a respected friend. I don't know if you know this, but just before she died, we presented her the Medal of Freedom—a well deserved recognition of her fantastic service.

Warm regards.

Sincerely,
George Bush

[Barbara did become ambassador at large for AmeriCares, and both of us have accompanied them on a number of relief missions, including to Bosnia, Guatemala, and Honduras.]

May 13, 1993
(Kennebunkport)

Dear Fred [Zeder],

I am thrilled you are willing to serve on our Presidential Library Board. We are going to have a fine Library up at A&M.

We'll be in touch later on; but, for now, many thanks.

Sincerely,
George

"paws up"? OK, but I really miss the guy!†

*Bob and I were friends and classmates at Andover. He has spent his life helping others through his wonderful AmeriCares relief organization.

†I was devastated when Ranger died of cancer just a few months after we got back to Houston. Leave it to Fred Zeder to make me smile about it.

By this time war had exploded in the Balkans and Milosevic's army was pounding Bosnia. My friend Sadruddin Khan sent me a "letter to the editor" he had written, critical of the West for sitting on its hands.

August 3, 1993

Dear Sadri,

I have read and re-read your July 28 FAX and it attachments. You are clearly right about the horror. I am unclear about the answer, however. . . .

I clearly remember a Colin Powell briefing, Sadri. He and the other chiefs told me that it would take 250,000 American troops, and then they could guarantee nothing other than keeping the supply lines open; and, that even with those huge number of forces, they could not guarantee limited loss of American life.

Let's hope the negotiations end the killing.

You are a most sincere compassionate friend; and I send this letter along not to argue but, once again, to point out the fact that there is no clear and easy call and at the same time to thank you for sending me your fine op-ed piece.

On a quieter and more pleasant subject, Bar and I set out on our first ever Mediterranean cruise next week. We start in Rabat and end up near Palma, spending 8 days or so on a friend's boat. We are excited to put it mildly. . . .

Warm regards and please keep sending me your views on these critical questions. I feel somewhat cut off, and your ideas are most welcome.

Love to Katie.

Most sincerely,
George

January 6 1994

For: Barbara Pierce
From: GHWB

Will you marry me? Oops, I forgot, you did that 49 years ago today! I was very happy on that day in 1945, but I am even happier today. You have given me joy that few men know. You have made our boys into men by bawling them out and then, right away, by loving them. You have helped Doro be the sweetest greatest daughter in the whole wide world. I have climbed perhaps the highest mountain in the world, but even that can not hold a candle to being Barbara's husband. Mum used to tell me: "Now, George, don't walk ahead". Little did she know I was only trying to keep up—keep up with Barbara Pierce from Onondaga Street in Rye New York. I love you!

_____

I saw my friend and former press secretary Sheila Tate during a visit to Washington, and she told me she thought I needed to get involved in a cause or a project.

February 27, 1994

Dear Sheila,

. . . Sheila, I need more time, more quiet time, more grandchild time, more time to forget **and** to remember. I have had lots of suggestions for things "big and important"; but, oddly, I don't have myself cast as a big and important person. I want to be a tiny point of light, hopefully a bright point of light, but I don't crave sitting at the head table; nor do I burn with desire to see that history is kind to us.

I'll figure it out but time is the key. In the meanwhile, having neglected my personal finances for many years, I am giving speeches. I'll do this for maybe 1½ more years. Then if something should happen to me—say when I am even more forgetful and Millie fails to return me to our house when we are out walking, then Bar will be in fair financial shape for her future. Once that's done maybe I'll do more forums, more chairing of meetings with "used-to-be" people, make more pronouncements on the Sahil or on fundamentalism or on ozone—who knows.

For now though—family, friends, be quiet, stay out of and away from the press, especially the talk shows—and oh yes count my many blessings for friends. That's where you fit in.

Con afecto,
GB

_____

March 22, 1995

Burton J. Lee, III, M.D.
Cambridge, Massachusetts 02139
Dear Burt,

I have no objection to your taking up the fight on the Gulf War syndrome,* but I must tell you that I find it difficult to believe that anyone in the Pentagon would want to cover up something of this nature. Why in God's name would a military officer not want to go to bat for his troops?

After the "60 Minutes" show, I talked to John Deutch,† who was on the

*Some Desert Storm veterans were complaining of strange, unexplained illnesses.
†John was deputy secretary of defense and had just been nominated by Clinton to be CIA director.

program. He told me in considerable detail what they had done to find out if there was any use of chemicals during Desert Storm. They were unable to find anything in spite of the drama of the "60 Minutes" program.

If there is some cover-up, which I strongly doubt, I would, of course, love to see the matter disposed of. I am disinclined to be put in a public position that shows me convinced that the military are not telling the truth. What you do is your business, though, Burt; and if you have some evidence on these matters, I'd love to take a look at it.

Good luck on all of this.

All's well for the Bushes, and I hope things are going well for you there at INTRACEL.

> Warm best wishes,
> George

April 16, 1995

Jean:*

It's Easter, and I am doing case work; for I answered the phone here in the office.

A Mr. Jesse Kirk, unemployed welder, called in. He wanted Barbara for he has a reading problem.

When queried, I told him "It is I".

He then told me his problem. A good welder, he cannot find work because his of his dyslexia and bad reading over all.

He is in construction and makes, sometimes, $15 per hour. Because of his reading failure he can't get work now.

He hates welfare. He doesn't want a hand out.

I gave him the usual disclaimer "out of office, unemployed myself, call the Congressman"

Can someone call him **Jesse Kirk 341 8105.**

Maybe BPB knows of an adult reading program. Just any call back might encourage the guy. Even if we said "We've checked, and have no suggestions".

Can we help Jesse?

> GB

[We called Jesse back and put him in touch with the Houston Read Commission.]

---

*Jean Becker, who became my chief of staff after Rose Zamaria retired. Up until then, she had worked for Barbara.

I wrote this after receiving an offensive fund-raising form letter from the National Rifle Association.

May 3, 1995

Mr. Thomas L. Washington, President
National Rifle Association
Fairfax, Virginia 22036
Dear Mr. Washington,

I was outraged when, even in the wake of the Oklahoma City tragedy,* Mr. Wayne La Pierre, Executive Vice President of NRA, defended his attack on federal agents as "jack-booted thugs." To attack Secret Service Agents or ATF† people or any government law enforcement people as "wearing Nazi bucket helmets and black storm trooper uniforms" wanting to "attack law abiding citizens" is a vicious slander on good people.

Al Whicher, who served on my USSS detail when I was Vice President and President, was killed in Oklahoma City. He was no Nazi. He was a kind man, a loving parent, a man dedicated to serving his country—and serve it well he did.

In 1993, I attended the wake for ATF agent Steve Willis, another dedicated officer who did his duty. I can assure you that this honorable man, killed by weird cultists,‡ was no Nazi.

John Magaw, who used to head the USSS and now heads ATF, is one of the most principled, decent men I have ever known. He would be the last to condone the kind of illegal behavior your ugly letter charges. The same is true for the FBI's able Director Louis Freeh. I appointed Mr. Freeh to the Federal Bench. His integrity and honor are beyond question.

Both John Magaw and Judge Freeh were in office when I was President. They both now serve in the current administration. They both have badges. Neither of them would ever give the government's "go ahead to harass, intimidate, <u>even murder</u> law abiding citizens." (Your words)

I am a gun owner and an avid hunter. Over the years I have agreed with most of NRA's objectives, particularly your educational and training efforts, and your fundamental stance in favor of owning guns.

However, your broadside against Federal agents deeply offends my own

---

*On April 19, 1995, a truck bomb exploded outside the federal office building in Oklahoma City, killing 168 people, including a number of federal law enforcement officials.

†The Bureau of Alcohol, Tobacco and Firearms.

‡Willis was one of four federal agents killed in an unsuccessful raid on the Branch Davidian cult headquarters near Waco, Texas. When federal agents tried to end the standoff fifty-one days later, the compound caught fire and burned down, killing seventy people inside. The Oklahoma City bombing was on the two-year anniversary of Waco.

sense of decency and honor; and it offends my concept of service to country. It indirectly slanders a wide array of government law enforcement officials, who are out there, day and night, laying their lives on the line for all of us.

You have not repudiated Mr. La Pierre's unwarranted attack. Therefore, I resign as a Life member of NRA, said resignation to be effective upon your receipt of this letter. Please remove my name from your membership list.

Sincerely,

George Bush

September 25, 1995

Mr. & Mrs. Charles Antone
Chesterfield, VA 23832
Dear Chuck and Connie,

Our caring son, Marvin, called today, broken hearted. He told me of your sadness, of the loss of your young son, of the terrible blow to you and to your many friends.

I know that at this, the moment of your anguish, there is little that words can do to console. I'll bet it does help a little, however, to know that you have so many loving friends who really care.

Long ago Barbara and I lost a tiny four year old to Leukemia. Of course we felt she was the most beautiful, wonderful little girl that God had ever put on this earth. We kept saying "Why? Why our Robin? Why our gentle child of smiles and innocence?"

Lots of people tried to help us find the answer. One woman wrote us and said, misquoting scripture, "Let the little children suffer so they can come unto me." Maybe she had it right, though.

I expect you are now saying "Why?"

Well I can't, even now, pretend to know the real answer; but let me tell you something that might help a little bit.

Only a few months after Robin died, the grief and the awful aching hurt began to disappear, to give way to only happy memories of our blessed child. Oh we'd shed a tear when we'd think of something she'd said or done; but the hurt that had literally racked our bodies literally went away—gone, vanished, replaced by happy thoughts.

Now, 40 years later, Robin brings us only happiness and joy—no sadness. She's never left us. The ugly bruises, trade marks of dread Leukemia, are gone now. We can't see them at all.

I'll bet your son, Chase, was the best kid ever. I hope your hurt goes away soon. I hope you will live the rest of your lives with only happy memories of that wonderful son who is now safely tucked in, God's loving arms around him.

Barbara and I send our most sincere condolences. And all of us in the Bush family send our love.

> Respectfully,
> George Bush

also known as Marvin's Dad

———————

September 27, 1995

The Honorable Ronald Reagan
Los Angeles, California 90024
Dear Ron,

. . . Barbara and I are very happy in our private lives. She still keeps up her interest in literacy and she loves being on the Board of Trustees of The Mayo Clinic. I am busy with our Library which will be up at Texas A&M. I am on the Board of our great M.D. Anderson Cancer Center, and I am still doing a lot of foreign travel.

On October 8-9 my Presidential Library, along with Brent Scowcroft's "Forum",* is sponsoring a meeting where old friends will be talking about the End of the Cold War; and, in the process, we will be talking fondly of you. The old friends are Thatcher, Mulroney, Gorbachev, and Mitterrand. I know that Ronald Reagan will properly get lots of credit for his key role in the End of the Cold War—you deserve that and much more.

I don't know how you feel, but I must say I do not miss politics at all; however, Barbara and I are, of course, very proud of our two sons who got into the Political arena last Fall. George is doing well as Governor of Texas; and Jeb, who ran so well in Florida though losing,† will probably run again in 1998. I hope so.

I seldom get to the Los Angeles area, but if I do come back I hope it will be OK if I drop by. You see I miss our lunches very much, and I miss you a lot.

Love to Nancy and the rest of the family.

> Sincerely,
> George

[I have visited my old friend a number of times during the last few years. Despite the fact he is suffering from Alzheimer's he still has his same wonderful sense of humor.]

———————

*The Forum for International Policy, Brent's foreign-policy think tank.

†George and Jeb both ran for governor of their respective states in 1994. George won; unfortunately, Jeb lost to the incumbent, Governor Lawton Chiles.

Ann Devroy was a tough, tenacious reporter for the Washington Post. *When I was President, she gave me heartburn many mornings when I opened the* Post *to find another infuriating Devroy piece. But when I found out she had cancer, I didn't hesitate to write her this note.*

July 26, 1996

Dear Ann,

. . . I feel a little funny writing this. Many on our team back in my employment days felt very close to you. I think of [Pete] Teeley and Jim Baker, I think of Margaret Tutwiler*—so many more. They used to hear me rant against some of your articles—mainly rant against those who fed you, those who leaked. They knew I hated the inside stories, and you were the best at those.

But they'd say "Ann is a good reporter, the best—tough, honest, penetrating but fair. She does her home work."

I admit I was hard to convince. You know that, for there was a tension; perhaps an inevitable tension, that clouded things between us—never a visceral dislike, but a tension. I was the out of touch President, the wimp; you were the beltway insider who thrived on who's up, who's down—who will be fired, who will win.

But now I am out of it, happy in my very private life, away from the arena; and you are on leave fighting a battle that far transcends the battles of the political wars.

Strangely, wonderfully, I feel close to you now. I want you to win this battle. I want that same toughness that angered me and frustrated me to a fare-thee-well at times to see you through your fight.

I want you to walk out of [M.D.] Anderson, victorious—having won the battle of your life. Because of the courage they tell me you are showing them out there every single day, you will do just that.

Fifty years ago there once was a strange little guy in my life. His name was Morris Greenberg, the greens keeper at Yale's magnificent baseball field. He was my friend. He hated it when I struck out. He hated it worse when a sports writer would knock me down. He knew when I was in the dumps. Others laughed at this funny little man who wore heavy overcoats when it was warm, whose accent was so thick that a lot of guys didn't even know what he was saying.

Once we lost a tough game. Morris knew I was hurting. He slipped a note under the door of our tiny apartment. It said "Don't ever give up. Fight hard. I'm wit 'ya!"

---

*Margaret was my scheduler in the 1980 campaign and then went to work for James Baker. She probably is best known for being the spokeswoman at the State Department during my administration.

I'm "wit 'ya", Ann, and I know you'll win this one.

> Affectionately
> George Bush

[She died October 23, 1997.]

> September 10, 1996

Dear Griffin,*

My, but you have an unusual name for a dog. At least it seems unusual to me, but today there are a lot of different, even strange, names around. How about if they had named you "Ng"—that's a real name. "Here, Ng, here boy, here Ng". It wouldn't have worked.

I knew a guy named U Thant. Suppose they had named you for him. "Here, U, Here U", Sam would have called out—and all the kids in the neighborhood would think that you didn't even have a name.

Anyway, Griffin is a nice name. The Griffins that I know about have the head and wings of an eagle and the body of a lion. Is that the way you look? What about your long tail?

Griffin, I don't mean to tease you about your name. I was a skinny guy most of my life but until the day he died my Dad Called me 'Fats". How would you like that?

I hear that you are a great puppy. I had a puppy once named Ranger. He made me very happy. He made me laugh a lot. He was a very fast dog and he could run like the wind through the woods at Camp David. Everyone at the White House loved Ranger. He was so fast he could catch squirrels when they were running their fastest. He never did catch a rabbit, but he tried hard to do that.

When we went back to Texas, Ranger died. I cried for two days. I cried because I loved him and knew I'd miss him; for he had made me the happiest dog owner in the whole world. I know that when you are an old guy you aren't supposed to cry, but I did. I hope you make Sam as happy as Ranger made me.

A lot of dogs like Halloween, because the kids in their house dress up in funny outfits; and they look different.

Here's a Halloween present for you—just what you need, an adjustable collar with jack-o-lanterns on it.

Good-bye, and "woof" for now.

> Devotedly,
> George Bush

Sam's Grandfather*
*I used to be President of the United States of America—no kidding, I was!

---

*The new dog at Doro's house. I really sent this letter to Sam.

November 6, 1996

Dear Jerry [Ford],

The election has come and gone. Bob Dole did far better percentage wise than CNN and all those pollsters and pundits were predicting for so many months. But he lost* and I'll bet he's hurting today. I know you must have hurt 20 years ago for I know how I felt 4 years ago.

I hope you don't think this letter is odd and strange.

In the House, from a back bench, I watched you lead. As President you gave me a chance to do interesting things. When I went to the White House you were always supportive.

So now, a little later in life, with more time to really sort out my own priorities, I write simply to say I am very proud to be your friend. This friendship matters a lot to me—it really does. As you and I drove across that Ohio countryside last week, it hit me like a ton of bricks, that too often we fail to tell our friends that we really care about them and are grateful to them.

Sincerely,

George

I wrote this short essay to be included in my Yale fiftieth reunion book. Our assignment was to say in a few words who we were after fifty years.

Well, I am a happy man, a very happy man. I used to be a government employee, holding a wide variety of jobs. So many, in fact, that my wife Barbara became fond of saying "Poor George, he cannot hold a job."

Now I am retired, unemployed. I do a lot of speaking—some for charity, some to pay the rent and buy the burgers. I travel abroad a lot for I like touching base with the world leaders with whom I used to work.

I used to love politics. Now I love politics no more. I love the fact two sons are involved in the "arena", but I am happy on the sidelines.

Yes, I am the George Bush that once was President of the United States of America. Now, at times, this seems hard for me to believe. All that is history and the historians in the future will sort out the bad things I might have done from the good things. My priorities now are largely friends, family, and faith.

I count my blessings every single day.

George Bush

*To President Clinton, in the 1996 presidential campaign. Jerry Ford and I traveled with Bob for a few days the week before the election.

February 10, 1997

Ms. Britnay Marie Mason
Jacksonville Beach, FL 32250
Dear Britnay,

You never knew your Dad. I didn't know him either.

When your Dad was killed I was President of the United States. I had to make the call that sent him into battle. Deciding to send someone's son or daughter into harm's way is the toughest decision a President has to make.

On December 19th 1989 I had to make such a decision. American lives were being threatened in Panama. Democracy had been ripped away from the people of Panama as an international drug lord took command of that country. Freedom was on the rocks and tyranny reigned in that friendly country; so upon the advice of many good people I decided that we had to act.

Your father was one of the ones that made the ultimate sacrifice. He gave his life. I think your Dad felt he might die in combat for he wrote a most beautiful letter to your grandmother, a letter that said among other things "I am frightened (by) what lays beyond the fog, and yet do not mourn for me. Revel in the life that I have died to give to you—Remember I joined the army to serve my country and ensure that you are free to do what you want and live your lives freely."

I shared this lovely letter with our entire nation, reading it as part of my State of the Union address on January 31, 1990. As I did so I choked up a bit, for I knew that your entire family was hurting, hearts broken over the loss of your Dad. But this letter made an impression all across our country, for America saw once again that it does indeed have good men willing to serve, willing to sacrifice.

Britnay, these are the words of a hero, a man clear of purpose who died loving his country and proud of wearing its uniform, proud of putting service ahead of self.

Today it is said we have no heroes. Not so. We do have heroes. Your Dad, Jim Markwell was one such man. The United States of America will always have him, treasuring his memory, giving thanks to God that such patriotic men are willing to serve.

I wish I had known your Dad personally. I think I would be a better man if I had known him, for his kind of courage lifts men up and inspires them.

May God bless you in your life ahead.

George Bush

––––––––––

I am including only excerpts from this letter since I wrote it over some six weeks and it got rather long.

February 11, 1997

Dear Kids,

Okay, so you might think I have lost it.

I plan to make a parachute jump. So there!

Yesterday I went to the International Parachute Association's annual meeting here in Houston. Asked to describe my [war] experience, I told them how terrified I was, how I pulled the rip cord and released my chest straps too early, and how I had sunk fairly deep when I hit the water.

As I recounted those errors, however, something happened. For some reason, I went back to a thought I had way in the back of my mind. It has been there, sleeping like Rip van Winkle, alive but not alive. Now it was quite clear.

I want to make one more parachute jump!

I was excited, but thought I better sleep on it—to give it a little time. This morning, however, I was more determined than ever, so I asked Chris Needels to come over. He brought Lt. Col. Danny Greene* and two other association people. They arrived bearing the kind of chute I would use, and began by explaining the safety features involved. That seemed appropriate.

"Piece of cake," thinks me.

The next move is up to them, but not entirely—for when I go home tonight I'll tell your Mom about this. She will not like it, but in the final analysis I will convince her (1) that it is safe and (2) that this is something I have to do, must do.

———————

February 12th

So far, so good. Last night at home, sitting in the den, I casually told your Mom, "Bar, I'm going to make a parachute jump."

"You're crazy," came the reply. She meant it, but she didn't sound angry.

I was firm. "This is something I must do."

"Sure, you must do it. Sure!" She could have well said, "Yeah, right!" That's what people say these days when they mean you're wrong.

Having clearly established my position, I changed the subject. "Another glass of Chardonnay, Bar? How'd the construction go today?"† Smart, for she answered both questions and never came back to the parachute jump.

———————

*Danny was then a member of the Golden Knights, the Army's elite parachute-jumping team. Chris is a former Golden Knight, now retired from the Army and running the United States Parachute Association.

†We were having some work done on our house.

February 27th

I attend a Desert Storm reunion party in Northern Virginia hosted by Prince Bandar.* It is in honor of his father, Prince Sultan, who is the number three man in the Saudi hierarchy.

As the dinner crowd readies to leave, Colin Powell,† with an amused look on his face, pulls me aside and asks: "Are you planning to jump from a plane? It's the talk of the Pentagon."

When I told him it was true, his only reaction was "Really?" Colin, too good a friend and far too polite to call me nuts, only smiled. I think I detected a shake of the head.

———————

February 28th

I called Colin.

This time he is armed with examples where men far younger than I had landed hard and were badly hurt.

I tell him the precautions we would be taking.

"Yes, but it isn't a question of the chute opening," he replies. "That will happen okay. It's the landing."

"The parachute guys tell me it's like stepping off a curb," I counter.

"Sure, but not if the wind does tricks."

Colin was not trying to talk me out of this, just pointing out some problems. "I know you look 45, but you're 72. How are your ankles, knees, etc.?"

"The ankle's better now. Knees in great shape—firm upper legs and buttock." Did I detect a smile by the good General?

Colin reports that the Pentagon can hardly believe this; and he confesses that Denny Reimer, the top General in the Army, had called him.‡

I assure Colin that I will fully understand if Reimer vetoes this, and ask him to have Reimer call me directly—promising to be light of heart.

So Colin goes into the fray not convinced of my sanity, certainly not a strong ally (understatement), but willing on his own to report back to Reimer that this is for real.

———————

*His Royal Highness Prince Bandar bin Sultan, Saudi Arabia's ambassador to the United States. We became good friends during Desert Storm.

†Colin was now retired from the Army.

‡Although the jump was sponsord by the U.S. Parachute Association, I wanted to jump with the Golden Knights, thus the involvement of the Army.

Has this shaken my determination? No it has not, but I will now make further inquiry. I do not want to do anything dumb, but I must complete my mission.

Why has this now become an obsession? I have everything in life, far more than I deserve. I want to finish my life as God would have it. I have never been happier, but I want to do this jump.

March 6th

Chris Needels calls. "All systems are go. General Reimer has agreed to permit the jump to go forward. No military plane, but the Knights can jump with the President at Yuma."*

I was so elated and caught off-guard that I'm afraid I made a ribald comment to Jean Becker. I told her that, if any press ends up covering the event, we should be sure not to give them the name of my laundry man. Should'na dunnit. Wasn't prudent. Wasn't nice. I'm a little ashamed.

Why did I do this? It goes back to my carrier days. We pilots would joke like this when we had a night landing or a rolling deck. "Only my laundry man will ever know!" we used to say. It helped to ease the tension.

Then I start to think that so much of this relates back to my pilot days—back to that dreadful day, September 2, 1944. I was scared then. Will I be scared again? I know I will not panic, but I expect to feel a touch of fright when I first look down from 12,500 feet—ready to jump.

I have a goal. I will achieve it. I will do it right.

March 7th

General Reimer, Chief of Staff US Army, calls. He asks if I was serious about the jump. I tell him I am, that it's a "matter of closure" for me. He went on to point out the risks involved, then he asked: "How does Mrs. Bush feel about all of this?" I said she was on board, though "unenthusiastic." The General then said, "I hope this doesn't lead to my getting a call from Strom Thurmond next week."

In any event, his phone call meant that all systems really were a "go," and from that point on Gen. Reimer was fully supportive of the jump.

*The Army base in Yuma, Arizona.

———————

March 14th—J Minus 11

Notification day for the kids. I first break the news to Marvin. "Are you kidding, Dad?" then becoming very supportive. "I can understand. I can see why you want to do this. Go for it!" He will talk to his Mother—to help put her at ease. I tell the Governor of Texas. Like Marv, there was the momentary "Are you kidding?" followed by enthusiasm. He was great about it, though he did add: "Don't tell anyone about your 18 year-old girlfriend."

Next was Jeb. He fully understood. Never one for idle chatter, Jeb says what he means and then hangs up. "Fine, Dad, but don't change your sexual preference." I put him down as positive.

Neil was abroad when I tried to reach him, but he was instantly supportive when told of the jump.

Finally I called Doro, who gasped upon hearing the news. I asked her not to tell anyone. She said, "You must be kidding. Do you think I'd tell anyone about *this*?" I felt Doro was ready to support me— tentative but okay.

———————

March 25th—J Day

I went with your Mother to the jump area. Then, wearing my Desert Storm boots, I was off to a final plane-side briefing and into my white Elvis suit (with white helmet and white gloves—the King would have approved) before boarding. We were off.

The jumpers inside were hyped, giving the parachute jumper's equivalent of the high five—two fists on top of the other guy's, then under, then knock the end of his fists, and finally index fingers point at each other (the signal for pulling the rip cord). I got caught up in the spirit of it all—totally hyped, too.

Nearing the exit zone, I was told to stand and back up towards the rear of the plane. My instructors kept saying, "Back up a little more, sir, a little more." It was only then that I felt a twinge of fear—not panic, but rather a halting feeling in the leg, groin, and gut.

Finally, it was time.

"Are you ready to sky dive?"

"Ready to go!"

Before I knew it, I was plummeting face down towards the desert at 120 mph, shoulders arched, pelvis out.

When I pulled the rip cord at 5000 feet, the jolt was far greater than I expected. Looking up, I saw the multi-colored canopy fully deployed. I grabbed the handles over my head for steering. I checked the altimeter on my left wrist, amazed at the slow and gentle descent. I practiced my turns and the flare.

I was at peace. Gone was the noise from the free fall. I was alone, floating gently towards earth, reveling in the freedom, enjoying the view. It was a marvelous sensation.

The floating to earth took longer than I thought, but I wish it could have gone on twice as long. At about 750 feet, the ground seemed to come up at me much faster—more so at 100 feet. I was anxious to flare properly so as to make a soft landing, and the order to do so came about 50 feet before hitting the ground.

Pulling down hard on the two shrouds gently softened the descent. I didn't hit hard, but a gust of wind seemed to pull me back. By then, my chute had been swarmed by the Golden Knights.

I was down. It had gone well. I had lived a dream.

Bar hugged me and smiled. All was well with the world.

Here are some excerpts from the speech I gave at my Greenwich Country Day reunion.

May 29, 1997

It is hard to believe that we are the old fogies (some of the more vulgar among us use a more descriptive term) that we used to watch march by and even laugh about at various reunions at various schools and various colleges over the years. Yet, we are them! (We are "they" Mr. Wierum—he was the guy that taught me English in 1934.)

And yet it doesn't feel that way. I don't feel old—bent over—out of it looking grumpily at life. Life is good and Barbara and I are very happy. "Blessed" might be a better word.

1929—the stock market crashed that year; and yet my classmates and I were privileged to enroll at GCDS in the fall of that very year. I'll never forget that year. The teacher wanted us all to write right handed. I was a lefty. I was not a rebelling little guy—I went along to get along, but this was too much. First the teacher wanted to call me "Walker" instead of Poppy, then she wanted to make me right handed. I won both minor skirmishes.

The depression came and persisted and yet my classmates and I were lucky—we lived in nice houses. We had loving parents who cared and who could pay the doctor when we were sick and could pay this school to give us the fine education that started us off in the <u>right</u> direction—in the process giving us "the <u>right</u> stuff."

Yes we were privileged.

Years later when I went into politics "privilege" was used against me. When I ran for the Presidency back in 1979-80 and then again in 1988 some adversarial reporters and elite editorialists used my background, my "privileged" background, to say 'how can this man, sheltered from the tough realities of this world, really understand the problems of America, really empathize with the poor, the homeless, the <u>underprivileged</u>?"

In a sense I could understand where they were coming from, for I was conservative by nature; and that, coupled with this life of "privilege", played into one of life's clichés and into the very 'id' and feelings of the liberals—"Rich, pampered conservatives simply cannot understand the problems and needs of this country." . . .

I rather defensively would say "You don't have to have cancer to be concerned about cancer". I made little headway with this stellar argument. . . .

But you know what the critics missed?

They missed "values"—the values we were taught at home—the values that were reinforced right here at GCDS. Our parents taught us to care—and the faculty here seemed to be intent on inculcating into us the fact that we had an obligation to care, indeed that we had an obligation to help others. Our critics called it Noblesse Oblige. I was later to call it being one of a 1000 Points of Light.

Society today is plagued by lack of values. Street crime, teen aged pregnancy, drugs, dishonor—you name it. The more outrageous your own actions, the better your books sell, the more TV talk shows you go on, the more fame you get. Vanity Fair will celebrate you.

The Internet is filled with a lot of good worthy things. Push a button and you can find the price of IBM, get the latest news. Know how the weather is in Phoenix or Phoenicia. Watch Tony Blair debate John Major. See Kabila march into Kinshasa, though the early adulation of Kabila as he ousted Mobutu reminds me a little of the NY Times treatment of Castro when he overthrew Batista.

Yes, in an instant on the tube or Internet you can watch the fundamentalist Talibans drive the women of Afghanistan back into the dark ages, you can learn how to garden, collect stamps, even <u>chat</u> with people about life its ownself, as my pal Dan Jenkins calls it. Or you can go back into history and watch the blimp Hindenburg blow up as it was about to land in New Jersey. . . .

But, lets face it, today the Internet and more broadly TV are adulating weird lifestyles, often just plain filth. Some of the lyrics in today's music are just plain sick—we don't want to offend any group or be against freedom of expression so we condone things that we know in our hearts we should condemn. And, if you are in politics, you've got to be careful about speaking out lest those protectors of the 1st Amendment who buy ink by the barrel and pay handsome blow dried men and women to tell you what you saw and what you should think will climb all over you like ugly on an ape and have you down as a puritanical censor.

Sadly, today's movies, not all but a lot of them, do the same thing—the more violent, sexy, and outrageous they are—the better they sell. I vigorously oppose censorship but I'd like to see the entertainment industry and, yes, much of the press become more accountable—I'd like to see them clean up their own act. Not just in terms of bad stuff being seen or written; but I'd like to see the press particularly take a look at themselves trying to find out why they are losing the confidence of the American people. Once great journals and magazines have become predictable adversarial gossip sheets—who's up, who's down—arrows, icons, gossip, mocking cartoons replacing the hard news that made them great way back when we were here.

I can't speak for these other old goats out there, but I can tell you what helped me a lot in life. Helped me through good times and bad. Helped me as my guide in private life and in public life too. Values. . . .

When I was President I often thought back to the advice given us all by Headmaster Minor, a kind and gentle man and Mr. Meadows, a not so kind and gentle man. They were disciplinarians and we never forgot when bawled out by them. Mr. Meadows would have made a good Singaporean. I always felt he'd like to cane us.

When I was President I often thought back, too, to the advice given me by my mother, she who always won the mother's race out here, and pitched and batted clean up on the mothers' baseball team.

My Dad led by example. We'd watch his leadership in business and community and we'd learn; but mother gave advice, nicely supplementing the values stuff we learned here.

Sometimes her advice was performance oriented. "You don't have a game yet. Get out and practice!" Mother was a perfectionist and a fierce competitor. . . . "Never quit! Never let 'em know you're hurting!"—values

Early on she'd give us profound advice. It sounds simple now but when I became President I knew just how sound it was.

Be honest. Tell the truth.

Be kind. "Compassionate" was too big a word for then, but that's what she meant.

Care about the other guy—help him.

Don't look down on anyone.

You have an obligation to help others.

Compete hard—play to win. Good winner—good loser, though.

Give the other guy credit.

And yes "Don't be a braggadocio."

Mother was never a lecturer. She could get pretty mad at times, but she preferred subtlety to bombast.

When I was V.P. and President I'd still get advice from her.

I was honored and blessed to be President of the USA, but I am dead certain that what truly matters in life is not the political office you hold or held, not the famous people you know, or the things that history might say you accomplished—what really matters are life's true values and your faith, and your family, and your friends. I am a very lucky man. . . .

After Tiger Woods's record-breaking win at the Master's golf tournament in 1997, I felt the media began nitpicking golf's newest and very young superstar. We had met before, and I liked Tiger very much, so I decided to write him a note:

May 31, 1997

Dear Tiger,

Meeting in that most pleasant brief encounter at the R & A* in Scotland like we did a couple of years ago does not really entitle me to be giving you advice; but perhaps genuine respect and affection for you, along with love of golf, does.

Politics is not unlike sports. The press can have you on a pinnacle one day, and then, in pack fashion, can be all over your case the next day. They can do it with carelessness, sometimes meanness. There is no accountability.

Barbara and I were watching the tube the other day, when on came some women golfers knocking your socks off, albeit rather gently, for practicing with Butch at Lochinvar.† You handled the matter with your usual class, but it burned me up and if you are human as I suspect you are it probably annoyed you.

You have earned the fame and fortune that have come your way, but because of that huge win at the Masters and those large endorsement contracts some in the press and, I am afraid, in golf itself want to see you fall down.

You won't though because you have the character that will keep you standing tall.

---

*The Royal and Ancient Golf Club.

†Tiger's coach was Butch Harmon, who was the pro at Houston's men-only Lochinvar course.

Herewith some truisms, some tidbits of advice—perhaps worth what you are paying for them.

When you lose, don't ever let anyone see that you hurt inside. I speak as one who has had his share of big defeats. And don't blame someone else. You never have, you never will.

Give the other guy the benefit of the doubt. You did that with Fuzzy.*

Keep being yourself. You are entitled to take time off, to miss an event, to be alone with your friends, to totally unwind. And you don't owe one single person an explanation when you do. The louses in the sporting press might carp and bitch; but be yourself. My friend Ted Williams stayed at war with the press most of his playing career, something you won't ever have to do. But Ted is still a legend and his critics are history.

If the columns go negative and some will or if some golfers give you grief like those women did—just flash that contagious smile. Barbara and I see that smile of yours and we think of our own kids—of their wins in life, of their kindness, of their caring. Others all across this great country must feel the same way when they see your smile and your inner light.

Invest wisely. Invest conservatively, avoiding the get rich quick schemes. Invest for tomorrow.

Stay close to your family. After all the glamorous walks up those 18th fairways end what will matter in life is your family. When you and your Dad hugged there at Augusta that said it all in terms of the values we Bushes hold dear. And when your great Mom looks at you with such pride and love every mother across America knows how much family matters.

Character matters, too. Decency matters. Honesty matters. You've got 'em all. Never change.

Enough. Forgive me for lecturing. I don't usually do this. But you are a special kid and I don't ever want to see you hurt. . . .

Sincerely,
George Bush

———

*Pro golfer Fuzzy Zoeller, known for his down-to-earth sense of humor, had teased Tiger about not asking for "fried chicken and collard greens" at the Master's Champions dinner, which is held the following year for the returning champion. Some people interpreted the remark as racist.

July 26, 1997

James R. Adriance*
North Andover, Mass. 01845
Dear Spike,

Bob Macauley, thoughtful guy that he is, sent me your address; so I thought I'd check in from up here at our own seaside Shangri La.†

First, I hope this finds you in good spirits and feeling OK.

Life has been great for Barbara and me since leaving the White house. We spend about 7+ months based out of our small but wonderful home in Houston, the rest up here where this place seems to be able to take a deep breath then accommodate thousands of kids, brothers, cousins, guests, and various unidentified strap hangers. The other day I went to go to bed and there watching TV in our room was a teenager I had never seen before. He wanted to watch the Astros while the other kids were in another part of the house watching the Rangers. Bar told him we were going to go to sleep so "Please turn down the volume on the TV." He was gone when we woke up the next morning.

The striped bass are here in large sizes, large numbers. This has been the greatest fishing summer of my 73 year old life.

Golf? Terrible, but I still enjoy it.

Health—Blessed! I pulled my Achilles tendon awhile back, so I now fast walk—4 miles @ less than 13 minutes per mile—good aerobics, no pounding on the joints. Rest of the old body functioning OK.

Macauley continues his great "Points of Light" work running, compassionately, AmeriCares. Bar and I try to do our part in various ways, helping various charities. My Presidential Library opens Nov. 6th at Texas A&M University—hooray! And a huge book on foreign policy and changes in the world when I was President that I am writing for Knopf with General Scowcroft is all but finished. Hooray for that, too!‡

But for us, Spike, life is good. I do not miss politics. That two of our sons, George and Jeb, are in the political arena (so described by Teddy Roosevelt) is all we need. . . . I avoid interviews. I miss the great White House staff, and I miss working with our military. I do not miss the politics or the Congress— no not at all.

George and Jeb both run next year. Jeb, you may recall, lost by a hair in '94. Now he shows to be a little ahead as he gets ready to run again for Governor of Florida.

---

*One of my teachers at Andover.
†I was writing him from Kennebunkport.
‡*A World Transformed* was published in September 1998.

George is doing a fine job as Governor of our state, and, of course, we are very proud of both those boys. The other three kids are getting along well, too. We are equally as proud of them.

Love from all the Bushes.

GB

————————

I wrote this letter for a charity auction to benefit Literacy Partners in New York.

Nov. 4, 1997

Dear Reader,

This is a letter about two of the great authors I have known and loved.

The first, our dog Millie. I used to be President of the USA. Millie, young and fast, then lived in the White House. She chased squirrels on the White House lawn. She ran like a dart through the lovely woods at Camp David, and climbed, sure footedly, on the rocks at Maine. And she wrote a best selling book, ably assisted by my wife.*

Then this summer she got cancer and died and we wept, for Millie had given us joy and love and we missed her.

The second author is Barbara Pierce Bush, the one who helped Millie write. Barbara is my wife—has been for almost 53 years. She wrote a Memoir. She helps our country know the importance of reading. She is down to earth. She loves grandkids, gardens, and dogs.

She is a grand writer but not scary like some authors. We laugh a lot together. We cry, too. We are two people, but we are one. I love her a lot—

Sincerely,
George Bush

————————

November 10, 1997

Dear Ashley,

Darn it! When your class is having that play on November 25, your old grandfather will be in Frankfurt, Germany, and Zurich, Switzerland, so I will have to miss it.

You were fantastic in the opera yesterday. I was very, very proud of you. I watched you through my binoculars. You did a wonderful job.

Devotedly,
Gampy

Millie's Book, published in 1990, earned more than $1 million for the Barbara Bush Foundation for Family Literacy.

Bob Woodward of the Washington Post *wrote and asked for an interview on a new book he was doing on post-Watergate presidents.*

———

February 12, 1998

Dear Bob,

. . . Let me be very frank—I am disinclined to have the conversation that you suggest. There are several reasons for this position.

First, I do not think you and I had a very pleasant relationship. You were the aggressive investigative reporter, I the office holder who knew that his every move, his every experience in business or personal life or politics no matter how long ago would come under intrusive scrutiny. In the old days this would not have influenced me. That aggressive adversarial relationship went with the territory.

Today, happily retired and trying to stay away from the beltway media, it does influence me.

Back then experts would tell me "You better talk to him/her, they'll write the story anyway and you better get your side of it told accurately." But now at 73 and having been through some ups and downs with the Washington Press I am inclined to stay out of the story, out of the interview business. Instead I favor letting the writers themselves make the call, letting the chips fall where they may without my spin.

Perhaps I am being unduly influenced by today's frenzy, a frenzy of sleaze and alleged tawdry behavior,* but for me my reluctance is far deeper than that.

When I read books by today's new school journalists I see my name in direct quotes, words in my mouth I never uttered. I talked to our publisher at Knopf† about this method. "Literary License" says he. But I don't like it.

Watergate was your watershed. For you it was an earthshaking event that made you a true media star—deservedly so. For me Watergate was a major event, for as you correctly point out, I was Chairman of the GOP during those tumultuous times. I am sure I learned from Watergate, but it did not have the major effect that your letter seems to imply. Watergate had absolutely nothing to do with how I conducted myself during the Iraq crises.

I think Watergate and the Vietnam war are the two things that moved beltway journalism into this aggressive, intrusive 'take no prisoners' kind of reporting that I can now say I find offensive.

The new young cynical breed wants to emulate you. But many of them to

---

*The Monica Lewinsky scandal had just broken.

†Ash Green at Knopf edited *A World Transformed*.

do that question the word and the integrity of all in politics. It is almost like their code is "You are guilty until proved innocent." . . .

Having said the above the bottom line is I really don't want to get into any of this with any reporter or writer any more than I want to discuss the current scandal about which I would inevitably be asked to comment.

Another reason for "just saying no" is that I do not want to try to direct history. I am not writing a Memoir. With Brent I have co-authored a book on several significant changes that took place in the world when I was President. Incidentally some of what we have written will agree with what you have written in the "Commanders"*—some will not.

Barbara's Memoir gave our family history and did it well. That's enough for me now. Oh there may be a handful of additional interviews but if they relive ancient history and reopen old wounds I'm sorry but I want no part of it.

I told the truth on Iran contra but I have been plagued by a press determination to prove otherwise. I listen to revisionistic leftists flail away against our action in Panama. I see respected columnists constantly criticize me for not "getting" Saddam Hussein, going in, finding him, killing him. They, of course, are free to do their thing; and I am free to do mine. Mine is to stay the hell out of Dodge and to do as the old Chinese mandarin adage says "Stand on sidelines hands in sleeves."

I hope you do not find this letter personally offensive. Out of office now, away from Washington, out of national politics I have a freedom now that I treasure. I am turned off by what you appropriately call a "climate of scandal and mistrust." I am deeply offended by much of what I read, having tried to show respect for the offices I was proud to hold. But I know that comments by me would not help change things, indeed would probably be seen as piling on by a poor loser. So, Bob, we better leave things as they are.

I suppose it might have a ring of hypocrisy if I, unwilling to pitch in, wish you well on your new project; but I do.

Sincerely,
George Bush

[Bob wrote me a nice letter back, saying "your shot has landed in Dodge . . . I appreciate your candor."]

———————

NBC anchorman Tom Brokaw asked me to answer some questions about World War II for a book he was writing about the war, The Greatest Generation, *which was published in the fall of 1998.*

*Woodward's book about Desert Storm.

March 9, 1998

Dear Tom,

I am glad to try to answer the questions you put to me in your letter of March 3rd.

1. I did indeed enlist on my 18th birthday, but back then, our country having been attacked at Pearl Harbor, one literally did not think about the danger that might ensue or the absence from home. The country was unified. It seemed that everyone wanted to do his part—do his duty. Having said that I did not really have any idea when I enlisted what kind of experiences lay ahead. I had never flown before, though I knew I wanted to be a Navy pilot. I had always loved the sea and the idea of flying off a carrier really appealed to me, But without much realization of the tests that lay ahead.

2. My combat experience, indeed my entire experience in the military, profoundly changed me. Coming out of a privileged background, I had had little exposure to the real world—to people from very different backgrounds. I went into the service as a gung ho kid, scared at times, becoming a Naval Aviator.

I experienced great joy and great sadness. I laughed a lot, and when my squadron mates were killed, and quite a few were, I wept. I was very close to some of the pilots in our squadron, VT-51. My roommate, Jim Wykes, was killed on his very first mission in hostile territory. Jim had become a very close friend.

I felt our nation's anger at Hitler and Hirohito. I wanted to fly off carriers. I never thought about risking my life—that was a given. That was my duty. How did I change. I went in a kid. I emerged a man. . . .

3. It was not difficult to return to civilian life. Barbara and I had gotten married—Jan. 6th 1945. I was sent to Virginia Beach, a Lt.J.G., part of a new Torpedo Squadron, VT 153. Soon we had orders for this new squadron to go back to the Pacific. But then in August the war ended, and shortly thereafter, given my combat service, I had enough "points" to get out of the service and to return to civilian life.

The transition was not hard. I applied to Yale University and was admitted to classes starting in October of 1945. There was little conversation of my own war experiences. Most of my friends had been through the same kinds of things. Some had had scarier combat experiences than I had endured. We wanted to shift gears, to get a good education and then a job. There was very little talk of what we had been through. . . .

Barbara and I lived in tiny apartments. The last one, next door to Yale President Charles Seymour, had once been occupied by one lady and a couple of people helping her in the house at 37 Hillhouse Ave. Yale, desperate for veteran housing, converted this house into apartments for 13 families. One requirement was that you had to have one child to live in this place. One family had twins, so 40 people lived in our little apartments, sharing the kitchen, sharing the bathrooms etc. . . .

4. I am not sure that my war time service had any effect whatsoever on my eventually entering politics. It did have a lot to do, in a very broad sense, with my conviction that service to country is honorable—that military service is honorable. I have great respect still for those who wear the uniform of any military service. I have contempt for those who, when called, fail to serve. I hated the Vietnam syndrome—when people who served were vilified and spat upon. Those who ducked and dodged and fled only to let some under-privileged take their places particularly offend my sense of honor. I have contempt for those who continually attack our military.

My own military experience honed my respect for "Duty, Honor, Country."

5. I am convinced that my own military experience was of enormous benefit to me when I became President. I knew first hand the horrors of combat. I had respect for the way the military operates, for what, if unfettered, our military could do. As President I knew it was my responsibility to do the diplomacy and the politics. But I was certain that once the battle began the politicians should not get in the way of letting the military do their job.

And yes I can think of times when my own experience way back in the 1940's "played a role in my thinking, my decision making." Certainly when I had to decide to use force in Panama and in Desert Storm and even in Somalia, a more benign environment, I was better able to make those decisions having served myself.

I still believe that the toughest decision a President ever has to make is when he has to send someone's son or daughter into combat—put their lives in harm's way. No one else can make this decision—only the President; and I am absolutely certain that my having been in the military, albeit years before, helped me make the right decisions regarding the use of force.

6. I do not think much about my WW II experiences. Until this experience became better known because of my entry into national politics I seldom reflected on it. I did think about the day I was shot down. Two friends flying with me were killed. I still think about that, wondering what else I might have done to help save their lives.

7. When I look back at my life I put my experience as a "combat Navy flier" right up at the top of the list of experiences that truly shaped my life.

I learned so much from my squadron mates, from our tough, quiet courageous skipper, Lt. Cmdr. Melvin. I learned that a wing man does not pull away from his leader. That was true in combat. That should be true in politics—I learned that courage is hard to define, but I saw it in fine young men almost on a daily basis.

Once having just landed on our carrier and standing next to the "island" on the carrier deck I saw the next plane to land make a bad landing. The pilot, trying to get back in the air and go around again, put the throttle to the fighter aircraft. The plane, in a stall, veered crazily to its right, crashed across the deck and plunged over the side. In the process the plane's propeller cut a deck hand in half. I was standing but a few feet from a severed leg. And than I saw a Chief Petty Officer, working the deck crew, swing into action. He rallied the shocked sailors. "God damn it, get back to work. Swab down the deck, clear the deck, get ready for the next plane." I will never forget how under great adversity this Chief took complete charge, rallied his men, kept on doing his job, doing his duty.

On San Jacinto the officers had to take turns censoring the enlisted men's mail to be sure no sensitive military information was inadvertently passed along through the mails. This experience gave me an insight into the lives of a wide array of men in our ships company. I learned a lot about being scared, missing loved ones, anticipating coming home. Heck I was only 19 or 20 and I learned a lot about people's sexual drives. We censors were not voyeurs, but as I did my duty and read the other guys' mail I learned a lot about life— about true love, about heartbreak, about fear and courage, about the diversity of our great country. The sailors would write their loved ones inquiring about the harvests, or fishing in the streams, or wondering if it was hot in the cities. When I would see a man whose letter I had censored I would look at him differently, look at him with much more understanding. I gained an insight into the lives of my ship mates and I felt richer.

8. In conclusion, Tom, you mention "what this nation owes the WW II generation." Perhaps there is a debt. But I don't look at it this way. I never will. I have never been sympathetic to those who feel they are owed something for having served. For me it was an honor to serve—a duty, yes—but truly an honor. I am afraid that some who go into the military feel that from the day they leave the service their country owes them something special. Let me put it this way—when this country is at war, certainly in a war as all encompassing as WW II, people should serve out of love of country, out of patriotism; and they ought not expect special treatment for ever more. Perhaps peace time service is different. There is a package of benefits to attract and keep good people. Fine. That is proper, but what is not proper in my view is the constant demand for more benefits by certain veteran organizations.

This is our great free country and everyone should feel some obligation to serve in some way at some time. That doesn't mean only military service—it means more broadly service to others. Everyone should feel some obligation to give something back. Everyone should find a time to do just that. My time was WW II. Serving was an honor, a privilege. I was a tiny part of something noble.

And then years later I was President—also a privilege—an honor. What are we "owed" those of us who have served. Nothing, not one damn thing. . . .

Tom, pardon the rambling nature of this letter. I will, of course, be glad to answer any further questions.

GB

———————

My journalist friend Vic Gold, after seeing an antimedia quote from me in the paper, wrote and told me it was "beneath me" to criticize the press so much.

May 18, 1998

Dear Vic,

It's tough. Withdrawal is very tough.

When I received your admonition last week about my criticism of the press I joined "Press Bashers Anonymous" (PBA), founded along the lines of Alcoholics Anonymous. I must confess that the withdrawal pains have been terrible, but so far I am clean.

I admit I was tempted to unleash a new blast against the media in my two graduation speeches at U. Conn—but I controlled myself.

In the meantime I received a letter from Sheila Tate saying "Rise above it. Don't bash the press". She had read the same beltway clipping you sent me.

I thought about writing Sheila back telling her that I liked bashing. That it felt good. That I loved the roar of the crowds when I criticized the unaccountable, overly intrusive, opinionated, self appointed stars of TV. I felt like telling Sheila that after years of saying "Thanks for that important question" when some bubble headed reporter tried to stick it in my ear, I now felt free, unconstrained, released and triumphant when I'd bash the media—better than the adrenaline rush from the parachute jump . . .

But I didn't do that. Instead I told her I had joined Press Bashers Anonymous; and that I was struggling to resist temptation.

But, Vic I have given several speeches since your letter—two at U. Conn, one at Duke, one at the Coast Guard Academy. No mention of the Press— none at all. But it's really hard. I miss the crowd reaction, frankly. I miss hearing Mr. and Mrs. Average American cheer as I attacked. No more wimp, no more nice guy—I was out there in the raw meat department stirring the passions of the crowd and old Average Joe is nodding and clapping. I was settling old scores. Dumping on those who rejoiced in dumping on me. Oh how I loved it.

But that's in the past. I think I can make it now. . . .

At our last meeting one member of PBA told me that Zen Buddhism is helping him get through withdrawal. Another got over her bashing days by going for more sex, ironically with a local newspaper man. An older man came to the last meeting and confessed that he has slipped off the wagon. At his Rotary Club meeting he called Mary McGrory an "Old _____" and he said he wasn't sorry he did. He has been dropped from the PBA roles. We all can't make it, Vic. . . .

I think I can make it.

Sincerely,
GB

———————

August 1, 1998

Dear George and Jeb,

. . . Your Mother tells me that both of you have mentioned to her your concerns about some of the political stories—the ones that seem to put me down and make me seem irrelevant—that contrast you favorably to a father who had no vision and who was but a place holder in the broader scheme of things.

I have been reluctant to pass along advice. Both of your are charting your own course, spelling out what direction you want to take your State, in George's case running on a record of accomplishment.

But the advice is this. Do not worry when you see the stories that compare you favorably to a Dad for whom English was a second language and for whom the word destiny meant nothing.

First, I am content with how historians will judge my administration—even on the economy. I hope and think they will say we helped change the world in a positive sense . . .

It is inevitable that the new breed journalists will have to find a hook in stories, will have to write not only on your plans and your dreams but will have to compare those with what, in their view, I failed to accomplish.

That can be hurtful to a family that loves each other. That can hurt you boys who have been wonderful to me, you two of whom I am so very proud. But the advice is don't worry about it. At some point both of you may want to say "Well, I don't agree with my Dad on that point" or "Frankly I think Dad was wrong on that." Do it. Chart your own course, not just on the issues but on defining yourselves. No one will ever question your love of family—your devotion to your parents. We have all lived long enough and lived in a way that demonstrates our closeness; so do not worry when the comparisons might be hurtful to your Dad for nothing can ever be written that will drive a wedge between us—nothing at all. . . .

And it's not just the journalists. There is the Washington Establishment. The far right will continue to accuse me of "Betraying the Reagan Revolution"—something Ronald Reagan would never do. Then they feed the press giving them the anti Bush quote of the day. I saw one the other day "No new Bushes" an obvious reference to no new taxes. . . .

Nothing that crowd can ever say or those journalists can ever write will diminish my pride in you both, so worry not. These comparisons are inevitable and they will inevitably be hurtful to all of us, but not hurtful enough to divide, not hurtful enough to really mean anything. So when the next one surfaces just say "Dad understands. He is at my side. He understands that I would never say anything much less do anything to hurt any member of our family".

So read my lips—no more worrying. Go on out there and, as they say in the oil fields, "Show 'em a clean one."

This from your very proud and devoted,

Dad

———————

Occasionally my friend and former speechwriter the very funny Chris Buckley asks me to write an essay for FYI *magazine, a publication of Forbes. I wrote this one on a subject near and dear to my heart.*

September 10, 1998

Dear Chris,

You asked me about fishing. Well, OK, here goes. I love it. . . .

Let me tell you about fishing for the little tinker mackerel right here in the bay by our house in Kennebunkport.

The mackerel was the first fish I ever went out for. Oh we caught pollock and cunners and I jigged some smelt, but my love of fishing started right about 1930 when I trolled for mackerel.

We used a silver jig tied to the end of a hand held hunk of green cord line. We put piece of white cloth on the jig and trolled behind the "Tomboy", my granddad's 33' boat that looked just like the Maine lobster boats of today.

Mackerel fishing is easy. When the fish are running you cannot miss. You can get five at once on a mackerel jig. They hit hard.

People on the ranches of Wyoming or Montana would kill to catch trout the size of our larger mackerel. But no one talks about mackerel back at the Links club—it's always rainbows, or browns, or cut throats.

Barbara likes to eat mackerel. I don't. They are too oily for me. They are beautiful fish. Caught on a fly they are really pretty good fighters.

The tinker mackerel, the smallest of the small, make great live bait for striped bass or blue fish. I catch them, put them in my live well, drive my boat in close to the rocks and then throw a mackerel, hooked through the back, in close to the rocks.

I like cleaning mackerel. I like seeing what they have been eating. It helps me predict when the bigger fish will be in. The blue fish chase the mackerel away, sometimes driving them right up on to our beach where they lay helplessly flopping around. The bad news is the blues have been very scarce recently.

The best mackerel fishing for me is when I take a couple of grandkids out in my new very fast boat. It is a 31', center console, Fountain fishing boat named Fidelity II.

I gave the old Fidelity, a 28' Cigarette, to my Presidential Library this year. It was exactly 25 years old. A lot of fascinating calls were made from that great boat—some on secure voice during Desert Storm. The press accused me of all things of vacationing". No, no. I was laboring away out on Fidelity. OK, so I did catch some fish at the same time.

Anyway my new Fountain flies and handles big Maine seas with ease. My grandkids love it when we speed to our fishing waters. They get restless if the mackerel don't bite. "C'mon, Gampy, let's go fast". They need to learn to calm down and to relax when we troll or cast. They need to learn the joy of just being out on the sea, watching the gulls, seeing the waves crash against the rocks, watching for a fish to break the water. They need to grow up, but I don't want them to do that.

When my grandson Walker pulls in 4 squirming mackerel and starts yelling "I got four—look at what I caught, Gampy," that is heaven for me. When this happens I remember exactly how I felt 68 years ago. I remember it so clearly. I can even see the smile on my grandfather's face.

I'm 74 now but I don't feel old. I meditate a lot when I am out fishing. I wonder how many more years I will have to fish with my sons, my grandkids.

I count my blessings of health and family. I want to keep on fishing.

I want to teach Gigi, our youngest grand child,* now 2½ years old, how to fish. When the fish aren't biting I want to listen to her tell me what makes her happy and what makes her cry. Maybe I can start next year.

I won't tell her I was President. I'll just try to tell her about the wonders of life and have her understand that our family is what matters. Out on the boat she is a captive. She can squirm but she can't hide.

I will tell her I love her.

And when she says "Are you crying"? I'll say "Yes but these are tears of joy. Older guys do that, Gigi."

See, you can do that kind of thing when you go fishing.

Though you are too young for the tears, Chris, be sure to take Conor and Caitlin out fishing.

Sincerely,
George Bush

---

*Since we left the White House, Doro and Bobby had blessed us with two more grandchildren, Robert and Gigi.

On election day, 1998, I wrote this note to my friend Hugh Sidey, who has had a long and distinguished career at Time *magazine:*

November 3, 1998

Dear Hugh,

It is 10:30 a.m. Within two hours the deadly exit polls will start rolling in. I should have the first cut on Florida at 12:30.

How does it feel? Well, I am nervous and I am proud.

My mind goes back to 6 years ago. I honestly thought I was going to win. No one else did. The polls had gone south after Mr. Walsh's indictment of Weinberger was handed down on the Friday before the election. But I still thought I'd win. I lost big time. And I hurt a lot. And I don't want either of my boys to hurt that much ever.

Now six years later I am here in my office—a different pace and tempo in my own life. I have nothing personally at stake, but then again I have everything.

Should Jeb lose in Florida I will be heartbroken—not because I want to be the former President with two Governor sons. No, heartbroken because I know how hurt Jeb will be.

Yesterday we attended George's final Houston rally. He was the rock star—Mr. Charisma. The rest of the ticket and some congressmen were all on stage when George entered. Then came Laura and Jenna, then Bar and me. The rest of the ticket became mere strap hangers. George was in command.

He is good, this boy of ours. He's uptight at time, feisty at other times—but who wouldn't be after months of grueling campaigning.

He includes people. He has no sharp edges on issues. He is no ideologue, no divider. He brings people together and he knows how to get things done. He has principles to which he adheres but he knows how to give a little to get a lot. He doesn't hog the credit. He's low on ego, high on drive.

All the talk about his wild youth days is pure nuts. His character will pass muster with flying colors.

Yesterday I told him—"George on November 4th things will be very different." He knew exactly what I meant. And, Hugh, it will be different. Though the national press has already focused on his potential and though the polls look good he will be in a different league come tomorrow. He is strong though—tough enough, too, to withstand the pressure.

As for Jeb, should he win today there is no question in my mind that he will become a major political figure in the country. He is passionate in his caring and in his beliefs. He speaks well and at 6'4" he is an impressive man. Take it from his proud Dad.

His opponent has tirelessly tried to tear down Jeb's character. Tried to make him into a shady business man. This is what has really hurt both Bar and me. It is so unfair, so untrue. Jeb is squeaky clean honest. . . .

So sad, so ugly, but that's how the game is played these days.

Anyway, as I type, it's nervous wreck time here at 10,000 Memorial Drive.

I didn't sleep a wink last night. I tossed and turned and got up and back down and took a Tylenol PM and nothing helped and I am very tired. When 5 a.m. rolled around I was ready to put Sadie* on her leash and walk down the block. The Secret Service guy said "How are you, sir?" I said "I am one pathetic nervous wreck."

If the early exit polls look even fairly good Barbara and I accompanied by Jean Becker will fly to Miami on a Westwind jet that I have chartered to surprise Jeb. The plan is to show up at his hotel rooms unannounced, unadvanced—just a mother and dad wanting to be with their boy. I love the thought.

Sally [Bradshaw], Jeb's campaign manager is all for it. So as not to hurt feelings I called both George and Laura about this. Both said "You must go." . . .

I don't want to be with Jeb if he loses. It would hurt him even more to have us there. But if he wins, we will do what I haven't done all year, make a public appearance with this wonderful son of ours. I will try not to be emotional. I think I can do it. I will walk out onto the stage and say "The next Governor of Florida, Jeb Bush."

Tomorrow I might well be the Dad of the Governors of the second and fourth largest states in the union. But there will be no feeling of personal vindication, no feeling of anything other than pride in two honest boys who, for the right reasons, want to serve—who fought the good fight and won.

People will call to congratulate us, but they will never begin to know the true depth of my feeling towards my sons. It will be what life is really all about for me right now.

Six years ago I was president of the United States of America. Tonight, maybe, the father of two governors. How great it is!

But then tomorrow a whole new life begins.

George Bush

Another note to Hugh Sidey:

March 29, 1999

Dear Hugh,

It's 11:05 a.m. here in Houston.

I feel horrible and alone—unloved and even scared.

*Sadie, our current English springer spaniel.

"Why?" might you ask. Well Michael* just rushed in and said our E-Mail must be closed down for 4 days. He announced, firmly almost defiantly, "Our server will be being turned off in exactly five minutes."

No time to notify family and friends, no time even to say goodbye to my wife of 54 years, Barbara. Cut off as if Norad† had told us a theater nuclear weapon was coming right here to suite 900, and here alone, in exactly five minutes. . . .

Michael was too busy rushing from office to office to explain why, but it has to do with a nationwide virus. Some evil little computer nerd out there is spreading a virus; and to hear Michael tell it, if we don't turn off our server and close out our own E-Mails in five minutes disaster could strike.

This virus might come right into my machine and wipe out all my files, all 'documents sent'. Michael tells me if it strikes, then virus laden messages will go out to everyone in my global file and in my Personal Address file. Every single person in those files will get a contagious message; and then their modems, their e-mails will crash. It's that serious. It's like Armageddon and there's nothing even Bill Gates can do about it.

It is a mean, unforgiving, penetrating virus and it sounds like it is coming my way.

Who will tell Little Jeb who owes me a 'reply' on this summer's fishing. Who will tell our two governors who e-mail me regularly or Quincy in New York or Brent, Ron or Kathy in Washington?‡ Who? Who will e-mail them that my modem is closed that nothing can get in it or out of it?

The answer "No one". There is no time. "Hurry up and turn off your e-mail." He's thinking, *Just because you were President of the United States that doesn't mean this virus won't strike you. Shut the damn thing down.*

Twelve months ago I was a Fax man or a phone man. Now I e-mail everyone in the office and tons of people outside the office. I am hooked. I know how to hit the "reply" button and to use the paper clip that let's me forward documents. I can spell check and thesaurus words. I can use color and different fonts to emphasize things and I can forward Monica Lewinsky jokes.

I even listen for the little chime that quietly sounds when an incoming e-mail hits my modem. When I hear it I look for that tiny little envelope icon on the bottom right hand corner of my IBM. It comes right on, saying by its very presence someone is writing you, someone cares.

*Michael Dannenhauer, my chief of staff.

†North American Aerospace Defense Command, based in Colorado.

‡Quincy Hicks, who used to work for us and now is at McGraw-Hill in New York; Brent Scowcroft; Ron Kaufman, who supported me in 1980 and then worked for me during the vice-presidential and White House years as a political adviser and advises me still today on politics; Kathy Super, whom I first met at the RNC and who has worked for me off and on for years. She was my scheduler at the White House and still does all my scheduling.

But that was five minutes ago. It has taken me longer than five minutes to write this cri de coeur and so right now I am a goner. . . .

It's 11:15 AM. We are now shut down, off line, disconnected from each other, alone in a world that is still tough in spite of the implosion of the Soviet Union.

When I was kid we didn't have TV. We didn't know about faxes or computers: and, of course, Al Gore hadn't even made his contribution to connectivity back then.

But then came E-mail right into my life. I resisted at first because our server in Kennebunkport kept mal-functioning; and I had not then discovered the absolute essentiality of e-mail, but our server has been down now for 6 minutes and I feel lonely and lost.

Call me—by phone. I'll let you know when I get back on line.

George

This letter is slightly out of chronological order, but I decided it was a good way to end this book as I approach age seventy-five. It's a letter about "life its ownself," and about a man who is very happily growing old.

September 23, 1998

Dear Kids,

This letter is about aging. Not about the President's Conference on Aging and how we should play lawn bowling, get discounts at the movies, turn into skin-conscious sunblockers, take Metamucil and grow old gracefully. No it's about me, about what happened between last year and this, between being 73 and 74. It's interesting—well, *fairly* interesting to you maybe, therapeutic to me for I know I am getting older now.

Last year I could drop the anchor on Fidelity and worry only a little bit about falling off the bow. This year if Bill Busch* or Neil isn't up there on the bow of Fidelity II to drop the anchor I can still do it; but I figure it's about a 75% chance that a wave will hit Fidelity, my balance will go and I'll be in the drink.

Last year I could fly fish on the end rocks at the Point, and not be too concerned about losing my balance. Oh, if I'd been casting at one target for a while way back in the summer of '97, my spike clad feet firmly placed on two rocks, and then I turned fast I'd feel a little—what's the word here—not "wobbly" but unbalanced"—that's the feeling.

This year if I turn fast, I wobble. I recover as I go from rock to rock, but I

*One of my Maine fishing buddies.

look like one of the Wallenza brothers going across Niagara Falls. Arms in the air are more important this year.

In August I was floating down the Bow River near Calgary in a 14' open fishing boat—the kind with the bow that goes up—not high up but up enough to keep the water out if you hit some rapids. Well we pulled in for a shore lunch, and I couldn't bend my legs enough to get them over the freeboard.

You may have noticed that in Greece* I leaned on the guys holding the rubber launch when we pulled into a beach or when in a chop I climbed back onto Alexander's gangway.

When I climb in or out of the Navigator I have to swing one leg in then lift the other with my hands. Last year—no problem!

Then there's memory. I'm still pretty good at faking it. "Well, I'll be darn, how in the heck are you?" or "long time no see!" or "What you been up to?" or if I want to gamble "How's your better half?" Careful of this last one at both 73 and 74 though. The better half crop is getting a little thinner. Death has claimed some 'better halfs' and over the years some have been dumped.

But no question my memory is getting worse. I was introduced up in Calgary by a guy named Sandy. I thanked him—then near the end of the speech I wanted to mention him again, ad lib him in, but I couldn't remember whether it was Sandy or Randy—so I go "And let me again thank all of you and especially our great host" at which point I gestured towards the spot in the totally darkened hall to which I thought Sandy had repaired after introducing me. When the lights came on, my speech finished, there was Sandy right near where I had pointed. What a country!

Memory? A definite problem now. The twins invited friends from Biddeford Pool over to Walker's Point this summer. Mystery guests in a way for they'd leave one day midst warm embraces and farewells only to mysteriously reappear the next.

Jenna introduced me to them on Day 1 and on Day 2—then gave up on me when failing to recall names I kept saying "Biddeford Girls—I am sure glad you came back. How long are you going to be with us?" They were very nice about it, and after a week of seeing them eating here they wedged into my heart—always room for more nice kids.

Near the end of their tenure when I needled them "Hey Biddeford girls, glad to see you could make it for ice cream" I almost wish I hadn't seen them exchange that 'who is this whacko?' look.

Sometimes humor works, it kind of obscures the memory thing. At a huge corporate gathering I had just met Kevin's wife. Kevin was my host and had

---

*For several summers I have taken the entire family on a Greek cruise, thanks to Greek shipping magnate Captain John Latsis, who lends us his beautiful ship, the *MY Alexander*.

been the question screener at a forum. When I went to bid farewell to Kevin and to his wife whose name suddenly escaped me I go "Kevin thanks a lot"— then patting his wife on the arm—a kind of farewell pat I go "You sure over-married, Kevin old boy." She never knew.

One last point on memory. I can remember things very clearly that hap-pened a long time ago. The longer ago, it seems, the clearer my recall.

Examples:

I can vividly remember the bottom of my mother's feet. Yes, she played a much younger woman named Peaches Peltz in tennis back in 1935 or so. Peaches was smooth. Mum was tenacious. Mother literally wore the skin off the bottom of her feet. But I can't remember whom I played tennis with last week.

I remember Uncle Johnny Walker back about 1945 telling me that Mr. Frank Parker, then a distinguished NYC lawyer of around 50, liked to stand in a cold shower and let ice cold water hit him in the crack of his buttocks. But I can't remember with any clarity what Gorbachev told me in 1991, or what Kohl said when the wall came down in '89. Incidentally I don't like what Mr. Parker liked. Warm water there—sure, but icy cold water no way.

I remember a lot of detail about all five of you when you were little—all happy memories I retain; but alas I am vague on recent details in your lives. I am passionately interested but factoids escape me.

This summer, one or two of you, I am sure in an effort to be helpful, said "get a hearing aid" or "try listening." I heard you. I also heard a family mem-ber (I won't say of which generation) go: "The old fogy is getting deaf." But I had clearly heard what had gone before and I heard that "old fogy" thing, too. Come to think back on it I am not sure the word used was "fogy"—not sure, not sure at all.

But on the hearing thing, here's my side of it. Each year I have my hearing checked at the Mayo Clinic. They keep telling me "very slight hearing loss—no need for a hearing aid." So there!

What happens this year unlike last is I just tune out more: because I do not want to know when they are all thinking of going to the movies and I don't want to sign off on having someone take them all the way to Portland. So, on purpose, I either look confused or simply proceed on my way pretending to have heard nary a sound. It works.

Many times this summer I'd walk by that cluttered room off the kitchen—the TV, Nintendo, sloppy pillows on the floor lolling around room. I'd hear a voice go "Gampster, can we"—-and I'd walk on by heading for the living room. The kids thought I was deaf when I was just in quest of tranquillity. I was tuning them out.

I sleep about the same as last year, but I find I am going to bed earlier but I wake up when the first sea gull, beak wide open, sends out his earliest screechiest call. Seagulls don't crow or scream, what is it they do? I forget.

This year I am more philosophical. I don't feel old at all, and I still love sports, but things are without a question different. I ache more after tennis— I mean I'm talking real hip and knee pain. Body parts hurt at night. Daytime is OK. . . . Golf's a problem—less distance this year. . . . Horseshoes, I can still hold my own. . . .

Desire—no aging in the desire department. I still want to compete. I still drive Fidelity II fast—very fast. My best so far—63 mph in a slight chop with one USSS agent on board.

I desire to play better golf, but I am allergic to practice, so I just tee it up and play fast. I can still volley but I can't cover behind me. I have the desire though. I love being out on the course or court with the greats of today or yesterday. It's more than name dropping. It's being close to excellence that I enjoy. No aging in the desire category.

If I try to read after dinner I fall asleep on the third page no matter how gripping the mystery. Read a briefing paper in bed? No way—Sominex time!

A very personal note. Three times this summer—once in June, twice in August someone has sidled up to me and whispered "Your zipper is down". Once I responded by quoting General Vernon Walters' memorable line: "An old bird does not fall out of the nest."

The other two times I just turned side ways, mumbled my thanks, and corrected the problem. But the difference is, 10 years ago I'd have been embarrassed. Now I couldn't care less. Tragic!

Actually I learned this zipper recovery technique from Italy's Prime Minister Andreotti. In the Oval Office one time George Shultz whispered to Andreotti that his zipper was down. Though speaking little English, Andreotti got the drift. Turning his back to all of us he stood up as if to examine the Gilbert Stuart picture of George Washington that was hanging behind President Reagan; and then with no visible concern zipped his pants up

Last year there was only a tiny sense of time left—of sand running through the glass. This year, I must confess, I am more aware of that. No fear, no apprehension, just a feeling like 'let's go—there's so much to do and there might not be a lot of time left.' And except for an ache here a pain there I feel like the proverbial spring colt. There is so much left to do

Your kids keep me young even if I don't bend as easily or run as fast or hear as well.

Maybe I am a little grumpier when there are a whole bunch of them together making funny sounds and having too many friends over who leave too many smelly sneakers around.

And, yes, I confess I am less tolerant about the 7-up can barely sipped—

left to get stale and warm or about all the lights left on or about the VCR's whose empty cases are strewn around, the tapes themselves off in another house—stuck into yet another VCR machine.

Though I try not to show it, I also get irritated now when I go to watch a tape and instead of the Hitchcock movie or my Costner film in the proper cover I find a tape of Bambi or of that horrible Simpson family—always a tape that needs rewinding, too.

This summer when he came to the Point, Kevin Costner his ownself gave me tapes of 7 of his movies. I now have 2 tapes in proper covers, empty cardboard covers for two others, the rest of the covers and the other 5 tapes gone—vanished—MIA. Am I being unreasonable here?

I have given up trying to assign blame. I did that when you all were young but I never had my heart and soul in the blame game. Now I find I tune out when someone says "Ask Jeb, he knows!" or "Gampy, I wasn't even in the boat when they hit the rock." Or after all five gallons of French vanilla turned to mush, the freezer door having been left open all night, "I didn't do it, and I'm not saying who did, but Robert took out two Eskimo Pies after dinner—honest!" I wasn't trying to find the culprit. I was trying to safeguard our future.

I realize "Keep the freezer door closed from now on and I mean it" lacks the rhetorical depth of "This will not stand" or "Read my lips", but back in the White House days Ramsey or George* worried about closing the freezer door while I worried about other problems. The lines were more clearly drawn back then.

No there is a difference now and maybe when we reconvene next year, you'll notice even more of a gentle slide. I hope not. I want to put this "aging" on hold for awhile now.

I don't expect to be on the A team any more; but I want to play golf with you. And I want to fish or throw shoes. And I want to rejoice in your victories be they political, or business, or family happiness victories.

And I want to be there for you if you get a bad bounce in life, and no doubt you will for the seas do indeed get rough.

When I say "be there" I don't mean just showing up—I mean in the game, in the lineup, viscerally involved in your lives even though I might be miles away.

I don't want you to pull your punches. If I call Lauren "Barbara" go ahead and give me your best shot—I can take it. But try not to say "C'mon, Alph, get with it."

If I shed tears easier now try not to laugh at me, because I'll lose more saline and that makes me feel like a sissy, and it might make my mouth dry

---

*James Ramsey and George Haney of the White House residence staff.

later on, and might be bad for digestion, too. And besides it's OK to cry if you are a man—a happy man (me) or a man faced with sadness or hurt (not me).

Hey, don't point the first finger at whom ever is shedding the tear because all Bushes cry easily when we're happy, or counting our blessings, or sad when one of gets bruised or really hurt inside.

As the summer finishes out and the seas get a little higher, the winds a little colder, I'll be making some notes—writing it down lest I forget—so I can add to this report on getting older. Who knows maybe they'll come out with a new drug that makes legs bend easier—joints hurt less, drives go farther, memory come roaring back, and all fears about falling off fishing rocks go away.

Remember the old song "I'll be there ready when you are." Well, I'll be there ready when you are, for there's so much excitement ahead, so many grandkids to watch grow. If you need me, I'm here.

Devotedly,
Dad

TIMELINE

June 12, 1924   Born in Milton, Massachusetts, to Prescott and Dorothy Walker Bush; family moved to Greenwich, Connecticut, six months later.

June 1942   Graduates from Philips Academy, Andover, Massachusetts.

June 12, 1942   Enlists in the United States Navy on eighteenth birthday.

June 9, 1943   Receives gold wings, becoming youngest naval aviator.

Sept. 2, 1944   While flying combat missions off the aircraft carrier USS *San Jacinto,* shot down near the island of Chichi Jima; rescued a few hours later by the submarine USS *Finback.*

Jan. 6, 1945   Marries Barbara Pierce in Rye, New York.

Sept. 18, 1945   Released from active duty.

July 6, 1946   Son George Walker Bush born in New Haven, Connecticut.

June 1948   Graduates Phi Beta Kappa from Yale University with bachelor's degree in economics.

June 1948   Moves to Odessa, Texas, to take job as equipment clerk for Dresser Industries/IDECO.

1948–51   As part of training program, holds variety of jobs for IDECO, including oil-field supply salesman and factory worker, moving from Odessa to California in 1949, then back to Midland, Texas, in 1950.

Dec. 20, 1949   Daughter Pauline Robinson Bush (Robin) born in Compton, California.

1951–53   Cofounder, with John Overbey, of Bush-Overbey Oil Development Company, in Midland.

Feb. 11, 1953   Son John Ellis Bush (Jeb) born in Midland.

Oct. 12, 1953   Robin dies of leukemia.

1953–59   Cofounder, with Hugh and Bill Liedtke, of Zapata Petroleum in Midland.

Jan. 22, 1955   Son Neil Mallon Bush born in Midland.

Oct. 22, 1956   Son Marvin Pierce Bush born in Midland.

August 1959   Moves to Houston, Texas, to run spin-off company, Zapata Offshore, a pioneering offshore drilling contractor.

Aug. 18, 1959   Daughter Dorothy Ellis Bush (Doro) born in Houston.

February 1963   Elected chairman of Harris County Republican Party.

Nov. 3, 1964   Loses Texas Senate race to Democratic incumbent Ralph Yarborough.

Nov. 5, 1966   Elected congressman from Texas's Seventh District; serves on House Ways and Means Committee.

Nov. 3, 1970   Loses Texas Senate race to Lloyd Bentsen.

February 1971   Sworn in as U.S. ambassador to the United Nations.

January 1973   Becomes chairman of the Republican National Committee.

October 1974   Moves to Beijing as chief of the U.S. Liaison Office in the People's Republic of China.

January 1976   Sworn in as director of Central Intelligence.

January 1977   Returns to private life in Houston.

May 1, 1979   Announces candidacy for President of the United States.

July 16, 1980   Becomes the running mate of former California governor Ronald Reagan.

Nov. 4, 1980   Elected Vice President of the United States, Reagan/Bush defeating Carter/Mondale.

March 30, 1981 Attempted assassination of President Reagan, who was seriously wounded.

October 1983   Visits Beirut after terrorist bombing of Marine barracks kills 241.

April 1984   Presents U.S. proposal for chemical convention at disarmament conference in Geneva.

Nov. 6, 1984   Reelected Vice President of the United States, Reagan/Bush defeating Mondale/Ferraro.

March 1985   Meets Mikhail Gorbachev for the first time while attending in Moscow the funeral of his predecessor, Konstantin Chernenko.

Nov. 8, 1988   Elected forty-first President of the United States, Bush/Quayle defeating Dukakis/Bentsen.

Feb. 9, 1989   Addresses joint session of Congress outlining administration's goals.

May 28, 1989   Attends NATO summit in Brussels.

July 9, 1989   Visits Poland and Hungary.

Sept. 27, 1989 Hosts Education Summit with all fifty governors in Charlottesville, Virginia.

Nov. 9, 1989   Berlin Wall falls.

Dec. 2, 1989   Meets with Gorbachev off Malta.

Dec. 20, 1989 Launches military operation in Panama to restore democracy and to capture renegade dictator and international drug trafficker Manuel Noriega.

May 31, 1990 Bush/Gorbachev first official summit meeting in Washington.

July 23, 1990 Nominates David Souter to Supreme Court.

July 26, 1990 Signs Americans with Disabilities Act.

Aug. 2, 1990 Iraq invades Kuwait.

Aug. 5, 1990 Announces, "This will not stand, this aggression against Kuwait."

Sept. 30, 1990 Announces a bipartisan federal budget agreement that breaks a budget deadlock and is first move toward reducing the federal deficit.

Oct. 3, 1990 West and East Germany are united.

Nov. 15, 1990 Signs the Clean Air Act.

Nov. 22, 1990 Spends Thanksgiving Day with the troops in Saudi Arabia.

Jan. 16, 1991 Orders the beginning of Operation Desert Storm to drive Iraqi forces out of Kuwait.

Feb. 27, 1991 Suspends combat operations in the Persian Gulf after Kuwait is liberated.

July 1, 1991 Nominates Clarence Thomas to the Supreme Court.

July 31, 1991 With Gorbachev, signs START I, reducing for the first time the strategic nuclear forces of the two superpowers.

Oct. 30, 1991 With Gorbachev, opens historic Middle East peace conference in Madrid.

Nov. 21, 1991 Signs the Civil Rights Act of 1991.

Dec. 25, 1991 Gorbachev resigns and the Soviet Union dissolves.

Nov. 3, 1992 Loses reelection bid for a second term, Clinton/Gore defeating Bush/Quayle.

Dec. 4, 1992 Announces Operation Restore Hope to relieve starvation in Somalia.

Jan. 3, 1993 With Boris Yeltsin, signs START II, banning the most destabilizing nuclear weapons in the superpower arsenals.

Jan. 20, 1993 Returns to private life in Houston.

Nov. 8, 1994 Son George W. Bush elected governor of Texas.

Jan. 6, 1995 Celebrates fifty years of marriage to Barbara Bush.

March 25, 1997 Fulfills a lifelong dream by making a second parachute jump.

Nov. 6, 1997 Dedication of the George Bush Presidential Library at Texas A&M University.

September 1998 *A World Transformed,* coauthored with Brent Scowcroft, published.

Nov. 3, 1998 Son Jeb Bush elected governor of Florida; George W. Bush elected to second term as governor of Texas.

May 14, 1999 Commencement ceremony for first master's-degree graduates from the George Bush School of Government and Public Service, Texas A&M.

ACKNOWLEDGMENTS

More people than we can probably mention here helped us put this book together, but a number of them deserve special recognition.

First, many, many thanks to Alicia Lee in my Houston office, who dutifully inputted every single word of the letters and diary entries into the computer. She was a key member of our team, and she is now one of the few people alive who can actually read my handwriting.

The book would not have been possible without the support, encouragement, and hard work of Dr. David Alsobrook, director of the George Bush Presidential Library. David guided us every step of the way on every aspect of the book. Special thanks also go to several members of his staff, especially Warren Finch, Gary Foulk, Bob Holzweiss, Mary Finch, and Deborah Bush.

Several close and trusted friends agreed to read the book, and they gave us invaluable advice that kept us on the right track. To Brent Scowcroft, Marlin Fitzwater, Don Rhodes, my attorney Terri Lacy, and my wife, Barbara: I hope you notice that we *almost* took out or added in everything you suggested.

Both Ginny Lampley and Pete Roussel helped in so many ways, including finding obscure documents and letters, fact-checking, and helping us cut through government red tape in getting certain documents declassified.

One of the reasons we decided to do this book was because of my reputation as a prodigious letter-writer. Although a majority of the letters in the book were either handwritten or self-typed, many of them (and thousands over the years) were produced with the help of my assistants. I have been blessed with the best, the brightest, and the most patient assistants over the years. This is a dangerous thing to do, to try to name them, but how can I do a book of letters and not try to thank them? Over the years they have included, in Midland, Juanita McBride Shannon; during the early Houston days, Vivian Flynn, Lee Goeppinger, and Velma Johnson; Aleene Smith, who was with me for years in Houston, on the Hill, and at the United Nations; also with me on the Hill, Mary Raether, Allie Matthews, Mary Lou Schwarzmann, and Mary Ann Fronce; Rose Zamaria, who oversaw the correspondence staff in Congress, at the RNC, and the White House, and then came to Houston as my chief of staff to set up my office in 1993; at the United Nations, Rita S. Brown; Jane

Kenny, who was with me at the United Nations and the RNC; Jane Johnson at the RNC; in China, Henrietta Morris; also in China, Jennifer Fitzgerald, my executive assistant, who then went to the CIA, the 1980 campaign, and my vice-presidential office; at the CIA, Karen Tillotson and Debbie Geer; back in Houston again, Margaret Wolfe and Darlene Brown; from 1978 until 1989 in Houston, Betty Green; in my vice-presidential office, Barbara Hayward, Patty Presock—who went on to be the Oval Office supervisor—and Susie Peake; at the White House, Bridget Montagne and Robin MacLean; and last but certainly not least, my current loyal assistant, Linda Casey Poepsel, who has been at my side for nineteen years, through the vice presidency, the White House, and up until the very end, I hope. To those of you I failed to mention, please forgive me and just know I was always grateful to have you at my side.

Most of the letters in the book came either from my personal collection or my presidential library. However, I would like to recognize the Richard M. Nixon Library and Birthplace, the Gerald R. Ford Library, the Jimmy Carter Library, the Ronald Reagan Library, the James A. Baker III Institute for Public Policy, the Virginia Historical Society (the FitzGerald Bemiss letters), and Yale University (Ethan Allen letters) for sharing their letter collections. We also owe a debt of gratitude to a small army of people at the United Nations and the State Department who helped track down my United Nations files, and to everyone at the CIA who first made it possible and then assisted us in looking through my classified CIA files.

Other letters in the book came from the personal collections of Martin Allday, the Reverend Jack Allin, Lee and Walter Annenberg, Marjorie Arsht, Thomas Ludlow Ashley, Robert W. Blake, David Bocskor, Jonathan Bush, Neil Bush, William Bush, Barber Conable, Flo Crichton, Trammell Crow, Mike Deland, Tom Devine, Vivian Flynn, Roy Goodman, Dick Jackman, His Highness Prince Sadruddin Aga Khan, Henry Knoche, Dorothy Koch, Dr. Burton Lee, Tom Lias, Allie Page Matthews, Fred McClure, Sally and William McKenzie, Robert Mosbacher, Sally Novetzke, Heinz Prechter, Sig Rogich, Peter Roussel, Brent Scowcroft, Raymond Siller, Alan Simpson, Debbie and Craig Stapleton, Janet Steiger, Joci and Joe Straus, Bob Strauss, Sheila Tate, Charles Untermeyer, and Fred Zeder.

Finally, a huge thank-you to everyone who sent us letters to be included in this book. We received literally hundreds of letters from all over the world, but unfortunately Lisa Drew would not let us print every single one of them. We are very grateful for the time you took to find and send us the letters. Reading them again reminded me of many happy memories and special friendships made over the years.

INDEX

Letters are indicated by **boldface** page numbers following the names of recipients.